June 1–3, 2015
Vienna, Austria

Association for Computing Machinery

Advancing Computing as a Science & Profession

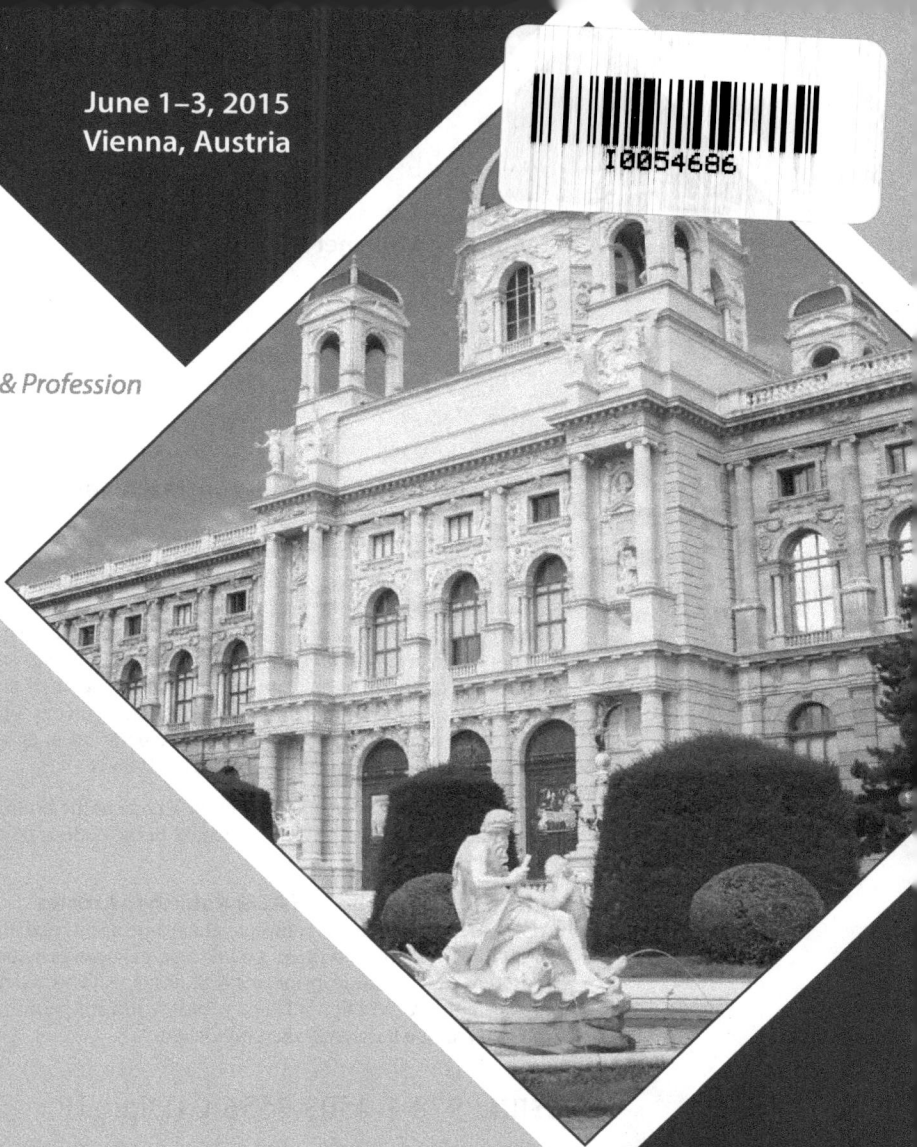

SACMAT'15

Proceedings of the 20th ACM
**Symposium on Access Control Models
and Technologies**

Sponsored by:
ACM SIGSAC

Supported by:
**SBA Research, Arizona State University,
and Society for ICT Knowledge Transfer**

Association for Computing Machinery

Advancing Computing as a Science & Profession

The Association for Computing Machinery
2 Penn Plaza, Suite 701
New York, New York 10121-0701

Notice to Past Authors of ACM-Published Articles
ACM intends to create a complete electronic archive of all articles and/or other material previously published by ACM. If you have written a work that has been previously published by ACM in any journal or conference proceedings prior to 1978, or any SIG Newsletter at any time, and you do NOT want this work to appear in the ACM Digital Library, please inform permissions@acm.org, stating the title of the work, the author(s), and where and when published.

ISBN: 978-1-4503-3556-0 (Digital)

ISBN: 978-1-4503-3866-0 (Print)

Additional copies may be ordered prepaid from:

ACM Order Department
PO Box 30777
New York, NY 10087-0777, USA

Phone: 1-800-342-6626 (USA and Canada)
+1-212-626-0500 (Global)
Fax: +1-212-944-1318
E-mail: acmhelp@acm.org
Hours of Operation: 8:30 am – 4:30 pm ET

Printed in the USA

Foreword

It is our great pleasure to welcome you to the *ACM Symposium on Access Control Models and Technologies (SACMAT 2015).* This year's symposium continues its tradition of being the premier forum for presentation of research results and experience reports on leading edge issues of access control, including models, systems, applications, and theory. The aims of the symposium are to share novel access control solutions that fulfil the needs of heterogeneous applications and environments, and to identify new directions for future research and development. SACMAT provides researchers and practitioners with a unique opportunity to share their perspectives with others interested in the various aspects of access control.

59 papers have been submitted from a variety of countries around the world. Submissions were anonymous; each paper has been reviewed by at least three reviewers who are experts in the field. Extensive online discussions took place to make the selections for the symposium. The program committee finally accepted 17 papers as full papers for presentation at the conference. The topics covered include policy analysis & management, specification & enforcement of access control in distributed environments, and applications of access control, but also expand into new areas such as software & systems security. The program contains a demo session with six additional demonstrations and a panel titled "Privacy and Access control, how are these two concepts related?". This year we are very happy to welcome two well-known keynote speakers:

- *Challenges in Making Access Control Sensitive to the "Right" Contexts,* Trent Jaeger (Pennsylvania State University, USA)
- *Post-Snowden Threat Models,* Bart Preneel (KU Leuven and iMinds, Belgium)

Putting together *SACMAT 2015* was a team effort. We first thank the authors for providing the content of the program. We are grateful to the program committee, who worked very hard in reviewing papers and providing feedback for authors. Special thanks go to Ting Yu and Anna Squicciarini (Panels Chairs), Andreas Schaad (Demonstrations Chair), Dongwan Shin (Webmaster), Jianwei Niu (Proceedings Chair) and Hongxin Hu (Publicity Chair) for their help in organizing and publicizing the symposium. We also thank the members of the steering committee and especially its chair, Gail-Joon Ahn, for providing valuable advice and support.

We would like to thank our sponsor, ACM SIGSAC, for their continued support of this symposium, to acknowledge Arizona State University for supporting the organization of the conference, and SBA Research for hosting and organizing it.

A different country hosts the conference every year. The 2015 edition takes place in Vienna, Austria. We are very happy to host the 20th edition of the Symposium in Vienna and we tried to put together a special social program for you, which will give you the opportunity to share ideas with other researchers and practitioners from institutions around the world and see all the beautiful sights of Vienna. A highlight will be our exclusive Conference Dinner in the middle of the vineyards. Finally we also thank Yvonne Poul for the great organization of social events and making Vienna one of the most enjoyable places for security conferences.

We hope that you will find this program interesting and thought-provoking. Enjoy SACMAT 2015 and Vienna!

Florian Kerschbaum
SACMAT 2015 Program Chair
SAP, Germany

Adam J. Lee
SACMAT 2015 Program Chair
University of Pittsburgh, USA

Edgar Weippl
SACMAT 2015 General Chair
SBA Research, Austria

Table of Contents

2015 ACM Symposium on Access Control Models and Technologies

General Chair: Edgar Weippl *(SBA Research, Austria)*

Program Co-Chairs: Florian Kerschbaum *(SAP, Germany)*
Adam J. Lee *(University of Pittsburgh, USA)*

Panels Co-Chairs: Anna Cinzia Squicciarini *(Pennsylvania State University, USA)*
Ting Yu *(Qatar Computing Research Institute, Qatar)*

Demonstrations Chair: Andreas Schaad *(Huawei European Research Center, Germany)*

Proceedings Chair: Jianwei Niu *(University of Texas at San Antonio, USA)*

Publicity Chair: Hongxin Hu *(Clemson University, USA)*

Treasurer: Basit Shafiq *(Lahore University of Management Sciences, Pakistan)*

Webmaster: Dongwan Shin *(New Mexico Tech, USA)*

Steering Committee Chair: Gail-Joon Ahn *(Arizona State University, USA)*

Steering Committee: Barbara Carminati *(University of Insubria, Italy)*
James Joshi *(University of Pittsburgh, USA)*
Axel Kern *(Beta Systems Software AG, Germany)*
Ninghui Li *(Purdue University, USA)*
Indrakshi Ray *(Colorado State University, USA)*
Bhavani Thuraisingham *(University of Texas at Dallas, USA)*

Program Committee: Rafael Accorsi *(University of Freiburg, Germany)*
Gail-Joon Ahn *(Arizona State University, USA)*
Vijay Atluri *(Rutgers University, USA)*
Lujo Bauer *(Carnegie Mellon University, USA)*
Elisa Bertino *(Perdue University, USA)*
Barbara Carminati *(University of Insubria, Italy)*
Mauro Conti *(University of Padua, Italy)*
Jason Crampton *(Royal Holloway, University of London, UK)*
Bruno Crispo *(University of Trento, Italy)*
Roberto Di Pietro *(Bell Labs, France)*
Elena Ferrari *(University of Insubria, Italy)*
Philip W. L. Fong *(University of Calgary, Canada)*
Hannes Hartenstein *(Karlsruhe Institute of Technology, Germany)*
Hongxin Hu *(Clemson University, USA)*

ACM SACMAT 2015 Sponsor & Supporters

Sponsors:

Supporters:

Post-Snowden Threat Models

Bart Preneel
COSIC KU Leuven and iMinds
Dept. Electrical Engineering-ESAT
Kasteelpark Arenberg 10 Bus 2452
B-3001 Leuven, Belgium
+32 16 32 11 48
bart.preneel@esat.kuleuven.be

ABSTRACT

In June 2013 Edward Snowden leaked a large collection of documents that describe the capabilities and technologies of the NSA and its allies. Even to security experts the scale, nature and impact of some of the techniques revealed was surprising. A major consequence is the increased awareness of the public at large of the existence of highly intrusive mass surveillance techniques. There has also been some impact in the business world, including a growing interest in companies that (claim to) develop end-to-end secure solutions. There is no doubt that large nation states and organized crime have carefully studied the techniques and are exploring which ones they can use for their own benefit. But after two years, there is little progress in legal or governance measures to address some of the excesses by increasing accountability. Moreover, the security research community seems to have been slow to respond to the new threat landscape. In this lecture we analyze these threats and speculate how they could be countered.

Categories and Subject Descriptors

K.6.5 [**Security and Protection**]: *Authentication, Invasive Software, Unauthorized access*

General Terms

Security

Keywords

Mass surveillance; threat models; information security; system security

ACKNOWLEDGMENTS

This work is supported in part by the Research Council of the KU Leuven through GOA/11/007, the Flemish Government through FWO G.0686.11 and FWO G.0360.11, and by the European Commission through the Horizon 2020 research and innovation programme under grant agreement No. 645421 ECRYPT-CSA.

Valued Workflow Satisfiability Problem

Jason Crampton
Information Security Group
Royal Holloway University of
London
Egham, Surrey, UK
jason.crampton@rhul.ac.uk

Gregory Gutin
Department of Computer
Science
Royal Holloway University of
London
Egham, Surrey, UK
gutin@cs.rhul.ac.uk

Daniel Karapetyan
School of Computer Science
University of Nottingham
Nottingham, NG8 1BB, UK
daniel.karapetyan@gmail.com

ABSTRACT

A workflow is a collection of steps that must be executed in some specific order to achieve an objective. A computerised workflow management system may enforce authorisation policies and constraints, thereby restricting which users can perform particular steps in a workflow. The existence of policies and constraints may mean that a workflow is unsatisfiable, in the sense that it is impossible to find an authorised user for each step in the workflow and satisfy all constraints. In this paper, we consider the problem of finding the "least bad" assignment of users to workflow steps by assigning a weight to each policy and constraint violation. To this end, we introduce a framework for associating costs with the violation of workflow policies and constraints and define the *valued workflow satisfiability problem* (VALUED WSP), whose solution is an assignment of steps to users of minimum cost. We establish the computational complexity of VALUED WSP with user-independent constraints and show that it is fixed-parameter tractable. We then describe an algorithm for solving VALUED WSP with user-independent constraints and evaluate its performance, comparing it to that of an off-the-shelf mixed integer programming package.

Categories and Subject Descriptors

D4.6 [**Operating Systems**]: Security and Protection—*Access controls*; F2.2 [**Analysis of Algorithms and Problem Complexity**]: Nonnumerical Algorithms and Problems; H2.0 [**Database Management**]: General—*Security, integrity and protection*

General Terms

Algorithms, Security, Theory

Keywords

workflow satisfiability, parameterized complexity, valued workflow satisfiability problem

1. INTRODUCTION

It is increasingly common for organisations to computerise their business and management processes. The coordination of the tasks or steps that comprise a computerised business process is managed by a workflow management system (or business process management system). A workflow is defined by the steps in a business process and the order in which those steps should be performed. A workflow is executed multiple times, each execution being called a *workflow instance*. Typically, the execution of each step in a workflow instance will be triggered by a human user, or a software agent acting under the control of a human user. As in all multi-user systems, some form of access control, typically specified in the form of policies and constraints, should be enforced on the execution of workflow steps, thereby restricting the execution of each step to some authorised subset of the user population.

Policies typically specify the workflow steps for which users are authorised, what Basin *et al.* call *history-independent* authorisations [2]. Constraints restrict which groups of users can perform sets of steps. It may be that a user, while authorised by the policy to perform a particular step s, is prevented (by one or more constraints) from executing s in a specific workflow instance because particular users have performed other steps in the workflow (hence the alternative name of *history-dependent* authorizations [2]). The concept of a Chinese wall, for example, limits the set of steps that any one user can perform [3], as does separation-of-duty, which is a central part of the role-based access control model [1]. We note that policies are, in some sense, discretionary, as they are defined by the workflow administrator in the context of a given set of users. However, constraints may be mandatory (and independent of the user population), in that they may encode statutory requirements governing privacy or separation-of-concerns or high-level organisational requirements.

It is well known that a workflow specification may be "unsatisfiable" in the sense that the combination of policies and constraints means that there is no way of allocating authorised users to workflow steps without violating at least one constraint. The workflow satisfiability problem is NP-hard [24] although relatively efficient algorithms have been developed on the assumption that the number of workflow steps is much smaller than the number of users that may perform steps in the workflow [7, 12, 18, 24]. Of course, the objectives of the business process associated with a workflow specification can never be achieved if the specification is unsatisfiable. Hence, it is interesting to consider an extended version of the workflow satisfiability problem that seeks the "best" allocation of users to steps in the event that the specification is unsatisfiable.

Accordingly, in this paper we study the *valued* workflow satisfiability problem (VALUED WSP). Informally, we associate constraint and authorisation violations with a cost, which may be regarded as an estimate of the risk associated with allowing those violations. We then compute an assignment of users to steps having minimal cost, this cost being zero when the workflow is satisfiable. In a sense, our work is related to recent work on risk-aware access control [4, 5, 13, 20], which seeks to compute the risk of allowing a user to perform an action, rather than simply computing an allow/deny decision, and ensure that cumulative risk remains within certain limits. However, unlike related work, we focus on computing user-step assignments of minimal cost, rather than access control decisions.

Our main contributions are: to define VALUED WSP and determine its complexity; to prove that VALUED WSP is fixed-parameter tractable for weighted user-independent constraints; to develop an algorithm to solve VALUED WSP with user-independent constraints; to provide a comprehensive experimental evaluation of our algorithm; and to demonstrate that the performance of our algorithm compares very favourably with an approach that uses the mixed integer programming solver CPLEX. Our experimental evaluation shows our algorithm enjoys a substantial advantage over CPLEX as the number of steps grows, with our algorithm being able to deal far better with problem instances containing more than 30 steps. Moreover, our algorithm is far better at solving instances that are unsatisfiable – precisely those instances for which VALUED WSP is relevant.

In the next section, we define VALUED WSP, having reviewed relevant concepts from the literature, including the workflow satisfiability problem and user-independent constraints. In Section 3, we prove that VALUED WSP is fixed-parameter tractable for user-independent constraints and describe an algorithm based on the concept of a *pattern*, which is, informally, a compact representation of a set of similar plans for a user-independent constraint. In Section 4, we present our experimental results. This section also includes a method of representing VALUED WSP as a mixed integer programming problem, which may be of use in subsequent research. We conclude the paper with a discussion of related work, a summary of contributions and some suggestions for future work.

2. BACKGROUND AND PROBLEM STATEMENT

We first briefly summarise relevant concepts from the literature, including *workflow authorisation schema*, *workflow constraints* and the *workflow satisfiability problem* (WSP). We then explain how a constrained workflow authorisation schema can be extended to assign costs to plans that do not satisfy the schema's policy and constraints. We conclude this section with a formal definition of VALUED WSP.

2.1 WSP

A directed acyclic graph $G = (V, E)$ is defined by a set of nodes V and a set of edges $E \subseteq V \times V$. The reflexive, transitive closure of a directed acyclic graph (DAG) defines a partial order, where $v \leqslant w$ if and only if there is a path

from v to w in G. We may write $v \geqslant w$ whenever $w \leqslant v$. We may also write $v < w$ whenever $v \leqslant w$ and $v \neq w$.

DEFINITION 1. *A workflow specification is defined by a directed, acyclic graph $G = (S, E)$, where S is a set of steps and $E \subseteq S \times S$. Given a workflow specification (S, E) and a set of users U, an* authorisation policy *for a workflow specification is a relation $A \subseteq S \times U$. A workflow authorisation schema is a tuple (G, U, A), where $G = (S, E)$ is a workflow specification and A is an authorisation policy.*

A workflow specification describes a sequence of steps and the order in which they must be performed when the workflow is executed, each such execution being called a *workflow instance*.[1] User u is authorised to perform step s only if $(s, u) \in A$.[2] We assume that for every step $s \in S$ there exists some user $u \in U$ such that $(s, u) \in A$ (otherwise the workflow is trivially unsatisfiable).

DEFINITION 2. *Let $((S, E), U, A)$ be a workflow authorisation schema. A* plan *is a function $\pi : T \to U$, where $T \subseteq S$. A plan π is* complete *if $T = S$.*

DEFINITION 3. *A workflow* constraint *has the form (T, Θ), where $T \subseteq S$ and Θ is a family of functions with domain T and range U. T is the* scope *of the constraint (T, Θ). A* constrained workflow authorization schema *is a pair $((S, E), U, A, C)$, where $((S, E), U, A)$ is a workflow authorization schema and C is a set of workflow constraints.*

Informally, a workflow constraint (T, Θ) limits the users that are allowed to perform a set of steps T in any given instance of the workflow. In particular, Θ identifies authorised (partial) assigments of users to workflow steps in T. More formally, let $\pi : S' \to U$, where $S' \subseteq S$, be a plan. Given $T \subseteq S'$, we write $\pi|_T$ to denote the function π restricted to domain T; that is $\pi|_T(s) = \pi(s)$ for all $s \in T$ (and is undefined otherwise). Then we say $\pi : S' \to U$ *satisfies* a workflow constraint (T, Θ) if $T \not\subseteq S'$ or $\pi|_T \in \Theta$.

DEFINITION 4. *Given a constrained workflow authorization schema $((S, E), U, A, C)$, we say a plan $\pi : S \to U$ is* valid *if it satisfies every constraint in C and, for all $t \in S$, $(t, \pi(t)) \in A$.*

In practice, we do not define constraints by enumerating all possible elements of Θ. Instead, we define different families of constraints that have "compact" descriptions. Thus, for example, we might define the family of simple separation-of-duty constraints, each of which is represented by a set

---

[1] In this paper, the ordering on the steps is not considered. Prior work has shown that the ordering is irrelevant to the question of satisfiability subject to certain assumptions about the constraints [12], assumptions that are satisfied by the constraints considered in this paper.

[2] In practice, the set of authorised step-user pairs, A, will not be defined explicitly. Instead, A will be inferred from other access control data structures. In particular, R^2BAC – the role-and-relation-based access control model of Wang and Li [24] – introduces a set of roles R, a user-role relation $UR \subseteq U \times R$ and a role-step relation $SA \subseteq R \times S$ from which it is possible to derive the steps for which users are authorised. For all common access control policies (including R^2BAC), it is straightforward to derive A. We prefer to use A in order to simplify the exposition.

$\{t_1, t_2\}$, the constraint being satisfied provided t_1 and t_2 are assigned to different users.

A constraint (T, Θ) is said to be *user-independent* if, for every $\theta \in \Theta$ and every permutation $\phi : U \to U$, $\phi \circ \theta \in \Theta$, where

$$\phi \circ \theta : T \to U \quad \text{and} \quad (\phi \circ \theta)(s) \stackrel{\text{def}}{=} \phi(\theta(s)).$$

Simple separation-of-duty constraints are user-independent, and it appears most constraints that are useful in practice are user-independent [7]. In particular, cardinality constraints and binding-of-duty constraints are user-independent. In this paper, we restrict our experimental evaluation to two particular types of user-independent constraints (in addition to separation-of-duty constraints):

- an *at-least-r counting* constraint has the form (T, r), where $r \leqslant |T|$, and is satisfied provided at least r users are assigned to the steps in T;

- an *at-most-r counting* constraint has the form (T, r), where $r \leqslant |T|$, and is satisfied provided at most r users are assigned to the steps in T.

It is important to stress that our approach works for any user-independent constraints. We chose to use counting constraints because such constraints have been widely considered in the literature (often known as cardinality constraints). Moreover, counting constraints can be encoded using mixed integer programming, so we can use off-the-shelf solvers to solve WSP and to compare with the performance of our bespoke algorithms.

We now introduce the workflow satisfiability problem, as defined by Wang and Li [24].

WORKFLOW SATISFIABILITY PROBLEM (WSP)
Input: A constrained workflow authorisation schema $((S, E), U, A, C)$
Output: A valid $\pi : S \to U$ or an answer that there exists no valid plan

---

2.2 Fixed-Parameter Tractability of WSP

A naïve approach to solving WSP would consider every possible assignment of users to steps in the workflow. There are n^k such assignments if there are n users and k steps, so an algorithm of this form would have complexity $O(mn^k)$, where m is the number of constraints. Moreover, Wang and Li showed that WSP is NP-hard, by reducing GRAPH k-COLORABILITY to WSP with separation-of-duty constraints [24, Lemma 3].

The importance of finding an efficient algorithm for solving WSP led Wang and Li to look at the problem from the perspective of *parameterised complexity*. Suppose we have an algorithm that solves an NP-hard problem in time $O(f(k)n^d)$, where n denotes the size of the input to the problem, k is some (small) parameter of the problem, f is some function in k only, and d is some constant (independent of k and n). Then we say the algorithm is a *fixed-parameter tractable* (FPT) algorithm. If a problem can be solved using an FPT algorithm then we say that it is an *FPT problem* and that it belongs to the class FPT [14, 21].

Wang and Li observed that fixed-parameter algorithmics is an appropriate way to study the problem, because the number k of steps is usually small and often much smaller than the number n of users.[3] Wang and Li [24] proved that, in general, WSP is W[1]-hard and thus is highly unlikely to admit an FPT algorithm. However, WSP is FPT if we consider only separation-of-duty and binding-of-duty constraints [24]. Henceforth, we consider special families of constraints, but allow arbitrary authorisations. Crampton *et al.* [12] obtained significantly faster FPT algorithms that were applicable to "regular" constraints, thereby including the cases shown to be FPT by Wang and Li. Subsequent research has demonstrated the existence of FPT algorithms for WSP in the presence of other constraint types [9, 10]. Cohen *et al.* [7] introduced the class of user-independent constraints and showed that WSP remains FPT if only user-independent constraints are included. Note that every regular constraint is user-independent and all the constraints defined in the ANSI RBAC standard [1] are user-independent. Results of Cohen *et al.* [7] have led to algorithms which significantly outperform the widely used SAT-solver SAT4J on difficult instances of WSP with user-independent constraints [6, 18].

2.3 Valued WSP

There has been considerable interest in recent years in making the specification and enforcement of access control policies more flexible. Naturally, it is essential to continue to enforce effective access control policies. Equally, it is recognised that there may well be situations where a simple "allow" or "deny" decision for an access request may not be appropriate. It may be, for example, that the risks of refusing an unauthorised request are less significant than the benefits of allowing it. One obvious example occurs in healthcare systems, where the denial of an access request in an emergency situation could lead to loss of life. Hence, there has been increasing interest in context-aware policies, such as "break-the-glass", which allow different responses to requests in different situations. Risk-aware access control is another promising line of research that seeks to quantify the risk of allowing a request, where a decision of "0" might represent an unequivocal "deny" and "1" an unequivocal "allow", with decisions of intermediate values representing different levels of risk.

Similar considerations arise very naturally when we consider workflows. In particular, we may specify authorization policies and constraints that mean a workflow specification is unsatisfiable. Clearly, this is undesirable from a business perspective, since the business objective associated with the workflow can not be achieved. There are two possible ways of dealing with an unsatisfiable workflow specification:(i) modify the authorization policy and/or constraints; (ii) find the "least bad" complete plan. Prior work by Basin, Burri and Karjoth considered the former approach [2]. They restricted their attention to modification of the authorisation policy, what they called *administrable authorizations*. They assigned costs to modifying different aspects of a policy and then computed a strategy to modify the policy of minimal cost.

We adopt a different approach and consider minimising the cost of "breaking" the policies and/or constraints. (We will compare our approach to Basin *et al.* in the related work section.) Informally, given a workflow specification, for each

---

[3] The SMV loan origination workflow studied by Schaad *et al.*, for example, has 13 steps and identifies five roles [22]. It is generally assumed that the number of users is significantly greater than the number of roles.

plan π, we define the total cost or weight associated with the plan $w(\pi)$. The problem, then, is to find the complete plan with minimum total cost.

More formally, let $((S, E), U, A, C)$ be a constrained workflow authorization schema. Let Π denote the set of all possible plans from S to U. Then, for each $c \in C$, we define a weight function $w_c : \Pi \to \mathbb{Z}$, where

$$w_c(\pi) \begin{cases} = 0 & \text{if } \pi \text{ satisfies } c, \\ > 0 & \text{otherwise.} \end{cases}$$

The pair (c, w_c) is a *weighted constraint*.

The intuition is that $w_c(\pi)$ represents the extent to which π violates c. Consider, for example, an at-most-r counting constraint (T, r). Then $w_c(\pi)$ depends only on the number of users assigned to the steps in T (and the penalty should increase as the number of users increases). Let $\pi(T)$ denote the set of users assigned to steps in T. Then $w_c(\pi) = 0$ if $|\pi(T)| \leqslant r$; for plans π and π', we have $w_c(\pi) = w_c(\pi')$ if $|\pi(T)| = |\pi(T')|$; and $0 < w_c(\pi) \leq w_c(\pi')$ if $r < |\pi(T)| \leq |\pi'(T)|$. Similarly, for an at-least-r constraint c with scope T, we would have $w_c(\pi) = 0$ if $|\pi(T)| \geqslant r$; for plans π and π', we have $w_c(\pi) = w_c(\pi')$ if $|\pi(T)| = |\pi(T)|$; and $0 < w_c(\pi) \leq w_c(\pi')$ if $|\pi(T)| \geq |\pi'(T)| > 0$.

Then we define

$$w_C(\pi) = \sum_{c \in C} w_c(\pi),$$

which we call the *constraint weight* of π. Note that $w_C(\pi) = 0$ if and only if π satisfies all constraints in C. Note also that $w_C(\pi)$ need not be defined to be the linear sum: $w_C(\pi)$ may be defined to be an arbitrary function of the tuple $(w_c(\pi) : c \in C)$ and Theorem 1 below would still hold. However, we will not use this generalisation in this paper, but simply remark that it is possible, if needed.

We next introduce a function $w_A : \Pi \to \mathbb{Z}$, which assigns a cost for each plan with respect to the authorisation policy. The intuition is that a plan in which every user is authorised for the steps to which she is assigned has zero cost and the cost of a plan that violates the policy increases as the number of steps that are assigned to unauthorised users increases. More formally,

$$w_A(\pi) \begin{cases} = 0 & \text{if } (\pi(t), t) \in A \text{ for all } t, \\ > 0 & \text{otherwise} \end{cases}$$

is the *authorisation weight* of π.

The definition of w_A can be arbitrarily fine-grained. We could, for example, associate a weight $\omega(t, u)$ with every pair (t, u), where a zero weight indicates that u is authorised for t, and define

$$w_A(\pi) = \sum_{t \in T} \omega(t, \pi(t)).$$

One particularly simple instantiation of this idea is to define a single weight $\omega > 0$ to be associated with every policy violation. In this case, $w_A(\pi) = a\omega$, where a is the number of steps that are assigned to unauthorised users. Alternatively, we might distinguish between different types of users, so that, for example, assigning steps to external contractors is associated with a higher weight ω_e than the weight ω_i associated with assigning steps to (internal) unauthorised staff members.

We may now define the valued workflow satisfiability problem, which will be the subject of the remainder of the paper.

> VALUED WSP
> *Input:* A constrained workflow authorisation schema $((S, E), U, A, C)$ with weights for constraints and authorisations, as above.
> *Output:* A plan $\pi : S \to U$ that minimises $w(\pi) = w_C(\pi) + w_A(\pi)$.

Before proceeding further, however, we introduce a weight function that is more fine-grained than those considered above, and the one that we shall use in the remainder of this paper. Specifically, for each user u and each subset T of S, we define a weight $\omega(T, u) \in \mathbb{Z}$, where

$$\omega(T, u) \begin{cases} = 0 & \text{if } (u, t) \in A \text{ for all } t \in T, \\ > 0 & \text{otherwise.} \end{cases}$$

We call $\omega : 2^S \times U$ the *(weighted) set-authorisation* function. Vacuously, we have $\omega(\emptyset, u) = 0$ for all $u \in U$. We write $\pi^{-1}(u)$ to denote the set of steps to which u is assigned by plan π. Then we define

$$w_A(\pi) = \sum_{u \in U} \omega(\pi^{-1}(u), u).$$

Clearly, this form of authorisation weight satisfies the required criteria.

We base w_A on weights of the form $\omega(T, u)$ because, in addition to allowing us to specify weights for every pair (t, u) if required, it allows us to express more complex ("non-linear") costs on plans. For example:

1. We can introduce a large penalty $\omega(T, u)$, effectively saying we prefer not to involve u in steps in T. (We use weights like this in our experimental work, described in Section 4.)

2. We can define a limit ℓ on the number of steps that can be executed by u, by setting a large penalty $\omega(T, u)$ for all T of cardinality greater than ℓ.

3. We can attempt to minimise the number of involved users by giving a small penalty for assigning a user to at least one step. This is similar to item 1 above, albeit with a different goal.

4. The weights associated with the same user executing different steps may not increase linearly. Once a user has performed one particular unauthorized step, the additional cost of executing a *related* unauthorized step may be reduced, while the additional cost of executing an *unrelated* unauthorized step may be the same as the original cost. Our formulation enables us to model this kind of situation.

5. We can implement separation-of-duty on a per-user basis, which is not possible with user-independent constraints. In particular, it may be acceptable for u_1 to perform steps s_1 and s_2, but not u_2, in which case $\omega(\{s_1, s_2\}, u_1)$ would be small, while $\omega(\{s_1, s_2\}, u_2)$ would be large.

The next claim is an important observation following directly from the definitions above.

PROPOSITION 1. *The optimal weight of an instance of* VALUED WSP *equals zero if and only if the corresponding WSP instance is satisfiable.*

3. SOLVING VALUED WSP WITH USER-INDEPENDENT CONSTRAINTS

In Section 3.1 we introduce the notion of weighted user-independent constraints and prove that VALUED WSP with only user-independent constraints is fixed-parameter tractable (FPT). In Section 3.2, we describe an FPT algorithm to solve VALUED WSP with user-independent constraints.

3.1 Weighted User-Independent Constraints and Patterns

A weighted constraint c is called *user-independent* if, for every permutation θ of U, $w_C(\pi) = w_C(\theta \circ \pi)$. Thus, a weighted user-independent constraint does not distinguish between users. Any (weighted) counting constraint for which the weight of plan π is defined in terms of the cardinality of the image of π is user-independent.

Given a plan $\pi : S' \to U$, where $S' \subseteq S$, the *pattern* $P(\pi)$ of π is the partition $\{\pi^{-1}(u) : u \in U, \pi^{-1}(u) \neq \emptyset\}$ of S' into non-empty sets. We say that two plans π and π' are *equivalent* if they have the same pattern. If all constraints are user-independent and π and π' are equivalent, then $w_C(\pi) = w_C(\pi')$. A pattern is said to be *complete* if $S' = S$.

Generalising the corresponding result for WSP with user-independent constraints [7, Theorem 2], we can prove the following theorem, which uses weighted set-authorisation. The proof uses ideas from [7] and [18]. We assume (i) that the weight of each assignment can be computed in time polynomial in the number of steps, users and constraints (denoted k, n and m, respectively); (ii) we can determine whether a plan satisfies a constraint in time polynomial in the number of steps and users.

THEOREM 1. VALUED WSP *in which all constraints are user-independent can be solved in time* $2^{k \log k}(k+n+m)^{O(1)}$. *Thus,* VALUED WSP *with user-independent constraints is FPT.*

PROOF. For a positive integer x, let $[x] = \{1, \ldots, x\}$. Recall that for equivalent complete plans π and π', we have $w_C(\pi) = w_C(\pi')$. However, $w_A(\pi) = \sum_{u \in U} w_A(\pi^{-1}(u), u)$ is, in general, different from $w_A(\pi')$ and so we must compute the minimum value of $w_A(\pi)$ among all equivalent complete plans π. To do so efficiently, for a complete plan π, we first construct a weighted complete bipartite graph G_π with partite sets $[p]$ and U, where $p = |P(\pi)|$ as follows. Let $P(\pi) = \{T_1, \ldots, T_p\}$. The weight of an edge $\{q, u\}$ is $\sum_{s \in T_q} \omega(s, u)$.

Now observe that $G_{\pi'} = G_\pi$ for every pair π, π' of equivalent complete plans and that $w_A(\pi)$ equals the weight of the corresponding matching of G_π covering all vertices of $[p]$. Hence, it suffices to find such a matching of G_π of minimum weight, which can be done by the Hungarian method [19] in time $O(n^3)$.

Observe that the number of partitions of the set $[k]$ into non-empty subsets, called the Bell number B_k, is smaller than $k!$ and there are algorithms of running time $O(B_k) = O(2^{k \log k})$ to generate all partitions of $[k]$ [15]. Thus, we can generate all patterns in time $O(2^{k \log k})$. For each of them we compute the corresponding complete plan of minimum weight, and, among all such plans, we choose the one of smallest weight. The total running time is $O(2^{k \log k}(k+n+m)^{O(1)})$. $\square$

Cohen *et al.* proved [7] that WSP with user-independent constraints cannot be solved in time $2^{o(k \log k)}(k+n+m)^{O(1)}$, unless the widely believed Exponential Time Hypothesis[4] fails. This and Proposition 1 imply that the FPT algorithm of Theorem 1 is optimal, in a sense.

3.2 Pattern Branch and Bound

We present a branch-and-bound algorithm (Algorithm 1) for the VALUED WSP. This algorithm is inspired by the Pattern Backtracking algorithm for the WSP [18]. However, the original algorithm solves a decision problem, whereas the VALUED WSP is an optimisation problem. Thus our algorithm for VALUED WSP requires a completely different algorithmic framework. We call our algorithm for the VALUED WSP Pattern Branch and Bound (PBB). Given a pattern P, we will write $T(P) = \bigcup_{p \in P} p$ to denote the set $T \subseteq S$ on which P is the partition.

Algorithm 1: Entry point of the PBB algorithm.

input : VALUED WSP instance W
output : The optimal complete plan for W
1   $\lambda \leftarrow \lambda(W)$, where $\lambda(W)$ is the global lower bound;
2   $\pi \leftarrow H(W)$, where $H(W)$ is a VALUED WSP heuristic;
3   **return** $explore(\emptyset, \pi, \lambda)$;

Algorithm 2: Recursive procedure $explore(P, \pi^*, \lambda)$ of the PBB algorithm.

input : Node P of the search tree; best plan π^* found so far; the global lower bound λ
output : The best plan found after exploring this branch of search
1   **if** P *is a complete pattern* **then**
2   Let π' be an optimal plan with pattern P;
3     $\pi'' \leftarrow \arg\min_{\pi \in \{\pi', \pi^*\}} w(\pi)$;
4   **else**
5     $\pi'' \leftarrow \pi^*$;
6   Select $s \in S \setminus T(P)$ maximising $I(P, s)$;
7   **forall the** *extensions* P' *of* P *with step* s **do**
8   **if** $L(P') < w(\pi'')$ *and* $w(\pi'') > \lambda$ **then**
9   Let $\pi' \leftarrow explore(P', \pi'', \lambda)$;
10        $\pi'' \leftarrow \arg\min_{\pi \in \{\pi', \pi''\}} w(\pi)$;
11   **return** π'';

The general idea of the algorithm follows the proof of Theorem 1. The algorithm explores the space of patterns with a depth-first search and for each complete pattern P seeks an optimal plan π such that $P(\pi) = P$ (recall that such a plan can be found efficiently). Each node of the search tree is a pattern, with the root being an empty pattern and leaves being complete patterns. In each non-leaf node P, the algorithm selects a step $s \in S$ such that $s \notin T(P)$ (line 6 of Algorithm 2), and generates one child node for each possibility to extend P with s (line 10). By extensions of P with step s we mean patterns P' obtained from P by adding s to one of the subsets $p \in P$ or adding a new subset $\{s\}$ to the partition; hence, there are $|P| + 1$ extensions of P.

---

[4] The Exponential Time Hypothesis claims there is no algorithm of running time $O^*(2^{o(n)})$ for 3SAT on n variables [17].

Like any branch-and-bound algorithm, PBB utilises a lower bound $L(P)$ for pruning branches. The lower bound $L(P)$ in a node P is computed as follows:

$$L(P) = \sum_{c \in C} L_c(P) + \sum_{p \in P} \min_{u \in U} \omega(p, u),$$

where $L_c(P)$ is the lower bound of $w_c(\pi)$, where π is an extension of a plan with pattern P. The implementation of $L_c(P)$ depends on the constraint type. For example, for a counting constraint c with the scope T and weight function $w_c(\pi) = \omega_c(|\pi(T)|)$, the lower bound can be computed as $L_c(P) = l(q, a)$, where $q = |\{p \in P : p \cap T \neq \emptyset\}|$, $a = |T \cap T(P)|$ and $l(q, a)$ is the following recursive function:

$$l(q, a) = \begin{cases} \omega_c(q) & \text{if } a = |T|, \\ \min\{l(q, a + 1), l(q + 1, a + 1)\} & \text{otherwise.} \end{cases}$$

Other speed-ups implemented in the PBB algorithm include a global lower bound $\lambda(W)$ (line 1 of Algorithm 1) and the heuristic $H(W)$ to obtain a good upper bound from the very beginning of the search (line 2 of Algorithm 1). In a simple implementation, the global lower bound $\lambda(W)$ could be a constant function $\lambda(W) = 0$; that would terminate the algorithm as soon as a complete plan satisfying all the constraints and authorisations is found. The heuristic algorithm can be as simple as a trivial plan assigning some user to all the steps S.

In our implementation, however, we translate the VALUED WSP instance W into WSP instances and solve them to obtain better global lower bound and upper bound. Let $WSP(W, x)$ be a WSP instance obtained from W by eliminating all the constraints and authorisations with penalties below x and converting the rest of the constraints and authorisations into hard constraints. By solving $WSP(W, x)$ we establish either the global lower bound or the upper bound. If $WSP(W, x)$ is unsatisfiable, we conclude that there exists no complete plan π such that $w(\pi) < x$ and, hence, $\lambda(W) = x$. Otherwise, the plan valid in $WSP(W, x)$ can be used for an upper bound in W.

We start from solving the $WSP(W, 1)$ and, if it turns out to be unsatisfiable, we solve the $WSP(W, M)$, where M is a large enough number, which usually gives us a good upper bound as it rules out plans that break highly-penalised constraints. We solve the WSPs using an improved version of the WSP algorithm of [18].

The order in which patterns are extended (a step at a time) makes no difference to the worst-case time complexity of the algorithm but is crucial to its performance in practice [18]. It is defined by the 'importance' function $I(P, s)$, the intention being to focus on the most important steps as early as possible to quickly prune fruitless branches of the search. The importance of a step mostly depends on the constraints that include the step in their respective scopes. For example, if a step is involved in several separation-of-duty constraints, adding it to the pattern may significantly reduce the search space and possibly result in increased penalties for some at-most constraints. Another example is if most of the steps of some constraint's scope are assigned, and adding the remaining steps to the pattern may have a severe effect on the penalty for that constraint. The 'importance' metric is context-dependent, i.e. the order of steps needs to be determined dynamically in each branch of the search tree.

The 'importance' function $I(P, s)$ is a heuristic expression which we parametrised and optimised by an automated parameter tuning method. Our function $I(P, s)$ takes into account the number and types of the constraints in which the step is involved. In addition, it accounts for the constraints with incomplete scopes. Finally, we check intersections of 'conflicting' constraints such as at-most and not-equals or at-most and at-least.

As shown in the proof of Theorem 1, finding the optimal assignment of users given a fixed pattern can be done in $O(n^3)$ time (if computing $w_C(\pi)$ takes $O(n^3)$ time and computing $\omega(T, u)$ takes $O(n^3/k)$ time). Each non-leaf node of the search tree has at least two child nodes and, hence, the size of the search tree is within $O(B_k)$. Then the worst case time complexity of the PBB algorithm is $O(B_k n^3)$.

With the exception of the 'step importance' function $I(P, s)$, which is easy to adjust for any type of instances, and the lower bound $L(P)$, our algorithm is a generic solver for the user-independent VALUED WSP. For example, it does not exploit the specifics of the counting constraints which could be used to preprocess problem instances [7]. This shows that our approach is generic, easy to implement and its performance can be further improved by implementing instance-specific speed-ups.

4. EXPERIMENTAL RESULTS

The pseudo-Boolean SAT solver SAT4J has been used to solve the WSP [24]. Recent work has demonstrated that a bespoke pattern-based algorithm can outperform SAT4J in solving WSP [6, 18]. Integer linear programming has been used by Basin *et al.* to solve the *allocation existence problem* [2], which is related to VALUED WSP. In this section, we describe the experimental work on VALUED WSP that we have undertaken. In particular, we will compare the performance of our PBB algorithm to that of the state-of-art commercial MIP solver in our computational experiments on VALUED WSP. We first describe the problem instances we used and how we represented VALUED WSP as a mixed integer programming (MIP) problem. We then present the results of our experiments.

4.1 Benchmark Instances

We use a pseudo-random instance generator to produce benchmark instances. Our generator is an extension of an existing instance generator for WSP [18]. The parameters of the generator are the number k of steps in the instance, the not-equals constraints density d in the range 0–100%, the multiplier α for the number of constraints and the seed value for initialisation of the pseudo-random number generator. The generator produces an instance with k steps and $10k + 10$ users: $10k$ employees U' and 10 external consultants U''. The penalty for assigning steps $T \subseteq S$ to an employee $u \in U'$ is given by

$$\omega(T, u) = |T \cap B| \cdot 10 + |T \setminus (A \cup B)| \cdot 10^6,$$

where $A \subset S$ and $B \subset S$ are selected uniformly at random from S, with $A \cap B = \emptyset$ and $|A|$ being selected uniformly at random from $[1, \lceil (k - 4)/2 \rceil]$, and $|B| = 2$. The penalty for assigning steps $T \subseteq S$ to an external consultant $u \in U''$ is given by

$$\omega(T, u) = \begin{cases} 0 & \text{if } T = \emptyset, \\ 20 & \text{if } T \neq \emptyset \text{ and } T \subseteq A, \\ 10^6 \cdot |T \setminus A| & \text{if } T \subseteq S \setminus A, \\ 10^6 \cdot |T \setminus A| + 20 & \text{otherwise,} \end{cases}$$

where $A \subset S$ is selected uniformly at random having selected $|A|$ uniformly at random from $[1, \lceil k/4 \rceil]$.

Further, $\lfloor (dk(k-1) + 1)/2 \rfloor$ distinct not-equals constraints are produced uniformly at random, each with penalty 10^6 for assigning one user to both steps. Finally, αk at-most-3 constraints and αk at-least-3 constraints are generated uniformly at random. The scopes of all the at-most-3 and at-least-3 constraints are set to 5 steps. The at-least-3 penalties are defined as $\omega_c(1) = 10^6$, $\omega_c(2) = 1$, $\omega_c(3) = \omega_c(4) = \omega_c(5) = 0$. The at-most-3 penalties are defined as $\omega_c(1) = \omega_c(2) = \omega_c(3) = 0$, $\omega_c(4) = 5$ and $\omega_c(5) = 10$.

The source code of our instance generator can be found at [11].

4.2 Mixed Integer Programming Formulation

In order to use an MIP solver, we propose an efficient MIP formulation of the VALUED WSP. Note that the MIP formulation is specific to the particular constraints present in the instances, unlike the PBB algorithm. In this section we describe an MIP formulation for the instances described in Section 4.1.

Let $C = C_{\leq} \cup C_{\geq}$, where $C_{\leq}$ is the set of at-most-r constraints and $C_{\geq}$ is the set of at-least-r constraints. (Note that not-equals constraints can be modelled as at-least-2 constraints with the scope of two steps.) For each constraint $c \in C$ we are given its scope $T_c \subseteq S$, the minimum (maximum, respectively) number r_c of users that can be assigned to $c \in C$ such that the at-most (at-least, respectively) constraint c is satisfied and the penalty $\omega_c(q)$ for assigning q distinct users to T_c (note that $\omega_c(r_c) = 0$).

For each employee $u \in U'$ and each step $s \in S \setminus A(u)$ we are given an additive weight $\omega_{su} > 0$ of assigning u to s, which models the penalties for steps in both $B(u)$ and $S \setminus (A(u) \cup B(u))$. For each consultant $u \in U''$ we are given a set of steps $A(u) \subseteq S$, any of which can be assigned to u for a penalty $\omega_u > 0$, and a weight $\Omega_u > 0$ for assigning a step $s \in S \setminus A(u)$ to u.

The complete plan in our formulation is defined by binary decision variables x_{su}, $s \in S$, $u \in U$. Variable x_{su} takes value 1 if step s is assigned to user u and 0 otherwise. The VALUED WSP is then encoded in (1)–(14):

$$\begin{aligned} \text{minimise} \quad & \sum_{c \in C_{\leq}} \sum_{q=r_c+1}^{|T_c|} (\omega_c(q) - \omega_c(q-1)) p_{cq} \\ & + \sum_{c \in C_{\geq}} \sum_{q=1}^{r_c-1} (\omega_c(q) - \omega_c(q+1)) p_{cq} \\ & + \sum_{u \in U'} \sum_{s \in S \setminus A(u)} \omega_{su} x_{su} \\ & + \sum_{u \in U''} \omega_u z_u + \sum_{u \in U''} \Omega_u \sum_{s \in S \setminus A(u)} x_{su} \end{aligned} \quad (1)$$

subject to

$$\sum_{u \in U} x_{su} = 1 \text{ for } s \in S, \quad (2)$$

$$\sum_{u \in U} y_{cu} - \sum_{q=r_c+1}^{|T_c|} p_{cq} \leq r_c \text{ for each } c \in C_{\leq}, \quad (3)$$

$$p_{cq} - p_{c,q+1} \geq 0 \text{ for } c \in C_{\leq} \text{ and } q = r_c+1, \ldots, |T_c| - 1, \quad (4)$$

$$\sum_{u \in U} y_{cu} + \sum_{q=1}^{r_c-1} p_{cq} \geq r_c \text{ for each } c \in C_{\geq}, \quad (5)$$

$$p_{cq} - p_{c,q+1} \leq 0 \text{ for } c \in C_{\geq} \text{ and } q = 1, 2, \ldots, r_c - 2, \quad (6)$$

$$y_{cu} - x_{su} \geq 0 \text{ for each } c \in C_{\leq}, \ u \in U \text{ and } s \in T_c, \quad (7)$$

$$y_{cu} - \sum_{s \in T_c} x_{su} \leq 0 \text{ for each } c \in C_{\geq} \text{ and } u \in U, \quad (8)$$

$$z_u - x_{su} \geq 0 \text{ for each } u \in U'' \text{ and } s \in A(u), \quad (9)$$

$$x_{su} \in \{0, 1\} \text{ for } s \in S \text{ and } u \in U, \quad (10)$$

$$0 \leq y_{cu} \leq 1 \text{ for } c \in C \text{ and } u \in U, \quad (11)$$

$$p_{cq} \in \{0, 1\} \text{ for } c \in C_{\leq} \text{ and } q = r_c+1, \ldots, |T_c|, \quad (12)$$

$$p_{cq} \in \{0, 1\} \text{ for } c \in C_{\geq} \text{ and } q = 1, 2, \ldots, r_c - 1, \quad (13)$$

$$0 \leq z_u \leq 1 \text{ for } u \in U''. \quad (14)$$

In addition to binary variables x_{su}, we introduce some other variables. Binary variables y_{cu}, $c \in C$, $u \in U$ determine if user u is assigned to some steps in the scope T_c of constraint c. Since y_{cu} for $c \in C_{\leq}$ is minimised and it is limited from below by binary expressions (7), its integrality constraint can be waived. Since y_{cu} for $c \in C_{\geq}$ is maximised and it is limited from above by binary expressions (8), its integrality constraint can also be waived. Similar logic applies to z_u, which indicates if the consultant $u \in U''$ is assigned any steps in $B(u)$. Finally, we introduce the binary variables p_{cq} for each $c \in C$ and $q \in \mathbb{N}$ such that $w_c(q) > 0$. These variables are responsible for the constraint penalties and (with appropriate limitations imposed on the instances, as our instance generator does) the integrality of p_{cq} and constraints (4) and (6) can be waived.

The objective function (1) is the weight of the plan defined by x_{su}, and thus our aim is to minimise it.

4.3 Experimental Results

We conducted a series of computational experiments to test the performance of the VALUED WSP solution methods. Our test machine is powered by two Intel Xeon CPU's E5-2630 v2 (2.6 GHz) and has 32 GB RAM installed. The PBB algorithm is implemented in C#, and the MIP formulation is solved with CPLEX 12.6. The source code of our implementation of the Pattern Branch and Bound algorithm can be found at [11]. In all our experiments, each solver run is allocated exactly one physical CPU core. Each result is reported as an average over 100 runs for 100 instances obtained by changing the random generator seed value.

Main computational results are reported in Table 1. The columns k, d and α indicate the parameters of the instances. For each combination of parameters, 100 instances were generated. The column "Sat." reports the percentage of the instances that are satisfiable. The column $w(\pi)$ shows the average weight of the optimal complete plans. The other columns compare the MIP-based solver to the PBB algo-

9

k	d	α	Sat.	w(π)	Solved		Time, sec		$w_C(\pi)$		$w_A(\pi)$		Best $w(\pi)$	
					PBB	MIP	PBB	MIP	PBB	MIP	PBB	MIP	PBB	MIP
20	10%	0.50	100%	0.0	100%	100%	0.0	5.9	0.0	0.0	0.0	0.0	—	—
20	20%	0.50	90%	0.4	100%	100%	0.0	19.8	0.4	0.4	0.2	0.0	—	—
20	30%	0.50	37%	4.0	100%	100%	0.0	65.0	3.8	4.0	0.2	0.0	—	—
20	10%	1.00	18%	4.4	100%	100%	0.1	556.0	4.3	4.2	0.1	0.2	—	—
20	20%	1.00	0%	14.2	100%	100%	0.1	532.9	13.5	13.8	0.7	0.4	—	—
20	30%	1.00	0%	24.3	100%	100%	0.1	469.9	23.4	23.5	0.9	0.8	—	—
25	10%	0.50	100%	0.0	100%	100%	0.0	32.0	0.0	0.0	0.0	0.0	—	—
25	20%	0.50	93%	0.4	100%	100%	0.0	102.2	0.4	0.4	0.0	0.0	—	—
25	30%	0.50	27%	5.0	100%	100%	0.0	319.3	5.0	5.0	0.0	0.0	—	—
25	10%	1.00	40%	2.3	100%	39%	0.3	?	2.3	?	0.0	?	—	4.1
25	20%	1.00	0%	14.3	100%	66%	0.8	?	13.7	?	0.6	?	—	14.9
25	30%	1.00	0%	29.9	100%	95%	2.0	?	28.9	?	1.0	?	—	29.9
30	10%	0.50	100%	0.0	100%	100%	0.0	72.2	0.0	0.0	0.0	0.0	—	—
30	20%	0.50	88%	0.6	100%	99%	0.0	?	0.6	?	0.0	?	—	0.6
30	30%	0.50	24%	5.7	100%	99%	0.1	?	5.7	?	0.0	?	—	5.7
30	10%	1.00	6%	5.8	100%	3%	5.1	?	5.7	?	0.1	?	—	14.9
30	20%	1.00	0%	22.8	100%	7%	36.3	?	22.4	?	0.4	?	—	31.5
30	30%	1.00	0%	43.5	100%	31%	173.7	?	43.2	?	0.3	?	—	52.8
35	10%	0.50	100%	0.0	100%	100%	0.0	195.9	0.0	0.0	0.0	0.0	—	—
35	20%	0.50	91%	0.4	100%	89%	0.2	?	0.4	?	0.0	?	—	0.6
35	30%	0.50	13%	7.7	100%	68%	18.5	?	7.7	?	0.0	?	—	8.0
35	10%	1.00	3%	6.2	100%	0%	64.7	?	6.2	?	0.0	?	—	33.5
35	20%	1.00	?	?	92%	0%	?	?	?	?	?	?	29.6	130071.1
35	30%	1.00	?	?	48%	0%	?	?	?	?	?	?	60.1	2990104.6

Table 1: Comparison of the PBB and MIP solvers, each being given one hour per instance A question mark shows that at least one of the runs failed for the MIP solver.

rithm. Each of them is given one hour for each instance. The "Solved" columns show the percentage of instances successfully solved within the one hour limit by each of the solvers. The "Time, sec" columns show the average time taken by each of the approaches. If at least one of the runs failed for a solver, a question mark is shown in the corresponding cell of the table. The $w_C(\pi)$ and $w_A(\pi)$ columns show the components of the weight corresponding to the constraints and the authorisations penalties, respectively. For those parameters where at least one of the runs failed, we use the "Best $w(\pi)$" columns to to report the average weight of the best plan obtained by each of the solvers.

For each k, Table 1 includes a range of instances starting from lightly constrained instances, which are mostly satisfiable, to highly constrained instances, none of which is satisfiable. Naturally, the most interesting instances from the perspective of VALUED WSP are those that are unsatisfiable (since it is necessary to find an optimal plan of non-zero weight for such instances). We are most interested in the unsatisfiable instances with moderate weights of the optimal complete plans. A small weight $w(\pi)$ indicates that only a few minor exceptions are needed to implement the complete plan π. With such a plan, it is easy to identify the bottleneck of the problem and refine it or accept the exceptions to the constraints as the exceptions are likely to be mild. The $w_C(\pi)$ and $w_A(\pi)$ columns show that in most of the cases the authorisations were not broken. In fact, there were only a few highly-constrained instances in which the the optimal complete plans assigned some steps to consul-

tants, as the penalty for doing that is relatively high in our instances.

The complexity of the instances depends to a great extent on the number of steps k and the parameters of the instances. While small lightly-constrained instances can be easily tackled by either of the solvers, other instances clearly require an efficient algorithm. The MIP solver succeeds with all the instances of size $k = 20$ but fails to solve many of the larger instances within an hour. The PBB algorithm demonstrates a much better performance, solving all the instances of size up to $k = 30$ and the majority of the instances of size $k = 35$. It is worth noting that the running time of the MIP solver can reach 10 minutes for $k = 20$ while the PBB solver solves all such instances within a fraction of a second.

Exact algorithms for solving hard optimisation problems will, necessarily, take a long time to compute results for certain instances. However, such an algorithm may find an optimum or near-optimum result long before the whole solution space has been searched and can thus be used to compute a reasonable solution for instances that do not run to completion. The Best $w(\pi)$ column in Table 1 clearly shows that MIP is far less suitable than PBB for this purpose.

To establish the practical limit on the problem size that each of the solvers can tackle within a reasonable time, we conducted another experiment to determine the number of instances that the two solvers could solve given at most one hour for each instance. Figure 1 shows the results of the experiment. Each result is averaged over 100 experiments for each instance.

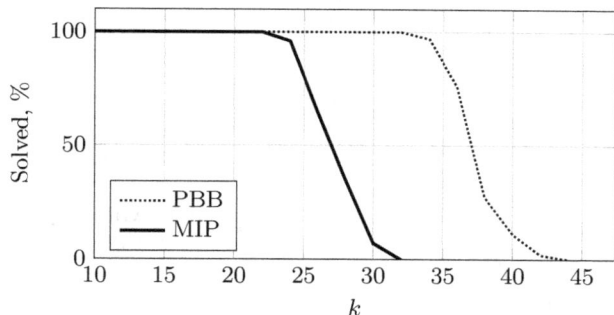

(a) $d = 20\%$ and $\alpha = 1.00$ (b) $d = 10\%$ and $\alpha = 0.75$

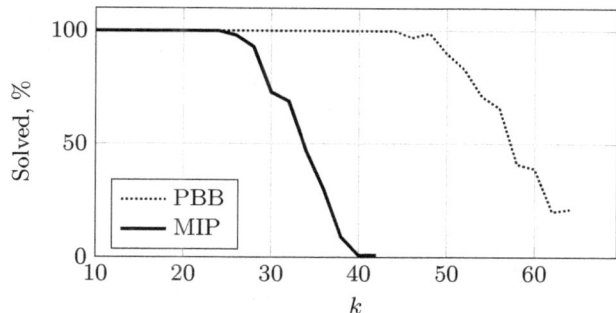

Figure 1: Comparison of the methods in terms of the ability to solve an instance within one hour

Figure 1a shows the performance of the methods on highly constrained instances. Being given one hour, PBB solves 100% of the instances of size up to $k = 32$. In contrast, MIP can only reliably manage instances for $k \leq 22$, and for $k = 32$ it fails to solve any instances at all. Figure 1b reports the results of the same experiment but for less constrained instances. The results are broadly similar, with PBB solving all the instances of up to $k = 44$, whereas MIP fails for some instances when $k > 24$. This experiment shows that the PBB algorithm significantly extends the range of solvable instances of VALUED WSP, something that will be important for large real-world workflow specifications. Considering that the running time of each of the methods grows exponentially with the size of the problem, large instances of VALUED WSP would require enormous computational power to be solved with MIP, while the PBB algorithm tackles them within minutes on a regular machine.

5. RELATED WORK

Recent work on workflow satisfiability has borrowed techniques from the literature on constraint satisfaction [7]. Indeed, WSP may be regarded as a constraint satisfaction problem, albeit with some unusual features which makes the study of WSP of interest in its own right. Recent work in the constraint satisfaction community has made a distinction between "hard" and "soft" constraints: the former must be satisfied, while the latter may be broken provided the "cost" of breaking the constraint is taken into account.

The *valued constraint satisfaction problem*, or VCSP for short, was introduced by Schiex, Fargier and Verfaillie [23] as a unifying framework for studying constraint programming with soft constraints. The study of a special case of VCSP, called *finite-valued* VCSP, was initiated by Cohen *et al.* [8]. In this case, useful for many applications, all weights are in $\mathbb{Z}$ (i.e., finite) and the objective function is the sum of appropriate weights. Valued CSP has influenced our framework for defining costs and VALUED WSP.

Recent work on WSP introduced the notion of a pattern for user-independent constraints, and bespoke algorithms, optimised to solve WSP using patterns, have been developed [7, 18]. The branch-and-bound algorithm in Section 3.2 is influenced by the work of Karapetyan, Gagarin and Gutin [18].

The most closely related work in the literature on access control in workflows is that of Basin, Burri and Karjoth [2], which considers the cost of modifying the authorisation pol-

icy when the workflow is unsatisfiable. They encode the problem of minimizing this cost as a integer linear programming problem and use off-the-shelf software to solve the resulting problem. We tackle the problem of an unsatisfiable workflow specification in a different way. We assume the constraints and authorisation policy are fixed and instead associate costs with breaking the constraints and/or policies. However, each violation will incur a cost and the goal of VALUED WSP is to minimise that cost. Thus our approach provides greater flexibility than that of Basin *et al.*: we can break constraints as well as override the existing authorisation policy. Obviously, there may be constraints (arising from statutory requirements, say) that cannot be broken. Violation of such a constraint is simply assigned the maximum cost. And of course, we can always refuse to implement a plan proposed by the algorithm.

Our work is also related to the growing body of research on risk-based and risk-aware access control [4, 5, 13, 20]. In such approaches, the decision returned by policy decision point for a given access request is not necessarily a simple "allow" or "deny". The decision may be a number in the range $[0, 1]$ indicating the risk associated with allowing the request, which allows the policy enforcement point to allow or deny the request on the basis of cumulative risk (either on a per-user or system basis). The decision may also include an obligation that must be fulfilled by the policy enforcement point or requester to ensure that the risk is recorded and/or mitigated appropriately.

There is little work in the security literature on risk-aware workflows. One exception is the MRARD framework of Han, Ni and Chen [16]. However, the emphasis of their work (and of similar work in the business processing literature) is on the modelling and computation of risk, rather than determining an optimal assignment of users to steps in a workflow given the risk metrics.

6. CONCLUDING REMARKS

We have established a framework that enables us to reason about unsatisfiable workflow specifications by associating costs with policy and constraint violations. This, in turn, enables us to formulate the VALUED WSP, whose solution provides an assignment of users to steps that minimises the total cost of violations. We have developed a bespoke algorithm for solving VALUED WSP and shown that its performance is far better than a generic solver, both in terms of the time taken to solve VALUED WSP and the range of instances that can be solved in a reasonable amount of time.

There are several interesting possibilities for future work. One obvious possibility is to move to a completely risk-based approach for the assignment of users to steps in workflows. Specifically, we retain the constraints but replace the authorisation policy with a risk matrix, associating each user-step pair with a risk. The goal would be to ensure that the risk associated with a workflow instance remains below some specified threshold.

A second possibility arises from the idea of associating each pair (T, u) with a cost, which provides the basis for an alternative "non-linear" approach to access control. Suppose that we consider a set of permissions P, as in conventional role-based access control, and we associate a cost $\omega(Q, u)$ with each pair, where u is a user and Q is a subset of P. Given an RBAC policy, expressed as a user-role relation $UA \subseteq U \times R$ and permission-role relation $PA \subseteq R \times P$, we write $P(u)$ to denote the set of permissions for which u is authorised: that is, $P(u) = \{p \in P : \exists r \in R, (u, r) \in UA, (r, p) \in PA\}$. Then we define the weight of the policy to be

$$w_A(UA, PA) = \sum_{u \in U} \omega(P(u), u).$$

This then raises some interesting questions that may have practical value. We might, for example, consider the following problem: given inputs U, P, $\{\omega(Q, u) : u \in U, Q \subseteq P\}$ and integer k, compute a set of roles of R of cardinality k and relations $UA \subseteq U \times R$ and $PA \subseteq R \times P$ such that at least one user is authorised for every permission and $w_A(UA, PA)$ is minimised. Alternatively, we may insist that a user session does not exceed a "budget", where the cost of a session in which user u invokes permissions Q is defined to be $\omega(Q, u)$.

7. ACKNOWLEDGMENTS

This research was partially supported by EPSRC grants EP/H000968/1 (for DK) and EP/K005162/1 (for JC and GG) and by Royal Society Wolfson Research Merit Award (for GG). The source codes of the algorithm and the instance generator are publicly available at [11].

8. REFERENCES

[1] American National Standards Institute. *ANSI INCITS 359-2004 for Role Based Access Control*, 2004.

[2] D. A. Basin, S. J. Burri, and G. Karjoth. Optimal workflow-aware authorizations. In V. Atluri, J. Vaidya, A. Kern, and M. Kantarcioglu, editors, *17th ACM Symposium on Access Control Models and Technologies, SACMAT'12, Newark, NJ, USA – June 20–22, 2012*, pages 93–102. ACM, 2012.

[3] D. F. C. Brewer and M. J. Nash. The Chinese Wall security policy. In *IEEE Symposium on Security and Privacy*, pages 206–214. IEEE Computer Society, 1989.

[4] L. Chen and J. Crampton. Risk-aware role-based access control. In C. Meadows and M. C. F. Gago, editors, *Security and Trust Management - 7th International Workshop, STM 2011, Copenhagen, Denmark, June 27–28, 2011, Revised Selected Papers*, volume 7170 of *Lecture Notes in Computer Science*, pages 140–156. Springer, 2011.

[5] P. Cheng, P. Rohatgi, C. Keser, P. A. Karger, G. M. Wagner, and A. S. Reninger. Fuzzy multi-level security: An experiment on quantified risk-adaptive access control. In *2007 IEEE Symposium on Security and Privacy (S&P 2007), 20–23 May 2007, Oakland, California, USA*, pages 222–230. IEEE Computer Society, 2007.

[6] D. Cohen, J. Crampton, A. Gagarin, G. Gutin, and M. Jones. Engineering algorithms for workflow satisfiability problem with user-independent constraints. In J. Chen, J. Hopcroft, and J. Wang, editors, *Frontiers in Algorithmics, FAW 2014*, volume 8497 of *Lecture Notes in Computer Science*, pages 48–59. Springer, 2014.

[7] D. Cohen, J. Crampton, A. Gagarin, G. Gutin, and M. Jones. Iterative plan construction for the workflow satisfiability problem. *J. Artif. Intel. Res.*, 51:555–577, 2014.

[8] D. A. Cohen, M. C. Cooper, P. G. Jeavons, and A. A. Krokhin. The complexity of soft constraint satisfaction. *Artif. Intell.*, 170(11):983–1016, Aug. 2006.

[9] J. Crampton, R. Crowston, G. Gutin, M. Jones, and M. S. Ramanujan. Fixed-parameter tractability of workflow satisfiability in the presence of seniority constraints. In M. R. Fellows, X. Tan, and B. Zhu, editors, *FAW-AAIM*, volume 7924 of *Lecture Notes in Computer Science*, pages 198–209. Springer, 2013.

[10] J. Crampton and G. Gutin. Constraint expressions and workflow satisfiability. In M. Conti, J. Vaidya, and A. Schaad, editors, *SACMAT*, pages 73–84. ACM, 2013.

[11] J. Crampton, G. Gutin, and D. Karapetyan. Source codes of the pattern branch and bound algorithm for the valued workflow satisfiability problem. DOI:10.6084/m9.figshare.1367470 retrieved 5 April 2015.

[12] J. Crampton, G. Gutin, and A. Yeo. On the parameterized complexity and kernelization of the workflow satisfiability problem. *ACM Trans. Inf. Syst. Secur.*, 16(1):4, 2013.

[13] N. Dimmock, A. Belokosztolszki, D. M. Eyers, J. Bacon, and K. Moody. Using trust and risk in role-based access control policies. In T. Jaeger and E. Ferrari, editors, *SACMAT 2004, 9th ACM Symposium on Access Control Models and Technologies, Yorktown Heights, New York, USA, June 2–4, 2004, Proceedings*, pages 156–162. ACM, 2004.

[14] R. G. Downey and M. R. Fellows. *Parameterized Complexity*. Springer Verlag, 1999.

[15] M. Er. A fast algorithm for generation set partitions. *The Computer Journal*, 31:283–284, 1988.

[16] W. Han, Q. Ni, and H. Chen. Apply measurable risk to strengthen security of a role-based delegation supporting workflow system. In *POLICY 2009, IEEE International Symposium on Policies for Distributed Systems and Networks, London, UK, 20–22 July 2009*, pages 45–52. IEEE Computer Society, 2009.

[17] R. Impagliazzo, R. Paturi, and F. Zane. Which problems have strongly exponential complexity? *J. Comput. Syst. Sci.*, 63(4):512–530, 2001.

[18] D. Karapetyan, A. Gagarin, and G. Gutin. Pattern backtracking algorithm for the workflow satisfiability problem. In *Frontiers in Algorithmics, FAW 2015*, volume to appear of *Lecture Notes in Computer Science*. Springer, 2015.

[19] H. W. Kuhn. The Hungarian method for the assignment problem. *Naval Research Logistics Quarterly*, 2(1-2):83–97, 1955.

[20] Q. Ni, E. Bertino, and J. Lobo. Risk-based access control systems built on fuzzy inferences. In D. Feng, D. A. Basin, and P. Liu, editors, *Proceedings of the 5th ACM Symposium on Information, Computer and Communications Security, ASIACCS 2010, Beijing, China, April 13–16, 2010*, pages 250–260. ACM, 2010.

[21] R. Niedermeier. *Invitation to Fixed-Parameter Algorithms*. Oxford University Press, 2006.

[22] A. Schaad, V. Lotz, and K. Sohr. A model-checking approach to analysing organisational controls in a loan origination process. In D. F. Ferraiolo and I. Ray, editors, *SACMAT 2006, 11th ACM Symposium on Access Control Models and Technologies, Lake Tahoe, California, USA, June 7–9, 2006, Proceedings*, pages 139–149. ACM, 2006.

[23] T. Schiex, H. Fargier, and G. Verfaillie. Valued constraint satisfaction problems: Hard and easy problems. In *Proceedings of the 14th International Joint Conference on Artificial Intelligence – Volume 1*, IJCAI'95, pages 631–637, San Francisco, CA, USA, 1995. Morgan Kaufmann Publishers Inc.

[24] Q. Wang and N. Li. Satisfiability and resiliency in workflow authorization systems. *ACM Trans. Inf. Syst. Secur.*, 13(4):40, 2010.

Mohawk+T: Efficient Analysis of Administrative Temporal Role-Based Access Control (ATRBAC) Policies

Jonathan Shahen
University of Waterloo
jmshahen@uwaterloo.ca

Jianwei Niu
University of Texas at San Antonio
niu@cs.utsa.edu

Mahesh Tripunitara
University of Waterloo
tripunit@uwaterloo.ca

ABSTRACT

Safety analysis is recognized as a fundamental problem in access control. It has been studied for various access control schemes in the literature. Recent work has proposed an administrative model for Temporal Role-Based Access Control (TRBAC) policies called Administrative TRBAC (ATRBAC). We address ATRBAC-safety. We first identify that the problem is **PSPACE**-complete. This is a much tighter identification of the computational complexity of the problem than prior work, which shows only that the problem is decidable. With this result as the basis, we propose an approach that leverages an existing open-source software tool called Mohawk to address ATRBAC-safety. Our approach is to efficiently reduce ATRBAC-safety to ARBAC-safety, and then use Mohawk. We have conducted a thorough empirical assessment. In the course of our assessment, we came up with a "reduction toolkit," which allows us to reduce Mohawk+T input instances to instances that existing tools support. Our results suggest that there are some input classes for which Mohawk+T outperforms existing tools, and others for which existing tools outperform Mohawk+T. The source code for Mohawk+T is available for public download.

Categories and Subject Descriptors

D.4.6 [**Operating Systems**]: Security and Protection—*Access controls*; D.2.4 [**Software Engineering**]: Software/Program Verification

General Terms

Security, Verification

Keywords

Role-Based Access Control; Administration; Temporal; Safety Analysis

1. INTRODUCTION

Access control deals with whether a principal, such as a user, may exercise a privilege, such as read or write, on a resource, such as a file. It is an important aspect of the security of a system. Whether an attempted access is permitted is customarily specified in a policy.

Effecting and intuiting the consequences of changes to an access control policy is called administration. An aspect of administration is delegation, with which a trusted administrator empowers another principal to change the policy in limited ways. Delegation is used so administrative efficiency can scale with the size of an access control system.

With delegation arises the need for safety analysis, which has been recognized as a fundamental problem in access control since the work of Harrison et al. [3]. The safety analysis problem takes three inputs: (1) a start-state, which is an instance of an access control policy, (2) a state-change rule, which is the set of administrative rules by which a policy can change, and, (3) a query, typically whether a particular user has a particular privilege.

The output is 'true' if the query can never become true, and 'false' otherwise. That is, the system is deemed to be unsafe if there exists a reachable state in which the user indeed has the privilege. The reason is that the user's acquisition of the privilege is presumably undesirable.

Safety analysis has been addressed for various access control schemes in the literature. Our focus is safety analysis in the context of Administrative Temporal Role-Based Access Control (ATRBAC) [12]. ATRBAC is an administrative scheme for Temporal Role-Based Access Control (TRBAC). TRBAC is Role-Based Access Control (RBAC) with temporal-extensions. In RBAC, rather than assigning a user directly to a permission, we adopt the indirection of a role. A user is authorized to a role, which in turn is authorized to a permission. In TRBAC, a user's authorization to a role is tempered by time-intervals during which the authorization is valid.

Furthermore, in TRBAC, a role may be annotated with time-intervals. The role is then said to be active during those time-intervals. A user is able to exercise permissions she acquires via a role when the role is active only.

In Figure 1, we show an example of an TRBAC policy. It can be seen as an example of an RBAC policy by simply ignoring the references to time periods such as "5 am – 8 pm." We show also an instances of administrative rules in ARBAC and ATRBAC. We discuss ATRBAC more precisely in Section 2.1. ATRBAC is an extension of Administrative RBAC (ARBAC) [7]. ARBAC is used to administer RBAC,

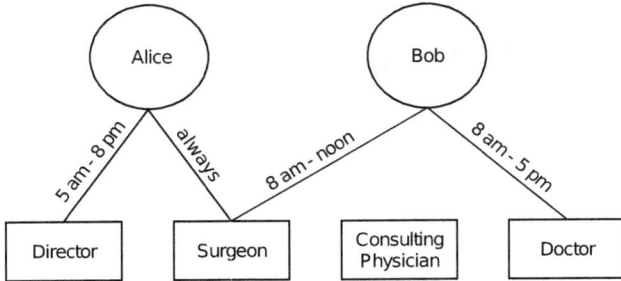

ARBAC rules:
can_assign:
⟨Director, Surgeon ∧ ¬Doctor, Consulting Physician⟩
can_revoke:
⟨Director, Doctor⟩

ATRBAC rules:
t_can_assign:
⟨Director, 8 am − 9 am, Surgeon ∧ ¬Doctor,
8 am − noon, Consulting Physician⟩
t_can_revoke:
⟨Director, 8 am − 9 am, true, 8 am − noon, Doctor⟩
t_can_enable:
⟨true, 6 am − 8 am, true, 8 am − 5 pm, Director⟩
t_can_disable is empty

Figure 1: An example of the *TUA* component of a TRBAC policy is to the left. We assume that no role is enabled. Ignoring the time periods on the edges gives us an example of the *UA* component of an RBAC policy. Example ARBAC and ATRBAC administrative rules are to the right. Figures 2 and 3 contain examples of safety queries.

i.e., without any temporal extensions. ATRBAC specifies how two components of a TRBAC access control policy can change: (1) the temporal assignment of a user to a role, and, (2) the temporal activation of a role.

In the example in Figure 1, as the caption for the figure says, with the RBAC policy in the figure as the start-state, the ARBAC safety query, "could Bob become a member of Consulting Physician?" is true. However, the safety query, "could Bob simultaneously be a member of Consulting Physician and Doctor?" is false.

Also, for the example in Figure 1, with the TRBAC policy as the start-state, the ATRBAC-safety query, "could Bob become a member of Consulting Physician between 8 am and noon?" is true. The sequence of actions that must occur for that query to become true, however, is somewhat different from the ARBAC case. In particular, the Director role must first be enabled, as the *t_can_assign* and *t_can_revoke* rules that must be exercised to make that query true have Director as the administrative role.

Prior work There is considerable prior work on safety analysis in various contexts. See, for example, the work of Harrison et al. [3]. It is beyond the scope of this paper to discuss all of those pieces of work. We are aware of two pieces of prior work on ATRBAC-safety. The work of Uzun et al. [12] is, to our knowledge, the first work to propose ATRBAC and pose the safety-analysis problem for it. In addition, that work discusses the design of two software tools, TREDROLE and TREDRULE to address instances in practice.

The work of Ranise et al. [6] syntactically generalizes some aspects of the version of ATRBAC from Uzun et al. [12]. It then presents a result on the computational-complexity of ATRBAC-safety — it proves that the problem is decidable. It then discusses the design, construction and evaluation of a different software tool, ASASPTIME, to address problem instances in practice.

Our work We make both theoretical and practical contributions in the context of ATRBAC-safety. We observe that prior work refers to a number of different versions of ATRBAC-safety. We carefully distinguish the various versions. This is important to validate prior claims regarding

the non-existence of an efficient reduction from one version to another, and for a meaningful empirical assessment. For our theoretical analysis, for each feature of the problem, we adopt the more general form across the two versions from prior work [6, 12].

Our main theoretical result is a much tighter identification of the complexity-class in which ATRBAC-safety lies than prior work — we show that it is **PSPACE**-complete. **PSPACE** is the class of decision problems that can be solved by a (deterministic) Turing machine given space only polynomial in the size of the input.

We show the upper-bound, i.e., that the problem is in **PSPACE**, by constructing a non-deterministic Turing machine that decides instances and uses space only polynomial in the size of the input, and then leveraging the corollary to Savitch's theorem that **NSPACE** = **PSPACE** [9]. **NSPACE** is the class of decision problems that can be solved by a non-deterministic Turing machine given space only polynomial in the size of the input. We infer the lower-bound, i.e., that the problem is **PSPACE**-hard, by observing that ATRBAC generalizes ARBAC, and user-role safety in ARBAC is known to be **PSPACE**-hard [5].

Our result that ATRBAC-safety is **PSPACE**-complete is also of practical consequence. It immediately suggests to us an approach that we can use for instances that arise in practice — model-checking that is complete for **PSPACE**. Mohawk [4] is an open-source tool for ARBAC-safety that leverages a state of the art model checker, and has additional features that are customized for the ARBAC-safety problem. As ARBAC-safety is **PSPACE**-hard and ATRBAC-safety is in **PSPACE**, we know that there exists an efficient, i.e., polynomial-time, reduction from the latter to the former.

Mohawk has been shown to scale to problem-instances that comprise tens of thousands of roles and hundreds of thousands of administrative rules. A thesis we seek to validate empirically is that Mohawk can be extended via an efficient reduction from ATRBAC-safety to ARBAC-safety to address ATRBAC-safety with scalability similar to what it demonstrates for ARBAC-safety instances. We call the tool that we have constructed in this manner, Mohawk+T. The version of ATRBAC-safety that Mohawk+T supports is the most general for each feature across the different tools

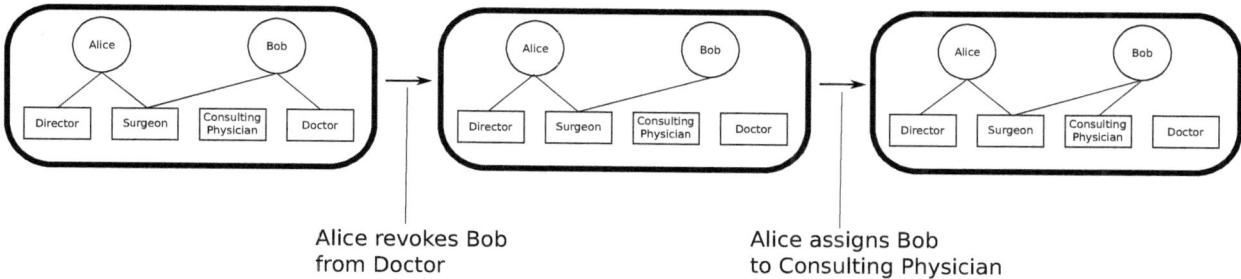

Figure 2: An ARBAC safety query for the example in Figure 1. We ignore the labels on edges that pertain to time-intervals to get an example of *UA* in RBAC. The ARBAC safety query, "could Bob become a member of the role Consulting Physician?," is true. Alice first revokes him from the role Doctor and then assigns him to the role Consulting Physician.

from prior work. Mohawk+T is available for public download [10].

We provide a thorough empirical assessment of Mohawk+T, and compare its performance to tools from prior work*. The versions of the problem that the tools from prior work support are syntactically incomparable to one another. As we adopt the most general from across those tools for each feature for Mohawk+T, to be able to meaningfully empirically compare the different tools on the same inputs, we efficiently reduce the Mohawk+T version to the others. Towards this, we present a "reduction toolkit". The toolkit comprises mappings to efficiently reduce from a version of the problem to another.

A composition of steps from the toolkit is also an efficient reduction, and different such compositions reduce the version of the problem that Mohawk+T supports to the other versions. This includes the version of ARBAC-safety that Mohawk supports. In this manner, we are able to perform an apples-for-apples empirical comparison with prior tools.

2. ATRBAC-SAFETY

In this section, we describe ATRBAC, and then pose the ATRBAC-safety problem. We do this in stages. We first introduce RBAC, ARBAC and a version of ARBAC-safety that is relevant to ATRBAC-safety. Then, we describe TR-BAC, ATRBAC and ATRBAC-safety. Figure 4 shows the relationship between RBAC, ARBAC, TRBAC and ATR-BAC.

We then clarify that various versions of ATRBAC- and ARBAC-safety are addressed in the literature, and discuss the choices we have made with regards to the various features of the problem. Specifically, that we have chosen the most general of each feature.

2.1 RBAC, ARBAC and ARBAC-Safety

ATRBAC addresses temporal extensions to RBAC and ARBAC. In this section we discuss RBAC, ARBAC and the version of safety analysis in ARBAC that we call ARBAC-safety that is relevant to our work on ATRBAC-safety.

RBAC RBAC is used to specify an authorization policy — who has access to what. An RBAC policy, in the context

of this work, is a set *UA*, the user–role assignment relation. An instance of *UA* is a set of pairs of the form $\langle u, r \rangle$, where u is a user and r is a role. A user u is authorized to the role r if and only if $\langle u, r \rangle \in UA$. RBAC has other constructs, such as role-permission assignment and a role-hierarchy, that are not relevant to ATRBAC-safety with which we deal in this paper. Indeed, a role-hierarchy can be flattened as a preprocessing step without affecting the correctness or efficiency of our techniques.

ARBAC ARBAC is a syntax for specifying the ways in which an RBAC policy may change. As our work deals with the *UA* component of an RBAC policy only, by ARBAC we mean its URA portion [7], via which users are authorized to and revoked from roles.

There are only two ways in which an instance of *UA* may change. One is the addition of an entry $\langle u, r \rangle$ to *UA*, which is the authorization of u to r. The other is the removal of an entry $\langle u, r \rangle$, which is the revocation of u's authorization to r. An instance of ARBAC is a collection of *rules*, and addresses two issues with regards to such changes to *UA*: who may carry out one of those operations, and under what conditions.

A set of *can_assign* rules controls additions to *UA*, and a set of *can_revoke* rules controls removals from *UA*. A *can_assign* rule is of the form $\langle a, C, t \rangle$, where a, t are roles and C is a precondition. The precondition C is a set in which each entry is either a role r, or its negation, $\neg r$. The semantics of the *can_assign* rule $\langle a, C, t \rangle$ is that a member of the role a may assign a user u to the role t provided u is already a member of every non-negated role in C and is not a member of any negated role in C.

In the *can_assign* rule in Figure 1 for example, a member of the role Director, e.g., Alice, may assign another user, e.g., Bob, to the role Consulting Physician provided he is already a member of the role Surgeon and is not a member of the role Doctor.

In a *can_assign* rule $\langle a, C, t \rangle$, the role a is called an administrative role and the role t is called a target role. A *can_revoke* rule has the form $\langle a, t \rangle$ where both a and t are roles. The semantics is that a member of the administrative role a is allowed to revoke a user's authorization from the target role t. The reason that a *can_revoke* rule has no

---

*We thank the creators of the prior tools [6, 12] for making their tools available to us and helping us with their use. We thank also Ranise et al. [6] for making all of their inputs from their empirical assessment available to us.

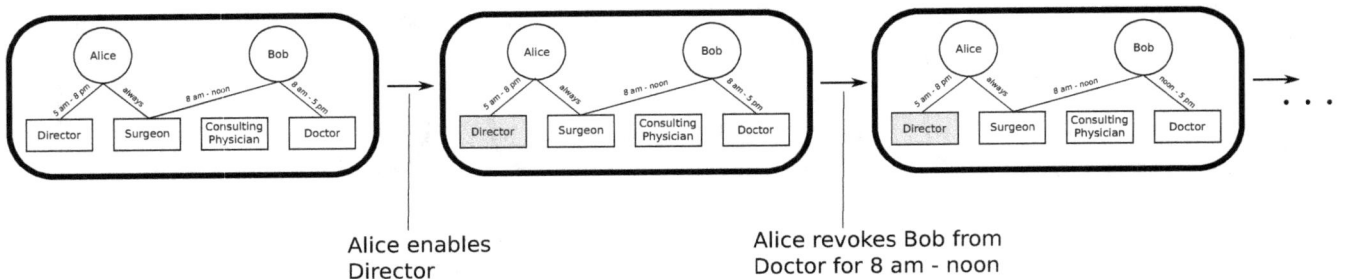

Figure 3: An ATRBAC safety query for the example in Figure 1. The ATRBAC safety query "could Bob become a member of the role Consulting Physician between 8 am and noon?," is true, provided we adopt a version of the problem that does not require the Consulting Physician role to be enabled. The role Director is first enabled (shown shaded in the second state in the figure). This allows Alice to carry out administrative tasks. Alice then exercises the _t_can_revoke_ rule so Bob is revoked from the Doctor role for 8 am − noon. She then is able to assign him to the Consulting Physician role for 8 am − noon. This last state-change is not shown in the above figure. "Could Bob become a member of the role Consulting Physician between 1 pm and 5 pm?," is an example of a safety query that is not true.

precondition is that revocation is seen as an inherently safe operation [7].

ARBAC-safety We now discuss a version of safety analysis in ARBAC that is relevant to our work. We call it ARBAC-safety. As our work deals with user-role authorization only, ARBAC-safety refers to that aspect only. More general versions of safety analysis for ARBAC have been considered in the literature [8], that reconcile not only the user-role authorizations, but also role-role relationships. Nevertheless, all the versions of safety analysis in ARBAC of which we are aware lie in the same complexity-class — they are all **PSPACE**-complete.

ARBAC-safety is a state-reachability problem. It takes three inputs. (1) A _query_, which is a pair $\langle u, r \rangle$, where u is a user and r is a role. (2) A current- or start-state, which is an instance of UA. (3) A state-change specification, which is an instance of ARBAC, i.e., instances of _can_assign_ and _can_revoke_ rules. The output of the ARBAC-safety instance is 'false,' if there exists a state that is reachable from the start-state in which the user u from the query is a member of the role r from the query. Otherwise, the output is 'true.' Figure 2 extends the example from Figure 1 with an example of ARBAC-safety.

ARBAC-safety is known to be **PSPACE**-complete [5]. Several techniques have been proposed to address instances that are likely to arise in practice. For example, Gofman et al. [2] propose a tool called RBAC-PAT, and Jayaraman et al. [4] propose a tool called Mohawk. We adopt the latter as the basis for the tool we build for ATRBAC-safety as it has been shown to scale well with the size of the input.

2.2 TRBAC, ATRBAC and ATRBAC-Safety

We now discuss the temporal extensions to RBAC and ARBAC that give us TRBAC and ATRBAC respectively. We discuss also the problem we address, ATRBAC-safety. We first present a model and encoding of time that is the basis for the syntax for temporality in ATRBAC. The version we adopt is the same as prior work [12].

Time An instant in time, m, can be thought of as represented by a real number. A time-slot represents some duration of time, and is represented as a non-negative integer. In an instance of ATRBAC-safety, no two distinct time-slots

overlap in time. Given time-slots i, j where $i < j$, the time-slot j is associated with a duration of time that occurs later than time-slot i. A time-instant m falls within a time-slot.

We assume that the earliest time-slot with which an instance of ATRBAC-safety is associated is 0, and there is some integer, $T_{\max}$, such that $T_{\max} - 1$ is the latest time-slot that pertains to the ATRBAC-safety instance. We discuss how time progresses under ATRBAC-safety below.

A generalization of a time-slot is a time-interval. A time-interval is a pair of integers $\langle i, j \rangle$ where $i \leq j$. It represents the set of time-slots $\{i, i + 1, \ldots, j\}$. We say that a time-instant m falls within a time-interval if m falls within one of the time-slots in that time-interval.

The mindset that underlies the above notions for time is that each time-slot represents some realistic, recurring, fixed time period, such as "9 AM − 10 AM." The particular such actual time periods to which time-slots in an instance of ATRBAC-safety map is irrelevant to the analysis.

TRBAC From the standpoint of our work, TRBAC generalizes RBAC in two, temporal ways. (1) The set UA is generalized to TUA, each of whose elements is a triple $\langle u, r, l_{u,r} \rangle$, where $l_{u,r}$ is a time-interval. The semantics is that u is a member of r during the time-interval $l_{u,r}$ only. (2) Each role r that appears in TUA is annotated with a time-interval, l_r. We say that l_r is the time-interval during which the role r is active. The semantics is that outside of the time-interval l_r, no user can exercise a permission that she acquires via the role r. The set of all pairs, $\langle r, l_r \rangle$, is denoted RS.

Thus, a TRBAC policy, and therefore a state in the verification problem we consider, is a 3-tuple, $\langle TUA, RS, m \rangle$, where TUA and RS are as described above, and m is a time-instant. A user u is authorized to a role r at the time-instant, m, if and only if there exists an entry $\langle u, r, l_{u,r} \rangle \in TUA$ such that m is within $l_{u,r}$. The entries in RS matter when a user attempts to make an administrative change, i.e., a change to the authorization state. We discuss this under ATRBAC below.

ATRBAC ATRBAC generalizes ARBAC by providing rules for changes to TRBAC policies. As we discuss under "Versions of the problem" below, the version we discuss generalizes prior versions. Under ATRBAC, there are two ways

18

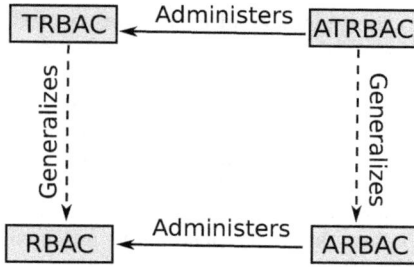

Figure 4: The relationship between RBAC, AR-BAC, TRBAC and ATRBAC. TRBAC syntactically generalizes RBAC with temporal extensions. Similarly, ATRBAC syntactically generalizes ARBAC. ARBAC is used to administer RBAC, and ATRBAC is used to administer TRBAC.

in which a state, which is a TRBAC policy, can change: (1) via an administrative action, or, (2) the passage of time.

Under (1), four kinds of administrative actions are possible to a TRBAC policy, $\langle TUA, RS, m \rangle$. It is possible to add an entry to, and remove an entry from TUA, and it is possible to add an entry to, and remove an entry from RS. The first two kinds of changes are called assign and revoke administrative actions, and the next two are called role enabling and disabling administrative actions. We have the corresponding sets of tuples t_can_assign, t_can_revoke, t_can_enable, and $t\_can\_disable$. (As in Uzun et al. [12], we employ the prefix "$t\_$" to distinguish clearly that these are rules for ATRBAC, rather than ARBAC.)

Each such set contains 5-tuples. Each tuple is of the form $\langle C_a, L_a, C_t, L_t, t \rangle$. The first two components, C_a, L_a are conditions on the administrator that seeks to effect the action. The next two components, C_t, L_t, are conditions on the user or role to which the rule pertains. The last component, t, is the target-role; the role that is affected by the action. C_a is either the mnemonic 'true,' or a condition, i.e., a set of negated and non-negated roles. L_a is a set of time-intervals. We specify their semantics below for each kind of administrative rule. The entry t is the target role, i.e., the role that is affected by the firing of the rule. C_t is a role-condition similar to C_a above. There are some important differences between C_a and C_t, however, and we discuss these below for each kind of rule. L_t is a set of time-intervals, similar to L_a above. We discuss the semantics of L_t below for each kind of rule as well.

Such a 5-tuple $\langle C_a, L_a, C_t, L_t, t \rangle$ applies when an administrator, say, Alice, attempts an administrative action at a particular time-instant, m. Each administrative action takes inputs, one of which is the administrator that attempts it, i.e., Alice, and others that we discuss below.

Role enabling: the inputs are Alice, a target role t, and a set of time-intervals, L. Alice succeeds in her attempt at enabling the role t if and only if there exists an entry $\langle C_a, L_a, C_t, L_t, t \rangle \in t\_can\_enable$ for which all of the following are true. (1) The time-instant, m, at which Alice attempts the action falls within some time-interval in L_a. (2) Alice and the current time-instant m together satisfy the administrative condition, C_a. That is, if p is a non-negated role in C_a, then Alice is a member of p at time-instant m in the current state, $\langle TUA, RS, m \rangle$, and p is active at the time-instant m. If n is a negated role in C_a, then either Alice is not a member of n at time-instant m in the current state, or the role n is not active, or both. If C_a is the mnemonic 'true,' then the rule may fire provided m is within some time-interval in L_a. (3) The set of time-intervals L is contained within the set of time-intervals L_t. That is, for every time-interval $l \in L$, there exists a time-interval $l_t \in L_t$ such that l is within l_t. (4) The set of time-intervals L satisfies the target condition C_t for every $l \in L$. That is, if p is a non-negated role in C_t, then for every $l \in L$, p is active during the time-interval l, in the current-state, i.e., RS. And if n is a negated role in C_t, then for every $l \in L$, n is not active during l, in the current-state.

The effect of a successful role enabling by Alice is that the component RS of the current-state is updated as follows to get a new state: $RS \leftarrow RS \cup \{\langle t, l \rangle : l \in L\}$.

Example: In Figure 1 Alice must first enable the role of "Director" so that she can later be allowed to exercise rules where the "Director" role is required by the administrative condition, C_a. Alice may exercise the t_can_enable rule during 6 am – 8 am as she satisfies C_a during that time. Once she enables it, Alice must wait before she exercises the t_can_revoke rule, where the "Director" role is required by t_can_revoke's C_a, until the current time falls within 8 am – noon.

Role disabling: the inputs are Alice, a target role t, and a set of time-intervals, L. Alice succeeds in disabling t via her action at time-instant m if and only if there exists an entry $\langle C_a, L_a, C_t, L_t, t \rangle \in t\_can\_disable$ for which all of the following are true. (1) The current time-instant, m, falls within some time-interval in L_a. (2) Alice and the current time-instant, m, together satisfy the administrative condition, C_a. (3) The set of time-intervals, L, is contained within the set of time-intervals, L_t. (4) The set of time-intervals L satisfies the target condition C_t for every $l \in L$.

The effect of a successful role disabling by Alice is that the component RS of the current-state is updated as follows to get a new state: $RS \leftarrow RS \setminus \{\langle t, l \rangle : l \in L\}$.

Example: Figure 1 does not provide a rule for $t\_can\_disable$. But an example case of this rule is to have a $t\_can\_disable$ rule: $\langle$true, 6 am – 6 pm, true, noon – 1 pm, Director$\rangle$. This rule allows for the "Director" role to be disabled during lunch time, which means that no changes to TUA can be done during lunch. Exercising the t_can_enable rule after this $t\_can\_disable$ rule will overwrite the changes and have the "Director" role enabled during noon – 1 pm.

User-role assignment: the inputs are the administrator, Alice, a user u, a target role t to which she seeks to assign u, and a set of time-intervals L. The assignment action that she attempts at time-instant m succeeds if and only if there exists an entry $\langle C_a, L_a, C_t, L_t, t \rangle \in t\_can\_assign$ for which all of the following are true. (1) The current time-instant, m, falls within some time-interval in L_a. (2) Alice and the current time-instant, m, together satisfy the administrative condition, C_a. (3) The set of time-intervals, L, is contained within the set of time-intervals, L_t. (4) The user u and the set of time-intervals L satisfy the target condition C_t for every $l \in L$. That is, if p is a non-negated role in C_t, then u is a member of p during every time-interval $l \in L$. If n is a negated role in C_t, then u is not a member of n in any time-interval $l \in L$. If C_t is the mnemonic 'true,' then there are no constraints on the current role-memberships of the user u.

The effect of a successful assignment by Alice is that the component TUA of the current-state is updated as follows to get a new state: $TUA \leftarrow TUA \cup \{\langle u, t, l \rangle : l \in L\}$.

Example: The example in Figure 1 shows that Alice is able to assign the "Consulting Physician" role to Bob during 8 am – noon. She is able to exercise this rule because Bob has the role "Surgeon," and does not have the role "Doctor" during 8 am – noon, and Alice satisfies the administrative condition by having the role "Director."

User-role revocation: the inputs are an administrator Alice, a user u that she seeks to revoke from a role, a target role, t from which she seeks to revoke u, and a set of time-intervals, L. The revocation action she attempts at some time-instant m succeeds if and only if there exists an entry $\langle C_a, L_a, C_t, L_t, t \rangle \in t\_can\_revoke$ for which all of the following are true. (1) The current time-instant, m, falls within some time-interval in L_a. (2) Alice and the current time-instant, m, together satisfy the administrative condition, C_a. (3) The set of time-intervals, L, is contained within the set of time-intervals, L_t. (4) The user u and the set of time-intervals L satisfy the target condition C_t for every $l \in L$. The effect of a successful revocation by Alice is that the component TUA of the current-state is updated as follows to get a new state: $TUA \leftarrow TUA \setminus \{\langle u, t, l \rangle : l \in L\}$.

Example: Alice may revoke Bob from the "Doctor" role during 8 am – noon using the t_can_revoke rule in Figure 1. If she does so, Bob retains membership of "Doctor" during noon – 5 pm, as we show in Figure 3.

Time-change: Another way that a state, $\langle TUA, RS, m \rangle$, can change is in its time component, m. The manner in which passage of time is modelled [6, 12] is simply by allowing the m component to increase without any change to the other two components, TUA and RS. That is, a possible state-change is from $\langle TUA, RS, m \rangle$ to a new state, $\langle TUA, RS, m' \rangle$, where $m' > m$.

An issue we clarify in this regard of passage of time is whether, once we reach the time-slot $T_{\max} - 1$ to which an instance of ATRBAC-safety pertains, the time-slot 0 recurs, followed by time-slot 1 and so on, forever. The assumption in prior work [12] is that it does. The reason regards the semantics of a time-slot — it maps to some realistic, recurring period of time. We refer to this property as periodicity, and revisit it in the context of the software tools.

Example: Time periodicity is what allows the rules in Figure 1 to be described by just the time of day. The intention of the rules is that they are contained within a day. Thus when a day ends and the next day begins, the rules should still apply to the new day.

ATRBAC-safety The safety analysis problem for ATRBAC takes three inputs. (1) A query, $\langle u, C, L, t \rangle$, where u is a user, C is a condition (set of negated and non-negated roles), L is a set of time-intervals and t is some units of time. (2) A start-state, $\langle TUA, RS, m \rangle$, which is an instance of TRBAC. (3) A state-change specification, which is an instance of ATRBAC, i.e., four sets of rules, t_can_assign, t_can_revoke, t_can_enable, and $t\_can\_disable$.

The output is 'false,' if there exists a TRBAC state $\langle TUA', RS', m' \rangle$ that is reachable from the start-state in which:

(i) the user u is a member of every non-negated role in C in every time-interval in L, and is not a member of any negated role in C in any time-interval in L, (ii) every non-negated role in C is active for every time-interval in L, and no negated role in C is active in any time-interval in L, and, (iii) the time-instant m' of this state is within t time-units of the time-instant of the start-state. Otherwise, the output is 'true.' We point out that it is possible to specify t that is large enough that the query pertains to any time-slot that pertains to the problem instance.

In Figure 3 we discuss two ATRBAC safety questions: "could Bob become a member of the role Consulting Physician between 8 am and noon?" and "could Bob become a member of the role Consulting Physician between 1 pm and 5 pm?". As the caption of the figure discusses, the former is true, provided we do not require the role Consulting Physician to be enabled when Bob becomes a member of it. The latter question is not true.

Versions of the problem Prior work that is relevant to our work refers to different versions of ATRBAC-safety. We broadly classify the various versions along two axes. One comprises the versions that are discussed theoretically, i.e., in prose, assertions and proofs only. The other comprises versions supported by software tools.

Correspondingly, from the work of Uzun et al. [12] we have the versions of ATRBAC-safety that we call TRED-THEORY, and the versions supported by their tools, TREDROLE and TREDRULE. They are so named because Ranise et al. [6] refer to their two software tools with the prefix TRED. Similarly, from Ranise et al. [6] we have ASASPTIME-THEORY, and the versions supported by their tools ASASPTIME-NSA and ASASPTIME-SA. The acronym "NSA" stands for Non-Separate Administration, and "SA" for "Separate Administration." They pertain to whether administrative roles are distinct from user roles. Finally, we refer to the version of ATRBAC-safety we discuss above as Mohawk+T-THEORY. We also have the version that is supported by our tool, Mohawk+T.

We address the differences between ASASPTIME-THEORY and TRED-THEORY, and our choices for Mohawk+T-THEORY here. We address the differences between the versions of the software tools in Section 4. A recognition of the differences of the theoretical versions is important from two standpoints. One is that Mohawk+T-THEORY syntactically generalizes both ASASPTIME-THEORY and TRED-THEORY. Thus, an upper-bound for the computational complexity of ATRBAC-safety for Mohawk+T-THEORY is an upper-bound for each of the other two as well.

Another reason a recognition of these different versions is important regards an assertion about the non-existence of an efficient reduction from ASASPTIME-THEORY to TRED-THEORY in prior work [6]. As we point out in the next section on computational complexity, the assertion is in error.

The differences between ASASPTIME-THEORY and TRED-THEORY pertain to (1) whether time-intervals are allowed, or only time-slots, (2) whether an administrative condition may be specified in a rule, or an administrative role only, and, (3) the kind of query that may be specified in an instance of safety. The differences are the following.

1. ASASPTIME-THEORY allows time-slot only, and not time-intervals. TRED-THEORY allows time-intervals. So, for this feature, ASASPTIME-THEORY is less gen-

eral than TRED-THEORY. We point out that naively encoding a time-interval as a set of time-slots is inefficient in the worst-case. Recall from our discussion above under "Time" that a time-interval is a set of consecutive time-slots $\{i, i+1, \ldots, i+n\}$, where $n \geq 0$. Encoding a time-interval as the pair $\langle i, i+n \rangle$ takes space $\leq 2\log(i+n)$ only. Encoding it as the set $\{i, i+1, \ldots, i+n\}$, however, takes space $\geq (n+1)\log(i)$. The latter is exponential in the former, in the worst-case.

2. ASASPTIME-THEORY allows a condition for the administrator in a rule, rather than an administrative role only. TRED-THEORY allows an administrative role only. For this feature, therefore, ASASPTIME-THEORY generalizes TRED-THEORY.

3. A query in ASASPTIME-THEORY is of the form $\langle u, C, L \rangle$ where u is a user, C is a role condition, and L is a set of time-slots. The semantics is: does there exist a reachable state in which (1) u satisfies C for L, i.e., is a member of every non-negated role for every time-slot in L and not a member of any negated role in C for any time-slot in L, and, (2) roles are enabled and disabled as C specifies for the time-slots in L.

   TRED-THEORY proposes two kinds of queries. One is of the form $\langle u, r, L \rangle$, which asks whether u can become a member of r in all the time-intervals L. This is less syntactically general than ASASPTIME-THEORY in that C is allowed to be a role only, but more general in that L is allowed to be a set of time-intervals, and not only a set of time-slots. The other kind of query is of the form $\langle u, r, L, t \rangle$, which asks whether u can become a member of r in all the time-intervals in L within t time-units of the start-state. This syntactically generalizes the version of the safety problem that allows the first kind of query only — there is a straightforward reduction from the safety problem that allows the first kind of query only, to one that allows the second kind of query.

   Thus, from the standpoint of the query, the two versions are incomparable to one another.

For Mohawk+T-THEORY that we describe earlier, for each of the three features above, we have chosen the more general. For example, the query allows a role condition, a set of time-intervals and the extra parameter t that limits the number of time units in which the query must become true. Also, we assume that all possible users that are allowed to exist in the system are part of the TUA component in the start-state. (It is easy to incorporate users that are not assigned to any role into TUA. Create a "dummy" role that does not appear in any of the administrative rules and assign all users to it in the start-state.)

The reason we have adopted such a general version is to emphasize our complexity result that we present in the next section — such a choice has no consequence to the upper-bound computational complexity of ATRBAC-safety.

3. COMPUTATIONAL COMPLEXITY

We now identify the computational complexity of ATRBAC-safety, for the version we call Mohawk+T-THEORY. In Theorem 1 below, we identify an upper-bound. Then, in Theorem 2, we identify a tight bound. We then identify that all

versions of ATRBAC-safety we address are **PSPACE**-complete. We then address the expressive power of ATRBAC and an assertion in prior work on the non-existence of a reduction.

THEOREM 1. *ARBAC-safety for Mohawk+T-THEORY is in* **PSPACE**.

The above theorem asserts an upper-bound on the hardness of safety analysis in ATRBAC. To prove it, we construct a non-deterministic Turing machine that terminates on every input with the correct 'safe' or 'unsafe' output, and runs with space only polynomial in the size of the input. Then, from the fact that **PSPACE** = **NSPACE**, which is a corollary to Savitch's theorem [9], we immediately infer that the problem is in **PSPACE**.

We point out that a similar non-deterministic Turing machine is constructed by Jha et al. [5] to show that their version of ARBAC-safety is in **PSPACE**. A main difference for us is that we need to reconcile the temporal aspect of ATRBAC-safety as well. Our non-deterministic Turing machine, M, is provided the three inputs: (1) a query, $q = \langle u, C, L, t \rangle$, (2) A start-state, $\langle TUA, RS, m \rangle$, and, (3) A set of state-change rules in ATRBAC, i.e., the four sets t_can_assign, t_can_revoke, t_can_enable and $t\_can\_disable$.

M first assembles a set S of all the time-intervals (some of which may be time-slots) that appear in any of the three components of the input. M then breaks up the time-intervals in S so none of them overlaps with any other. It does this using the algorithm in Figure 5. The input set S is at worst linear in the size of the input ARBAC-safety instance. The output from the algorithm in Figure 5, call it S', is at worst quadratic in the size of input S – the caption in Figure 5 provides a reasoning.

The reason M does this is that it only has to maintain one of these time-intervals as the current time. The exact value of the current time, or even time-slot, no longer matters. For convenience, M could rewrite the input ATRBAC rules so each mentions only entries from S' and not S. M then maintains the following state. (1) The current values for the sets TUA and RS. (2) The current time-interval from S' within which the current time instant falls. (3) The number of time units that have elapsed.

M performs its moves as follows. M first checks whether the query q is satisfied. It can do so from the state information it maintains. If yes, it halts with output 'unsafe.' If not, it checks whether it has exceeded t from the query q. If yes, it halts with output 'safe.' Otherwise, it assembles all the administrative rules that are enabled, i.e., for which the administrative and role conditions are met. It also includes an update of the current time-interval to the next time-interval as an option. It non-deterministically picks an option from those, updates its state, and continues.

M ensures that it terminates — we know that the input instance is unsafe if and only if the non-deterministic Turing machine halts with an output of 'unsafe' within 2^n transitions, where n is the size of the input. The Turing machine can keep a count of its transitions with space $\log_2(2^n) = n$. Thus, if M has not determined that the instance is unsafe after 2^n transitions, it outputs 'safe' and halts. We point out also that M maintains state that is at worst quadratic in the size of the input.

THEOREM 2. *ATRBAC-safety for Mohawk+T-THEORY is* **PSPACE***-complete.*

Input: a set of time-intervals, S

1: From the entries of S that have not been considered before, pick one of smallest duration.
2: If any entry in S overlaps with the entry chosen in Line (1) other than itself, break it up into at most 3 non-overlapping entries and add those back to S.
3: If all entries have been considered, halt.
4: Else goto Line 1.

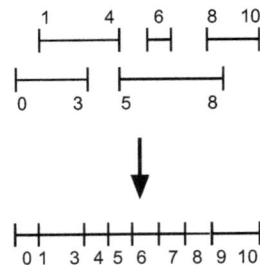

Figure 5: To the left is an algorithm to break up input time-intervals into non-overlapping time-intervals. An example of an input and output is shown to the right. The algorithm is used by the non-deterministic Turing machine in Section 3, and as part of our Reduction Toolkit in Section 4. The algorithm takes as input S, a set of time-intervals. The algorithm is guaranteed to terminate as no entry is chosen more than once in Line (1), and at most a constant number of entries is added in Line (2) for every entry chosen in Line (1). The algorithm runs in time at-worst quadratic in the size of the input S because for every entry chosen in Line (1), each entry in S is broken up into at most a constant number of entries in Line (2). In the example to the right, the input is the 5 time-intervals, $\{\langle 0,3 \rangle, \langle 1,4 \rangle, \langle 5,8 \rangle, \langle 6,6 \rangle, \langle 8,10 \rangle\}$. The output is the 8 non-overlapping time-intervals, $\{\langle 0,0 \rangle, \langle 1,3 \rangle, \langle 4,4 \rangle, \langle 5,5 \rangle, \langle 6,6 \rangle, \langle 7,7 \rangle, \langle 8,8 \rangle, \langle 9,10 \rangle\}$. To represent the time interval $\langle 0,3 \rangle$, from the input set S, in non-overlapping time intervals we would use: $\{\langle 0,0 \rangle, \langle 1,3 \rangle\}$.

We infer the above theorem from the fact that ARBAC-safety is **PSPACE**-hard [5]. As ATRBAC-safety for Mohawk+T-THEORY generalizes that version of ARBAC-safety, the **PSPACE**-hard lower bound applies to ATRBAC-safety for Mohawk+T-THEORY as well. Given Theorem 1, we thus prove Theorem 2.

THEOREM 3. *All the versions of ATRBAC-safety we consider in this paper are* **PSPACE**-*complete. They are: ASASPTIME-THEORY, TRED-THEORY, Mohawk+T-THEORY, and the versions supported by the tools ASASPTIME-NSA, ASASPTIME-SA, TREDROLE, TREDRULE, Mohawk+T and Mohawk.*

To prove the theorem, we first oberve that the version of ARBAC-safety, which can be perceived as a special case of ATRBAC-safety with only 1 time-slot, supported by Mohawk, is **PSPACE**-complete. We comment on this more in Section 4 under Item (4), "Admin role is 'true' only," in our Reduction Toolkit. All the other versions generalize the version supported by Mohawk, and therefore are **PSPACE**-hard. And, all the versions are at most as general as Mohawk+T-THEORY, and therefore are in **PSPACE**.

3.1 Expressive power of ATRBAC

We can interpret the hardness of ATRBAC-safety as a measure of the expressive power of ATRBAC. The fact that ATRBAC-safety is no harder than ARBAC-safety, within a polynomial factor, suggests that ATRBAC is no more expressive than ARBAC.

Indeed, in this context, one can point to some seeming deficiencies in the syntax of ATRBAC. It is not possible, for example, to directly express a rule such as the following: "if a user is a member of the role Surgeon between 8 am and 9 am, then allow the user to be assigned to the role Consulting Physician between noon and 5 pm." The reason is that the set of time-intervals L_t in a rule $\langle C_a, L_a, C_t, L_t, t \rangle$ serves two purposes. It is used as a precondition to check the current temporal role-memberships of the user along with C_t, and, it is used to limit the time-intervals for which the user can acquire membership in the target role t.

A straightforward way to extend the syntax of ATRBAC to account for such use cases is to allow C_t to be a set of pairs, each of the form $\langle c, l \rangle$, where c is either a non-negated or negated role, and l is a time-interval. This separates the two purposes mentioned above. Nonetheless, ATRBAC-safety for this version of ATRBAC is also **PSPACE**-complete. That is, from the standpoint of computational complexity of safety analysis, nothing has changed. This means that this new version can be reduced efficiently to the original.

Another issue in this context regards an assertion from prior work [6] regarding the non-existence of an efficient reduction from ASASPTIME-THEORY to TRED-THEORY. Theorem 3 invalidates the assertion. The erroneous reasoning in that work is that to support an administrative condition in an ATRBAC rule rather than only an administrative role, one must introduce exponentially many new roles.

An efficient reduction, however, can be constructed as follows. We introduce a new role for every administrative condition. Thus, the number of new roles is at worst linear in the ATRBAC-safety instance. We then introduce *t_can_assign* rules with the condition as a role precondition to assign a user to the new role. There are additional details we need which we omit here, for example to account for when a user no longer satisfies a condition in a future state.

4. EMPIRICAL ASSESSMENT

We have designed and built a software tool that we call Mohawk+T for ATRBAC-safety. Mohawk+T has been built as a wrapper to Mohawk [4], an open-source tool for ARBAC-safety. Mohawk reduces ARBAC-safety to model-checking and employs an off-the-shelf model checker, NuSMV. In addition, Mohawk employs within it domain-specific heuristics called abstraction-refinement and bound-estimation for increased efficiency. The empirical results that have been reported for Mohawk suggest that it scales well for large input instances, for example, $40,000$ roles and $200,000$ rules.

Our intent here is to validate the thesis that we can wrap Mohawk in a manner that we preserve its scalability for ATRBAC policies. Thus, Mohawk+T would scale significantly better than what has been shown for existing tools for

	Time-intervals or time-slots only	Enable/disable rules supported	Query	Administrative roles supported or 'true' only
ASASPTIME-NSA	Time-slots only	Yes	$\langle r, l \rangle$ — can some user become a member of r in time-slot l?	Yes
ASASPTIME-SA	Time-slots only	No	$\langle r, l \rangle$ — see above	No — 'true' only
TREDROLE, TREDRULE	Allows time-interval in administrative condition	No	$\langle R \rangle$ — can the same user become a member of all roles in R in the same time-slot?	No — 'true' only
Mohawk+T	Allows time-interval in administrative condition	Yes	$\langle R, l \rangle$ — can the same user become a member of all roles in R in the time-slot l?	Yes
Mohawk	No temporal support	No	$\langle u, r \rangle$ — can the user u become a member of role r?	No — 'true' only

Table 1: Feature-support of the various existing tools, and our design choice for Mohawk+T. For Mohawk+T, we have chosen the most general version of a feature from amongst existing tools for ATRBAC-safety. We show also the support Mohawk offers. As a tool for ARBAC-safety only, Mohawk expectedly has no support for temporality. There is also no notion of enable/disable rules in ARBAC-safety. When we say "'true' only" for administrative roles, we mean that every rule is enabled in every state.

ATRBAC-safety [6, 12]. The manner in which Mohawk+T wraps Mohawk is an efficient reduction from ATRBAC-safety to ARBAC-safety. That is, given as input an instance of ATRBAC-safety, the wrapper in Mohawk+T maps this to an instance of ARBAC-safety that it provides as input to Mohawk. The mapping is a reduction, and therefore Mohawk's 'safe' or 'unsafe' output can immediately be adopted as Mohawk+T's output.

We had to address some technical challenges in realizing and assessing Mohawk+T. One is that we had to choose a version of ATRBAC-safety that Mohawk+T would support. So far in this paper, we have discussed what we have called theoretical versions of ATRBAC-safety. None of the prior tools, ASASPTIME-NSA, ASASPTIME-SA, TREDROLE and TREDRULE supports its corresponding theoretical version. ASASPTIME-NSA, for example, supports administrative roles only, and not administrative conditions. Another example is that TREDROLE allows only a set of time-slots, and not a time-interval, as the role condition.

As with their theoretical counterparts, the two sets of existing tools are incomparable to one another from the standpoint of generality. We have investigated the various features that the existing tools allow for their input, and chosen for Mohawk+T the more general for each feature. We discuss this in more detail below.

Another technical challenge we had to address is that we had to devise an efficient reduction from the version of ATRBAC-safety that Mohawk+T supports to the version of ARBAC-safety that Mohawk supports. In this context, we point out that Mohawk also has a corresponding theoretical version [5] that is more general. Mohawk, for example, allows only 'true' for the administrative role in a rule. We discuss our reduction in Section 4, once we introduce our Reduction Toolkit.

We devised our Reduction Toolkit not only to reduce the version of ATRBAC-safety that Mohawk+T supports to the version of ARBAC-safety that Mohawk supports, but also so we can conduct a meaningful empirical comparison with existing tools for ATRBAC-safety. As Mohawk+T syntactically generalizes all existing tools, we cannot directly pro-

vide as input to an existing tool an input designed for Mohawk+T.

So we can perform apples-for-apples comparisons on inputs, we have devised and implemented efficient reductions from the version of ATRBAC-safety that Mohawk+T supports to the version that each of the existing tools supports. Thus, we need 4 reductions in total — to (1) ASASPTIME-NSA, (2) ASASPTIME-SA, (3) TREDROLE and TREDRULE, and, (4) Mohawk. We observed that the reductions have commonalities, which motivated us to devise our Reduction Toolkit. Composing particular reductions from the toolkit provides us with each of the 4 reductions we seek.

Versions that tools support Table 1 expresses the support for various features in existing tools, and our design choice for Mohawk+T. We list only those features for which the tools differ. As the table shows, for Mohawk+T, we have chosen the most general for each feature in existing tools. We show in the table also the support in Mohawk. We show this to indicate what our reduction from Mohawk+T's version of ATRBAC-safety must address. We point out, in addition to the information in the table, that none of the existing tools for ATRBAC-safety supports administrative conditions. They also do not support periodicity of time. Therefore, neither does Mohawk+T. These are features that are supported by the theoretical versions we discuss earlier in the paper.

4.1 A "Reduction Toolkit"

There are some common transformations we effect in our efficient reductions from Mohawk+T to ASASPTIME-NSA, ASASPTIME-SA, TREDROLE and TREDRULE, and Mohawk. In this section, we discuss six mappings, each of which transforms some component of the problem efficiently (in polynomial time). Then, in subsequent sections, we mention which ones we need for each of the four reductions. Each of our transformations from an input to Mohawk+T to one of the other tools composes some of these transformations from our toolkit. As each of these transformations is an efficient reduction, so is any of those compositions. We provide more details in [11].

Reduction (1) in our toolkit maps a Mohawk+T query, which is of the form $\langle R, l \rangle$, to what we call a Type 1, 2 or 3 query. Type 1 is of the form $\langle r', l' \rangle$, which is supported by AsaspTime-Nsa and AsaspTime-Sa. We create a new role r' and a new t_can_assign rule with it as target. The roles in R are the precondition. We also identify to which time-slot l', the time-slot l maps from Reduction (2) of the toolkit. A query of Type 2 is of the form $\langle R' \rangle$, which is supported by TredRole and TredRule. We do something similar to Type 1 — create a new role r', a new t_can_assign rule for it, and set $R' = \{r'\}$. The Type 3 query is of the form $\langle u', r' \rangle$ and is supported by Mohawk. For this mapping, we first remove temporality using Reduction (5) from the toolkit. Then, we create a can_assign rule as for Types 1 and 2, and also ensure that a user u' exists by mentioning it in Mohawk's input.

Reduction (2) maps time-intervals to time-slots only. Recall from our discussion in Section 2.2 that naively enumerating the time-slots that comprise a time-interval is not efficient. For this reduction, we run the algorithm from Figure 5. We then adopt each time-interval in the output as a time-slot.

Reduction (3) produces an output with no t_can_enable or $t\_can\_disable$ rules. This is needed to map Mohawk+T inputs to AsaspTime-Sa, TredRole, TredRule and Mohawk. (For Mohawk, we also need to remove temporality using Reduction (5) below.) The manner in which we remove t_can_enable and $t\_can\_disable$ rules is to introduce, for every role r, a new role r_e. The user's membership in r_e indicates enablement. A $t\_can\_enable/t\_can\_disable$ rule with r as target or precondition becomes a $t\_can\_assign/t\_can\_revoke$ rule with r_e as target or precondition respectively.

Reduction (4) produces an output with admin role set to the mnemonic 'true' only. That is, every rule is enabled in every state. It may seem surprising that an efficient reduction exists from Mohawk+T's version of the problem that allows arbitrary administrative roles in rules to this one. We point out that the **PSPACE**-hardness reduction of Jha et al. [5], maps to instances of ARBAC-safety that has such rules only. The way to do this is to first observe that the maximum number of administrative users we need is $A \times L$, where A is the set of all administrative roles and L is the set of time-intervals in the input. We transform the administrator in a rule, which can be seen as a constraint, to a role precondition. The way to do this is to allow the same, single user to act as each administrator. We need to do this carefully, however, to ensure that it is a reduction. See [11] for more details.

Reduction (5) produces an output with no temporality. This can be seen as a version of the problem with one time-slot only. We need this to reduce to Mohawk's version, which is for ARBAC-safety. We map every entry in $R \times L$ to a role in Mohawk, where R is the set of all roles and L is the set of all time-intervals in the Mohawk+T input.

Reduction (6) produces an output with no preconditions in can_revoke rules. This is needed to reduce to Mohawk — we assume that temporality has been removed using Reduction (5) above. Given a can_revoke rule $\langle a, C, t \rangle$, we

first rewrite it as $\langle a, t \rangle$. Then, we add a new role t' and a can_assign rule, $\langle a, \neg t \wedge C, t' \rangle$. We replace a role precondition $\neg t$ with $\neg t \wedge t'$. See [11] for the reasoning.

Reductions to versions To reduce from Mohawk+T's version to AsaspTime-Nsa, we compose Reductions (1) and (2). To reduce to AsaspTime-Sa, we compose Reductions (1)–(4). To reduce to TredRole and TredRule, we compose Reductions (1), (3) and (4). To reduce to Mohawk's version, we compose (1), and (3)–(6).

5. EMPIRICAL RESULTS

We have conducted empirical assessments on the three benchmark classes from prior work [6]. In addition, we have converted the input instances that were used in the empirical assessment of Mohawk [4] to ATRBAC-safety instances, and tried them as well on the tools. The conversion of Mohawk inputs is trivial — we adopt a single time-slot for the policy. Our results are shown in Figures 6, 7 and 8. The curves interpolate the average of 5 runs. The error-bars show the standard deviation from the average.

We observe that the results are mixed with regards to favoring Mohawk+T. For Benchmark Class (a), which is shown in Figure 6, the existing tools for ATRBAC-safety outperform Mohawk+T. Mohawk+T completes in a few seconds, while existing tools complete in less than a second each. Our investigation reveals that the policies in this benchmark are always safe, given the way they are generated. Mohawk's static slicing does a good job of paring large policies (e.g., 2,000 roles, 100,000 rules) down to a much smaller size (e.g., 150 roles and rules). However, its bound estimator estimates a bound that is linear in the number of roles for these policies, e.g., 150. While this is certainly much better than the worst-case estimate of 2^{150}, it still results in Mohawk+T taking several seconds.

For Benchmark Class (b), which is shown in Figure 7, and Mohawk inputs, which is shown in Figure 8, however, Mohawk+T significantly outperforms the existing tools. Furthermore, the existing tools are unable to withstand the input instances from Mohawk [4] beyond a certain threshold. For the polynomial-time verifiable sub-class, for example, which is Test Suite 1 in Figure 8, none of the existing tools is able to handle inputs beyond 20,000 roles and 80,000 rules.

For Benchmark Class (c), which is shown in Figure 7, AsaspTime-Nsa outperforms Mohawk+T. Note that as in prior work [6], we did not try this Benchmark Class on the other existing tools.

Thus, we have the somewhat interesting situation that no single tool can be said to be good with all the input ATRBAC-safety instances we have tried. Further investigation is warranted to carefully identify the structure of input instances, and what features a universally good tool needs to have.

6. CONCLUSIONS

We have addressed the safety analysis problem in the context of Administrative Temporal Role-Based Access Control (ATRBAC-safety). We have shown that the problem is **PSPACE**-complete, and also that various versions of the problem from the literature are **PSPACE**-complete. As the complexity class is the same as ARBAC-safety, we have investigated an approach to dealing with practical instances via reduction to ARBAC-safety, and the leveraging an exist-

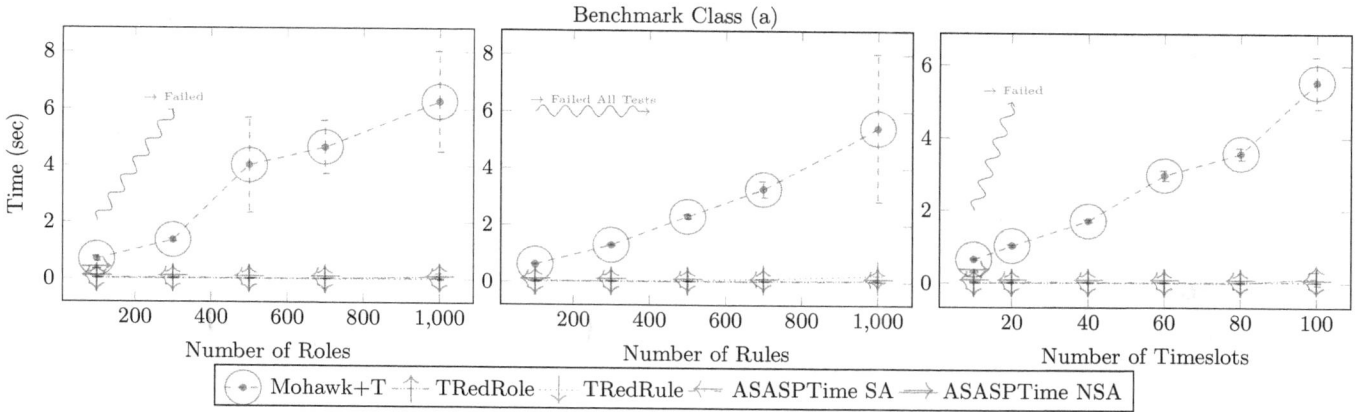

Figure 6: Results on all tools for Benchmark Class (a). It comprises random input instances from a generator from Uzun et al. [12]. The curves interpolate averages, and the error-bars show the standard deviation.

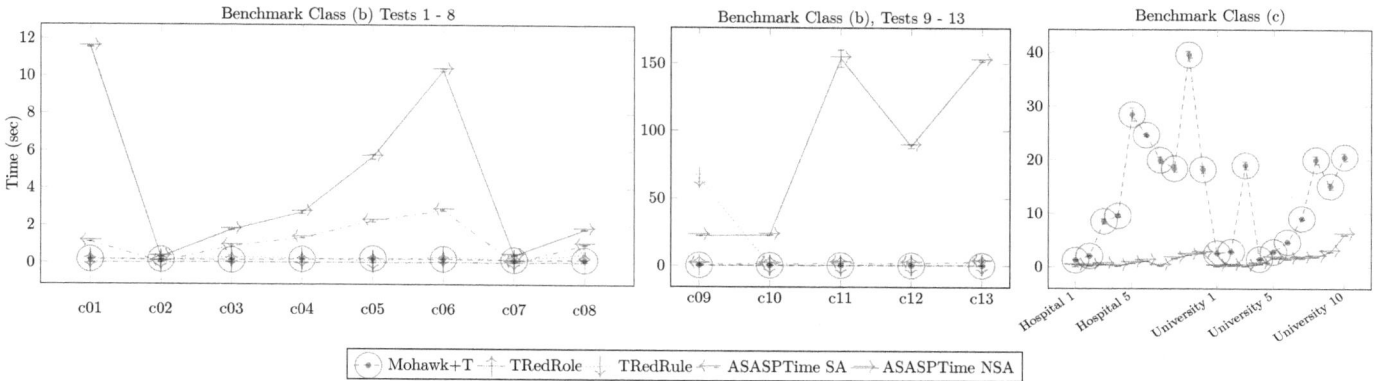

Figure 7: Results for Benchmark Class (b) (two graphs to the left), and Benchmark Class (c) (right). These comprise input instances from the work of Ranise et al. [6].

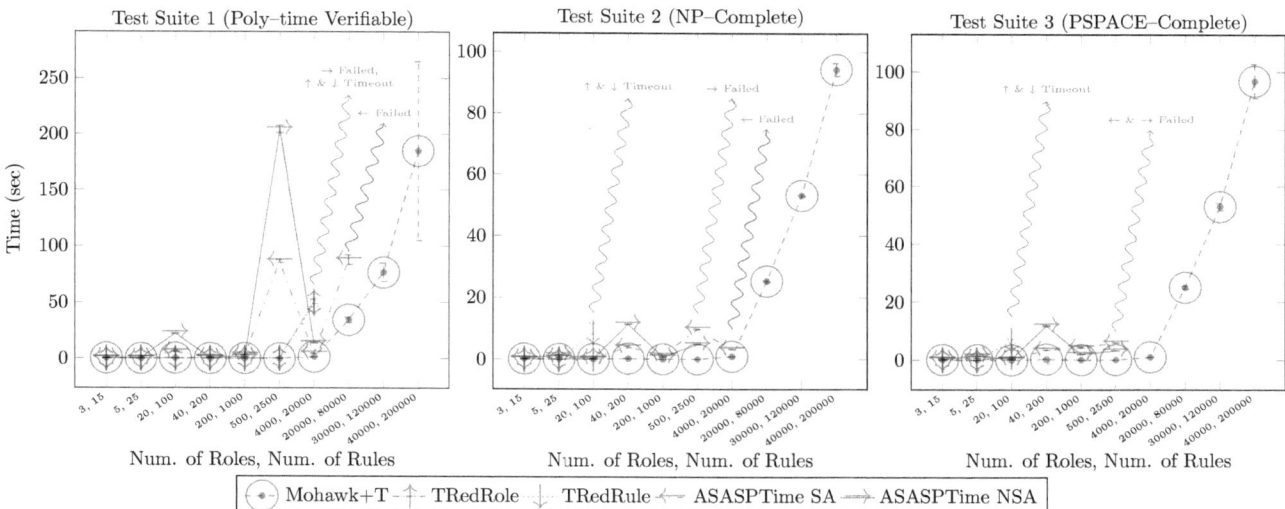

Figure 8: Results for inputs used in the empirical assessment of Mohawk [4]. We trivially converted the Mohawk inputs to ATRBAC-safety instances — there is one time-slot only. The graph to the far left is for inputs with non-negated preconditions only. The middle graph is for inputs with no revoke rules. To the right is the hardest class, in which both negated and non-negated preconditions are allowed, as are revoke rules. Some of the curves are truncated because the corresponding tools crash at those inputs sizes and beyond.

25

ing tool that has been shown to scale well — Mohawk. For an apples-for-apples comparison with existing tools, we have also come up with a Reduction Toolkit. Compositions of reductions from the toolkit allow us to reduce Mohawk+T's more general version of ATRBAC-safety to other versions. We have conducted a thorough empirical assessment. Our results are that there are some classes of inputs for which exiting tools outperform Mohawk+T, and others for which Mohawk+T outperforms existing tools.

7. REFERENCES

[1] MiniSat. http://minisat.se/, Feb 2015.
[2] M. Gofman, R. Luo, A. Solomon, Y. Zhang, P. Yang, and S. Stoller. Rbac-pat: A policy analysis tool for role based access control. In S. Kowalewski and A. Philippou, editors, *Tools and Algorithms for the Construction and Analysis of Systems*, volume 5505 of *Lecture Notes in Computer Science*, pages 46–49. Springer Berlin Heidelberg, 2009.
[3] M. A. Harrison, W. L. Ruzzo, and J. D. Ullman. Protection in operating systems. *Commun. ACM*, 19(8):461–471, Aug. 1976.
[4] K. Jayaraman, M. Tripunitara, V. Ganesh, M. Rinard, and S. Chapin. Mohawk: Abstraction-refinement and bound-estimation for verifying access control policies. *ACM Trans. Inf. Syst. Secur.*, 15(4):18:1–18:28, Apr. 2013.
[5] S. Jha, N. Li, M. Tripunitara, Q. Wang, and W. Winsborough. Towards formal verification of role-based access control policies. *Dependable and Secure Computing, IEEE Transactions on*, 5(4):242–255, Oct 2008.
[6] S. Ranise, A. Truong, and A. Armando. Scalable and Precise Automated Analysis of Administrative Temporal Role-based Access Control. In *Proceedings of the 19th ACM Symposium on Access Control Models and Technologies*, SACMAT '14, pages 103–114, New York, NY, USA, 2014. ACM.
[7] R. Sandhu, V. Bhamidipati, and Q. Munawer. The arbac97 model for role-based administration of roles. *ACM Trans. Inf. Syst. Secur.*, 2(1):105–135, Feb. 1999.
[8] A. Sasturkar, P. Yang, S. D. Stoller, and C. R. Ramakrishnan. Policy analysis for administrative role based access control. *Theoretical Computer Science*, 412(44):6208–6234, Oct. 2011.
[9] W. J. Savitch. Relationships between nondeterministic and deterministic tape complexities. *Journal of Computer and System Sciences*, 4(2):177 – 192, 1970.
[10] J. Shahen. Mohawk+T: Source Code. https://ece.uwaterloo.ca/~jmshahen/mohawk+t/, Jun 2015.
[11] J. Shahen. Mohawk+T: Efficient Analysis of Administrative Temporal Role-Based Access Control (ATRBAC) Policies. Master's thesis, University of Waterloo, 2016. Available from https://uwspace.uwaterloo.ca/.
[12] E. Uzun, V. Atluri, S. Sural, J. Vaidya, G. Parlato, A. L. Ferrara, and M. Parthasarathy. Analyzing Temporal Role Based Access Control Models. In *Proceedings of the 17th ACM Symposium on Access Control Models and Technologies*, SACMAT '12, pages 177–186, New York, NY, USA, 2012. ACM.

Automated Inference of Access Control Policies for Web Applications

Ha Thanh Le, Cu D. Nguyen, and
Lionel Briand
Interdisciplinary Centre for Security, Reliability
and Trust (SnT Centre)
University of Luxembourg, Luxembourg
{hathanh.le,duy.nguyen,lionel.briand}@uni.lu

Benjamin Hourte
HITEC Luxembourg S.A.
L-1458 Luxembourg
benjamin.hourte@hitec.lu

ABSTRACT

In this paper, we present a novel, semi-automated approach to infer access control policies automatically for web-based applications. Our goal is to support the validation of implemented access control policies, even when they have not been clearly specified or documented. We use role-based access control as a reference model. Built on top of a suite of security tools, our approach automatically exercises a system under test and builds access spaces for a set of known users and roles. Then, we apply a machine learning technique to infer access rules. Inconsistent rules are then analysed and fed back to the process for further testing and improvement. Finally, the inferred rules can be validated based on pre-specified rules if they exist. Otherwise, the inferred rules are presented to human experts for validation and for detecting access control issues. We have evaluated our approach on two applications; one is open source while the other is a proprietary system built by our industry partner. The obtained results are very promising in terms of the quality of inferred rules and the access control vulnerabilities it helped detect.

Categories and Subject Descriptors

D.2.5 [**Software Engineering**]: Testing and Debugging; D.2.7 [**Software Engineering**]: Distribution, Maintenance, and Enhancement

Keywords

Access Control Policies, Inference, Machine Learning

1. INTRODUCTION

Broken access control is a widely recognised security issue in web applications; it leads to unauthorised accesses to sensitive data and system resources. The consequences can be dramatic, from information leakage to business services being shut down. According to a recent report by

OWASP[1], broken access control is involved in three out of the top ten vulnerabilities: *A7 – Missing Function Level Access Control, A4 – Insecure Direct Object References,* and *A2 – Broken Authentication and Session Management* [9]. Due to a lack of proper access enforcement, many web applications check access rights before making functionality or system resources visible (via web links, for example). However, the same check must be carried out on the server side when a functionality or a resource is accessed. Otherwise, attackers can forge requests to get access to the resource without being authorised (A7). The second vulnerability (A4) refers to the exposure of direct references to internal resources (such as files). If such internal resources are not adequately protected, they can be maliciously accessed. The third vulnerability (A2) relates to the authentication and session management of an access control mechanism. If they are implemented improperly, attackers can compromise user credentials or impersonate other users to access their private resources.

As web applications are integrating and providing more services to increasingly diverse entities (users, devices, or other service providers – which often have different functionalities and data), they are becoming complex. As a result, access control engineering for web applications becomes increasingly challenging. Broken access control is a likely risk if the access control model of a system is not designed and documented properly or the access control implementation is not adequately tested. For this reason, access control testing and validation is crucial to decrease the level of risk.

In general, access control (AC) consists of two artefacts: *AC policy specifications* and *AC mechanisms* that implement and enforce AC policies [10]. AC policies can be specified explicitly using models [4], such as RBAC (Role-Based Access Control) [21], or rules, such as XACML [18]. Such AC models must be correctly implemented and supported by runtime verification mechanisms. Moreover, regardless of the types of AC model or implementation, we have to ensure the coverage of AC policies and implementation. It is often the case that *not all resources that need access protection are properly covered by the policies and that such policies are not enforced by the implementation.* Another problem is that, in practice, many systems use hard-coded AC policies in their business logic code and do so without documentation. This implies that, more often than not, there is no AC policy specification available for testing and validation.

---

[1] https://www.owasp.org

As a result, testing requires more human effort and its cost increases.

In this paper, we propose a semi-automated approach to the inference of AC policies for web applications. Taking advantage of a suite of security tools, our approach automatically exercises a target system and builds access spaces for a set of known users and roles. An access space of a specific user consists of discovered resources and the permissions the user has to these resources. Different abstraction techniques can be applied to the resources in order to group them into a higher level representation. Then, we are in a position to apply a machine learning to infer access rules for resources , at the chosen level of abstraction and roles. Certain rules may appear to be "Inconsistent", that is not consistently granting access to a resource for different users having a given role. They are then subject to further testing and analysis for refinement. Finally, the inferred rules can be validated against the specification of policies if they exist. Otherwise, they are presented to human experts for validation. The output rules help pinpoint AC problems, including: (i) resources that are left unprotected by the AC implementation, (ii) mismatch between the actual AC enforcement and the expected AC policies. Also, such rules, once validated, might be used in regression AC testing of future releases of web applications to detect regression faults in access control.

We have carried out an experimental evaluation of the proposed approach on two web applications, iTrust– an open source prototype for electronic health care management, and ISP– a crisis management system developed by our industry partner. The obtained results show that our approach is effective in discovering resources, determining access permissions, and inferring AC policies as expected. Furthermore, such policies help detect many AC problems including AC vulnerabilities that might lead to privilege escalation attacks and resources that are unprotected by AC implementation.

The remainder of the paper is organised as follows. Section 2 provides background concepts and discusses related work. Section 3 introduces a motivating example, followed by Section 4 where we discuss in detail the proposed approach. Section 5 shows the evaluation of the approach and analyses the outcome. Finally, Section 6 concludes the paper and outlines our ongoing work.

2. BACKGROUND AND RELATED WORK

2.1 Background

Access Control is a pervasive security mechanism which is used in virtually all systems [7]. It is concerned with authorising the right resource access permissions to users. The fundamental concepts in an access control model include *users*, *subjects*, *objects*, and *permissions*. *User* refers to human users who interact with a computer system. *Subject* refers to a process or program acting on behalf of a user. *Object* refers to resources accessible from a system, *Object* and *resource* are used interchangeably. *Permission* refers to the authorisation to perform some actions (e.g., read, update) on objects. In some systems, the notion of *Access Context* is also important, it concerns properties of subjects (e.g., location, age) who access, states of objects being accessed (e.g., a *paper* cannot be modified after the proceeding has been published), contextual factors when the access is taking place (e.g., working time or holiday), and access methods (e.g, using a trusted device or not). Over

the past decade, a number of access control models have been proposed. Among them, the Role-based Access Control (RBAC) model [8] is the most widely adopted. *Role* is the most important concept in RBAC and refers to different privileges on a system. Users and permissions are assigned to roles; these assignments govern users' accesses to resources.

Web Crawling, also referred to as *Web Spidering*, is a technique for the retrieval of web resources. Its basic process is rather straightforward, starting from one or a few seeding (entry) pages, a web crawler (also called spider) extracts hyperlinks from the contents of the pages and then iteratively navigates the web pages addressed by those links [19]. Advanced web crawlers can identify and submit web forms to achieve more thorough exploration of web applications. Recent advances in web technologies (i.e., Web 2.0), where Javascript is used extensively to render user interfaces, implement navigation, and to enable asynchronous communications with web servers, have brought great challenges to web crawling as discussed in [23]. Unfortunately, only limited research attention has been paid to improve web crawlers to support Web 2.0, e.g., [16, 6].

Web crawling is used for a variety of purposes, such as web archiving, building search engines [19], or reverse engineering of web applications where models of web systems are reconstructed and used for maintenance or testing [5]. In security contexts, it helps scanning the "attack surface" of web applications, through which security test inputs, i.e., attacks, can be submitted to applications.

2.2 Related Work

Our work belongs to the research family of applying dynamic analysis to infer program specifications for detecting security vulnerabilities. In the area of access control analysis, a technique called "differential analysis" has been proposed to detect authorisation vulnerabilities in web applications [1]. It involves crawling a system under test using different authenticated users' sessions and unauthenticated ones in order to determine which portions of the system are accessible from which users. Our approach also involves web crawling with a set of user credentials, but we improve such a technique to account for Javascript and "unlinked" areas of web applications. Moreover, the goal of our approach is different, we aim at recovering AC policies for web applications. We consider different resource abstractions and apply machine learning to infer AC policies for roles, not users. As a result, our approach is more scalable to deal with complex web applications.

Noseevich et al. extended the differential analysis with the role concept and the notion of user cases, which represents roles' actions and their dependencies [17]. These are inputs defined by a human operator. The approach, then, considers sequences of use cases, iterates through these sequences and applies differential analysis for each user case in order to detect insufficient access control. Our approach differs in a number of aspects. First, our goal is to infer AC policies that, on the one hand, can be validated to detect AC issues. On the other hand, such inferred AC policies can be used for other purposes, e.g., regression testing or software maintenance. Second, we deal with Javascript and unlinked resources, which are omitted in the related work.

Alalfi et al. have conducted a number of work on the reverse engineering of RBAC models for web applications.

Source code transformation and instrumentation techniques and tools were proposed to recover UML-based structural models and behavioural models [2]. Such models act as inputs for another model transformation technique to construct RBAC models that can be used to check against security properties [3]. Our approach uses a proxy to obtain access traces, hence, we do not need to modify application source code. In addition, we take into account all types of server resources, including static files (e.g., PDF documents, images), which are not considered in Alalfi's approach.

On a larger scope, Slankas et al. [22] proposed an approach to extract access control policies from natural language text. Natural language processing techniques are used to extract access control concepts like subjects, actions, and resources. One of our applications used for evaluation is also used in [22]. Xiao et al. [25] proposed an approach, called Text2Policy, to extract automatically AC policies in XACML format from software documents and resource access information written in natural language.

Outputs of our approach are Role-based AC policies inferred along with execution logs that contain concrete web requests and responses. Our subsequent work will investigate an approach to transform them into models used for test case generation. Existing work on model-based test generation for access control testing, e.g., [12, 20, 13, 26], can be applied or extended towards the goal of having a complete and effective automated test generation for AC.

3. MOTIVATING EXAMPLE

We consider a simple web-based document management (SDM) system, depicted in Figure 1, as a motivating example for our approach. Its server-side code consists of five server pages: *LogIn*, *Main*, *viewDocument*, *manageDocument*, and *manageUser*; they are located in the following folders: *root*, *root*, *root/user*, *root/manager*, *root/admin*, respectively. The folder *root* is the root server directory of SDM. When a user accesses to the system, she is sent to the *Login* page and, once authenticated, she is redirected to the *Main* page in which she will be provided links to the *viewDocument* and *manageDocument* pages, depending on her roles in the system. *viewDocument* has two parameters, *path* and *id*, which indicate the path to a file and document identifier, respectively.

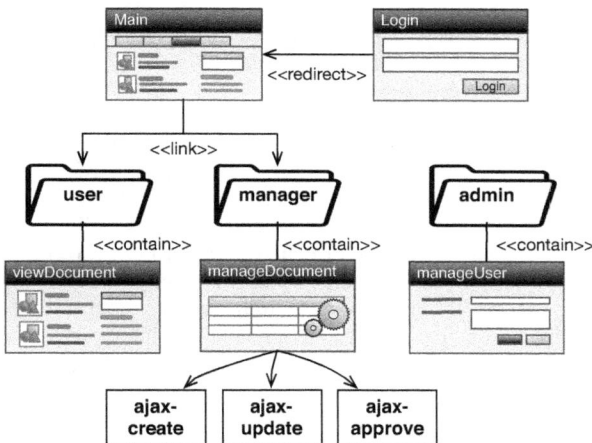

Figure 1: A simple web-based document management system.

In particular, the page *manageDocument* has three Ajax-based functions, namely *ajax-create*, *ajax-update*, and *ajax-approve* to create, update, and approve documents. These functions are also enabled based on users' roles and, once triggered, they open dynamic forms through which documents can be uploaded and updated.

The administrator of the system has to enter the *admin* suffix manually to the URL of SDM in order to access the administrative zone. The page *manageUser* allows him to create, update, delete, and assign roles to users. There is no direct link to the admin area from the *Main* page.

SDM adopts a role-based access control model to restrict accesses to the functionality of the system. Five roles are pre-defined: *adminRole*, *userRole*, *managerRole*, *authorRole*, and *guestRole*. Access permissions are assigned to roles as follows:

Role	can access
userRole	viewDocument
managerRole	manageDocument/ajax-approve
authorRole	manageDocument/ajax-create
	manageDocument/ajax-update
adminRole	manageUser

By design, all users can access the *Login* page while only authenticated users can access the *Main* page. From there, depending on the roles of a user, authorised functions (i.e., links) will be provided. Moreover, users of a given role *userRole* can only view their documents. Let us discuss some of the commonly encountered issues in web applications using SDM as an example:

Wrong Assumption: Once logged in, a user is redirected to the *Main* page. In this page, only links to the allowed pages are displayed. For example, assuming a malicious user named Mallory has been assigned to *userRole*, only a list of links of the form *viewDocument?path=...* are displayed on his browser. The developer makes an assumption that by displaying only authorised links a user like Mallory cannot access other pages. However, this assumption is wrong because based on indexing and suggesting tools like Google, by looking at a browser's history, or by simple guessing, Mallory can easily access other web pages if proper access enforcement is not in place. A malicious user can also try to guess and add some commonly used nouns like *admin*, *backup*, *config* to the main URL, in order to access sensitive areas of a web application. In the case of SDM, if only the administrator is assumed to know the *admin* suffix and no access control is in place, then unauthorised access is likely to occur.

Missing Protection: Since web clients can send direct HTTP requests to SDM, a malicious user can create requests to trigger the Ajax-based functions. If accesses are enforced only at the web pages, unauthorised accesses to these functions will occur.

Path Traversal: The *path* parameter of the *viewDocument* page can easily be tampered with illegitimate values. For example, a malicious user can enter a value such as */etc/passwd*, trying to compromise the server. Based on the naming scheme of the parameter an attacker can guess and access other users' documents. For example, if the values of the path parameter for Mallory are *mallory/1* and *mallory/2*, the pattern cam be inferred and Mallory can try the *alice/[0-9]+* pattern in order to view the documents of the user *alice*.

In the next section, we discuss our approach and how it aims at discovering resources in web applications like SDM, learning access permissions for different roles in an automated fashion, and pointing out AC issues.

4. APPROACH

Our approach, as illustrated in Figure 2, consists of five main steps: (1) *automated exploratory access testing*, (2) *resource access analysis*, (3) *inferring access rules*, (4) *rule assessment*, and (5) *targeted incremental access testing*. Our approach takes as input a set of credentials of different users who belong to different roles in a system under test (SUT). In the first step, we leverage a suite of security tools to explore (crawl) the SUT dynamically in order to generate access logs (HTTP requests/responses) for each user. During the second step, we perform resource extraction from the access logs and determine access permissions for users. In the third step, based on data about users' accesses obtained from the second step, we use machine learning to infer a decision tree that characterises access control policies. Step 4 assesses the decision tree to identify inconsistent rules. Step 5 performs additional access tests for the inconsistent rules that require more training data and refinement before iterating to the second step. Finally, we report the inferred rules to a human expert for validation and identification of AC problems. In the subsequent sections, we discuss each step in detail.

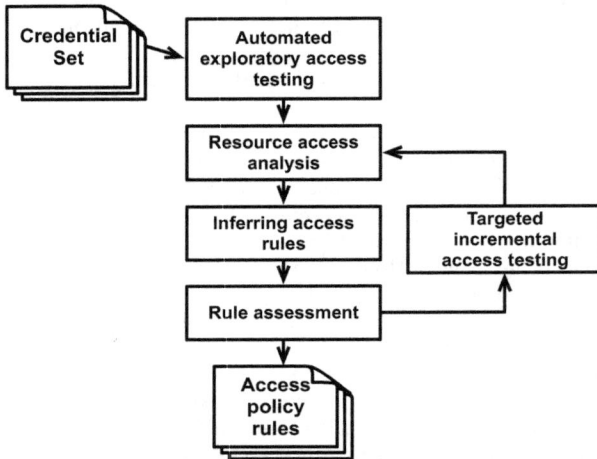

Figure 2: An overview of the proposed approach.

4.1 Automated Exploratory Access Testing

The goal of this step is to determine user access space for a given set of users. Depending on the assigned roles and roles' permissions, each user is *allowed* to access to some resources and is *denied* to access to the other unauthorised resources. We define the user access space of the SUT as a tuple $AS = \{U, G, R, C, p\}$, where U is a set of users; G is a set of roles; R set of resources of the SUT; C is a set of access contexts; and finally p is *allowed* or *denied*.

Figure 3 depicts our approach and the tools that we use for exploring a SUT and generate resource access logs. In our approach, we make use of a security tool suite called *BurpSuite*[2] to determine user access space. The BurpSuite's spider is used to discover the SUT's resources the users can access. It takes users' credentials and automatically analyses web contents for forms and links, submits the forms

[2]http://portswigger.net/burp

or follows the links to further explore the SUT. The chosen spider shows good crawling capability in most of the applications we used for evaluation. However, it needs support to deal with Javascript codes so that the dynamically rendered contents (e.g., menu links created with Javascript) can be explored. This is important because modern web applications use Javascript and asynchronous communication extensively to update the content, including links and forms, of web pages. In our motivating example, the three Ajax-based resources can only be discovered if Javascript is executed.

In addition, a chain of automated security tools (other spiders with different crawling capabilities or web scanners like Nikto2[3]) or testers, using a browser with Javascript enabled, can interact with the SUT. The SUT's discovery results, including HTTP requests and responses, are captured by BurpSuite's proxy.

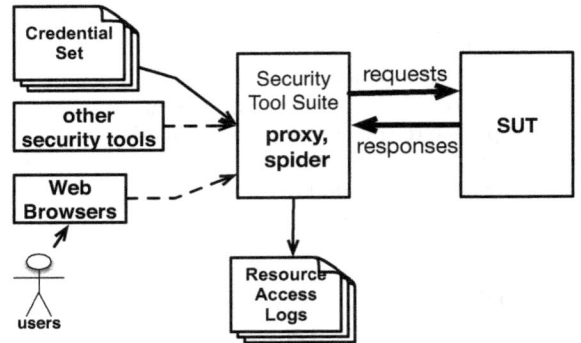

Figure 3: Automated exploration of resource accesses for a SUT.

Taking the intercepted responses as entry points and user's provided data in their requests, the spidering tool can explore the SUT more thoroughly for hidden resources that are unlinked or are accessible only with specific data and/or by following some business flows. For example, considering our motivating example, since the administration pages are isolated from the main page, the spider alone may not detect them. However, if an entry point to those pages is provided by a user and captured by the proxy, the spider can use the entry point to explore the pages for resources. Moreover, when the SUT has Web test cases (such as Selenium[4] tests), which access the SUT via Web interface, we can execute such tests over the proxy to provide more entry points and valid data to the spider. This will help the spider quickly uncover more resources.

It is worth noticing that there are other commercial or open source security tool suites that provide similar features, such as WebInspect[5] and Acunetix WVS[6]. Since our approach analyses the standard HTTP requests and responses, it can be easily integrated with those tools as well. We selected BurpSuite because of it has shown good performance and is more affordable compared to other commercial tools. Besides, it also has a free community version for limited adoption.

Each user is considered separately in our exploration approach. Her credential is fed to the security tool suite, which

[3]https://cirt.net/Nikto2
[4]http://www.seleniumhq.org
[5]https://download.hpsmartupdate.com/webinspect/
[6]http://www.acunetix.com/vulnerability-scanner/

will then automatically crawl the SUT until no new resource access is discovered. During the session, the developer can optionally access the SUT so as to provide meaningful input data and more entry points to aid the crawling process. Once all users have been considered, we combine all the discovered resource URLs and their corresponding requests to perform user-resource access testing for each user and all the resources that were not discovered within her exploratory session. The goal is to check the access permissions of each user on all resources.

Moreover, we need to provide the crawling tool with one or more entry (i.e., seeding) pages so that the crawling process can start from them. For the SUTs that do not provide access to their server directories, we can use the usual spidering method that is provided with the home/login page as the only entry point. We name this method *single-entry* exploration.

For SUTs that have their server directories accessible for analysis, we propose an exploration method called *all-entry*, in which we consider all server static resources, including server pages, images, folders, and all other files located in the server directory, as entry points for spidering. The goal is to improve the crawler's performance by providing it with more seeding pages. In fact, for *all-entry*, we can easily scan the server directory for all static resources (e.g., all JSP pages using the Linux *find* command) and issue HTTP requests to access them. Such requests and their responses are captured by the proxy and served as entry points for the spider.

The outputs of this phase are *resource access logs* that contain detailed data about all the issued HTTP requests (resource URLs, parameters, etc.) and server HTTP responses. The next phase focuses on analysing these logs for determining meaningful access spaces.

4.2 Resource Access Analysis

Resource access logs contain session identifiers, HTTP requests, and HTTP responses. From them, we need to extract important information for access control analysis, including *user*, *target resource*, and *access permission*. Since in the previous phase each user has a separate exploratory session, mapping the log entries to users is straightforward. Hence, this section discusses in detail two tasks: (1) extracting resources, and (2) determining access permissions on the identified resources.

4.2.1 Extracting Resources

We propose to extract resources that need to be considered in access control from the logged HTTP requests, especially from the URIs (Uniform Resource Identifiers) of the GET requests and from the URIs combined with the message body contents of the POST requests [24]. The URI of a GET request is composed of a path to a server resource and a query, which is specified as pairs of parameters and their values. The URIs of POST requests often contain only paths to server pages; the content of the request is also specified as pairs of parameters and their values. We name the path section of a URI of any HTTP request as *base URI*. In general, a base URI indicates a web element, for example, a server page/servlet/CGI script, a directory, or a file. They are often resources that need to be protected. However, in addition to the base URIs, some applications also use request parameters to identify resources and, in such cases,

relevant parameters and concrete values must be taken into account in extracting resources.

We propose two levels of resource identification: *base-URI-resource*, and *full-resource*. At the base-URI-resource level, we consider the base URIs as resources, stripping out all parameters. At the full-resource level, we are interested in controlling access to specific resources that are identified based on request parameters. Therefore, we have to consider also the parameters and their values as provided in the requests that help identifying resources. For example, the parameter *id* of the page *viewDocument* can have multiple integer values in the access logs, each identifying a specific document that can only be accessed by the owner of the document and users belonging to the *managerRole* role. The challenge at this level is to know which parameters are relevant for determining resources. For example, the requests that point to the URI *manageDocument/ajax-update* could have a number of parameters such as *id*, *title*, *date*, where only the first one is relevant for resource identification. In this work, we need to involve the developer to provide a list of parameters that can have an impact on access control policies. Future work will look into automated solutions to identify such parameters.

By default, our approach considers the base-URI-resource level. Since our approach is iterative, in subsequent steps, if we find inconsistent AC rules for some resources because of missing parameters, we will go back to this step and consider the full-resource level for them. Base-URI resources will be decomposed into more concrete resources, taking into account relevant parameters and values. The output of this extraction task is the set of identified resources R.

4.2.2 Determining Access Permission

This task focuses on determining access contexts C and granted permissions P for the identified resources. We analyse the information available in the access logs, specifically the HTTP requests and responses, to decide in which context a resource is requested, and the permissions the SUT grants to the user who is accessing the resource.

Various factors can contribute to determining access contexts, such as *resource states*, *access methods*, and *access history*. Each resource may have its own set of states, identifying them and determining their roles in access control automatically is non-trivial. As a result, we reserve resource states for future work. Access methods are the standard HTTP request methods [24], including *GET*, *POST*, and *DELETE*. Access history is a list of requests prior to the current resource accesses and reflects the sequence of activities characterising how a user interacted with the SUT. Such a sequence of activities is often governed by the business process model of the SUT and might affect whether a request is allowed or denied. For example, a *payment* request is allowed only if some items were previously added to a shopping cart.

In this work, access context includes access methods and the *referrer* attribute of HTTP requests that indicates the prior page that links to the current resource being requested. This attribute, to a limited extent, captures access history. Future work will investigate more complex definitions of context.

Access permission of a user to a resource is determined based on HTTP responses, more specifically the standard HTTP status codes [24] and the HTML contents. In addition to using HTTP status codes, some web systems gracefully deny unauthorised accesses with an "OK Status" web page (HTTP code = 200) stating "Access is not allowed". These denial messages usually follow one or a few specific patterns and we, therefore, attempt to use regular expressions to match HTML contents and classify them into *denial* or *normal*. The former indicates that its corresponding request was denied while the latter implies otherwise. Following are the rules to determine access permission:

Condition	Permission
HTTP Code = 4xx,5xx,301, any content	denied
HTTP Code = 200,302,304, *denial* content	denied
HTTP Code = 200,302,304, *normal* content	allowed

4.3 Inferring Access Rules

After resource access logs have been analysed from the previous steps we obtain a data corpus characterising the access space $AS = \{U, G, R, C, p\}$. It can be presented as a table with the following columns (attributes): user, role, resource, context-method (i.e., HTTP access methods), context-referrer (i.e., referrers in HTTP requests), and permission.

Since the number of resources is often large, their combinations with other attributes tend to yield large tables preventing manual analysis. We propose to apply a classification technique called *decision tree*, from machine learning, which is widely used in many fields to infer rules. The goal is to aid the analyst to infer quickly access rules from the data collected, check the rules against expectations, and identify potential issues and inconsistencies.

We employ a machine classifier implemented in Weka[7], a popular machine-learning tool suite. Specifically, we use the *RandomTree* classifier because its output decision trees are interpretable. Furthermore, in our preliminary study about alternative classification methods, we have found that *RandomTree* yields good classification precision and recall when processing our data. Attribute *permission*, which takes the value *allowed* or *denied*, acts as the class (or label) in the data samples. A learned decision tree can be graphically represented as a tree (e.g., Figure 4) in which the root and intermediate nodes are the predictor attributes, outgoing edges from the nodes are specific values for these attributes, and each leaf node represents a predicted class label (allowed or denied in this context). For example, in Figure 4, the root node is the resource attribute and if resource is r_1 then the next decision node is the role attribute. If role is $role_1$ and then the next node is the context attribute. Finally, if context is c_1 then the access is allowed.

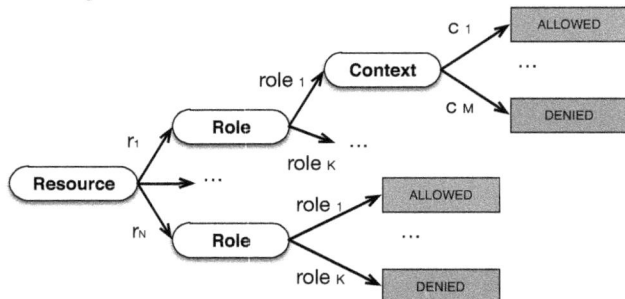

Figure 4: Graphical representation of decision trees learned to infer access rules.

More interestingly, the paths from the root to the leaves represent classification rules. In our context, they are the

[7]http://www.cs.waikato.ac.nz/ ml/weka

AC policy rules that we need to infer. It is important to note that the user attribute is not in the tree and rules since, in most systems (e.g., those that use the RBAC model), access permissions are assigned to roles. Therefore, the user attribute does not participate in decision-making and is not accounted for by the classifier. However, in some cases where the concept of ownership is relevant, i.e., only owners of some resources can access them, the user attribute may be accounted for and appear in the decision tree and rules. Following example shows three concrete rules that we inferred from the experimental systems. Rule 1 states that everyone is allowed to access the 'login.jsp' page. Rule 2 states that users of the role 'guest' cannot access the 'admin.jsp' page. Rule 3 states that users of role *author* can edit documents only when their status is 'draft'.

```
RULE 1:
      resource = 'login.jsp' : allowed
RULE 2:
      resource = 'admin.jsp'
   |    role = 'guest'
   |    |    method = 'GET' : denied
RULE 3:
      resource = 'edit.jsp'
   |    role = 'author'
   |    |    docStatus = 'draft' : allowed
   |    |    docStatus = 'post' : denied
```

The next section discusses how we assess the inferred rules, improve them if necessary, and finally help the analyst to validate the rules.

4.4 Rule Assessment

Apart from the learned decision tree and rules, the classifier provides the *prediction confidence* at each leaf node of the tree. This measure indicates the homogeneity of the data sample that forms the leaf node, in terms of percentages of accesses that are allowed or denied. We define *consistent* rules as those that predict allowed or denied with 100% confidence level, whereas the other rules are referred to as *inconsistent*, meaning that in their corresponding leaf nodes corresponding some accesses are allowed while others are denied. In the context of access control, such inconsistent rules may indicate potential problems in the access control implementation, or alternatively a lack of information regarding the attempted accesses (e.g., history, parameters), as further discussed below.

One possible reason for inconsistent rules is the abstraction process when extracting resources, where details of parameters are abstracted away to help scale the analysis. As a result, some resources considered in our analysis may actually represent groups of concrete resources for which different users may have different access permissions, even if they have the same role. This is due to some systems using request parameters to specify access operations (e.g., read, update, delete) or relying on the concept of ownership (e.g., users can edit the resources they create) or user profile (e.g., customers being 18 or older can purchase wine) to implement access control.

To deal with inconsistency we employ a step called *targeted incremental access testing* (see Figure 2). In this phase, we first select inconsistent rules and identify resources and roles that are involved in these rules. Identified resources and roles will help trace back to their original users, requests, and responses. The full-resource level of resource extraction should then be considered for such resources. Let us consider our motivating example. If we consider the URI *user/viewDocument* as a target resource, different users of the role *userRole* can hold different access permissions since, during the exploratory phase, they access different documents identified by the id parameter. Therefore, for *user/viewDocument* we need to consider its full-resource level, i.e., including the id parameter and its values. As a result, instead of having *user/viewDocument* as the only resource, we have to consider *user/viewDocument?id=1*, *user/viewDocument?id=2*, etc., assuming 1 and 2 are two example values of id.

In the step *Targeted incremental access testing*, we currently involve the developer to identify relevant parameters and their input values for the resources involved in the inconsistent rules. Then, requests accessing these resources are generated by combining their base URI and those parameter values. A t-way test combinatorial technique [11] can be applied to reduce the number of combinations to be exercised in such new requests. The generated requests are submitted to the SUT for every user (among those selected), and then the obtained access logs are analysed again to update the access space and the inferred policy rules. This iterative process is repeated until inconsistent rules are resolved. Finally, the obtained policy rules are validated by the developer.

All the inferred rules should be checked to pinpoint AC problems and discrepancies with expected AC requirements. However, since their number could be large, we suggest the developer should, first, pay special attention to the following types of resources and their corresponding access rules:

- Resources that allow access to all users; we have observed many cases where such resources have been left unprotected by the implemented AC mechanism.

- Resources that are related to database, configuration, installation, backup files, and other static documents. The development team might have forgotten to clean them up or properly protect them before deployment, and there could potentially be insecure direct accesses (without authentication) to them.

- Resources with corresponding inconsistent AC rules. In practice, AC policies might be governed by other factors, such as subject profiles or resource states. We may have to limit incremental access testing iterations because of time constraints, hence not fully resolving all inconsistent rules. In such cases, the developer should check whether inconsistency is due to AC implementation mistakes or other reasons that affect access control.

5. EXPERIMENTS AND RESULTS

In this section, we discuss the experiments that were carried out to evaluate our approach. We investigate whether the proposed approach is effective in discovering resources and inferring correct AC rules. We also assess whether such rules are helping to detect AC vulnerabilities. More specifically, we aim at addressing the following research questions:

RQ1: *Does the proposed approach effectively discover resources for inferring AC rules?*

RQ2: *What is the quality in terms of correctness and consistency of the inferred AC rules?*

RQ3: *How useful are the inferred AC rules in detecting AC issues?*

In what follows, we present the applications selected for the experiments, the experimental procedure, and the results we obtained.

5.1 Applications

Our criteria to select web-based systems for our evaluation are twofold. First, they must implement an access control mechanism that supports the basic concepts of *user*, *role*, *resource*, and *permissions* of roles to access resources. Second, we must know beforehand the users, roles, and user-role assignments in selected systems, which is a pre-requisite to be able to learn access control rules.

We have selected two systems, ISP and iTrust, for our experimental evaluation. ISP is a complex crisis management system under development by an industry partner involved in this work. (The full name of the system and the name of the company are omitted because of the anonymity requirement of the conference.) ISP is used in disaster relief and humanitarian missions to manage and process sensitive data. It involves mobile teams that are deployed on the field to collect data and synchronise them with crisis management centres via satellite communications. In the system, users are assigned to different roles (for example, *ground-team*, *mission-lead*) that have different access permissions to resources, e.g., missions. ISP implements an AC administration module where users and roles can be defined at run-time. ISP distinguishes 49 groups of resources, called *logical* resources so that administrators of the system can efficiently assign access permissions to roles. In addition, from a technology standpoint, Javascript is extensively used in ISP to render the user interface and for Ajax communications with the web server.

iTrust is a feature-rich prototype and open source system for electronic health care management [15]. It has been developed at North Carolina State University to provide software engineering students with an educational project that is relevant and has enough depth and complexity. Moreover, it also provides an educational testbed for understanding the importance of security and privacy requirements. iTrust has been used in previous studies related to access control [14, 22].

iTrust predefines eight roles including *doctor*, *patient*, and *staff*. The definition of roles and role access permissions are carried out at design time. Authorised users of a role can access resources in specific folders. For example, the users with role *patient* are allowed to access resource files under the */auth/patient/* and */auth/* folders. These access control rules are specified in the configuration file (WEB-INF/web.xml) of iTrust and enforced by the web container where iTrust is deployed, e.g., apache-tomcat[8]. We use this configuration as a baseline of comparison ("gold standard") when evaluating inferred access rules for iTrust.

5.2 Tool and Experiment

We have developed a tool that works in tandem with BurpSuite to support our approach. The tool takes as inputs configuration files that specify user credentials and content patterns, which are used in the determination of access permissions as discussed in Section 4.2. It interacts with BurpSuite to feed login credentials, to start spidering sessions, and to send requests to web servers through BurpSuite's proxy so that requests and responses can be captured and

---

[8]http://tomcat.apache.org

used for analysis. Once the spidering process is finished, the tool can analyse the log data of BurpSuite for identifying resources and determining access permissions. This tool is available for download[9].

Since ISP needs roles to be defined at run-time (except the most privileged *admin* role), we created five roles having different sets of permissions on resources. Then, for each application we prepared a set of users and assigned them to roles: 15 users for iTrust, and 14 users for ISP. As for correctly classifying access permissions, we defined five content patterns for iTrust. For example, the pattern *"your role is invalid"* is used to classify accesses as denied if it is contained in their corresponding responses. Similarly, we defined ten additional content patterns for ISP. The definition of such patterns is straightforward; we can try some unauthorised accesses to learn the response patterns or we can simply ask the developer for the coding convention of denial messages.

Users' credentials (*username* and *password*) and content patterns are fed into our tool, which exercises the web applications and return the user access space, i.e., the data corpus ready for applying machine learning. Finally, the developer can assess the inferred AC rules, following the guidelines discussed in the rule assessment step of our approach, and perform additional access testing to refine inconsistent rules where needed.

To answer the research questions, we rely on the following experimental data: (1) the number and percentage of discovered resources in comparison with static resources when applicable, (2) the correctness and completeness of inferred AC rules when compared to the gold standard, and (3) the number of AC issues detected and their cause.

5.3 Results

In this section, we present in turn the experimental results obtained from iTrust and ISP.

5.3.1 iTrust

Regarding iTrust, we used the base-URI-resource extraction level, and consequently no request parameters were considered. When applying the single-entry exploration technique, only the home page of iTrust was fed into our framework. As a result, it was able to discover 130 out of a total of 248 resources. When all-entry exploration was performed, all 248 resources were detected. However, among them, 44 resources returned Java exception error pages because of implementation errors or due to the fact they were not intended to be accessed directly but only through other pages. For example, *header.jsp* or *footer.jsp* are included in all other web pages. In terms of access control, these 44 resources are considered to be vulnerabilities (of the type *A4 – Insecure Direct Object References*) since their direct access are allowed to all users, and even worse, source code and database information is disclosed in the error pages. We exclude them from the next step, AC rule inference, as it is clear that they are accessible to all users. Since the results of all-entry subsumes the results of single-entry in terms of resources, inferred AC rules, as well as issues found, in the following we analyse the results of all-entry only.

Based on the 207 discovered resources that remain for further analysis, our technique has inferred 1518 AC rules for resources, roles, and permissions. Among them, 1441 are correct with respect to the gold standard AC rules of iTrust.

[9]URL removed for anonymity.

These inferred rules encompass all the gold standard rules thus reaching the maximum completeness of 100%. The remaining 77 inferred AC rules for 43 resources need further validation. Analysing them we found that:

- 38 resources are uncovered by the implemented AC rules (*A7 – Missing Function Level Access Control*). In other words, they are not checked for authorisation. Most of them are located in the *util*, *errors*, and *DataTables* folders. These resources can leak important information, such as showing database tables or transactional logs, or can lead to privilege escalation. We realised that only some of them are intended for end users, while the others are for development purposes only. This is the reason why there are so many resources that are left unprotected.

- Five resources are false positives. Three of them are intended to be accessible without authentication (*/privacyPolicy.jsp*, */j_security_check*, */css.jsp*), while the other two are system files that should be ignored by our tool as their access is controlled by the web server (*/WEB-INF/web.xml*, and */META-INF/context.xml*).

Among the unprotected resources for end users, we found three privilege vulnerabilities: (1) */util/resetPassword.jsp* allows any user (even a guest without authentication) to change passwords. It has a simple question-answering scheme, and no old password is required. As a result, it is very easy to change the passwords of other users, including the admin user, to gain access to the system. (2) The */util/getUser.jsp* page is designed to be invoked from other pages where the developer assumed that authorisation has already been enforced. However, it is also accessible independently and does not re-enforce authorisation in such a case. As a result, any user can query private data from other users. (3) The */errors/reboot.jsp* page allows anyone to reboot the web server, which might render the system inaccessible to all users. The first and second vulnerability can be categorised as *A2 – Broken Authentication and Session Management*, while the third one belongs to *A7 – Missing Function Level Access Control*.

Among the 1441 correctly-inferred AC rules, 11 AC rules (0.8%) for seven resources are inconsistent. We have performed one iteration of incremental access testing to resolve the inconsistencies by refining relevant branches of the decision tree. No parameter of these seven resources is relevant to determine more resources or access permissions. As a result, we applied our *Resource Access Analysis* step, refining a content filter, to correct the access permissions of the requests to six (out of seven) resources, which were classified as "denied" due to an application error (*index out of bound*), while the correct permission should have been "allowed". The AC rules of the last resource, */auth/patient/addTelemedicineData.jsp*, remains inconsistent:

```
RULE:
      resource = patient/addTelemedicineData.jsp
   |    role = Patient
   |    |    method = GET : denied (75.0
   |    |    method = POST : allowed (62.5
```

Investigating this resource we found that there is no relevant parameter that participates in AC. Also, according to the gold standard, all requests from the role *Patient* should be allowed, which is not the case in this rule where 75% GET and 37.5% POST requests are denied. The reason is that iTrust implements an additional AC policy that controls access based on patient profiles: access permission is only allowed to patients that have a specific profile regarding their *blood pressure, glucose level, height, and weight*. To make this rule consistent, we would have to take into account different classes of patients according to such a profile.

Looking more carefully at the rule, we find that the permissions determined for POST and GET are different. This indicates a potential flaw in the implementation. We looked further into the source code of the resource and confirmed that this is indeed an AC vulnerability. The AC check based on patient profiles is missing for POST requests, and as a consequence, many direct POST requests were allowed even if they came from patients that did not have the required profile.

In summary, in the evaluation on iTrust, our approach discovered 130 and 248 resources (i.e., 100%), respectively, with single-entry and all-entry exploration. All-entry is provided with more seeding pages for crawling. As a result, it is more effective than single-entry. Our approach inferred 1518 AC rules in which 1441 (94.92%) are correct compared to the gold standard. The remaining 5.08% need further inspections since their corresponding resources are not protected by the AC implementation. Our approach has also indicated many AC issues in iTrust: 44 resources show compilation errors revealing source code and valuable information for malicious exploitation; 38 resources are uncovered by access control implementation leading to three AC vulnerabilities; one resource (pertaining to an inconsistent AC rule) is improperly protected given that access is driven by patient profiles. This resource is vulnerable to privilege escalation attacks since a patient could change other patients' data.

5.3.2 ISP

Regarding ISP, we could only apply the single-entry exploration technique since we had limited access to the system at the time of running the evaluation. However, thanks to the support of the proxy, we could also use web browsers during the crawling process to access ISP so that interfaces were rendered and Javascript-based navigation was used by the crawler. This helped discover more resources.

We compared two runs of the exploratory step: one is completely automated by BurpSuite (i.e., no Javascript is executed) while the other is enhanced with Javascript execution. For the latter, we had involved one developer using a web browser to traverse ISP pages in a depth-first manner, through the exploratory session of an admin user (who can access to all resources). It took him four working hours to complete the task, which is reasonable compared to the effort that can be saved using the technique. The run without Javascript support returned 353 resources. The run with Javascript support discovered 680 resources, which is significantly higher than the number of resources discovered when Javascript execution is ignored. This shows the importance of considering Javascript, which our approach does, in resource discovery.

After excluding Javascript, CSS, and unimportant (with respect to information disclosure) image files from the discovered 680 resources, there were 399 resources left for analysis. We inferred and analysed AC rules for a subset of 131 randomly selected resources since their mapping to logical resources required substantial manual effort among system engineers. In what follows we discuss three interesting and representative situations.

- There were 15 CSV and JSON files that were unprotected from direct accesses (*A4 – Insecure Direct Object References*). Unauthorised users can access them if they know the URLs.

- Five resources have accesses that are specified by 15 inconsistent rules. Inspecting them, we detected a number of discrepancies between the defined AC rules, using the ISP's AC administration module, and the inferred AC rules. This was due to access control enforcement being different from the defined rules. For example, according to the defined AC rules, some users are allowed to create new data records while in reality their accesses to such a function are denied. ISP developers have confirmed these issues after discussion.

- 80 resources can be mapped to 16 logical resources based on their names. All 240 rules inferred for them are consistent. However, since the mapping has not been checked by the ISP developers due to time constraints, the correctness of the inferred AC rules is yet to be confirmed.

To support the analyst in inspecting inferred AC rules, our tool can filter rules of interest, including those that are inconsistent or allow/deny accesses from any user. We present them graphically as a decision tree in Freemind[10]. Figure 5 depicts an example of the graphical format of the inferred AC rules for ISP, where the analyst can expand/collapse and navigate the tree to check the inferred access permissions of roles to resources. Note that the leaves of the decision tree are labelled with the corresponding classification and confidence level.

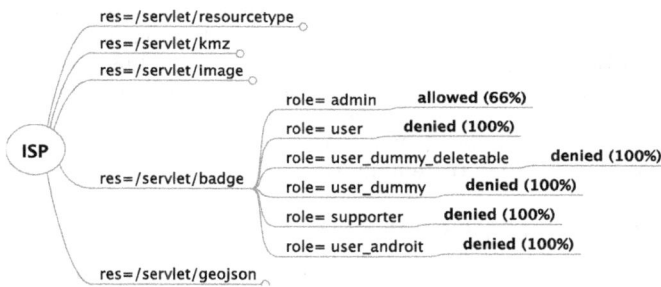

Figure 5: Examples of AC rules inferred for ISP.

5.4 Discussion

Based on the results presented above, we find that our approach is effective in discovering resources for inferring AC rules, especially with the all-entry exploration (**RQ1**). This technique discovered all iTrust resources considered in access control management. In the case of ISP, the single-entry exploration, augmented with the use of interactive web browsers for Javascript, has also resulted in a high number of resources being discovered.

> *RQ1: The proposed approach is effective in discovering resources when considering all-entry exploration and supporting Javascript.*

The proposed technique yielded a high ratio of correctly inferred AC rules (**RQ2**): 94.92% (1441/1518) of the rules in the gold standard for iTrust. The remaining rules are not

---

[10]http://freemind.sourceforge.net/

necessarily incorrect since they were not specified. They pertain mostly to resources that are left unprotected by the AC mechanism in place. Among the correctly inferred AC rules, only about 0.8% (11/1441) were inconsistent and needed further refinement. The reason for inconsistency, as we have discussed earlier, is due to the misclassification of access permissions for six resources (due to incomplete content patterns) and an AC vulnerability for one resource. The former can be resolved by completing our list of content patterns and the latter requires to fix the AC implementation.

> *RQ2: The proposed approach can infer a high ratio of correct AC rules that highly, though not completely, encompass the gold standard.*

Resources that are left unprotected by the AC implementation or have access permissions specified by inconsistent rules have a high probability of being affected by AC vulnerabilities. As the results we obtained for both applications have shown, unprotected resources can lead to leakage of valuable information or AC privilege escalation vulnerability. Apart from inferring AC rules, our technique can help detecting such problems as well (**RQ3**).

> *RQ3: Inconsistency in the inferred AC rules are helpful in detecting AC issues.*

Though presenting many advantages, our approach is not fully automated yet. First, it involves manual effort in identifying parameters that are relevant for resource identification and inputs for incremental access testing. However, our approach is easier to apply when dealing with systems like iTrust in which access control is mainly done on the level of server files and folders, or systems that have a limited number of request parameters participating in AC. Second, the mapping between discovered resources and logical resources also requires manual effort. We are currently extending our work to address these limitations.

6. CONCLUSION

Broken access control is a widely recognised security issue in web applications. As web applications are becoming increasingly complex , access control (AC) vulnerabilities become significant threats. Testing and validation to detect AC problems are thus crucial but usually rely on predefined and regularly updated AC specifications. In practice, however, it is common for such specifications to be missing or outdated. For many systems, AC policies are hard-coded in the business logic code without proper documentation.

We propose in this paper a semi-automated, bottom-up approach to infer AC rules for web applications. The proposed approach rests on an integration of a spider, a web proxy, and web browsers for dealing with Javascript and user inputs. It first exercises a target system automatically and builds access spaces for a set of known users and roles. Then, machine learning is applied to infer AC rules. Problematic resources are identified if the accesses to them are specified by inconsistent or incorrect rules (checked by the developer) or they are left unprotected accidentally.

We have evaluated our approach and its supporting tool on two web applications, one open source and the other a proprietary system developed by our industrial partner. The results are very promising: our approach can effectively discover resources, determine and correctly infer access permissions and AC rules. It is also helpful in pinpointing many AC vulnerabilities, including insecure direct access to resources, privilege escalation, and faulty implementation of AC policies. In our ongoing work, we aim at addressing the limitations of this work with incremental testing and rule refinement. We will also investigate an approach to map actual resources to logical ones. These two extensions will help reducing the amount of manual effort that is needed with the current solution.

7. REFERENCES

[1] *Hacking Exposed Web Applications: Web Application Security Secrets and Solutions.* McGraw-Hill, 3rd edition, 2011.

[2] M. Alalfi, J. Cordy, and T. Dean. Automated reverse engineering of uml sequence diagrams for dynamic web applications. In *Software Testing, Verification and Validation Workshops, 2009. ICSTW '09. International Conference on*, pages 287–294, April 2009.

[3] M. Alalfi, J. Cordy, and T. Dean. Recovering role-based access control security models from dynamic web applications. In M. Brambilla, T. Tokuda, and R. Tolksdorf, editors, *Web Engineering*, volume 7387 of *Lecture Notes in Computer Science*, pages 121–136. Springer Berlin Heidelberg, 2012.

[4] N. Damianou, A. Bandara, M. Sloman, and E. Lupu. A survey of policy specification approaches. *Department of Computing, Imperial College of Science Technology and Medicine, London*, 2002.

[5] G. Di Lucca, M. Di Penta, G. Antoniol, and G. Casazza. An approach for reverse engineering of web-based applications. In *Reverse Engineering, 2001. Proceedings. Eighth Working Conference on*, pages 231–240, 2001.

[6] C. Duda, G. Frey, D. Kossmann, and C. Zhou. Ajaxsearch: Crawling, indexing and searching web 2.0 applications. *Proc. VLDB Endow.*, 1(2):1440–1443, Aug. 2008.

[7] D. Ferraiolo, D. R. Kuhn, and R. Chandramouli. *Role-based access control - 2nd edition.* Artech House, 2007.

[8] D. Ferraiolo and R. Kuhn. Role-based access control. In *In 15th NIST-NCSC National Computer Security Conference*, pages 554–563, 1992.

[9] T. O. Foundation. Owasp 10 most critical web application security risks. Technical report, OWASP, 2013.

[10] J. Hwang, E. Martin, T. Xie, and V. C. Hu. Testing access control policies. In *Encyclopedia of Software Engineering*, pages 673–683. 2010.

[11] R. Kuhn, R. Kacker, Y. Lei, and J. Hunter. Combinatorial software testing. *Computer*, 42(8):94 –96, aug. 2009.

[12] E. Martin. Automated test generation for access control policies. In *Companion to the 21st ACM SIGPLAN Symposium on Object-oriented Programming Systems, Languages, and Applications,*

OOPSLA '06, pages 752–753, New York, NY, USA, 2006. ACM.

[13] A. Masood, R. Bhatti, A. Ghafoor, and A. P. Mathur. Scalable and effective test generation for role-based access control systems. *Software Engineering, IEEE Transactions on*, 35(5):654–668, 2009.

[14] A. K. Massey, P. N. Otto, L. J. Hayward, and A. I. Antón. Evaluating existing security and privacy requirements for legal compliance. *Requirements engineering*, 15(1):119–137, 2010.

[15] A. Meneely, B. Smith, and L. Williams. itrust electronic health care system: A case study.

[16] A. Mesbah, A. van Deursen, and S. Lenselink. Crawling Ajax-based web applications through dynamic analysis of user interface state changes. *ACM Transactions on the Web (TWEB)*, 6(1):3:1–3:30, 2012.

[17] G. Noseevich and A. Petukhov. Detecting insufficient access control in web applications. In *SysSec Workshop (SysSec), 2011 First*, pages 11–18, July 2011.

[18] OASIS. Extensible access control markup language (xacml). Technical report, OASIS, 2003.

[19] C. Olston and M. Najork. Web crawling. *Foundations and Trends in Information Retrieval*, 4(3):175–246, 2010.

[20] A. Pretschner, T. Mouelhi, and Y. Le Traon. Model-based tests for access control policies. In *Software Testing, Verification, and Validation, 2008 1st International Conference on*, pages 338–347. IEEE, 2008.

[21] R. S. Sandhu, E. J. Coyne, H. L. Feinstein, and C. E. Youman. Role-based access control models. *Computer*, 29(2):38–47, 1996.

[22] J. Slankas and L. Williams. Access control policy extraction from unconstrained natural language text. In *Social Computing (SocialCom), 2013 International Conference on*, pages 435–440, Sept 2013.

[23] P. Tonella and F. Ricca. Dynamic model extraction and statistical analysis of web applications: Follow-up after 6 years. In *Web Site Evolution, 2008. WSE 2008. 10th International Symposium on*, pages 3–10, Oct 2008.

[24] W3C. Hypertext transfer protocol – http/1.1, 1999.

[25] X. Xiao, A. Paradkar, S. Thummalapenta, and T. Xie. Automated extraction of security policies from natural-language software documents. In *ACM SIGSOFT FSE'12*, page 12. ACM, 2012.

[26] D. Xu, L. Thomas, M. Kent, T. Mouelhi, and Y. Le Traon. A model-based approach to automated testing of access control policies. In *Proceedings of the 17th ACM symposium on Access Control Models and Technologies*, pages 209–218. ACM, 2012.

Commune: Shared Ownership in an Agnostic Cloud

Claudio Soriente
ETH Zurich, Switzerland
claudio.soriente@inf.ethz.ch

Ghassan O. Karame
NEC Laboratories Europe, Germany
ghassan.karame@neclab.eu

Hubert Ritzdorf
ETH Zurich, Switzerland
hubert.ritzdorf@inf.ethz.ch

Srdjan Marinovic
The Wireless Registry Inc, USA
srdjan@wirelessregistry.com

Srdjan Capkun
ETH Zurich, Switzerland
srdjan.capkun@inf.ethz.ch

ABSTRACT

Cloud storage platforms promise a convenient way for users to share files and engage in collaborations, yet they require all files to have a single owner who unilaterally makes access control decisions. Existing clouds are, thus, agnostic to shared ownership. This can be a significant limitation in many collaborations because, for example, one owner can delete files and revoke access without consulting the other collaborators.

In this paper, we first formally define a notion of *shared ownership* within a file access control model. We then propose a solution, called Commune, to the problem of distributed enforcement of shared ownership in agnostic clouds, so that access grants require the support of an agreed threshold of owners. Commune can be used in existing clouds without modifications to the platforms. We analyze the security of our solution and evaluate its performance through an implementation integrated with Amazon S3.

Categories and Subject Descriptors

C.2.0 [**Computer-Communication Networks**]: General – Security and protection.

Keywords

Cloud security; Shared ownership; Distributed enforcement

1. INTRODUCTION

Even though the cloud promises a convenient way for users to share files and effortlessly engage in collaborations, it still retains the notion of *individual* file ownership. That is, each file stored in the cloud is owned by a single user, who can *unilaterally* decide whether to grant or deny any access request to that file. However, the individual ownership is not suitable for numerous cloud-based applications and collaborations. Consider a scenario where a number of research organizations and industrial partners want to set up a shared cloud repository to collaborate on a joint research project. If all participants contribute their research efforts to the project, then they may want to share the ownership over the collaboration files so that all access decisions are agreed upon among the owners. There are two main arguments why this may be preferred to individual ownership. First, a sole owner can abuse his rights by unilaterally making access control decisions. The community features a number of anecdotes where malicious users revoke access to shared files from other collaborators. Second, even if owners are willing to elect and trust one of them to make access control decisions, the elected owner may not want to be held accountable for collecting and correctly evaluating other owners' policies. For example, incorrect evaluations may incur negative reputation or financial penalties.

In contrast to individual ownership, we introduce a novel notion of *shared ownership* where n users jointly own a file and each file access request must be granted by a pre-arranged threshold of t owners. We remark that existing cloud platforms, such as Amazon S3 and Dropbox, provide no support for shared ownership policies, and offer only basic access control lists. In short, they are *agnostic* to the concept of shared ownership. Furthermore, state-of-the-art trust management systems that can support shared ownership policies (e.g., SecPAL [9], KeyNote [12], Delegation Logic [22]) make all access decisions using a *centralized* Policy Decision Point (PDP). This is not suitable for enforcing our shared ownership model, because the user who administrates the PDP can arbitrarily change the policy rules set by the owners and enforce his own policies.

In this paper, we address the problem of *distributed enforcement of shared ownership within an agnostic cloud*. By distributed enforcement, we mean enforcement where access to files in a shared repository is granted if and only if t out of n owners separately support the grant decision. To tackle this problem, we first introduce the Shared-Ownership file access control Model (SOM) to define our notion of shared ownership, and to formally state the given enforcement problem. We then propose our solution, called Commune, that enforces shared ownership policies in a distributed fashion. Commune can be used within a third-party cloud without any modifications to the platform. It only requires that the cloud offers basic access control lists, as is the case with current platforms. We integrate a prototype implementation of Commune within Amazon S3 [1] and we show that its performance scales well with the file size and with the number of users.

To the best of our knowledge, Commune is the first solution to distributed enforcement of shared ownership in an agnostic cloud. We summarize our contributions as follows:

- We formalize the notion of shared ownership within a file access control model named SOM, and use it to define a novel access control problem of distributed enforcement of shared ownership in an agnostic cloud.
- We propose a solution, called Commune, which distributively enforces SOM and can be deployed in an agnostic cloud platform. Commune ensures that *(i)* a user cannot read a file from a shared repository unless that user is granted read access by at least t of the owners, and *(ii)* a user cannot write a file to a shared repository unless that user is granted write access by at least t of the owners.
- We build a prototype of Commune and evaluate it within Amazon S3. We show that our solution scales well with the file size and the number of users.

The rest of the paper is organized as follows. Section 2 introduces our notion of shared ownership in a file access control model. Section 3 details Commune and analyzes its security. Section 4 evaluates the performance of Commune through an implementation within Amazon S3. Section 5 reviews related work, and Section 6 provides concluding remarks.

2. SOM: SHARED-OWNERSHIP FILE ACCESS CONTROL MODEL

In this section, we first formalize our notion of Shared Ownership within a file access control Model named SOM. We then discuss the main shortcoming of centralized enforcement, and we define the problem of SOM's distributed enforcement.

2.1 Syntax and Semantics

For simplicity, we do not consider directories (or other file groupings). A file is created with the following request

$$U \text{ reqs } \text{Create}(F, t, \mathcal{O}).$$

Upon receiving this request, SOM creates a file F, assigns a user U and all the users in $\mathcal{O}$ as F's owners, and sets the file's threshold to t. SOM grants requests for file creation to authenticated users if the new file name is unique.

To access a file, a user submits a request with an action he wishes to perform on the file

$$U \text{ reqs } \text{Action}(F).$$

SOM does not instantiate concrete file actions, these are left to implementations, and we use Action(F) to denote a generic file access action on a file F.

If an owner O wishes to grant an action to U over F, then he issues a credential of the form

$$O \text{ says } U \text{ can } \text{Action}(F).$$

Intuitively, a credential is a certificate by an owner to support a user action. The full credential and request grammar is:

$$
\begin{aligned}
credential &::= u(i) \textbf{ says } u(j) \textbf{ can } \text{Action}(f) \\
request &::= u \textbf{ reqs } \text{Create}(f, t, o_1, \ldots, o_n) \\
request &::= u \textbf{ reqs } \text{Action}(f) \\
u, f, o &::= String \\
t &::= \mathbb{N}
\end{aligned}
$$

File access requests are granted if and only if t out of n owners issue the corresponding credentials. For example, if the threshold for F is 2, then U can perform Action on F if the following credentials are present: O **says** U **can** Action(F) and O' **says** U **can** Action(F), where O and O' are two of F's owners.

The SOM access control policy, Π_{SOM}, is a mapping from the set of all requests $\mathcal{R}$ and the set of all credentials $\mathcal{C}$ into the $\{grant, deny\}$ decision set, such that the file threshold is always respected.

Definition 1 (Shared Ownership Access Control Policy). *The SOM access control policy, denoted Π_{SOM}, is a mapping $\mathcal{R} \times \mathcal{C} \to \{grant, deny\}$ such that:*

$$\Pi_{SOM}(U \textbf{ reqs } \text{Action}(F), Creds) \mapsto grant \quad iff$$
$$\{(O_1 \textbf{ says } U \textbf{ can } \text{Action}(F)), \ldots,$$
$$(O_t \textbf{ says } U \textbf{ can } \text{Action}(F))\} \subseteq Creds,$$
$$O_1 \neq \cdots \neq O_t \text{ and } \quad O_1 \in \mathcal{O}, \ldots, O_t \in \mathcal{O},$$

where t is F's threshold, and $\mathcal{O}$ is the set of F's owners.

We say that SOM grants a file access to a given request r and its accompanying credentials C if and only if $\Pi_{SOM}(r, C) = grant$. Note that by Definition 1, SOM treats owners only as sources of credentials, and does not implicitly grant them any additional access rights.

2.2 Centralized vs. Distributed Enforcement

Existing credential-based access control systems have the following enforcement model. A Policy Enforcement Point (PEP) has one designated Policy Decision Point (PDP), which collects all the required credentials and evaluates an access control policy (such as Π_{SOM}) for a given request. The PDP has one user who can administrate its access control policy. We refer to this enforcement model as *centralized* since a single policy decision point grants all access requests. Note that even if a PEP used multiple PDP components (managed by different users), it would still require an additional PDP to centrally decide how these decisions are combined. In Appendix A, we show how SOM can be centrally enforced. We do this by specifying the SOM access control policy as a Datalog logic program. A Datalog interpreter can then act as the PDP. Using Datalog interpreters as PDPs is also common in state-of-the-art access control systems (e.g., [9], [22]).

The key shortcoming of centralized enforcement is that the PDP's access decision is solely sufficient for granting access requests. The administrator, responsible for managing the rules stored at the PDP, can therefore change the policy rules to grant requests that lack the necessary credentials. In practice, this means that the shared ownership policy agreed upon by the owners can always be bypassed, and thus the notion of shared ownership nullified. The natural question to consider is how to enforce the SOM policy so that the agreed thresholds cannot be bypassed. We refer to such an enforcement solution as *distributed* because it must grant access if and only if t owners separately support the grant decision.

When considering a cloud as a collaboration platform, this enforcement issue is even more difficult because a cloud platform does not allow deployment of additional enforcement components. A cloud platform only supports basic access control policies via Access Control Lists (ACLs). We frame these concerns as the SOM distributed enforcement problem.

| Enforcement | Ownership | |
	Individual	Shared
Centralized	ACLs	Datalog-based Systems
Distributed	—	Commune

Table 1: Solutions for ownership enforcement in a cloud. Note that Datalog-based systems require modifications to the cloud platform.

Problem Statement: How can the SOM access control policy be distributively enforced within a cloud platform that supports only ACL-based PDPs?

We summarize the state-of-the-art with respect to this problem in Table 1.

3. COMMUNE: DISTRIBUTED ENFORCEMENT OF SHARED OWNERSHIP

This section presents Commune, a solution for distributed enforcement of the SOM access control policy in an agnostic cloud. As SOM does not specify concrete file access operations, we instantiate Commune with write and read actions. Before introducing our solution, we outline our cloud and attacker model.

3.1 Cloud and Attacker Model

We focus on a cloud storage platform, S, where a set of users U have personal accounts onto which they upload files. For example, users might set up their own personal clouds [5, 6], or might create personal accounts in existing public clouds. A user $U \in U$ can unilaterally decide who has access to files stored on his account. In particular, S allows each user to define access control policies of the type $p : U \times \{write, read\} \rightarrow \{grant, deny\}$. We also assume that S correctly enforces individual access control policies. This model reflects the functionalities provided by existing cloud platforms, such as Amazon S3.

Since we assume that S authenticates users, we only focus on internal adversaries. An adversary may try to gain read access to a file even if fewer than t owners have issued the corresponding credentials. We refer to this adversary as a "malicious reader". Alternatively, an adversary, who has been granted write access by fewer than t owners, may try to publish a file F as if F were authored by a user had been granted write access by t or more owners. We refer to this adversary as a "malicious writer". We also consider sets of users who collude to escalate their access rights.

3.2 Overview of Commune

Before describing Commune, we make the following observations:

Observation 1. Commune's files cannot be stored on a single user account.

Following the discussion regarding the centralized enforcement, a single user must not be charged with making unilateral grant and deny decisions. Otherwise, that user may abuse his rights and take unilateral access control decisions. A naïve solution where a file is encrypted (e.g., using a key shared among the owners) and the ciphertext is stored on a single account, allows that account holder to, for example,

unilaterally deny read access to the ciphertext. If the ciphertext cannot be read, any mechanism to distribute or recover the encryption key is of no help. We argue, therefore, that Commune cannot use a centralized repository because the repository owner can unilaterally grant or deny access to the files stored therein. Our alternative is to use a "shared repository", which is an abstraction built on top of the owners' personal accounts on S.

Observation 2. Commune cannot support in-place writing.

If Commune were to allow in-place writing, then users who are granted write access could overwrite a file with "garbage". This would equate to granting users the right to unilaterally delete the file, thus nullifying our efforts to prevent such scenarios. A standard alternative to in-place writing is to introduce "copy-on-write" mechanisms whereby a new file is created upon each file write operation. To optimize performance, Commune implements versioning and splits files into *units* (i.e., the unit of granularity of versioning) so that writing a new version of an existing file, only requires updating the units that have changed with respect to the previous version.

Observation 3. Commune cannot prevent users from disseminating a file through an out-of-band channel.

Access control solutions cannot prevent a user from distributing content through an out-of-band channel. For example, a user who rightfully reads a file can leak it to third parties. Similarly, a malicious writer can write a file and disseminate it through an out-of-band channel. For example, a user can publish files on his account on S and make them available for others to read. We cannot prevent such behaviour. Commune, however, must at least allow honest readers, who abide to the protocol specification, to distinguish between the content written by malicious writers and the content written by honest writers.

Given these observations, Commune unfolds as follows. At system setup, users define the set of n owners O and the threshold t (with $t \leq n$).[1] Commune abstracts the storage space of the owners' accounts on S as the "shared repository". Each owner grants/denies read and write access on his account to users (including other owners) according to his individual access control policy. The distributed enforcement of the SOM access control policy then follows from the enforcement of the individual access policies set by each owner.

To write a file to the shared repository, the writer encodes the file in *tokens* and distributes the tokens to the owners' accounts. A file is written to the shared repository if and only if the writer successfully distributes the file's tokens onto at least t owners' accounts. That is, a user has write access granted to the shared repository if and only if he has write access granted to at least t of the owners' accounts. We refer to such a user as an "authorized writer".

To read a file from the shared repository, the reader must fetch the file's tokens from at least t distinct owners' accounts. Therefore, a user has read access granted to the file if and only if he has read access granted to the file's

---

[1] Mechanisms to select the set of owners and the threshold t are outside of our scope. In settings like scientific collaboration scenarios, owners and thresholds are agreed by the partners.

41

Algorithm 1 AON-FFT($K, f_1, \ldots, f_m$)

1: Parse $f_1, \ldots, f_m$ as $f_1^0, \ldots, f_m^0$
2: **for** $r \leftarrow 1$ to $\log_2 m$ **do**   ▷ round counter
3:   **for** $i \leftarrow 0$ to $\frac{m}{2^r} - 1$ **do**
4:     **for** $j \leftarrow 1$ to 2^{r-1} **do**
5:       $f_{j+i\cdot 2^r}^r \| f_{j+i\cdot 2^r + 2^{r-1}}^r \leftarrow E(K, f_{j+i\cdot 2^r}^{r-1}, f_{j+i\cdot 2^r + 2^{r-1}}^{r-1})$
6:     **end for**
7:   **end for**
8: **end for**
9: **return** $f_1^r \ldots, f_m^r$ as $\bar{f}_1 \ldots, \bar{f}_m$

---

tokens by at least t owners. We refer to such a user as an "authorized reader".

To securely enforce shared ownership policies, Commune is designed to fulfil the following properties.

- **P1:** A malicious writer (i.e., a user who has been granted write access by fewer than t owners), must not be able to publish a file F as if F were authored by an authorized writer.

- **P2:** A malicious reader (i.e., a user who has been granted read access to a file F by fewer than t owners), must not be able to recover the file content. This property must also hold in case of *revocation*. Assume that, at the time τ_1, U has read access to F granted by at least t owners. Also assume that, at the time $\tau_2 > \tau_1$, U has his access rights revoked. This happens if, at the time τ_2, some of the owners decide to revoke read access to U so that U is left with fewer than t read grants. We must ensure that, starting from time τ_2, U cannot recover meaningful bits of F. We remark that, as is common for access control systems, we cannot prevent U from storing a local copy of F at the time t_1 and reading it even after his read right has been revoked.

  Commune must also provide *collusion resistance*. That is, coalitions of users—where no single user is an authorized reader—must not be able to pool their credentials to escalate their read access rights.

Property P1 ensures protection against malicious writers who try to disseminate content despite lacking the required credentials. Property P2 guarantees that malicious readers cannot read content written to the shared repository.

Commune fulfils property P1 by design, through the abstraction of the shared repository and the copy-on-write mechanism (see Section 3.5). Property P2 is fulfilled through two cryptographic building blocks: Secure File Dispersal (SFD), and Collusion Resistant Secret Sharing (CRSS). SFD ensures that malicious readers cannot acquire any information about a file, even if they previously had access to the file and were later revoked. CRSS builds atop SFD and ensures that coalitions of users where no single user has enough credentials to read the file, cannot pool their credentials in order to escalate their read access rights.

In the following, we describe and analyze SFD (Section 3.3) and CRSS (Section 3.4). In Section 3.5, we detail the integration of both building blocks in Commune.

3.3 Secure File Dispersal (SFD)

Information dispersal algorithms [24] encode a file in n chunks so that any t chunks (where $t \leq n$) are sufficient to decode it. However, information dispersal algorithms do not provide any security guarantees if the number of available chunks is smaller than t: any party with fewer than t chunks may still recover meaningful information about the original file's content.

Previous work on securing information dispersal algorithms [25] combines erasure codes with All-Or-Nothing Transforms (AONT) [26]. The latter is an efficient block-wise transformation that maps an n-block bitstring in input to an n'-block bitstring in output (with $n' \geq n$). AONTs are designed in such a way that, unless all the n' output blocks are available, it is hard to recover any of the input blocks.

Existing AONTs [13, 26] leverage block ciphers and rely on the secrecy of a cryptographic key that is embedded within the output blocks. Given all AONT output blocks, the key can be recovered; once the key is known, individual blocks can be reverted, independently of other blocks. Current AONTs, therefore, preserve their all-or-nothing property only for *one time*: knowledge of the cryptographic key allows to revert single output blocks and to recover parts of the original data. This is at odds with our security requirements. As argued before, we cannot prevent users from caching a local copy of the file and reading it at later time when their read rights may have been revoked. However, we still want to provide revocation of a user who only stored the encryption key at the time when he had read access to the file.

We therefore introduce a new scheme, called Secure File Dispersal (SFD), that combines information dispersal algorithms with an AONT that preserves its all-or-nothing property even if the adversary has the encryption key.

Definition. An SFD scheme consists of the following algorithms:

$\{c_1, \ldots, c_n\} \leftarrow$ SFD.Encode(t, n, F, K, λ). Encodes a file F into n chunks, such that F can be correctly decoded using any t chunks; K denotes a key used in the encoding process and λ is a security parameter.

$F' \leftarrow$ SFD.Decode($K, \mathcal{C}, \lambda$). Takes as input a key K, a set of chunks $\mathcal{C}$, and security parameter λ; it outputs a file F'.

Correctness. Given $\{c_1, \ldots, c_n\} \leftarrow$ SFD.Encode(t, n, F, K, λ) and $F' \leftarrow$ SFD.Decode($K, \mathcal{C}, \lambda$), we require that if $\mathcal{C} \subseteq \{c_1, \ldots, c_n\}$ and $|\mathcal{C}| \geq t$, then $F' = F$.

Security. We define the advantage of adversary $\mathcal{A}$ as follows:

$$
\begin{aligned}
\mathrm{Adv}_{SFD}(\mathcal{A}) = \Pr[&f \leftarrow \mathcal{A}(K, \mathcal{C}) | K \leftarrow \{0,1\}^l, l \geq \lambda, \\
&F = f_1, \ldots, f_m \leftarrow \{0,1\}^{m\lambda}, \\
&\{c_1, \ldots, c_n\} \leftarrow \text{SFD.Encode}(t, n, F, K, \lambda), \\
&\mathcal{C} \subset \{c_1, \ldots, c_n\}, |\mathcal{C}| < t, f \subseteq F, |f| \geq \lambda].
\end{aligned}
$$

where $f \subseteq F$ refers to a substring of F. We say that SFD is secure if, for any p.p.t. adversary, its advantage is negligible in the security parameter, i.e., $\mathrm{Adv}_{SFD}(\mathcal{A}) \leq negl(\lambda)$. Our security definition captures the scenario where, at an earlier time, $\mathcal{A}$ was given enough chunks to decode F and has cached a copy of the key K, while at current time he is only given fewer than t chunks. Even if $\mathcal{A}$ has the key K, we require the probability that $\mathcal{A}$ recovers any λ consecutive bits of F to be negligible in the security parameter.

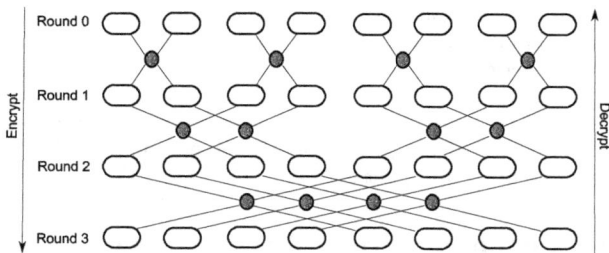

Figure 1: Sketch of the AON-FFT scheme where the input consists of $m = 8$ input blocks. Solid circles refer to the block cipher $E(\cdot)$, while empty circles depict its input/output blocks.

Instantiation. Our SFD scheme combines information dispersal techniques with AON-FFT, an all-or-nothing transformation inspired by Fast Fourier Transform.

Let $E : \{0,1\}^{4\lambda} \to \{0,1\}^{2\lambda}$ be a semantically secure block cipher (e.g., $E(\cdot)$ could correspond to 256-bit Rijndael [17], with $\lambda = 128$).[2] AON-FFT takes as input a symmetric key K (of size 2λ) and m input blocks $f_1, \ldots, f_m$ (each of size λ). It executes in $\log_2 m$ rounds and, at each round, applies $E(\cdot)$ to pairs of blocks. Each round is fed with the output of the previous round. The original input $f_1, \ldots, f_m$ is treated as the output of round 0; the final output of the algorithm is the output of round $\log_2 m$ (cf. Figure 1). The pseudo-code of AON-FFT is shown in Algorithm 1. We omit the details of the decryption algorithm since it is specular to encryption.

Given the pseudo-code of AON-FFT, our SFD scheme unfolds as follows:

$c_1, \ldots, c_n \leftarrow$ SFD.Encode(t, n, F, K, λ). Parse F as $f_1, \ldots, f_m$ where each f_i has size λ.
Run $\bar{f}_1 \ldots, \bar{f}_m \leftarrow$ AON-FFT$(K, f_1, \ldots, f_m)$. Use the information dispersal encoder to encode $\bar{f}_1 \ldots, \bar{f}_m$ in n chunks with reconstruction threshold t.[3]

$F' \leftarrow$ SFD.Decode(K, C, λ). Given a set of at least t chunks C and key K, use the information dispersal decoder to decode blocks $\bar{f}'_1, \ldots, \bar{f}'_m$. Run $f'_1 \ldots, f'_m \leftarrow$ AON-FFT$(K, \bar{f}'_1, \ldots, \bar{f}'_m)$.

Correctness. If $\{c_1, \ldots, c_n\} \leftarrow$ SFD.Encode(t, n, F, K, λ), any subset of at least t chunks $\{c_{i_1}, \ldots, c_{i_t}\}$ can be decoded into the whole output of AON-FFT, namely $\bar{f}_1 \ldots, \bar{f}_m$. Given K, the output of AON-FFT can be decrypted to recover $F = f_1, \ldots, f_m$.

Security. Given the construction of our AON-FFT scheme, it is easy to see that each input block depends on all output blocks and on the encryption key. Furthermore, assuming that $E(\cdot)$ is a semantically secure block cipher, for any p.p.t. algorithm $\mathcal{A}$, we have $\text{Adv}_{SFD}(\mathcal{A}) \leq negl(\lambda)$. We provide a security argument in the Appendix.

Note that a construct similar to AON-FFT, was first mentioned by Rivest [26] and later on used as a "proof of storage"

---
[2]The key size is 2λ and the input/output size is also 2λ, totalling 4λ size of input.
[3]SFD can leverage any information dispersal algorithm (e.g., Reed-Solomon codes [30]).

in [29]. Nevertheless, the construction proposed therein can use any pseudo-random permutation in the FFT network. Our AON-FFT requires a keyed permutation, hence a block-cipher. Furthermore, the goal of the adversary in [29] is to recover, in a given amount of time, all *output* blocks. In contrast, the goal of our adversary is to recover any *input* block. This entails different security definition and analysis.

3.4 Collusion Resistant Secret Sharing (CRSS)

We now introduce our second building block, called Collusion Resistant Secret Sharing (CRSS). Similar to threshold secret-sharing schemes, CRSS allows one party to distribute a secret among a set of designated shareholders, so that any subset of shareholders of size equal to or greater than the threshold can reconstruct the secret. Furthermore, CRSS allows shareholders to issue to other users *delegation* to reconstruct the secret. If a user collects enough (i.e., above the threshold) delegations, he can rightfully reconstruct the secret. However, users cannot pool their delegations to reconstruct the secret, unless one of them has collected enough delegations. In Commune, CRSS is used to secret-share the key K used in SFD, in order to achieve collusion resistance.

CRSS is inspired by decentralized Attribute Based Encryption [21] where shares of a secret are *blinded* with shares of 0, such that, if a user collects enough shares for his identity, the blinding cancels out and the secret can be reconstructed.

Definition. Our definition of CRSS builds on top of a *standard* threshold secret-sharing scheme SS with algorithms SS.Share$(\cdot)$ and SS.Combine$(\cdot)$, to share and reconstruct a secret, respectively. We assume SS to be secure according to the **Game Priv** definition by Rogaway et al. [27]. That is, we assume that an adversary has only negligible advantage in identifying which out of two values was (t, n) secret-shared using the SS.Share$(\cdot)$ algorithm, even if the adversary can corrupt up to $t - 1$ shareholders and access their shares.

CRSS defines the following algorithms:

$\{s_1, \ldots, s_n\} \leftarrow$ CRSS.Share(s, t, n). Shares secret s in a set of n shares $\{s_1, \ldots, s_n\}$ with reconstruction threshold t.

$d_{i,j} \leftarrow$ CRSS.Delegate(s_i, U_j). Takes as input a share s_i and an user identity U_j. The output is a *delegation* $d_{i,j}$.

$s' \leftarrow$ CRSS.Combine$(\{d_{i_1,j}, \ldots, d_{i_l,j}\})$. Combines delegations $\{d_{i_1,j}, \ldots, d_{i_l,j}\}$ into s'.

Correctness. Given $\{s_1, \ldots, s_n\} \leftarrow$ CRSS.Share(s, t, n) and $s' \leftarrow$ CRSS.Combine$(\{d_{i_1,j}, \ldots, d_{i_l,j}\})$, we require that if $d_{i_p,j} \leftarrow$ CRSS.Delegate(s_{i_p}, U_j), for $1 \leq p \leq l$ and $l \geq t$, then $s' = s$.

Security. We model the security of CRSS using an adaptation of the **Game Priv** of [27] and we denote the refined game by **Game Priv***:

Init. The adversary $\mathcal{A}$ submits two messages x_0, x_1 of equal length. The challenger flips an unbiased coin b and runs $\{s_1, \ldots, s_n\} \leftarrow$ CRSS.Share(x_b, t, n).

Find. $\mathcal{A}$ can submit two types of queries. In Type-1 queries, the adversary can corrupt up to $t' \leq t - 1$ shareholders and receives their shares. At this time, $\mathcal{A}$

picks t' indexes $i_1, \ldots, i_{t'}$ and receives $\{s_{i_1}, \ldots, s_{i_{t'}}\}$. In Type-2 queries, for any fresh identity U_j, the adversary can ask for up to t'' delegations, as long as $t' + t'' \leq t - 1$. $\mathcal{A}$ submits an identity U_j and t'' indexes $i_1, \ldots, i_{t''}$, and receives delegations $\{d_{i_1,j}, \ldots, d_{i_{t''},j}\}$.

Guess. The adversary outputs his guess b' and wins if $b' = b$.

We define the advantage of the adversary as the probability of its winning minus a half. That is, $\mathrm{Adv}_{CRSS}^{\mathtt{Priv*}}(\mathcal{A}) = Prob[\mathtt{Priv*}^{\mathcal{A}}] - \frac{1}{2}$. Therefore, we say that CRSS is secure if any p.p.t. algorithm $\mathcal{A}$ has only negligible advantage in winning **Game Priv***.

The above **Game Priv*** models a scenario where a set of malicious users, including up to t' shareholders, collects up to t'' delegations for each of their identities. If $t' + t'' \geq t$, the malicious shareholders can produce the missing delegations for any of the colluding user identities, so that the secret can be reconstructed by means of CRSS.Combine($\cdot$). Otherwise, colluding users must not be able to retrieve the secret.

Instantiation. Our CRSS scheme is based on the threshold secret-sharing scheme proposed in [15], which is defined as follows:

$g^x, \{x_1, \ldots, x_n\} \leftarrow$ SS.Share$(-, t, n)$. Pick a cyclic group G of prime order q where the discrete logarithm assumption holds; let $\langle g \rangle = G$. Pick a random $x \in Z_q$ and set the secret to g^x. Pick a random $t - 1$-degree polynomial X with coefficients in Z_q, such that $X(0) = x$. Set the i-th share to $x_i = X(i)$.

$s' \leftarrow$ SS.Combine$(\{x_{i_1}, \ldots, x_{i_l}\})$. Given shares $\{x_{i_1}, \ldots, x_{i_l}\}$, use polynomial interpolation to recover the secret. That is $s' = g^{\sum_{p=1}^{p=l} x_{i_p} \lambda_p}$ where $\lambda_p = \prod_{1 \leq k \leq l}^{k \neq p} \frac{x_{i_k}}{x_{i_k} - x_{i_p}}$.

Note that in the above scheme, the secret is not given as input to the Share algorithm; rather, it is set to g^x for a randomly chosen x. Given the above algorithms, our CRSS scheme unfolds as follows:

$\{s, s_1, \ldots, s_n\} \leftarrow$ CRSS.Share$(-, t, n)$. Run SS.Share$(-, t, n)$ to obtain $g^x, \{x_1, \ldots, x_n\}$. Pick $H(\cdot) : \{0, 1\}^* \rightarrow G$ to be a cryptographic hash function that maps random strings in G. Pick a random $t - 1$-degree polynomial Y with coefficients in Z_q, such that $Y(0) = 0$, and denote $y_i = Y(i)$. The secret is set to $s = g^x$ while each share is set to $s_i = (x_i, y_i)$.

$d_{i,j} \leftarrow$ CRSS.Delegate(s_i, U_j). Parse $s_i = (x_i, y_i)$ and output $d_{i,j} = g^{x_i} H(U_j)^{y_i}$.

$s' \leftarrow$ CRSS.Combine$(\{d_{i_1,j_1}, \ldots, d_{i_l,j_l}\})$. Run $s' \leftarrow$ SS.Combine$(\{d_{i_1,j_1}, \ldots, d_{i_l,j_l}\})$.

Correctness. If $l \geq t$, then CRSS.Combine$(\{d_{i_1,j}, \ldots, d_{i_l,j}\})$ outputs

$$
\begin{aligned}
s' &= \prod_{p=1}^{p=l} (d_{i_p,j_p})^{\lambda_{i_p}} = \prod_{p=1}^{p=l} (g^{x_i} H(U_j)^{y_i})^{\lambda_{i_p}} = \\
&= g^{\sum_{p=1}^{p=l} \lambda_{i_p} x_{i_p}} H(U_j)^{\sum_{p=1}^{p=l} \lambda_{i_p} y_{i_p}} = \\
&= g^k H(U_j)^0 = g^k = s.
\end{aligned}
$$

Security. The security of CRSS is based on the fact that, in the random oracle model, delegations for different identities cannot be combined to remove the blinding factor from the secret. Assuming that $H(\cdot)$ is modeled as a random oracle and that the discrete logarithm assumption holds in G, we can show that any p.p.t. algorithm $\mathcal{A}$ has only negligible advantage in winning **Game Priv***.

3.5 Commune: Protocol Specification

Recall that Commune leverages a shared repository, which is an abstraction of the owners' storage space on $\mathcal{S}$. The shared repository uses a versioning system so that content cannot be overwritten but only new content can be added. In particular, Commune optimizes performance by splitting a file in smaller *units*, and encoding/decoding each unit separately. Therefore, when a new file version is written to the shared repository, the writer only needs to upload the units that have changed from the previous version.

Files written to the repository are encoded in *tokens* and distributed across the owners' accounts. Leveraging the basic ACLs of $\mathcal{S}$, owners exert their individual policy on the tokens they store on their accounts. The distributed enforcement of the SOM policy is implied by the enforcement of each owner's individual policy on his tokens by $\mathcal{S}$.

Encoding must guarantee both correctness and security of reading operations. Hence, users who are authorized to read at least t tokens must be able to decode the original file; users who are granted read access on fewer than t tokens must not be able to recover its content. Furthermore, users must not be able to pool their credentials to escalate their access rights.

Create a File. File creation requires one user, the file creator, to "bootstrap" the system and write the initial version of the file into the repository. For this reason, we assume that—at the file creation time—the file creator has been granted the right to write new data to each of the owner's accounts on $\mathcal{S}$.

The file creator first divides the file F into k fixed-sized units. For each unit F_i ($i \in [1, \ldots, k]$), he runs $\{s_i, s_{i1}, \ldots, s_{in}\} \leftarrow$ CRSS.Share$(-, t, n)$ to produce a fresh secret s_i and n of its shares. Secret s_i is used as a symmetric key to encode the unit F_i in n chunks using SFD. That is, the file creator runs $\{c_{i1}, \ldots, c_{in}\} \leftarrow$ SFD.Encode$(t, n, F_i, s_i, \lambda)$. The token of the unit F_i for the owner O_j is set to (c_{ij}, s_{ij}) (i.e., one chunk outputted by SFD.Encode$(\cdot)$ and one secret-share outputted by CRSS.Share$(\cdot)$). Finally, for each owner O_j, the file creator writes $\{(c_{ij}, s_{ij})\}_{i \in [1, \ldots, k]}$ to O_j's account on $\mathcal{S}$. Each owner, therefore, receives one token for each unit that constitutes F.

Grant/Deny Write Rights. An owner O_j grants write rights to a user U_l by granting to U_l the right to write new data (i.e., tokens) to O_j's account. Similarly, O_j denies write rights to U_l by denying U_l the right to write new data to O_j's account.

Update a File. Assume U_l wants to write a new version of a file F. For simplicity, assume that the new version differs from the previous one by only one unit F_i (the case where the old and the new versions differ in several units is handled in a similar fashion). At this point, some owners may allow U_l to write tokens to their accounts while others may not.

Let $\mathcal{O}^+$ be the subset of owners who grant to U_l write rights to their accounts. Similarly, let $\mathcal{O}^-$ be the subset of owners who deny to U_l write rights to their accounts. U_l can, therefore, only distribute tokens to owners in $\mathcal{O}^+$. This scenario is equivalent to the case where U_l distributes tokens to all owners in $\mathcal{O}$, but the ones in $\mathcal{O}^-$ decide to reject the version produced by U_l and make the received tokens unavailable.

U_l is an authorized writer and his version accepted (i.e., considered as written to the shared repository) if and only if $|\mathcal{O}^+| \geq t$. In this case, there are at least t tokens for the new unit, so it may be decoded by users who collect enough credentials. If $|\mathcal{O}^+| < t$, user U_l is not authorized to write and his version is rejected (i.e., considered as not written to the repository), since there are not enough tokens to decode the unit produced by U_l.

Grant/Deny Read Rights. Recall that for each unit F_i, an owner O_j receives the token (c_{ij}, s_{ij}). O_j can grant to U_l read access to that unit by *endorsing* the token for U_l and granting to U_l read access on the endorsed token. Token endorsement requires O_j to run $d_{ij,l} \leftarrow \text{CRSS.Delegate}(s_{ij}, U_l)$. The endorsed token $(c_{ij}, d_{ij,l})$ is then made available by O_j for U_l to read. If a file consists of multiple units, O_j must endorse all relative tokens for U_l and grant to U_l read access on all endorsed tokens.

O_j can revoke read rights that were previously granted, by denying to U_l the right to read the previously endorsed tokens.

Read a File. If the original file spans several units, U_l must decode each unit separately in order to read the entire file. That is, for each unit, he uses the set of endorsed tokens he can fetch to recover the secret key via CRSS.Combine($\cdot$) and then uses the secret key to decode the unit via SFD.Decode($\cdot$). Note that for an authorized reader to read version x of file F, he must fetch the latest endorsed tokens created up to (and including) version x, for each unit that comprises the file. Assume user U_l is granted read access to $\{(c_{ij_1}, d_{ij_1,l}), \ldots, (c_{ij_t}, d_{ij_t,l})\}$. To recover F_i that user runs $s_i \leftarrow \text{CRSS.Combine}(\{d_{ij_1,l}, \ldots, d_{ij_t,l}\})$ and then $F_i \leftarrow \text{SFD.Decode}(s_i, \{c_{ij_1}, \ldots, c_{ij_t}\}, \lambda)$. U_j proceeds in a similar way in order to recover all units of F that he has access to.

Security analysis. From Sections 3.3 and 3.4, it follows that given t tokens of a file unit F_i (endorsed for a unique user identity), it is possible to recover both the secret key used to encode F_i and its AON-FFT ciphertext, so that the original file can be decrypted. That is, users can read files written by honest writers, if they are granted such right by at least t out of n owners.

Property P1 (cf. Section 3.2) is fulfilled as follows. First, Commune uses copy-on-write to prevent writers from overwriting content in the shared repository with garbage. Second, malicious writers (i.e., writers who have been granted write access by fewer than t owners) are unable to distribute a file without honest readers detecting it. In other words, a file is considered as written if and only if it is correctly encoded in tokens and those tokens are distributed to and endorsed by at least t out of n owners. Any content distributed through other means (e.g.,out of band channels) is easily recognized as malicious by honest readers. We argue that detection of unauthorized files is the only solution for

Parameter	Default Value
w	128 B
t	4
n	10
$|F_i|$	10 MiB

Table 2: Default parameter used during the evaluation.

protecting honest readers, because there are no mechanisms to deter malicious writers from disseminating arbitrary content (cf. Observation 3). We also stress that honest readers can easily detect writers that distribute polluted (i.e., non-decodable) tokens. Denial-of-service attacks are, nevertheless, out of the scope of this work.

Property P2 is satisfied by combining CRSS and SFD. The former ensures that coalitions of users, where no single user has enough tokens endorsed for his identity, cannot pool their endorsed tokens in order to escalate their access rights. The latter addresses the case where at a time τ_1 a user has access to t or more endorsed tokens of a file unit F_i, but at a time $\tau_2 > \tau_1$, his access rights are revoked. That is, at the time τ_2, the user has access to fewer than t endorsed tokens. SFD ensures that even if, at the time τ_1 the user may have cached the key used to encode F_i in tokens, he will not be able at the time τ_2 to decode parts of F_i. Note that, once a user has access to the file, then he can locally store any plaintext content of his choice. Similar to other access control schemes, Commune cannot deter this behavior.

Finally, given the guarantees that Commune makes for enforcing the write and read actions, it follows that Commune is a (correct) solution for distributed enforcement of the SOM access control policy (see Definition 1).

4. PROTOTYPE DESIGN & EVALUATION

We implement a prototype of Commune integrated with Amazon S3 [1]. In this section, we describe the implementation and evaluate its performance.

4.1 Implementation Setup

We leverage Amazon S3 to instantiate $\mathcal{S}$: for each user in $\mathcal{U}$, we create personal accounts in Amazon S3, into which users can upload content and define arbitrary access control policies. In our implementation, we use Amazon S3 access control features to distribute tokens from the file creator to the set of owners $\mathcal{O} \subseteq \mathcal{U}$. In particular, we assume that each user sets up *(i)* one "temporary" folder where other peers are granted write access, and *(ii)* one "main" folder where endorsed tokens are stored and retrieved. When the file creator wants to distribute a token to owner O_j, he writes the token to O_j's temporary folder. Since no other user apart from O_j has read access to the temporary folder, the new token is protected from unauthorized access. At this point, O_j can endorse the token for another user U_l, store the endorsed token in his main folder, and grant read access rights on the endorsed token to U_l.

Our prototype, implemented in Java, is a multi-threaded client-side interface to repositories hosted on Amazon S3. The client runs on a user's machine and uploads/downloads content to/from the repositories. For the evaluation, we use an Intel Core i5-2400 (at 3.10 GHz), where up to 4 GB of RAM are allocated to the OpenJDK VM.

	Peak Throughput (Mbps)
Write	43.39
Read	29.52

Table 3: Peak throughput. We assume the default parameters of Table 2. Each data point is the average of 20 measurements.

The implementation of SFD leverages Rijndael [17] (implemented using the Bouncy Castle Java library [4]) as the underlying block cipher for AON-FFT and systematic Reed-Solomon codes [30] (implemented using the Jerasure library [2, 23]) for information dispersal. We chose a symbol size of 16 bytes, and a security parameter $\lambda = 128$ bits. Our implementation of CRSS leverages the secretsharejava library [3] with a 386-bit modulus.

To optimize performance, our prototype handles file unit operations at a smaller granularity, called *pieces*. During the creation of any file unit, the unit is split into pieces that are processed in parallel. A token for each unit contains one output chunk of SFD for each piece that composes the unit. The piece size w is chosen such that $t\lambda | w$, where λ is the security parameter and t is the required reconstruction threshold. This condition ensures that (i) a piece can be encrypted in an integer number of ciphertext blocks of λ bits, (ii) an encrypted piece can be divided into an integer number of input chunks for the Reed-Solomon encoder, and (iii) the size of each chunk of the Reed-Solomon encoder/decoder is at least λ bits.

4.2 Evaluating Single Unit Write/Read

We evaluate the performance of Commune for a single file unit write and read, with respect to (i) the piece size w, (ii) the reconstruction threshold t, (iii) the number of owners n, and (iv) the size of the file unit $|F_i|$. We assume the default parameter values shown in Table 2.[4] We then change one variable at a time, to assess its impact on the system performance. For each configuration, we measure the time required (i) to create and upload F_i (denoted by *Unit Write* in our plots), and (ii) to retrieve F_i (denoted by *Unit Read*). These times are measured from the initiation of the operation until the output is available either in the repositories (for unit write) or on a local disk (for unit read). We control for the effect of caching by uploading random binary streams at each run.

During *Unit Read*, our client fetches endorsed tokens from t randomly chosen owners. Recall that a (t, n) systematic erasure code outputs t data chunks and $n - t$ parity chunks. Since data chunks need not be decoded, our evaluation accounts for the average-case scenario where the probability that a token contains a data chunk is bounded by $\frac{t}{n}$. Note that we do not evaluate the time required to grant read rights (i.e., the time required to endorse a token), since it does not depend on any of the considered parameters.

Our results are depicted in Figure 2. Each data point is averaged over 20 runs; where appropriate, we also provide the corresponding 95% confidence intervals. We also monitor the runtime of the intermediate steps for a number of configurations (Figure 3).

---

[4]Since our SFD scheme requires that the number of plaintext blocks input to AON-FFT is a power of 2, we also set w, λ, and t to be powers of 2, in order to ensure that $t\lambda | w$.

Our evaluation shows that writing a new unit (*Unit Write*) is less expensive than reading it (*Unit Read*). This is due to the overhead of thread synchronization on a single file descriptor when storing decoded pieces on the local disk.

Impact of the Piece Size: Figure 2(a) shows the impact of the piece size w on the performance of Commune. Smaller w leads to a smaller number of input blocks to the AON-FFT scheme, which results in better performance. Recall that AON-FFT requires $\log_2 m$ rounds of encryption over all the m input blocks. However, we experience higher latencies for very small values of w, especially in the *Unit Read* operation. This is due to the overhead incurred by different threads that must synchronize on the single file descriptor in order to write data to disk. Throughout the rest of the evaluation, we set $w = 128$ bytes, since it offers a good performance trade-off for both file read and write operations.

Impact of the Reconstruction Threshold: Figure 2(b) shows the impact of the reconstruction threshold t on the system's performance. As t decreases, the chunk size of the Reed-Solomon encoder increases; this results in larger chunk upload and download times. Figure 3 also shows that a smaller value of t results in longer encoding and decoding times. On the one hand, during *Unit Write*, small values of t result in larger encoding overhead since the size of the encoding matrix increases. On the other hand, during *Unit Read*, small values of t decrease the probability of recovering data chunks (w.r.t. the probability of recovering parity chunks), which makes decoding slower (cf. Figure 3).

Impact of the Number of Owners: Figure 2(c) shows that latency increases for both *Unit Write* and *Unit Read* as the number of owners grows. During *Unit Write*, this increase is caused by the distribution of tokens from the file creator to the set of owners. Latency increase during *Unit Read* is due to an higher probability of fetching parity codes that take more time to be decoded by the Reed-Solomon decoder.

Impact of the Unit Size: Figure 2(d) shows Commune's performance for different unit sizes. In particular, we vary the number of pieces, that comprise a file unit. Our results show that the time required to write/read a unit increases almost linearly with the unit size. (Note that Figure 2(d) uses semi-logarithmic axes.) The time required to read a 10 MB unit is roughly 4.47 seconds. In this case, the effective throughput of our prototype is close to 18 Mbps.

To optimize the performance, the choice of the unit size should depend on the user update patterns. Larger unit sizes mean that users have to upload larger amounts of data when updating any part of the file. Smaller unit sizes result in smaller upload times for small updates. Small unit sizes, however, incur considerable overhead when a user updates significant parts of the file (i.e., when the update affects a large number of units). In the following, we study the performance of writing and reading multiple units.

4.3 Multiple units

We now assess the performance of writing/reading multiple units of a file. In particular, we measure the peak throughput exhibited by our prototype implementation. We increase the number of units that are concurrently written/read to/from Amazon S3 until the throughput is sat-

(a) Impact of the piece size.

(b) Impact of the reconstruction threshold.

(c) Impact of the number of owners.

(d) Impact of the unit size.

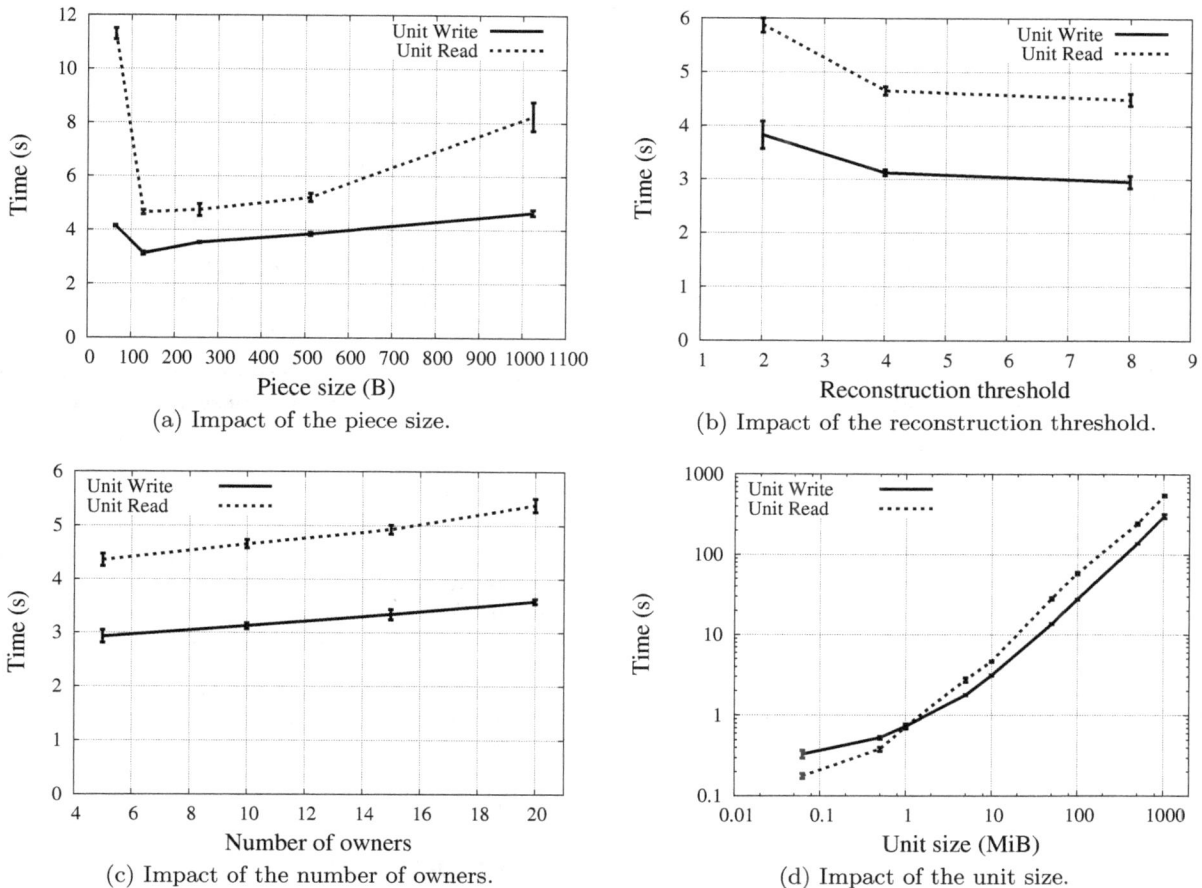

Figure 2: Performance evaluation of our prototype implementation. The system parameters are chosen from Table 2. Each data point is averaged over 20 measurements; where appropriate, we also provide the corresponding 95% confidence intervals.

urated. We then compute the peak throughput as the maximum aggregated amount of data (in bits) that can be written/read per second to/from Amazon S3. Table 3 shows that the peak throughput is above 29 Mbps for both write and read operations.

In summary, we conclude that Commune's overhead can be tolerated in applications scenarios like authoring applications, where users work on content on their local machines and periodically upload/download content to/from the cloud. Furthermore, in a practical use case, users bear the full cost of file write/read only once. Thanks versioning, once a user has uploaded/downloaded the entire file, subsequent updates can be made to individual units.

5. RELATED WORK

Secret Sharing and Information Dispersal: Secret sharing schemes [10] allow a dealer to distribute a secret among a number of shareholders, such that only authorized subsets of shareholders can reconstruct the secret. In threshold secret sharing schemes [15, 28], the dealer defines a threshold t and each set of shareholders of cardinality equal to or greater than t is authorized to reconstruct the secret. Secret sharing guarantees security (i.e., the secret cannot be recovered) against a non-authorized subset of shareholders; however, they incur a high computation/storage cost, which makes them impractical for sharing large files.

Rabin [24] proposed an information dispersal algorithm with smaller overhead than that of [28], however, his proposal does not provide any security guarantees when a small number of shares (fewer than the threshold) are available. Krawczyk [19] combines both Shamir's [28] and Rabin's [24] approaches; in [19] a file is first encrypted using AES and then dispersed using the scheme in [24], while the encryption key is shared using the scheme in [28].

Information dispersal based on erasure codes [30] are effective tools to enhance the reliability of cloud-based storage systems [7, 8, 20, 31]. Ramp schemes [11] constitute a trade-off between the security guarantees of secret sharing and the efficiency of information dispersal algorithms.

All or Nothing Transformations: All-or-nothing transformations were first introduced in [26] and later investigated in [13, 16]. The majority of AONTs leverage a secret key that is embedded in the output blocks. Once all output blocks are available, the key can be recovered and single

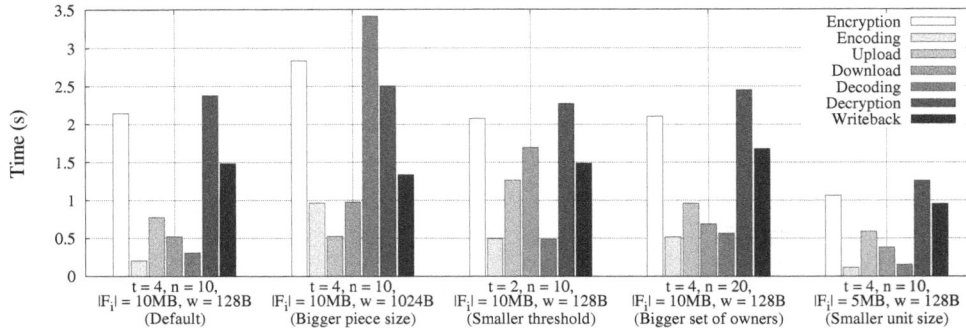

Figure 3: Runtime analysis for five different configurations of our prototype implementation. The label "Writeback" denotes the operation of writing the data back on disk onto the file descriptor (during Unit Read).

blocks can be reverted. Rivest [26] also mentioned a transformation that is inspired by Fast Fourier Transform. Van Dijk et al. [29] later on leveraged Rivest's transformation to construct a "proof of encryption" of files in the cloud. In this paper, we extend the use of Rivest's transformation to construct an AONT scheme, that keeps its all-or-nothing property even if the adversary is given the secret key. Resch et al. [25] combine AONT and information dispersal to provide both fault-tolerance (i.e., decoding requires only t out of n shares) and data secrecy (i.e., confidentiality is guaranteed w.r.t. parties that collect fewer than t shares), in the context of distributed storage systems. In [25], however, an adversary who caches the encryption key can still decode single shares. In [18], Karame *et al.* showed that by first encrypting the data then post-processing it using a linear transform, one can construct an *encryption mode* which provides similar guarantees as all or nothing transforms, and with comparable performance.

Access Control Systems: Current state-of-the-art access control systems, such as SecPAL [9], KeyNote [12], and Delegation Logic [22], can in principle express t out of n policies. These languages, however, rely on the presence of a centralized PDP component to evaluate their policies. Furthermore, their PDPs cannot be deployed within a third-party cloud platform. As explained in Section 2, these access control systems rely on an administrator to define and manage access control policies. In our setting, this means that a set of owners has to elect one enforcer who has unilateral powers over their files.

6. CONCLUSION

Even though existing clouds platforms are used as shared repositories, they surprisingly do not support any notion of shared ownership. We consider this to be a severe limitation because parties which contribute data to the repository cannot jointly decide how their resources are used. The problem of enforcing shared ownership in the cloud is even more difficult since a cloud platform does not allow deployment of a third-party enforcement component.

In this paper, we introduced a novel concept of shared ownership and we described it through a formal access control model, called SOM. We also proposed our scheme, Com-

mune, that distributively enforces SOM. Commune can be used in existing clouds without any modifications to the platforms. We implemented and evaluated the performance of our solution within Amazon S3. Our results show that Commune scales well with the file size and with the number of users.

Given the rise of personal clouds (e.g., [5, 6]), we argue that Commune finds direct applicability in setting up shared repositories that are distributively managed atop of the various personal clouds owned by users. We therefore hope that our findings motivate further research in this area.

7. REFERENCES

[1] Amazon Simple Storage Service (Amazon S3). http://aws.amazon.com/s3/.

[2] Github—Jerasure. https://github.com/tsuraan/Jerasure.

[3] Shamir's Secret Share in Java (secretsharejava). http://sourceforge.net/apps/trac/secretsharejava/wiki.

[4] The Legion of the Bouncy Castle. http://www.bouncycastle.org/java.html.

[5] The Respect Network. https://www.respectnetwork.com/.

[6] WD My Cloud. http://www.wdc.com/en/products/products.aspx?id=1140.

[7] M. Abd-El-Malek, G. R. Ganger, G. R. Goodson, M. K. Reiter, and J. J. Wylie. Fault-Scalable Byzantine Fault-Tolerant Services. In *ACM Symposium on Operating Systems Principles (SOSP)*, pages 59–74, 2005.

[8] M. K. Aguilera, R. Janakiraman, and L. Xu. Using Erasure Codes Efficiently for Storage in a Distributed System. In *International Conference on Dependable Systems and Networks (DSN)*, pages 336–345, 2005.

[9] M. Y. Becker, C. Fournet, and A. D. Gordon. SecPAL: Design and Semantics of a Decentralized Authorization Language. In *Journal of Computer Security (JCS)*, pages 597–643, 2010.

[10] A. Beimel. Secret-sharing schemes: A survey. In *Third International Workshop on Coding and Cryptology (IWCC)*, pages 11–46, 2011.

[11] G. R. Blakley and C. Meadows. Security of ramp schemes. In *Advances in Cryptology (CRYPTO)*, pages 242–268, 1984.

[12] M. Blaze, J. Ioannidis, and A. D. Keromytis. Trust Management for IPsec. In *ACM Transactions on Information and System Security (TISSEC)*, pages 95 – 118, 2002.

[13] V. Boyko. On the Security Properties of OAEP as an All-or-nothing Transform. In *Procedings of CRYPTO*, pages 503–518, 1999.

[14] S. Ceri, G. Gottlob, and L. Tanca. What you always wanted to know about Datalog (and never dared to ask). In *Knowledge and Data Engineering, IEEE Transactions on*, pages 146 –166, 1989.

[15] C. Charnes, J. Pieprzyk, and R. Safavi-Naini. Conditionally secure secret sharing schemes with disenrollment capability. In *ACM Conference on Computer and Communications Security (CCS)*, pages 89–95, 1994.

[16] A. Desai. The security of all-or-nothing encryption: Protecting against exhaustive key search. In *Advances in Cryptology (CRYPTO)*, pages 359–375, 2000.

[17] J. Daemen, and V. Rijmen. AES Proposal: Rijndael. http://csrc.nist.gov/archive/aes/rijndael/Rijndael-ammended.pdf.

[18] G. O. Karame, C. Soriente, K. Lichota, and S. Capkun. Securing cloud data in the new attacker model. *IACR Cryptology ePrint Archive*, 2014:556, 2014.

[19] H. Krawczyk. Secret Sharing Made Short. In *International Conference on Advances in Cryptology*, 1993.

[20] J. Kubiatowicz, D. Bindel, Y. Chen, S. E. Czerwinski, P. R. Eaton, D. Geels, R. Gummadi, S. C. Rhea, H. Weatherspoon, W. Weimer, C. Wells, and B. Y. Zhao. OceanStore: An Architecture for Global-Scale Persistent Storage. In *International Conference on Architectural Support for Programming Languages and Operating Systems (ASPLOS)*, pages 190–201, 2000.

[21] A. B. Lewko and B. Waters. Decentralizing Attribute-Based Encryption. In *International Conference on the Theory and Application of Cryptographic Techniques (EUROCRYPT)*, pages 568–588, 2011.

[22] N. Li, B. N. Grosof, and J. Feigenbaum. Delegation logic: A Logic-based Approach to Distributed Authorization. In *ACM Transactions on Information and System Security (TISSEC)*, pages 128–171, 2003.

[23] J. S. Plank, S. Simmerman, and C. D. Schuman. Jerasure: A library in C/C++ facilitating erasure coding for storage applications. Technical report, 2007.

[24] M. O. Rabin. Efficient Dispersal of Information for Security, Load Balancing, and Fault Tolerance. In *Journal of the Association for Computing Machinery*, pages 335–348, 1989.

[25] J. K. Resch and J. S. Plank. AONT-RS: Blending Security and Performance in Dispersed Storage Systems. In *USENIX Conference on File and Storage Technologies (FAST)*, pages 191–202, 2011.

[26] R. L. Rivest. All-or-Nothing Encryption and the Package Transform. In *International Workshop on Fast Software Encryption (FSE)*, pages 210–218, 1997.

[27] P. Rogaway and M. Bellare. Robust computational secret sharing and a unified account of classical secret-sharing goals. In *ACM Conference on Computer and Communications Security (CCS)*, pages 172–184, 2007.

[28] A. Shamir. How to Share a Secret? In *Communications of the ACM*, pages 612–613, 1979.

[29] M. van Dijk, A. Juels, A. Oprea, R. L. Rivest, E. Stefanov, and N. Triandopoulos. Hourglass Schemes: how to prove that cloud files are encrypted. In *ACM Conference on Computer and Communications Security (CCS)*, pages 265–280, 2012.

[30] J. H. van Lint. *Introduction to Coding Theory*. Springer-Verlag New York, Inc., Secaucus, NJ, USA, 1982.

[31] H. Xia and A. A. Chien. RobuSTore: a Distributed Storage Architecture with Robust and High Performance. In *ACM/IEEE Conference on High Performance Networking and Computing (SC)*, page 44, 2007.

APPENDIX

A. DATALOG ENCODING OF THE SOM ACCESS CONTROL POLICY

To show that SOM can be centrally enforced, we present its encoding in the Datalog logic-programming language.

We represent a file system state as a Datalog database [14] that has a set of relations describing each file's owners and its threshold. We translate requests and credentials into Datalog clauses (rules), which are then evaluated over the current state together with the SOM policy. We first give a brief overview of Datalog (see [14] for a more extensive survey). A Datalog program is a finite set of clauses of the form: $S \leftarrow L_1, \ldots, L_n$, where S and L_i are function-free first-order literals of the form $predicate(arg_1, \ldots, arg_n)$. We refer to S as the head of the clause, and to L_i as a body literal. We adopt the following notation: a variable starts with the ? character, a constant starts with a capital letter, and a predicate name starts with a lower-case letter. A clause with no body literals is called a *fact*. All clauses are safe: all variables that appear in a head literal also appear in at least one body literal. A Datalog program can be split into two sets of clauses: *EDB* and *IDB*. *EDB* is a set of facts whose head literals do not appear as head literals in any other clause. All other clauses are in the *IDB* set. Intuitively, we think of an *EDB* as an input for computing all implied facts by the clauses in the *IDB* set. The declarative semantics of a Datalog program interpret each clause as a first-order sentence: $\forall \bar{x} L_1 \wedge \cdots \wedge L_i \rightarrow S$, and take a whole program to be a conjunction of its clauses. For each program $\mathcal{P} = IDB \cup EDB$, let $\sigma(IDB, EDB) = \{atom \mid \mathcal{I}(\mathcal{P}) \models atom\}$, where $\mathcal{I}(\mathcal{P})$ is the first-order translation of $\mathcal{P}$, and $\models$ is the logical implication.

A SOM state s is a tuple (*Files, Users, Owns, Thresholds*) where *Files* denotes a set of strings representing file names, *Users* is a set of users, *Owns* is a subset of $2^{Users \times Files}$, and *Thresholds* is a mapping from *Files* into $\mathbb{N}$. For a state s, we define a set EDB_s containing all ground atoms: *file(File)*, *user(User)*, *owns(User, File)*, and *threshold(File, N)*. A request r is a tuple $(R, \mathcal{C})$, where R is a request credential submitted by a user, and $\mathcal{C}$ is a set of available credentials.

Credentials can be either submitted by a user, or kept in a separate storage and appended to each request. Given a request, $\mathcal{T}(C)$ generates the following set of Datalog rules IDB_r:

$$\mathcal{T}(O \textbf{ says } U \textbf{ can } actionOp(\text{F})) = says(O, U, actionOp, F)$$

The translation of R is similar, except that we do not generate *says* facts but Datalog queries:

$$\mathcal{T}(U \textbf{ reqs } actionOp(\text{F}) = can(U, actionOp, F)$$

The set $\mathcal{A}_s$ is a set of Datalog rules *parameterized* on s, that enforces the shared ownership:

$$
\begin{aligned}
can(?U, actionOp, ?F) &\leftarrow file(?F), user(?U), \\
&threshold(?F, ?T), \\
&[[says(?O_1, ?U, actionOp, ?F), \dots, \\
&\quad says(?O_{?T}, ?U, actionOp, F), \\
&owns(?O_1, ?F), \dots, owns(?O_T, ?F), \\
&?O_1 \neq ?O_2, \dots, ?O_1 \neq ?O_{?T}, \dots, ?O_{?T-1} \neq ?O_{?T}]]
\end{aligned}
$$

Intuitively, the given rule is a *template* rule that instantiates the necessary clauses for all *actionOp* operations. The variable $?T$ denotes a threshold, and $?U$ denotes a user. The reason for doing so is to correctly enforce the current (for the given state s) threshold t for a particular file. In short, we need to generate the correct number of $?O_i$ variables for each file and its threshold in s. To represent this *dynamic* part of a clause, we enclose it within $[[$ and $]]$ brackets.

Finally, given a SOM state s, and a request (R, C), we say that SOM's Datalog-based Policy Decision Point (PDP) grants R if and only if: $\mathcal{I}(EDB_s \cup \mathcal{A}_s \cup \mathcal{T}(\mathcal{C})) \models \mathcal{T}(R)$

B. SECURITY ANALYSIS OF SFD

We treat the information dispersal encoder of SFD.Encode($\cdot$) as a ramp scheme [11]. In particular, to maximize the code rate, we assume a $(0, t, n)$-ramp scheme, with t as reconstruction threshold and 0 as privacy threshold. This means that any single chunk leaks information about the encoded input. Let $\bar{F}$ denote the input to the information dispersal encoder. Hence, at least t chunks are necessary to reconstruct $\bar{F}$; however, each single chunk leaks some information about $\bar{F}$. More specifically, if the adversary $\mathcal{A}$ is given l out of n chunks outputted by SFD.Encode(t, n, F, K, λ), then:

$$H(\bar{F}|\mathcal{A}) = \begin{cases} \frac{l}{t} H(\bar{F}) & \text{if } l < t \\ 0 & \text{if } l \geq t \end{cases}$$

where $H(\cdot)$ denotes the entropy. Since $\bar{F}$ is the output of AONT (which is essentially a block cipher) we can assume $H(\bar{F}) = m\lambda$. Therefore, if $\mathcal{A}$ is given $l = t - 1$ chunks, $H(\bar{F}|\mathcal{A}) = \frac{m}{t}\lambda$. For simplicity, we assume that when $m = t$ and given $t - 1$ SFD encoded chunks, $\mathcal{A}$ can decode all but one block of the AONT output.

We are left to show that, given K and $\bar{f}_{i_1}, \dots, \bar{f}_{i_{m-1}}$, $\mathcal{A}$ has negligible advantage in recovering $f \subseteq F$, i.e., a substring of F of size λ. We note that the security of the underlying block-cipher prevents the adversary from recovering partial bits of any cleartext block. That is, the adversary can only learn entire blocks of cleartext. Therefore, we focus our analysis on an adversary that tries to recover any cleartext block $f_i \in F$. Furthermore, in our definition the adversary is not allowed to store any blocks of ciphertext/cleartext nor

is she allowed to store any intermediate block produced by AON-FFT. We argue that if an adversary were to store any block of data, then she would store blocks the actual file to easily access it despite revocation. No mechanism can cater for effective revocation if the adversary has a local copy of the resource.

We prove the security of AON-FFT by induction. Denote with AON-FFT(4) the graph that defines the operations of AON-FFT when $m = 4$. Clearly, recovering any input block of AON-FFT(4) requires all 4 output blocks. Recall that each output block is λ-bit in size and has high-entropy (since it is the output of a block-cipher). Therefore, given all but one output block, $\mathcal{A}$ has only negligible advantage in guessing the missing block and recovering any input block. Similarly, an AON-FFT(8) graph has two AON-FFT(4) subgraphs (one left and one right), plus an additional round of encryption. Recovering any input block of AON-FFT(8) requires one input blocks of each of the two AON-FFT(4) subgraphs which, in turn, require all their output blocks. Therefore, recovering any input block of AON-FFT(8) requires all 8 output blocks. By iterating this analysis for larger graph sizes, we can easily prove that for any m, recovering any input block of AON-FFT(2^m) requires all 2^m output blocks.

C. SECURITY ANALYSIS OF CRSS

We now prove the security of our CRSS scheme (Section 3.4). More specifically, we show that a p.p.t. algorithm $\mathcal{A}$ that has non-negligible advantage in winning `Game Priv*` of Section 3.4, can be used by p.p.t. algorithm $\mathcal{B}$ as an internal routine to break the security of the threshold secret sharing scheme in [15]. That is, $\mathcal{B}$ is challenged by a challenger C to find the secret g^x given only $t - 1$ shares as output by $g^x, \{x_1, \dots, x_n\} \leftarrow$ SS.Share($-, t, n$). On the other hand, $\mathcal{B}$ challenges $\mathcal{A}$ to break the security of CRSS. Simulation starts with $\mathcal{A}$ who submits two messages x_0, x_1 of equal length. Those are forwarded by $\mathcal{B}$ to C that flips an unbiased coin b and secret-shares x_b. Given our particular secret sharing scheme, we assume that the secret to be reconstructed is g^{x_b}. At this time, $\mathcal{B}$ also picks a random polynomial Y of degree $t - 1$, such that $Y(0) = 0$ and computes $y_i = Y(i)$, for $1 \leq i \leq n$.

During Type-1 queries, $\mathcal{A}$ submits indexes $i_1, \dots, i_{t'}$. $\mathcal{B}$ forwards them to C that replies with $\{x_{i_1}, \dots, x_{i_{t'}}\}$. $\mathcal{B}$ then sends to $\mathcal{A}$ shares $\{s_{i_1}, \dots, s_{i_{t'}}\}$ where $s_{i_l} = (x_{i_l}, y_{i_l})$, for $1 \leq l \leq t'$.

Similarly, during a Type-2 query $\mathcal{A}$ submits a fresh identity U_j and t'' indexes $i'_1, \dots, i'_{t''}$. For each identity U_j, $\mathcal{B}$ picks at random $h_j \in Z_q$ and sets $H(U_j) = g^{h_j}$. If an index i'_l has been submitted during type-1 query, $\mathcal{B}$ knows $x_{i'_l}$ and can compute the delegation $d_{i'_l, j} = g^x_{i'_l} H(U_j)^{y_{i'_l}}$. Otherwise, $\mathcal{B}$ asks C for share $x_{i'_l}$ and computes the corresponding delegation.

Note that $\mathcal{A}$ can submit a Type-2 query if only if $t' < t - 1$. Therefore $\mathcal{B}$ can still ask C for the missing shares. During the guess stage, $\mathcal{A}$ will output his guess b' and $\mathcal{B}$ will use it as its own guess towards C. Since $H(\cdot)$ is a random oracle and $\mathcal{A}$ has a non-negligible advantage in guessing b, then B has the same advantage in breaking the security of [15], thus concluding our proof.

SecLoc: Securing Location-Sensitive Storage in the Cloud

Jingwei Li[*]
Nankai University
Tianjin, P.R. China
lijw1987@gmail.com

Anna Squicciarini
Pennsylvania State University
PA, USA
asquicciarini@ist.psu.edu

Dan Lin
Missouri University of Science
& Technology, MO, USA
lindan@mst.edu

Shuang Liang
Nankai University
Tianjin, P.R. China
nkliangshuang@gmail.com

Chunfu Jia[†]
Nankai University
Tianjin, P.R. China
cfjia@nankai.edu.cn

ABSTRACT

Cloud computing offers a wide array of storage services. While enjoying the benefits of flexibility, scalability and reliability brought by the cloud storage, cloud users also face the risk of losing control of their own data, in partly because they do not know where their data is actually stored. This raises a number of security and privacy concerns regarding one's sensitive data such as health records. For example, according to Canadian laws, data related to personal identifiable information must be stored within Canada. Nevertheless, in contrast to the urgent demands, privacy requirements regarding to cloud storage locations have not been well investigated in the current cloud computing market, fostering security and privacy concerns among potential adopters. Aiming at addressing this emerging critical issue, we propose a novel secure location-sensitive storage framework, called SecLoc, which offers protection for cloud users' data following the storage location restrictions, with minimum management overhead to existing cloud storage services. We conduct security analysis, complexity analysis and experimental evaluation on the proposed SecLoc system. Our results demonstrate both effectiveness and efficiency of our mechanism.

Categories and Subject Descriptors

D.4.3 [**File System Management**]: Distributed file systems; D.4.6 [**Security and Protection**]: Cryptographic controls

---

[*]Jingwei Li is currently with The Chinese University of Hong Kong.

[†]Chunfu Jia is also with Information Security Evaluation Center of Civil Aviation, Civil Aviation University of China, China

Keywords

Cloud Storage; Location Sensitive; Access Control; Attribute-based Encryption

1. INTRODUCTION

Cloud computing offers a wide array of storage services which brings numerous benefits such as flexibility, scalability and reliability. While enjoying these benefits, cloud users also face underlying security and privacy risks due to the limited control they can exercise once their own data is stored in the cloud [4, 20]. Specifically, the cloud provider typically takes care of data management, storage and recovery to relieve the burden previously opposed on data owners. This seemingly attractive feature, however, makes it extremely hard for the cloud users, an individual user or a government organization, to prevent their sensitive data (e.g., health records, criminal records) from being copied to risky locations that can potentially be exposed to cyber attacks or information leakage. For example, Canadian law has clearly specified that data related to personal identifiable information must be stored within Canada. With the cloud storage services in current cloud computing market, there is no way to guarantee that cloud user's data is stored according to the privacy laws.

To mitigate the above security and privacy issue, a common approach is to ask cloud users to encrypt their sensitive data and then upload the encrypted data to the cloud [13]. The cloud providers do not know the encryption key and will not be able to decrypt the encrypted data. Although such approach ensures that the user data is fully secured, it sacrifices the powerful processing capability brought by the cloud computing technology since very limited number of queries can be implemented over encrypted data, and these queries are also very time consuming [11, 15]. On the other hand, if the user provides decryption keys to the cloud storage nodes that will process his/her data, he/she cannot prevent the storage nodes from sharing the keys with other nodes that are not qualified.

In order to address the cloud users' security and privacy concerns incurred by the storage location constraints while also allowing cloud users to take advantage of computing services offered by the cloud, we propose a novel *Secure Location-sensitive storage* (SecLoc) framework. SecLoc can achieve data confidentiality, location-sensitivity and computing efficiency. Specifically, SecLoc ensures that the cloud user's data is stored and can be processed only at locations that satisfy user specified location constraints (e.g., within Canada). If the cloud providers (unintentionally) copy the user data to nodes outside the expected regions, the user data will become unaccessible at those ineligible locations. This is realized through our proposed new cryptographic primitive, namely transformable Attribute-Based Encryption (tABE). Details of tABE will be introduced later in the paper. Our security analysis has shown that SecLoc can withstand a variety of attacks, and our complexity and experimental evaluation demonstrates that SecLoc impose minimum overhead on top of existing cloud storage services.

The rest of the paper is organized as follows. Section 2 reviews the related works. Section 3 introduces some preliminary backgrounds. Section 4 gives an overview of the proposed SecLoc, followed by the detailed construction scheme in Section 5. Section 6 analyzes the security of the proposed SecLoc system. Section 7 describes the extension of SecLoc with data re-storage capabilities. Section 8 reports both the theoretical complexity analysis and the experimental evaluation. Finally, Section 9 concludes the paper.

2. RELATED WORKS

Many research efforts have been devoted into preserving confidentiality and integrity of cloud storage services. For example, in [12], Juels et al. proposed the proof of retrievability technique to check the integrity of cloud data without downloading the data itself; in [13], Kamara et al. described a cryptographic cloud that combines the functions of integrity checking, data confidentiality and fine-grained access control.

However, very few existing works have investigated how to ensure the storage locations of user data in the cloud. One of the first few works that tackles location sensitivity was by Peterson et al. [19] who proposed to couple data authenticity and geographical location in the cloud and defined the notion of data sovereignty. They employ a MAC-based possession technique for this, which however incurs a large amount of additional communication cost. Later, Watson et al. [22] proposed a proof of location (PoL) system that delegates the location verification to landmarks and the landmarks execute proof of retrievability protocols to check the encoded data is stored in specified locations. The PoL system can only prove that cloud nodes at agreed locations have the copies of the user data, but does not consider any protections on the user data being copied to other ineligible locations. Noman et al. [17] presented a data location assurance service (DLAS) solution in the cloud under the "honest-but-curious" threat model. Specifically, they store location information of user's data in a database and only allow users with certain credentials to retrieve the location information for verification. Unlike our approach which aims to preserve the privacy of user's data, the DLAS is mainly for preserving confidentiality of the location information of the data.

More recently, Paladi et al. [18] proposed a high-level architecture for a trusted, geolocation-based mechanism for data placement control in distributed cloud storage systems. Fu et al. [9] leveraged the trusted computing technology to provide a strong validation of geolocation of cloud data. Their approaches require the cloud service to be equipped with a fully trusted component, namely Trusted Platform Module (TPM), to detect any malicious software. Unlike their approach, our proposed system does not need the fully trusted module equipped in the cloud server.

3. PRELIMINARIES

We briefly review some basic encryption techniques that serve as the foundation of our approach, namely Key-Policy Attribute-Based Encryption (KP-ABE) [10], and bilinear map [7].

3.1 Key-Policy Attribute-Based Encryption

Key-Policy Attribute-Based Encryption (KP-ABE) [10] is an important type of Attribute-Based Encryption (ABE) which has been widely employed to impose fine-grained access control on encrypted data [10]. In KP-ABE, ciphertexts are labeled with sets of attributes, and private keys are associated with access structures that determine which user can decrypt which ciphertext. The following is an overview of the main algorithms of KP-ABE primitive.

- Setup(λ) : The setup algorithm takes as input a security parameter λ, and outputs (pk, msk), where pk denotes the public key and msk denotes the master secret key of the KP-ABE system.

- KeyGen($\mathcal{P}, msk$) : The key generation algorithm takes as input an access control policy $\mathcal{P}$ and the master secret key msk, and outputs the decryption key dk which is associated with the policy $\mathcal{P}$.

- Encrypt(m, ω) : The encryption algorithm takes as input a message m and an attribute set ω, in which the attributes are pre-defined in an attribute universe for describing the access requirements, and outputs the ciphertext ct of m with respect to attribute set ω.

- Decrypt(ct, dk) : The decryption algorithm takes as input a ciphertext ct embedded with the attribute set ω, and the decryption key dk with respect to access control policy $\mathcal{P}$. It outputs the original message m if and only if ω satisfies $\mathcal{P}$.

3.2 Bilinear Map

Bilinear map [7] is the common tool for designing the aforementioned KP-ABE primitives. In this subsection, we give the definition of the bilinear map, which will be used in this paper.

DEFINITION 1 (BILINEAR MAP). *Denote* $\mathbb{G}, \mathbb{G}_T$ *as cyclic groups of prime order* p, *writing the group action multiplicatively.* g *is a generator of* $\mathbb{G}$. *Let* $e : \mathbb{G} \times \mathbb{G} \to \mathbb{G}_T$ *be a map with the following properties:*

- *Bilinearity:* $e(g_1^a, g_2^b) = e(g_1, g_2)^{ab}$ *for all* $g_1, g_2 \in \mathbb{G}$, *and* $a, b \in_R \mathbb{Z}_p$;

- *Non-degeneracy: There exists* $g_1, g_2 \in \mathbb{G}$ *such that* $e(g_1, g_2) \neq 1$, *in other words, the map does not send all pairs in* $\mathbb{G} \times \mathbb{G}$ *to the identity in* $\mathbb{G}_T$;

- *Efficiency: There exists an efficient polynomial time algorithm to compute the bilinear map* $e(\cdot, \cdot)$.

4. OVERVIEW OF SECLOC SYSTEM

In this section, we first present the system design goals and threat model. Then, we give an overview of our proposed SecLoc system.

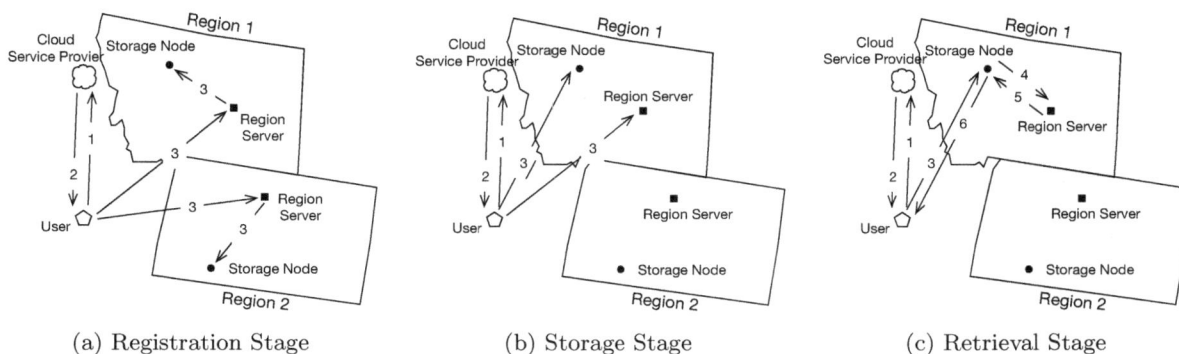

(a) Registration Stage   (b) Storage Stage   (c) Retrieval Stage

Figure 1: Stages in SecLoc

4.1 Design Goals and Threat Model

In our work, we consider three types of entities:

- *Cloud service providers*: This includes cloud vendors and their storage nodes. Storage nodes may be located in different regions and are uniquely identifiable by their cloud vendor.

- *Cloud users:* Cloud users mainly refer to the users who use the cloud storage services. They may have specific requirements on which regions are allowed to store their data and only the storage nodes located in these regions can process their data.

- *Region servers:* These servers are independent of the cloud service providers. Each server is in charge of a region and responsible for authenticating the storage nodes in its controlled regions.

The overarching goal of the SecLoc framework is to prevent storage nodes outside the user specified regions from accessing the content of the user data. More specifically, the SecLoc framework has the following unique features:

- *Location-sensitive access control*: The cloud user's data will only be accessible to the cloud storage nodes that satisfy user specified location constraints. Storage nodes outside the expected regions will not be able to obtain the plaintext of the user data.

- *Content-based access control*: Even the storage nodes assigned to store the user data will only be given access to the content of the data that is allowed by the user specified access control policies. For example, users can store fully encrypted data at the storage node and the storage node will only be able to compute the decryption key for *only a portion of* the data that is allowed to be processed.

- *Keyless*: Unlike many traditional key-based security [5], cloud users in our SecLoc system do not need to maintain a large number of keys, which helps avoid the potential risk of key leakage or abuse.

- *Cost effectiveness*: Our proposed SecLoc system introduces minimum overhead on top of existing cloud storage services, which will ensure its wide adoption in the real world applications.

The SecLoc framework is developed based on the following assumptions and threat model. First, we assume that the cloud storage architecture is static, and each storage node in this architecture is globally identifiable. Second, we assume that the region servers are developed as a minimally trusted third-party service. By minimally trusted, we mean that the region servers are able to reliably authenticate the storage nodes in their controlled regions so long as they are not compromised by attackers. Third, we do not trust the cloud service providers and their storage nodes, either of which could be compromised to extract user's (encrypted) data. Fourth, we assume that the storage nodes and region servers in the same region will not be compromised simultaneously. We argue that this assumption is realistic, because the storage nodes (belonging to cloud service providers) and region servers are maintained by different parties, and it rarely occurs when multiple parties' servers are compromised by the same attacker at the same time.

Under the above threat model, we consider two types of attacks: 1) The cloud service provider might provide a tampered list of candidate nodes to the user, misleading the user to store data in a wrong place; 2) The storage nodes might collude with each other, or even with some compromised region servers, to extract user's (encrypted) data.

4.2 SecLoc Framework

We now give an overview of our proposed Secure Location-sensitive (SecLoc) storage framework. The SecLoc consists of three stages:

- **Registration Stage.** This stage generates system parameters and assignments. As shown in Figure 1(a), initially the user requests a storage service from the cloud service provider (highlighted by workflow 1 in Figure 1(a)). The cloud service provider assigns several storage nodes for this requested service and returns the list of candidate storage nodes to the user (highlighted by workflow 2 in Figure 1(a)). Note that these candidate storage nodes may be located in different regions and they are just a small subset of storage nodes maintained by the cloud service provider. Any tamper to the list of candidate nodes can be easily prevented using public key infrastructure whereby the list can be encrypted with the user's public key and opened by the user using the corresponding secret key. After receiving the list of the candidate storage nodes, the user will verify the location of the storage nodes with the aid of the region server. This verification can be done by leveraging the distance bounding protocol (e.g., [8]), which enables a verifier (i.e., user and region server) to establish an upper bound on the physical distance to a prover (i.e., storage node). Then, the user assigns a piece of decryption key (dk_1 in our construction) to each qualifying candidate storage node. Meanwhile, the user also assigns a control seed (sd in our construction) to each involved region server, which is used for generating the other piece of decryption key dk_2 in future (highlighted by workflow 3 in Figure 1(a)).

- **Storage Stage.** Once a user has successfully registered the service with the cloud service provider, the user can proceed to store his/her data in the cloud. Specifically, the user first needs to send a "`storage`" request to the cloud service provider (highlighted by workflow 1 in Figure 1(b)). The cloud service provider will then return a list of available storage nodes (a subset of the candidate nodes) to the user (highlighted by workflow 2 in Figure 1(b)). The user encrypts its data and uploads it to the preferred storage nodes from the available node list provided by the cloud service provider (highlighted by workflow 3 in Figure 1(b)), and also sends a receipt to the corresponding region server to indicate the storage of data in this region.

- **Retrieval Stage.** When a user needs to retrieve the data stored in the cloud, he/she will send a "`retrieve`" request (i.e., a data query) to the cloud service provider (highlighted by workflow 1 in Figure 1(c)), which retrieves and returns the address of storage nodes having the requested portion of the data (highlighted by workflow 2 in Figure 1(c)). Then, the user will send the data retrieval request to these storage nodes. Upon receiving the request from the user, the storage nodes need to be authenticated by the local region server. Only qualified storage nodes will be able to reconstruct the entire decryption key to decrypt the requested portion of the stored user data and return it to the user (highlighted by workflow 4 and 5 in Figure 1(c)).

5. CONSTRUCTING SECLOC SYSTEM

In order to realize the design goals of the SecLoc system, we propose a new cryptographic primitive, namely transformable Attribute-Based Encryption (tABE for short). In what follows, we will present the details of the tABE and how it is used to construct the SecLoc system.

5.1 The Work Flow in SecLoc

For better understanding, we will first treat the tABE as a black box and introduce the overall work flow in the SecLoc system. Figure 2 illustrates the overview of the key components of tABE and how they function in the SecLoc. The detailed description is the following.

- **Registration Stage.** After the cloud user registered the cloud service (corresponding to workflow 1 and 2 in Figure 1(a)), the user initiates the tABE's Setup algorithm which takes as input the security parameter λ and outputs a pair of public key and master secret key (pk, msk). pk is published outside and msk is kept secret by user.

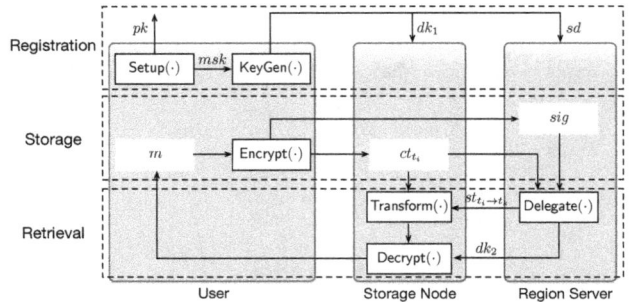

Figure 2: Components of tABE

Next, the user will produce a decryption key for each candidate storage node returned by the cloud service provider. Specifically, suppose that there exists n regions, respectively uniquely identified by the attribute $u_1, \ldots, u_n$. For the ith region in which there exists a candidate storage node, the user executes the tABE's KeyGen algorithm that takes the master secret key msk, the region identity u_i and a randomly selected state parameter t_0 ($t_0 \in_R \mathbb{Z}_p$, will be explained in the Section 5.2) as input, to generate a partial decryption key (denoted as $dk_{1,i}$) and the seed sd_i. Then, the user sends the decryption key $dk_{1,i}$ to the corresponding candidate storage node, and sends the seed sd_i to the region server in the ith region (corresponding to workflow 3 in Figure 1(a)). Note that, the partial key alone is not sufficient for the candidate storage node to decrypt the user data. After this stage, the master secret key msk could be destroyed by user to achieve keyless security [16].

- **Storage Stage.** During this stage, the users will upload their data to the cloud. Suppose that the user has a data item with identifier `dID` to be stored in region i[1]. The user will encrypt the data item twice before uploading to the cloud. First, the user encrypts the plaintext (denoted as m) of the data item with a random symmetric key sk ($sk \in_R \{0,1\}^\lambda$), and generates the ciphertext ct_m. Then, the user further encrypts the ct_m using the tABE's Encrypt algorithm to encapsulate the symmetric key sk, i.e., $(ct_{sk,t_0}, sig) = $ tABE.Encrypt($\{u_i\}, sk, t_0$), where sig is a receipt of the ciphertext, u_i is the identifier of the ith region, and t_0 is the state parameter in tABE.

Finally, the ciphertext ($\texttt{dID}, i, ct_m, ct_{sk,t_0}$) is uploaded to the assigned storage node in region i (corresponding to the workflow 3 in Figure 1(b)). It is worth noting that our tABE guarantees that only the storage node that has been verified to be in the correct region would be able to receive the user data. This will be further discussed in our security analysis in Section 6. Meanwhile, the pair ($\texttt{dID}, sig$) is sent to the region server in region i to indicate that a data identified by `dID` has been stored in this region. After the storage stage, the state t_0 is allowed to be dropped by the user as well.

---

[1]Notice that here we omit the steps that user contacts with cloud service provider to get the available storage nodes in region i which corresponds to the workflow 1 and 2 in Figure 1(b).

- **Retrieval Stage.** When a user wants to retrieve or query a data item identified by dID from the cloud, the user will first contact the cloud service provider to obtain the address of the storage node that stores this data item (corresponding to workflow 1 and 2 in Figure 1(c)). Then, the user sends the data retrieval/query request[2] to the corresponding storage node (corresponding to workflow 3 in Figure 1(c)). Given dID, the storage node will retrieve its ciphertext $(\text{dID}, i, ct_m, ct_{k,t_0})$. In order to conduct queries or data analysis on the user's data item, the storage node needs to decrypt the data item. Since the storage node has only part of the decryption key which is $dk_{1,i}$, the storage node will request the second part of the decryption key from the ith region server (corresponding to workflow 4 in Figure 1(c)). The region server first verifies the location of the storage node using the distance bounding protocol [8]. If the location of the storage node is correct, the region server retrieves the receipt sig corresponding to the requested data item dID and runs the tABE's Delegate algorithm to produce and return the transformation variable $st_{t_0 \to t_k}$ and the other piece of decryption key $dk_{2,i}$ (corresponding to workflow 5 in Figure 1(c)).

Upon receiving the information from the region server, the storage node will first transform the key encapsulated ciphertext ct_{sk,t_0} from temporal state t_0 to that under the temporal state t_k. The transformed ciphertext ct_{sk,t_k} is then decrypted using the combined decryption key $dk_{1,i}$ and $dk_{2,i}$. Finally, this storage node could use the sk to decrypt the user's data item, conduct the query processing, and return the query results to the user (corresponding to workflow 6 in Figure 1(c)). Note that, the tABE guarantees that only the storage nodes that satisfy user specified access control policies will be allowed to view and process the user's data, which will be elaborated shortly in the following subsection.

5.2 Transformable Attribute-Based Encryption

We now proceed to elaborate the mechanism inside the transformable attribute-based encryption (tABE). The tABE is designed to offload the key management to the cloud so as to ease the users' computing burden. It is developed based on policy-based encryption/decryption in ABE, with several new features tailored for the SecLoc framework. More specifically, the tABE allows the user to specify what portion of the user data can be accessed by what storage nodes in what region using access control policies. The access control policies are implemented using access tree in the tABE construction as described in the following.

An access tree [10] is a tree structure used to represent an access control policy. Each interior node of the access tree represents a threshold gate (i.e., AND or OR gates) described by its children and a threshold value, while each leaf node is associated with an attribute of potential data requesters. In this paper, we use the following notations for the access tree.

[2]In practice, user needs to along send request with authentication information (e.g., signature) on retrieval. We omit the description of these steps for the sake of simplicity and readability.

- num_x denotes the number of children of an interior node x. Let y be the child of node x, we denote index(y) as a unique number in $[1, num_x]$ associated with the node y.

- k_x denotes the threshold value of an interior node x. In other words, when $k_x = 1$, the threshold gate at x is OR gate and when $k_x = num_x$, that is an AND gate.

- The function parent(x) returns the parent of the node x in the tree; and the function attr(x) returns the subscript of attribute associated with the leaf node x.

Let $\mathcal{P}$ be an access tree, and $\mathcal{P}_x$ be a subtree of $\mathcal{P}$ with root x. For an attribute set ω, $\mathcal{P}_x(\omega) = 1$ if ω satisfies $\mathcal{P}_x$. Otherwise, $\mathcal{P}_x(\omega) = 0$. Obviously $\mathcal{P}(\cdot)$ equals $\mathcal{P}_x(\cdot)$ if x is the root node of the access tree $\mathcal{P}$. We can evaluate $\mathcal{P}_x(\cdot)$ recursively as follows: If x is an interior node, evaluate $\mathcal{P}_\cdot(\omega)$ on all the children of x; If x is a leaf node, $\mathcal{P}_x(\omega) = 1$ if attr(x) $\in \omega$.

Next, we present the detailed algorithms for each component in tABE. As shown in Figure 2, the tABE consists of six main algorithms: Setup($\cdot$), KeyGen($\cdot$), Encrypt($\cdot$), Delegate($\cdot$) and Decrypt($\cdot$). Note that although we elaborate tABE here in a generic form, $\mathcal{P}$ is an access tree and ω is a set of attributes, the application of tABE in SecLoc is just in a special case: $\mathcal{P}$ includes a single attribute node, and ω consists of one attribute indicating the region user wants to store in.

- Setup(λ) : It takes as input the security parameter λ and outputs a pair of public key and master secret key (pk, msk). Specifically, we denote the Lagrange coefficient $\Delta_{i,S}$ for $i \in \mathbb{Z}_p$ and a set S of elements in $\mathbb{Z}_p$:

$$\Delta_{i,S}(x) = \prod_{j \in S, j \neq i} \frac{x - j}{i - j}. \qquad (1)$$

Then, we define a bilinear group $\mathbb{G}$ with prime order p and generator g. We randomly pick an integer $l_i \in_R \mathbb{Z}_p$ for each attribute $u_i \in \{u_1, u_2, \ldots, u_n\}$, where n is the total number of regions. Finally, the public key $pk = (\{g^{l_i}\}_{i=1}^n, e(g,g)^\alpha)$ is published, and the master secret key $msk = (\{l_i\}_{i=1}^n, \alpha)$ is kept secret.

- KeyGen($msk, \mathcal{P}, t_i$) : This piece-wise key generation algorithm takes as input the master key msk, the user specified policy $\mathcal{P}$ and a state t_i, and outputs a piece of decryption key dk_1 and a seed sd. Specifically, we first randomly pick $\alpha_1, \alpha_2 \in_R \mathbb{Z}_p$ with $\alpha_1 + \alpha_2 = \alpha$. Then, for each node x in the access tree $\mathcal{P}$, we choose a $(k_x - 1)$-degree polynomial $q_x(\cdot)$ in a top-down manner, with the restriction that $q_x(0) = \alpha_1$ if x is the root node of $\mathcal{P}$, and $q_x(0) = q_{\text{parent}(x)}(\text{index}(x))$ otherwise. Finally we output $dk_1 = \{g^{q_x(0)/l_i}\}$ where x here is used to denote the leaf node in $\mathcal{P}$, $i = \text{attr}(x)$ is the attribute stored in x, and $sd = (t_i, \alpha_2)$.

- Encrypt(ω, m, t_i) : The encryption algorithm takes as input the attribute set ω, a plaintext m and a state t_i, and outputs the ciphertext ct_{t_i} and the corresponding receipt sig identifying this ciphertext. In particular, to encrypt a message $m \in \mathbb{G}_T$ with an attribute set ω at the state t_i, we first pick a random number $s \in_R \mathbb{Z}_p$.

Then, we compute the ciphertext at state t_i as $ct_{t_i} = (m \cdot e(g,g)^{\alpha s}, g^s, \{g^{l_i \cdot s}\}_{i \in \omega}, g^{t_i \cdot s}, g^{r \cdot s})$ and $sig = g^{1/r}$, where $r \in_R \mathbb{Z}_p$. Note that since the user will use a symmetric key sk which is encoded as a binary string, the construction in the SecLoc needs to be revised as follows. Specifically, the message component of ct_{sk,t_0} is changed from $sk \cdot e(g,g)^{\alpha s}$ to $sk \oplus \mathsf{H}(e(g,g)^{\alpha s})$ to adapt the format of sk, where $\mathsf{H} : \mathbb{G}_T \rightarrow \{0,1\}^\lambda$ is a hash function.

- Delegate(sd, sig, t_i) : The delegation algorithm takes as input the seed sd, a receipt sig and a state t_i, and outputs the other piece of the decryption key dk_2 at the state t_k as well as a transformation variable $st_{t_i \rightarrow t_k}$. The transformation variable $st_{t_i \rightarrow t_k}$ is used for transforming the ciphertext identified by sig at state t_i to that at a random state t_k. To achieve this, we randomly pick $\alpha_{21}, \alpha_{22} \in_R \mathbb{Z}_p$ with $\alpha_{21} + \alpha_{22} = \alpha_2$ mod p, and compute the state transformation variable $st_{t_i \rightarrow t_k} = t_k/t_i$ and the other piece of decryption key $dk_2 = (g^{\alpha_{21}/t_k}, g^{\alpha_{22}/r})$, where $t_k \in_R \mathbb{Z}_p$.

- Transform$(st_{t_i \rightarrow t_k}, ct_{t_i})$: The ciphertext transformation algorithm takes as input the transformation variable $st_{t_i \rightarrow t_k}$ and a ciphertext ct_{t_i} at the state t_i, and outputs the ct_{t_k}, which is the original ciphertext but at state t_k. This is implemented as follows. We first pick the state identification part (i.e., $g^{t_i \cdot s}$) in ct_{t_i}. Then, we compute $(g^{t_i \cdot s})^{t_k/t_i} = g^{t_k \cdot s}$. Finally, we output the ciphertext $ct_{t_k} = (m \cdot e(g,g)^{\alpha s}, \{g^{l_i}\}_{i \in \omega}, g^{t_k \cdot s}, g^{r \cdot s})$ at state t_k.

- Decrypt(dk_1, dk_2, ct_{t_j}) : The decryption algorithm takes as input two matching pieces of the decryption key, i.e., dk_1 and dk_2, where dk_2 is at state t_j, and a ciphertext ct_{t_j} at the same state t_j, and outputs the corresponding plaintext m if $\mathcal{P}$ is satisfied by ω. In particular, the decryption is executed in the following three steps:

  1. Use dk_1 for decryption: For each attribute $i \in \omega$ corresponding to the attribute stored in leaf node x in $\mathcal{P}$, compute $F_x = e(g^{q_x(0)/l_i}, g^{l_i \cdot s}) = e(g,g)^{sq_x(0)}$ where $i = \mathsf{attr}(x)$; For each interior node x in $\mathcal{P}$, let S_x be an arbitrary k_x-sized set of child nodes y such that $F_y \neq \perp$, if no such set exists then the node is not satisfied and the function returns $\perp$, otherwise recursively compute

$$F_x = (\prod_{y \in F_x} F_y)^{\Delta_{i, S_x}(0)}$$
$$= (e(g,g)^{\sum_{y \in S_x} sq_y(0)})^{\Delta_{i, S_x}(0)} = e(g,g)^{sq_x(0)}.$$

  Finally obtain $F_R = e(g,g)^{s\alpha_1}$ where R is the root of $\mathcal{P}$.

  2. Use dk_2 for decryption: Compute

$$e(g^{t_k \cdot s}, g^{\alpha_{21}/t_k}) \cdot e(g^{r \cdot s}, g^{\alpha_{22}/r})$$
$$= e(g,g)^{(\alpha_{21}+\alpha_{22})s} = e(g,g)^{\alpha_2 s}.$$

  3. Final decryption: compute

$$m \cdot e(g,g)^{\alpha s}/(e(g,g)^{\alpha_1 s} \cdot e(g,g)^{\alpha_2 s}) = m.$$

To summarize, the tABE not only inherits the basic property of policy-based encryption/decryption in ABE, but also

adds new features of *stateful* and *piece-wise key generation* [21, 14]. Specifically, based on basic ABE [10], we embed *state* into ABE ciphertext and decryption key, such that a decryption key can decrypt a ciphertext only when 1) the policy associated with decryption key is satisfied by the attributes in ciphertext, and 2) both the decryption key and ciphertext are in the same state (stateful). Moreover, we produce the ABE decryption in a piece-wise way. Two pieces of decryption keys are produced in *well-form* in the key generation of tABE, and decryption is allowed to be executed only when two matching pieces of decryption keys are involved. Note that the "matching" means both pieces decryption keys are produced together (piece-wise key generation).

6. SECURITY ANALYSIS

Recall in our threat model we mainly consider two types of attacks: 1) The cloud service provider might return a tampered list of candidate storage nodes, misleading user to store data in a cheating place; 2) The storage nodes might collude with each other, or even with the region servers to extract underlying information in user's data. Since the first type of attack could be easily verified by user as described in Section 4.2, we focus on the second attack here. We firstly analyze the security of the tABE primitive, and then reduce the security of SecLoc to that of the underlying tABE scheme.

6.1 Security Analysis of tABE

6.1.1 Security Definition

We first formalize the security goals we want to achieve in tABE. Recall that we have made an assumption that the region servers and storage nodes in the same region would not be compromised simultaneously. So, given the target region in which user has stored data for challenge, we can classify the second type of attack into two adversaries $\mathcal{A}_I$ and $\mathcal{A}_{II}$. 1) $\mathcal{A}_I$ models a set of "curious" storage nodes (not within the target region) colluding with some compromised region servers, which attempt to decrypt the ciphertext intended to be stored in the target region. 2) $\mathcal{A}_{II}$ models the (qualified) storage node in the target region colluding with storage nodes and (compromised) region servers in other regions, which attempt to decrypt the ciphertext under its control. We then define some notations and respectively model the game for $\mathcal{A}_I$ and $\mathcal{A}_{II}$.

We use m to denote the querying message, x to denote the regions in which both "curious" storage nodes and "corrupted" servers locate, $*$ to denote the target storage region. We model the game for $\mathcal{A}_I$ as follows. Note that, since the definition is for tABE and works in a generic case, the $\mathcal{P}_*$ and $\mathcal{P}_x$ are tree-based policies respectively satisfied by the subset set ω_* and ω_x of $\{u_1, u_2, \ldots, u_n\}$. $\mathcal{P}_* = u_*, \omega_* = \{u_*\}$ and $\mathcal{P}_x = u_x, \omega_x = \{u_x\}$ are specific to the location-sensitive storage scenario.

Line 1-3 model the registration stage in $\mathcal{A}_I$'s game: the user runs Setup$(\cdot)$ and assigns secret keys to all the storage nodes and region servers. Line 4-5 denote functions for message encryption m and store the ciphertext in a preferred region. Note that the preferred region could be chosen arbitrarily. Line 6-7 describe the challenge in $\mathcal{A}_I$'s game. Intuitively, $\mathcal{A}_I$ models a collusion in a set of "curious" nodes and the region servers. Thus, it can access $(sd_*, sig_*, sd_x, sig_x)$ from all the region servers and $(dk_{1,x}, ct_{m,t,x})$ from "curi-

1 $(pk, msk) \leftarrow \mathsf{Setup}(\lambda), t \in_R \mathbb{Z}_p$;
2 $(dk_{1,*}, sd_*) \leftarrow \mathsf{KeyGen}(\mathcal{P}_*, msk, t)$;
3 $(dk_{1,x}, sd_x) \leftarrow \mathsf{KeyGen}(\mathcal{P}_x, msk, t)$;
4 $(ct_{m,t,*}, sig_*) \leftarrow \mathsf{Encrypt}(\omega_*, m, t)$;
5 $(ct_{m,t,x}, sig_x) \leftarrow \mathsf{Encrypt}(\omega_x, m, t)$;
6 $(m_0, m_1) \leftarrow \mathcal{A}_I(pk, sd_*, sig_*, dk_{1,x}, ct_{m,t,x}, sd_x, sig_x)$;
7 $b' \leftarrow \mathcal{A}_I(\mathsf{Encrypt}(\omega_*, m_b, t)), b \in_R \{0, 1\}$;

ous" nodes, and outputs two challenge messages m_0 and m_1 which have not ever been "stored" declared in line 4-5. After providing the tABE ciphertext of m_b in the target region $*$, $b \in_R \{0, 1\}$, $\mathcal{A}_I$ finally outputs a bit b' which is the guess of b.

As with the definition of $\mathcal{A}_I$, we use $*$ to denote the target region. In this type of attack, we allow this "dishonest" node in a target region to collude with any other entity except the region server in the same region. We model the game of $\mathcal{A}_{II}$ as follows.

1 $(pk, msk) \leftarrow \mathsf{Setup}(\lambda), t \in_R \mathbb{Z}_p$;
2 $(dk_{1,*}, sd_*) \leftarrow \mathsf{KeyGen}(\mathcal{P}_*, msk, t)$;
3 $(dk_{1,x}, sd_x) \leftarrow \mathsf{KeyGen}(\mathcal{P}_x, msk, t)$;
4 $(ct_{m,t,*}, sig_*) \leftarrow \mathsf{Encrypt}(\omega_*, m, t)$;
5 $(ct_{m,t,x}, sig_x) \leftarrow \mathsf{Encrypt}(\omega_x, m, t)$;
6 $(m_0, m_1) \leftarrow$ $\mathcal{A}_{II}(pk, dk_{1,*}, ct_{m,t,*}, dk_{1,x}, sd_x, sig_x, ct_{m,t,x})$;
7 $b' \leftarrow \mathcal{A}_{II}(\mathsf{Encrypt}(\omega_*, m_b, t)), b \in_R \{0, 1\}$;

The operations in line 1-5 are identical to the same operations of the game for $\mathcal{A}_I$. The difference is in the operation reported in line 6, in which $\mathcal{A}_{II}$ can access the tuple $(dk_{1,x}, ct_{m,t,x}, sd_x, sig_x)$ from the compromised nodes and servers in region x and $ct_{m,t,*}$ from the node itself, and outputs the challenge messages m_0 and m_1. Finally, after receiving the encryption of m_b, $b \in_R \{0, 1\}$, $\mathcal{A}_{II}$ outputs the guess b' of b.

We can then define the advantage of $\mathcal{A}_I$ and $\mathcal{A}_{II}$ as

$$\mathsf{Adv}(\mathcal{A}_i) = \mathsf{Pr}[b' = b]$$

where $i = \mathrm{I}, \mathrm{II}$.

DEFINITION 2. *A tABE scheme is secure if all polynomial time adversaries in types of $\mathcal{A}_I$ and $\mathcal{A}_{II}$ have at most a negligible advantage in the corresponding games.*

6.1.2 Security Proof

We now turn to analyze the security of our proposed instantiation against Definition 2. We firstly introduce a new computational assumption, namely strong Decisional Bilinear Diffie-Hellman (sDBDH) assumption, and show it is at least *not stronger than* the weak Decisional Bilinear Diffie-Hellman Inversion (wDBDHI) assumption, investigated in [6]. Then, we prove our tABE proposal is secure under the sDBDH assumption.

We describe both assumptions as follows.

DEFINITION 3 (wDBDHI ASSUMPTION). *Suppose a challenger chooses $a, b \in_R \mathbb{Z}_p$ at random where p is a large prime. The l-wDBDHI assumption is that no polynomial-time adversary can distinguish $(g, g^a, \ldots, g^{a^l}, g^b, e(g, g)^{a^{l+1}b})$*

from the tuple $(g, g^a, \ldots, g^{a^l}, g^b, e(g, g)^z)$ with more than a negligible advantage, where $g \in \mathbb{G}$ and $z \in_R \mathbb{Z}_p$.

DEFINITION 4 (sDBDH ASSUMPTION). *Suppose a challenger chooses $a, b, c, z \in_R \mathbb{Z}_p$ at random where p is a large prime. The sDBDH assumption is that no polynomial-time adversary can distinguish the tuple $(g, g^a, g^b, g^{1/b}, g^c, e(g, g)^{abc})$ from the tuple $(g, g^a, g^b, g^c, e(g, g)^z)$ with more than a negligible advantage, where $g \in \mathbb{G}$ and $z \in_R \mathbb{Z}_p$.*

THEOREM 1. *sDBDH assumption is at least not stronger than wDBDHI assumption.*

PROOF. Suppose there exists a problem solver $\mathcal{S}_{\mathrm{sDBDH}}$ which can solve the sDBDH problem in polynomial time. We then describe how to construct $\mathcal{S}_{\mathrm{wDBDHI}}$ for solving the 2-wDBDHI problem.

Given the 2-wDBDHI tuple $(g, g^x, g^{x^2}, g^y, Z)$, $\mathcal{S}_{\mathrm{wDBDHI}}$ sets $h = g^x$ and calls the sDBDH problem solver $\mathcal{S}_{\mathrm{sDBDH}}$ with the input $(h, h^{y/x}, h^x, h^{1/x}, h^x, Z)$, which implicitly fixes the variables in sDBDH tuple as $a = y/x, b = x$ and $c = x$. Then if $\mathcal{S}_{\mathrm{sDBDH}}$ guesses $Z = e(h, h)^{abc}$, $\mathcal{S}_{\mathrm{wDBDHI}}$ guesses $Z = e(g, g)^{x^3 y}$; otherwise $\mathcal{S}_{\mathrm{wDBDHI}}$ guesses $Z = e(g, g)^z$, $z \in_R \mathbb{Z}_p$. Since $e(h, h)^{abc} = e(g^x, g^x)^{xy} = e(g, g)^{x^3 y}$, we can say, if $\mathcal{S}_{\mathrm{sDBDH}}$ solves sDBDH problem, $\mathcal{S}_{\mathrm{wDBDHI}}$ can solve wDBDHI problem with the same advantage of $\mathcal{S}_{\mathrm{sDBDH}}$. $\square$

From Theorem 1, we can see the introduced sDBDH problem is at least *not easier than* wDBDHI problem, for which the best known algorithm is to solve the standard Discrete Logarithm Problem (DLP) [3]. Thus, we can say the sDBDH assumption is at least *not stronger than* DLP assumption, and directly use it in the security proof of the tABE instantiation.

THEOREM 2. *Our proposed tABE scheme in Section 5.2 is secure against $\mathcal{A}_I$ under the sDBDH assumption.*

PROOF. Suppose there exists an adversarial algorithm $\mathcal{A}_I$ attacking our proposed tABE instantiation with advantage ϵ. To prove this theorem, our aim is to utilize $\mathcal{A}_I$ to construct a sDBDH problem solver (say $\mathcal{S}$), which is able to solve sDBDH problem with similar advantage. Precisely, on input the sDBDH tuple $(A = g^a, B = g^b, B' = g^{1/b}, C = g^c, Z = e(g, g)^z)$, the problem solver $\mathcal{S}$ sets up the tABE world for the adversary $\mathcal{A}_I$ with the goal of using $\mathcal{A}_I$ to decide whether $z = abc$. We let a variable $\mu = 0$ for the case of $z = abc$, or $\mu = 1$ for the case of $z \in_R \mathbb{Z}_p$. We construct $\mathcal{S}$ as follows.

To begin, $\mathcal{S}$ outputs the global parameters pk to $\mathcal{A}_I$. Here, we let $\mathcal{S}$ assign pk in the following way: 1) For all the attribute $u_i \in \mathcal{U}$, if $u_i \in \omega_*$ (recall ω_* is the target region) randomly pick $r_i \in_R \mathbb{Z}_p$ and set $g^{l_i} = g^{r_i}$; otherwise (i.e., $u_i \notin \omega_*$) pick $\beta_i \in_R \mathbb{Z}_p$ and set $g^{l_i} = (B)^{\beta_i} = g^{\beta_i b}$. 2) Set $e(g, g)^\alpha = e(A, B) = e(g, g)^{ab}$. Finally the public key is given to $\mathcal{A}_I$. Thus, we can think of ab as the master secret key of user.

Before simulating $\mathcal{A}_I$'s queries, we define two procedures.

- PolicySatis$(\mathcal{P}, \omega, \lambda)$ is to assign the root node of a *satisfied* tree-based policy $\mathcal{P}$ (by ω_*) with a polynomial. Suppose the root node of $\mathcal{P}$ is R and k_R is the threshold value of R. This procedure randomly picks a $(k_R - 1)$-degree polynomial $q_R(\cdot)$ with $q_R(0) = \lambda$. Then for each child node (say R') of R, denote the tree-based sub-policy rooted at R' as $\mathcal{P}_{R'}$, and recursively call the procedure PolicySatis$(\mathcal{P}_{R'}, \omega, q_R(\mathsf{index}(R')))$.

- PolicyUnSatis($\mathcal{P}, \omega, g^\lambda$) is to assign the root node of an *unsatisfied* tree-based policy $\mathcal{P}$ (by ω_*) with a polynomial. Similarly we denote R as the root node of $\mathcal{P}$ and k_R as the threshold value of R. This procedure implicitly picks a (k_R-1)-degree polynomial $q_R(\cdot)$ with $q_R(0) = \lambda$. Then, for each child node R', if its sub-policy $\mathcal{P}_{R'}$ (rooted at R') is satisfied by ω_*, call PolicySatis($\mathcal{P}, \omega, q_R(\text{index}(R'))$); otherwise if its sub-policy $\mathcal{P}_{R'}$ is not satisfied by ω_*, call the procedure PolicyUnSatis($\mathcal{P}_{R'}, \omega, g^{q_R(\text{index}(R'))}$).

Then, after randomly picking $t \in_R \mathbb{Z}_p$, we can simulate $\mathcal{A}_{\text{I}}$'s queries as follows.

- $(dk_{1,x}, sd_x)$, a node and region server in region x corrupted by $\mathcal{A}_{\text{I}}$ in registration. $\mathcal{S}$ picks $\alpha_2 \in_R \mathbb{Z}_p$ and runs PolicyUnSatis($\mathcal{P}_x, \omega^*, A(B')^{-\alpha_2}$). As defined above the polynomial $q_N(\cdot)$ could be fixed for each node N of $\mathcal{P}$. $\mathcal{S}$ defines the final polynomial $Q_N(\cdot) = bq_N(\cdot)$, which would implicitly set $Q_R(0) = ab - \alpha_2$, where R is the root node of $\mathcal{P}$. For any leaf node N of $\mathcal{P}$ and its attribute subscript $i = \text{attr}(N)$ (the corresponding attribute is u_i), and $\mathcal{S}$ can simulate and return the seed $sd_x = (\alpha_2, t)$ and decryption key as $dk_{1,x} = \{D_i\}$ where

$$
D_i = \begin{cases} g^{\frac{Q_N(0)}{l_i}} = g^{\frac{bq_N(0)}{r_i}} = B^{\frac{q_N(0)}{r_i}} & \text{if } u_i \in \omega_* \\ g^{\frac{Q_N(0)}{l_i}} = g^{\frac{bq_N(0)}{b\beta_i}} = g^{\frac{q_N(0)}{\beta_i}} & \text{otherwsie} \end{cases} \quad (2)
$$

- sd_*, a region server in the target region $*$ corrupted by $\mathcal{A}_{\text{I}}$ in registration. $\mathcal{S}$ randomly picks $\alpha_2 \in_R \mathbb{Z}_p$ and returns $sd_* = (\alpha_2, t)$.

- $(ct_{m,t,x}, sig_x)$, a node and server in region x corrupted by $\mathcal{A}_{\text{I}}$ in storage. For querying message m, $\mathcal{S}$ returns $(ct_{m,t,x}, sig_x) = \text{Encrypt}(pk, \omega_x, m)$.

- sig_x, a region server in the target region $*$ corrupted by $\mathcal{A}_{\text{I}}$ in storage. For querying message m, $\mathcal{S}$ obtains $(ct_{m,t,*}, sig_*) = \text{Encrypt}(pk, \omega_*, m)$ and returns sig_*.

Eventually, $\mathcal{A}_{\text{I}}$ must output a challenge (m_0, m_1) where $m_0 \neq m_1$. $\mathcal{S}$ randomly picks $b \in \{0, 1\}$ and simulates the ciphertext $ct_* = (m_b \cdot e(A, B)^s, g^s, \{g^{r_i \cdot s}\}_{u_i \in \omega_*}, g^{t \cdot s}, g^{r \cdot s})$ and $sig_* = g^{1/r}$ where $r \in_R \mathbb{Z}_p$. 1) If $b = 0$, $\mathcal{S}$ implicitly set the randomness $s = c$. In this case, ct_* is a *valid* encryption of m_b. 2) If $b = 1$, $\mathcal{S}$ picks $s \in_R \mathbb{Z}_p$ at random. In this case, $m_b \cdot e(A, B)^s$ would be a random element in $\mathbb{G}_T$ from $\mathcal{A}_{\text{I}}$'s vew and the rest of ciphertext contains no information about m_b.

$\mathcal{S}$ runs $\mathcal{A}_{\text{I}}$ to get the guess b'. If $b' = b$, $\mathcal{S}$ guesses $\mu' = 0$ (i.e., it is given the $Z = e(g,g)^{abc}$); Otherwise, $\mathcal{S}$ guesses $\mu' = 1$ (i.e., it is given a random element in $\mathbb{G}_T$).

In the case that $\mathcal{S}$ is given $e(g,g)^{abc}$ (i.e., $\mu = 0$), $\mathcal{A}_{\text{I}}$ sees the encryption of m_b. The advantage of adversary in tABE is ϵ by definition. Therefore, we have $\Pr[b = b'|\mu = 0] = 1/2 + \epsilon$. Since $\mathcal{S}$ guesses $\mu' = 0$ when $b = b'$, we have $\Pr[\mu' = \mu|\mu = 0] = 1/2 + \epsilon$.

In the case that $\mathcal{S}$ is given $e(g,g)^z$ (i.e., $\mu = 1$), where $z \in_R \mathbb{Z}_p$, $\mathcal{A}_{\text{I}}$ gains no information about b. Since $\mathcal{S}$ guesses $\mu' = 1$ when $b \neq b'$, we have $\Pr[\mu' = \mu|\mu = 1] = \Pr[b' \neq b|\mu = 1] = 1/2$.

Finally, we can get the overall advantage of the simulator $\mathcal{S}$ in sDBDH problem is $|\Pr[\mu' = \mu|\mu = 0]/2 + \Pr[\mu' = \mu|\mu =$

$1]/2 - 1/2| = \epsilon$. In other words, the fact that an adversary $\mathcal{A}_{\text{I}}$ has non-negligible advantage in attacking tABE schema would result that a simulator $\mathcal{S}$ has the *same* advantage in solving sDBDH problem. $\square$

THEOREM 3. *Our proposed tABE scheme in Section 5.2 is secure against $\mathcal{A}_{\text{II}}$ under sDBDH assumption.*

PROOF. The proof is similar to that of Theorem 2. The only difference is that $\mathcal{A}_{\text{II}}$ can access $dk_{1,*}$ from the storage node in a target region. We just provide the simulation of $dk_{1,*}$ as follows. Note that we abuse $\mathcal{S}$ here to denote the problem solver utilizing $\mathcal{A}_{\text{II}}$ to solve the sDBDH problem.

- $dk_{1,*}$, a node in the target region $*$ corrupted by $\mathcal{A}_{\text{II}}$ in registration. $\mathcal{S}$ randomly picks $\alpha_1 \in_R \mathbb{Z}_p$ and runs PolicySatis($\mathcal{P}_*, \omega_*, \alpha_1$) to obtain $dk_{1,*} = \{D_i\}$. Finally, $\mathcal{S}$ returns $dk_{1,*}$ back to $\mathcal{A}_{\text{II}}$.

The rest of proof is identical to that of Theorem 2. $\square$

Based on Theorem 2 and Theorem 3, we prove the security of proposed tABE instantiation.

6.2 Security Analysis of SecLoc

The following theorem allows us to reduce the security of SecLoc to that of the underlying primitive tABE.

THEOREM 4. *If the underlying primitives SE and tABE are secure, our proposed construction SecLoc achieves the goals of location-sensitive and content-based access control.*

PROOF. To prove this theorem, our aim is to respectively reduce the goal of *location-sensitive access control* and *content-based access control* to the security of underlying primitive tABE resistant to $\mathcal{A}_{\text{I}}$ and $\mathcal{A}_{\text{II}}$.

Since the data is encrypted with a two-layered encryption (i.e., the inner symmetric encryption and the outer tABE encryption), to access the data m, the adversary should decrypt ct_{sk,t_0} to retrieve the symmetric key sk. However such a key is protected by tABE. Thus, the goal of data privacy can be reduced to the security of tABE.

Regarding the goal of *location-sensitive access control*, the adversary considered in our threat model includes the storage nodes at unexpected regions colluding with all the region servers. We argue that this attack could be generalized as the first type adversary $\mathcal{A}_{\text{I}}$, because it could be modeled as the storage nodes accessing a set of decryption keys and controlling seed from the region servers (as per our definition in Section 6.1.1). Since tABE is secure against $\mathcal{A}_{\text{I}}$, SecLoc achieves location-sensitive access control.

Regarding the goal of *content-based access control*, the adversary considered in our threat model is the storage node in qualified regions colluding with the nodes and servers in unqualified regions. This attack could be modeled as the second type adversary $\mathcal{A}_{\text{II}}$, which is allowed to access its own piece of decryption, but attempts to decrypt the unspecified ciphertext (as our definition in Section 6.1.1). Since tABE is secure against $\mathcal{A}_{\text{II}}$, SecLoc achieves content-based access control. $\square$

7. DATA RE-STORAGE CAPABILITIES

A limitation of SecLoc proposal in Section 5.1 is that it only allows for storing data *all at once*. In other words, the storage stage in SecLoc is ran only once, and after its execution SecLoc does not support uploading or storing data again. We point out that this limitation originates from the *keyless* goal. Since we want to achieve a keyless system, a user cannot memorize any secret information including the *state*. Nevertheless, in the storage stage of SecLoc, the state variable (i.e., t_i) is a necessary input of tABE encryption algorithm. The lack of a state would lead to failing the tABE.Encrypt$(\cdot)$ protocol. One option is that the user communicates with the region servers to re-obtain the state variable t_i for encryption. However, region servers might return back an incorrect t_i, and as a result the retrieval stage will not be executed successfully.

In order to extend SecLoc to support data re-storage, we extend SecLoc as follows: 1) After the initial storage at state t_0, for each time of data re-storage, we allow users to specify a new (random) state and encrypt data at this new specified state. In other words, as long as the storage stage occurs, a new state would be involved. 2) We introduce a new stage, say Transformation Stage, into SecLoc. The transformation stage is triggered after each execution of storage stage (except the first execution), and transforms the cloud data encrypted under the old states into the same data with the new state.

We describe the extended SecLoc as follows. Since registration and retrieval stages are identical with those of basic SecLoc, we only discuss the storage stage and newly introduced transformation stage.

- **Storage Stage.** Suppose a data item identified by dID $\in \mathbb{Z}_p$ is to be stored in the storage node in region i. The user contacts cloud vendor to get the available storage nodes in region i. Then, the user performs a two-layered encryption to encapsulate m as with the basic SecLoc. The only difference is that, if the storage stage is executed for the first time, t_0 is used as the state for tABE encryption (as with the basic SecLoc); otherwise a random picked state t_i is used. After uploading ciphertext (dID, $i, v_{t_i}, ct_m, ct_{sk,t_i}$) and *sig* to the assigned storage nodes and local region server, user broadcasts t_i to all the region servers, which store t_i for state transformation in future. Note that even when the region servers have received and stored t_i, they should not drop the old state t_{i-1}.

- **Transformation Stage.** When the $(i+1)$th time of storage stage ends, where $i = 1, 2, \ldots$, the transformation stage is triggered. In this stage, storage nodes make "transformation" request to local region servers, which respond with the transformation variable $st_{t_{i-1} \to t_i} = t_i / t_{i-1}$. The storage nodes update the ciphertexts (dID, $i, ct_m, ct_{sk,t_{i-1}}$) at the old state t_{i-1}, by updating the component $ct_{sk,t_{i-1}}$ to ct_{sk,t_i} and by running tABE.Transform$(st_{t_{i-1} \to t_i}, ct_{sk,t_{i-1}})$.

8. PERFORMANCE STUDY

In this section, we firstly analyze the computational complexity of our proposed (basic) SecLoc, and then we evaluate its performance.

8.1 Complexity Analysis

We analyze the computational complexity for the the core stages of SecLoc, as they are defined in Section 4: Registration, Storage and Retrieval Stage.

Stage	Computation Overhead
Registration Stage	$(2n+1)\mathrm{E}_\mathbb{G} + 1\mathrm{P}$
Storage Stage	$(|\omega|+4)\mathrm{E}_\mathbb{G} + 1\mathrm{E}_{\mathbb{G}_T} + \xi_1|m|$
Retrieval Stage	$2\mathrm{E}_\mathbb{G}$ (for region server)
	$1\mathrm{E}_\mathbb{G} + 3\mathrm{P} + \xi_2|m|$ (for storage node)

Table 1: Computation Overhead in SecLoc

During the registration stage, the user registers to a service offered by the cloud vendor, and initializes the underlying bilinear groups, the public key pk and master secret key msk. The user also needs to assign parameters $dk_{1,i}$ and sd_i respectively to the storage nodes and region servers. As described in Section 5.2, the main computation overhead for initialization is introduced by the $n+1$ modular exponentiations in $\mathbb{G}$ and 1 bilinear pairing, while the main computation overhead for assignment is n modular exponentiations.

During the storage stage, the main computation overhead incurred by the user is the encryption of the data using the symmetric data encryption key sk as well as the encryption of sk using tABE. The complexity of the former depends on the size of the underlying data file. The overhead for the latter consists of $|\omega| + 4$ modular exponentiations in $\mathbb{G}$ and 1 modular exponentiation in $\mathbb{G}_T$, where ω denotes the set of regions in which data is expected to be stored in.

Finally, at retrieval stage, most of the operations are carried out between region servers and storage nodes. The region servers need to generate the piece of decryption key dk_2 as well as the transformation variable, which represents two modular exponentiations in $\mathbb{G}$. The storage nodes' main computation overhead is caused by the execution of algorithm Transform$(\cdot)$ and Decrypt$(\cdot)$. The former accounts for 1 modular exponentiation in $\mathbb{G}$, while the latter costs 3 bilinear pairings.

We summarize the main computational overhead of our proposed SecLoc in Table 1. Notice that in Table 1, $\mathrm{E}_\mathbb{G}$ and $\mathrm{E}_{\mathbb{G}_T}$ respectively denotes the modular exponentiation in $\mathbb{G}$ and $\mathbb{G}_T$; P denotes the bilinear pairing operation; $\xi_1|m|$ and $\xi_2|m|$ respectively denotes the time cost for encrypting and decrypting data m, both of which are depended on the size of m.

8.2 Experimental Evaluation

We simulated our approaches using the Polarssl cryptographic library [2] and the Pairing-Based Cryptography library [1]: the data encryption algorithm used in SecLoc used AES. We used our local machine, a Mac OS X machine with processor of 1.7 GHz Intel Core i7 and memory of 8 GB 1600 MHz DDR3, as users. The storage nodes and region servers are implemented as the T2 Micro Servers in Amazon EC2 platform.

We adopted the trivial method as a baseline approach, in which user encrypts file expected to be stored in one region per key. Compared with our approach in functionality, this baseline approach does not reduce the number of keys, which not only introduces significant overhead for key management, but also might lead to the underlying risk of key exposure.

Table 2 shows the time cost of SecLoc in registration stage, which is clearly growing linearly with the number of global regions, validating the complexity analysis in Table 1. Note that, the baseline approach does not need the process of

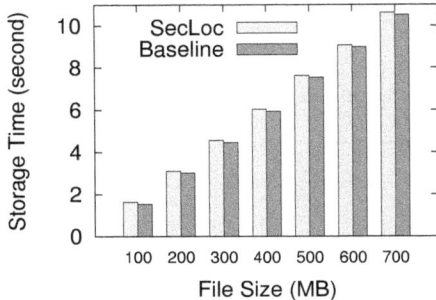

(a) Performance of Storage Stage

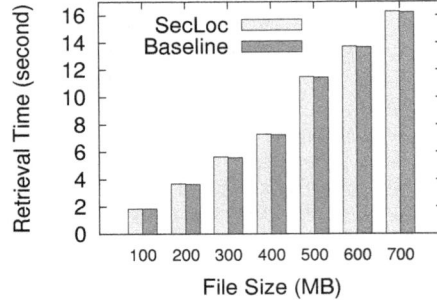

(b) Performance of Retrieval Stage

Figure 3: Performance of Storage and Retrieval Stage

Number of Regions	Registration Time (sec.)
10	2.553
20	3.816
30	4.189
40	6.114
50	6.505

Table 2: Cost of Registration Stage

parameters assignment (i.e., respectively assign dk_1 and sd to each storage node and region server), and the time cost of registration is negligible.

Figure 3(a) and Figure 3(b) respectively compares the time cost of SecLoc and baseline approach in terms of storage and retrieval stage varying the files size. Note that the retrieval cost in SecLoc includes the time cost per region server and that for storage nodes. It is not surprising to see that SecLoc takes (slightly) more time than the baseline approach. This is because, SecLoc utilizes the tABE as underlying primitive to encapsulate (storage stage) and decapsulate (retrieval stage) the symmetric data key.

To sum up, our proposed SecLoc is slower than the baseline approach due to two main reasons: 1) SecLoc requires a (relative) "heavy" registration stage for parameter assignments; 2) SecLoc takes more time for encapsulating and decapsulating key. However, we argue that the former overhead is required only once for initialization, while the latter could be restricted on millisecond level, which is negligible when the file size is large enough. Thus, we conclude that, compared with the baseline approach, SecLoc introduces small overhead, and achieves the goal of securing location-sensitive storage, while simplifying the key management.

9. CONCLUSION

Aiming at addressing the emerging critical issue of location-sensitive storage, we propose the SecLoc framework. SecLoc guarantees that cloud user's data is stored and can be processed only at locations that satisfy user specified location constraints. Further, even if the cloud providers (unintentionally) copy user data to nodes outside the desired regions, the user data will become unaccessible at those ineligible locations. Our SecLoc construction is based on the tABE primitive which enjoys the features of stateful and piece-

wise key generation. The security of tABE scheme relies on a new introduced computational assumption sDBDH, which is shown to be at least not stronger than the non-standard wDBDHI assumption and the standard DLP assumption. Extensions of SecLoc for supporting data re-storage have also been discussed. Finally, both complexity and experimental analysis demonstrate the effectiveness of SecLoc.

Acknowledgements

We would like to thank our anonymous reviewers and shepherd Adam J. Lee for their insightful comments that helped improve the paper. The work of Anna Squicciarini is funded by the National Science Foundation (NSF-1250319). The work of Dan Lin is funded by the National Science Foundation (NSF-DGE-1433659). The work of Chunfu Jia is funded by the National Key Basic Research Program of China (Grant No. 2013CB834204), the National Natural Science Foundation of China (Grant No. 61272423), the Natural Science Foundation of Tianjin (Grant No. 14JCYBJC15300), and the Open Project Foundation of Information Security Evaluation Center of Civil Aviation, Civil Aviation University of China (Grant No. CAAC-ISECCA-201403).

10. REFERENCES

[1] Pairing-based cryptography library. http://crypto.stanford.edu/pbc/.

[2] PolarSSL library. https://polarssl.org.

[3] Final report on main computational assumptions in cryptography. http://www.ecrypt.eu.org/documents/D.MAYA.6.pdf, 2013.

[4] ARMBRUST, M., FOX, A., GRIFFITH, R., JOSEPH, A. D., KATZ, R., KONWINSKI, A., LEE, G., PATTERSON, D., RABKIN, A., STOICA, I., AND ZAHARIA, M. A view of cloud computing. *Communications of the ACM 53*, 4 (Apr. 2010), 50–58.

[5] BELLARE, M., DESAI, A., JOKIPII, E., AND ROGAWAY, P. A concrete security treatment of symmetric encryption. In *Proceedings of the 38th Annual Symposium on Foundations of Computer Science* (Oct 1997), pp. 394–403.

[6] BONEH, D., BOYEN, X., AND GOH, E.-J. Hierarchical identity based encryption with constant size ciphertext. In *Advances in Cryptology – EUROCRYPT*

2005, vol. 3494 of *Lecture Notes in Computer Science*. Springer Berlin Heidelberg, 2005, pp. 440–456.

[7] BONEH, D., AND FRANKLIN, M. Identity-based encryption from the weil pairing. In *Advances in Cryptology — CRYPTO 2001*, vol. 2139 of *Lecture Notes in Computer Science*. Springer Berlin Heidelberg, 2001, pp. 213–229.

[8] CREMERS, C., RASMUSSEN, K., SCHMIDT, B., AND CAPKUN, S. Distance hijacking attacks on distance bounding protocols. In *IEEE Symposium on Security and Privacy (SP)* (2012), pp. 113–127.

[9] FU, D. L., PENG, X. G., AND YANG, Y. L. Trusted validation for geolocation of cloud data. *The Computer Journal* (2014).

[10] GOYAL, V., PANDEY, O., SAHAI, A., AND WATERS, B. Attribute-based encryption for fine-grained access control of encrypted data. In *Proceedings of the 13th ACM Conference on Computer and Communications Security* (New York, NY, USA, 2006), CCS '06, ACM, pp. 89–98.

[11] HAHN, F., AND KERSCHBAUM, F. Searchable encryption with secure and efficient updates. In *Proceedings of the 2014 ACM Conference on Computer and Communications Security* (New York, NY, USA, 2014), CCS '14, ACM, pp. 310–320.

[12] JUELS, A., AND KALISKI, JR., B. S. Pors: Proofs of retrievability for large files. In *Proceedings of the 14th ACM Conference on Computer and Communications Security* (New York, NY, USA, 2007), CCS '07, ACM, pp. 584–597.

[13] KAMARA, S., AND LAUTER, K. Cryptographic cloud storage. In *Financial Cryptography and Data Security*, vol. 6054 of *Lecture Notes in Computer Science*. Springer Berlin Heidelberg, 2010, pp. 136–149.

[14] LI, J., CHEN, X., LI, J., JIA, C., MA, J., AND LOU, W. Fine-grained access control system based on outsourced attribute-based encryption. In *Computer Security – ESORICS 2013*, J. Crampton, S. Jajodia, and K. Mayes, Eds., vol. 8134 of *Lecture Notes in Computer Science*. Springer Berlin Heidelberg, 2013, pp. 592–609.

[15] LI, J., WANG, Q., WANG, C., CAO, N., REN, K., AND LOU, W. Fuzzy keyword search over encrypted data in cloud computing. In *Proceedings IEEE INFOCOM* (March 2010), pp. 1–5.

[16] LI, M., QIN, C., LEE, P. P. C., AND LI, J. Convergent dispersal: Toward storage-efficient security in a cloud-of-clouds. In *6th USENIX Workshop on Hot Topics in Storage and File Systems (HotStorage 14)* (Philadelphia, PA, June 2014), USENIX Association.

[17] NOMAN, A., AND ADAMS, C. Providing a data location assurance service for cloud storage environments. *Journal of Mobile Multimedia 8*, 4 (June 2012), 265–286.

[18] PALADI, N., AND MICHALAS, A. "one of our hosts in another country": Challenges of data geolocation in cloud storage. In *4th International Conference on Wireless Communications, Vehicular Technology, Information Theory and Aerospace Electronic Systems (VITAE)* (May 2014), pp. 1–6.

[19] PETERSON, Z. N. J., GONDREE, M., AND BEVERLY, R. A position paper on data sovereignty: The importance of geolocating data in the cloud. In *Proceedings of the 3rd USENIX Conference on Hot Topics in Cloud Computing* (Berkeley, CA, USA, 2011), HotCloud'11, USENIX Association.

[20] REN, K., WANG, C., WANG, Q., ET AL. Security challenges for the public cloud. *IEEE Internet Computing 16*, 1 (2012), 69–73.

[21] SAHAI, A., SEYALIOGLU, H., AND WATERS, B. Dynamic credentials and ciphertext delegation for attribute-based encryption. In *Advances in Cryptology – CRYPTO 2012*, vol. 7417 of *Lecture Notes in Computer Science*. Springer Berlin Heidelberg, 2012, pp. 199–217.

[22] WATSON, G. J., SAFAVI-NAINI, R., ALIMOMENI, M., LOCASTO, M. E., AND NARAYAN, S. LoSt: Location based storage. In *Proceedings of the 2012 ACM Workshop on Cloud Computing Security Workshop* (New York, NY, USA, 2012), CCSW '12, ACM, pp. 59–70.

Mitigating Multi-Tenancy Risks in IaaS Cloud Through Constraints-Driven Virtual Resource Scheduling

Khalid Bijon
Institute for Cyber Security
Univ of Texas at San Antonio
khalid.bijon@utsa.edu

Ram Krishnan
Institute for Cyber Security
Univ of Texas at San Antonio
ram.krishnan@utsa.edu

Ravi Sandhu
Institute for Cyber Security
Univ of Texas at San Antonio
ravi.sandhu@utsa.edu

ABSTRACT

A major concern in the adoption of cloud infrastructure-as-a-service (IaaS) arises from multi-tenancy, where multiple tenants share the underlying physical infrastructure operated by a cloud service provider. A tenant could be an enterprise in the context of a public cloud or a department within an enterprise in the context of a private cloud. Enabled by virtualization technology, the service provider is able to minimize cost by providing virtualized hardware resources such as virtual machines, virtual storage and virtual networks, as a service to multiple tenants where, for instance, a tenant's virtual machine may be hosted in the same physical server as that of many other tenants. It is well-known that separation of execution environment provided by the hypervisors that enable virtualization technology has many limitations. In addition to inadvertent misconfigurations, a number of attacks have been demonstrated that allow unauthorized information flow between virtual machines hosted by a hypervisor on a given physical server. In this paper, we present attribute-based constraints specification and enforcement as a mechanism to mitigate such multi-tenancy risks that arise in cloud IaaS. We represent relevant properties of virtual resources (e.g., virtual machines, virtual networks, etc.) as their attributes. Conflicting attribute values are specified by the tenant or by the cloud IaaS system as appropriate. The goal is to schedule virtual resources on physical resources in a conflict-free manner. The general problem is shown to be NP-complete. We explore practical conflict specifications that can be efficiently enforced. We have implemented a prototype for virtual machine scheduling in OpenStack, a widely-used open-source cloud IaaS software, and evaluated its performance overhead, resource requirements to satisfy conflicts, and resource utilization.

Categories and Subject Descriptors

K.6.5 [**Management of Computing and Information Systems**]: Security and Protection

General Terms

Security

Keywords

Cloud IaaS; Virtual-Resource Scheduling; VM Migration; Multi-Tenancy; Constraint; VM Co-Residency Management

1. INTRODUCTION

Enterprises are increasingly driven by economics and flexibility to utilize computing resources provided by cloud infrastructure-as-a-service (IaaS) [32]. A major impediment to wider adoption of cloud IaaS stems from an enterprise's loss of direct control over their virtual resources in cloud IaaS relative to the customary level of control over physical (or virtual) resources in an enterprise-managed data center [22]. In cloud IaaS, the physical resources in a datacenter are logically arranged by the cloud service provider (CSP) and virtual resources are hosted on those logical collections of physical resources. This is illustrated in figure 1 where a rack, for example, is a collection of a specific set of physical servers and network hosts. Other resources such as physical storage volumes may be associated with those compute hosts in the rack. This is shown as physical resource to physical resource mapping (PR-to-PR) in the figure. The single and double-headed arrows indicate the usual "one-to" and "many-to" mappings respectively. Tenants obtain a number of separate pieces of virtual computing resources (or simply resources), e.g. virtual machines, virtual networks, etc., from the CSP. The cloud IaaS system should have suitable policy specification capabilities so that tenants can dynamically manage and arrange these resources to build a particular computing environment based on their needs. For instance, tenants can systematically control specific virtual hardware (e.g. RAM, disk) assignment to virtual machines based on certain properties (e.g. purpose, running work-load type, sensitivity). This is shown as virtual resource to virtual resource mapping (VR-to-VR) in the figure and several mechanisms have been proposed [10, 11] to manage it.

More significantly, in cloud IaaS, physical hardware is also shared by multiple virtual resources for maximizing utilization and reducing cost. IaaS public or community cloud providers allow multi-tenancy which multiplexes virtual resources of multiple enterprises upon same hardware. This includes co-location of virtual machines from different tenants on a single physical host, sharing physical disk storage, etc. This is illustrated as virtual resource to physical resource mapping (VR-to-PR) in figure 1. This raises many secu-

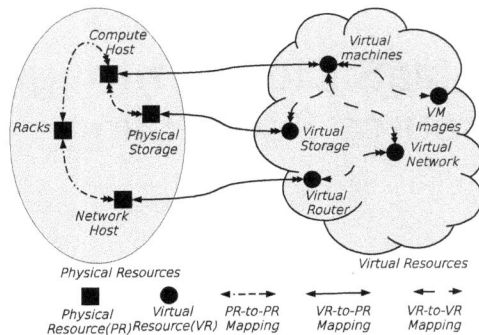

Figure 1: Cloud Resources Mapping Relation

rity and performance considerations for a tenant's workload in the cloud. For instance, a tenant's virtual machines can be attacked by co-located malicious virtual machines of an adversary tenant. Similarly, highly cpu-intensive co-located virtual machines may disrupt each other's expected performance. The work of Ristenpart et al [31, 36, 40, 41] has demonstrated such co-location vulnerabilities in real-world clouds. In particular, they show that preventing targeted co-location of virtual machines from different tenants on the same physical server is unlikely to be successful. Their conclusion is that "the best solution is simply to expose the risk and placement decisions directly to users" (i.e. tenants) [31]. The main objective of this paper is to address this goal where the tenants and the cloud system are able to schedule virtual resources on the physical resources consistent with high-level and fine-grained constraints.

In this respect, even the leading IaaS service providers offer minimal support to their tenants. In particular, tenants have very little influence in how their resources are scheduled. Of course, certain coarse-grained and static preferences for disaster management are supported. For instance, the Amazon Web Services cloud infrastructure is hosted at multiple locations worldwide where a location comprises of multiple geographically isolated datacenters called a 'Region' [1]. Each 'Region' also has multiple, isolated locations known as 'Availability Zones'. As a client, a tenant can at best specify the 'Availability Zone' of its virtual resources and specify backup Availability Zones for a premium. This concerns engineering for fail-safety but does not concern co-location of a tenant's resources with those of others in a given physical server or a rack. This article explores a highly dynamic and fine-grained technique for scheduling virtual resources based on high-level constraints specified by tenants in order to mitigate security threats (several of which are discussed in [5]) due to the co-residency of virtual resources.

We present the design, implementation, and evaluation of an attribute-based constraints specification framework which enables tenants to express several essential properties of their resources as attributes and to specify values of those attributes that conflict for the purpose of co-locating virtual resources on a given physical resource. A constraints enforcement engine schedules virtual resources on the physical resources while respecting the conflicts specified using attributes of those resources. For instance, consider two attributes of a virtual machine: a `tenant` attribute that represents the owning enterprise of that virtual machine, and a `sensitivity` attribute that represents the sensitivity level of the data processed by that virtual machine. An example of

a high-level co-location constraint is that virtual machines of different tenants may co-locate in a physical server as long as the `sensitivity` is not 'high'. As we will see, enforcing constraints in general in large-scale systems such as IaaS cloud is computationally inefficient. Moreover, it negatively impacts physical resource requirements and their utilization—directly impacting the bottom line of IaaS CSPs.

The contributions of this paper are summarized below which aligns with its general outline.

• We present a design of an attribute-based framework for specifying co-location constraints of virtual resources scheduled on given physical resources (section 2).

• Given that co-location constraints can drastically affect physical resource utilization, we propose a host optimization process while enforcing constraints (section 3). Note that, host optimization (i.e., optimizing the number of hosts necessary for scheduling the vms in a conflict-free manner) is an important requirement for achieving energy-efficient datacenter which is also a major concern for the CSPs for cost optimization [7]. We establish that, in general, the algorithms for host optimization while enforcing such constraints are NP-Complete (section 3). We demonstrate a subset of attribute conflicts that are of practical significance in varied application domains and cloud deployment scenarios (public, private, community, etc.), which can be efficiently enforced in polynomial-time (section 3).

• We develop a prototype of the conflict-free virtual machine scheduling framework in OpenStack [3] and rigorously evaluate the framework on various aspects, e.g., resource requirements, resource utilizations, etc. (section 4).

We analyze issues that arise due to the incremental changes of conflicts over time. A discussion of the security risks in this approach, some related works and conclusion are given in section 6, 7 and 8 respectively.

2. CONFLICT-FREE VIRTUAL RESOURCE SCHEDULING

Intuitively, an attribute captures a property of an entity in the system, expressed as a name:value pair. In the context of cloud IaaS, attributes can represent a virtual machine's owner tenant, sensitivity-level, cpu intensity-level of workloads, etc. For simplicity, we restrict the scope of the paper as follows. We confine our attention to virtual to physical resource mapping in the context of virtual machines and physical compute servers. Then we briefly discuss the possible extension of this approach to other virtual and physical resources. In the rest of the article we refer to physical compute host and virtual machine as `host` and `vm` respectively. We restrict the kind of constraint to "must not co-locate" constraint where the specified conflicts are co-location conflicts that state whether two vms can be co-located in the same `host` or not. In this section, we formally define the components of `hosts` allocation for the vms, which we refer as `host`-to-`vm` allocation, in the presence of various co-location conflicts. Note that, a vm may have multiple attributes each with its own values. Attribute value of a vm can be assigned either manually by a user or automatically by the system. For instance, when an enterprise user creates a vm, an appropriate value is assigned to the *tenant* attribute of the vm automatically whereas, the user may need to explicitly specify the value for a *sensitivity* attribute based on sensitivity of data processed in that vm. Developing administration models for such attribute assignments is beyond the scope of this paper. We assume that vms are assigned with proper attribute values. For our purpose, the values of an attribute can conflict with each other and the goal is to allow the vms to co-locate in same host only if their assigned attribute-values do not conflict. For general and in-depth understanding about various types of attribute conflicts we suggest to read the articles of Bijon et al [8, 9].

2.1 Scheduling Components Specification

The scheduling components include two sets called HOST and VM that contain the existing hosts and vms respectively. There are attributes of vm that characterize different properties of a vm and are modeled as functions. For each attribute function, there is a set of finite constant values that represents the possible values of that attribute. For our purpose, we assume values of attributes to be atomic.[1] Therefore, for a particular vm, the name of the attribute function maps to one value from the set. For convenience attribute functions are referred to as attributes. Also, values of an attribute can have conflicts with each other and these conflicts are specified in a conflict-set of the attribute. Conflicts are specified on values of each attribute independent of other attributes. Formally these components are defined as follows.

- HOST is the finite set of hosts (physical servers).

- VM is the finite set of vms.

- Each host $\in$ HOST has a capacity, represented as a function called W_{HOST}, that maps a host to a value greater than 1.0 to a maximum value of the host capacity[2]. The capacity restricts the number of vms that a host can contain based on the accumulated capacity of the vms. Value of it for a host remains constant unless explicitly modified, e.g., increasing RAM size.

- Similar to the capacity of host, each vm $\in$ VM has a capacity represented by a function called W_{VM} where, W_{VM} : VM $\to$ k where $0.0 < k \leq 1.0$. Also, capacity of a vm remains constant unless explicitly modified.

- ATTR$_{VM}$ is the set of attribute functions of vm.

- For each $att \in$ ATTR$_{VM}$, the domain of the function is the VM and the codomain is the values of att written as SCOPE$_{att}$ which is a set of atomic values. Formally, att: VM $\to$ SCOPE$_{att}$, for each $att \in$ ATTR$_{VM}$.

The values in SCOPE$_{att}$ of an $att \in$ ATTR$_{VM}$ that conflict with each other is specified as a relation called ConSet$_{att}$.

---

[1] An example of an atomic attribute is *sensitivity* where the values are high, medium and low. A vm can only get one of the three values for *sensitivity*. However, some cases might require set-valued attributes for which a vm may take multiple values. For our purpose, we only consider atomic attributes, however, it can easily extend to set-valued one.

[2] Multi-dimensional weights of a host, e.g., RAM, CPU, can be reduced to one single normalized weight. In OpenStack [3], hosts are mapped to a single weight which is calculated by the *weighted_sum* method that takes weighted average of different metrics of a host e.g., RAM, workload.

ConSet$_{att}$ is reflexive and symmetric, but not transitive. Hence, each element in ConSet$_{att}$ is an unordered pair. For each $att \in$ ATTR$_{VM}$, ConSet$_{att}$ is defined as follows.

- ConSet$_{att}$ is the set of conflicts of the values of each $att \in$ ATTR$_{VM}$. Formally,
  ConSet$_{att} \subseteq \{\{x,y\} \mid x \neq y$ and x,y $\in$ SCOPE$_{att}\}$

Part I in figure 2 shows two attributes, *tenant* and *sensitivity*, and their respective scopes. Some conflicts among values of *tenant* and *sensitivity* attributes are also shown representing conflicts among their values. For instance, $\{\{tnt_1, tnt_2\}, \{tnt_2, tnt_3\}, \{tnt_4, tnt_6\}\}$ in ConSet$_{tnt}$ specifies that vms with tnt_1 and tnt_2, tnt_2 and tnt_3, and tnt_4 and tnt_6 conflict with each other and, hence, cannot be co-located. Also, part IV shows an example of attribute assignment for vms. For instance, for vm1, $tenant(vm1) = tnt_3$ and $sensitivity(vm1)$ = high. Also note that the value 0.6 denotes the capacity requirement of that vm. That is, $W_{VM}(vm1)=0.6$.

2.2 Conflict-Free Host to VM Allocation

Given that the ConSet$_{att}$ specifies conflicting values for an attribute $att \in$ ATTR$_{VM}$, the conflict-free host to vm allocation is concerned about allocation of a host to a group of vms that do not conflict with each other. There are 4 steps in this process as illustrated in figure 2. Step 1 is to *partition* the values of each attribute (i.e., SCOPE$_{att}$ of an $att \in$ ATTR$_{VM}$), into a family of subsets where the elements in each subset do not conflict with each other. We refer to such *partition* as "Conflict-Free Partition of Attribute-Values".

Definition 1. (Conflict-Free Partition of Attribute-Values) *A conflict-free partition of attribute-values of each $att \in$ ATTR$_{VM}$ is specified as PARTITION$_{att}$ that partitions the values in SCOPE$_{att}$ where the values of each element in PARTITION$_{att}$ do not conflict with each other, i.e., for each $x \in$ PARTITION$_{att}$ and for each $y \in$ ConSet$_{att}$, $|x \cap y| \leq 1$*

We can state that, for an attribute att, a PARTITION$_{att}$ partitions SCOPE$_{att}$ where (1) PARTITION$_{att}$ does not contain $\emptyset$, (2) elements in PARTITION$_{att}$ are pairwise disjoint, (3) the union of the elements in PARTITION$_{att}$ is SCOPE$_{att}$, and (4) the values in a set-element of PARTITION$_{att}$ do not conflict with each other, i.e. no more than one value from that set-element belongs to the same element in ConSet$_{att}$.

Part II in figure 2 shows examples of conflict-free partitions, Partition$_{tenant}$ and Partition$_{sensitivity}$, for ConSet$_{tenant}$ and ConSet$_{sensitivity}$ given in part I. For example, $\{tnt_1, tnt_3, tnt_6\}$ in Partition$_{tenant}$ means these values do not conflict with each other. Note that, there can be multiple candidate PARTITION$_{att}$ for a given ConSet$_{att}$ of an attribute $att \in$ ATTR$_{VM}$. Section 3 shows that the selection of an appropriate PARTITION$_{att}$ is important for the host optimization.

Step 2 combines the *conflict-free partitions of attribute-values* of all attributes. We define a *conflict-free segment* that consists one element of PARTITION$_{att}$ of each attribute $att \in$ ATTR$_{VM}$. We will see later that vms, mapped to a conflict-free segment, do not conflict with that of others, hence, can co-locate. Note that a vm can get any value from the scope of an attribute. Therefore, conflict-free segments should be generated in such a way so that it can map all possible assigned values to the attributes of the vms. A cartesian product of the PARTITION$_{att}$ for all $att \in$ ATTR$_{VM}$ generate all possible segments of conflict-free values of the attributes that can a vm based on its assigned attribute values.

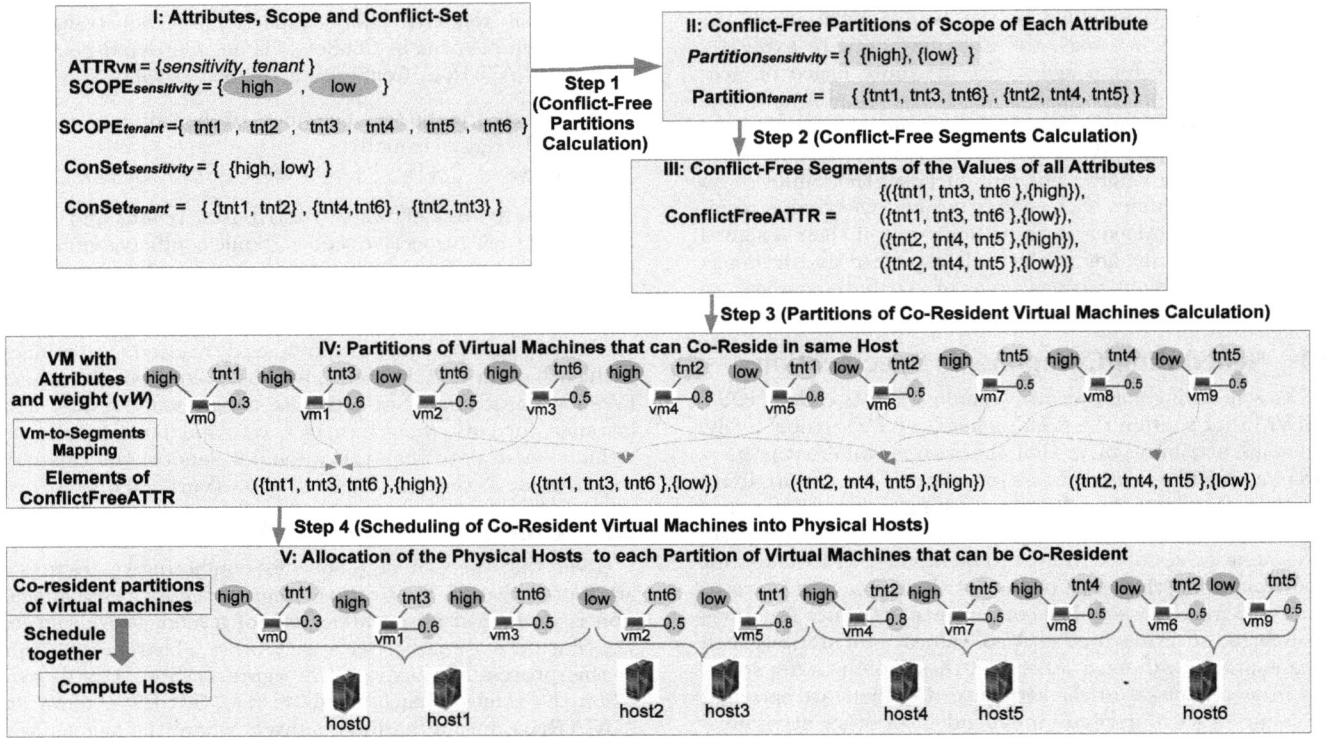

Figure 2: Conflict-Free vm-host Allocation

Definition 2. (Conflict-Free Segments of the Values of Attributes) *The* conflict-free segments of the values of attributes *is a set, called **ConflictFreeATTR**, of n-tuples where* $n = |ATTR_{VM}|$ *and each tuple is a result of the cartesian product of* $PARTITION_{att}$ *of all* $att \in ATTR_{VM}$, *i.e.,*

$$ConflictFreeATTR = \prod_{att \in ATTR_{VM}} PARTITION_{att}$$

Each element $conFval \in$ ConflictFreeATTR is an ordered pair which is written as $\langle X_{att_1}, ..., X_{att_n} \rangle$ where $\{att_1, ..., att_n\} = $ ATTR$_{VM}$ and $X_{att_i} \in$ PARTITION$_{att_i}$. We assume that elements of each $conFval \in$ ConflictFreeATTR can be accessed by the notation $conFval[att]$ for each $att \in$ ATTR$_{VM}$.

Part III in figure 2 shows an example ConflictFreeATTR which is produced from the Cartesian product of conflict-free partitions Partition$_{tenant}$ and Partition$_{sensitivity}$. A tuple $(\{tnt_1, tnt_3, tnt_6\}, \{high\})$ is an element in ConflictFreeATTR since $\{tnt_1, tnt_3, tnt_6\}$ and $\{high\}$ are members of Partition$_{tenant}$ and Partition$_{sensitivity}$ respectively.

Step 3 partitions the set VM such that vms of each element of the partition can be co-located. This is achieved by partitioning VM in a way such that each element of the partition can be mapped to an element of ConflictFreeATTR.

Definition 3. (Co-Resident Partition of VM) *The* Co-Resident Partition of VM, *specified as **CoResidentVM-Grp**, is a partition of **VM** where the assigned values to att* $\in$ *ATTR$_{VM}$ of all vms in an element of the partition map to the same segment in* **ConflictFreeATTR**, *i.e.,*

for all $X \in$ *CoResidentVMGrp and for all* $vm_i \neq vm_j \in X$,

$$\bigvee_{conFval \in ConflictFreeATTR} SetResidence(vm_i, vm_j, conFval, ATTR_{VM}))$$

where, $SetResidence(vm_i, vm_j, conFval, ATTR_{VM}) =$

$$\bigwedge_{att \in ATTR_{VM}} (att(vm_i) \in conFval[att] \land att(vm_j) \in conFval[att])$$

CoResidentVMGrp partitions VM if vms in an element of CoResidentVMGrp are assigned to the values, for all $att \in$ ATTR$_{VM}$, that belong to the same element in ConflictFreeATTR.

Part IV in figure 2 shows an example of CoResidentVM-Grp calculation of 10 vms where vms are mapped to different elements of ConflictFreeATTR based on their attributes. For instance, vm1 is mapped to the segment $(\{tnt_1, tnt_3, tnt_6\}, \{high\})$ since it is assigned with 'tnt$_3$' and 'high' for *tenant* and *sensitivity* attributes. Also, vm1 and vm3 belong to the same partition of CoResidentVMGrp since they are both mapped to the segment $(\{tnt_1, tnt_3, tnt_6\}, \{high\})$.

Finally, step 4 allocates hosts for the vms of each partition in CoResidentVMGrp. A host cannot contain vms from multiple partitions of CoResidentVMGrp. Also, combined capacity of the allocated vms must satisfy the capacity (W_{HOST}) of the host. Therefore, for each partition of vms in CoResidentVMGrp, multiple hosts might be required depending on the combined weight of the vms in that partition.

Definition 4. (Conflict-Free Host to VM Allocation) *Given VM, HOST, ATTR$_{VM}$, CoResidentVMGrp, W_{HOST} and W_{VM}, the* Conflict-Free Host to VM Allocation *is a mapping function called allocate that finds a set of hosts, HOST$' \subseteq$ HOST, to allocate all $vm \in$ VM where the vms that reside in a host form a subset of an element of CoResidentVMGrp such that their combined weight does not exceed the weight of host, i.e., allocate : HOST$' \hookrightarrow \mathcal{P}(VM)$ where, if chost $\in$ HOST$'$ and allocate(chost) = lvm, then,*

$$lvm \subseteq VM \land \bigvee_{x \in CoResidentVMGrp} lvm \subseteq x \land \left(\sum_{vm \in lvm} W_{VM}(vm) \right) \leq W_{HOST}(cs)$$

Part V in figure 2 shows an example of Conflict-Free Host to VM Allocation where the total number of vms is 10 and they are partitioned into 4 co-resident sets. Note that, here,

66

Host0 and Host1 are allocated to one co-resident partition of vms containing {vm0, vm1, vm3} since their combined weight is more than the weight of a single host.

2.3 Conflict-Free Scheduling of Other Virtual Resources to Physical Resources

The process of sections 2.1 and 2.2 can also apply for the scheduling of other virtual resources (shown in figure 1) with the following modifications.

In physical storage to virtual storage allocation, two sets VM and HOST, defined in section 2.1, are substituted by sets VS and PS that specifies virtual storage volumes and physical volumes in the system respectively. Similar to the capacity functions of vm and host, two functions can be defined for virtual and physical resources that can map their respective capacities where the capacity can be a single metric calculated by weighted sum of different properties of a storage system. Such properties include size, storage i/o speed, etc. Now, similar to the $ATTR_{VM}$, a set can represent the attributes of the virtual storage volumes. Also, $ConSet_{att}$ and definition 1-4 can be modified accordingly for the physical storage to virtual storage allocations.

A similar approach can be followed to derive the network host to virtual router allocation. Here, two sets called NH and VR can specify network hosts and virtual routers in the system respectively. Now the capacity could be the limit of network bandwidth of a network host and the bandwidth of a virtual router. One motivation of scheduling virtual router across different network hosts is for load-balancing of the network traffic and ensuring availability. Here, similar to the virtual machines, necessary attributes of the virtual routers can be generated. $ConSet_{att}$ and definition 1-4 can be modified for network host to virtual router allocations.

3. OPTIMIZATION PROBLEM DEFINITION AND SOLUTION ANALYSIS

In this system, the specified conflicts restrict certain vms from co-locating in the same host. Hence, some hosts cannot schedule vms that conflict with currently scheduled vms in these hosts, despite having the required capacity. That increases the required number of hosts than a system without conflicts. Hence, it is desirable to schedule vms in a way that minimizes the number of hosts while satisfying the conflicts leading to an optimization problem.

Definition 5. (Host Optimization Problem) *The* Host optimization problem *seeks to minimize the number of* hosts *in the mapping,* allocate : $HOST' \hookrightarrow \mathcal{P}(VM)$, *specified in* Conflict-Free Host to VM Allocation (Definition 4).

This section investigates algorithms for definition 1 through 4 in order to solve the Host Optimization Problem.

3.1 MIN_PARTITION: Minimum Conflict-Free Partitions of Attribute-Values

More than one $PARTITION_{att}$ can be generated for a given $ConSet_{att}$. In figure 2, for the given $ConSet_{tenant}$, candidate $Partition_{tenant}$ sets could be {{tnt1, tnt3}, {tnt2, tnt6}, {tnt4, tnt5}} and {{tnt1,tnt3,tnt6},{tnt2,tnt4,tnt5}} with 3 and 2 elements in the sets respectively. Here, each element of a $PARTITION_{att}$ contains the conflict-free attribute-values of *att*. Number of elements in $PARTITION_{att}$ affects the total number of conflict-free segments (definition 2) where the vms

mapped to same conflict-free segment can co-exist. A partition, with minimum number of elements, reduces the number of conflict-free segments. It also reduces the elements in CoResidentVMGrp that also minimizes the required number of hosts. We call such a partition as MIN_PARTITION.

Finding a MIN_PARTITION is similar to the graph-coloring problem that partitions the vertices of a graph G(V,E) into minimum color classes so that no two adjacent vertices, such as {v1,v2} ∈ E, fall in the same class. Graph-coloring problem is NP-Complete given that graph coloring *decision* problem, called k-coloring, is NP-Complete, which states that given a graph G(V, E) and a positive integer k ≤ |V|, can the vertices in V be colored by k different colors?

We show that MIN_PARTITION is NP-Complete by showing that the MIN_PARTITION *decision* problem, which we refer to as K_PARTITION, is NP-Complete. The problem states that given $SCOPE_{att}$ and $ConSet_{att}$ of an $att \in ATTR_{VM}$, and a positive integer k ≤ |$SCOPE_{att}$|, can the values in $SCOPE_{att}$ be partitioned into k sets?

THEOREM 1. *K_PARTITION is NP-Complete.*

PROOF. We prove that K_PARTITION is NP-Complete by polynomial-time reduction of k-coloring to K_PARTITION.

An *instance* of k-coloring is a graph G(V, E) and an integer k. We construct $SCOPE_{att} \leftarrow V$ and $ConSet_{att} \leftarrow E$ and feed $SCOPE_{att}$, $ConSet_{att}$, and k to K_PARTITION. The complexity of this conversion is |V| × |E|.

Now we show that an *yes instance* of k-coloring maps to an *yes instance* of K_PARTITION and vice versa.
⟹ Assume G is an *yes instance* of k-coloring and there exists a set of colors C of size k in G. Thus, for all u ∈ V, color(u) ∈ C and for any u, v ∈ V, color(u)=color(v) only if {u, v} ∉ E. Also, for all u ∈ $SCOPE_{att}$, u belongs to cfs ∈ CFS where #CFS is k, and for any u, v ∈ $SCOPE_{att}$, u, v belongs to the same cfs ∈ CFS, if {u, v} ∉ $ConSet_{att}$. Thus, G is an *yes instance* of K_PARTITION.
⟸ Assume $SCOPE_{att}$, $ConSet_{att}$ is an *yes* instance of K_PARTITION and there exists a family of CFS of size k. Thus, for all u ∈ $SCOPE_{att}$, u belongs to a cfs ∈ CFS, and for any u, v ∈ $SCOPE_{att}$, u, v belongs to the same cfs ∈ CFS, if {u, v} ∉ $ConSet_{att}$. Thus, the vertices in same cfs ∈ CFS can be colored by the same color and there will be k number of colors to color all the vertices in G. Thus, G is an *yes instance* of k-coloring.
Thus, K_PARTITION is NP-Complete. □

Therefore, MIN_PARTITION is also NP-Complete. However, there are a number of *approximate* graph-coloring algorithms that can be applied to MIN_PARTITION. The algorithms are approximate in the sense that they may not provide the minimum size of $PARTITION_{att}$, i.e., MIN_PARTITION may not be optimal. This is useful, although not optimal, because the conflicts are still satisfied. In appendix A, we discuss approximate algorithms for graph-coloring and their applications to MIN_PARTITION. We also develop an exact algorithm, shown in algorithm 1, based on backtracking. The complexity of this algorithm is NP since it is an adaptation of the general backtracking algorithm for the graph-coloring [6]. However, for attributes whose size of the scope is small enough (e.g. *sensitivity*), the algorithm computes the partition relatively fast. In algorithm 1, the MAKE_PARTITION procedure is called with scope $SCOPE_{att}$ of an attribute $att \in ATTR_{VM}$, $ConSet_{att}$, and a partition

Algorithm 1 Conflict-Free Partition using Backtracking

1: **procedure** CHECK_VALIDITY(attval, ConSet$_{att}$, CSet)
2:     **for all** attval$_i$ ∈ CSet **do**
3:         **if** {attval, attval$_i$} ∈ ConSet$_{att}$ **then**
4:             Return False
5:         **end if**
6:     **end for**
7:     Return True
8: **end procedure**
9: **procedure** MAKE_PARTITION(SCOPE$_{att}$, ConSet$_{att}$, PARTITION$_{att}^{k}$)
10:     **if** attval ∈ SCOPE$_{att}$ **then**
11:         **for all** par ∈ PARTITION$_{att}^{k}$ **do**
12:             **if** CHECK_VALIDITY(attval, ConSet$_{att}$, par) **then**
13:                 par = par ∪ attval
14:                 **if** MAKE_PARTITION(SCOPE$_{att}$-{par},
15:             ConSet$_{att}$,PARTITION$_{att}^{k}$) **then**
16:                     Return True
17:                 **end if**
18:                 par = par − attval
19:             **end if**
20:         **end for**
21:     **end if**
22:     Return False
23: **end procedure**

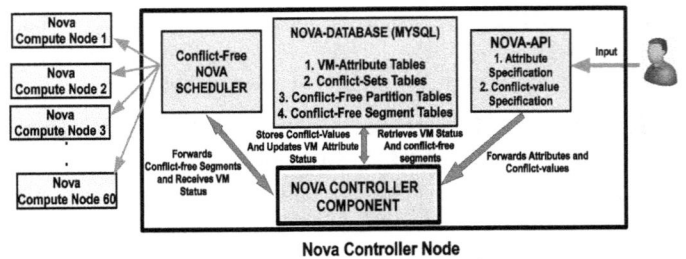

Figure 3: Experimental Setup in OpenStack

PARTITION$_{att}^{k}$ that can contain k elements. It uses a recursive backtracking algorithm that tries all possible combinations of k partitions and returns true if there is a valid conflict-free k partition of a given ConSet$_{att}$. Before adding an attribute value to a partition, MAKE_PARTITION calls CHECK_VALIDITY that verifies if the attribute value to be added is indeed free of conflict with respect to ConSet$_{att}$. In section 4, we analyze the performance of this algorithm for various sizes of attribute scopes and conflict sets.

Certain graphs such as perfect graphs have polynomial graph-coloring solutions. We identify that certain restricted versions of attribute conflict specification generates such graphs. For example, like in a Chinese-Wall policy, an organization can have a conflict-of-interest with certain other organizations. For instance, all banking tenants of a *CSP* may have a conflict-of-interest with each other. Similarly, all the oil-company tenants may conflict. A *CSP* can generate an attribute called *tenant* that represents a particular tenant name in the system, e.g, bank-of-america, and the values of *tenant* can be categorized into mutually disjoint conflict-of-interest classes. The conflict-set generates disjoint cliques of attribute values which can be solved in polynomial-time [18]. Appendix B discusses several such restricted conflicts.

3.2 ConflictFreeATTR Generation

This is a trivial algorithm that calculates the values of ConflictFreeATTR specified in definition 2. The algorithm takes as input PARTITION$_{att}$ for all att ∈ ATTR$_{VM}$, and returns ConflictFreeATTR which is a Cartesian product of PARTITION$_{att}$ for all att. It also stores the calculated ordered tuples in ConflictFreeATTR. The complexity is $O(n \times m)$ where n and m are the size of ATTR$_{VM}$ and PARTITION$_{att}$.

3.3 Co-Resident VM Partitions Generation

This algorithm takes ConflictFreeATTR and VM sets as input, creates a family of sets, called CoResidentVMGrp (definition 3), where each set contains a subset of vms that can co-reside. The number of sets in CoResidentVMGrp is equal

to the number of elements in ConflictFreeATTR, where the algorithm maps an element of ConflictFreeATTR to an element in CoResidentVMGrp and the mapping is one-to-one and onto. The vms that map to the same element in ConflictFreeATTR belong to the same partition. The complexity of this algorithm is $O(\text{VM} \times \text{ConflictFreeATTR} \times \text{ATTR}_{\text{VM}})$. This algorithm works for both *offline* and *online* versions of VM scheduling. In offline, the total number of vms is fixed and are given before the algorithm runs. In *online*, the scheduling request for a vm arrives one at a time. For both versions, the algorithm takes one vm and maps it to an element in ConflictFreeATTR and adds the vm to a corresponding element in CoResidentVMGrp.

3.4 Scheduling VMs to Hosts

This algorithm takes CoResidentVMGrp, and schedules the vms that belong to each element in CoResidentVMGrp, together in one or more hosts. For vms of each element in CoResidentVMGrp, this process might need one or more hosts based on the combined capacity of the vms. If the total capacity exceeds the capacity of a single host then it will need multiple hosts. This scheduling problem is similar to the bin-packing [16] problem which is NP-Hard. However, there are a number of known heuristic approaches that can be applied here [30]. The scheduling of vms in an optimal way based on capacity is orthogonal to MIN_PARTITION since MIN_PARTITION is solved before this scheduling begins.

4. IMPLEMENTATION AND EVALUATION

We implement and evaluate our conflict-free vm to host scheduling framework. Since our work concerns scheduling, to conduct realistic experimentation, we need exclusive access to a large-scale cloud infrastructure with 100s of physical hosts to meaningfully study resource requirements and its utilization. First, we setup an IaaS cloud environment using a set of 5 physical machines (each of them is a Dell-R710 with 16 cores, 2.53 GHz and 98GB RAM). We now treat each of the vms that this cloud provides as a physical host. These vms are configured with 4 cores and 3 GB of RAM. We now create a DevStack-based cloud framework [2], a quick installation of OpenStack ideal for experimentation, using those vms as physical hosts to create a virtual cloud for the purpose of experimentation. Now, we create the second-level of vms to get a virtual IaaS cloud and the configuration of these vms are varied based on the experiment we perform.

We implemented our host-to-vm scheduling on the testbed described above. Figure 3 illustrates our experiment setup. In OpenStack, the component that takes care of vm management and scheduling is the Nova service. We created a cloud cluster with 61 hosts where one of them is the Nova controller node and another 60 are the Nova compute nodes.

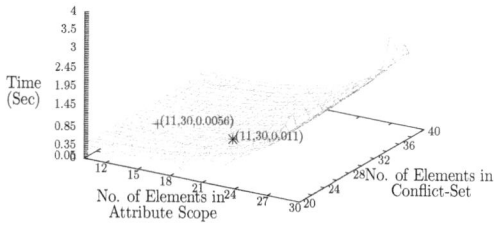

Figure 4: Required Time for Small Scope and Confilct-Set

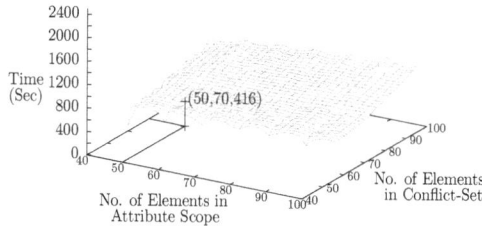

Figure 5: Required Time for Large Scope and Conflict-Set

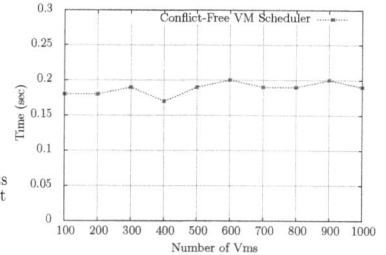

Figure 6: Latency for Conflict-free Scheduling

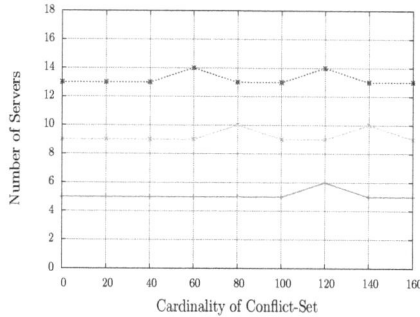

Figure 7: Required Number of hosts for Varying Number of Elements in Conflict-Set

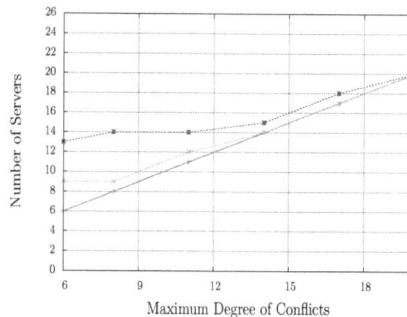

Figure 8: Required Number of hosts for Max Degree of Conflicts

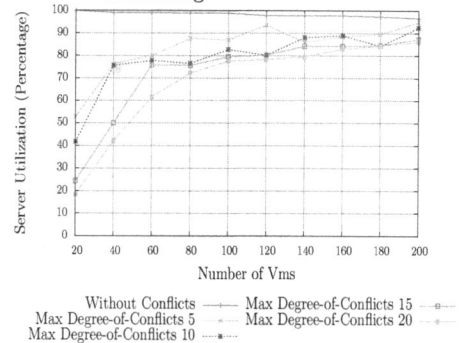

Figure 9: *Host Utilization Overhead*

The Controller node provides main services, e.g. database, message queues, etc., while the compute nodes only contain components such as hypervisor and nova-compute that are required for running vms. We deployed the prototype in the nova controller node. Our python-based implementation of conflict specification allows tenant admins to specify attribute conflict values and the ability to store conflict values in nova database (MySQL) (part I in figure 2). Our python based conflict free segments calculation process (steps 1 and 2 in figure 2) has 153 lines of code. Finally, our implementation of conflict-free host to vm scheduling (steps 3 and 4 in figure 2) has 170 lines of code that maps a vm to a conflict-free segment based on conflicting-values and assigned attribute values of the vm which are retrieved from the nova database. For the conflict-free segment, designated hosts are identified and weighed based on default Nova weighing factors and the vm is scheduled to the suitable host.

Experiment 1 - *Upper Bound of Algorithm 1.* This experiment analyzes the runtime of Algorithm 1. Since the complexity is in NP, here, we identify the maximum size of scope and conflict set for which required runtime of the algorithm remains feasible. First, we conduct the experiment with a small size of scope of an attribute and respective conflict set. We vary scope size from 10 to 40, and for each scope size, we vary the size of conflict set from 20 to 40. For each scope and a particular size of the conflict set, we randomly create elements in conflict set and execute the algorithm. Figure 4 shows the results where, for a small scope and conflict set, runtime is very low, e.g., 0.011s for a scope and conflict set size of 18 and 30 respectively. However, for bigger scope and conflict set sizes, it increases drastically, e.g, for scope size 30 and conflict set size 35 it becomes approximately 4s. We also conduct the same experiment for

large scope and conflict sets where we vary the size from 40 to 100 and 60 to 100 respectively. Figure 5 shows the results where the runtime is very high as expected. For instance, for a scope and conflict set size of 50 and 70 respectively, the execution time is more than 7mins. Note that, a high runtime may be acceptable, since conflict-free partitions are created before starting the scheduling of vms and hence it does not impact the scheduler's performance drastically. This experiment gives an estimation of delay the *CSP* might face before scheduling the vms if it wants to create conflict-free partitions for a given scope and conflict set size.

Experiment 2 - *Scheduling Latency.* In the second experiment, we analyzed the timing overhead of our conflict-free host-to-vm scheduler once that conflict-free partitions are calculated by algorithm 1. In figure 6, we study how the amount of time the scheduler takes to schedule a single vm varies with increasing number of vms that have already been scheduled. A value of 500 in the x-axis, for example, indicates that 499 vms have already been scheduled and the corresponding value in the y-axis (0.19s) indicates the time to schedule one new vm. The attribute values of the pre-scheduled vms were randomly assigned. The scheduler takes a fairly fixed amount of time to schedule a single vm regardless of the number of conflict-free pre-scheduled vms.

Experiment 3 - *Required Number of Hosts.* Our third experiment concerns the impact of satisfying conflicts on the resource requirements. In our case, the conflict set of a given attribute can be varied in two significant ways to evaluate the number of physical hosts that are necessary. In figure 7, we vary the number of elements in the conflict set while fixing the maximum degree of conflict to a constant value. The highest number of values that conflict with each other in the conflict set is referred to as the maximum degree of conflict for that conflict set. In figure 7, we fix the maximum degree to 2. In figure 8, we vary the maximum degree of conflicts with a fixed attribute scope. Given the server memory capacity to be 3 GB, the vm capacity is varied between 512 MB and 1024 MB. The experiment confirms our intuition that that the maximum degree of conflict dominates the server requirement to schedule vms. Note that minor spikes and drops (for example between 100 and 140 on the x-axis for scheduling 100 vms) are due to the randomness of the workload we automatically generate and some variability in Devstack. However, overall, our observation holds true.

Experiment 4 - *Host Utilization.* Finally, this experiment concerns the impact of conflict-free scheduling on the overall utilization level of all the physical servers. Since we know from experiment 2 that resource requirements are predominantly impacted by maximum degree, in figure 9, in the x-axis we vary maximum degree while scheduling a varied number of vms. The y-axis specifies the aggregate percentage of utilization of all the servers after scheduling the vms in a conflict-free manner. For example, given N number of servers, 80% utilization means that 20% of N servers in total is not utilized. We can see, server utilization dramatically increases with the number of vms that are scheduled. This is because since the max degree dictates server requirements, for smaller number of vms, a minimum of max degree number of servers remain heavily under-utilized. Once the vms scale toward real-world numbers, the utilization is above 80% even with a very high degree of conflict.

5. INCREMENTAL CONFLICTS

So far, our conflict-free scheduling approach has assumed that conflicts can be pre-specified and remains unchanged. However, in practice, conflicts may change, and may be specified incrementally as new tenants join the cloud. We now explore this fundamentally hard problem—if two vms that did not conflict at a certain time happen to be co-located in a server, but later develop a conflict due to an update of conflict specification, it is necessary to migrate one of those vms from that server, to remain conflict free.

5.1 Types of Conflict Change

In general, a conflict-set changes if a new conflict is added or an existing conflict is removed. Given a ConSet_{att} and a $\mathsf{PARTITION}_{att}$ of an $att \in \mathsf{ATTR}_{\mathsf{VM}}$, ConSet_{att} can change to a new conflict set ConSet'_{att} (a new partition $\mathsf{PARTITION}'_{att}$ can be calculated accordingly) in three different ways.

- Δ_1—this type of change involves operations that only remove an element from ConSet_{att} where $|\mathsf{PARTITION}'_{att}| < |\mathsf{PARTITION}_{att}|$. Evidently, it does not add new conflicts, hence, the scheduled vms need not migrate.
- Δ_2—this type of change involves operations that add an element to ConSet_{att}. However, $\mathsf{PARTITION}_{att}$ remains unchanged. If addition of a new conflict results in no change in conflict-free partition, scheduled vms need not be migrated.
- Δ_3—this type of change adds an element to ConSet_{att} where $\mathsf{PARTITION}'_{att} \neq \mathsf{PARTITION}_{att}$. Evidently, certain vms need to be migrated if they need to remain conflict-free.

Consider an attribute $att \in \mathsf{ATTR}_{\mathsf{VM}}$ and $\mathsf{SCOPE}_{att} = \{a1,a2,a3,a4,a5,a6\}$, where the initial conflict-set $\mathsf{ConSet}_{att} = \{\{a1,a2\},\{a1,a4\}, \{a2,a4\}, \{a1,a5\}, \{a2,a6\}, \{a4,a6\}\}$ and the corresponding partition set which is calculated using al-

gorithm 1 is $\mathsf{PARTITION}_{att}=\{\{a1,a3,a6\},\{a2,a5\},\{a4\}\}$.

Consider a change of type Δ_1 that removes $\{a2,a4\}$ from ConSet_{att} where resultant conflict set $\mathsf{ConSet}^1_{att}=\{\{a1,a2\}, \{a1,a4\},\{a1,a5\},\{a2,a6\},\{a4,a6\}\}$ and $\mathsf{PARTITION}^1_{att}=\{\{a1,a3,a6\}, \{a2,a4,a5\}\}$. Here, $\#\mathsf{PARTITION}^1_{att} < \#\mathsf{PARTITION}_{att}$ and it does affect already scheduled vms.

Consider a change of type Δ_2 that adds $\{a2,a3\}$ to ConSet_{att} where new conflict set $\mathsf{ConSet}^2_{att}=\{\{a1,a2\}, \{a1,a4\}, \{a2,a4\}, \{a2,a3\}, \{a1,a5\}, \{a2,a6\}, \{a4,a6\}\}$ and $\mathsf{PARTITION}^2_{att}= \{\{a1,a3,a6\}, \{a2,a5\},\{a4\}\}$ which is equal to the previous partition set $\mathsf{PARTITION}_{att}$.

Consider a change of type Δ_3 that adds $\{a1,a6\}$ to ConSet_{att} where $\mathsf{ConSet}^3_{att}= \{\{a1,a2\}, \{a1, a4\}, \{a2,a4\}, \{a1,a5\},\{a2,a5\},\{a2,a6\},\{a4,a6\},\{a1,a6\}\}$ and $\mathsf{PARTITION}^3_{att} = \{\{a1,a3\},\{a2\},\{a4\},\{a6\}\}$. This clearly affects the previously scheduled VMs because, from $\mathsf{PARTITION}_{att}$, vms with attribute value a4 are co-located with vms with attribute values a1 or a3. Now, those vms with a4 need to migrate since they cannot co-locate with a1 or a3.

5.2 Cost Analysis

In this section, we analyze the cost of continuing to satisfy the conflicts as they change, when the change is of type Δ_3. We calculate the cost based on the number of migrations that are necessary when conflicts change. Based on experimentation, we gain insights on the strategies for minimizing the cost while handling this type of change.

We define an incremental plan, or simply plan, as a sequence of operations that adds a number of conflicts to the current conflict-set resulting in a Δ_3-type change (i.e., requires migration). Our strategy for minimizing cost is as follows. Consider an element $\{a1, a2, a3, a4\}$ of a conflict-free partition set $\mathsf{PARTITION}_{att}$ of attribute att. Since attribute values $a1$ through $a3$ are conflict-free, the scheduler is free to co-locate vms that have those attribute values in a given server. We refer to this as *promiscuous* conflict-free scheduling because it maximizes the mixing of vms in a given server so long as they do not conflict. In contrast, a *conservative* approach minimizes the co-location of vms even though their attribute values do not conflict. For instance, vms with values $a1$ or $a2$ may be co-located in one server, and those with values $a3$ or $a4$ may be co-located in another. In this case, if values $a3$ and $a1$ were to develop a conflict in the future, the migration cost can be minimal (zero in this scenario). Promiscuous scheduling can have better resource utilization but higher cost for managing conflict changes. Conservative scheduling can minimize cost when conflict changes more frequently, at the expense of lower resource utilization.

We conduct an experiment to evaluate the impact of conflict change on the number of migrations for different levels of conservative scheduling. The steps of the experiment are: (step-1) We consider a single vm attribute called att where we vary the size of SCOPE_{att} from 10 to 35 with an increment of 5. (step-2) For each SCOPE_{att}, initially, we randomly populate ConSet_{att} with 5 to 50 elements and calculate $\mathsf{PARTITION}_{att}$. We repeatedly perform this step for 50 times for every step 1. (step-3) For each step-2, we schedule X number of vms where we vary X from 500 to 5000. We also schedule them using a promiscuous approach and four conservative approaches where VMs of same host can not have

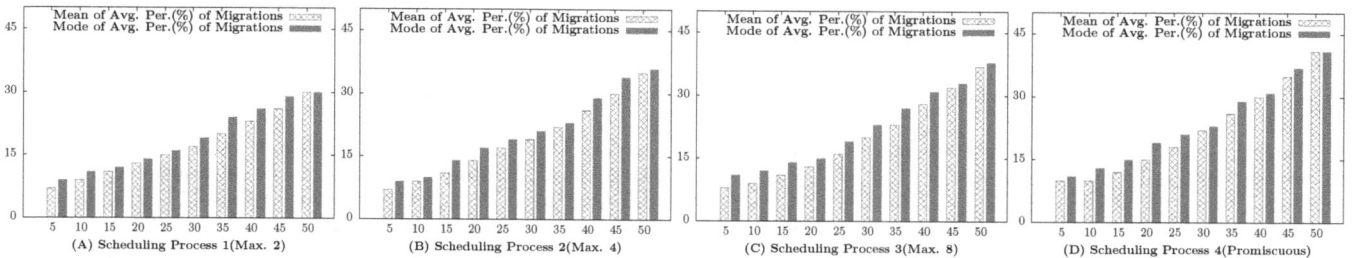

Figure 10: Cost Analysis: X-axis(% of the Total Conflicts for Given Scopes), Y-axis(% of Total VMs that Require Migrations)

more than 1, 2, 4, and 8 different values from a conflict-free partition respectively. Also, each vm is randomly assigned a value to its *att*. We repeat each scheduling process for 30 times. We also randomly assign vm memory capacity to 512 and 1024 MB, and host capacity to 3GHz. (step-4) Finally, we measure migrations for 5 different plans where the plans gradually add random 5%, 10%, 15%, 20%, 25%, 30%, 35%, 40%, 45% and 50% of the total number of conflicts to ConSet$_{att}$ respectively. For each plan, step-4 is repeated for 50 times and we count the migrations. Note that these numbers (the number of times a particular step is repeated) provide sufficient variations, and are primarily dictated by amount of time it takes to perform these steps.

Figure 10 shows the result of our analysis. Parts (A), (B) and (C) are results of different degrees of conservative scheduling. For example, in part (A), if attribute values {a1, a2, ..., a8} are conflict free, we at most schedule vms with one of two possible conflict-free values in any given server (e.g. vms with a1 or a2 are co-located, and those with a3 and a4 are co-located in a different server, etc.). Similarly, in part (B), we co-locate vms with either of a1, a2, a3 or a4 in one server and those with a5, a6, a7 or a8 in a different server. Part (D) is the result of promiscuous scheduling.

We found that the percentage of the migrating vms does not necessarily increase with the increasing number of vms, rather, it depends on the percentage of total number of conflicts that are newly added. For instance, in figure 10(A), for varying number of vms from 500 to 5000, mean value of the average percentage of vms that need to migrate is 29% when number of newly added conflicts is 35%. Also, the mode is 27%. We found that the average difference between the mean and mode values from all cases is no more than 0.5%. The percentage of migrations remain constant with respect to the size of the attribute scope and it does not depend on the initial conflicts for which the vms are scheduled. Finally, we found that it is always better to schedule vms with conservative scheduling with minimum degree. For instance, there is no migration using scheduling process #1 where a host can only contain vms with same attribute value. Also, we notice that addition of a large % of conflicts at a time costs less than combined cost of multiple additions of comparatively small % of conflicts. For instance, in Figure 10(C), 50% conflicts cost 79% migrations, where 10 different 5% conflicts cost 10×9%=90% migrations.

5.3 Reachability Heuristics

Besides analyzing the cost of a plan that leads to a particular conflict set, it is also important to find the steps of a plan where each step adds a particular conflict. For instance, identifying steps of a plan helps to design operations for maintaining conflicts and their authorization process, al-

though, we consider the designing of such front-end operational model as future work. Here, we define this problem as plan reachability problem where for a given attribute, its scope, and an initial conflict-set, what are the steps with a particular cost that will reach target plan with specific values in conflict-set? This problem can be viewed as finding a path from an initial state to a goal state in a weighted state-transition directed graph where each edge of the graph is the cost for adding one conflict to the conflict-set. Here, a simple algorithm can construct the state-transition graph and uses a weighted shortest path algorithm to find a plan in $O(nlogn)$ time [14]. However, it is infeasible due to a very large number of states where, for a size of scope N, the number of conflicts is $\binom{N}{2}$ and possible states are $2^{\binom{N}{2}}$. Instead, it is possible to use a search algorithm to construct regions as needed. Proper heuristics can intelligently search for steps and some well-known heuristics such as k-lookahead based heuristics may be applied in this domain [14].

6. SECURITY ISSUES AND LIMITATIONS

In terms of applicability, an attribute of a vm can be applied to represent properties of a single tenant or multiple tenants. We refer such attributes as intra-tenant and inter-tenant respectively. In figure 2, *tenant* and *sensitivity* are inter-tenant and intra-tenant attributes respectively since values of *tenant* can represent different tenant in the system, while, *sensitivity* can be very particular to a tenant. We analyze the following security concerns for specifying conflicts of the inter-tenant attributes in a multi-tenant cloud.

• *Privacy of a Tenant.* As seen in section 2.1, a conflict is specified between a pair of values of an attribute. However, for an inter-tenant attribute, the values of the conflict can belong to different tenants. For instance, in public cloud, values of the *tenant* attribute of figure 2 represent each tenant in the system and each tenant should not know values of *tenant* attribute except their own value for privacy of other tenant in this system. Specifying conflicts of such attributes can be very tricky where a tenant should be able to specify the conflicts with other tenants without, basically, knowing them. The *CSP* could take the initiative to develop a privacy preserving conflict specification process for inter-tenant attribute. A simple approach could be the classification of attribute-values based on some class, as shown in section 3.1 for conflict-of-interest classes, and a tenant can only mention the class of their attribute values where conflicts will be generated automatically with other values of the same class.

• *Disrupt Multi-tenancy:* In public cloud, multiplexing is to share a physical host among the vms of multiple tenants. However, if a tenant can specify conflicts with all other tenants in the system, then its vms cannot co-locate with any other tenant. This process disrupts the multi-tenancy in the system and, basically, creates a private cloud for the tenant. The *CSP* should restrict such specifications of conflicts.

We discuss following limitations on expressive-power of the generated conflicts by our mechanism.

- *Homogeneous and Non-hierarchical.* Generated conflicts in a conflict-set are treated equally and they do not have any hierarchical relationships. In figure 2, three different conflicts are specified in ConSet$_{sensitivity}$ of attribute *sensitivity*. Here, each conflict has the same semantics, which is a binary relation between two values of *sensitivity*. Also, generated conflicts of the values of two different attributes are independent and bear equal meaning. In figure 2, the values of ConSet$_{sensitivity}$ and ConSet$_{tenant}$ do not have any connection and have equal significance.

- *Conflicts between the Virtual Resources only.* Our scheduling mechanism does not consider any host property, such as location or trust-level of a host, for the scheduling decisions. Rather, it only focuses on generating attribute and their conflicts only for the vms and schedule them accordingly. Also, it does not consider any relationship between hosts and vms for the scheduling. Such type of relations between hosts and vms are specified in [25]. A potential future extension is to consider conflicts between hosts and vms for the scheduling decisions while optimizing the number of hosts.

7. RELATED WORK

Generally scheduling problems are NP-Complete. However, these problems are well-studied by the research community where they proposed various heuristic and approximate approaches for addressing different issues. For instance, the goal of resource-constrained multi-project scheduling problem is to minimize average delay per project. A number of efforts have been made in this scheduling problem including the priority rule based analysis [13, 27] where they propose heuristics, such as first-come-first-served, and shorted operation first, to minimize average delay. Another scheduling problem is to minimize number of bins, while scheduling a number of finite items in it. This problem is called bin packing. There are one and multi capacity bin packing based on multiple requirements for scheduling and approaches have been proposed in [28]. Multi-capacity bin packing is also applied in resource scheduling in grid computing [33, 34]. One variation of bin packing problem is called bin-packing with conflicts that packs items in a minimum number of bins while avoiding joint assignments of items that are in conflict. This problem is analogous to the problem we address in this paper. Several bin-packing with conflict algorithms [23, 24] are proposed where it is assumed that items can be conflicting in random manner. However, we investigated the nature of various conflicts for scheduling items (vms) where the items do not have direct conflict with each other, rather the attributes of the item have conflicts.

Different performance and security issues exist in cloud IaaS for unorganized multiplexing of resources and several of which are summarized in [17, 21, 35]. Recently, articles have been published exposing the vulnerability of state-of-art co-residency system in public cloud IaaS system [39, 40]. However, the virtual resources schedulers designed by the

commercial IaaS clouds such as Amazon and IBM mainly aim to address performance management or load balancing related issues rather than security conflicts that we address in this article. Developing proper vm placement algorithms recently drew attention from the research community. Bobroff et al [12] propose an algorithm that proactively adapts to demand changes and migrates virtual machines between physical hosts. Yang et al [38] also propose a load-balancing approach in vm scheduling process. Calcavecchia et al [15] develop a process to select candidate host for a vm by analyzing past behaviors of a host and deploy the request, and Gupta et al [19] propose a process for scheduling HPC related vms together. Li et al [29] propose vm-placement that maximizes a hosts cpu and bandwidth utilization. Also, Mastroianni et al [30] propose a probabilistic approach for vm scheduling for maximizing CPU and RAM utilization of the hosts. The main focus of these efforts is scheduling vms either for the purpose of high-performance computing or load balancing. Our approach is to capture different properties of vms by means of assigned attributes, and scheduling them while respecting conflicts expressed over those attributes.

8. CONCLUSION

We presented a generalized attribute-based constraint specification framework for virtual resource to physical resource scheduling in IaaS clouds. The mechanism also optimizes the number of physical resources while satisfying the conflicts. A potential future work is to extend this mechanism to address the limitations discussed in section 6. Another future research is to develop a suitable front-end application program interface for specification and management of the conflicts. Our vision is to expose resource management capabilities to the tenants.

9. ACKNOWLEDGEMENT

This research is partially supported by NSF Grants (CNS-1111925 and CNS-1423481).

10. REFERENCES

[1] AWS availabiltiy-zones. *http://docs.aws.amazon.com/ AWSEC2/latest/using-regions-availability-zones.html/.*

[2] Devstack. *https://wiki.openstack.org/wiki/DevStack.*

[3] Openstack. *http://docs.openstack.org/.*

[4] Amazon and CIA ink cloud deal. In *http://fcw.com/ articles/2013/03/18/amazon-cia-cloud.aspx*, 2013.

[5] Y. Azar, S. Kamara, I. Menache, M. Raykova, and B. Shepard. Co-location-resistant clouds. In *Proceedings of the 6th edition of the ACM Workshop on Cloud Computing Security*, pages 9–20. ACM, 2014.

[6] E. A. Bender and H. S. Wilf. A theoretical analysis of backtracking in the graph coloring problem. *Journal of Algorithms*, 6(2):275–282, 1985.

[7] A. Berl et al. Energy-efficient cloud computing. *The computer journal*, 53(7):1045–1051, 2010.

[8] K. Bijon, R. Krishman, and R. Sandhu. Constraints specication in attribute based access control. *ASE Science Journal*, 2(3), 2013.

[9] K. Bijon, R. Krishnan, and R. Sandhu. Towards an attribute based constraints specfication language. In *Proc. of the International Conference on Privacy, Security, Risk and Trust.* IEEE, 2013.

[10] K. Bijon, R. Krishnan, and R. Sandhu. A formal model for isolation management in cloud infrastructure-as-a-service. In *Proceedings of the Network and System Security*, pages 41–53. Springer, 2014.

[11] K. Bijon, R. Krishnan, and R. Sandhu. Virtual resource orchestration constraints in cloud infrastructure as a service. In *Proceedings of the 5th ACM Conference on Data and Application Security and Privacy*, pages 183–194. ACM, 2015.

[12] N. Bobroff et al. Dynamic placement of virtual machines for managing sla violations. In *Integrated Network Management*, pages 119–128. IEEE, 2007.

[13] T. R. Browning and A. A. Yassine. Resource-constrained multi-project scheduling: Priority rule performance revisited. *International Journal of Production Economics*, 2010.

[14] D. Bryce and S. Kambhampati. A tutorial on planning graph based reachability heuristics. *AI Magazine*, 2007.

[15] N. M. Calcavecchia et al. Vm placement strategies for cloud scenarios. In *IEEE Cloud*, 2012.

[16] E. G. Coffman Jr et al. Approximation algorithms for bin packing: A survey. In *Approximation algorithms for NP-hard problems*. PWS Publishing Co., 1996.

[17] W. Dawoud, I. Takouna, and C. Meinel. Infrastructure as a service security: Challenges and solutions. In *IEEE INFOS*, pages 1–8, 2010.

[18] M. C. Golumbic. *Algorithmic graph theory and perfect graphs*, volume 57. Elsevier, 2004.

[19] A. Gupta et al. HPC-aware vm placement in infrastructure clouds. In *IEEE Intl. Conf. on Cloud Engineering*, volume 13, 2013.

[20] M. M. Halldórsson. A still better performance guarantee for approximate graph coloring. *Information Processing Letters*, 45(1):19–23, 1993.

[21] K. Hashizume et al. An analysis of security issues for cloud computing. *Journal of Internet Services and Applications*, 4(1):1–13, 2013.

[22] S. Iyer. Top 5 challenges to cloud computing. *Cloud Computing Central, https://www.ibm.com/*, 2011.

[23] K. Jansen. An approximation scheme for bin packing with conflicts. In *Algorithm Theory—SWAT*. 1998.

[24] K. Jansen. An approximation scheme for bin packing with conflicts. *Combinatorial Optimization*, 3(4), 1999.

[25] R. Jhawar, V. Piuri, and P. Samarati. Supporting security requirements for resource management in cloud computing. *IEEE CSE*, 0:170–177, 2012.

[26] D. Karger et al. Approximate graph coloring by semidefinite programming. In *35th Annual Symp. on Foundations of Computer Science*, pages 2–13, 1994.

[27] I. S. Kurtulus and S. C. Narula. Multi-project scheduling: Analysis of project performance. *IIE Transactions*, 1985.

[28] W. Leinberger et al. Multi-capacity bin packing algorithms with applications to job scheduling under multiple constraints. In *Proc. of ICPP*, 1999.

[29] K. Li et al. Elasticity-aware virtual machine placement for cloud datacenters. In *IEEE 2nd Int. Conf. on Cloud Networking*, pages 99–107, Nov 2013.

[30] C. Mastroianni et al. Probabilistic consolidation of virtual machines in self-organizing cloud data centers. *IEEE Tran. on Cloud Computing*, 1(2):215–228, 2013.

[31] T. Ristenpart et al. Hey, you, get off of my cloud: exploring information leakage in third-party compute clouds. In *Proc. of the ACM CCS*, 2009.

[32] J. Rivera. Gartner identifies the top 10 strategic technology trends for 2014. *http://www.gartner.com*.

[33] M. Stillwell et al. Resource allocation using virtual clusters. In *IEEE/ACM Int. Symp. on Cluster Computing and the Grid*, pages 260–267, May 2009.

[34] M. Stillwell et al. Dynamic fractional resource scheduling for HPC workloads. In *IEEE Int. Symp. on Parallel Distributed Processing*, pages 1–12, 2010.

[35] H. Takabi, J. B. Joshi, and G.-J. Ahn. Security and privacy challenges in cloud computing environments. *IEEE Security and Privacy*, 8(6):24–31, 2010.

[36] V. Varadarajan, T. Kooburat, B. Farley, T. Ristenpart, and M. M. Swift. Resource-freeing attacks: Improve your cloud performance (at your neighbor's expense). In *ACM CCS*, 2012.

[37] A. Wigderson. Improving the performance guarantee for approximate graph coloring. *JACM*, 30(4), 1983.

[38] C.-T. Yang et al. A dynamic resource allocation model for virtual machine management on cloud. In *Grid and Distributed Computing*. Springer, 2011.

[39] Y. Zhang et al. Homealone: Co-residency detection in the cloud via side-channel analysis. In *IEE S&P*, 2011.

[40] Y. Zhang et al. Cross-vm side channels and their use to extract private keys. In *ACM CCS*, 2012.

[41] Y. Zhang et al. Cross-tenant side-channel attacks in paas clouds. In *ACM CCS*, 2014.

APPENDIX
A. APPROXIMATE ALGORITHMS

Present literature contains a number of approximate algorithms for the graph-coloring problem which also can be used for solving the MIN_PARTITION problem. For instance, an approximate graph-coloring algorithm given in [37]. Their Algorithm B takes as input a graph G(V, E) and a variable k, and returns *true* if G is k-colorable. Then algorithm C finds colors for the vertices in G using a binary search. It is shown that if the chromatic number (i.e., the minimum number of colors for coloring the graph) of a graph G(V, E) of n vertices is denoted $\mathcal{X}(G)$, the approximate colors generated by their algorithms is $2 \times \mathcal{X}(G) \times \lceil n^{1-1/(\mathcal{X}(G)-1)} \rceil$ (where n is the number of vertices) and the running time of the algorithm is $\mathcal{O}((|V| + |E|) \times \mathcal{X}(G) \times log\mathcal{X}(G))$. Therefore, for a given ConSet_{att} of an $att \in \mathsf{ATTR_{VM}}$, if the minimum number of conflict-free partitions is p, this algorithm will generate $2 \times p \times \lceil \mathsf{SCOPE}_{att}^{1-1/(p-1)} \rceil$ number of conflict-free partitions. A few other approximate approaches include [20, 26].

B. RESTRICTED CONFLICT GRAPHS

This section explores restricted graphs having polynomial-time solutions and demonstrate their usage scenarios for private, public, and community cloud deployment scenarios.

B.1. Public Cloud

A public cloud provides compute services to multiple tenants. We present two scenarios where tenants may need isolation depending on the kind of data the vm's process.

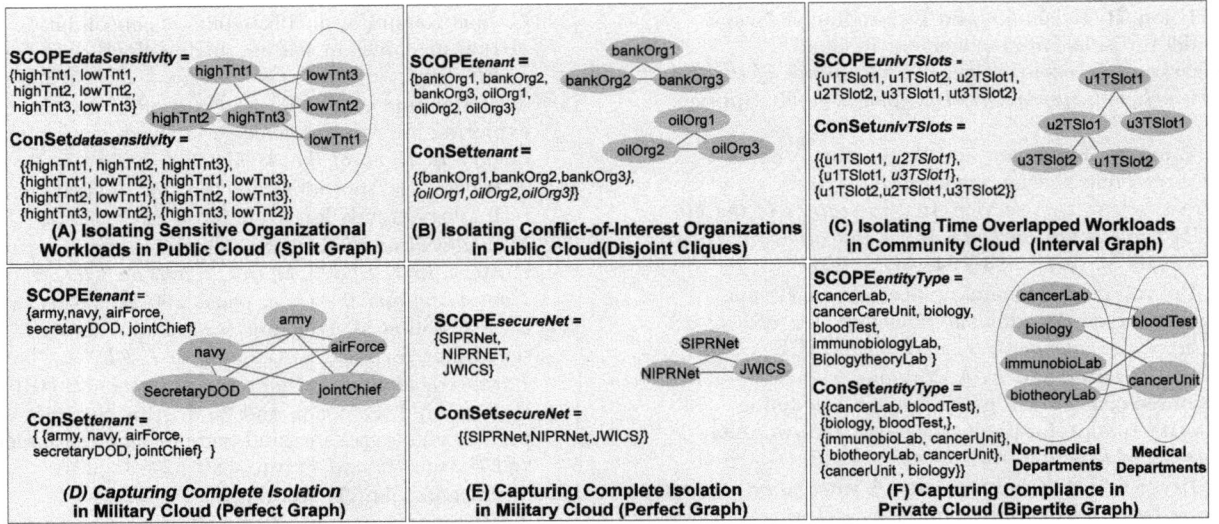

Figure 11: Conflicts of different Systems and Corresponding Conflict Graphs

1. Sensitive Organizational Data: Suppose an e-commerce organization moves to a public cloud. An expectation could be that the vm's that run the general website may be co-located with other tenants while those that process sensitive data such as customer's credit card information or PII should not be co-located. This is infeasible in current public clouds since a tenant can only manually choose to avail services from clouds and carefully distribute the vm's across those clouds based on data sensitivity.

Such scenarios can be easily automated using our conflict specification framework. In this situation (figure 11-A), the cloud provider generates an attribute called *dataSensitivity* and for each tenant it includes two values, e.g., highTnt$_i$ and lowTnt$_i$ for tenant$_i$, to represent the high and low sensitivity of data that will be respectively processed by the vms. When a tenant creates a vm it assigns an appropriate value to the *dataSensitivity* attribute. Here, a vm with highTnt$_i$ would conflict with all the vms of other tenants, however, it does not conflict with vms of own tenant. Conflict-Set of this attribute is a split graph, hence, can be solved in polynomial-time [18].

2. Conflict-of-Interest: Please refer back to section 3.1 and figure 11-B for conflict-of-interest use cases.

B.2. Community Cloud

In a community cloud, the infrastructure is typically shared between enterprises with a common interest. One example of a community cloud is a scientific computing cloud infrastructure that is shared between, say, a set of universities. Figure 11-C illustrates an example where compute resources of participating universities must be isolated if the time-slot assigned to those universities happen to overlap. If there is no overlap in the time-slot, university 1, for example, can use the same physical host that was allocated to university 2 (though at a different time). Such a scenario forms an interval graph for which can be solved in polynomial-time [18].

B.3. Private Cloud

A private cloud has a single owner and thus does not share infrastructure with other tenants. The cloud infrastructure is typically hosted and operated in-house by the tenant or sometimes outsourced to a service provider. A great example is the private cloud operated by Amazon for the CIA [4].

1. Sensitivity in Military Cloud: Consider a large-scale cloud for the US Department of Defense (DoD). A fundamental principle in DoD's move to IaaS cloud from their current IT infrastructure could be that the different military organizations including army, navy and air-force, and their operations need to be isolated from each other consistent with the current operational status of each organization (currently, most of each organization's infrastructure is isolated from each other). To this end, a vm attribute *military-Org* can be created where SCOPE$_{militaryOrg}$={army, navy, airForce, secretaryDoD, jointChief} and all values of *militaryOrg* would conflict with each other. The graph generated from this conflict-set is a complete graph as illustrated in figure 11-D which can be solved in polynomial-time [18].

Figure 11-E illustrates another DoD example resulting in a complete graph where vm's processing data belonging to different networks (such as SIPRNet, NIPRNet and JWICS) in the DoD need to be isolated from each other.

2. Compliance in Healthcare Cloud: For the compliance scenario, consider a *hybrid entity* in Health Insurance Portability and Accountability Act (*HIPAA*) that provides both healthcare and non-healthcare related services. An example of such entity is a university that includes a medical center that provides health-care services to the general public and also research labs in the university that conduct healthcare-related research internally. HIPAA rule mandates that such a hybrid entity should maintain a strict separation between those departments while handling protected health information (PHI). In order to comply strictly with HIPAA, virtual resources processing PHI need to be isolated. Such a scenario is illustrated in figure 11-D where blood-Test and cancerUnit are departments that provide health-care and hence utilize compute services that process PHI. Those compute services need to be isolated from compute services of non-medical departments such as immunobiologyLab. This scenario forms a bipartite graph which has polynomial-time [18] coloring.

A Logical Approach to Restricting Access in Online Social Networks

Marcos Cramer
University of Luxembourg

Jun Pang
University of Luxembourg

Yang Zhang
University of Luxembourg

ABSTRACT

Nowadays in popular online social networks users can black-list some of their friends in order to disallow them to access resources that other non-blacklisted friends may access. We identify three independent binary decisions to utilize users' blacklists in access control policies, resulting into eight access restrictions. We formally define these restrictions in a hybrid logic for relationship-based access control, and provide syntactical transformations to rewrite a hybrid logic access control formula when fixing an access restriction. This enables a flexible and user-friendly approach for restricting access in social networks. We develop efficient algorithms for enforcing a subset of access control policies with restrictions. The effectiveness of the access restrictions and the efficiency of our algorithms are evaluated on a Facebook dataset.

Categories and Subject Descriptors

K.6.5 [**Management of Computing and Information Systems**]: Security and Protection

Keywords

Online social networks; hybrid logic; access control; blacklist

1. INTRODUCTION

Online social networks (OSNs) have been the dominating applications in the Internet during the past few years. Leading actors, including Facebook, Twitter and Instagram, have a large number of users. Facebook has more than one billion monthly active users, 500 million tweets are published on Twitter everyday, and Instagram users share more than 70 million photos and videos on a daily base. Nowadays, OSNs have become an indispensable part of people's life.

A user can perform a lot of activities in OSNs, such as building his profile, articulating social relationships and publishing photos and statuses. In addition, OSNs have provided access control schemes for users to decide who can

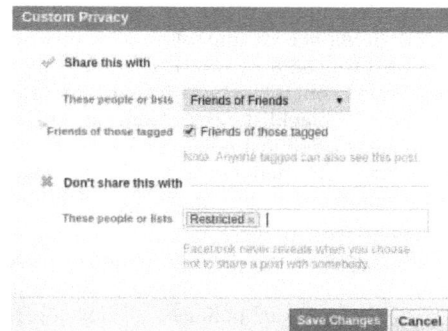

Figure 1: Access control with blacklist in Facebook

view their resources. The access control schemes in OSNs are relationship-based. In simple terms, a user can define access control policies to allow others who are in a certain relationship with him to access his resources.

With more personal information published in OSNs, sometimes a user can be bothered by others, e.g., due to harassment or different political views. To deal with this, major OSN companies have provided functionalities to allow a user to put someone on his *blacklist.*[1] Those who are on a user's blacklist are still his friends but they are forbidden automatically to access his resources. For example, in Facebook, if a user only allows his friends to view his profile, then friends on his blacklist are disallowed to access his profile directly.[2] In this way, blacklists can be treated as orthogonal to access control policies. Figure 1 shows that a Facebook user can define a policy to share his post with his friends of friends but not with those on his blacklist.

However, to the best of our knowledge, the use of blacklists for restricting access in OSNs has not been well-understood and formally studied. For instance, suppose Alice and Bob are friends and Charlie is on Bob's blacklist. If Alice wants to share her photo with her friends of friends, should she *also* consider Bob's blacklist to deny Charlie's access? To address such research problems, we propose a logical approach to formalizing blacklist and its utilization in access control policies.

---

[1]It is called *Restricted list* in Facebook and *list of muted accounts* in Twitter.
[2]Note that adding someone into a blacklist is different from blocking him. This later is referred as *unfriending* in Facebook and *unfollowing* in Twitter, while blacklists do not change any relationship.

Our contributions. We summarize our main contributions in this paper as follows.

- We adopt a hybrid logic [12, 4] to specify access control policies in OSNs (Section 2). In order to better describe blacklist in policies, we propose a new path semantics for the logic and prove that it is equivalent to the original semantics of the logic (Section 3).

- Depending on different requirements, we classify three dimensions on how blacklists can be considered, namely *globality*, *generality* and *strength*. Each dimension is a binary decision, giving rise to eight flexible restrictions for users to use blacklists in their policies (Section 4).

- Since each policy can be affiliated with eight different blacklist-restrictions, in order to free users from the burden of defining access control policies precisely and correctly, we propose a syntactical transformation to rewrite an access control formula into its corresponding formula under a blacklist-restriction. In this way, a user only needs to define a policy and a restriction, our transformation will then generate the corresponding formula for enforcement automatically (Section 5).

- Most access control policies in OSNs mainly concentrate on the length of the path between the owner and the requester. Therefore, to improve the evaluation efficiency of this type of policies, we develop new algorithms for finding paths between the owner and the requester under different blacklist-restrictions. Experiments on a real-life social network dataset demonstrate their efficiency (Section 6 and Section 7).

- We perform experiments to study the effect of blacklist-restrictions on access control policies. We find that the restriction from the *strength* dimension is more powerful than from the other two dimensions. In order for a requester to access the owner's information, we also find that he should have different social closeness to the owner for different blacklist-restrictions (Section 7).

2. A HYBRID LOGIC

In this section we present the hybrid logic introduced in [12, 4] for relationship-based access control in OSNs.

An online social network (OSN) is modeled as a directed graph, called *social graph*, and is denoted by $\mathcal{G} = (\mathcal{U}, \mathcal{E})$, where the set $\mathcal{U}$ of nodes consists of the users in the OSN, and the set $\mathcal{E}$ of labeled edges represents the relationships between the users. We use $\mathcal{R} = \{\alpha_1, \ldots, \alpha_m\}$ to denote a (finite) set of relationship types supported in the OSN. The semantics of each relationship type can be defined as $\alpha_i \subseteq \mathcal{U} \times \mathcal{U}$. For two users $u, u' \in \mathcal{U}$, if they are in a relationship of $\alpha_i \in \mathcal{R}$, we say $(u, u') \in \alpha_i$. Moreover, each user is affiliated with some basic information which are treated as attributes of the user. Figure 2 depicts a sample social graph.

For every resource, the owner of the resource can specify an access control policy for determining which users have access to the resource. In the logic [12, 4], we have two distinguished variables own and req for referring to the owner of the resource in question and the user requesting access.

Syntax. The syntax of the hybrid logic is given below.

$$t ::= n \mid x$$
$$\phi ::= t \mid p \mid \neg\phi \mid (\phi_1 \wedge \phi_2) \mid (\phi_1 \vee \phi_2) \mid \langle\alpha_i\rangle\phi \mid @_t\phi \mid \downarrow_x \phi$$

In order to explain the meaning of the symbols and oper-

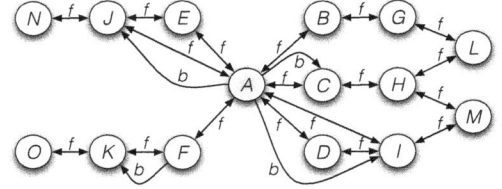

Figure 2: A social graph example

ators informally, we first need to point out that a formula is always evaluated at some user in the graph. The logic supports two kinds of atoms, namely nominals (n) that represent a user's name in the social graph, and variables(x). Terms can function as formulas; they express that the user at which the formula is being evaluated is identical to the user referred to by the term. Propositional symbols (p) are used for representing attributes of the user at which they are evaluated. Negation ($\neg$), conjunction ($\wedge$) and disjunction ($\vee$) have their usual meanings. The intended meaning of the modal operator $\langle\alpha_i\rangle\phi$ is that $\langle\alpha_i\rangle\phi$ is true at a user u iff ϕ is true at some user u' such that u and u' stand in relationship α_i. The hybrid logic operator $@_t$ specifies that the formula following it should be evaluated at the user that the term t refers to. $\downarrow_x$ assigns the user at which the formula is evaluated to the variable x.

The set of formulas of the hybrid logic is denoted by L. We write $(\phi \rightarrow \psi)$ as an abbreviation for $(\neg\phi \vee \psi)$, and follow the usual conventions for dropping brackets in formulas.

Semantics. A *model* Γ is a triple $(\mathcal{G}, W, V)$, where $\mathcal{G}$ is a social graph, for every nominal n, $W(n)$ is a user in $\mathcal{G}$, and for every propositional variable p, $V(p)$ is a set of users that have the attribute as specified by p. A *valuation* is a map from variables to $\mathcal{U}$. The formulas of the logic are evaluated on triples Γ, u, τ, where $u \in \mathcal{U}$ and τ is a valuation:

$$
\begin{array}{lll}
\Gamma, u, \tau \vDash x & \text{iff} & u = \tau(x) \\
\Gamma, u, \tau \vDash n & \text{iff} & u = W(n) \\
\Gamma, u, \tau \vDash p & \text{iff} & u \in V(p) \\
\Gamma, u, \tau \vDash \neg\phi & \text{iff} & \Gamma, u, \tau \nvDash \phi \\
\Gamma, u, \tau \vDash \phi_1 \wedge \phi_2 & \text{iff} & \Gamma, u, \tau \vDash \phi_1 \wedge \Gamma, u, \tau \vDash \phi_2 \\
\Gamma, u, \tau \vDash \phi_1 \vee \phi_2 & \text{iff} & \Gamma, u, \tau \vDash \phi_1 \vee \Gamma, u, \tau \vDash \phi_2 \\
\Gamma, u, \tau \vDash \langle\alpha_i\rangle\phi & \text{iff} & \exists\, u' \in \mathcal{U} \text{ s.t. } (u, u') \in \alpha_i \wedge \Gamma, u', \tau \vDash \phi \\
\Gamma, u, \tau \vDash @_n\phi & \text{iff} & \Gamma, u', \tau \vDash \phi, \text{ where } W(n) = u' \\
\Gamma, u, \tau \vDash @_x\phi & \text{iff} & \Gamma, \tau(x), \tau \vDash \phi \\
\Gamma, u, \tau \vDash \downarrow_x \phi & \text{iff} & \Gamma, u, \tau[x \mapsto u] \vDash \phi
\end{array}
$$

Access control policies. The formulas in the hybrid logic are used to express an *access control policy* that specifies the conditions under which the access requester gets access to a resource depending on his relation to the owner of the resource. We define a subset of formulas of the hybrid logic which can be meaningfully applied for this purpose:

Definition 1. Let $L(\text{own}, \text{req})$ be the set of formulas of the hybrid logic that

- contain at most own and req as free variables, and
- are Boolean combinations of formulas of the two forms $@_{\text{own}}\phi$ and $@_{\text{req}}\phi$.

An element of $L(\text{own}, \text{req})$ is called an *access control policy*.

A user u can specify a policy ϕ for every resource he owns. For determining whether a user u' gets access to the resource, it needs to be checked whether $\Gamma, u, \tau \models \phi$. We use u_{own} to denote the owner and u_{req} to denote the requester. In the following discussions, we often refer to the policies $@_{\text{own}}\langle f\rangle\langle f\rangle\text{req}$ and $@_{\text{own}}\langle f\rangle\langle f\rangle\langle f\rangle\text{req}$. The first one expresses that u_{req} is a friend of a friend of u_{own}, we call this policy the *2-depth policy*. The second one expresses that u_{req} is three *friend* steps away from u_{own}, and is called the *3-depth policy*.

3. PATH SEMANTICS

In this section, we introduce a new definition of the semantics of the hybrid logic, which we call *path semantics*. It is equivalent to the standard semantics (see Theorem 1 below), but it allows us to refer to the set of paths in the social graph that makes a formula true. Being able to refer to this set of paths is important for defining the different ways in which blacklists can be used for restricting access.

When a formula is satisfied, there is a set of paths in the social graph that witnesses the truth of the formula. In Figure 2, taking A as the owner and M as the requester, the formula $@_{\text{own}}(\langle f\rangle\langle f\rangle\text{req} \land \langle f\rangle\langle f\rangle\langle f\rangle\text{req})$ is satisfied, and this satisfaction is witnessed by the set $\{(A, I, M), (A, D, I, M)\}$ (path (A, I, M) witnesses $@_{\text{own}}\langle f\rangle\langle f\rangle\text{req}$, path (A, D, I, M) witnesses $@_{\text{own}}\langle f\rangle\langle f\rangle\langle f\rangle\text{req}$). This notion of a set of paths witnessing a formula can be formalized by defining the semantics of hybrid logic with reference to sets of paths.

For formalizing this new path semantics, we first define a path π to be a sequence of edges $\langle e_0, e_1, \ldots, e_n\rangle$, where $e_i \in \mathcal{E}$ for $0 \le i \le n$.[3] For such a path π, $\pi[k]$ denotes e_k, $\pi[1:]$ denotes $\langle e_1, \ldots, e_n\rangle$ and $e \circ \pi$ denotes $\langle e, e_0, e_1, \ldots, e_n\rangle$. For a set Π of paths, $\Pi[1:]$ denotes $\{\pi[1:] \mid \pi \in \Pi\}$. The path semantics for the hybrid logic is given as follows:

$$
\begin{array}{ll}
\Gamma, u, \Pi, \tau \models x & \text{iff } \Pi = \{\langle\rangle\} \land u = \tau(x) \\
\Gamma, u, \Pi, \tau \models n & \text{iff } \Pi = \{\langle\rangle\} \land u = W(n) \\
\Gamma, u, \Pi, \tau \models p & \text{iff } \Pi = \{\langle\rangle\} \land u \in V(p) \\
\Gamma, u, \Pi, \tau \models \neg\phi & \text{iff } \Pi = \{\langle\rangle\} \land \nexists \Pi' \text{ s.t. } \Gamma, u, \Pi', \tau \models \phi \\
\Gamma, u, \Pi, \tau \models \phi_1 \land \phi_2 & \text{iff } \exists \Pi_1, \Pi_2 \text{ with } \Pi_1 \cup \Pi_2 = \Pi \text{ s.t.} \\
& \quad \Gamma, u, \Pi_1, \tau \models \phi_1 \land \Gamma, u, \Pi_2, \tau \models \phi_2 \\
\Gamma, u, \Pi, \tau \models \phi_1 \lor \phi_2 & \text{iff } \Gamma, u, \Pi, \tau \models \phi_1 \lor \Gamma, u, \Pi, \tau \models \phi_2 \\
\Gamma, u, \Pi, \tau \models \langle\alpha_i\rangle\phi & \text{iff } \exists u' \in \mathcal{U} \text{ s.t. } \Gamma, u', \Pi[1:], \tau \models \phi \land \\
& \quad (u, u') \in \alpha_i \land \forall \pi \in \Pi, \pi[0] = (u, u') \\
\Gamma, u, \Pi, \tau \models @_n\phi & \text{iff } \Gamma, u', \Pi, \tau \models \phi, \text{ where } W(n) = u' \\
\Gamma, u, \Pi, \tau \models @_x\phi & \text{iff } \Gamma, \tau(x), \Pi, \tau \models \phi \\
\Gamma, u, \Pi, \tau \models \downarrow_x \phi & \text{iff } \Gamma, u, \Pi, \tau[x \mapsto u] \models \phi
\end{array}
$$

The following theorem, which we prove in the appendix, establishes that the path semantics is equivalent to the standard semantics for the hybrid logic presented in Section 2.

THEOREM 1. *For every $u \in \mathcal{U}$, $\Gamma, u, \tau \models \phi$ iff there is a set of paths Π such that $\Gamma, u, \Pi, \tau \models \phi$.*

4. RESTRICTING ACCESS IN OSNS

As stated in Section 1, adding a friend into a user's blacklist is a very useful way in OSNs for restricting the friend to access some resources of the user. Blacklists can be treated

---

[3]Normally the paths have the property that the end node of an edge e_i is the start node of the next edge e_{i+1} in the path. But the hybrid logic is very expressive, and for some special formulas, which in practice would hardly be used as access control policies, the satisfaction of the formula can be witnessed by a disconnected path, i.e., a path where some edge does not start where the previous edge ended.

orthogonal to access control policies. In this section, we give a straightforward model of blacklists in OSNs and formally study their usage in relationship-based access control.

4.1 Blacklist in OSNs

We use a relationship type, called b, to model blacklists. If $(u, u') \in b$, then u' is on u's blacklist. For example, in Figure 2, users C and A are friends, but C is on A's blacklist.

Suppose that u_{own} has an access control policy without considering blacklist, we call this policy *non-restricted*. If he wants to restrict the policy by systematically adding the blacklist relationship to it, we say that u_{own} *blacklist-restricts* the access control policy, and the policy is a *restricted policy*.

In the examples used to motivate and illustrate our approach, we assume that the only relationships in place are *friend* (f) and *blacklist* (b). However, all our formal definitions are phrased in such a way that they apply equally when the OSN supports more relationships than these two.

4.2 Three Dimensions

Having defined the blacklist relationship in our social network model, next we focus on how to blacklist-restrict access control policies. The basic requirement is that u_{req} should never be on u_{own}'s blacklist. Beyond this requirement, there exist other decisions to make when blacklist-restricting access control policies. For instance, suppose that Alice and David share two friends Bob and Charlie, and David is on Bob's blacklist. If Alice wants to share her photo with her friends of friends and meantime forbids the access of users on her friends' blacklists, then David on one hand cannot view the photo due to his relationship with Bob, while on the other hand David can still access the photo via Charlie as he is not on Charlie's blacklist. This example shows that it is necessary to identify and precisely define how blacklists are used to restrict access in OSNs. Thanks to the path semantics of the hybrid logic in Section 3, we can classify blacklist-restrictions into three dimensions by considering the following questions: (1) whose blacklist should be used, (2) where blacklists should be applied, and (3) how many paths need to be considered. Each dimension leads to a binary decision and is defined with the reference to the paths witnessing the truth of the access control logic formula.

Whose blacklists should be used? It is clear that the blacklist of u_{own} should always be considered for blacklist-restricting policies, i.e., the user following u_{own} on a path from u_{own} to u_{req} cannot be on u_{own}'s blacklist. Besides, other users' blacklists can be considered as well. In the social graph depicted in Figure 2, suppose that user A wants to share his photo with his friends of friends. If A only considers his blacklist, then N cannot access the photo as J is on A's blacklist. If A considers the blacklists of everyone on the path, then K's access is also denied as he is on F's blacklist.

If u_{own} wants the blacklists of everyone on the path to be considered for blacklist-restricting an access control policy, u_{own} should *globally* blacklist-restrict the policy (GL). If on the other hand u_{own} only wants his own blacklist to be considered, he should *locally* blacklist-restrict the access control policy (LO). We name this restriction dimension *globality*.

Where blacklists should be applied? It is natural to require that u_{req} should never be on u_{own}'s blacklist. Besides, u_{own} may want no one on a path from him to u_{req} to be on his blacklist, i.e., he may want to consider his blacklist on the whole path. In Figure 2, suppose that A defines a 3-depth policy. If A does not consider his blacklist on the whole path, N can access the resource due to the path (A, E, J, N). However, if A considers his blacklist on the whole path, then N's access is denied as J is on A's blacklist.

If u_{own} wants no one on a path in the set of paths witnessing the access control policy to be on his blacklist, he should perform a *general* blacklist-restriction to the policy (GE). If on the other hand u_{own} only wants u_{req} not to be on his blacklist, he should perform a *limited* blacklist-restriction to the policy (LI). We name this restriction dimension *generality*.

How many paths need to be considered? Having fixed the decisions for the previous two dimensions, u_{own} has determined which set of paths are *free of blacklist problems*. There can still be several paths from u_{own} to u_{req}, some of which are free of blacklist problems while others are not. In Figure 2, there are two 3-depth paths from A to L ((A, C, H, L) and (A, B, G, L)). Under the 3-depth policy, if A requires only one path that is free of blacklist problems, L can access the resource because of (A, B, G, L); if A requires all the paths from him to u_{req} to be free of blacklist problems, L's access is denied as (A, C, H, L) does not satisfy the local restriction.

If u_{own} just wants there to be some set of paths free of blacklist problems witnessing the access control policy, he should *weakly* blacklist-restrict the access control policy (W). If on the other hand he wants that every set of paths witnessing the policy should be free of blacklist problems, he should *strongly* blacklist-restrict the access control policy (S). We name this restriction dimension *strength*.

We now formally define the three dimensions in terms of the path semantics (Section 3). For every triple (X, Y, Z) with $X \in \{\text{Lo}, \text{Gl}\}$, $Y \in \{\text{Li}, \text{Ge}\}$ and $Z \in \{\text{W}, \text{S}\}$ and every access control policy ϕ, we define the intended semantics of the *blacklist-restricted access control policy* $\phi_{(X,Y,Z)}$ by defining the conditions under which access is granted to u_{req} according to this blacklist-restricted access control policy. For defining these conditions, we first need to define the predicate $Valid_{(X,Y)}(\Pi)$, whose intended semantics is that the set Π of paths is free of blacklist problems according to the choice (X, Y) of values for the first two dimensions.

Definition 2. Let $\Gamma = (\mathcal{G}, W, V)$ be a model and τ be a valuation. For $X \in \{\text{Lo}, \text{Gl}\}$, $Y \in \{\text{Li}, \text{Ge}\}$ and a set Π of paths, we define $Valid_{(X,Y)}(\Gamma, \Pi, \tau)$ to hold iff the following four properties are satisfied:

- If $X = \text{Lo}$, then for every $u \in \mathcal{U}$ such that $(\tau(\mathsf{own}), u)$ is an element of some $\pi \in \Pi$, $(\tau(\mathsf{own}), u) \notin b$.
- If $X = \text{Gl}$, then for all $u, u' \in \mathcal{U}$ such that (u, u') is an element of some $\pi \in \Pi$, $(u, u') \notin b$.
- If $Y = \text{Li}$, then $(\tau(\mathsf{own}), \tau(\mathsf{req})) \notin b$.
- If $Y = \text{Ge}$, then $(\tau(\mathsf{own}), \tau(\mathsf{req})) \notin b$, and for all $u, u' \in \mathcal{U}$ such that (u, u') is an element of some $\pi \in \Pi$, $(\tau(\mathsf{own}), u) \notin b$ and $(\tau(\mathsf{own}), u') \notin b$.

The set of formulas not involving $\langle b \rangle$ is denoted by L'.

Definition 3. $L'(\mathsf{own}, \mathsf{req})$ is defined to be $L' \cap L(\mathsf{own}, \mathsf{req})$, i.e., the set of access control policies not containing the modality $\langle b \rangle$.

The following definition formally defines the intended semantics of the restricted access control policy $\phi_{(X,Y,Z)}$:

Definition 4. Let $\Gamma = (\mathcal{G}, W, V)$ be a model, $u \in \mathcal{U}$ and τ a valuation. Suppose $X \in \{\text{Lo}, \text{Gl}\}$, $Y \in \{\text{Li}, \text{Ge}\}$ and $Z \in \{\text{W}, \text{S}\}$, and suppose $\phi \in L'(\mathsf{own}, \mathsf{req})$.

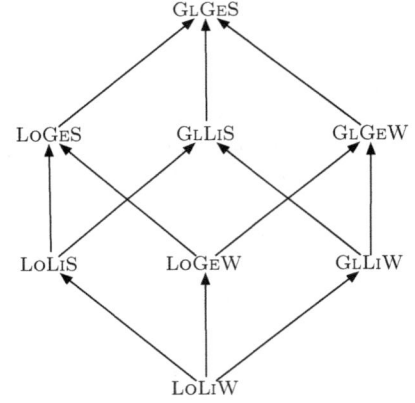

Figure 3: Black-restriction lattice

- If $Z = \text{W}$, then $\Gamma, u, \tau \vDash \phi_{(X,Y,Z)}$ iff there is a set Π of paths such that $\Gamma, u, \Pi, \tau \vDash \phi$ and $Valid_{(X,Y)}(\Pi)$.
- If $Z = \text{S}$, then $\Gamma, u, \tau \vDash \phi_{(X,Y,Z)}$ iff there is a set Π of paths such that $\Gamma, u, \Pi, \tau \vDash \phi$, and for every set Π of paths such that $\Gamma, u, \Pi, \tau \vDash \phi$, $Valid_{(X,Y)}(\Pi)$.

The eight ways of forming blacklist-restricted policies establish a lattice as shown in Figure 3. In the figure, we use, for instance, GlGeS to present a restriction when the decisions in each of the three dimensions are fixed as $X = \text{Gl}$, $Y = \text{Ge}$, and $Z = \text{S}$. If a user's access is denied by one of the blacklist-restricted policies, then the same user's access is denied by any restricted policy above this policy in the lattice. The following theorem, which we prove in the appendix, expresses this statement formally:

THEOREM 2. *Let $\Gamma = (\mathcal{G}, W, V)$ be a model, $u \in \mathcal{U}$, τ a valuation and $\phi \in L'(\mathsf{own}, \mathsf{req})$. Let (X_1, Y_1, Z_1) and (X_2, Y_2, Z_2) be two triples with $X_1, X_2 \in \{\text{Lo}, \text{Gl}\}$, $Y_1, Y_2 \in \{\text{Li}, \text{Ge}\}$ and $Z_1, Z_2 \in \{\text{W}, \text{S}\}$. If $(X_1, Y_1, Z_1) \leq (X_2, Y_2, Z_2)$ in the blacklist-restriction lattice, then we have that $\Gamma, u, \tau \vDash \phi_{(X_2,Y_2,Z_2)}$ implies $\Gamma, u, \tau \vDash \phi_{(X_1,Y_1,Z_1)}$.*

To illustrate the eight different blacklist-restrictions, we use the social graph in Figure 2 to present an example. We assume that the owner is A and the policy is a 3-depth policy. Under the non-restricted policy, five users including L, H, M, N and O can access the resource. Under different restrictions, different users' access are denied (see Table 1). In the following, for each restriction we explain why some users are granted and others are denied access. The complete information in Table 1 follows from these explanations by Theorem 2.

Restriction	Denied users	Restriction	Denied users
LoLiW	H	LoLiS	H, L, M
LoGeW	H, M, N	LoGeS	H, L, M, N
GlLiW	H, O	GlLiS	H, L, M, O
GlGeW	H, M, N, O	GlGeS	H, L, M, N, O

Table 1: Denied users under different blacklist-restrictions

1. LoLiW. Under this blacklist-restriction, H's access is denied. The only path of length 3 from A to H is (A, I, M, H), but I is on A's blacklist, so this path violates the restriction for Lo.

78

2. LoGeW. M's access is denied. There are two paths from A to M. On the path (A, C, H, M), C is on A's blacklist which violates the restriction for Lo; on (A, D, I, M), I is on A's blacklist which violates the restriction for Ge. N's access is also denied. The only path from A to N is (A, E, J, N). On this path, J is on A's blacklist which violates the restriction for Ge.

3. GlLiW. O's access is denied. On the only path from A to O, namely (A, F, K, O), there exists a blacklist relation, namely $(F, K) \in b$, thus this path does not satisfy the restriction for Gl. M can access the resource. There is one path from A to M, namely (A, D, I, M), that does not violate the restrictions for Gl and Li.

4. GlGeW. L can access the resource. There is one path from A to L, namely (A, B, G, L), that does not violate the restrictions for Gl and Ge.

5. LoLiS. M's access is denied. There are two paths from A to M. On the path (A, C, H, M), C is on A's blacklist which violates the restriction for Lo. Since the restriction is S, M cannot access the resource. L's access is also denied. There are two paths from A to L; the path (A, C, H, L) violates the restriction for Lo, as C is on A's blacklist. Since the restriction is S, L cannot access the resource.

6. LoGeS. O can access the resource. The only path from A to O, namely (A, F, K, O), does not violate the restrictions for Lo and Ge.

7. GlLiS. N can access the resource. The only path from A to N, namely (A, E, J, N), does not violate the restrictions for Gl and Li.

8. GlGeS. No one can access the resource.

5. SYNTACTICAL TRANSFORMATION

In Section 4, we give a semantic characterization of the three dimensions for blacklist-restricting an access control policy ϕ by defining the conditions under which $\phi_{(X,Y,Z)}$ is satisfied in a given context. In this section we define an algorithm which – given an access control policy $\phi \in L'(\mathsf{own}, \mathsf{req})$ and a choice X, Y, Z of values for the three dimensions – syntactically transforms ϕ to a policy $\phi[X, Y, Z] \in L(\mathsf{own}, \mathsf{req})$ such that $\phi[X, Y, Z]$ is satisfied in precisely the same contexts as $\phi_{(X,Y,Z)}$. The model-checking algorithm from [4] can then be applied for evaluating the blacklist-restricted access control policy $\phi[X, Y, Z]$.

5.1 The Transformation Algorithm

Before presenting the algorithm that syntactically transforms ϕ to produce $\phi[X, Y, Z]$, we need to define the notion of a strictly positive subformula:

Definition 5. A subformula ψ of ϕ is *strictly positive* iff it is not in the scope of a negation symbol in ϕ.

Next we give Algorithm 1 for transforming a formula into disjunctive form, which means pulling out all strictly positive occurrences of $\vee$ in ϕ. The algorithm takes a hybrid logic formula as input and returns a list of disjuncts.

In both Algorithm 1 and Algorithm 2 for syntactically transforming ϕ, we have **for**-loops referring to subformulas of ϕ. The only requirement on the order of the iterations of these **for**-loops is that the iteration for a subformula χ of ϕ must come after the iterations of all strict subformulas of χ. Namely, we proceed from deeper to higher subformulas.

Algorithm 1 Disjunctive Form

Input: $\phi \in L$
Output: a list $DF(\phi)$ of formulas in L
1: **for** χ a strictly positive subformula of ϕ **do**
2:   **if** χ is of the form $\psi_1 \wedge (\psi_2 \vee \psi_3)$ **then**
3:     replace χ in ϕ by $(\psi_1 \wedge \psi_2) \vee (\psi_1 \vee \psi_3)$
4:   **else if** χ is of the form $(\psi_1 \vee \psi_2) \wedge \psi_3$ **then**
5:     replace χ in ϕ by $(\psi_1 \wedge \psi_3) \vee (\psi_2 \wedge \psi_3)$
6:   **else if** χ is of the form $@_n(\psi \vee \chi)$ **then**
7:     replace χ in ϕ by $@_n\psi \vee @_n\chi$
8:   **else if** χ is of the form $@_x(\psi \vee \chi)$ **then**
9:     replace χ in ϕ by $@_x\psi \vee @_x\chi$
10:   **else if** χ is of the form $\langle \alpha_i \rangle(\psi \vee \chi)$ **then**
11:     replace χ in ϕ by $\langle \alpha_i \rangle\psi \vee \langle \alpha_i \rangle\chi$
12:   **else if** χ is of the form $\downarrow_x(\psi \vee \chi)$ **then**
13:     replace χ in ϕ by $\downarrow_x\psi \vee \downarrow_x\chi$
14: $DF(\phi) \leftarrow \{\psi \mid \psi$ is a disjunct of $\phi\}$

Algorithm 2 takes a formula ϕ as input and syntactically transforms it to $\phi[X, Y, Z] \in L(\mathsf{own}, \mathsf{req})$. The transformation is defined separately for weak blacklist-restrictions (lines 2-12) and strong blacklist-restrictions (lines 13-27). In both cases, we insert $\downarrow_{x_k}$'s and $\downarrow_{y_k}$'s into the formula (lines 3 and 15) in order to be able to refer to the nodes of the paths satisfying the formula. We then use the bound variables x_k, y_k to formulate the conditions of Definition 2 to ensure that the specified blacklist-restriction in $[X, Y, Z]$ is satisfied.

The following theorem, whose proof is sketched in the appendix, establishes the equivalence between the syntactical transformation $\phi[X, Y, Z]$ and the semantically defined satisfaction conditions for $\phi_{(X,Y,Z)}$:

THEOREM 3. *Let* $\Gamma = (\mathcal{G}, W, V)$ *be a model,* $u \in \mathcal{U}$, τ *a valuation and* $\phi \in L'(\mathsf{own}, \mathsf{req})$. *Let* $X \in \{\mathrm{Lo}, \mathrm{Gl}\}$, $Y \in \{\mathrm{Li}, \mathrm{Ge}\}$ *and* $Z \in \{\mathrm{W}, \mathrm{S}\}$. *Then* $\Gamma, u, \tau \models \phi[X, Y, Z]$ *iff* $\Gamma, u, \tau \models \phi_{(X,Y,Z)}$.

We illustrate the syntactical transformation by showing its results for some typical policies and blacklist-restrictions:

$@_{\mathsf{own}}\langle f \rangle\langle f \rangle\mathsf{req}[\mathrm{Gl}, \mathrm{Li}, \mathrm{W}] =$
$@_{\mathsf{own}} \downarrow_{x_1} \langle f \rangle \downarrow_{y_1}\downarrow_{x_2} \langle f \rangle \downarrow_{y_2} (\mathsf{req} \ \wedge \neg@_{x_1}\langle b \rangle y_1 \wedge$
$\neg@_{x_2}\langle b \rangle y_2) \wedge \neg@_{\mathsf{own}}\langle b \rangle\mathsf{req}$

$@_{\mathsf{own}}\langle f \rangle\langle f \rangle\mathsf{req}[\mathrm{Lo}, \mathrm{Ge}, \mathrm{S}] =$
$@_{\mathsf{own}}\langle f \rangle\langle f \rangle\mathsf{req} \wedge \neg@_{\mathsf{own}} \downarrow_{x_1} \langle f \rangle \downarrow_{y_1}\downarrow_{x_2} \langle f \rangle \downarrow_{y_2} (\mathsf{req} \ \wedge$
$((@_{\mathsf{own}}x_1 \wedge @_{x_1}\langle b \rangle y_1) \vee (@_{\mathsf{own}}x_2 \wedge @_{x_2}\langle b \rangle y_2) \vee @_{\mathsf{own}}\langle b \rangle x_1 \vee$
$@_{\mathsf{own}}\langle b \rangle y_1 \vee @_{\mathsf{own}}\langle b \rangle x_2 \vee @_{\mathsf{own}}\langle b \rangle y_2)) \wedge \neg@_{\mathsf{own}}\langle b \rangle\mathsf{req}$

5.2 Blacklist-restriction in Practice

Allowing the users to write access control policies in a hybrid logic gives them a lot of flexibility in the specification of the policies. But in practice, if one has in mind an OSN whose users are not all computer scientists, logicians or mathematicians, one cannot expect users to be or become competent in writing formulas in hybrid logic. Instead, we envisage an OSN to provide a tool to the users that allows them to specify an access control policy in an easy-to-understand and hence user-friendly way. This tool would produce a hybrid logic formula to be used internally. Such a tool would give the user various options for considering various information in the access control policy and for

Algorithm 2 Syntactical Transformation

Input: $\phi \in L'(\mathsf{own}, \mathsf{req})$, $X \in \{\mathrm{Lo}, \mathrm{Gl}\}$, $Y \in \{\mathrm{Li}, \mathrm{Ge}\}$, $Z \in \{\mathrm{W}, \mathrm{S}\}$

1: let $x_1, y_1, x_2, y_2, \ldots$ be variables not occurring in ϕ
2: **if** $Z = \mathrm{W}$ **then**
3:      replace every strictly positive subformula of ϕ of the form $\langle \alpha_i \rangle \psi$ by $\downarrow_{x_k} \langle \alpha_i \rangle \downarrow_{y_k} \psi$.
4:      **for** χ a strictly positive subformula of ϕ of the form x, n, p or $\neg\psi$ **do**
5:          $K_\chi \leftarrow \{k \mid \text{some subformula } \downarrow_{x_k} \psi \text{ of } \phi \text{ contains } \chi\}$
6:          **if** $X = \mathrm{Lo}$ **then**
7:              replace every strictly positive subformula χ of ϕ of the form x, n, p or $\neg\psi$ by $\chi \wedge \bigwedge_{k \in K_\chi} (@_{\mathsf{own}} x_k \to \neg@_{x_k} \langle b \rangle y_k)$
8:          **if** $X = \mathrm{Gl}$ **then**
9:              replace every strictly positive subformula χ of ϕ of the form x, n, p or $\neg\psi$ by $\chi \wedge \bigwedge_{k \in K_\chi} \neg@_{x_k} \langle b \rangle y_k$
10:          **if** $Y = \mathrm{Ge}$ **then**
11:              replace every strictly positive subformula χ of ϕ of the form x, n, p or $\neg\psi$ by $\chi \wedge \bigwedge_{k \in K_\chi} (\neg@_{\mathsf{own}} \langle b \rangle x_k \wedge \neg@_{\mathsf{own}} \langle b \rangle y_k)$
12:      $\psi \leftarrow \phi \wedge \neg@_{\mathsf{own}} \langle b \rangle \mathsf{req}$
13: **if** $Z = \mathrm{S}$ **then**
14:      **for** $\phi_i \in (DF(\phi))$ **do**
15:          replace every strictly positive subformula of ϕ_i of the form $\langle \alpha_i \rangle \psi$ by $\downarrow_{x_k} \langle \alpha_i \rangle \downarrow_{y_k} \psi$.
16:          **for** $\chi_{i,j}$ a strictly positive subformula of ϕ_i of the form x, n, p or $\neg\psi$ **do**
17:              $K_{\chi_{i,j}} \leftarrow \{k \mid \text{some subformula } \downarrow_{x_k} \psi \text{ of } \phi \text{ contains } \chi\}$
18:              **if** $X = \mathrm{Lo}$ **then**
19:                  $\psi_{i,j} \leftarrow \bigvee_{k \in K_{\chi_{i,j}}} (@_{\mathsf{own}} x_k \wedge @_{x_k} \langle b \rangle y_k)$
20:              **if** $X = \mathrm{Gl}$ **then**
21:                  $\psi_{i,j} \leftarrow \bigvee_{k \in K_{\chi_{i,j}}} @_{x_k} \langle b \rangle y_k$
22:              **if** $Y = \mathrm{Ge}$ **then**
23:                  $\psi_{i,j} \leftarrow \psi_{i,j} \vee \bigvee_{k \in K_{\chi_{i,j}}} (@_{\mathsf{own}} \langle b \rangle x_k \vee @_{\mathsf{own}} \langle b \rangle y_k)$
24:          $\phi_{i,j} \leftarrow$ result of replacing $\chi_{i,j}$ in ϕ_i by $\chi_{i,j} \wedge \psi_{i,j}$
25:          $\overline{\phi_i} \leftarrow \bigwedge_j \neg\phi_{i,j}$
26:      $\overline{\phi} \leftarrow \phi \wedge \bigwedge_i \overline{\phi_i}$
27:      $\psi \leftarrow \overline{\phi} \wedge \neg@_{\mathsf{own}} \langle b \rangle \mathsf{req}$
28: $\phi[X, Y, Z] \leftarrow \psi$

Algorithm 3 Path Policy Evaluation

Input: $u_{\mathsf{own}}, u_{\mathsf{req}}, \mathcal{G}, \phi \in L'(\mathsf{own}, \mathsf{req})$, $X \in \{\mathrm{Lo}, \mathrm{Gl}\}$, $Y \in \{\mathrm{Li}, \mathrm{Ge}\}$, $Z \in \{\mathrm{W}, \mathrm{S}\}$
Output: access permission

1: **if** $(u_{\mathsf{own}}, u_{\mathsf{req}}) \in b$ **then**
2:      access denied
3: **else**
4:      **if** $Z = \mathrm{W}$ **then**
5:          **for** each path policy ϕ' of ϕ **do**
6:              extract rp and n from ϕ'
7:              $satisfied_{\phi'} \leftarrow \mathsf{Weak}(u_{\mathsf{own}}, u_{\mathsf{req}}, \mathcal{G}, rp, n, X, Y)$
8:              **if** $satisfied_{\phi'} = 1$ **then**
9:                  access granted, **return**
10:          **if** access permission is not set **then**
11:              access denied
12:      **else if** $Z = \mathrm{S}$ **then**
13:          **for** each path policy ϕ' of ϕ **do**
14:              extract rp and n from ϕ'
15:              $(nopath_{\phi'}, satisfied_{\phi'}) \leftarrow$
                     $\mathsf{Strong}(u_{\mathsf{own}}, u_{\mathsf{req}}, \mathcal{G}, rp, n, X, Y)$
16:              **if** $satisfied_{\phi'} = 0$ **then**
17:                  access denied, **return**
18:          **if** $\bigwedge_{(\phi' \text{ of } \phi)} nopath_{\phi'} = 1$ **then**
19:              access denied
20:          **else**
21:              access granted

---

is much more complex than ϕ. Possibly in combination with some tool for producing the basic formula ϕ, our approach can be used for allowing users to flexibly use the information from the blacklists for restricting their access control policies without the need to write complex hybrid logic formulas. This makes our approach a *user-friendly* framework for restricting access in social networks.

6. PATH EVALUATION ALGORITHMS

In practice, especially in the most popular OSNs such as Facebook, a user normally focuses on the length of the path between him and the potential requesters when defining his access control policies. In Facebook one could define a policy to allow his friends or friends of friends to view his profile. In the hybrid logic, the policy can be represented as $@_{\mathsf{own}} \langle f \rangle \mathsf{req} \vee @_{\mathsf{own}} \langle f \rangle \langle f \rangle \mathsf{req}$.

To evaluate this formula under a blacklist-restriction, we can follow the procedure as described in Section 5 to transform the policy into a blacklist-restricted policy. Then we apply the local model-checking algorithm of Bruns et al. [4] to evaluate the resulting policy on a social network model. However, as we have seen with the two examples in Section 5, after the transformation the size of the new formula is usually getting larger, which in turn will make the evaluation using model-checking inefficient: The model checking algorithm needs to go through the structure of the formula (see details in [4]).

In fact, to evaluate a policy that only focuses on the path length from u_{own} to u_{req}, we can first decompose it into several sub-policies, e.g., $@_{\mathsf{own}} \langle f \rangle \mathsf{req}$ and $@_{\mathsf{own}} \langle f \rangle \langle f \rangle \mathsf{req}$ for the above policy, and evaluate each sub-policy by finding the qualified path(s) from u_{own} to u_{req}. During the path-finding process, we can perform optimizations such as filtering out the users who are on u_{own}'s blacklist on-the-fly. In the end,

making the policy more stringent or more lax. One of the decisions that a user has to make is whether and how to use the information from his and other users' blacklists. The three dimensions discussed in the previous section constitute three binary choices of how to use blacklist information in the policy. We believe that these three binary choices are simple enough to make them comprehensible to non-expert users.

As we have seen in first part of this section, for every access control policy ϕ not involving the modality $\langle b \rangle$ and any choice of X, Y, Z for the three dimensions, there is an access control policy $\phi[X, Y, Z] \in L(\mathsf{own}, \mathsf{req})$ such that $\phi[X, Y, Z]$ is satisfied in precisely the same contexts as $\phi_{(X,Y,Z)}$. In other words, the three dimensions for blacklist-restriction do not allow us to express any policy that is not already expressible in the hybrid logic with the help of the modality $\langle b \rangle$. But even if we assume the users to have some competence in writing hybrid logic formulas, it would be cumbersome for the users to write $\phi[X, Y, Z]$ themselves, for often $\phi[X, Y, Z]$

Algorithm 4 Weak

Input: u_{own}, u_{req}, $\mathcal{G}$, rp, n, $X \in \{\text{Lo}, \text{Gl}\}$, $Y \in \{\text{Li}, \text{Ge}\}$
Output: *satisfied*
1: $ulist \leftarrow \{u \mid (u_{\text{own}}, u) \in rp(1) \wedge (u_{\text{own}}, u) \notin b\}$
2: **if** $[X, Y] = \text{LoLi}$ **then**
3:    **for** $i = 2 : n-1$ **do**
4:       **for** $u \in ulist$ **do**
5:          add $\{u' \mid (u, u') \in rp(i)\}$ into $ulist$
6:          delete u from $ulist$
7:    **for** $u \in ulist$ **do**
8:       **if** $(u, u_{\text{req}}) \in rp(n)$ **then**
9:          $satisfied \leftarrow 1$, **break**
10: **else if** $[X, Y] = \text{LoGe}$ **then**
11:    **for** $i = 2 : n-1$ **do**
12:       **for** $u \in ulist$ **do**
13:          add $\{u' \mid (u, u') \in rp(i) \wedge (u_{\text{own}}, u') \notin b\}$ into $ulist$
14:          delete u from $ulist$
15:    **for** $u \in ulist$ **do**
16:       **if** $(u, u_{\text{req}}) \in rp(n) \wedge (u_{\text{own}}, u_{\text{req}}) \notin b$ **then**
17:          $satisfied \leftarrow 1$, **break**
18: **else if** $[X, Y] = \text{GlLi}$ **then**
19:    **for** $i = 2 : n-1$ **do**
20:       **for** $u \in ulist$ **do**
21:          add $\{u' \mid (u, u') \in rp(i) \wedge (u, u') \notin b\}$ into $ulist$
22:          delete u from $ulist$
23:    **for** $u \in ulist$ **do**
24:       **if** $(u, u_{\text{req}}) \in rp(n) \wedge (u, u_{\text{req}}) \notin b$ **then**
25:          $satisfied \leftarrow 1$, **break**
26: **else if** $[X, Y] = \text{GlGe}$ **then**
27:    **for** $i = 2 : n-1$ **do**
28:       **for** $u \in ulist$ **do**
29:          add $\{u' \mid (u, u') \in rp(i) \wedge (u, u') \notin b \wedge (u_{\text{own}}, u') \notin b\}$
         into $ulist$
30:          delete u from $ulist$
31:    **for** $u \in ulist$ **do**
32:       **if** $(u, u_{\text{req}}) \in rp(n) \wedge (u, u_{\text{req}}) \notin b \wedge (u_{\text{own}}, u_{\text{req}}) \notin b$
      then
33:          $satisfied \leftarrow 1$, **break**
34: **if** $satisfied$ is not set **then**
35:    $satisfied \leftarrow 0$

Algorithm 5 Strong

Input: u_{own}, u_{req}, $\mathcal{G}$, rp, n, $X \in \{\text{Lo}, \text{Gl}\}$, $Y \in \{\text{Li}, \text{Ge}\}$
Output: *nopath*, *satisfied*
1: $path \leftarrow \text{BFS}(u_{\text{own}}, u_{\text{req}}, \mathcal{G}, rp, n)$
2: **if** $path$ is empty **then**
3:    $nopath \leftarrow 1$, $satisfied \leftarrow 1$
4: **else**
5:    $nopath \leftarrow 0$
6:    **if** $[X, Y] = \text{LoLi}$ **then**
7:       **for** $p \in path$ **do**
8:          **if** $(u_{\text{own}},$ the first user on $p) \in b$ **then**
9:             $satisfied \leftarrow 0$, **break**
10:    **else if** $[X, Y] = \text{LoGe}$ **then**
11:       **for** $p \in path$ **do**
12:          **if** $\exists$ a user u on p s.t. $(u_{\text{own}}, u) \in b$ **then**
13:             $satisfied \leftarrow 0$, **break**
14:    **else if** $[X, Y] = \text{GlLi}$ **then**
15:       **for** $p \in path$ **do**
16:          **if** $\exists (u, u')$ is part of p s.t. $(u, u') \in b$ **then**
17:             $satisfied \leftarrow 0$, **break**
18:    **else if** $[X, Y] = \text{GlGe}$ **then**
19:       **for** $p \in path$ **do**
20:          **if** $\exists u$ on p s.t. $(u_{\text{own}}, u) \in b \vee \exists (u, u')$ is part of p
         s.t. $(u, u') \in b$ **then**
21:             $satisfied \leftarrow 0$, **break**
22:    **if** $satisfied$ is not set **then**
23:       $satisfied \leftarrow 1$

---

access permission is made by the result of the boolean function connecting the results of each sub-policy. In this way, for policies of such simple form, we can avoid syntactical transformation as well as model-checking, and design more efficient algorithms for policy evaluation.

The policies we consider here can be written as the disjunctions of several *path policies*, and each path policy has the form of @$_{\text{own}}\langle\alpha_1\rangle \ldots \langle\alpha_n\rangle$req, representing a certain depth path from u_{own} to u_{req}. Among the three dimensions, both *globality* and *generality* concentrate on how blacklists are used on a single path while *strength* takes into account all the paths from u_{own} to u_{req}. When the policy's blacklist-restriction is weak, u_{req} can access u_{own}'s resource as long as there exists a path that satisfies the restrictions from the other two dimensions. Therefore, during the process of finding paths from u_{own} to u_{req}, we can directly skip the unqualified edges. On the other hand, when the restriction is strong, we need to make sure that all the possible paths from u_{own} to u_{req} are free of blacklist problems. Since the processes

for evaluating weak and strong restrictions are different, we treat them separately.

Our evaluation algorithm is listed in Algorithm 3. Its input consists of u_{own}, u_{req}, a policy ϕ and a blacklist-restriction X, Y, Z. Due to the restriction of the *generality* dimension, we first check whether u_{req} is on u_{own}'s blacklist. If he is, then we directly deny his access (lines 1-2). Otherwise, we check path policies one by one. Depending on the strength restriction of each path policy, we use the corresponding algorithm (lines 4-17). Each path policy represents a relation path denoted by rp. Here, $rp = (\alpha_1, \ldots \alpha_n)$ is tuple with each item as the corresponding relationship type specified in the path policy and it is indexed by $rp(i)$. Moreover, n is the length of the path (lines 6 and 12). Under the weak restriction, once a path policy's evaluation result is positive ($satisfied_{\phi'} = 1$), u_{req}'s access is granted (lines 8-9). Under the strong restriction, if there exists no path (specified in all the path policies) from u_{own} to u_{req}, u_{req}'s access is denied (lines 18-19). Otherwise, all the existing paths from u_{own} to u_{req} have to satisfy the restrictions from the other two dimensions. If one path policy is not satisfied, then the access is denied and the algorithm is finished (lines 16-17).

Algorithm 4 is used for evaluating path policies under weak restrictions. Here, we perform breadth first search (BFS) to find paths from u_{own} to u_{req} in the social graph $\mathcal{G}$. We first add u_{own}'s $rp(1)$ relations who are not on his blacklist into a list $ulist$, thus the local restriction is implemented. Then, depending on the chosen restriction, different processes are conducted. For example, when the restriction is LoGeW, for each user, to traverse his friends, we only consider the ones that are not on u_{own}'s blacklist (line 13). Note that in the last step, once there is a qualified path from a user in *ulist* to u_{req}, the access is directly granted (*satisfied* $\leftarrow$ 1) (e.g., lines 15-17).

Algorithm 5 presents the process for evaluating the policies under strong restrictions. In the beginning, we exploit BFS to find all the paths from u_{own} to u_{req}. If there is no path from u_{own} to u_{req}, then *nopath* is set to 1 (line 3). Otherwise, we begin to evaluate the paths. Under strong restrictions, once we find an unqualified path from u_{own} to u_{req}, we can directly deny u_{req}'s access without considering other paths anymore (*satisfied* $\leftarrow$ 0). For example, under restriction LoLiS, as long as there exists one path whose first user is on u_{own}'s blacklist, the access is denied (lines 8-9).

7. EVALUATION

As introduced in Section 6, our path evaluation algorithms only consider access control policies that are composed by one or several path policies and each path policy represents a relation path from u_{own} to u_{req}. For empirical evaluation, we focus on the 2-depth policy and the 3-depth policy.

7.1 Algorithm Efficiency

Experiment setup. To evaluate the performance of our proposed algorithms in Section 6, we check the time difference between evaluating restricted and non-restricted policies. The metric we adopt is defined as $time\_ratio[X, Y, Z] = t[X, Y, Z]/t$, where t is the time for checking a non-restricted policy and $t[X, Y, Z]$ is the time for checking the corresponding restricted policy. Here, to enforce a non-restricted policy, we perform BFS to find whether there exists a path from u_{own} to u_{req} satisfying the policy. Since major OSN companies such as Facebook do not disclose their algorithms for enforcing access control policies, we simply choose BFS for the purpose to evaluate the performance of our algorithms. Other algorithms for path-finding can be used as well.

The dataset we use to conduct our experiments is collected by McAuley and Leskovec [17], it is a Facebook dataset that contains 4,039 users and 88,234 edges. For each user, we randomly sample five different ratios, i.e., 1%, 5%, 10%, 20% and 30% of his friends to be on his blacklist. The ratio is called the *blacklist ratio*. The algorithms are implemented on a machine with Intel core i7 processor and 8GB RAM.

Experimental results. For each blacklist-restriction, we plot the metric *time_ratio* as a function of blacklist ratio in Figure 4. The performance of algorithms is quite different for weak and strong restrictions.

Weak restrictions. As shown in Figures 4a, 4b, 4c and 4d, with the increase of blacklist ratio, checking path policies under weak restrictions is getting faster. This is because during the path-finding process, Algorithm 4 filters out all the unqualified edges which saves a lot of operations. On the other hand, for non-restricted policies, the algorithm cannot skip any edges until it finds a path. Due to the same reason, evaluating weak restrictions is faster than evaluating strong ones. We also notice that, in Figures 4b, 4c, 4d, the curves for 3-depth policies (blue) are far below the curves for 2-depth ones (red). The reason is that longer paths our algorithm traverses, more edges it filters out, thus more operations are saved compared to running non-restricted policies. On the other hand, the difference between the two curves in Figure 4a is small since running LoLiW only filters out the users that are on u_{own}'s blacklist in the first step.

Strong restrictions. As depicted in Figures 4e, 4f, 4g and 4h, time for running 3-depth policies with strong restrictions is almost twice as much as running non-restricted policies. This indicates that the most time-consuming operations are for finding paths. On the other hand, checking 2-depth strong policies only requires around 30% overhead.

7.2 Power of Blacklist-restrictions

It is interesting to learn what is the impact of different restrictions on access control. We focus on two questions.

Which restrictions are relatively powerful? The "power" of a blacklist-restriction is quantified by the number of users denied by it. We first define a metric, *access_ratio*, representing the fraction of the number of qualified requesters under an owner's restricted policy and the number of qualified requesters under the same non-restricted policy. When a user's *access_ratio* under a blacklist-restriction is high, it means that he *cannot* forbid many users with the restriction.

As we can see from Figure 5, the power of all the eight blacklist-restrictions is consistent with the lattice presented in Figure 3. GLGeS which is the supremum in the lattice is the most powerful blacklist-restriction. When the blacklist ratio is 20%, the average *access_ratio* is only 20% (40%) for the 3-depth (2-depth) case (see Figure 5h). On the other hand, LoLiW is the least powerful one. When the blacklist ratio is 20%, the average *access_ratio* is around 85% for the 3-depth case (see Figure 5a). For each edge of the lattice in Figure 3, the restriction of the source node always denies less users than the one of the target node, e.g., LoGeW denies less users than LoGeS (Figure 5b vs. Figure 5f).

We notice that among all the three dimensions, shifting the *strength* dimension from weak to strong denies many more users' access than shifting the other two dimensions. For example, the difference between the curves in Figure 5f (LoGeW) and Figure 5b (LoGeS) is much bigger than the difference between Figure 5b (LoGeW) and Figure 5d (GLGeW). This is because the strong restriction requires all the paths from u_{own} to u_{req} to be free of blacklist problems, while the weak restriction only needs one qualified path. On the other hand, shifting the *globality* dimension from local to global denies more users than shifting the *generality* from limited to general. For example, by shifting the blacklist-restriction from GLLiW to GLGeW, the *access_ratio* barely changes (see Figure 5c and Figure 5d), while the difference between LoLiS and GLLiS is more notable (see Figure 5e and Figure 5g). The reason is that the global restriction considers the blacklist of everyone on the path from u_{own} to u_{req} while the general restriction only focuses on u_{own}'s blacklist.

Which users are relatively easily to be forbidden? To precisely answer this question, we study the social strength between the owner and the qualified requesters under different blacklist-restrictions. The social strength between two users is quantified by three metrics including embeddedness, Jaccard index and Adamic-Adar score [1]. If two users' embeddedness (as well as Jaccard index and Adamic-Adar score) is high, then they are considered to have a strong relationship. We compute the average value of the three metrics between the qualified requesters and the corresponding owners under different blacklist-restrictions. As shown in Figure 6, the three metrics give us similar results. Qualified requesters under weak restrictions are more socially close to the corresponding owners than the qualified requesters under strong ones. This is because higher social strength implies more

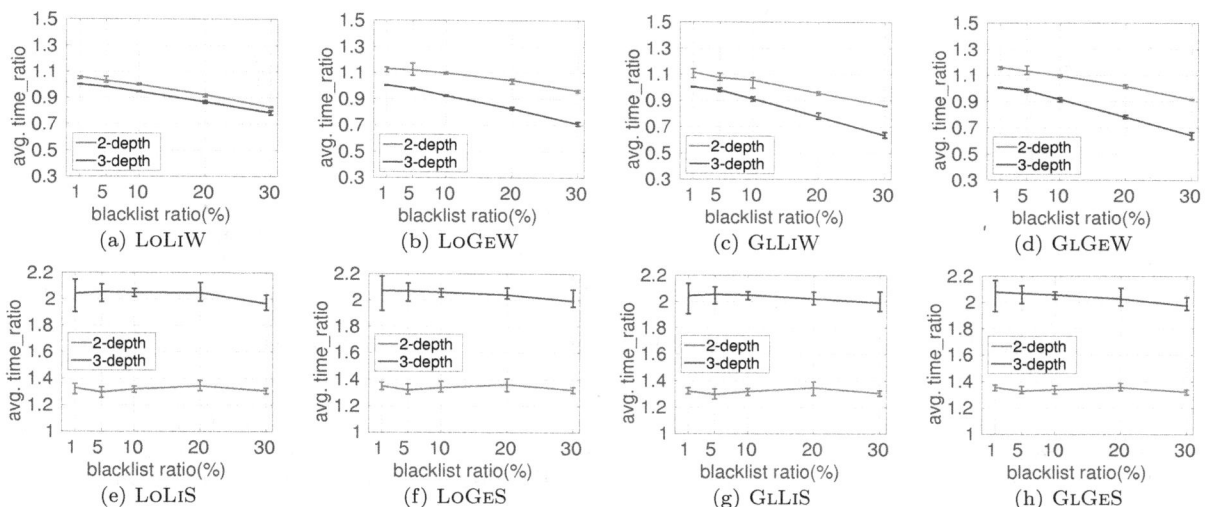

Figure 4: Average *time_ratio* under eight blacklist-restrictions

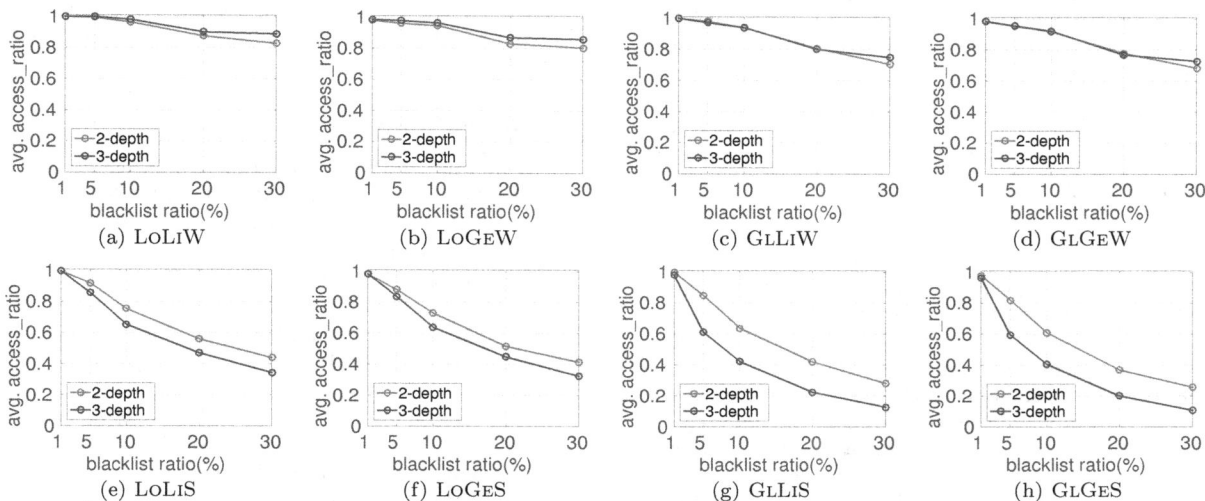

Figure 5: Average *access_ratio* under eight blacklist-restrictions

paths. Therefore, there is a better chance for the requester to be qualified under weak restrictions. However, to access the resource under a strong blacklist-restriction, the requester is better *not* to be socially close with the owner, which seems counter-intuitive. This is because the strong restriction considers all the paths from u_{own} to u_{req}.

8. RELATED WORK

Blacklists have been used in a wide range of applications, such as spam detection [7, 19] and sybil defense [22, 11]. In this work, we focus on the use of blacklists in relationship-based access control.

Relationship-based access control is first proposed in [14], it states that the data owner can control the access to his data based on the relationship between him and the requester. Following this work, several papers have focused on modeling relationship-based access control systems. In [6], Carminati et al. interpret the access decision in terms of three conditions including relationship, depth and trust level between the owner and the requester. In [13], the authors

model the relationship-based access control into a two-stage process where the requester needs to first be able to reach the owner and then applies for access. Besides proposing different models, defining and specifying access control policies have also been studied in the literature. In [5], the authors exploit the use of semantic web to define policies. Moreover, they propose three system-level policies including authorization, admin and filtering policies. Fong et al. [13] propose several topology-based policies such as k-common friends and clique. Later, the authors of [12, 4] exploit hybrid logics to specify these fine-grained policies. Their logic is quite expressive and has been used in several other systems [20, 21, 18], and we adopt the same logic to specify restricted access. In [8], Cheng et al. consider not only user-to-user, but also user-to-resource and resource-to-resource relationships in OSNs, which enables them to express new types of policies such as users who are tagged in the same photo with the owner can view his profile can be expressed. Crampton and Sellwood [10] apply the ideas of relationship-based access control on general computing systems. They propose

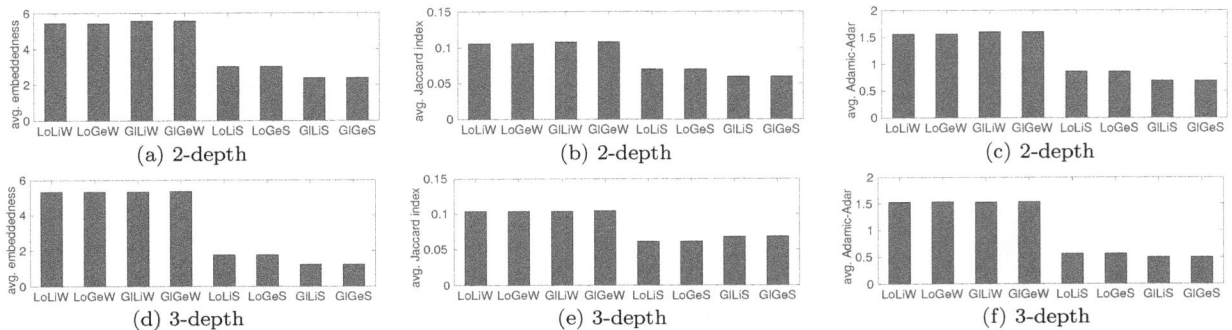

Figure 6: Embeddedness, Jaccard index and Adamic-Adar score between users and the owner (blacklist ratio = 10%)

path conditions to specify policies and principal matching for evaluation. However, to the best of our knowledge, exploring blacklists for restricting access has not been discussed in relationship-based access control. Moreover, it is the first time to model and formally define different blacklist-restrictions in a hybrid logic.

Delegation means that one active entity in a system delegates its authority to another entity in the systems to carry out some functions; it has been extensively studied in access control (e.g., see [23, 16, 2, 9]). Fong [12] explicitly points out that relationship-based access control supports delegation – the use of other users' social relations (and blacklists) to regulate access control in OSNs can be naturally considered as a delegation process. Revocation is an important issue that has been studied with delegation [23], which has been formally categorized and defined in [3, 15]. When a user blacklist-restricts a policy, it can be treated as revoking other users' privileges that they are delegated under the corresponding non-restricted policy. For example, under the restriction GLLIW, a user can only delegate privileges to his friends that are not on his blacklist. Different from revocation which takes away all the delegated users' privileges, blacklist-restrictions can be considered a "partial" revocation since a user can still delegate the privilege to others if the blacklist-restrictions are not violated. The formal relation between blacklist-restriction and revocation deserves further investigations, and we leave it for our future work.

9. CONCLUSION

In this paper, we have focused on blacklists, which already exist in popular OSNs such as Facebook, for the purpose of restricting access. We treated blacklists as a special relationship among OSN users. This allows us to build our work naturally on an exiting social network model and a hybrid logic for specifying relationship-based access control policies. We have identified three different dimensions of applying blacklists. Each dimension provides a binary choice, resulting into eight types of blacklist-restrictions. The meaning of the choices are intuitive for the users to understand. We formally defined the blacklist-restrictions, using a new path semantics for the hybrid logic. To release users from the task of precisely writing their policies with blacklist-restrictions and in order to make our approach user-friendly, we also provided a procedure to syntactically rewrite a non-restricted policy into a policy under a user specified blacklist-restriction. To enforce policies which require the witness of a relation path from the owner to the requester, we designed efficient algorithms for blacklist-restrictions and evaluated

their performance on a Facebook dataset. In addition, we have made a few interesting observations on the impact of the blacklist-restrictions for access control in OSNs.

10. ACKNOWLEDGEMENTS

The work of Marcos Cramer was supported by the FNR INTER project *Specification logics and Inference tools for verification and Enforcement of Policies*.

11. REFERENCES

[1] L. Adamic and E. Adar. Friends and neighbors on the web. *Social Networks*, 25(3):211–230, 2003.

[2] M. Alam, X. Zhang, K. Khan, and G. Ali. xDAuth: a scalable and lightweight framework for cross domain access control and delegation. In *Proc. SACMAT*, pages 31–40. ACM, 2011.

[3] E. Barka and R. S. Sandhu. Framework for role-based delegation models. In *Proc. ACSAC*, pages 168–176. IEEE CS, 2000.

[4] G. Bruns, P. W. L. Fong, I. Siahaan, and M. Huth. Relationship-based access control: its expression and enforcement through hybrid logic. In *Proc. CODASPY*, pages 117–124. ACM, 2012.

[5] B. Carminati, E. Ferrari, R. Heatherly, M. Kantarcioglu, and B. Thuraisingham. A semantic web based framework for social network access control. In *Proc. SACMAT*, pages 177–186. ACM, 2009.

[6] B. Carminati, E. Ferrari, and A. Perego. Rule-based access control for social networks. In *Proc. IFIP WG 2.12 and 2.14 Semantic Web Workshop (OTM)*, volume 4278 of *LNCS*, pages 1734–1744. Springer, 2006.

[7] C. Castillo, D. Donato, A. Gionis, V. Murdock, and F. Silvestri. Know your neighbors: web spam detection using the web topology. In *Proc. SIGIR*, pages 423–430. ACM, 2007.

[8] Y. Cheng, J. Park, and R. S. Sandhu. Relationship-based access control for online social networks: beyond user-to-user relationships. In *Proc. PASSAT*, pages 646–655. IEEE CS, 2012.

[9] J. Crampton and C. Morisset. An auto-delegation mechanism for access control systems. In *Proc. STM*, volume 6710 of *LNCS*, pages 1–16. Springer, 2011.

[10] J. Crampton and J. Sellwood. Path conditions and principal matching: a new approach to access control. In *Proc. SACMAT*, pages 187–198. ACM, 2014.

[11] P. W. L. Fong. Preventing sybil attacks by privilege attenuation: a design principle for social network systems. In *Proc. S&P*, pages 263–278. IEEE CS, 2011.

[12] P. W. L. Fong. Relationship-based access control: protection model and policy language. In *Proc. CODASPY*, pages 191–202. ACM, 2011.

[13] P. W. L. Fong, M. M. Anwar, and Z. Zhao. A privacy preservation model for Facebook-style social network systems. In *Proc. ESORICS*, volume 5789 of *LNCS*, pages 303–320. Springer, 2009.

[14] C. E. Gates. Access control requirements for Web 2.0 security and privacy. In *Proc. IEEE Workshop on Web 2.0 Security and Privacy (W2SP)*, 2007.

[15] A. Hagstrom, S. Jajodia, F. Parisi-Presicce, and D. Wijesekera. Revocations-a classification. In *Proc. CSFW*. IEEE CS, 2001.

[16] J. Joshi and E. Bertino. Fine-grained role-based delegation in presence of the hybrid role hierarchy. In *Proc. SACMAT*, pages 81–80. ACM, 2006.

[17] J. J. McAuley and J. Leskovec. Learning to discover social circles in ego networks. In *Proc. NIPS*, pages 548–556. NIPS, 2012.

[18] J. Pang and Y. Zhang. A new access control scheme for Facebook-style social networks. In *Proc. ARES*, pages 1–10. IEEE CS, 2014.

[19] A. Ramachandran, N. Feamster, and S. Vempala. Filtering spam with behavioral blacklisting. In *Proc. CCS*, pages 342–351. ACM, 2007.

[20] E. Tarameshloo and P. W. L. Fong. Access control models for geo-social computing systems. In *Proc. SACMAT*, pages 115–126. ACM, 2014.

[21] E. Tarameshloo, P. W. L. Fong, and P. Mohassel. On protection in federated social computing systems. In *Proc. CODASPY*, pages 75–86. ACM, 2014.

[22] H. Yu, P. B. Gibbons, M. Kaminsky, and F. Xiao. Sybillimit: A near-optimal social network defense against sybil attacks. In *Proc. S&P*, pages 3–17. IEEE CS, 2008.

[23] L. Zhang, G.-J. Ahn, and B.-T. Chu. A rule-based framework for role-based delegation and revocation. *ACM TIST*, 6(3):404–441, 2003.

APPENDIX

A. PROOF OF THEOREM 1

We proof the theorem by induction over the length of ϕ.

- $\phi = x$:
  Left-to-right: Suppose $\Gamma, u, \tau \vDash x$, i.e. $u = \tau(x)$. Set $\Pi := \{\langle\rangle\}$. Then $\Gamma, u, \Pi, \tau \vDash x$.
  Right-to-left: Trivial.

- $\phi = n$: Similar to the case $\phi = x$

- $\phi = p$: Similar to the case $\phi = x$

- $\phi = \neg\psi$:
  Left-to-right: Suppose $\Gamma, u, \tau \vDash \neg\psi$, i.e. $\Gamma, u, \tau \nvDash \psi$. By the inductive hypothesis, there is no set of paths Π' s.t. $\Gamma, u, \Pi', \tau \vDash \phi$. Set $\Pi := \{\langle\rangle\}$. It now follows that $\Gamma, u, \Pi, \tau \vDash \neg\psi$.
  Right-to-left: Suppose $\Gamma, u, \Pi, \tau \vDash \neg\psi$, i.e. $\Pi = \{\langle\rangle\}$ and there is no set of paths Π' s.t. $\Gamma, u, \Pi', \tau \vDash \phi$. By the inductive hypothesis, $\Gamma, u, \tau \vDash \neg\psi$.

- $\phi = \psi_1 \wedge \psi_2$:
  Left-to-right: Suppose $\Gamma, u, \tau \vDash \psi_1 \wedge \psi_2$, i.e. $\Gamma, u, \tau \vDash \psi_1$ and $\Gamma, u, \tau \vDash \psi_2$. By the inductive hypothesis, $\Gamma, u, \tau \vDash \psi_1$ implies that there is a set Π_1 of paths s.t. $\Gamma, u, \Pi_1, \tau \vDash \psi_1$, and $\Gamma, u, \tau \vDash \psi_2$ implies that there is a set Π_2 of paths s.t. $\Gamma, u, \Pi_2, \tau \vDash \psi_2$. Set $\Pi := \Pi_1 \cup \Pi_2$. Then $\Gamma, u, \Pi, \tau \vDash \psi_1 \wedge \psi_2$.
  Right-to-left: Suppose $\Gamma, u, \Pi, \tau \vDash \psi_1 \wedge \psi_2$, i.e. there are sets Π_1, Π_2 of paths with $\Pi_1 \cup \Pi_2 = \Pi$ s.t. $\Gamma, u, \Pi_1, \tau \vDash \psi_1$ and $\Gamma, u, \Pi_2, \tau \vDash \psi_2$. By the inductive hypothesis $\Gamma, u, \tau \vDash \psi_1$ and $\Gamma, u, \tau \vDash \psi_2$.

- $\phi = \psi_1 \vee \psi_2$: Similar to the case $\phi = \psi_1 \wedge \psi_2$

- $\phi = \langle\alpha_i\rangle\psi$:
  Left-to-right: Suppose $\Gamma, u, \tau \vDash \langle\alpha_i\rangle\psi$, i.e. there is a $u' \in \mathcal{U}$ s.t. $(u, u') \in \alpha_i$ and $\Gamma, u', \tau \vDash \psi$. By the inductive hypothesis, there is a set Π' of paths s.t. $\Gamma, u', \Pi', \tau \vDash \psi$. Set $\Pi := \{(u, u') \circ \pi \mid \pi \in \Pi'\}$. Then $\Pi' = \Pi[1 :]$ and $\forall \pi \in \Pi\ \pi[0] = (u, u')$. So $\Gamma, u, \Pi, \tau \vDash \langle\alpha_i\rangle\psi$.
  Right-to-left: Suppose $\Gamma, u, \Pi, \tau \vDash \langle\alpha_i\rangle\psi$, i.e. there is a $u' \in \mathcal{U}$ s.t. $\Gamma, u', \Pi[1 :], \tau \vDash \psi$, $(u, u') \in \alpha_i$. By the inductive hypothesis $\Gamma, u, \tau \vDash \langle\alpha_i\rangle\psi$.

- $\phi = @_n\psi$:
  Left-to-right: Suppose $\Gamma, u, \tau \vDash @_n\psi$, i.e. $\Gamma, u', \tau \vDash \psi$, where $W(n) = u'$. By the inductive hypothesis, there is a set Π of paths s.t. $\Gamma, u', \Pi, \tau \vDash \psi$. Then $\Gamma, u, \Pi, \tau \vDash @_n\psi$.
  Right-to-left: Suppose $\Gamma, u, \Pi, \tau \vDash @_n\psi$, i.e. $\Gamma, u', \Pi, \tau \vDash \psi$, where $W(n) = u'$. By the inductive hypothesis $\Gamma, u', \tau \vDash \psi$, and therefore $\Gamma, u, \tau \vDash @_n\psi$.

- $\phi = @_x\psi$: Similar to the case $@_n\psi$

- $\phi = \downarrow_x \psi$:
  Left-to-right: Suppose $\Gamma, u, \tau \vDash \downarrow_x \psi$, i.e. $\Gamma, u, \tau[x \mapsto u] \vDash \psi$. By the inductive hypothesis, $\Gamma, u, \Pi, \tau[x \mapsto u] \vDash \psi$, i.e. $\Gamma, u, \Pi, \tau \vDash \downarrow_x \psi$.
  Right-to-left: Suppose $\Gamma, u, \Pi, \tau \vDash \downarrow_x \psi$, i.e. $\Gamma, u, \Pi, \tau[x \mapsto u] \vDash \psi$. By the inductive hypothesis, $\Gamma, u, \tau[x \mapsto u] \vDash \psi$, i.e. $\Gamma, u, \tau \vDash \downarrow_x \psi$.

B. PROOF OF THEOREM 2

First, we need to prove the following lemma:

LEMMA 1. *Let* $\Gamma = (\mathcal{G}, W, V)$ *be a model,* τ *a valuation and* Π *a set of paths in* $\mathcal{U}$. *Let* $X_1, X_2 \in \{\text{Lo}, \text{Gl}\}$ *and* $Y_1, Y_2 \in \{\text{Li}, \text{Ge}\}$ *be s.t.* $(X_1, Y_1, \text{W}) \leq (X_2, Y_2, \text{W})$ *in the blacklist-restriction lattice. Then* $Valid_{(X_2, Y_2)}(\Gamma, \Pi, \tau)$ *implies* $Valid_{(X_1, Y_1)}(\Gamma, \Pi, \tau)$.

PROOF. Suppose $Valid_{(X_2, Y_2)}(\Gamma, \Pi, \tau)$. We want to show that $Valid_{(X_1, Y_1)}(\Gamma, \Pi, \tau)$. For this we have to show that the four conditions from Definition 2 are satisfied for X_1, Y_1. We call the first two conditions the globality conditions and the other two the generality conditions.

Since $(X_1, Y_1, \text{W}) \leq (X_2, Y_2, \text{W})$, we know that it is not the case that $X_1 = \text{Gl}$ and $X_2 = \text{Lo}$. If $X_1 = X_2$, the globality conditions are satisfied for X_1 since they are satisfied for X_2. So all we have to show is that the globality conditions are satisfied for X_1 if $X_1 = \text{Lo}$ and $X_2 = \text{Gl}$. Of course, since $X_1 \neq \text{Gl}$, the second globality condition is trivially satisfied. Since $X_2 = \text{Gl}$, we have that for all $u, u' \in \mathcal{U}$ s.t. (u, u') is an element of some $\pi \in \Pi$, $(u, u') \notin b$. So in particular, for every $u \in \mathcal{U}$ s.t. $(\tau(\text{own}), u)$ is an element of some $\pi \in \Pi$, $(\tau(\text{own}), u) \notin b$. Therefore, the first globality condition is satisfied for X_1.

Similarly, it is enough to show that the first generality condition is satisfied for $Y_1 = \text{Li}$ and $Y_2 = \text{Ge}$. But since $Y_2 = \text{Ge}$, we know by the second generality condition for Y_2 that $(\tau(\text{own}), \tau(\text{req})) \notin b$, so that the first generality condition for Y_1 is satisfied. $\square$

We now proceed to proving Theorem 2. Let $X_1, X_2 \in \{\text{Lo}, \text{Gl}\}$, $Y_1, Y_2 \in \{\text{Li}, \text{Ge}\}$ and $Z_1, Z_2 \in \{\text{W}, \text{S}\}$ be s.t. $(X_1, Y_1, Z_1) \leq (X_2, Y_2, Z_2)$ in the blacklist-restriction lattice. Suppose $\Gamma, u, \tau \vDash \phi_{(X_2, Y_2, Z_2)}$. We need to show that $\Gamma, u, \tau \vDash \phi_{(X_1, Y_1, Z_1)}$. Since $(X_1, Y_1, Z_1) \leq (X_2, Y_2, Z_2)$, we know that it is not the case that $Z_1 = \text{S}$ and $Z_2 = \text{W}$. We consider the other three possible values for Z_1, Z_2 separately:

- $Z_1 = Z_2 = \text{W}$:
Since we have $Z_2 = \text{W}$, $\Gamma, u, \tau \vDash \phi_{(X_2, Y_2, Z_2)}$ implies that there is a set Π of paths s.t. $\Gamma, u, \Pi, \tau \vDash \phi$ and $Valid_{(X_2, Y_2)}(\Pi)$. Since $(X_1, Y_1, \text{W}) \leq (X_2, Y_2, \text{W})$, Lemma 1 implies that $Valid_{(X_1, Y_1)}(\Pi)$. Hence, $\Gamma, u, \tau \vDash \phi_{(X_1, Y_1, Z_1)}$.

- $Z_1 = Z_2 = \text{S}$:
In this case, $\Gamma, u, \tau \vDash \phi_{(X_2, Y_2, Z_2)}$ implies that (i) there is a set Π of paths s.t. $\Gamma, u, \Pi, \tau \vDash \phi$, and (ii) for every set Π of paths s.t. $\Gamma, u, \Pi, \tau \vDash \phi$, $Valid_{(X_2, Y_2)}(\Pi)$. For showing that $\Gamma, u, \tau \vDash \phi_{(X_1, Y_1, Z_1)}$, it is enough to show that for every set Π of paths s.t. $\Gamma, u, \Pi, \tau \vDash \phi$, $Valid_{(X_1, Y_1)}(\Pi)$. So let Π be a set of paths s.t. $\Gamma, u, \Pi, \tau \vDash \phi$. It is now enough to show that $\Gamma, u, \Pi, \tau \vDash \phi$, $Valid_{(X_1, Y_1)}(\Pi)$. By (ii), $Valid_{(X_2, Y_2)}(\Pi)$. $(X_1, Y_1, \text{S}) \leq (X_2, Y_2, \text{S})$ implies that $(X_1, Y_1, \text{W}) \leq (X_2, Y_2, \text{W})$. This together with Lemma 1 implies that $Valid_{(X_1, Y_1)}(\Pi)$, as required.

- $Z_1 = \text{W}$ and $Z_2 = \text{S}$:
Since $Z_2 = \text{S}$, $\Gamma, u, \tau \vDash \phi_{(X_2, Y_2, Z_2)}$ implies that (i) there is a set Π of paths s.t. $\Gamma, u, \Pi, \tau \vDash \phi$, and (ii) for every set Π of paths s.t. $\Gamma, u, \Pi, \tau \vDash \phi$, $Valid_{(X_2, Y_2)}(\Pi)$. (i) and (ii) together imply that there is a set Π of paths s.t. $\Gamma, u, \Pi, \tau \vDash \phi$ and $Valid_{(X_2, Y_2)}(\Pi)$. $(X_1, Y_1, \text{W}) \leq (X_2, Y_2, \text{S})$ implies that $(X_1, Y_1, \text{W}) \leq (X_2, Y_2, \text{W})$. This together with Lemma 1 implies that $Valid_{(X_1, Y_1)}(\Pi)$. Hence, $\Gamma, u, \tau \vDash \phi_{(X_1, Y_1, Z_1)}$.

C. SKETCH OF PROOF OF THEOREM 3

First note by inspection of the definition of the path semantics that a path in a set of paths satisfying a formula ϕ corresponds to a branch in the syntax tree of ϕ starting at the root (which is labeled by ϕ) and ending in a node labeled by a strictly positive subformula of ϕ of the form x, m, p or $\neg \psi$. The edges in this branch that connect a node labeled $\langle \alpha_i \rangle \psi$ to ψ correspond to the edges of the path.

Note that in Definition 2, where we defined which sets of paths are free of blacklist problems, the first, second and fourth condition actually refer to the set Π of paths, whereas the third condition does not refer to this set and hence is independent of the choice of Π. For this reason, Algorithm 2 handles the restrictions imposed by this condition somewhat differently from the restrictions imposed by the other three conditions. To refer to the restrictions imposed by the other three conditions, we define $v_{(X, Y)}(\Gamma, \Pi, \tau)$ as follows:

Definition 6. Let $\Gamma = (\mathcal{G}, W, V)$ be a model and τ be a valuation. For $X \in \{\text{Lo}, \text{Gl}\}$, $Y \in \{\text{Li}, \text{Ge}\}$ and a set Π of paths, we define $v_{(X, Y)}(\Gamma, \Pi, \tau)$ to hold iff the following four properties are satisfied:

- If $X = \text{Lo}$, then for every $u \in \mathcal{U}$ s.t. $(\tau(\text{own}), u)$ is an element of some $\pi \in \Pi$, $(\tau(\text{own}), u) \notin b$.

- If $X = \text{Gl}$, then for all $u, u' \in \mathcal{U}$ s.t. (u, u') is an element of some $\pi \in \Pi$, $(u, u') \notin b$.

- If $Y = \text{Ge}$, then $(\tau(\text{own}), \tau(\text{req})) \notin b$, and for all $u, u' \in \mathcal{U}$ s.t. (u, u') is an element of some $\pi \in \Pi$, $(\tau(\text{own}), u) \notin b$ and $(\tau(\text{own}), u') \notin b$.

We first sketch how to prove the theorem for $Z = \text{W}$: The insertion of $\downarrow_{x_k}$'s and $\downarrow_{y_k}$'s into ϕ in line 3 of algorithm does not affect which sets of paths satisfy ϕ, but makes it possible to refer to the nodes of these paths. The new subformulas, which in lines 6-11 of Algorithm 2 get conjuncted to strictly positive subformulas χ of ϕ of the form x, m, p or $\neg \psi$, make use of this possibility to refer to the nodes of the paths in order to express the conditions for $v_{(X, Y)}(\Gamma, \Pi, \tau)$ within ϕ. In line 12 we ensure that if $Y = \text{Li}$, then $(\tau(\text{own}), \tau(\text{req})) \notin b$. Hence the modifications performed on ϕ in case $Z = \text{W}$ ensure that $\phi[X, Y, Z]$ is satisfied precisely by those sets of paths Π that satisfy ϕ and $Valid_{(X, Y)}(\Gamma, \Pi, \tau)$, i.e. precisely by those sets of paths that satisfy $\phi_{(X, Y, Z)}$.

Now we sketch how to prove the theorem for $Z = \text{S}$: Note that for a set Π of paths to satisfy a formula ϕ of the form $\psi_1 \vee \psi_2$, it is enough that it satisfies ψ_1 or ψ_2. Hence, concerning the correspondence mentioned in the first paragraph of this proof sketch, only the branches of the syntax tree of one of ψ_1 and ψ_2 correspond to paths in Π, while the branches in the syntax tree of the other are not reflected in the structure of Π at all. In general, we can say that the correspondence is only a one-to-one correspondence, if ϕ is a formula that does not have a strictly positive subformula of the form $\psi_1 \vee \psi_2$. This is why for the case $Z = \text{S}$, Algorithm 2 makes use of the Disjunctive Form $DF(\phi)$ of ϕ: The modifications made to the disjuncts ϕ_i depend on the correspondence between paths and branches of the syntax tree being one-to-one.

Furthermore, note that one can easily prove by an induction over the length of ϕ that every hybrid logic formula ϕ is equivalent to its Disjunctive Form.

In lines 18-23 of Algorithm 2, we define – for each strictly positive subformula $\chi_{i,j}$ of ϕ_i of the form x, m, p of $\neg \psi$ – a formula $\psi_{i,j}$ that expresses that the conditions for $v_{(X, Y)}(\Gamma, \{\pi\}, \tau)$ are not satisfied, where π is the path corresponding to the syntax tree branch ending at $\chi_{i,j}$. Hence, $\phi_{i,j}$ as defined in line 24 has the following property: $\Gamma, u, \tau \vDash \phi_{i,j}$ iff there is a set Π of paths s.t. $\Gamma, u, \Pi, \tau \vDash \phi_i$ and it is not the case that $v_{(X, Y)}(\Gamma, \{\pi\}, \tau)$ (where $\pi \in \Pi$ is the path corresponding to the syntax tree branch ending at $\chi_{i,j}$). This implies that $\Gamma, u, \tau \vDash \neg \phi_{i,j}$ iff for every set Π of paths s.t. $\Gamma, u, \Pi, \tau \vDash \phi_i$, we have $v_{(X, Y)}(\Gamma, \{\pi\}, \tau)$. Hence, $\overline{\phi_i}$ as defined in line 25 has the following property: $\Gamma, u, \tau \vDash \overline{\phi_i}$ iff for every set Π of paths with $\Gamma, u, \Pi, \tau \vDash \phi_i$, $v_{(X, Y)}(\Gamma, \{\pi\}, \tau)$ holds for every path in $\pi \in \Pi$, i.e. $v_{(X, Y)}(\Gamma, \Pi, \tau)$.

Now the equivalence between ϕ and $DF(\phi)$ together with the property of $\overline{\phi_i}$ that we just established implies the following property for the $\overline{\phi}$ defined in line 26: $\Gamma, u, \tau \vDash \overline{\phi}$ iff $\Gamma, u, \tau \vDash \phi$ and for every set Π of paths with $\Gamma, u, \Pi, \tau \vDash \phi$, we have $v_{(X, Y)}(\Gamma, \Pi, \tau)$. Concerning the ψ defined in line 27, this implies that $\Gamma, u, \tau \vDash \psi$ iff $\Gamma, u, \tau \vDash \phi$ and for every set Π of paths with $\Gamma, u, \Pi, \tau \vDash \phi$, we have $Valid_{(X, Y)}(\Gamma, \Pi, \tau)$, i.e. $\Gamma, u, \tau \vDash \psi$ iff $\Gamma, u, \tau \vDash \phi_{(X, Z, Y)}$, as required.

Preventing Information Inference in Access Control

Federica Paci
University of Southampton
f.m.paci@soton.ac.uk

Nicola Zannone
Eindhoven University of Technology
n.zannone@tue.nl

ABSTRACT

Technological innovations like social networks, personal devices and cloud computing, allow users to share and store online a huge amount of personal data. Sharing personal data online raises significant privacy concerns for users, who feel that they do not have full control over their data. A solution often proposed to alleviate users' privacy concerns is to let them specify access control policies that reflect their privacy constraints. However, existing approaches to access control often produce policies which either are too restrictive or allow the leakage of sensitive information. In this paper, we present a novel access control model that reduces the risk of information leakage. The model relies on a data model which encodes the domain knowledge along with the semantic relations between data. We illustrate how the access control model and the reasoning over the data model can be automatically translated in XACML. We evaluate and compare our model with existing access control models with respect to its effectiveness in preventing leakage of sensitive information and efficiency in authoring policies. The evaluation shows that the proposed model allows the definition of effective access control policies that mitigate the risks of inference of sensitive data while reducing users' effort in policy authoring compared to existing models.

Categories and Subject Descriptors

D.4.6 [**Operating Systems**]: Security and Protection—*Access controls*; K.6.5 [**Management of Computing and Information Systems**]: Security and Protection; D.2.8 [**Software Engineering**]: Metrics—*complexity measures, performance measures*

General Terms

Security, Theory

Keywords

Inference control; information leakage; semantic approach; XACML; comparison study

1. INTRODUCTION

Today individuals live in a digital world where everything they do happens online: they use their personal devices to check their email, read their favorite blogs, look for restaurants and jobs, read their friends' social network profiles, buy services and goods, tweet their locations, and more. However, everything individuals do online leaves a huge amount of information about them online. This makes it easy for companies and government agencies to collect this information as well as use analytic models to infer who a user is and what he does. For example, it is possible to discover the dietary preferences of an individual from the recipes she searches online; or to predict if she is pregnant based on her purchase habits. This information is considered highly sensitive, and an individual might want to disclose this information only to a restrict audience. Thus, the online proliferation of personal information raises significant privacy concerns for individuals.

Several studies have shown that individuals' privacy concerns are alleviated when they have a greater sense of control over the disclosure and subsequent use of their personal information [2, 13, 30]. A solution proposed to empower individuals with control over their personal information is to let them specify fine-grained policies that define which personal information they are willing to disclose and to whom it can be disclosed [4, 11, 16, 17, 39].

However, policy authoring has been proven to be a time consuming and error prone task [16, 20]. This is mainly due to the significant cognitive burden required by existing languages for policy authoring. In fact, in order to specify a policy, users need to have a deep and comprehensive knowledge of the application domain. To illustrate this issue, imagine a patient defining a policy to protect her Electronic Healthcare Record (EHR). Suppose that the patient wants to reveal that she is HIV-positive only to her treating doctor. To this end, she defines a policy explicitly restricting the access to this information, leaving other information in her EHR unrestricted. Based on this policy, no one except her treating doctor can read the HIV status in the patient's EHR. However, despite this policy, a nurse can read information concerning AIDS in the patient's EHR and, thus, infer that the patient is HIV-positive.

The main problem is that the disclosure of data, which a user may not consider sensitive and thus he leaves unrestricted, can allow the inference of sensitive information that the user wants to keep private [1, 3, 7, 18, 37]. A cause of this undesirable behavior is that users often ignore the semantic relation between data when specifying their policies [12, 34, 41]. Without such a knowledge, users can end up with policies that do not reflect their privacy inclinations: policies can be either too restrictive or expose them to the risk of disclosing their personal information to a much wider audience than intended. However, users often have only a limited knowledge of the application domain. For instance, an "average" patient unlikely has knowledge of all medical terms and the relations between them, which is necessary to specify accurate and effective access control policies to protect information in an EHR.

This observation motivates our research question: *How to facilitate users in the specification of access control policies that effectively protect them against inference of sensitive information?*

In this paper we make three contributions to the authoring and enforcement of access control policies able to capture users' privacy constraints. First, we propose an access control model that prevents inference of sensitive information caused by the semantic relations between data. In particular, the access control model is based on a semantic approach which leverages knowledge about the application domain for access decision making. We represent domain knowledge along with the semantic relations between data in a data model. Intuitively, the data model organizes data within an application domain in a hierarchical structure as well as it makes semantic inference relations between data explicit. Based on these relations, it is possible to reason on situations in which access control policies grant access to data which make it possible to infer sensitive information a user would like to keep private. To this end, we study how information can be inferred through semantic relations between data and define authorization propagation rules that prevent the inference of information to be protected. These propagation rules form an inference control mechanism. Such a mechanism mitigates the impact of mistakes that users can make in the specification of their policies due to inaccurate or partial knowledge they have about the application domain. The access control model does not require users to define the data model and, thus, to have a deep knowledge of the application domain. We show how existing domain specific ontologies can be leveraged for the representation of domain knowledge, relieving users of the burden of its definition.

Second, we demonstrate that the proposed access control model can be implemented using existing access control mechanisms. In particular, we show that the model can be automatically translated in XACML [33], the de facto standard for the specification and enforcement of access control policies. To this end, we provide an encoding of the access control model and reasoning over the data model in XACML.

Last, we compare the effectiveness and efficiency of existing access control models with respect to our model. Our findings show that access control models that do not consider semantic relations between data as the basis for authorization decision making do not fully protect users from inference of sensitive information and require significant efforts in writing policies. In contrast, our access control model prevents semantic inference of sensitive information while reducing users' effort in policy authoring in that it minimizes the number of policy statements a user has to specify.

The remainder of the paper is structured as follows. Section 2 introduces the basic notation used to formalize the proposed model. Section 3 reviews existing access control models and presents their formalization using the notation introduced in Section 2. Then, Section 4 presents the proposed access control model. Section 5 illustrates how the policies and the reasoning on the data model can be encoded in XACML. Section 6 compares the effectiveness and efficiency of various access control models. Finally, Section 7 reviews related work, and Section 8 concludes the paper providing directions for future work.

2. BASIC NOTATION

In this section we introduce the basic concepts underlying our approach. First, we present a simple notation for the representation of access control policies that suffices for the purpose of this work. Then, we introduce a formal definition of access control model.

An access control policy specifies the permissions that are granted or denied for each subject, i.e. which actions a subject can perform on an object. Our notation distinguishes *positive authorizations* and *negative authorizations* to allow easy management of exceptions in policy definition.

DEFINITION 1. *Let S be a set of subjects, A a set of actions, D a set of data elements and $R = \{+, -\}$ the set of rulings. An access control policy is a tuple $\langle s, a, d, r \rangle$ with $s \in S$, $a \in A$, $d \in D$, and $r \in R$. We refer to access control policies of the form $\langle s, a, d, + \rangle$ as positive policies and to policies of the form $\langle s, a, d, - \rangle$ as negative policies.*

The first three elements of a policy (i.e., subject, action and object) define the target of the policy. Intuitively, the target of a policy represents the applicability space of the policy, i.e. to which access requests the policy is applicable. The ruling defines the effect of the policy where $+$ indicates Permit and $-$ indicates Deny. A positive policy $\langle s, a, d, + \rangle$ states that subject s is allowed to execute action a on data element d. Similarly, a negative policy $\langle s, a, d, - \rangle$ states that subject s is not allowed to execute action a on data element d. Hereafter, we denote $\mathcal{P}$ the set of access control policies, $\mathcal{P}^+ \subseteq \mathcal{P}$ the set of positive policies in $\mathcal{P}$, and $\mathcal{P}^- \subseteq \mathcal{P}$ the set of negative policies in $\mathcal{P}$.

EXAMPLE 1. *An example of positive policy is*

$$\langle doctor, read, medical\ record, + \rangle$$

with subject "doctor", action "read", object "medical record" and ruling "+". The policy should be read: "a doctor is allowed to read a medical record".

The effectiveness of a policy depends on the access control model used for its evaluation. In fact, an access control model determines how policies are evaluated based on the data structures used to organize and reason on the policy elements in the target. We define formally an access control model as follows. Note that, as the focus of this work is on information inference, in the definition we only consider the data structure used to represent data elements. However, the definition can be easily extended to consider data structures for subjects (e.g., role hierarchies) and actions.

DEFINITION 2. *An access control model is a tuple $\langle \mathcal{Q}, \mathcal{P}, \mathcal{DS}, [\![\cdot]\!]_{\mathcal{DS}} \rangle$ where $\mathcal{Q} \subseteq S \times A \times D$ is a set of access requests, $\mathcal{P}$ is a set of policies, $\mathcal{DS}$ is a data structure encoding the relationships between data elements, and $[\![\cdot]\!]_{\mathcal{DS}} : \mathcal{Q} \times \wp(\mathcal{P}) \rightarrow \{\text{Permit, Deny, NotApplicable}\}$ is an evaluation function mapping an access request to an access decision based on $\mathcal{P}$ and $\mathcal{DS}$.*

An evaluation function should determine the applicability of policies for a given access request and, based on the applicable policies, map the request to an access decision. We use the predicate $match(q, \mathcal{P})$ to denote that there is a policy $P \in \mathcal{P}$ that directly matches a request $q \in \mathcal{Q}$, i.e. the elements in the request match the elements in the policy. The predicate $match$ can be defined in the straightforward way over the target of a policy. In this work, we are mainly interested to study the behavior of access control models with respect to data elements. Thus, abusing notation, we will write $[\![d, \mathcal{P}]\!]_{\mathcal{DS}}$ to represent the evaluation of an access request for data element d against a set of policies $\mathcal{P}$, and $match(d, \mathcal{P})$ to represent there exists a policy $P \in \mathcal{P}$ that matches a request for d.

The combined use of both positive and negative authorizations can lead to conflicts when conflicting policies are applicable for

Reference Model	Data Structure	Evaluation Function		Existing Models
$\mathcal{AC}_{\mathcal{NR}} = \langle \mathcal{Q}, \mathcal{P}, \mathcal{NR}, [\![\cdot]\!]_{\mathcal{NR}} \rangle$	$\mathcal{NR}$: No relations	$[\![d, \mathcal{P}]\!]_{\mathcal{NR}} = \begin{cases} & \\ & \\ & \end{cases}$	Deny — if $match(d, \mathcal{P}^-)$ Permit — if $match(d, \mathcal{P}^+) \wedge [\![d,\mathcal{P}]\!]_{\mathcal{NR}} \neq$ Deny NotApplicable — otherwise	System R [6]
$\mathcal{AC}_{\mathcal{DH}_1} = \langle \mathcal{Q}, \mathcal{P}, \mathcal{DH}, [\![\cdot]\!]_{\mathcal{DH}_1} \rangle$	$\mathcal{DH}$: Data Hierarchy	$[\![d, \mathcal{P}]\!]_{\mathcal{DH}_1} =$	Deny — if $\exists d_i \in D$ s.t. $d_i \in d^\uparrow \wedge match(d, \mathcal{P}^-)$ Permit — if $(\exists d_i \in D$ s.t. $d_i \in d^\uparrow \wedge match(d, \mathcal{P}^+))$ $\wedge [\![d,\mathcal{P}]\!]_{\mathcal{DH}_1} \neq$ Deny NotApplicable — otherwise	FAF [23] WDAP [36] PBAC [11] Lee et al. [27] Masoumzadeh et al. [28]
$\mathcal{AC}_{\mathcal{DH}_2} = \langle \mathcal{Q}, \mathcal{P}, \mathcal{DH}, [\![\cdot]\!]_{\mathcal{DH}_2} \rangle$	$\mathcal{DH}$: Data Hierarchy	$[\![d, \mathcal{P}]\!]_{\mathcal{DH}_2} =$	Deny — if $\exists d_i \in D$ s.t. $d_i \in d^\downarrow \wedge match(d, \mathcal{P}^-)$ Permit — if $(\exists d_i \in D$ s.t. $d_i \in d^\uparrow \wedge match(d, \mathcal{P}^+))$ $\wedge [\![d,\mathcal{P}]\!]_{\mathcal{DH}_2} \neq$ Deny NotApplicable — otherwise	Rabitti et al. [35]
$\mathcal{AC}_{\mathcal{DH}_3} = \langle \mathcal{Q}, \mathcal{P}, \mathcal{DH}, [\![\cdot]\!]_{\mathcal{DH}_3} \rangle$	$\mathcal{DH}$: Data Hierarchy	$[\![d, \mathcal{P}]\!]_{\mathcal{DH}_3} =$	Deny — if $\exists d_i \in D$ s.t. $d_i \in d^\updownarrow \wedge match(d, \mathcal{P}^-)$ Permit — if $(\exists d_i \in D$ s.t. $d_i \in d^\uparrow \wedge match(d, \mathcal{P}^+))$ $\wedge [\![d,\mathcal{P}]\!]_{\mathcal{DH}_3} \neq$ Deny NotApplicable — otherwise	EPAL [4] DPAL [5]
$\mathcal{AC}_{\mathcal{DM}} = \langle \mathcal{Q}, \mathcal{P}, \mathcal{DM}, [\![\cdot]\!]_{\mathcal{DM}} \rangle$	$\mathcal{DM}$: Data Model	$[\![d, \mathcal{P}]\!]_{\mathcal{DM}} =$	Deny — if $\big(\exists d_i \in D$ s.t. $d_i \in d^\downarrow \wedge match(d_i, \mathcal{P}^-)\big) \vee$ $\big(\exists d_i \in D$ s.t. $d_i \in d^\infty \wedge match(d_i, \mathcal{P}^-)\big)$ Permit — if $\exists d_i \in D$ s.t. $(d_i \in d^\uparrow \wedge match(d_i, \mathcal{P}^+))$ $\wedge [\![d,\mathcal{P}]\!]_{\mathcal{DM}} \neq$ Deny NotApplicable — otherwise	this work

Table 1: Overview of access control models

the same data element. Several conflict resolution strategies have been proposed in the literature [4, 23, 29]. As our goal is to prevent leakages of sensitive information, we assume that an evaluation function combines conflicting (applicable) policies using a deny-overrides strategy, where negative authorizations override positive authorizations.

3. REVIEW OF ACCESS CONTROL MODELS

Several access control models have been proposed in the literature to regulate the access to sensitive information. Access control models use an evaluation function to determine the policies that apply to a given access request and, based on the applicable policies, make an authorization decision. The definition of such an evaluation function depends on the data structure used by the access control model to reason on the elements in the target of a policy. In the remainder of this section, we review a number of existing access control models, focusing on the data element as the main decision criterion. An overview of the considered models is presented in Table 1. Note that, for the sake of comparison, we limit our study to access control models that explicitly support both positive and negative authorizations.

Early access control models like the one presented in [6] do not consider relationships between data elements for decision making. In these models, a policy is applied to an access request for a data element only if the policy has been explicitly specified for that data element. Hereafter, $[\![\cdot]\!]_{\mathcal{NR}}$ denotes a policy evaluation function that does not use relations between data elements to make access decision, and $\mathcal{AC}_{\mathcal{NR}}$ access control models that use such a function (a formal definition of $[\![\cdot]\!]_{\mathcal{NR}}$ and $\mathcal{AC}_{\mathcal{NR}}$ is given in Table 1).

To effectively reduce the number of permission assignments (and thus reducing the cost of policy administration), several access control models [4, 11, 23, 38, 35] represent and reason on data elements in a policy using hierarchical structures.

DEFINITION 3. *A data hierarchy $\mathcal{DH}$ is a pair $\langle D, \uparrow \rangle$ where*

- *D is a set of data elements;*
- *$\uparrow \subseteq D \times D$ a partial order on D.*

A data hierarchy $\mathcal{DH}$ organizes data elements in direct acyclic graph (DAG). Hierarchy relations represent a specialization relationship between data elements, i.e. $(d', d) \in \uparrow$ denotes that d' is

a specialization of d. Based on hierarchy relations we define the descendants and ancestors of a node d. A data element d' is a *descendant* of a data element d if d' is either a child of d (i.e., $(d', d) \in \uparrow$) or the child of some descendants of d. A data element d' is an *ancestor* of a data element d if d' is either a parent of d (i.e., $(d, d') \in \uparrow$) or the parent of some ancestors of d. The set of descendants of a data element d, including the data element itself, is denoted $d^\downarrow$. The set of ancestors of a data element d, including the data element itself, is denoted $d^\uparrow$. $d^\updownarrow$ denotes the set of ancestors or descendants of d, i.e. $d^\updownarrow = d^\downarrow \cup d^\uparrow$.

Different propagation rules over data hierarchies have been proposed for policy evaluation. Some access control models (e.g., [23, 27, 28, 36]) assume that both positive and negative authorizations are propagated down the data hierarchy.[1] Intuitively, positive and negative authorizations propagate to the descendants of the data element specified in a policy. Byun and Li [11] annotate data elements with intended purpose labels (representing the allowed and prohibited intended usage of data), and use these labels to control access to data elements. To determine the effective intended purpose of data elements, they present a purpose inference mechanism that propagates the intended purpose of a data element to its child elements, thus propagating authorizations down the data hierarchy.[2] We use $[\![\cdot]\!]_{\mathcal{DH}_1}$ to denote the evaluation function using these propagation rules and $\mathcal{AC}_{\mathcal{DH}_1}$ the corresponding access control models (see Table 1 for their formalization).

Other access control models (e.g., [35]) use different propagation rules for negative authorizations. In particular, these models propagate negative authorizations up the data hierarchy, i.e. negative authorizations are propagate to the ancestors of the data ele-

---

[1]Note that a number of propagation policies are presented in [23], namely *no propagation*, *no overriding*, *most specific overrides* and *path overrides*. In this work, we consider the *no overrides* policy in which all the authorizations of a node are propagated to its child nodes, regardless of the presence of other contradicting authorizations. However, it is worth noting that the other policies also propagate authorizations down the data hierarchy.

[2]The work in [11] also uses propagations rules which support the inheritance of negative authorizations up the hierarchy like in [4, 5]. However, these rules are limited to the reasoning over the purpose hierarchy and are not used to reason over the data hierarchy.

ments for which a negative policy is defined.[3] In the remainder, we denote $[\![\cdot]\!]_{\mathcal{DH}_2}$ the evaluation function based on these propagation rules and $\mathcal{AC}_{\mathcal{DH}_2}$ the corresponding access control models. Their formalization is given in Table 1.

Some access control models like EPAL [4] and DPAL [5], combine the propagation rules underlying $\mathcal{AC}_{\mathcal{DH}_1}$ and $\mathcal{AC}_{\mathcal{DH}_2}$. These models propagate positive authorizations down the data hierarchy. On the other hand, negative authorizations are inherited both up and down the data hierarchies. Intuitively, negative authorizations are propagated to the ancestors and descendants of the data element for which a negative policy is defined. In the remainder, we denote $[\![\cdot]\!]_{\mathcal{DH}_3}$ the evaluation function based on these propagation rules and $\mathcal{AC}_{\mathcal{DH}_3}$ the corresponding access control models. Their formalization is given in Table 1.

4. PREVENTING INFORMATION INFERENCE

The access control models discussed in the previous section are not able to protect end-users from situations in which other users can infer sensitive information from information to which they have legitimate access. The main reason is that they do not account for the semantic relations between data elements when making authorization decisions. For example, it is possible to infer whether a patient is HIV-positive by knowing that the patient has AIDS or the T-helper cell count[4]. Thus, an access control model that does not rely on the semantic relation between data elements, will inevitably lead to information leakage.

To address these issues, we propose a semantic approach which enables to reason on the information that can be inferred from the disclosure of a data element. The approach is based on a data model that augments a data hierarchy with inference relations between data elements.

DEFINITION 4. *A data model* $\mathcal{DM}$ *is a tuple* $\langle D, \uparrow, \rightarrow \rangle$ *where*

- *D is a set of data elements;*
- $\uparrow \subseteq D \times D$ *is a partial order on D;*
- $\rightarrow \subseteq D \times D$ *represents an inference relation on D.*

Intuitively, a data model encodes the domain knowledge, making the semantic relation between data elements within the application domain explicit. As discussed in Section 3, hierarchy relations represent the specialization relation between data elements. Inference relations $(d', d) \in \rightarrow$ indicate that by knowing a data element d', a user knows data element d. We denote $\rightarrow^R$ the reflexive closure of $\rightarrow$. We say that a data element d' is *reachable* from a data element d, denoted $(d, d') \in \rightsquigarrow$, if and only if $\exists d_i \in d^{\uparrow}$ s.t. $(d_i, d') \in \rightarrow^R$. We denote $\rightsquigarrow^*$ the transitive closure of $\rightsquigarrow$. d^{∞} denotes the set of data elements that are reachable from a data element d, i.e. $d^{\infty} = \bigcup_{(d,d_i) \in \rightsquigarrow^*} d_i^{\uparrow}$.

It is worth noting that our approach does not require policy authors to define the data model and thus to have a deep knowledge of the application domain. Domain knowledge is often represented using an ontology, and several ontologies are currently available for a large range of application domains, e.g. FOAF[5] for social networks, GoodRelations [19] and CContology [24] for e-commerce,

---

[3] The access control model in [35] uses special actions, e.g. *Read Definition*, for which positive authorizations are propagated up the data hierarchy and negative authorizations are propagated down the hierarchy. We do not consider these actions in our model.

[4] The HIV virus attacks T-helper cells, destroying them.

[5] http://www.foaf-project.org

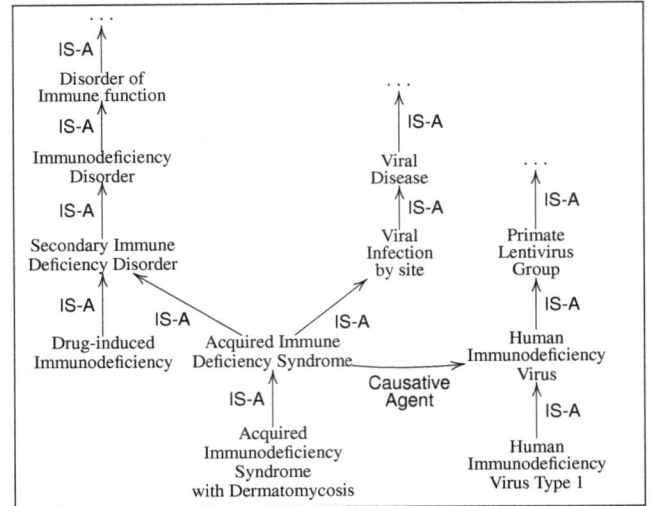

(a) Fragment of SNOMED-CT

Data Model	SNOMED-CT
Nodes	Concepts
Hierarchy relations (↑)	IS-A relationship
Inference relations (→)	Attribute relationships

(b) Mapping of the data model to SNOMED-CT

Figure 1: Data model instantiation in the healthcare domain.

and many others. These ontologies can be used as a representation of the data model. Next, we show an exemplification of how the data model can be implemented through an ontology within the healthcare domain.

EXAMPLE 2. *Let us illustrate how the proposed data model can be instantiated in the healthcare domain using SNOMED Clinical Terms (SNOMED-CT) [21], one of the most complete and used medical ontologies. SNOMED-CT provides a comprehensive and structured collection of medical terms often used in electronic health records along with relations between them. SNOMED-CT includes terms related to clinical findings, symptoms, diagnoses, procedures, body structures, organisms and other etiologies, substances, pharmaceuticals, devices and specimen. Fig. 1a presents a fragment of SNOMED-CT, and Fig. 1b the mapping of the data model to SNOMED-CT. In SNOMED-CT a concept is a clinical meaning identified by a unique identifier. The meaning of concepts is defined in terms of the relationships with other concepts. SNOMED-CT uses the* IS-A *relationship to represent hierarchical associations between entity types (i.e., generalization/specialization relationship). In particular, this relationship organizes concepts into DAGs where concepts can have multiple parent nodes. For instance, the term* Acquired Immune Deficiency Syndrome *(AIDS) is child of both terms* Secondary Immune Deficiency Disorder *and* Viral Infection by site*. SNOMED-CT also provides a number of attribute relationships which define interrelationships between concepts. In particular, an attribute relationship is an association between two concepts describing an intrinsic property of the concepts. Attribute relationships can be used to infer additional information about a data element. For instance, SNOMED-CT relates the term* Acquired Immune Deficiency Syndrome *to the term* Human Immunodeficiency Virus *(HIV) using attribute relationship* Causative Agent*; knowing that a patient has AIDS reveals that she is HIV-positive.*

90

Given a data model $\mathcal{DM}$, we are interested in an access control model $\langle \mathcal{Q}, \mathcal{P}, \mathcal{DM}, \llbracket \cdot \rrbracket_{\mathcal{DM}} \rangle$ which uses $\mathcal{DM}$ to make authorization decisions. To this end, we have to define an evaluation function $\llbracket \cdot \rrbracket_{\mathcal{DM}}$ which allows propagation of positive and negative authorizations along with hierarchical and inference relations in the data model. For the propagation through data hierarchies, we adopt the approach proposed in [4, 5]. As shown in Section 6, other propagation rules over data hierarchies do not capture user intention properly and/or require additional effort for policy authoring.

Inference relationships only propagate negative authorizations (in the opposite direction of the inference). The reason is that by explicitly denying the access to a data element a policy author intends to restrict the access to such a data element. Therefore, the access to all data elements that allow its inference should be restricted. On the other hand, allowing the access to a data element does not imply that the access to data elements from which it can be inferred should be allowed. We can observe that the set of data elements that can be inferred by a data element is the set of data elements reachable from that data element. Indeed, by definition, a data element is reachable from another data element if the former can be inferred by the latter. Moreover, reachability is defined over bottom-up propagation of negative authorizations through data hierarchies. This is motivated by the fact that knowledge of a data element makes it possible to infer information on the ancestors of that data element. Conversely, knowledge of a data element does not imply a leakage of information about the descendants of that data element. For instance, knowing that a patient has Disorder of Immune function does not allow a nurse to infer that the patient has Acquired Immune Deficiency Syndrome. Indeed the patient might be affected by Drug-induced Immunodeficiency or other diseases (not represented in Fig. 1a).

The following definition formally defines the evaluation function $\llbracket \cdot \rrbracket_{\mathcal{DM}}$.

DEFINITION 5. *Let* $\mathcal{DM} = \langle D, \uparrow, \rightarrow \rangle$ *be a data model and* $\langle \mathcal{Q}, \mathcal{P}, \mathcal{DM}, \llbracket \cdot \rrbracket_{\mathcal{DM}} \rangle$ *an access control model using* $\mathcal{DM}$ *for decision making. Given a request for data element* $d \in D$, *the evaluation function* $\llbracket \cdot \rrbracket_{\mathcal{DM}}$ *is*

$$
\llbracket d, \mathcal{P} \rrbracket_{\mathcal{DM}} = \begin{cases} \text{Deny} & \begin{aligned} &\textit{if } match(d, \mathcal{P}^-) \vee \\ &(\exists d_i \in D \textit{ s.t. } d_i \in d^{\updownarrow} \wedge \\ &match(d_i, \mathcal{P}^-)) \vee \\ &(\exists d_i \in D \textit{ s.t. } d_i \in d^{\infty} \wedge \\ &match(d_i, \mathcal{P}^-)) \end{aligned} \\ \text{Permit} & \begin{aligned} &\textit{if } \big[match(d, \mathcal{P}^+) \vee \\ &\exists d_i \in D \textit{ s.t. } \big(d_i \in d^{\uparrow} \wedge \\ &match(d_i, \mathcal{P}^+) \big) \big] \wedge \\ &\llbracket d, \mathcal{P} \rrbracket_{\mathcal{DM}} \neq \text{Deny} \end{aligned} \\ \text{NotApplicable} & \textit{otherwise} \end{cases}
$$

The definition of the evaluation function $\llbracket \cdot \rrbracket_{\mathcal{DM}}$ explicitly encodes the propagation rules discussed above. It is worth noting that such a definition is redundant. For instance, by definition $d^{\updownarrow}$, $d^{\updownarrow}$ and d^{∞} include data element d. Moreover, $d^{\updownarrow}$ and d^{∞} are not disjoint, i.e. $d^{\updownarrow} \cap d^{\infty} = d^{\uparrow}$. Based on these observations, the evaluation function $\llbracket \cdot \rrbracket_{\mathcal{DM}}$ can be rewritten as shown at the end of Table 1.

EXAMPLE 3. *Consider an Electronic Healthcare Record (EHR) whose fields and entries are defined over SNOMED-CT. Let us suppose that the record belongs to a patient named Alice who is affected by AIDS. Alice is highly concerned about revealing she has contracted a virus in the primate lentivirus group. Thus, she defines a negative authorization stating that access to her status concerning* Primate Lentivirus Group *in her EHR is denied to any nurse.*

At the same time, Alice allows nurses working in the hospital where she is hospitalized to access information about Immunodeficiency Disorder *in order to receive proper treatment. These authorizations are represented by the following policies*

$$P_1 = \langle nurse, read, \text{Primate Lentivirus Group}, - \rangle$$
$$P_2 = \langle nurse, read, \text{Immunodeficiency Disorder}, + \rangle$$

If only data hierarchies are used to evaluate access requests, a nurse is allowed to know that the patient has AIDS. Indeed, the positive authorization defined by policy P_2 *is propagated to the descendants of* Immunodeficiency Disorder *and, thus, to* Acquired Immune Deficiency Syndrome. *This, however, allows the nurse to infer that Alice has contracted a virus in the primate lentivirus group, violating policy* P_1. *Reasoning over inference relationships makes it possible to propagate the negative authorization associated with* Primate Lentivirus Group *to* Acquired Immune Deficiency Syndrome. *As authorizations are combined using deny-overrides, the access to* Acquired Immune Deficiency Syndrome *is denied and, thus, the actual permissions on the data element comply with Alice's privacy constraints.*

We remark that the aim of this work is the design of an access control model that prevents inference of sensitive information due to explicit inference relations between data elements. In this setting, the absence of an inference relation does not necessarily indicate that a data element cannot be inferred, for instance using statistical methods.

5. POLICY ENCODING AND ENFORCING IN XACML

In this section we demonstrate how the proposed access control model can be implemented using existing access control mechanisms. In particular, we present an encoding of the access control model in eXtensible Access Control Markup Language (XACML) [33], the de facto standard for the specification and enforcement of access control policies. The advantage of encoding the access control model in XACML is that there exist several XACML policy engines, many of which are free to use. These engines usually support basic functionalities needed for policy evaluation like the matching of access requests against policies.

Next, we first present the encoding of authorization policies defined using the notation presented in Section 2; then, we present how these policies are combined to support the reasoning on the data model presented in Section 4.

5.1 Encoding Policies in XACML

We show here how authorization policies written in the notation introduced in Section 2 can be easily transformed into enforceable policies written in XACML. Here we only discuss the elements needed to encode our access control model and refer to [33] for the complete XACML policy language specification.

Positive and negative authorizations are represented using the `<Rule>` element whose `Effect` attribute is set respectively to `Permit` and `Deny`. Intuitively, the `Effect` attribute encodes the ruling of a policy (Definition 1). The subject s and action a are represented as attributes and, thus, mapped to `<Match>` elements in `<Target>` of the `<Rule>` element. The encoding of data element d requires considering the propagation rules; its encoding is presented in the next section.

Rules, however, are not intended to be evaluated in isolation by the policy decision point (PDP) in XACML. The basic unit of policy used by the PDP for evaluation is the `<Policy>` element [33,

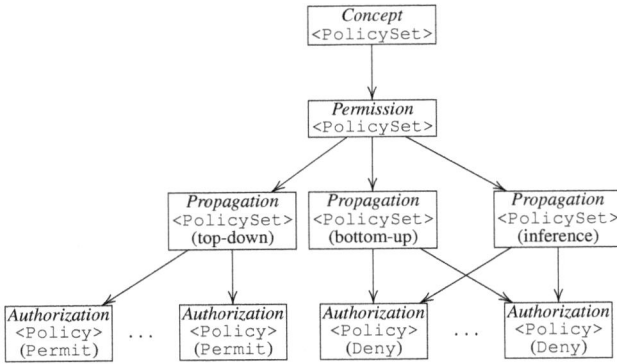

Figure 2: Policy Structure

Section 2.2]. To this end, we wrap each `<Rule>` element into a `<Policy>` element (with an empty `<Target>`). In the next section, we discuss how these policies are combined.

5.2 Encoding the Data Model in XACML

A natural choice to represent data hierarchies in XACML would be to adopt the XACML Hierarchical Resource Profile [32], which illustrates how to specify XACML policies for resources that are structured as hierarchies. However, this profile does not distinguish the propagation of positive and negative authorizations, which is necessary to implement the propagation strategy over the data model. To this end, we represent the data model in terms of the policy structure along the lines suggested in the XACML RBAC Profile [31] to deal with role hierarchies. This profile distinguished between *Permission* `<PolicySet>`, which contains the actual permissions associated with a role, and *Role* `<PolicySet>`, which associates the role with the corresponding permissions. A Permission `<PolicySet>` can contain references to the Permission `<PolicySet>` elements associated with other roles, thus enabling permission propagation through role hierarchies.

We use a similar approach to enable the permission propagation over the data model. Every data element in the data model is associated with a XACML policy encoding all the policies specified for the data element. These XACML policies consist of four parts (Fig. 2): a *Concept* `<PolicySet>` element, a *Permission* `<PolicySet>` element, *Propagation* `<PolicySet>` elements, and *Authorization* `<Policy>` elements. The Concept `<PolicySet>` specifies the data element to which the policy applies, while the Permission `<PolicySet>` is used to manage the actual authorizations over such a data element. The data element is specified as an attribute (i.e., a `<Match>` element) in the `<Target>` element of a Concept `<PolicySet>`; the Concept `<PolicySet>` element references a single Permission `<PolicySet>`, which in turn contains references to Propagation `<PolicySet>` elements. In turn, Propagation `<PolicySet>` elements reference Authorization `<Policy>` elements which encode the actual authorizations over the data element as described in Section 5.1. The extra layer given by the Propagation `<PolicySet>` elements is needed to prevent loops in the policy structure due to up and down inheritance through data hierarchies and thus to properly implement the evaluation function $[\![\cdot]\!]_{\mathcal{DM}}$.

The XACML policy associated with a data element contains three Propagation `<PolicySet>` elements, one for top-down inheritance over data hierarchies, one for bottom-up inheritance over data hierarchies and one for inference (defined in terms of reachability). The top-down Propagation `<PolicySet>` contains references to

the positive Authorization `<Policy>` elements, i.e. to `<Policy>` elements that only contain a `Permit` rule.[6] In addition, it contains a policy reference to the top-down Propagation `<PolicySet>` associated with the parent node(s) in the data model. This way, the data element inherits the (positive) policies of the parent node(s). The bottom-up and inference Propagation `<PolicySet>` elements are only linked to negative Authorization `<Policy>` elements, i.e. to `<Policy>` elements that only contain a `Deny` rule. This construction guarantees that only the propagation of negative authorizations can occur up a hierarchy or through inference relations. To inherit the negative authorizations of the child node(s), the bottom-up Propagation `<PolicySet>` also contains a policy reference to the bottom-up Propagation `<PolicySet>` of the child node(s) in the data model. Inference relations and top-down propagation of negative authorizations are encoded in a similar way. Let x be the node for which the policy is defined. For each inference relation $(x, y) \in \rightarrow$, a policy reference to the inference Propagation `<PolicySet>` associated with the node y is added to the inference Propagation `<PolicySet>` associated with x. The inference Propagation `<PolicySet>` also contains a reference to the inference Propagation `<PolicySet>` of the parent node(s). This combination of inference and hierarchical relations captures the notion of reachability, thus allowing the inheritance of the (negative) authorizations associated with the data elements that can be inferred from the disclosure of the data element.

To enable propagation through data hierarchies and inference relations, the `<Target>` element of Permission `<PolicySet>` elements should not constraint the data element to which the policy element applies. Consequently, Permission `<PolicySet>`, Propagation `<PolicySet>` and Authorization `<Policy>` elements cannot be root policies, i.e. they cannot be directly evaluated by the PDP. Policy elements are combined using the `deny-overrides` combining algorithm. Intuitively, if one of these policies evaluates `Deny`, the access to the data element is denied.

Encoding the evaluation function within the policy structure makes it possible to build a simple and automated procedure for the construction of XACML policies implementing the evaluation function $[\![\cdot]\!]_{\mathcal{DM}}$. In addition, this approach provides the flexibility necessary to support the adoption of different strategies for policy evaluation. For instance, it allows the implementation of an evaluation strategy based on the specificity level of policies [23, 29]. Intuitively, this strategy gives higher priority to policies that are more specific. Specificity can be implemented using the `first-applicable` combining algorithm. In particular, the policies associated with a data element and with the data elements that can be inferred from it can be combined using `deny-overrides`. The resulting policy can be combined with the policies of the parent node(s) using `first-applicable`. This ensures that the policy of parent node(s) is evaluated only if the policies specific for the data element are not applicable.

It is worth noting that, although the proposed encoding requires the definition of a XACML policy for each data element in the application domain, only the Concept `<PolicySet>` concerning the requested data element is applicable. Thus, only the applicable Concept `<PolicySet>` and the policy elements reachable from it are evaluated, making policy evaluation independent from the size of the application domain in terms of data elements.

---

[6]Remark that in our construction Authorization `<Policy>` elements contain a single rule.

6. EVALUATION AND COMPARISON

In this section we analyze the effectiveness and efficiency of the access control models in Table 1 with respect to $\mathcal{AC}_{\mathcal{DM}}$. In particular, we study the impact of using inference relations on the specification and evaluation of access control policies. *Effectiveness* characterizes the completeness and accuracy of access control policies, while *efficiency* characterizes the effort (in relation to the completeness and accuracy) needed to specify the policies [22].

Evaluation Framework.

To measure the effectiveness and efficiency of an access control model, we introduce an evaluation framework consisting of a number of metrics. These metrics are defined in terms of *explicitly protected data* and *intended protected data*. To formally define the metrics, we introduce the following notation.

Let $\mathcal{DM} = \langle D, \uparrow, \rightarrow \rangle$ be a data model and $\mathcal{P}$ a set of policies. The set of data elements explicitly protected by $\mathcal{P}$ is the set of data elements for which a policy is defined. Specifically, we have $D_{Exp}^{\mathcal{P}^+} = \{d : match(d, \mathcal{P}^+)\}$ and $D_{Exp}^{\mathcal{P}^-} = \{d : match(d, \mathcal{P}^-)\}$. The set of intended protected data is the set of data elements whose access needs to be regulated in order to capture a user's privacy constraints according to the domain knowledge encoded in $\mathcal{DM}$. Specifically, we have $D_{Int}^{\mathcal{P}^-} = \{d_i : d_i \in d^{\downarrow} \wedge d \in D_{Exp}^{\mathcal{P}^-}\} \cup \{d_i : d_i \in d^{\infty} \wedge d \in D_{Exp}^{\mathcal{P}^-}\}$ and $D_{Int}^{\mathcal{P}^+} = \{d_i : d_i \in d^{\uparrow} \wedge d \in D_{Exp}^{\mathcal{P}^+}\} \setminus D_{Int}^{\mathcal{P}^-}$. In other words, the set of intended protected data correspond to the evaluation function $[\![\cdot]\!]_{\mathcal{DM}}$.

Let $\mathcal{AC} = \langle \mathcal{Q}, \mathcal{P}, \mathcal{DS}, [\![\cdot]\!]_{\mathcal{DS}} \rangle$ be an access control model. The *accuracy* of $\mathcal{AC}$ is assessed using the following metrics:

(M_1) Number of cases where a user intends to deny the access to a data element, while access is not denied by the access control model.

$$M_1 = \left| D_{Int}^{\mathcal{P}^-} \setminus \{d \in D : [\![d, \mathcal{P}]\!]_{\mathcal{DS}} = \mathsf{Deny}\} \right|$$

(M_2) Number of cases where a user intends to permit the access to a data element, while access is not granted by the access control model.

$$M_2 = \left| D_{Int}^{\mathcal{P}^+} \setminus \{d \in D : [\![d, \mathcal{P}]\!]_{\mathcal{DS}} = \mathsf{Permit}\} \right|$$

(M_3) Number of cases where data elements could be leaked.

$$M_3 = \left| D_{Int}^{\mathcal{P}^-} \cap \{d \in D : [\![d, \mathcal{P}]\!]_{\mathcal{DS}} = \mathsf{Permit}\} \right|$$

(M_4) Number of cases where the availability of data elements is not guaranteed.

$$M_4 = \left| D_{Int}^{\mathcal{P}^+} \cap \{d \in D : [\![d, \mathcal{P}]\!]_{\mathcal{DS}} = \mathsf{Deny}\} \right|$$

These metrics aims to verify to what extent a policy evaluated with respect to a given access control model is able to capture a user's intention. In particular, M_1 checks whether a policy is less restrictive than what the user wants, while M_2 checks whether a policy is more restrictive than what the user wants. M_3 refines M_1 by checking whether access that should be denied is instead permitted. Similarly, M_4 refines M_2 by checking whether access that should be permitted is instead denied. In order to achieve accuracy, the objective of an access control model is to minimize these metrics.

The *completeness* of $\mathcal{AC}$ is assessed by measuring the coverage of $\mathcal{P}$. Coverage is evaluated using the following metric:

(M_5) Fraction of data elements that are correctly protected by $\mathcal{P}$ over the set of intended protected data.

$$M_5 = \frac{\left| \left(D_{Int}^{\mathcal{P}^+} \cap \{d \in D : [\![d, \mathcal{P}]\!]_{\mathcal{DS}} = \mathsf{Permit}\} \right) \cup \left(D_{Int}^{\mathcal{P}^-} \cap \{d \in D : [\![d, \mathcal{P}]\!]_{\mathcal{DS}} = \mathsf{Deny}\} \right) \right|}{\left| D_{Int}^{\mathcal{P}^+} \cup D_{Int}^{\mathcal{P}^-} \right|}$$

Intuitively, coverage determines to what extent a policy evaluated in a given access control model is able to capture the set of intended protected data. In order to achieve completeness, the objective of an access control model is to maximize this metric.

The *efficiency* of $\mathcal{AC}$ is measured by the following metric:

(M_6) Number of policies to be specified by a user in order to capture her intention.

$$M_6 = \min \left\{ \mid D_{Ext}^{\mathcal{P}^+} \mid + \mid D_{Ext}^{\mathcal{P}^-} \mid \text{ s.t. } M_5 = 1 \right\}$$

The number of policies explicitly specified by a user quantifies the effort that the user has to spend to cover the set of intended protected data. Higher is the number of policies, higher is the complexity of specifying policies for the user. Therefore, in order to achieve efficiency, the objective of an access control model is to minimize this metric.

Evaluation Settings.

We have compared a number of existing access control models with $\mathcal{AC}_{\mathcal{DM}}$. In particular, we have analyzed the impact of the data model on the specification and evaluation of access control policies with respect to other data structures and propagation rules (Table 1). Recall that $\mathcal{AC}_{\mathcal{NR}}$ is representative of access control models that do not use relations between data elements, while $\mathcal{AC}_{\mathcal{DH}_1}$, $\mathcal{AC}_{\mathcal{DH}_2}$ and $\mathcal{AC}_{\mathcal{DH}_3}$ are representative of models which use data hierarchies. As discussed in Section 3, these models differ in the way negative authorizations are propagated.

The access control models in Table 1 and the evaluation framework have been implemented in Datalog. In particular, the Datalog program encodes the evaluation function (i.e., propagation rules and combining algorithm) for each access control model as well as the metrics M_1 to M_6.

To evaluate and compare the completeness, accuracy and efficiency of the access control models, we generated three sets of policies $\mathcal{P}_1, \mathcal{P}_2, \mathcal{P}_3$ protecting access to an EHR specified over a vocabulary consisting of 100 terms (taken from the SNOMED-CT ontology). Each set of policies $\mathcal{P}_i$ ($i = 1, \dots, 3$) defines the set of data elements to which access is explicitly permitted (i.e., $D_{Ext}^{\mathcal{P}_i^+}$) and denied (i.e., $D_{Ext}^{\mathcal{P}_i^-}$) by a user. From these sets, we computed the sets of intended protected data $D_{Int}^{\mathcal{P}_i^+}$ and $D_{Int}^{\mathcal{P}_i^-}$. Sets $D_{Int}^{\mathcal{P}_i^+}$ and $D_{Int}^{\mathcal{P}_i^-}$ have been used as a reference model for the evaluation.

To study the efficiency of access control models and their ability to capture user intention, for every set of policies $\mathcal{P}_i$ ($i = 1, \dots, 3$) and access control model $\mathcal{AC}_j$ ($j = \mathcal{NR}, \mathcal{DH}_1, \mathcal{DH}_2, \mathcal{DH}_3, \mathcal{DM}$), we specified a policy set $\mathcal{P}_i^j$ that captures $D_{Int}^{\mathcal{P}_i^+}$ and $D_{Int}^{\mathcal{P}_i^-}$ using the minimal number of policy statements with respect to $\mathcal{AC}_j$. When an access control model is not able to fully cover both $D_{Int}^{\mathcal{P}_i^+}$ and $D_{Int}^{\mathcal{P}_i^-}$, we defined the minimal policy set that fully cover $D_{Int}^{\mathcal{P}_i^-}$ while maximizing the coverage of $D_{Int}^{\mathcal{P}_i^+}$. This represents the minimal policy set that prevent the risk of data leakage with respect to the access control model.

The three policy sets were passed as an input to the Datalog program which evaluated them with respect to the access control models in Table 1 and returned the metrics M_1 to M_6 for each access control model.

$\mathcal{P}_i$	AC_{NR}						AC_{DH_1}						AC_{DH_2}						AC_{DH_3}						AC_{DM}					
	M_1	M_2	M_3	M_4	M_5	M_6	M_1	M_2	M_3	M_4	M_5	M_6	M_1	M_2	M_3	M_4	M_5	M_6	M_1	M_2	M_3	M_4	M_5	M_6	M_1	M_2	M_3	M_4	M_5	M_6
$\mathcal{P}_1^{DM}$	56	5	1	0	0.13		29	0	12	0	0.58		51	0	13	0	0.27		24	0	12	0	0.66		0	0	0	0	1	10
$\mathcal{P}_1^{DH_3}$	42	5	1	0	0.33		4	0	0	0	0.94		38	2	7	2	0.43		0	2	0	2	0.97	24	–	–	–	–	–	–
$\mathcal{P}_1^{DH_2}$	12	5	0	0	0.76		6	0	0	0	0.91		0	2	0	2	0.97	64	–	–	–	–	–	–	–	–	–	–	–	–
$\mathcal{P}_1^{DH_1}$	39	5	1	0	0.37		0	4	0	4	0.94	27	38	2	7	2	0.43		–	–	–	–	–	–	–	–	–	–	–	–
$\mathcal{P}_1^{NR}$	0	0	0	0	1	70	–	–	–	–	–	–	–	–	–	–	–	–	–	–	–	–	–	–	–	–	–	–	–	–
$\mathcal{P}_2^{DM}$	64	14	2	0	0.11		27	0	24	0	0.69		60	0	26	0	0.32		23	0	22	0	0.74		0	0	0	0	1	12
$\mathcal{P}_2^{DH_3}$	57	14	1	0	0.19		2	0	0	0	0.97		54	3	21	3	0.35		0	3	0	3	0.97	19	–	–	–	–	–	–
$\mathcal{P}_2^{DH_2}$	16	14	2	0	0.66		6	0	4	0	0.93		0	3	0	3	0.97	62	–	–	–	–	–	–	–	–	–	–	–	–
$\mathcal{P}_2^{DH_1}$	55	14	1	0	0.21		0	11	0	11	0.88	21	54	3	21	3	0.35		–	–	–	–	–	–	–	–	–	–	–	–
$\mathcal{P}_2^{NR}$	0	0	0	0	1	88	–	–	–	–	–	–	–	–	–	–	–	–	–	–	–	–	–	–	–	–	–	–	–	–
$\mathcal{P}_3^{DM}$	75	13	6	0	0.08		47	0	31	0	0.51		69	0	35	0	0.28		41	0	27	0	0.57		0	0	0	0	1	14
$\mathcal{P}_3^{DH_3}$	58	13	4	0	0.26		6	0	4	0	0.94		46	2	15	2	0.50		0	2	0	2	0.98	31	–	–	–	–	–	–
$\mathcal{P}_3^{DH_2}$	22	13	4	0	0.64		6	0	4	0	0.94		0	2	0	2	0.98	70	–	–	–	–	–	–	–	–	–	–	–	–
$\mathcal{P}_3^{DH_1}$	55	13	3	0	0.29		0	7	0	7	0.93	34	46	2	15	2	0.50		–	–	–	–	–	–	–	–	–	–	–	–
$\mathcal{P}_3^{NR}$	0	0	0	0	1	96	–	–	–	–	–	–	–	–	–	–	–	–	–	–	–	–	–	–	–	–	–	–	–	–

Table 2: Comparison of Access Control Models

Results.

Table 2 provides an overview of the results. For each policy set $\mathcal{P}_i^j$ (with $i \in \{1, \ldots, 3\}$ and $j \in \{NR, DH_1, DH_2, DH_3, DM\}$), the table reports the metrics M_1 to M_6 computed when the policy set is evaluated with respect to AC_{NR}, AC_{DH_1}, AC_{DH_2}, AC_{DH_3} and AC_{DM}. Note that we did not evaluate $\mathcal{P}_i^{DH_3}$ within AC_{DM}; $\mathcal{P}_i^{DH_1}$ and $\mathcal{P}_i^{DH_2}$ within AC_{DH_3} and AC_{DM}; and $\mathcal{P}_i^{NR}$ within AC_{DH_1}, AC_{DH_2}, AC_{DH_3} and AC_{DM}. This is because AC_{DM} has full coverage (i.e., $M_5 = 1$) for $\mathcal{P}_i^{DM}$, AC_{DH_3} has full coverage of $D_{Int}^{\mathcal{P}_i}$ for $\mathcal{P}_i^{DH_3}$, AC_{DH_2} has full coverage of $D_{Int}^{\mathcal{P}_i^-}$ for $\mathcal{P}_i^{DH_2}$, and AC_{DH_1} has full coverage of $D_{Int}^{\mathcal{P}_i^-}$ for $\mathcal{P}_i^{DH_1}$.

We can observe in the table that AC_{DM} achieves the best trade-off between *coverage* (M_5) and *efficiency* (M_6). In fact, AC_{DM} covers the set of intended protected data with a significantly less number of policies than AC_{NR}, AC_{DH_1}, AC_{DH_2} and AC_{DH_3}. For instance, $\mathcal{P}_1^{NR}$ consists of 70 policy statements, $\mathcal{P}_1^{DH_1}$ of 27 statements, $\mathcal{P}_1^{DH_2}$ of 64 statements and $\mathcal{P}_1^{DH_3}$ of 24 statements, while $\mathcal{P}_1^{DM}$ is formed by only 10 policy statements. In particular, to define a policy that covers the full set of intended protected data in AC_{NR}, a user has to define a policy for each data element in the set. However, the user can only do that if he has a deep knowledge of the application domain, which is rarely the case for an average user. In contrast, AC_{DM} relieves users of this burden by relying on a data model encoding the domain knowledge for decision making. Moreover, the results show that AC_{DH_2} requires the specification of a policy for a larger number of data elements compared to AC_{DH_1} and AC_{DH_3} in order to prevent the leakage of sensitive information. This is due to the fact that, when using AC_{DH_2}, policies have to be defined for leaf nodes, and in a data hierarchy the number of nodes in a stratum is usually larger than the number of nodes in the stratum immediately above it.

It is worth noting that it may not be possible to obtain full coverage of the set of intended protected data within AC_{DH_1}, AC_{DH_2} and AC_{DH_3}, i.e. there may not exist policy sets $\mathcal{P}_i^{DH_1}$, $\mathcal{P}_i^{DH_2}$ and $\mathcal{P}_i^{DH_3}$ respectively, such that $M_5 = 1$. In order to define a policy capturing their privacy constraints, users should know the data elements that allow the inference of the data elements to which they wants to restrict the access and define negative authorizations for those data elements explicitly. However, these negative authorizations are not correctly interpreted by AC_{DH_2} and AC_{DH_3}. In particular, they are propagated both up and down the hierarchy in

AC_{DH_3} and up the hierarchy in AC_{DH_2}, thus restricting the access to data elements which the user wants to disclose. On the other hand, when a negative authorization is defined for a data element, AC_{DH_1} requires the specification of a negative authorization for the root elements of the data hierarchy. This, by propagation, might prevent access to data elements for which access should be allowed. Consequently, policies expressed in access control models only relying on a data hierarchy, result to be more restrictive than what the user aims at as indicated by M_4.

The experiments also show that AC_{NR}, AC_{DH_1}, AC_{DH_2} and AC_{DH_3} do not fully protect a user from data leakages without a comprehensive knowledge of the application domain. This becomes evident when we evaluate $\mathcal{P}_i^{DM}$ with respect to these models. When $\mathcal{P}_i^{DM}$ is evaluated within AC_{DH_1}, AC_{DH_2} and AC_{DH_3}, there may be situations in which the user would like to deny access but these models do not (M_1), or even worse, situations in which the access should be denied while AC_{DH_1}, AC_{DH_2} and AC_{DH_3} grant access (M_3), thus allowing inference of user sensitive data. Indeed, the propagation of positive authorizations through hierarchies increases the number of data elements for which permission is allowed: those permissions grant access to user's information that should be protected, leading to leakages of sensitive information. Similar situations happen when $\mathcal{P}_i^{DM}$ is evaluated with respect to AC_{NR}. Since the user relies on her (limited) knowledge of the application domain to define a policy set that covers the whole set of intended protected data, the defined policies might not reflect her constraints on the disclosure of sensitive information. Indeed, there are several cases where the user would like to deny access but AC_{NR} does not (M_1) or vice versa (M_2). Moreover, a user may explicitly grant access to a data element that allows the inference of a data element to which the user has explicitly denied the access (M_3). Comparing AC_{NR}, AC_{DH_1}, AC_{DH_2} and AC_{DH_3} with respect to the evaluation of $\mathcal{P}_i^{DM}$, we can observe that, in general, AC_{DH_3} better captures a user's intention than AC_{DH_1} and AC_{DH_2}; in turn, AC_{DH_1} and AC_{DH_2} better capture a user's intention than AC_{NR} (M_1 and M_2). However, AC_{DH_1}, AC_{DH_2} and AC_{DH_3} are more prone to data leakages when a user does not have a sufficient knowledge of the application domain and, in particular, of inference relations (M_3).

Note that AC_{DH_2} can achieve the same level of accuracy offered by AC_{DH_3}. This can be explained by the fact that the it is always possible to define a policy $\mathcal{P}_i^{DH_2}$ which evaluated using AC_{DH_2}

behaves as a policy $\mathcal{P}_i^{\mathcal{DH}_3}$ evaluated using $\mathcal{AC}_{\mathcal{DH}_3}$. However, such a policy requires a larger amount of policy statements compared to the corresponding policy for $\mathcal{AC}_{\mathcal{DH}_3}$. On the other hand, the maximum level of accuracy that can be reached by $\mathcal{AC}_{\mathcal{DH}_1}$ (i.e., for $\mathcal{P}_i^{\mathcal{DH}_1}$) is lower than the maximal accuracy that can be reached by $\mathcal{AC}_{\mathcal{DH}_2}$ and $\mathcal{AC}_{\mathcal{DH}_3}$. Moreover, one can observe that $\mathcal{P}_i^{\mathcal{DH}_1}$ and $\mathcal{P}_i^{\mathcal{DH}_3}$ behave in a similar way with respect to $\mathcal{AC}_{\mathcal{DH}_2}$. This can be explained by the fact that policy $\mathcal{P}_i^{\mathcal{DH}_1}$ can be seen as an extension of $\mathcal{P}_i^{\mathcal{DH}_3}$. In other words, it can be obtained from $\mathcal{P}_i^{\mathcal{DH}_3}$ by adding the statements needed to reduce the number of cases in access is not properly denied (i.e., M_1).

Based on these observations, we can conclude that $\mathcal{AC}_{\mathcal{DM}}$ performs better than existing access control models in that it provides full protection from data leakages with lower efforts on the user side. In particular, it minimizes the number of policies a user has to write while allowing full coverage of the intended protected set.

7. RELATED WORK

In this paper we have investigated the problem of preventing inference of sensitive information in access control. Inference control aims to prevent indirect access to sensitive information where a user learns sensitive information from non-sensitive one. Access control, instead, prevents direct access to sensitive information.

In the remainder of this section, we discuss approaches that focus on inference control and approaches that focus on the combination of inference control and access control.

Inference Control.

Several approaches to inference control have been proposed in the literature [1, 15, 18, 37], especially for database systems [3, 7]. The inference problem in databases occurs when sensitive information is disclosed indirectly by combining the answers to a sequence of non-sensitive queries. For this reason, most of the proposed approaches focus on controlling query execution at runtime. For instance, Biskup and Bonatti [7] propose a technique for controlled query evaluation, which modifies the ordinary query evaluation by distorting answers if necessary to preserve confidentiality with respect to a given confidentiality policy.

However, these techniques are computationally inefficient. Thus, Biskup et al. [8, 9, 10] propose to reduce the problem of inference control to access control. These approaches are based on introducing constraints which represent a combination of attribute values in a tuple to be kept secret. If the constants in a query match the constraints, the query asks for a secret value and therefore is not allowed. These approaches are complementary to our approach because they consider inference deriving from the combination of different attribute values. In our work instead we tackle the inference problem by adopting a semantic approach in which inference is prevented on the basis of hierarchical and inference relations between data elements.

Inference and Access Control.

Only few works have considered the issue of information inference in access control [25, 34]. For instance, Katos et al. [25] present an approach based on the concept of inference control by design. They model inference channels between attributes in a data schema as a disclosure matrix that, for each attribute, represents the probability of an attribute revealing other attributes. This matrix is used to compute an access leakage matrix capturing the effective access control. The access leakage matrix is used to define an access control policy that avoids inference channels using separation of duty constraints. However, inference is only analyzed at

the attribute level, thus limiting the granularity of the analysis. In contrast, our approach enables to reason on information inference at any level of the data hierarchy. In particular, we have tackled the problem of inference control by proposing an access control model that adopts semantic inference relationship among data and defines on top of these relationship authorization propagation rules that prevent inference of sensitive information.

The key role played by semantic relationships among data in making access control decisions has been recognized in earlier work [12, 34, 41]. Crampton and Sellwood [12] propose a generic access control model using relationships among entities as the basis to specifying authorization rules. An access request is evaluated with respect to two types of rules: principal matching rules and authorization rules. The former express conditions on the relationships that form a path between a subject s and an object o in an access request (s, o, a); the latter specify the actions that the subject s can/cannot perform on the object o. Similarly, in our approach we consider (semantic) relations between data as the basis of the evaluation of authorization policies. These relations can be considered as a special case of the relations among entities used in [12] to define principal matching rules.

Vavilis et al. [41] use inference relations to reason on data sensitivity and quantify the severity of data leakages. Similarly to [41], our approach is based on a data model which considers both hierarchical and inference relations between data elements. Leveraging these two types of relations makes it possible to detect situations in which access control policies permit access to data from which it is possible to infer sensitive information the user would not like to disclose.

The closest work to ours is the one of Qin et al. [34]. This work presents an access control model for Semantic Web, which allows the specification of authorizations over concepts defined in ontologies and their enforcement upon data instances annotated by concepts. The model makes use of semantic relationships among concepts to define authorization propagation policies that prevent inference of sensitive information. The authors also show how policies can be represented in an OWL-based access control language.

As in [34], we use domain knowledge (possibly represented using an ontology) and, in particular, the semantic relationship between data elements to define propagation rules that prevent leakage of sensitive information. However, there are significant differences between our work and the one in [34]. First, we discriminate between hierarchical relations and inference relations in the definition of authorization propagation rules while Qin et al. do not make this distinction. In particular, Qin et al. classify the relations that can occur in an ontology (including hierarchical relations) in three categories, namely inferable, partially inferable and non-inferable. Based on this classification they propose four propagation rules. These rules are used to propagate both positive and negative authorizations regardless of the type of relations (except non-inferable relations that do not propagate authorizations). In contrast, the definition of our propagation rules is driven by the observation that granting access to a data element does not imply granting access also to the data elements from which it can be inferred. As a consequence, the propagation rules proposed in [34] allow the access to information to a wider audience than intended. Moreover, Qin et al. propose their own language based on OWL to express access control policies, which requires the development of an ad-hoc engine for policy evaluation. In contrast, we encode policies and data model in XACML, thus making our model directly implementable using any existing XACML-compliant engine. More importantly, OWL-based policy languages have inherent limitations in the expressiveness of the policies that can be enforced due to the fact that

OWL with rules is undecidable if unrestricted [26]. On the other hand, our approach can leverage the expressivity and extensibility of XACML for the specification of access control policies, resulting in a larger set of policies that can be supported by our access control model.

8. CONCLUSION

In this paper we have presented an access control model that uses a semantic approach to prevent inference of sensitive information. The model is based on a data model that encodes domain knowledge. In particular the data model organizes domain knowledge in a hierarchical structure and makes inference relations between data explicit. These relations are used to define authorization propagation rules that prevent inference of sensitive information.

We acknowledge that the proposed access control model can only prevent inference of sensitive information based on the inference relations that are explicit in the data model. Thus, our approach is complementary to non-semantic approaches to inference control that consider inference of sensitive information as combination of non-sensitive one.

We have evaluated and compared the proposed access control model with existing access control models which either do not consider relations among data or rely only on data hierarchies to determine applicable policies. The experiments show that our model overcomes the limitations of existing access control models in that it provides protection against explicit secondary data leakages and reduces the effort required by a user to specify a policy expressed in term of number of statements that the user has to specify.

The work presented in this paper poses the basis for several directions for future work. The aim of the proposed access control model is to prevent inference of sensitive information. This, however, may result in users not being fully conscious about the side effects that defining a certain policy may lead to. To this end, the access control model can be complemented with transparency tools that help users in the understanding of the consequences of the defined policies. Transparency tools can be used either to analyze users' policies at design time, for instance based on policy analysis approaches [20, 40], or at run time to provide feedback to users when the access decision differs from the authorizations they have explicitly specified in their policies [14].

Moreover, we are planning to conduct an extensive evaluation of our approach with respect to different aspects. First, we want to evaluate the effectiveness and efficiency of our approach in a controlled experiment in which users specify an access control policy using the proposed access control model, an access control model that do not consider relations among data and one that makes use of data hierarchies. Second, since the proposed access control model relies on the representation of the application domain for the decisional process, we want to study the impact of the representation of the application domain has on the effectiveness of the access control model. To this end, we plan to perform experiments in which different domain specific ontologies like FOAF for social networks, GoodRelations [19] and CContology [24] for e-commerce are used to instantiate the data model.

Acknowledgments

This work has been partially funded by the ITEA2 projects FedSS and M2MGrid, the EDA project IN4STARS2.0, the Dutch national program COMMIT under the THeCS project, the EU under grant agreement n.285223 (SECONOMICS) and the SESAR JU WPE under contract 12-120610-C12 (EMFASE).

9. REFERENCES

[1] R. Accorsi and G. Muller. Preventive inference control in data-centric business models. In *Proceedings of Security and Privacy Workshops*, pages 28–33. IEEE, 2013.

[2] A. Acquisti and R. Gross. Imagined communities: Awareness, information sharing, and privacy on the facebook. In *Privacy Enhancing Technologies*, LNCS 4258, pages 36–58. Springer, 2006.

[3] K. Arkoudas and A. Vashist. A model-theoretic approach to data anonymity and inference control. In *Proceedings of Conference on Data and Application Security and Privacy*, pages 249–256. ACM, 2012.

[4] M. Backes, G. Karjoth, W. Bagga, and M. Schunter. Efficient comparison of enterprise privacy policies. In *Proceedings of Symposium on Applied Computing*, pages 375–382. ACM, 2004.

[5] A. Barth and J. C. Mitchell. Enterprise privacy promises and enforcement. In *Proceedings of Workshop on Issues in the Theory of Security*, pages 58–66. ACM, 2005.

[6] E. Bertino, P. Samarati, and S. Jajodia. An extended authorization model for relational databases. *IEEE Trans. on Knowl. and Data Eng.*, 9(1):85–101, 1997.

[7] J. Biskup and P. Bonatti. Controlled query evaluation for enforcing confidentiality in complete information systems. *International Journal of Information Security*, 3(1):14–27, 2004.

[8] J. Biskup, D. W. Embley, and J. Lochner. Reducing inference control to access control for normalized database schemas. *Inf. Process. Lett.*, 106(1):8–12, 2008.

[9] J. Biskup, S. Hartmann, S. Link, and J.-H. Lochner. Efficient inference control for open relational queries. In *Data and Applications Security and Privacy XXIV*, LNCS 6166, pages 162–176. Springer, 2010.

[10] J. Biskup and J.-H. Lochner. Enforcing confidentiality in relational databases by reducing inference control to access control. In *Information Security*, LNCS 4779, pages 407–422. Springer, 2007.

[11] J.-W. Byun and N. Li. Purpose based access control for privacy protection in relational database systems. *The VLDB Journal*, 17(4):603–619, 2008.

[12] J. Crampton and J. Sellwood. Path conditions and principal matching: A new approach to access control. In *Proceedings of Symposium on Access Control Models and Technologies*, pages 187–198. ACM, 2014.

[13] M. J. Culnan and P. K. Armstrong. Information privacy concerns, procedural fairness, and impersonal trust: An empirical investigation. *Organization Science*, 10(1):04–115, 1999.

[14] S. Damen, J. den Hartog, and N. Zannone. CollAC: Collaborative access control. In *Proceedings of International Conference on Collaboration Technologies and Systems*, pages 142–149. IEEE, 2014.

[15] J. Domingo-Ferrer. A Survey of Inference Control Methods for Privacy-Preserving Data Mining. In *Privacy-Preserving Data Mining*, Advances in Database Systems 34, pages 53–80. Springer, 2008.

[16] M. Egea, F. Paci, M. Petrocchi, and N. Zannone. PERSONA - A Personalized Data Protection Framework. In *Proceedings of IFIP WG 11.11 International Conference on Trust Management*, IFIP Advances in Information and Communication Technology 401, pages 272–280. Springer, 2013.

[17] P. Guarda and N. Zannone. Towards the development of privacy-aware systems. *Information & Software Technology*, 51(2):337–350, 2009.

[18] R. Heatherly, M. Kantarcioglu, and B. M. Thuraisingham. Preventing private information inference attacks on social networks. *IEEE Trans. Knowl. Data Eng.*, 25(8):1849–1862, 2013.

[19] M. Hepp. GoodRelations: An Ontology for Describing Products and Services Offers on the Web. In *Proceedings of International Conference on Knowledge Engineering: Practice and Patterns*, LNCS 5268, pages 329–346. Springer, 2008.

[20] G. Hughes and T. Bultan. Automated Verification of Access Control Policies Using a SAT Solver. *Int. J. Softw. Tools Technol. Transf.*, 10(6):503–520, 2008.

[21] IHTSDO. SNOMED CT – The Global Language of Healthcare. http://www.ihtsdo.org/snomed-ct.

[22] ISO/IEC 25010:2011. Systems and software engineering - Systems and software Quality Requirements and Evaluation (SQuaRE) - System and software quality models, 2011.

[23] S. Jajodia, P. Samarati, M. L. Sapino, and V. S. Subrahmanian. Flexible support for multiple access control policies. *ACM Trans. Database Syst.*, 26(2):214–260, 2001.

[24] M. Jarrar. *Towards Effectiveness and Transparency in e-Business Transactions, An Ontology for Customer Complaint Management*, chapter 7. Idea Group Inc., 2009.

[25] V. Katos, D. Vrakas, and P. Katsaros. A framework for access control with inference constraints. In *Proceedings of Computer Software and Applications Conference*, pages 289–297. IEEE, 2011.

[26] M. Krötzsch, S. Rudolph, and P. Hitzler. Description logic rules. In *Proceedings of European Conference on Artificial Intelligence*, Frontiers in Artificial Intelligence and Applications 178, pages 80–84. IOS Press, 2008.

[27] J.-G. Lee, K.-Y. Whang, W.-S. Han, and I.-Y. Song. The dynamic predicate: integrating access control with query processing in XML databases. *The VLDB Journal*, 16(3):371–387, 2007.

[28] A. Masoumzadeh and J. Joshi. PuRBAC: Purpose-Aware Role-Based Access Control. In *On the Move to Meaningful Internet Systems*, LNCS 5332, pages 1104–1121. Springer, 2008.

[29] I. Matteucci, P. Mori, and M. Petrocchi. Prioritized Execution of Privacy Policies. In *Data Privacy Management and Autonomous Spontaneous Security*, LNCS 7731, pages 133–145. Springer, 2012.

[30] G. R. Milne and M.-E. Boza. Trust and concern in consumers' perceptions of marketing information management practices. *Journal of Interactive Marketing*, 13(1):5 – 24, 1999.

[31] OASIS XACML Technical Committee. XACML v3.0 Core and Hierarchical Role Based Access Control (RBAC) Profile Version 1.0. Committee specification, OASIS, 2010.

[32] OASIS XACML Technical Committee. XACML v3.0 Hierarchical Resource Profile Version 1.0. Committee specification, OASIS, 2010.

[33] OASIS XACML Technical Committee. eXtensible Access Control Markup Language (XACML) Version 3.0. Oasis standard, OASIS, 2013.

[34] L. Qin and V. Atluri. Concept-level access control for the semantic web. In *Proceedings of ACM Workshop on XML Security*, pages 94–103. ACM, 2003.

[35] F. Rabitti, E. Bertino, W. Kim, and D. Woelk. A model of authorization for next-generation database systems. *ACM Trans. Database Syst.*, 16(1):88–131, 1991.

[36] C. Ruan and S. Shahrestani. Logic based authorization program and its implementation. In *Proceedings of International Conference on Security of Information and Networks*, pages 87–94. ACM, 2011.

[37] A. Sabelfeld and A. C. Myers. Language-based information-flow security. *IEEE Journal on Selected Areas in Communications*, 21(1):5–19, 2006.

[38] R. Sandhu, E. Coyne, H. Feinstein, and C. Youman. Role-based access control models. *Computer*, 29(2):38–47, 1996.

[39] A. Squicciarini, F. Paci, and S. Sundareswaran. PriMa: a comprehensive approach to privacy protection in social network sites. *Annales des Télécommunications*, 69(1-2):21–36, 2014.

[40] F. Turkmen, J. den Hartog, S. Ranise, and N. Zannone. Analysis of XACML Policies with SMT. In *Principles of Security and Trust*, LNCS 9036, pages 115–134. Springer, 2015.

[41] S. Vavilis, M. Petkovic, and N. Zannone. Data leakage quantification. In *Data and Applications Security and Privacy*, LNCS 8566, pages 98–113. Springer, 2014.

On Missing Attributes in Access Control: Non-deterministic and Probabilistic Attribute Retrieval*

Jason Crampton
Royal Holloway, University of London
jason.crampton@rhul.ac.uk

Charles Morisset
Newcastle University
charles.morisset@ncl.ac.uk

Nicola Zannone
Eindhoven University of Technology
n.zannone@tue.nl

ABSTRACT

Attribute Based Access Control (ABAC) is becoming the reference model for the specification and evaluation of access control policies. In ABAC policies and access requests are defined in terms of pairs attribute names/values. The applicability of an ABAC policy to a request is determined by matching the attributes in the request with the attributes in the policy. Some languages supporting ABAC, such as PTaCL or XACML 3.0, take into account the possibility that some attributes values might not be correctly retrieved when the request is evaluated, and use complex decisions, usually describing all possible evaluation outcomes, to account for missing attributes. In this paper, we argue that the problem of missing attributes in ABAC can be seen as a non-deterministic attribute retrieval process, and we show that the current evaluation mechanism in PTaCL or XACML can return a complex decision that does not necessarily match with the actual possible outcomes. This, however, is problematic for the enforcing mechanism, which needs to resolve the complex decision into a conclusive one. We propose a new evaluation mechanism, explicitly based on non-deterministic attribute retrieval for a given request. We extend this mechanism to probabilistic attribute retrieval and implement a probabilistic policy evaluation mechanism for PTaCL in PRISM, a probabilistic model-checker.

Categories and Subject Descriptors

D.4.6 [**Security and Protection**]: Access Controls; D.2.4 [**Software Software/Program Verification**]: Model checking

*This work has been partially funded by the EPSRC/GCHQ funded project ChAISe (EP/K006568/1), the project "Data-Driven Model-Based Decision-Making", part of the NSA funded Centre on Science of Security at University of Illinois at Urbana-Champaign, the EDA project IN4STARS2.0 and by the Dutch national program COMMIT under the THeCS project.

General Terms

Security, Theory

Keywords

Policy evaluation; missing attribute; probabilistic model-checking; PTaCL

1. INTRODUCTION

In recent years there has been considerable interest in attribute-based access control (ABAC), resulting in the development of languages such as XACML [11] and PTaCL [5]. Such languages have moved away from the "classical" view of access control, which was based on (authenticated) users and their respective identities. In the classical view, an access request was modelled as a triple (s, o, a), where s denoted a subject (corresponding to a user identity), o denoted an object (corresponding to the identity of some protected resource) and a denoted an access mode (such as read or write). In ABAC, an access request is modelled as a collection of attribute name-value pairs. ABAC is particularly suitable in "open" computing environments where the user population is not known in advance and access is allowed or denied on the basis of user characteristics, rather than identities.

One problem that arises in ABAC is that a request may not present all the relevant information to the policy decision point (PDP) and different decisions may be generated, depending on the information that is presented. Equally, an ABAC policy may not be able to produce a conclusive decision (an allow or deny) for a given request because the policy is under-specified. Conversely, an ABAC policy may be over-specified and different components of the policy may both allow and deny the request. Finally, a request may be malformed and policy evaluation may fail unexpectedly. Thus, the PDP may return an inconclusive result, indeterminate results, or inconsistent results. XACML and PTaCL handle such possibilities by extending the set of possible decisions that the PDP may return and allowing the PDP to return a subset of that decision set. XACML, for example, introduces the "not-applicable" and "indeterminate" decisions: the former is returned when the policy does not evaluate to any conclusive decision; the latter is used to indicate some error or inconsistency occurred during policy evaluation. PTaCL uses the equivalent of a "not-applicable", but models evaluation errors by returning a set of possible decisions that might have been returned if no errors had occurred.

However, the policy enforcement point (PEP) must, ultimately, take one of two actions, either allowing or denying an access request. In this paper we investigate whether the PEP should (or can) rely on the decision(s) returned by the PDPs defined for XACML and PTaCL. In particular, we focus on the case where inconclusive decisions are sets of possible decisions, which may be generated by considering attributes that may not have been included in the request (perhaps because the requester deliberately withheld them). We will show that the set of possible decisions returned by the PDP is not always meaningful and, therefore, the PEP should not rely on it. We also show that, under certain conditions, the PEP should not even rely on a single conclusive decision returned by the PDP. Of course, this raises the question of why existing PDPs are designed in the way they are. Thus, we establish a new way of thinking about request evaluation and alternative designs for PDPs in ABAC systems. In particular, we make the following contributions.

- We first show that the decision sets returned by a PTaCL/XACML policy do not necessarily correspond with an intuitive interpretation of what those decisions mean.

- We then propose a declarative evaluation mechanism for PTaCL which matches this intuition. The mechanism is based on a *non-deterministic* evaluation [14], which simulates the non-determinism of retrieving the attributes forming the request: if a value for an attribute is missing from a request, we do not know whether it should be in it or not[1].

- Finally, we extend this non-deterministic evaluation to a probabilistic one, and we show how they can be mixed.

- The concepts presented in this paper are supported by an automatic translation of PTaCL policies into PRISM, which is a probabilistic model-checker.

In the next section we briefly review related work and summarize the PTaCL language. In Section 3, we introduce a new way of reasoning about requests in the presence of uncertainty about the inclusion of attributes. We then consider non-deterministic and probabilistic attribute retrieval in Sections 4 and 5, respectively. We conclude with a summary of our contributions and some ideas for future work.

2. BACKGROUND AND RELATED WORK

Our work relies clearly on the PTaCL language [5] together with the definition of the ATRAP tool [7], which automatically analyses the safety of PTaCL policies. The notion of reducing complex decisions to simple, conclusive ones is also addressed in recent work [10], which focuses on decisions and operators, whereas we focus here on attribute retrieval. In terms of methodology, our approach follows that of Tschantz and Krishnamurthi [14], since we first establish some requirement for an access control evaluation mechanism, and we then analyse an existing language against those requirements.

Model-checking has been used in the past for access control, for instance Zhang et al. [18] propose a tool checking whether a particular goal can be reached within an access control policy; Fistler et al. [6] defined the tool Margrave, which can analyse role-based access-control policies; more recently, Ranise et al. [12, 13] have used model checking to analyse the safety problem with administrative policies. In this work, we mostly focus on the attribute retrieval problem rather than on the policy evaluation/analysis problem (although they are quite related). To the best of our knowledge, we are the first to investigate probabilistic attribute retrieval in access control.

In the remainder of this section, we recall the language PTaCL [5], after a brief introduction to 3-valued logic, to establish the notations used throughout the paper.

2.1 3-valued Logic

The truth values in Boolean logic are 0 and 1, where 1 represents *true* and 0 represents *false*; 3-valued logic extends it by considering an additional value $\bot$ [8]. There can be multiple interpretations of this extra symbol, for instance, the *weak conjunction* and *weak disjunction* operators, defined in Fig. 1 by $\sqcap$ and $\sqcup$, respectively, consider $\bot$ as absorbing; on the other hand, the *strong* conjunction and disjunction operators, defined by $\tilde{\sqcap}$ and $\tilde{\sqcup}$ consider $\bot$ as being either 1 or 0, and therefore try to "resolve" $\bot$ as much as possible. Another interpretation is to "ignore" the symbol $\bot$ as much as possible, for instance with the operators $\triangledown$ and $\triangle$, which correspond to the XACML operators permit-overrides and deny-overrides, respectively. Finally, we also consider the negation operator $\neg$, where $\neg 1 = 0$, $\neg 0 = 1$ and $\neg\bot = \bot$; and the "weakening" operator $\sim$, where $\sim\bot = \sim 0 = 0$ and $\sim 1 = 1$.

2.2 PTaCL

PTaCL is attribute-based, which means that a request is a set of attribute name-value pairs $\{(n_1, v_1), \ldots, (n_k, v_l)\}$. For instance, in a healthcare context, the request $\{(\mathsf{r}, \mathsf{nurse}), (\mathsf{emg}, true)\}$ represents a request made by a nurse during an emergency. In addition, PTaCL uses policy targets [1, 2, 4, 11, 17], which specify the requests to which the policy is applicable.

- An *atomic target* is a pair (n, v), where n is an attribute name and v is an attribute value.
- A *composite target* has the form $\mathsf{op}(t_1, \ldots, t_n)$, where op represents an n-ary 3-valued logical operator. For the sake of simplicity, we focus here on the unary and binary operators defined in Fig. 1.

Given a request, a target evaluates to a single value in $\{1, 0, \bot\}$, intuitively indicating if the request matches, does not match, or does not contain the attributes required to evaluate its applicability, respectively. More formally, the semantics of an atomic target (n, v) for a request $q = \{(n_1, v_1), \cdots, (n_k, v_l)\}$ is given as:

$$[\![(n, v)]\!]_{\mathrm{P}}(q) = \begin{cases} 1 & \text{if } (n, v') \in q \text{ and } v = v', \\ \bot & \text{if } (n, v') \notin q, \\ 0 & \text{otherwise.} \end{cases}$$

Composite targets are inductively evaluated by applying the operator to the result of the evaluation of the sub-targets. Note that the unary operator $\sim$ deals with the absence of an attribute as if the attribute does not match the value[2].

An *authorisation policy* can be:

---

[1]We assume non-forgeability of attribute values: if a value for an attribute belongs to a request, then it is genuine.

[2]In other words, PTaCL expects all attributes to be present by default, in XACML terminology, but the "indetermi-

Table 1: Binary operators on the set $\{1,0,\bot\}$

d_1	d_2	$d_1 \mathbin{\tilde\sqcap} d_2$	$d_1 \sqcap d_2$	$d_1 \triangle d_2$	$d_1 \mathbin{\tilde\sqcup} d_2$	$d_1 \sqcup d_2$	$d_1 \triangledown d_2$
1	1	1	1	1	1	1	1
1	0	0	0	0	1	1	1
1	$\bot$	$\bot$	$\bot$	1	1	$\bot$	1
0	1	0	0	0	1	1	1
0	0	0	0	0	0	0	0
0	$\bot$	0	$\bot$	0	$\bot$	$\bot$	0
$\bot$	1	$\bot$	$\bot$	1	1	$\bot$	1
$\bot$	0	0	$\bot$	0	$\bot$	$\bot$	0
$\bot$	$\bot$	$\bot$	$\bot$	$\bot$	$\bot$	$\bot$	$\bot$

Table 2: Policy evaluation with $\llbracket \cdot \rrbracket_\mathrm{P}$.

Request	Policy			
	p_d	p_e	p_c	p_1
$\emptyset$	$\{1,\bot\}$	$\{\bot\}$	$\{\bot\}$	$\{1,\bot\}$
$\{(\mathbf{r}, \text{phys})\}$	$\{1\}$	$\{\bot\}$	$\{\bot\}$	$\{1\}$
$\{(\mathbf{r}, \text{phys}), (\mathbf{cf}, true)\}$	$\{1\}$	$\{\bot\}$	$\{0\}$	$\{0\}$
$\{(\mathbf{r}, \text{nurse})\}$	$\{\bot\}$	$\{\bot\}$	$\{\bot\}$	$\{\bot\}$
$\{(\mathbf{r}, \text{nurse}), (\mathbf{emg}, true)\}$	$\{\bot\}$	$\{1\}$	$\{\bot\}$	$\{1\}$

- a single decision, i.e., either 1 (allow) or 0 (deny);
- a targeted policy (t, p), where t is a target;
- a composite policy $\mathsf{op}(p_1, \ldots, p_n)$, where op is a n-ary operator. Here again, we focus on the operators defined in Fig. 1.

In general, for a given request, an attribute can be completely missing (for instance, an visitor might not have any official role in a hospital), have exactly one value, or have multiple values (for instance, a nurse might be training as a physician, and in some contexts, activate both roles). However, because it is not necessarily known in advance the number of values an attribute can take for a particular request, it is impossible to know whether some values have been removed or not. PTaCL handles such situations by considering that if the target of a policy (t, p) evaluates to $\bot$, p must evaluate as if the target evaluates to both 1 and 0. More formally, the evaluation of a targeted policy (t, p) for a request q is given by:

$$\llbracket (t,p) \rrbracket_\mathrm{P}(q) = \begin{cases} \llbracket p \rrbracket_\mathrm{P}(q) & \text{if } \llbracket t \rrbracket_\mathrm{P}(q) = 1, \\ \{\bot\} & \text{if } \llbracket t \rrbracket_\mathrm{P}(q) = 0, \\ \{\bot\} \cup \llbracket p \rrbracket_\mathrm{P}(q) & \text{otherwise.} \end{cases}$$

where $\bot$ represents the not-applicable decision, $\llbracket p \rrbracket_\mathrm{P}(q) = 1$ if p is the authorisation policy 1 (allow) and $\llbracket p \rrbracket_\mathrm{P}(q) = 0$ if p is 0 (deny). It is worth emphasising that even though the evaluation of both targets and policies uses the set $\{1, 0, \bot\}$, these values have a different interpretation in each case: they stand for "match", "non-match" and "indeterminate" when evaluating targets, and for "allow", "deny" and "not-applicable" when evaluating policies.

In order to illustrate PTaCL, we define the following policy for an electronic health record: a physician can access it; a nurse can access it if there is an emergency; but in all cases, it cannot be accessed if the requester has a conflict of interest (e.g., the physician is a relative of the patient). These three policies correspond to the PTaCL policies p_d, p_e and p_c defined below. The global policy formed by combining p_d, p_e and p_c is defined by p_1.

$$p_d = ((\mathbf{r}, \text{phys}), 1)$$
$$p_e = ((\mathbf{r}, \text{nurse}) \mathbin{\tilde\sqcap} \sim(\mathbf{emg}, true), 1)$$
$$p_c = (\sim(\mathbf{cf}, true), 0)$$
$$p_1 = (p_d \triangledown p_e) \triangle p_c$$

The evaluation of these policies for different requests is given in Table 2, where each row contains a request q, and the evaluation of $\llbracket p \rrbracket_\mathrm{P}(q)$, for $p \in \{p_d, p_e, p_c, p_1\}$.

---

nate" value $\bot$ can always be transformed into the non-match value 0.

3. ACCESS CONTROL WITH INCOMPLETE REQUESTS

Thus, ABAC introduces the possibility that some attributes might be missing from a request. Moreover, missing attributes cannot always be automatically detected. PTaCL addresses this possibility by letting targets evaluate to $\bot$ when an attribute required by the target is missing, which, in turn, can cause a policy to return multiple values.

In this section, we first introduce some general characterisation of requests, after which we establish some requirements for policy evaluation mechanisms. Then, we show that PTaCL does not necessarily meet them and propose an abstract mechanism satisfying them.

3.1 Characterising Missing Information

The major issue with missing information is that it is not necessarily syntactically detectable. Indeed, some attributes might simply not exist in a particular context, or the number of values expected for a given attribute is not necessarily known in advance. For instance, the request $\{(\mathbf{r}, \text{nurse})\}$ has all required information if the subject submitting is only a nurse, but is missing information if she has multiple roles. Similarly, the empty request is missing information if the subject has a role, but is not if the subject is not member of the hospital staff.

Tschantz and Krishnamurthi [14] introduce an ordering relation $\sqsubseteq$ over requests, such that if $q \sqsubseteq q'$, "then q' contains all the information contained in q and possibly more". This relation is used to define policy safety, such that a policy p is safe when, given two requests q and q', if $q \sqsubseteq_p q'$, then $\llbracket p \rrbracket(q) \leq \llbracket p \rrbracket(q')$. For the sake of generality, they deliberately under-specify the ordering relations over requests, but claim that "informally, in a safe language, undue access is impossible provided that requests tell no lies; whereas, in an unsafe language, the requests must additionally tell the whole truth."

3.2 Well-formed and complete requests

Given an attribute n, a value v and a request q, three cases are possible:

1. it is certain that n has the value v in q;
2. it is certain that n does not have the value v in q;
3. we do not know whether n has the value v in q or not.

In this work, we assume attributes are unforgeable, and therefore, if $(n, v) \in q$, we are in the first case. However, the main idea behind ABAC with incomplete information is to say that if $(n, v) \notin q$, we could be either in the second or the third case. This is typically handled in PTaCL and XACML at the policy level, by considering indeterminate target evaluations as non-matching ones. However, we know that with these approaches, policies are in general unsafe.

We propose here to address this problem at the request level. More precisely, we suggest to consider *negative* attribute values $\overline{v}$, such that for any values v and v', $\overline{v} \neq v'$. Intuitively, a negative attribute value $\overline{v}$ explicitly indicates that an attribute cannot have value v in a given context. In order to avoid any contradiction, we say that a request q is *well-formed* if it does not contain both (n, v) and $(n, \overline{v})$, for any attribute n and any value v, and in this case we write $\mathsf{wf}(q)$.

In other words, the negative value $\overline{v}$ never matches any atomic target, but ensures that the "positive" value v cannot be added to the request. We can now define the three cases above as:

1. (n, v) belongs to q;
2. $(n, \overline{v})$ belongs to q;
3. neither (n, v) nor $(n, \overline{v})$ belong to q.

Intuitively, in the third case, the value v for n has not been retrieved for q yet. Hence, q could either correspond to $q \cup \{(n, v)\}$ or to $q \cup \{(n, \overline{v})\}$. This leads to the idea of *non-deterministic attribute retrieval*: the value for the attribute must be retrieved, but we do not know whether it is going to be positive or negative.

We say that a request q is *complete* when, for any attribute n and any value v, either $(n, v) \in q$ or $(n, \overline{v}) \in q$. In this case, adding a new value to q would create request that is not well-formed. In addition, given a request q, we write $\overline{q}$ for the request where we add the negative values when the positive value is not already present:

$$\overline{q} = q \cup \{(n, \overline{v}) \mid (n, v) \notin q\}$$

Clearly, $\overline{q}$ is complete, and well-formed if q is well-formed.

3.3 Requirements

We are now in position to establish some intuitive requirements for a general evaluation function $[\![\cdot]\!]$, such that given a policy p and a request q, $[\![p]\!](q)$ returns a set of decisions. The first requirement expresses the fact that any decision returned for a request in which information is missing corresponds to a decision that would be returned had the missing information been provided.

REQUIREMENT 1. *For any request q, if $d \in [\![p]\!](q)$, then there exists a well-formed request $q' \supseteq q$ such that $[\![p]\!](q') = \{d\}$.*

The second requirement is the converse of the first one, and expresses that if a decision can be returned when all information in a request is provided, then evaluating the same request but with missing information should at least return that decision.

REQUIREMENT 2. *Given a request q and a decision d, if there exists a well-formed request $q' \supseteq q$ such that $[\![p]\!](q') = \{d\}$, then $d \in [\![p]\!](q)$.*

Intuitively, these two requirements could correspond to the notions of correctness and completeness, respectively. Indeed, Requirement 1 implies that no incorrect decision can be returned when information is missing, i.e., no decision that could not have been returned had all information been provided. A trivial evaluation mechanism satisfying this requirement is one that always returns the empty set of decisions for any request (i.e., a mechanism that never returns an incorrect decision). Conversely, Requirement 2 implies that *all* the correct decisions are returned when information is

missing (and potentially more). A trivial mechanism satisfying this requirement is that returning all possible decisions for any query.

Suppose the PEP receives the decisions $\{d_1, \ldots, d_n\}$ from the PDP. If the PEP knows that the PDP is meeting these two requirements, then it can deduce that all d_i are potentially correct decisions, had all information been provided, and that any decision different from any d_i is not a potentially correct decision. It can therefore reduce its choice to selecting a decision in $\{d_1, \ldots, d_n\}$. In particular, when the set returned by the PDP is reduced to a unique decision, then the PEP can be certain that this decision is the correct one.

3.4 PTaCL Analysis

We now show that PTaCL satisfies neither Requirement 1 nor Requirement 2.

Firstly, consider the policy $p_3 = ((\mathbf{r}, \mathsf{nurse}), 1) \triangle ((\mathbf{r}, \mathsf{nurse}), 0)$, where $\triangle$ stands for the deny-overrides operator. If we evaluate for the empty request, we have

$$[\![(\mathbf{r}, \mathsf{nurse}), 1)]\!]_{\mathrm{P}}(\emptyset) = \{1, \bot\}$$
$$[\![(\mathbf{r}, \mathsf{nurse}), 0)]\!]_{\mathrm{P}}(\emptyset) = \{0, \bot\}$$
$$[\![p_3]\!]_{\mathrm{P}}(\emptyset) = \{1, 0, \bot\}.$$

However, it is easy to see that there is no request q such that $[\![p_3]\!]_{\mathrm{P}}(q) = \{1\}$: if $((\mathbf{r}, \mathsf{nurse}), 1)$ evaluates to 1, then $((\mathbf{r}, \mathsf{nurse}), 0)$ necessarily evaluates to 0. As these policies are combined in p_3 using a deny-overrides operator, even though $1 \in [\![p_3]\!]_{\mathrm{P}}(q)$, there is no request $q' \supseteq q$ such that $[\![p_3]\!](q') = \{1\}$. Thus, PTaCL does not satisfy Requirement 1.

Let us now consider the policy p_1, defined in Section 2.2, the requests $q = \{(\mathbf{r}, \mathsf{phys})\}$ and $q' = \{(\mathbf{r}, \mathsf{phys}), (\mathbf{cf}, \mathit{true})\}$. As described before, we have $[\![p_1]\!]_{\mathrm{P}}(q) = \{1\}$, while $[\![p_1]\!]_{\mathrm{P}}(q') = \{0\}$. In other words, the decision returned by the extended request q' does not appear in the set returned by the request q, and we can conclude that PTaCL does not satisfy Requirement 2. Note that this kind of situation is described in [5] as an *attribute hiding attack*, where an attacker can gain some advantage by hiding information.

In other words, the decision set received by an access control resolver is not necessarily helpful to make a conclusive decision, and it is worth observing that these two observations also hold for XACML 3.0. One possibility is to constrain the policy language: if the policy is constructed using some specific constraints, then some monotonicity results can be shown [5]. In this paper, we propose a new approach by designing an evaluation function explicitly relying on the non-determinism of the attribute requests.

4. NON-DETERMINISTIC RETRIEVAL

We now introduce a new method for computing the set of decisions returned by the evaluation of a PTaCL policy (t, p) for a request q. Informally, we remove any indeterminism from the evaluation of targets, instead evaluating a set of associated requests (specifically those that are extensions of q). We therefore present two new abstract evaluation functions: $[\![\cdot]\!]_{\mathrm{C}}$, which evaluates a request without considering missing attributes, and $[\![\cdot]\!]_{\mathrm{N}}$, which evaluates a request by considering all possible extensions, and suggest that the function $[\![\cdot]\!]_{\mathrm{N}}$ should be used instead of the function $[\![\cdot]\!]_{\mathrm{P}}$ defined above. We then explain how to use the PRISM model-checker to compute $[\![\cdot]\!]_{\mathrm{N}}$.

4.1 Abstract evaluation

Intuitively, we define $\llbracket \cdot \rrbracket_{\mathrm{C}}$ such that the evaluation of a target is either 0 or 1, where 1 is returned if there exists a matching attribute and 0 is returned otherwise. More formally, we first define an evaluation function $\llbracket \cdot \rrbracket_{\mathrm{C}}$ as follow:

$$\llbracket (n, v) \rrbracket_{\mathrm{C}}(q) = \begin{cases} 1 & \text{if } (n, v') \in q \text{ and } v = v', \\ 0 & \text{otherwise;} \end{cases}$$

and composite targets are evaluated in a similar fashion than with $\llbracket \cdot \rrbracket_{\mathrm{P}}$. The evaluation of a request with respect to a policy p guarded by a target t is $\perp$ if the evaluation of the target is 0 (that is, the policy is not applicable to the request), otherwise the result of evaluating p is returned.

$$\llbracket (t, p) \rrbracket_{\mathrm{C}}(q) = \begin{cases} \llbracket p \rrbracket_{\mathrm{C}}(q) & \text{if } \llbracket t \rrbracket_{\mathrm{C}}(q) = 1, \\ \perp & \text{otherwise.} \end{cases}$$

Composite policies are evaluated by applying the corresponding operators to the results of evaluating their respective operands. We can observe that for any policy p and any well-formed request q, we have $\llbracket p \rrbracket_{\mathrm{C}}(q) = \llbracket p \rrbracket_{\mathrm{C}}(\overline{q})$. In other words, $\llbracket \cdot \rrbracket_{\mathrm{C}}$ corresponds to the evaluation of the query assuming it is complete and that any value not explicitly provided is not in the request.

Given a request q, we define the set of extensions to q, denoted by $Ext(q)$ to be $\{q' \in Q \mid q \subseteq q' \wedge \mathsf{wf}(q')\}$. For the sake of simplicity, we assume here that for a given request q, $Ext(q)$ is finite, and we leave for future work the study of infinite sets of request extensions. Then

$$\llbracket p \rrbracket_{\mathrm{N}}(q) = \{\llbracket p \rrbracket_{\mathrm{C}}(q') : q' \in Ext(q)\}.$$

Thus, we have non-determinism in request evaluation, as with the original evaluation method used in PTaCL. However, the non-determinism now arises because we consider all possible related requests and the decisions associated with those requests.

Table 3 illustrates the evaluation of $\llbracket \cdot \rrbracket_{\mathrm{N}}$ for the policies defined in Section 2.2, and the same requests than those in Table 2. Clearly, $\llbracket \cdot \rrbracket_{\mathrm{N}}$ introduces much more indeterminism in the evaluation, for instance the request $\{(\mathbf{r}, \mathsf{phys})\}$ now evaluates to $\{1, 0\}$, instead of $\{1\}$ according to $\llbracket \cdot \rrbracket_{\mathrm{P}}$, since if the attribute value $(\mathbf{cf}, \mathit{true})$ is missing, this request would evaluate to $\{0\}$. However, when a conclusive decision is returned, for instance with the request $\{(\mathbf{r}, \mathsf{phys}), (\mathbf{cf}, \mathit{true})\}$, then there is no doubt that this is the only possible decision.

On the other hand, if we evaluate the policy p_3 defined in Section 3.4, we can see that $\llbracket p_3 \rrbracket_{\mathrm{N}}(\emptyset) = \{0, \perp\}$, which corresponds to the fact that there is no request in $Ext(\emptyset)$ that evaluates to the decision 1.

In the following proposition, we show that this new evaluation method satisfies Requirements 1 and 2.

PROPOSITION 1. *For any decision d, any policy p and any request q, $d \in \llbracket p \rrbracket_{\mathrm{N}}(q)$ if and only if there exists a well formed request $q' \supseteq q$ such that $\llbracket p \rrbracket_{\mathrm{N}}(q') = \{d\}$.*

PROOF. $\Rightarrow$) Let d be a decision in $\llbracket p \rrbracket_{\mathrm{N}}(q)$. By definition of $\llbracket \cdot \rrbracket_{\mathrm{N}}$, there exists $q' \in Ext(q)$ such that $\llbracket p \rrbracket_{\mathrm{C}}(q') = d$. As observed above, $\llbracket p \rrbracket_{\mathrm{C}}(q') = \llbracket p \rrbracket_{\mathrm{C}}(\overline{q'})$. It follows that $\llbracket p \rrbracket_{\mathrm{N}}(\overline{q'}) = \{d\}$, since $Ext(\overline{q'}) = \{\overline{q'}\}$. By definition, q' is well-formed, and thus so is $\overline{q'}$, and since $\overline{q'} \supseteq q$, we can conclude.

$\Leftarrow$) Let $q' \supseteq q$ be a well-formed request such that $\llbracket p \rrbracket_{\mathrm{N}}(q') = \{d\}$. Since q' is well-formed, we know that

$q' \in Ext(q')$, and by definition of $\llbracket \cdot \rrbracket_{\mathrm{N}}$, it follows that $\llbracket p \rrbracket_{\mathrm{C}}(q') = d$. Since $q' \supseteq q$, we have $q' \in Ext(q)$, and we can conclude that $d \in \llbracket p \rrbracket_{\mathrm{N}}(q)$. $\square$

It is worth observing at this point that it is possible to construct $Ext(q)$ by inspection of the PTaCL policy and q. Morisset and Griesmeyer showed that it is sufficient to only consider requests comprising attribute name-value pairs that explicitly occur in the PTaCL policy [7]. In particular, it is not necessary to consider (n, v) for every possible value of v that n can take.

4.2 Evaluation using model-checking

Model-checking [3], in a nutshell, consists in(i) abstracting a system as a finite state machine, where each state s contains some atomic propositions that are true for that state; and (ii) checking whether some properties holds for this model. These properties can be *temporal*, when they are expressed over the paths of the model, the intuition being that a path represents an execution sequence.

For instance, given a path $(s_0, \ldots, s_n)$, where each s_i represents a state, and a property φ over states, $\mathsf{F}\varphi$ (also denoted as $\Diamond \varphi$ in the literature) holds if there exists i such that for any $j \geqslant i$, $\varphi(s_j)$ holds. We also use here the operator E, such that given a state s and a path property ϕ, $\mathsf{E}\phi$ holds if there exists a path from s such that ϕ holds.

Intuitively, our encoding of the function $\llbracket \cdot \rrbracket_{\mathrm{N}}$ relies on the following key points:

- each state of the model corresponds to a single request;
- each transition from one state to another corresponds to adding some (n, v) or some $(n, \overline{v})$;
- the evaluation of a policy according to $\llbracket \cdot \rrbracket_{\mathrm{C}}$ is expressed as a property over states;
- the evaluation of a policy according to $\llbracket \cdot \rrbracket_{\mathrm{N}}$ is expressed as a path property, starting from the state corresponding to request, and checking for each decision whether there exists a state for which $\llbracket \cdot \rrbracket_{\mathrm{C}}$ evaluates to that decision.

The model does not strictly depend on the policy, but only on the attribute values, and all possible requests are modelled, not only the one we want to evaluate.

More precisely, each state contains, for any attribute value (n, v), two atomic Boolean propositions, $\iota_{n,v}$ and $\alpha_{n,v}$. These propositions characterise the request q corresponding to that state:

- $\iota_{n,v}$ is false when neither (n, v) nor $(n, \overline{v})$ belongs to q;
- $\iota_{n,v}$ is true and $\alpha_{n,v}$ is false when $(n, \overline{v})$ belongs to q;
- $\iota_{n,v}$ is true and $\alpha_{n,v}$ are true when (n, v) belongs to q.

For instance, if we only consider the attribute values $(\mathbf{r}, \mathsf{phys})$ and $(\mathbf{cf}, \mathit{true})$, a state is a tuple $(\iota_{\mathbf{r},\mathsf{phys}}, \alpha_{\mathbf{r},\mathsf{phys}}, \iota_{\mathbf{cf},\mathit{true}}, \alpha_{\mathbf{cf},\mathit{true}})$, and the request $\{(\mathbf{r}, \overline{\mathsf{phys}})\}$ corresponds to the state $(\mathit{true}, \mathit{false}, \mathit{false}, \mathit{false})$, while

Table 3: Policy evaluation with $\llbracket \cdot \rrbracket_{\mathrm{N}}$

| Request | Policy | | | |
	p_d	p_e	p_c	p_1
$\emptyset$	$\{1, \perp\}$	$\{1, \perp\}$	$\{0, \perp\}$	$\{1, 0, \perp\}$
$\{(\mathbf{r}, \mathsf{phys})\}$	$\{1\}$	$\{1, \perp\}$	$\{0, \perp\}$	$\{1, 0\}$
$\{(\mathbf{r}, \mathsf{phys}), (\mathbf{cf}, \mathit{true})\}$	$\{1\}$	$\{1, \perp\}$	$\{0\}$	$\{0\}$
$\{(\mathbf{r}, \mathsf{nurse})\}$	$\{1, \perp\}$	$\{1, \perp\}$	$\{0, \perp\}$	$\{1, 0, \perp\}$
$\{(\mathbf{r}, \mathsf{nurse}), (\mathbf{emg}, \mathit{true})\}$	$\{1, \perp\}$	$\{1\}$	$\{0, \perp\}$	$\{1, 0\}$

the request $\{(\mathbf{cf}, true)\}$ corresponds to the state $(false, false, true, true)$.

The transition function is defined such that, given two states $s = (\iota_{n_1,v_1}, \alpha_{n_1,v_1}, \ldots, \iota_{n_k,v_l}, \alpha_{n_k,v_l})$ and $s' = (\iota'_{n_1,v_1}, \alpha'_{n_1,v_1}, \ldots, \iota'_{n_k,v_l}, \alpha'_{n_k,v_l})$, there is a transition from s to s' if, and only if, there exists an attribute value (n, v) such that $\iota_{n,v}$ is false and $\iota'_{n,v}$ is true ($\alpha'_{n,v}$ can be either true or false), and the propositions for all other attribute values are identical in both states. In other words, a transition corresponds to the non-deterministic retrieval of exactly one attribute value.

The evaluation of a policy according to $[\![\cdot]\!]_C$ can be mapped directly from the request to the state using the definition in Section 4.1. Given a policy p and a decision d, we write $\delta_{p,d}$ for the predicate over states such that given a state s, $\delta_{p,d}(s)$ holds if, and only if, $[\![p]\!]_C(q_s) = d$ holds, where q_s is the request corresponding to the state s.

PROPOSITION 2. *Given a policy p, a decision d and a request q, $d \in [\![p]\!]_N(q)$ if and only if the path property $\mathsf{EF}\delta_{p,d}$ holds from the state corresponding to q.*

4.3 PRISM Encoding

4.3.1 PRISM

We only present the basic PRISM elements used for our encoding, and refer the reader to the manual[3] for further details. Intuitively, a PRISM model consists of several modules. Each module can contain some variables, and describes the possible transitions at each step. A transition has the following general form:

```
[] g → p₁:(post₁) + ... + pₙ:(postₙ)
```

where g is a boolean expression representing the guard of the transition, and p_i is the probability that the post-condition (i.e., some conditions on the variables) post_i is selected. For instance, a very simple example of a module representing a coin toss can be defined as:

```
module coin_toss
  head : bool init false;
  [] true → 0.5:(head'=true) + 0.5:(head'=false);
endmodule
```

where (head'=true) is a post-condition, indicating that the value of the variable head after the transition (which is indicated by the apostrophe) is true. In this particular example, the coin is fair and the probability of setting head to true is the same than that of setting head to false, which effectively corresponds to obtaining tail. In general, when several transitions are enabled within a given module, one is non-deterministically selected.

It is worth observing that there is a fundamental difference between probabilistic and non-deterministic transitions. For instance, in the above example, if we trigger the coin toss multiple times, in average, we will have as many heads as tails. On the other hand, if we were to define the two following transitions:

```
[] true → (head'=true);
[] true → (head'=false);
```

then either transition can be triggered. This would correspond to having a coin potentially biased, for which we do not know the bias. In this paper, we first use only non-deterministic transitions, and we mix both types of transitions in the next section.

4.3.2 Attribute retrieval

We define one module for each attribute value (n, v), which encodes the propositions $(\iota_{n,v})$ and $(\alpha_{n,v})$.

```
module att_n_v
  n_v: bool init false;
  r_n_v: bool init false;

  [] !r_n_v → (n_v'=true) & (r_n_v'=true);
  [] !r_n_v → (n_v'=false) & (r_n_v'=true);
endmodule
```

The variable n_v corresponds to the proposition $\alpha_{n,v}$ and r_n_v corresponds to $\iota_{n,v}$ (the prefix r_ denotes that (n, v) has been retrieved).

In addition, the completeness of a request is encoded with the formula complete, which holds when all r_n$_i$_v$_j$ are true.

4.3.3 Target and Policies

Following the definition of the function $[\![\cdot]\!]_C$, a target evaluates to a boolean value: an atomic target (n, v) is true if and only if the variable n_v is true, and composite targets are evaluated by applying their corresponding boolean operators on the evaluation of the sub-targets.

Policies evaluate to a value in $\{0, 1, \bot\}$, and therefore we cannot encode a policy directly as a boolean formula. Instead, we encode the set $\{0, 1, \bot\}$ as the integer values 0, 1 and 2, respectively, and we adapt the logical operators accordingly. We also use the PRISM ternary operator c ? e1 : e2 which evaluates to e1 is c is true and to e2 otherwise. Given a PTaCL policy p, we note $\widehat{p}$ the PRISM expression corresponding the encoding of the policy p, which is defined as follows:

$$\widehat{0} \triangleq 0$$
$$\widehat{1} \triangleq 1$$
$$\widehat{\neg p} \triangleq (\widehat{p} = 2) \; ? \; 2 : (1 - \widehat{p})$$
$$\widehat{\sim p} \triangleq \mathrm{mod}(\widehat{p}, 2)$$
$$\widehat{p_1 \sqcap p_2} \triangleq (\widehat{p_1} = 2 \mid \widehat{p_2} = 2) \; ? \; 2 : (\widehat{p_1} * \widehat{p_2})$$
$$\widehat{p_1 \sqcup p_2} \triangleq \max(\widehat{p_1}, \widehat{p_2})$$
$$\widehat{p_1 \tilde{\sqcap} p_2} \triangleq \min(\widehat{p_1} * \widehat{p_2}, 2)$$
$$\widehat{p_1 \tilde{\sqcup} p_2} \triangleq (\widehat{p_1} = 1 \mid \widehat{p_2} = 1) \; ? \; 1 : \max(\widehat{p_1}, \widehat{p_2})$$
$$\widehat{(t, p)} \triangleq \widehat{t} \; ? \; \widehat{p} : 2$$

For instance, we give below the PTaCL definition for the policy p_1 defined in Section 2.2, using the syntax of the tool ATRAP [7], where Ptar is the constructor for target policies, Ppov for the operator $\triangledown$, Pdov for the operator $\triangle$, Topt for the operator $\sim$ and Tstrongand for the operator $\tilde{\sqcap}$:

```
p_d : (Ptar (Tatom "role" "phys") (Patom one))
p_e : (Ptar (Tstrongand
              (Tatom "role" "nurse")
              (Topt (Tatom "emergency" "1")))
        (Patom one))
p_c : (Ptar (Topt (Tatom "conflict" "1"))
        (Patom Zero))

p3 : Ppov p_d p_e
p4 : Pdov p3 p_c
```

[3]Available at http://www.prismmodelchecker.org/

The intermediary policies are introduced for the sake of readability. This policy is automatically translated to the following PRISM model (for the sake of conciseness, we only detail the module for the attribute value $(\mathbf{r}, \mathsf{nurse})$, the other modules being analogous):

```
module att_role_nurse
    role_nurse: bool init false;
    r_role_nurse: bool init false;
    [] !r_role_nurse → (role_nurse'=true) &
        (r_role_nurse'=true);
    [] !r_role_nurse → (role_nurse'=false) &
        (r_role_nurse'=true);
endmodule

module att_role_phys ... endmodule
module att_emergency_1 ... endmodule
module att_conflict_1 ... endmodule

formula p_d = role_phys? 1: 2;

formula p_e = (role_nurse & emergency_1) ? 1: 2;
formula p_c = conflict_1 ? 0: 2;

formula p3 = (p_d = 1 | p_e = 1)? 1 : min(p_d, p_e);
formula p4 = min(p3, p_c);
```

4.3.4 Policy evaluation

As stated in Proposition 2, in order to evaluate whether $d \in [\![p]\!]_N(q)$, we need to evaluate the path property $\mathsf{EF}\widehat{p_d}$ from the state corresponding to the request q. Based on the previous definition, the path property $\mathsf{EF}\delta_{p,d}$ can be expressed in PRISM as $\mathsf{E} [\mathsf{F} \ \widehat{p} = d]$.

However, PRISM starts by default from the initial state, which, in our model, corresponds to the empty request (i.e., the state with all propositions set to false). In order to "reach" first the state corresponding to the request q, we first define $\widetilde{q}$, which is the conjunction of all attributes retrieved in q:

$$\widetilde{q} = \begin{cases} true & \text{if } q = \emptyset, \\ \mathsf{r\_n\_v} \ \& \ \mathsf{n\_v} \ \& \ \widetilde{q'} & \text{if } q = q' \cup \{(n,v)\} \\ \mathsf{r\_n\_v} \ \& \ !\mathsf{n\_v} \ \& \ \widetilde{q'} & \text{if } q = q' \cup \{(n,\overline{v})\} \end{cases}$$

We can use the command filter, such that filter(op, prop, states) computes the value of the property prop for each state satisfying states, and combines these values using the operator op. In this case, we use the operator first, which evaluates prop on the first state that matches states, starting from the initial state and following a lexicographic ordering, where false is less than true.

Finally, we can check if the path property $\mathsf{EF}\delta_{p,d}$ holds (and thus evaluate $[\![\cdot]\!]_N$, according to Proposition 2) by checking whether the PRISM property filter(first, $\mathsf{E} [\mathsf{F} \ \widehat{p} = d]$, $\widetilde{q}$) holds over the generated model.

5. PROBABILISTIC RETRIEVAL

Consider the policy p_1 defined in Section 3.4: $[\![p_1]\!]_N(\{\mathbf{r}, \mathsf{phys}\}) = \{1, 0\}$, whereas, according to the original PTaCL semantics, $[\![p_1]\!]_P(\{\mathbf{r}, \mathsf{phys}\}) = \{1\}$. The indeterminacy in the evaluation of $[\![\cdot]\!]_N$ is due to the fact that depending on the value of the attribute $\mathbf{cf}$, the decision could be either 1 or 0, and thus both decisions are returned.

In practice, it could be argued that the likelihood for a physician to be in conflict with a patient is quite low, and

even though it is useful to know that this possibility exists, the final decision might take into account this likelihood. In this section, we describe how the attribute values can be associated with a given probability. Intuitively, we propose the following approach:

- an attribute value can be either non-deterministic (as in the previous section) or probabilistic;

- we want to know the probability of reaching a decision from a given request rather than just checking whether this decision is reachable;

- before calculating this probability, we need to resolve first the retrieval of non-deterministic attribute values, which leads to multiple probabilities for each decision, one for each possible resolution.

5.1 Attribute value probability

The probability of an attribute value can be modelled with a partial function $\Pr : \mathcal{N} \times \mathcal{V} \mapsto [0, 1]$, such that if $\Pr(n, v)$ is defined, then $\Pr(n, \overline{v})$ is also defined and $\Pr(n, \overline{v}) = 1 - \Pr(n, v)$. If $\Pr(n, v)$ is undefined, then the retrieval of this attribute value remains non-deterministic. Hence, we do not assume that all attribute values are associated with a probability, instead we propose to include probabilities in the decision evaluation when they are defined. We however assume that all probabilities are independent, and do not depend on non deterministic attributes, and we leave for future work the study of more complex probabilistic models. Let us also point out that the probability does not effectively appear in the request, which means that the previous evaluation functions can still be applied. In other words, probabilities can always be ignored if they are not relevant.

As described above, the first step for the probabilistic evaluation of a request is to retrieve the non-deterministic attribute values. Given a request q, we define $\mathsf{ND}(q)$ to be the set of requests which corresponds to q with each non-deterministic attribute value retrieved. More precisely, $\mathsf{ND}(q)$ is the set of requests $q' \supseteq q$ such that for any (n, v) where $\Pr(n, v)$ is undefined, either (n, v) or $(n, \overline{v})$ belongs to q', and for any (n, v) where $\Pr(n, v)$ is defined, (n, v) belongs to q' if and only if (n, v) belongs to q. If no attribute is probabilistic, then $\mathsf{ND}(q)$ corresponds to the set of complete and well-formed requests that include q.

For instance, consider the previous policy p_1 where we define $\Pr(\mathbf{emg}, true) = 0.1$ and $\Pr(\mathbf{cf}, true) = 0.05$. Given the requests $q_1 = \{(\mathbf{r}, \mathsf{phys})\}$ and $q_2 = \{(\mathbf{cf}, true)\}$, we have:

$$\mathsf{ND}(q_1) = \{ \{(\mathbf{r}, \mathsf{phys}), (\mathbf{r}, \mathsf{nurse})\}, $$
$$\{(\mathbf{r}, \mathsf{phys}), (\mathbf{r}, \overline{\mathsf{nurse}})\}\}$$
$$\mathsf{ND}(q_2) = \{ \{(\mathbf{cf}, true), (\mathbf{r}, \mathsf{phys}), (\mathbf{r}, \mathsf{nurse})\}, $$
$$\{(\mathbf{cf}, true), (\mathbf{r}, \mathsf{phys}), (\mathbf{r}, \overline{\mathsf{nurse}})\}\}$$
$$\{(\mathbf{cf}, true), (\mathbf{r}, \overline{\mathsf{phys}}), (\mathbf{r}, \mathsf{nurse})\}\}$$
$$\{(\mathbf{cf}, true), (\mathbf{r}, \overline{\mathsf{phys}}), (\mathbf{r}, \overline{\mathsf{nurse}})\}\}$$

For q_1, the only non-deterministic value is $(\mathbf{r}, \mathsf{nurse})$, and we can add both corresponding values, but we do not add any probabilistic value. For q_2, since $(\mathbf{cf}, true)$ is already retrieved, we do not remove it, but we retrieve instead all possible values for $(\mathbf{r}, \mathsf{phys})$ and $(\mathbf{r}, \mathsf{nurse})$.

Now, given a request in $\mathsf{ND}(q)$, we need to explore all possible extensions with the probabilistic attribute values, and to check the probability with which each decision can be returned. Intuitively, we add all possible probabilistic values not already retrieved, and we multiply the corresponding probability of these values. Hence, given a request $q' \in \mathsf{ND}(q)$, we define $\mathsf{NDP}(q')$ to be the set of requests q'' such that $q'' \supseteq q'$ and q'' is complete and well-formed (i.e., $\mathsf{NDP}(q')$ corresponds to all possible retrieval for the probabilistic values not already in q'). Each q'' is associated with a probability defined as the product of the probabilities of all probabilistic values (n, v) (where v can either be a positive or negative value) belonging to q'' but not to q', which we denote $\mathsf{Pr}(q'' \mid q')$. More formally:

$$\mathsf{Pr}(q'' \mid q') = \prod \{\mathsf{Pr}(n, v) \mid (n, v) \in (q'' \setminus q')\}$$

For instance, for each request in $q' \in \mathsf{ND}(q_1)$ defined above, we can defined $\mathsf{NDP}(q')$ as the set of $q' \cup pv_i$, where the sets pv_i are defined as:

- $pv_1 = \{(\mathbf{emg}, true), (\mathbf{cf}, true)\}$, with the probability $0.1 * 0.05 = 0.005$;

- $pv_2 = \{(\mathbf{emg}, true), (\mathbf{cf}, false)\}$, with the probability $0.1 * 0.95 = 0.095$;

- $pv_3 = \{(\mathbf{emg}, false), (\mathbf{cf}, true)\}$, with the probability $0.9 * 0.05 = 0.045$;

- $pv_4 = \{(\mathbf{emg}, false), (\mathbf{cf}, false)\}$, with the probability $0.9 * 0.95 = 0.855$.

Similarly, we can add to each request in $\mathsf{ND}(q_2)$ defined above either the set $pv_5 = \{(\mathbf{emg}, true)\}$ with the probability 0.1 or the set $pv_6 = \{(\mathbf{emg}, false)\}$ with the probability 0.9.

Finally, we can define the probability of a decision d to be reached from a request $q' \in \mathsf{ND}(q)$ by aggregating the probability of the requests in $\mathsf{NDP}(q')$ for which d is returned, which we defined as $\mathsf{Pr}(d \mid q')$:

$$\mathsf{Pr}(d \mid q') = \sum \left\{\mathsf{Pr}(q'' \mid q') \mid q'' \in \mathsf{NDP}(q') \wedge [\![p]\!]_{\mathrm{C}}(q'') = d\right\}.$$

For instance, in the above example, consider the request $q_{11} = \{(\mathbf{r}, \mathsf{phys}), (\mathbf{r}, \mathsf{nurse})\}$ in $\mathsf{ND}(q_1)$. We have:

$$[\![p_1]\!]_{\mathrm{C}}(q_{11} \cup pv_1) = [\![p_1]\!]_{\mathrm{C}}(q_{11} \cup pv_3) = 0$$
$$[\![p_1]\!]_{\mathrm{C}}(q_{11} \cup pv_2) = [\![p_1]\!]_{\mathrm{C}}(q_{11} \cup pv_4) = 1$$

and it follows that

$$\mathsf{Pr}(0 \mid q_{11}) = 0.005 + 0.095 = 0.05$$
$$\mathsf{Pr}(1 \mid q_{11}) = 0.095 + 0.855 = 0.95$$
$$\mathsf{Pr}(\bot \mid q_{11}) = 0$$

The same results hold for $\{(\mathbf{r}, \mathsf{phys}), (\mathbf{r}, \overline{\mathsf{nurse}})\}$, which corresponds with the fact that if $(\mathbf{r}, \mathsf{phys})$ belongs to the requests, then the request can only be denied if there is a conflict of interest, which can happen with a probability 0.05, otherwise it is granted. In this case, the retrieval of the attribute value $(\mathbf{r}, \mathsf{nurse})$ has no impact.

However, if we consider the request $q_3 = \{(\mathbf{r}, \mathsf{nurse})\}$, the probability of reaching each decision depends on the retrieval of the non-deterministic attribute value $(\mathbf{r}, \mathsf{phys})$. Indeed, consider first the request $q_{31} = \{(\mathbf{r}, \mathsf{nurse}), (\mathbf{r}, \mathsf{phys})\} \in \mathsf{ND}(q_3)$. Clearly, $q_{31} = q_{11}$ and therefore the previous probabilities of reaching each decisions are the same as above.

Table 4: Evaluation of p_1 with $\mathsf{Pr}(\mathbf{emg}, true) = 0.1$ and $\mathsf{Pr}(\mathbf{cf}, true) = 0.05$, where for each q in the first column, the value in the column d corresponds to $[\![p_1]\!]_{\min}(q, d), [\![p_1]\!]_{\max}(q, d)$.

| | decision d | | |
Request	0	1	$\bot$
$\emptyset$	[0.05,0.05]	[0,0.95]	[0,0.95]
$\{(\mathbf{r}, \mathsf{phys})\}$	[0.05,0.05]	[0.95,0.95]	[0,0]
$\{(\mathbf{r}, \mathsf{phys}), (\mathbf{cf}, true)\}$	[1,1]	[0,0]	[0,0]
$\{(\mathbf{r}, \mathsf{nurse})\}$	[0.05,0.05]	[0.095,0.95]	[0,0.855]
$\{(\mathbf{r}, \mathsf{nurse}), (\mathbf{emg}, true)\}$	[0.05,0.05]	[0.95,0.95]	[0,0]

However consider now the request $q_{32} = \{(\mathbf{r}, \mathsf{nurse}), (\mathbf{r}, \overline{\mathsf{phys}})\} \in \mathsf{ND}(q_3)$

$$[\![p_1]\!]_{\mathrm{C}}(q_{32} \cup pv_1) = [\![p_1]\!]_{\mathrm{C}}(q_{32} \cup pv_3) = 0$$
$$[\![p_1]\!]_{\mathrm{C}}(q_{32} \cup pv_2) = 1$$
$$[\![p_1]\!]_{\mathrm{C}}(q_{32} \cup pv_4) = \bot$$

and it follows that

$$\mathsf{Pr}(0 \mid q_{32}) = 0.005 + 0.095 = 0.05$$
$$\mathsf{Pr}(1 \mid q_{32}) = 0.095$$
$$\mathsf{Pr}(\bot \mid q_{32}) = 0.855$$

Hence, the probability of reaching the decisions 1 and $\bot$ depend on the retrieval of the attribute value $(\mathbf{r}, \mathsf{phys})$. Since this value is non-deterministic, the probabilities $\mathsf{Pr}(1 \mid q_{31})$ and $\mathsf{Pr}(1 \mid q_{32})$ correspond to different possible futures, and thus cannot be "merged" together. We therefore define here two new evaluation functions, $[\![\cdot]\!]_{\min}$ and $[\![\cdot]\!]_{\max}$, which compute the minimal and the maximal probability to reach a given decision d from a given query q. More formally:

$$[\![p]\!]_{\min}(q, d) = \min_{q' \in \mathsf{ND}(q)} \mathsf{Pr}(q' \mid d)$$
$$[\![p]\!]_{\max}(q, d) = \max_{q' \in \mathsf{ND}(q)} \mathsf{Pr}(q' \mid d)$$

Table 4 summaries the evaluation of the policy p_1 for the different requests previously considered. It is worth pointing out that the resolution of the non-determinism used to calculate the minimal/maximal probability for a decision can change from one decision to another, so the minimal/maximal probabilities do not necessarily add up to 1.

It is also worth noting that $[\![\cdot]\!]_{\min}$ and $[\![\cdot]\!]_{\max}$ are consistent with $[\![\cdot]\!]_{\mathrm{N}}$, i.e., for any policy p, any request q and any decision d, $[\![p]\!]_{\min}(q, d) = [\![p]\!]_{\max}(q, d) = 0$ if and only if $d \notin [\![p]\!]_{\mathrm{N}}(q)$. The interest of $[\![\cdot]\!]_{\min}$ and $[\![\cdot]\!]_{\max}$ therefore lies with decision that have non null probabilities.

When $[\![p]\!]_{\min}(q, d) = [\![p]\!]_{\max}(q, d)$, the probability of reaching a decision is the same regardless of the resolution of non-determinism, which provides useful information to reach a conclusive decision. For instance, for the request $\{(\mathbf{r}, \mathsf{phys})\}$, it could be a reasonable choice to select the conclusive decision 1, since it is the one with the highest probability.

However, when $[\![p]\!]_{\min}(q, d) \neq [\![p]\!]_{\max}(q, d)$, deciding a conclusive decision can be more complex. For instance, with the empty request, we can observe that the minimal probability for the decision 0 is not null, even though this decision is not returned in the basic PTaCL evaluation (see Table 2). On the other hand, there are some non-deterministic retrieval for which the probability of 1 is null. Clearly, there is no easy way to solve this particular request, and probabilistic

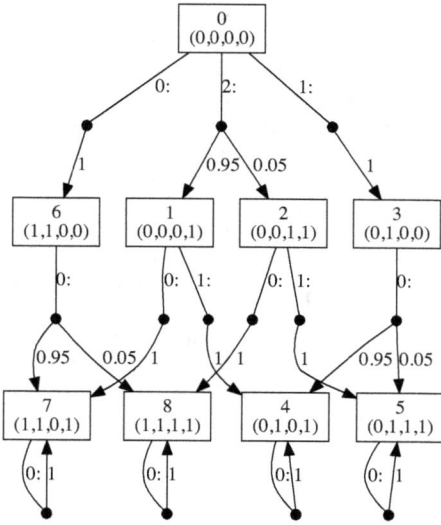

Figure 1: PRISM transition matrix with the values $(\mathbf{r}, \mathsf{phys})$ and $(\mathbf{cf}, true)$, and $\Pr(\mathbf{cf}, true) = 0.05$.

5.2 PRISM encoding

For any attribute value (n, v) such that $\Pr(n, v) = p_{nv}$, we change the generated PRISM module to:

```
const double p_n_v = pnv;

module att_n_v
  n_v: bool init false;
  r_n_v: bool init false;
  [] !r_n_v → p_n_v:(n_v'=true) & (r_n_v'=true)
    + (1 − p_n_v):(n_v'=false) & (r_n_v'=true);
endmodule
```

The encoding of non-deterministic attribute values and of target and policies is identical to the previous section.

For instance, Figure 1 is automatically generated from the PRISM model containing the values $(\mathbf{r}, \mathsf{phys})$ and $(\mathbf{cf}, true)$[4]. Each state is therefore a tuple (r_role_phys, role_phys, r_cf_true, cf_true), transitions with a label i: corresponds to non-deterministic choices (note that there is no actual ordering between these transitions, the label only serve for identification purposes), while the other transitions are labelled with their associated probability. The label inside each square corresponds to the lexicographic ordering of the states.

In order to compute the function $[\![\cdot]\!]_{\min}$ and $[\![\cdot]\!]_{\max}$, we use the PRISM operators Pmin and Pmax, respectively. Given a path property ϕ, Pmin =? ϕ and Pmax =? ϕ returns the minimum and maximum probabilities of this property to hold, after resolving non-determinism.

PROPOSITION 3. *Given a policy p, a request q and a decision d, we have:*

$$[\![p]\!]_{\min}(q, d) = \mathsf{filter}(\mathsf{first}, \mathsf{Pmin} =? \ [\mathsf{F} \ \mathsf{complete} \ \& \ \widehat{p} = d], \widetilde{q})$$

$$[\![p]\!]_{\max}(q, d) = \mathsf{filter}(\mathsf{first}, \mathsf{Pmax} =? \ [\mathsf{F} \ \mathsf{complete} \ \& \ \widehat{p} = d], \widetilde{q})$$

---

[4] Any larger model is too large to be meaningfully presented here.

Figure 2: Performance analysis of $[\![\cdot]\!]_N$ (blue triangles) and $[\![\cdot]\!]_{\min} + [\![\cdot]\!]_{\max}$ (green triangles) for randomly generated PTaCL policies.

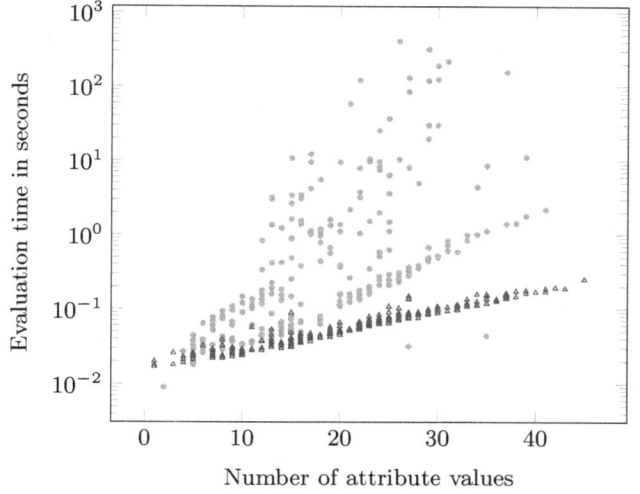

PROOF. The combination of first and $\widetilde{q}$ ensures that we only consider paths starting from the state corresponding exactly to the request q. Since we impose in the path property for complete to hold, we know that we only check the decision on complete requests that extend q. Finally, the operators Pmin and Pmax automatically resolve the non-determinism by considering all possible non-deterministic retrievals. □

6. PERFORMANCE EVALUATION

In order to measure the performances of our PRISM encoding, we have generated 261 random PTaCL policies, with a number of attribute values included between 1 and 42, such that some attribute values are associated with a random probability, while the others are defined as non-deterministic.

For each policy p, we first measure the time required to compute $[\![p]\!]_N(\emptyset)$. Note that the empty request is the request requiring the most space exploration. These values are depicted with the blue triangle points in Figure 2, and have been measured with PRISM v4.2.beta1 and the MTBDD engine, and a Macbook Air with 2 GHz Intel Core i7 and 8 GB or RAM. We can observe that the computation time of $[\![\cdot]\!]_N$, although exponentially increasing with the number of attribute values (the y axis uses a logarithmic scale), is consistently below 0.1 second.

For each policy, we then compute $[\![p]\!]_{\min}(\emptyset, d)$ and $[\![p]\!]_{\max}(\emptyset, d)$, for all $d \in \{0, 1, \bot\}$, and each green circle in Figure 2 represents the sum of the evaluation of all corresponding PRISM properties. We can observe that the evaluation time also increases exponentially with the number of attribute values. There is more variety in the evaluation time compared to $[\![\cdot]\!]_N$, and for some policy, it can take more than 100 seconds to evaluate the empty requests. However, it is worth pointing out that 88 out 261 policies evaluated under 0.1 seconds, 189 under 1 second and 240 under 10 seconds. Finally, for each policy, the time required by PRISM by building and loading in memory the model is very close to that required to compute $[\![\cdot]\!]_N$, and therefore is not shown in Figure 2. Note that this time is the same, regardless of the evaluation function chosen.

These results show first that that $[\![\cdot]\!]_N$ is relatively efficient, with little variation, while $[\![\cdot]\!]_{min}$ and $[\![\cdot]\!]_{max}$ can be still practical, but can also be very long to compute. However, it is also worth pointing out that concrete access control policies tend to be more structured than randomly generated ones, and as such, model checking can be more efficient. In addition, some decisions can be cached [16]. Hence, these results should not necessarily be interpreted as providing an average computation time based on the size of the policy, but rather as an indication that $[\![\cdot]\!]_N$ can be first used for evaluation, since it is relatively fast, and in case of indeterminacy, $[\![\cdot]\!]_{min}$ and $[\![\cdot]\!]_{max}$ can be used to try to decide on a conclusive decision based on the probabilities of the decisions. Of course, as illustrated in the previous section, these probabilities are not necessarily sufficient to decide on a conclusive decision, but our approach consists in providing as much meaningful information as possible.

7. DISCUSSION – CONCLUSION

In the previous sections, given a policy p and a request q, we have defined several evaluation functions, each computing a different set of decisions for the same request:

- $[\![p]\!]_P(q)$ is the original PTaCL definition, which follows the XACML definition, and which considers that if an attribute value (n, v) is required by the target of a sub-policy of p, but the n is not present at all in q, then the target evaluation fails and the sub-policy evaluates both to $\bot$ and to the value the policy would have returned had (n, v) been present in q.

- $[\![p]\!]_C(q)$ considers that in the case described above, the target evaluation should not fail, and the policy should simply evaluate to $\bot$.

- $[\![p]\!]_N(q)$ returns all the possible decisions reachable by adding all missing attributes in q.

- $[\![p]\!]_{min}(q, d)$ and $[\![p]\!]_{max}(q, d)$ consider that some attribute values can be probabilistic and return the minimum and maximum probability, respectively, to reach the decision d by adding all missing attributes in q, for any possible retrieval of the non-deterministic attribute values.

We have shown in Section 3.4 that $[\![\cdot]\!]_P$ can be counter intuitive, because it can return some decisions that are not reachable, and not return some decisions that are reachable, where $[\![\cdot]\!]_N$ returns exactly all reachable decisions. $[\![\cdot]\!]_{min}$ and $[\![\cdot]\!]_{max}$ are equivalent to $[\![\cdot]\!]_N$ when there is no probabilistic attribute value, and can provide more information of the reachability of the decisions otherwise.

However, although these new evaluation functions are somehow more accurate than $[\![\cdot]\!]_P$, they are also more computationally intensive, since they must explore the space of possible request extensions, as shown in the previous section.

An interesting and general question concerns whether probabilities can be meaningfully used in security systems, and this question can be split in two parts. Firstly, is it possible to define the probabilities for attribute values? Clearly, in general, it is not possible to know the probability of all possible attribute values. However, we believe

that a strength of our approach is its ability to mix non-deterministic and probabilistic attribute retrieval, which allows for a "best effort" strategy: by specifying the information we know, we can get a somehow more accurate analysis.

Secondly, can the resolution mechanism use these probabilities to make a final decision? This aspect is particularly important when the resolution mechanism is done by human users, who are known not to be particularly good at understanding probabilities when making choices [15]. In other words, the way we present the result from the function $[\![\cdot]\!]_{min}$ and $[\![\cdot]\!]_{max}$ can have an impact on the final choice made by a user, as suggested in [9].

In addition, more complex policy analyses could be considered from the angle of non-deterministic and probabilistic attribute retrieval, such as policy safety [7], or the integration of administrative policies.

8. REFERENCES

[1] P. Bonatti, S. De Capitani Di Vimercati, and P. Samarati. An algebra for composing access control policies. *ACM Transactions on Information and System Security*, 5(1):1–35, 2002.

[2] G. Bruns and M. Huth. Access control via Belnap logic: Intuitive, expressive, and analyzable policy composition. *ACM Transactions on Information and System Security*, 14(1):9, 2011.

[3] E. M. Clarke, O. Grumberg, and D. Peled. *Model checking*. MIT press, 1999.

[4] J. Crampton and M. Huth. An authorization framework resilient to policy evaluation failures. In *ESORICS*, LNCS 6345, pages 472–487, 2010.

[5] J. Crampton and C. Morisset. PTaCL: A language for attribute-based access control in open systems. In *POST*, LNCS 7215, pages 390–409, 2012.

[6] K. Fisler, S. Krishnamurthi, L. A. Meyerovich, and M. C. Tschantz. Verification and change-impact analysis of access-control policies. In *Proceedings of the 27th International Conference on Software Engineering*, pages 196–205. ACM, 2005.

[7] A. Griesmayer and C. Morisset. Automated certification of authorisation policy resistance. In *ESORICS*, LNCS 8134, pages 574–591. Springer, 2013.

[8] S. Kleene. *Introduction to Metamathematics*. D. Van Nostrand, Princeton, NJ, 1950.

[9] C. Morisset, T. Groß, A. P. A. van Moorsel, and I. Yevseyeva. Nudging for quantitative access control systems. In *Human Aspects of Information Security, Privacy, and Trust*, LNCS 8533, pages 340–351. Springer, 2014.

[10] C. Morisset and N. Zannone. Reduction of access control decisions. In *Proceedings of the 19th ACM Symposium on Access Control Models and Technologies*, pages 53–62. ACM, 2014.

[11] OASIS. *eXtensible Access Control Markup Language (XACML) Version 3.0*, 2010. Committee Specification.

[12] S. Ranise and A. T. Truong. Incremental analysis of evolving administrative role based access control policies. In *Data and Applications Security and Privacy*, LNCS 8566, pages 260–275. Springer, 2014.

[13] S. Ranise, A. T. Truong, and A. Armando. Scalable and precise automated analysis of administrative temporal role-based access control. In *Proceedings of*

19th Symposium on Access Control Models and Technologies, pages 103–114. ACM, 2014.

[14] M. C. Tschantz and S. Krishnamurthi. Towards reasonability properties for access-control policy languages. In *Proceedings of 11th ACM Symposium on Access Control Models and Technologies*, pages 160–169. ACM, 2006.

[15] A. Tversky and D. Kahneman. The framing of decisions and the psychology of choice. *Science*, 211(4481):453–458, 1981.

[16] Q. Wei, J. Crampton, K. Beznosov, and M. Ripeanu. Authorization recycling in hierarchical RBAC systems. *ACM Trans. Inf. Syst. Secur.*, 14(1):3, 2011.

[17] D. Wijesekera and S. Jajodia. A propositional policy algebra for access control. *ACM Transactions on Information and System Security*, 6(2):286–235, 2003.

[18] N. Zhang, M. Ryan, and D. P. Guelev. Evaluating access control policies through model checking. In *ISC*, LNCS 3650, pages 446–460, 2005.

Challenges in Making Access Control Sensitive to the "Right" Contexts

Trent Jaeger
Pennsylvania State University
Systems and Internet Infrastructure Security (SIIS) Lab
University Park, PA USA
tjaeger@cse.psu.edu

ABSTRACT

Access control is a fundamental security mechanism that both protects processes from attacks and confines compromised processes that may try to propagate an attack. Nonetheless, we still see an ever increasing number of software vulnerabilities. Researchers have long proposed that improvements in access control could prevent many vulnerabilities, many of which capture contextual information to more accurately detect obviously unsafe operations. However, developers are often hesitant to extend their access control mechanisms to use more sensitive access control policies. My experience leads me to propose that it is imperative that an access control systems be able to extract context accurately and efficiently and be capable of inferring any non-trivial policies. In this talk, I will discuss some recent research that enforces context-sensitive policies by either extracting process context, integrating code to extract context from programs, or extracting user context. We find that context-sensitive mechanisms can prevent some obviously unsafe operations from being authorized efficiently and discuss our experiences in inferring access control policies. Based on this research, we are encouraged that future research may enable context-sensitive access control policies to be produced and enforced to prevent vulnerabilities.

Categories and Subject Descriptors

D.4.6 [**Software**]: Operating Systems—*Security and Protection*

General Terms

Access controls, Information flow controls

Keywords

Context sensitivity, capabilities, program analysis

1. ACKNOWLEDGMENTS

This material is based upon work supported by the National Science Foundation under Grant Nos. CNS-1408880 and CNS-1117692. This material is based on research sponsored by the Air Force Office of Sponsored Research (AFOSR), under agreement number FA9550-12-1-0166. The U.S. Government is authorized to reproduce and distribute reprints for Governmental purposes notwithstanding any copyright notation thereon.

Relationship-Based Access Control for an Open-Source Medical Records System

Syed Zain R. Rizvi   Philip W. L. Fong
University of Calgary
Alberta, Canada
{szrrizvi, pwlfong}@ucalgary.ca

Jason Crampton   James Sellwood
Royal Holloway, University of London
Egham, United Kingdom
jason.crampton@rhul.ac.uk
james.sellwood.2010@live.rhul.ac.uk

ABSTRACT

Inspired by the access control models of social network systems, Relationship-Based Access Control (ReBAC) was recently proposed as a general-purpose access control paradigm for application domains in which authorization must take into account the relationship between the access requestor and the resource owner. The healthcare domain is envisioned to be an archetypical application domain in which ReBAC is sorely needed: e.g., my patient record should be accessible only by my family doctor, but not by all doctors.

In this work, we demonstrate for the first time that ReBAC can be incorporated into a production-scale medical records system, OpenMRS, with backward compatibility to the legacy RBAC mechanism. Specifically, we extend the access control mechanism of OpenMRS to enforce ReBAC policies. Our extensions incorporate and extend advanced ReBAC features recently proposed by Crampton and Sellwood. In addition, we designed and implemented the first administrative model for ReBAC. In this paper, we describe our ReBAC implementation, discuss the system engineering lessons learnt as a result, and evaluate the experimental work we have undertaken. In particular, we compare the performance of the various authorization schemes we implemented, thereby demonstrating the feasibility of ReBAC.

Categories and Subject Descriptors

D.4.6 [**Security and Protection**]: Access Control

Keywords

Medical records system, relationship-based access control, authorization graph, authorization principal, administrative model

1. INTRODUCTION

OpenMRS [4] is a production-scale, open-source electronic medical records system that has been deployed in many countries, including South Africa, Kenya, Rwanda, India,

China, United States, Pakistan, the Phillipines, etc. Despite its tremendous success and wide deployment, OpenMRS has a limitation in its access control mechanism, which is an instantiation of *Role-Based Access Control (RBAC)*. This limitation is the topic of the following posting in the developer forum [28].

> The RBAC system provides a reasonably robust mechanism for restricting access to system behaviours; however, we do not yet have a mechanism for restricting access to specific data (e.g., you can see data for patient X, but not patient Y; or, you can see your patient's data except for specific lab results).

An interpretation of the above limitation is that, while it is possible to restrict access of patient records to the role of doctors, it is not possible to restrict access of *my* patient record to *my* family doctor. RBAC satisfies the access control requirements of business domains in which data objects are "owned" by the organization, and thus all qualified personnel (i.e., of a certain role) may be granted access. In application domains in which privacy is a concern, the data objects are sometimes "owned" by individuals. There is now a need for finer-grained access control: e.g., my patient record shall only be accessible by the clinicians who are actually treating me. That is, access is granted on the basis of how the requestors are related to me.[1]

The above access control challenge is one of the primary motivations for the recently proposed *Relationship-Based Access Control (ReBAC)* models. Originally inspired by the access control models of social network systems (e.g., Facebook), ReBAC grants access based on how the access requester is related to the resource owner (e.g., friends, friends-of-friends). This is in contrast with RBAC, in which access is granted by considering the attributes of the requestor. Fong *et al.* proposed a series of general-purpose ReBAC models [19, 21, 10], in which ReBAC is envisioned to be applied to application domains other than social computing, with the healthcare domain being an archetypical example. While the idea of ReBAC has undergone a number of recent extensions in the literature [14, 13, 6, 16, 20, 33], *what remains to be seen is the adoption of ReBAC in a production-scale system for an application domain other than social computing. And this is the gap we attempt to bridge by extending the access control subsystem of OpenMRS to include an implementation of a ReBAC model.*

---

[1]Further examples of relationships are given in §7 and §9.

In this paper, we report our experience of extending the access control subsystem of OpenMRS with a ReBAC model. The "diff" between our extension and the original OpenMRS code base consists of 25,754 lines (with no context lines). The extension involves 113 new files, 26 new database tables, and 15 web pages. Our contributions are the following.

1. We demonstrated for the first time that ReBAC can be incorporated into a production-scale medical records system, and did so with backward compatibility to the legacy RBAC mechanism.

2. We identified system engineering issues that one needs to address when one is to cleanly and efficiently implement ReBAC in a large system (§4, §5, §6 and §10).

3. We adapted, extended and implemented the advanced features of ReBAC that were recently proposed by Crampton and Sellwood [16]. The implemented features include a generalization of social graphs called authorization graphs (§5), a ReBAC analogue of roles called authorization principals (§7), and a Unix-style authorization mechanism for authorization principals (§8). Because OpenMRS supports a rich mechanism of privilege matching, the notions of authorization principals and authorization algorithms as proposed in [16] must be either adapted (§7) or extended (§8). Our novel extensions involve the proposal of two semantics of authorization (strict-grant vs liberal-grant), as well as a highly efficient principal matching algorithm based on the idea of lazy evaluation (lazy-match). What is pleasantly surprising is that, even after extensive adjustments in our implementation, the basic spirit of Crampton and Sellwood's design is preserved, thereby demonstrating the robustness of their proposals.

4. We designed and implemented an administrative model for ReBAC (§9). To the best of our knowledge, this is the first such implementation.

5. We empirically evaluated the performance of the various authorization schemes in item 3 above (§10). The evaluation is performed on a social network of 1.6 million nodes and 30 million directed edges. The lazy-match algorithm is found to offer competitive performance.

2. RELATED WORK

It has long been observed that the health domain requires an access control model that takes into account the relationship between the resource owner and the access requestor when an authorization decision is made [9, 29]. That was partly the reason that led to the proposal of an extension of OpenMRS to incorporate parameterized roles [18].

Relationship-Based Access Control was a term coined independently by Gates [22] and Carminati and Ferrari [11] to refer to a paradigm of access control in which authorization decisions are based on whether the resource owner and the access requestor are related in a certain way. Initially, ReBAC was envisioned to be applied to the domain of social computing. A seminal work with this application in mind was that of Carminati et al. [12].

Fong et al. proposed a series of general-purpose ReBAC models [19, 21, 10], and advocated the adoption of ReBAC for application domains outside of social computing. The health domain was envisioned to be an application domain in which ReBAC is particularly suited. ReBAC protection states are social networks. Modal logic and hybrid logic were

proposed as policy languages for specifying ReBAC policies [19, 21, 10].

In UURAC (user-to-user relationship-based access control) [14], a policy is specified in a regular expression-based policy language. Access is granted if the resource owner and the access requestor are connected by a path made up of a sequence of edge labels satisfying the regular expression. An algorithm for finding a path that honors the regular expression is formulated. In a subsequent work [13], the protection states were extended to track relationships between user and resources (U2R) as well as between resources and resources (R2R). Another innovation is the provision for multiple policies to be applicable to the protection of a resource, and the design of conflict resolution policies (conjunctive, disjunctive and precedence) to arbitrate authorization decisions. The work proposes to employ ReBAC to regulate administrative activities, but does not provide details on how that is achieved. The administrative actions we proposed in §9 has clear semantics of how they are protected by security preconditions, and how their executions affect the protection state.

In [20], a temporal dimension is introduced into ReBAC, so that access control policies require entities to be related in a certain way in the past. The goal of this extension is to support the expression of social contracts in online communities. In [33], ReBAC is extended to account for geo-social network systems, and the hybrid logic policy language is extended to impose relationship constraints over people located in a certain geographical neighbourhood.

Crampton and Sellwood recently proposed a series of extensions to ReBAC [16]. The protection state is an authorization graph that tracks relationships among users, resources, as well as other abstract entities relevant to access control (e.g., groups, roles, etc). They also proposed a ReBAC analogue of roles called authorization principals. The run-time semantics of authorization principals are specified through path conditions, a language akin to regular expressions. An XACML-style conflict resolution mechanism was proposed to arbitrate authorizations when the access requestor is associated with authorization principals that grant conflicting authorizations. A UNIX-inspired authorization procedure serves as a framework for binding these technologies together. Our implementation has adopted the ideas of authorization graphs, authorization principals, and the UNIX-style authorization procedure. Yet we employ hybrid logic rather than path conditions for specifying the denotation of authorization principals. Detailed comparison with [16] will be given in the rest of this paper.

It has long been recognized that any practical access control system must provide ways to modify the authorization state or policy [24, 30]. While administrative access control models, which control modifications to policies, have been widely studied for the protection matrix and RBAC, this is a relatively unexplored area in the context of ReBAC. Fong's ReBAC model allows for changes to the protection state through the use of contexts [19], but we are not aware of any implementation of administrative features for ReBAC.

3. ReBAC GOES OPEN SOURCE

This section reviews the background materials needed for understanding the rest of the paper.

3.1 An Overview of ReBAC

In a series of papers [19, 21, 10], Fong *et al.* proposed a general-purpose access control model for Relationship-Based Access Control (ReBAC). This work is mainly based on the variant of the model discussed in [10].

The protection state of ReBAC is an edge-labelled, directed graph: directed edges represent interpersonal relationships, and each edge is labelled with a relation identifier to signify the type of relation (e.g., patient-of). In the original conception of ReBAC, vertices represent users, and thus the protection state is a social network. (In §5, we follow the proposal of [16], and generalize the social network to an authorization graph.)

A *graph predicate* determines whether particular conditions, relating the vertices in a graph, hold or not. We might, for example, define a predicate that returns true if two vertices are connected by an edge having a particular label. More formally, a *graph predicate of arity* k is a Boolean-valued function $GP(G, x_1, \ldots, x_k)$, where G is a graph that defines the current protection state of the system, and each x_i is a vertex in G. GP evaluates to 1 if and only if $(x_1, \ldots, x_k)$ belongs to a k-ary relation defined over G. A graph predicate of arity 2 is said to be a *relationship predicate*. The relationship predicate friend-of-friend(G, x_1, x_2), for example, returns 1 iff there exists a path of length two or less in G connecting x_1 and x_2, where both edges in the path are labelled with the relationship type friend.

A ReBAC policy has the form "*grant access to r if RP evaluates to 1*", where r is a resource and RP is a relationship predicate [10]. An access request has the form (v, r), where user v wishes to access resource r. Access is permitted if $RP(G, u, v)$ evaluates to 1, where u is the owner of resource r. (In §7, we adopt a recent idea due to Crampton and Sellwood [16], and formulate ReBAC policies in terms of authorization principals — a ReBAC analogue of roles.)

A graph predicate $GP(G, x_1, \ldots, x_k)$ (with a relationship predicate as a special case) can be syntactically specified as a Hybrid Logic formula ϕ [10] with k free variables.[2] A local model checker is an algorithm that takes as input (i) a hybrid logic formula ϕ with k free variables, (ii) a protection state G, and (iii) k vertices $v_1, \ldots, v_k$, and then decides whether the k-ary graph predicate represented by ϕ is satisfied by $v_1, \ldots, v_k$ in G.

In the rest of this paper, knowledge of hybrid logic is not necessary for appreciating the contributions of this work. Nevertheless, examples of hybrid logic formulas will be shown to convey the realism of our design. Readers who are unfamiliar with hybrid logic can safely skip those examples.

3.2 The ReBAC Java Library

A reusable Java library of ReBAC technologies was released under open-source terms [8]. The library was developed and maintained separately from OpenMRS. The library was also packaged as a Maven module for easy integration with large projects.

A main feature of the ReBAC library is the implementation of a local model checker for the hybrid logic policy language of [10]. This model checker is a cornerstone of the authorization mechanism in our OpenMRS extension, allowing us to determine membership in authorization principal (§7), as well as to test if an administrative action is enabled and/or applicable (§8).

Recall that the inputs to a local model checker include a graph and the abstract syntax tree (AST) of a hybrid logic formula. To allow the model checker to interoperate with different representations of graphs, we have defined a Java interface for graphs. For example, in the case of OpenMRS, relationship edges may come from three different sources (§5). A concrete class that makes appropriate queries to check for existence of each of the three kinds of relationships will implement the graph interface, thereby allowing the model checker to interoperate with OpenMRS.

Similarly, Java interfaces are declared for the AST nodes of hybrid logic formulas. This allows the model checker to work with different representations of hybrid logic formulas. One may ask why there is a need for different representations of hybrid logic formulas. A motivating example comes from OpenMRS. In OpenMRS, all data objects are stored as persistent objects (via Hibernate [25]). That includes AST nodes of hybrid logic formulas. Consequently, there are concrete representational demands on how AST node classes are declared (e.g., must be a subclass of a certain superclass). Declaring interfaces for AST nodes allows our model checker to interoperate with such representational idiosyncrasies.

Other features of the library include an XML parser for hybrid logic formulas that are stored as XML files.

4. ARCHITECTURE OF OpenMRS

This section introduces the architecture of OpenMRS, and explains how ReBAC is built on top of this architecture.

4.1 Interposition via AOP

Our ReBAC implementation is based on the source code of OpenMRS 1.10.[3] OpenMRS is built on the Spring Framework, which is a Java-based web application framework [32]. Core functionalities of OpenMRS are exposed as *service-layer methods* on the web application server. The HTML pages invoke the service-layer methods in order to query application data or alter application state. Access control is achieved by limiting access to the service-layer methods.

Each service-layer method is annotated with either one of two kinds of guard.[4] Intuitively, a guard is a specification of privilege requirements that must be satisfied by the requestor in order for the invocation of the service-layer method to be allowed.

1. one-of(P): Here P is a set of privileges (i.e., positive permissions). The intended meaning is that the invoker of this method must have been granted one of the privileges in P in order for method invocation to be authorized.

2. all-of(P): The invoker must have all of the privileges in P.

---

[2]More specifically, a graph predicate of arity k can be represented by a hybrid logic formula ϕ with k free variables, such that ϕ is a Boolean combination of *anchored formulas*. Each anchored formula is one in which the top-level operator is @$_x$, where x is one of the free variables. This is a generalization of the syntactic restriction adopted in [10] for relationship predicates (i.e., arity 2).

[3]The latest stable version of OpenMRS is 2.0, released on February 26, 2014.

[4]Annotation is achieved via the Java custom annotation mechanism [23, §9.7].

Formally, we write $Q \models g$ for a set Q of privileges and a guard g whenever Q *satisfies* g in the following sense:

$$Q \models \texttt{one-of}(P) \quad \text{iff} \quad P \cap Q \neq \emptyset$$
$$Q \models \texttt{all-of}(P) \quad \text{iff} \quad P \subseteq Q$$

Intuitively, if a requestor u has been "*granted*" a set Q of privileges, and $Q \models g$, where g is the guard of the method that u attempts to invoke, then invocation is authorized. (As we shall see in §8, there are two ways to interpret the word "*granted*", thereby yielding two authorization semantics.)

Spring uses aspect-oriented programming (AOP) [26] to implement interposition of authorization checks. The original authorization checking code is implemented as an "advice" (more precisely, a "before advice") that is "weaved" into the entry point of each service-layer method, thereby introducing additional behaviour on method entry. Thus every method invocation is intercepted by the RBAC authorization mechanism. To implement ReBAC, we introduced an additional authorization advice. The ReBAC authorization advice is an "around advice", which introduces additional behaviour at both the entry and exit of a method. Consequently every method invocation as well as method return is intercepted by the ReBAC authorization mechanism.

LESSON 1. *Physically localizing all authorization checks in an identifiable code unit (e.g., module, reference monitor, aspect, etc) greatly eases the extension of the authorization mechanism to incorporate ReBAC.*

In fact, the above lesson applies generally to all software systems that anticipate future evolution in their authorization mechanisms (incorporating ReBAC is but one possible evolution), and we have very positive experience with AOP in this regard.

4.2 Combining RBAC and ReBAC

Unmodified, OpenMRS enforces a Role-Based Access Control (RBAC) model [31], although the notion of sessions is not implemented. That is, all roles assigned to a user are activated when the user logs into the system. The likely reason is that the notion of role activation is probably too exotic for medical professionals, and the extra step of role activation in every log-in attempt would degrade care delivery efficiency. It has also been pointed out that the support for sessions is not essential to core RBAC implementations in certain application domains [27].

As discussed in §4.1, the original RBAC authorization checks are implemented as an advice. We implemented ReBAC authorization checks as a separate advice. The configuration is that the RBAC authorization checks are conducted first, and only when access is granted by RBAC will the ReBAC authorization checks be conducted. In summary, access is granted when both the RBAC and ReBAC mechanisms authorize access. We have also tailored configuration files in such a way that system administrators who do not use the new ReBAC features will not observe any difference between the original implementation and the extended one.

LESSON 2 (BACKWARD COMPATIBILITY). *Care must be taken to ensure that ReBAC features are backward compatible with the legacy access control model of the system.*

Crampton and Sellwood proposed a way of "encoding" RBAC in their extended ReBAC model [16]. This suggests an alternative means for integrating ReBAC and RBAC: implement only a ReBAC model, and simulate RBAC with ReBAC. Such an approach would be particularly fitting if the software application is written from scratch with a requirement to support both access control models.

4.3 Protection and Application State

In an application with a traditional access control model (e.g., RBAC), the protection state (e.g., role hierarchy, user-role assignment, etc) of the system is separate from its application state (i.e., application data). This is true of the original architecture of OpenMRS.

In social computing systems, however, the above is not necessarily true. For example, the interpersonal relationships articulated by users in a social network system is both application data and part of the protection state: authorization is granted based on the relationship between the resource owner and requestor. Inspired by social computing applications, ReBAC inherits this overlapping of protection and application state.

The above overlap is also present in the ReBAC extension of OpenMRS. Included in a patient record is a set of users (e.g., family members) related to the patient, as well as their relationships. This, for example, allows clinicians to anticipate hereditary conditions, or to identify compatible blood, organ and tissue donors. These relationships obviously belong to the application state of OpenMRS. Yet, as we shall see below, ReBAC authorization checks also make use of such relationships when an authorization decision is computed. That is, these relationships constitute part of the protection state.

The above overlap creates something of a dilemma. In the original OpenMRS architecture, patient relationships are accessible only via service-layer methods, thereby ensuring complete mediation. Yet, the ReBAC authorization advice also needs to access patient relationships. The advice will therefore need to invoke service-layer methods in order to access the relationships. As invocations of service-layer methods are intercepted by the authorization advice, this inevitably leads to an infinite loop.

All patient data, including patient relationships, are stored as Hibernate persistent objects [25]. These persistent objects are made accessible via Data Access Objects (DAOs). To break the infinite loop, we created direct access paths to patient relationships by configuring DAOs specifically for the ReBAC authorization advice, so that the latter may access patient relationships without mediation of authorization checks. The above experience leads to the articulation of the following general lesson for ReBAC systems.

LESSON 3 (APPLICATION AND PROTECTION STATE). *Data belonging to both the application and protection state of a system must be held in a data store which exposes two Application Programming Interfaces (APIs). One is mediated by authorization checks, the other is not. The mediated API is invoked by users, while the unmediated one is utilized internally for authorization.*

5. AUTHORIZATION GRAPH

In the early conception of ReBAC [10], the protection state is a social network of users: an edge-labelled, directed graph in which vertices represent users and edges model their interpersonal relationships. Crampton and Sellwood proposed an extension of ReBAC in which the protection state is an *authorization graph* [16]. The vertices model not only users, but also resources as well as other entities that are relevant to access control (e.g., groups). The edges capture relationships among users, objects and the aforementioned entities. Our ReBAC adaptation of OpenMRS implements the idea of authorization graphs.

When one applies ReBAC to an enterprise application domain (i.e., a domain other than social computing), a frequently raised question is: Where do the relationships come from? This rest of this section reports our answer to this question, as shaped by our experience with OpenMRS.

In OpenMRS, domain objects are all instances of the root class `BaseOpenmrsObject`, which has two subclasses `BaseOpenmrsData` and `BaseOpenmrsMetadata`. The instances of `BaseOpenmrsData` include users, patient records and their components, etc. Therefore, we take all instances of `BaseOpenmrsData` as the vertices of the authorization graph.

The authorization graph tracks binary relationships among instances of `BaseOpenmrsData`. During our development of the ReBAC extensions for OpenMRS, we identified three categories of relationships.

1. *User-managed relationships.* These are relationships that are explicitly articulated and managed by end users. An example is friendship in Facebook.

    As we mentioned in §4.3, OpenMRS enables a clinician to document in a patient record the relatives of the patient. These interpersonal relationships are considered part of the authorization graph. More specifically, `BaseOpenmrsData` has a subclass `Person`. Recorded interpersonal relationships between instances of `Person` are considered to be edges in the authorization graph.

2. *System-induced relationships.* The data structures of the system may contain relationships that are relevant to authorization. Examples include organizational structures, object ownership, object containment and provenance relationships. End users are not allowed to directly manipulate these relationships.

    In our ReBAC adaptation of OpenMRS, we have created an extension mechanism for administrators to introduce new system-induced relationships. Specifically, a system-induced binary relation is implemented as a Java class that performs queries into the run-time data structures of OpenMRS. Such a class implements the `ImplicitRelationIdentifier` interface, which defines a standard calling convention for performing relationship queries. At run-time, such a class will be dynamically loaded into the Java Virtual Machine, an instance of that class is created, and an appropriate method of that instance will be invoked when the authorization mechanism needs to check the system-induced relation. The administrator can install an extension class for each type of system-induced relationship.

    In our ReBAC adaptation of OpenMRS, a system-induced relation relates instances of `BaseOpenmrsData`, meaning that such relationships are not only among users, but they may also relate resources to resources, or persons to resources. As an example of the last case, we implemented resource ownership (owner) as a system-induced relation, relating a resource to its owner(s).

3. *Access control relationships.* There are relationships that belong solely to the protection state: they

are tracked solely for the purpose of access control, and have no relevance to the business logic of the application. Examples of access control relationships include role or group membership, records of access events (e.g., for implementing history-based policies, as in [20]), etc.

In our ReBAC adaption of OpenMRS, access control relationships are defined among instances of the `Person` class. Manually adding or removing access-control edges in the authorization graph is an error-prone step. To reduce the cognitive burden of users, we have implemented an administrative model for ReBAC, thereby supporting a principled way for adding or removing access control relationships. See §9 for details.

For example, say the family doctor of a patient may refer the patient to a specialist. Such a capability is only allowed if patient and a clinician are related by an access control relationship family-doctor. Once the referral is confirmed, the patient and the specialist will be related by the access control relationship referred-clinician, thereby enabling the specialist to access the patient's record.

LESSON 4. *In a ReBAC system, relationships come from three sources. Some relationships belong purely to the protection state (i.e., access control relationships): these are managed by system administrators. Other relationships are shared between the application state and the protection state. This latter kind may be further classified into (i) relationships that are explicitly articulated and managed by end users, and (ii) relationships that are induced by the system data structure (and thus cannot be manipulated directly by users and administrators).*

6. ACCESS REQUESTS

The ReBAC authorization advice needs three pieces of information to compute an authorization decision: (a) the resource r to which access is required, (b) the user u who wishes to have access (aka the "requestor"), and (c) the guard g of the service-layer method being invoked. Therefore, an access request in OpenMRS is characterized by a triple (r, u, g).

The ReBAC authorization advice can discover the identity of the requestor (u) and the service-layer method that is being invoked.[5] Using the Java Reflection API, the ReBAC authorization advice can then extract the guard (g) of the service-layer method. The last component of the access request, namely the resource r, is not directly available. OpenMRS was originally designed to use RBAC for authorization, and that explains why the identity of the resource is not explicitly made available for the authorization mechanism. In the following, we discuss how the requested resource r is identified in a systematic manner for the ReBAC authorization advice.

The ReBAC authorization advice has access to the arguments that are passed to the service-layer method, as well as the return value of that invocation. Depending on the

---

[5] The requestor can be identified by calling a public static method of the `Context` class in OpenMRS. The ReBAC authorization method is passed an argument of type `Method-Invocation`, which in turn provides access to the identity of the service-layer method that is being invoked.

kind of service-layer method, the target resource may be either (a) an argument or (b) the return value. There are two kinds of service layer methods in OpenMRS:

1. A **setter** method is one that operates on a given resource, which appears as one of the method arguments. That is, a setter produces side effects on the application state. The argument for which side effect is targeted is the resource that requires access control.

2. A **getter** method retrieves patient information (e.g., searching for the records of all patients with a given family name). The return value of a getter method is either (a) a single piece of patient information, or (b) a collection or a map of patient information. In the former case, the returned patient datum is the resource that requires access control, and in the latter case, every returned patient datum requires access control.

In the original design of OpenMRS, a naming convention is adopted to differentiate getter and setter methods, but there is no way for the ReBAC authorization advice to recognize which argument of a setter requires access control.

To address the above problem, we designed a custom annotation `@Resource` for identifying (a) whether a service-layer method is a setter or a getter, and (b) the target resource for each kind. In the case of setter methods, the `@Resource` annotation can be applied to a method parameter to indicate that that parameter corresponds to a protected resource.

$$T \ m(T_1 \ x_1, \ \texttt{@Resource} \ T_2 \ x_2, \ T_3 \ x_3) \ \{ \ \dots \ \}$$

The `@Resource` annotation is applied above to explicitly declare that the parameter x_2 of method m is a controlled resource. We systematically annotated the setter methods in the OpenMRS code base using the above annotation.

When the authorization advice is invoked, it employs the Java Reflection API to discover if any of the parameters of the invoked method is annotated by `@Resource`. If so, then it will pass the request (r, u, g) through the authorization procedure, where r is the value of the annotated parameter. Invocation of the method is only granted if authorization is successful.

Similarly, the `@Resource` annotation can also be applied to the method as a whole to declare that the method is a getter and thus the return value requires access control.[6]

$$\texttt{@Resource} \ T \ m(T_1 \ x_1, \ T_2 \ x_2, \ \dots) \ \{ \ \dots \ \}$$

Again, we systematically annotated the getter methods in the OpenMRS code base using the above annotation.

Before an invoked method returns, the ReBAC authorization advice will check if the method has the `@Resource` annotation. If so, it will perform authorization checks on the return value. If the return value is a single piece of patient information r, then the request (r, u, g) will be subject to the authorization procedure, and a security exception will be raised if authorization fails. Otherwise, the return value is either a collection or a map of patient information. For every member r in the returned collection (resp. map), the request (r, u, g) will be subject to authorization check. A

collection (resp. map) containing only those rs that pass authorization will be returned.

LESSON 5. *The legacy authorization subsystem of some applications may not have direct access to both the requestor and the resource of an access request. A ReBAC extension of such applications will need to provide means for run-time identification of these two entities.*

7. AUTHORIZATION PRINCIPALS

In an early conception of ReBAC [10], a ReBAC policy has the form "*grant access to r if RP*", where r is a resource and RP is a relationship predicate. There are two limitations to this design. First, access to resource r may be performed via many different forms of operations, and thus finer grained access control based on permissions (i.e., privileges in OpenMRS) is desirable. Second, there is no provision of permission abstraction (i.e., such as roles in RBAC) to ease administration. To overcome these limitations, Crampton and Sellwood [16] proposed an extension of ReBAC that is based on permission granting, and invented the notion of **authorization principals**, which could be seen as a ReBAC analogue of roles, to ease administration. In our ReBAC extension of OpenMRS, we have adopted a variant of Crampton and Sellwood's proposal. In the following, we will first describe the scheme that we actually implemented, and then discuss how it differs from the original proposal of Crampton and Sellwood.

An authorization principal is defined via a principal matching rule of the form (AP, RP), where AP is the identifier of the authorization principal, and RP is a relationship predicate. Unlike a role in RBAC, in which membership in a role is defined statically (via the user-role assignment relation UA), the semantics of an authorization principal is dynamic. When a request to access resource r is issued (at run time), AP denotes the set of users u for which r and u satisfy RP, the relationship predicate that is associated with AP. This notion of authorization principals is actually familiar to us. For example, in Unix, there are three built-in authorization principals: "owner", "group", "other" (aka "world"); in Facebook, there are four built-in authorization principals: "me", "friend", "friend-of-friend", "everyone".

Note again that, in the original conception of ReBAC [10], the relationship predicate in a ReBAC policy specifies a desired relation between the resource owner and the access requestor. In contrast, the relationship predicate in a principal matching rule specifies a desired relation between the resource itself and the requestor. For example, the following principal matching rule specifies the principal treating-clinician.

$$\Big(\text{treating-clinician},$$
$$@_{\text{resource}} \langle \text{owner} \rangle \big(\langle \text{family-doctor} \rangle \text{requestor} \ \vee$$
$$\langle \text{referred-clinician} \rangle \text{requestor} \big) \Big)$$

The rule says that the requestor is a treating clinician if she is either the family doctor or a referred specialist of the resource's owner. Note that the two free variables resource and requestor identifies the two parameters of the relationship predicates.

In our implementation, there is only one principal matching rule for each authorization principal AP: i.e., the princi-

---

[6]The annotation of getter methods is not absolutely necessary, as the above-mentioned naming convention already identifies getter methods. The annotation is performed as a convenience for the ReBAC authorization advice. The annotation of setter methods, however, is necessary in order for the ReBAC authorization advice to function properly.

pal matching rule defines a functional mapping from authorization principals to their corresponding relationship predicates. We write RP_{AP} for the relationship predicate of the authorization principal AP.

Permission abstraction is achieved by authorization rules of the form (AP, P), where AP is the identifier of an authorization principal, and P is a set of privileges. The meaning is analogous to the permission assignment relation PA in RBAC. That is, at run time, the members of authorization principal AP is granted permissions in P.

In our implementation, there is only one authorization rule for each authorization principal. We write P_{AP} for the set of privileges granted to authorization principal AP.

The scheme we implemented differs from the original proposal of Crampton and Sellwood in the following manners.

- Crampton and Sellwood use a formalism called path conditions to specify the relationship predicate RP. In our implementation, RP is specified via a hybrid logic formula. Path conditions and hybrid logic have incomparable expressiveness. There are certain relationship predicates that are expressible in hybrid logic but not path conditions, and vice versa. Extending our implementation to accommodate other specification formalisms for relationship predicates is a modular task.

- In Crampton and Sellwood's proposal, an authorization rule may grant either positive or negative permissions (i.e., allow or deny). Complying to the original design of OpenMRS, our implementation supports only positive permissions. Without negative permissions, the conflict resolution strategies proposed in [16] are not needed and thus not implemented. Extension of our implementation to accomodate negative permissions and conflict resolution is a tractable endeavour.

- An authorization rule of Crampton and Sellwood has an explicitly specified scope of applicability. Specifically, a rule is either applicable to all resources, or it is applicable only to a specific resource r. Our implementation supports only the first possibility (applicable to all resources).

A number of user interface elements have been introduced to ease the administration of authorization principals and privilege assignment. First, the specification of principal matching rules and the specification of authorization rules are performed in two separate web pages. Each web page is protected by separate privileges. This separation of duty allows a different group of administrators to be responsible for specifying each kind of rules. Second, we have developed a Javascript-based structure editor for specifying Hybrid Logic formulas (e.g., as relationship predicates in principal matching rules).

8. AUTHORIZATION MECHANISM

Inspired by the UNIX access control model [15], Crampton and Sellwood proposed an authorization mechanism for determining when a request is to be granted. We adapted their proposal for OpenMRS. Given an access request (r, u, g) directed against a protection state (i.e., an authorization graph) G, an authorization principal AP is said to be **enabled** iff $RP_{AP}(G, r, u) = 1$. Intuitively, the requestor u is a member of the enabled principals for the present access request. Thus, requestor u is granted the privileges in P_{AP}, for each enabled principal AP. Such privileges are then used for satisfying the privilege requirement of guard g.

On top of the above adaptations, we propose two novel extensions to their scheme: (a) liberal- and strict-grant semantics, and (b) eager- and lazy-match strategies.

Authorization Semantics. The presence of guards of the form `all-of(P)` present ambiguities in the precise manner in which authorization should be conducted. We therefore extend the proposal of Crampton and Sellwood by differentiating between two semantics of authorization.

1. *Liberal-grant semantics*.
   - Let $\mathcal{E}$ be the set of all enabled principals.
   - Let $Q = \bigcup_{AP \in \mathcal{E}} P_{AP}$. That is, Q is the set of all privileges that are granted by at least one enabled principal.
   - Authorization is granted iff $Q \models g$.

   In liberal-grant authorization, the privileges required by g may come from any enabled principals. The assumption is that the requestor u can simultaneously "be" all the enabled principals.

2. *Strict-grant semantics*.
   - Let $\mathcal{E}$ be the set of all enabled principals.
   - Authorization is granted iff there exists $AP \in \mathcal{E}$ such that $P_{AP} \models g$.

   In strict-grant authorization, the privileges required by g must originate from only one enabled principal. The idea is that the privilege requirements of g are satisfied only if there is an enabled principal who can "single-handedly" satisfy it.

The two semantics produce identical behaviour if the guard g is of the form `one-of(P)`.[7] They differ in behaviour only if the guard is of the form `all-of(P)`.[8] If a request is authorized in the strict-grant semantics then it is authorized in the liberal-grant semantics.[9]

Principal Matching Strategies. For each of the above semantics, we also developed two principal matching strategies.

1. *Eager-match strategy*. This is the straightforward implementation of the two semantics, in which the set of all enabled principals is computed before an authorization decision is produced.

2. *Lazy-match strategy*. This is an optimized implementation of the two semantics. The core idea is that the testing of relationship predicates during principal matching (i.e., determining which principals are enabled) is an expensive operation, and thus such checks should be avoided whenever possible. This idea is materialized in two ways. First, two principals may share the same relationship predicate. There is no point re-evaluating the predicate for both principals. When we determine what principals are enabled, the same relationship predicate is evaluated only once. Second, rather than computing the set of all enabled authorization principals, they are computed one at a time, and only for the principals that are relevant. If the

---

[7] If $g = $ `one-of(P)`, then $P \cap (\bigcup_{AP \in \mathcal{E}} P_{AP}) \neq \emptyset$ iff there exists $AP \in \mathcal{E}$ such that $P \cap P_{AP} \neq \emptyset$. That is, the two semantics agree in their authorization decisions.

[8] Suppose $g = $ `all-of({p_1, p_2})`. Suppose further $\mathcal{E} = \{AP_1, AP_2\}$. Say $P_{AP_1} = \{p_1\}$ and $P_{AP_2} = \{p_2\}$. Then liberal grant semantics will allow access but strict grant semantics will deny access.

[9] Suppose strict-grant allows access. There exists $AP \in \mathcal{E}$ such that $P_{AP} \models g$. In that case, $\bigcup_{AP \in \mathcal{E}} P_{AP} \models g$ as well, since $\models$ is monotonic. Thus, liberal grant allows access also.

Algorithm 1: Lazy-match, liberal-grant authorization of access request (r, u, g) against authorization graph G.

```
1  let P be such that g is either all-of(P) or one-of(P);
2  Q := ∅;
3  foreach AP do
4      if (P_AP \ Q) ∩ P ≠ ∅ then
5          if RP_AP(G, r, u) has been evaluated then
6              reuse previous value;
7          else
8              compute value;
9          if value is true then
10             Q := Q ∪ P_AP;
11             if Q ⊨ g then
12                 return "allow";
13 return "deny";
```

Algorithm 2: Lazy-match, strict-grant authorization of access request (r, u, g) against authorization graph G.

```
1  foreach AP do
2      if P_AP ⊨ g then
3          if RP_AP(G, r, u) has been evaluated then
4              reuse previous value (which must be false);
5          else
6              compute value;
7          if value is true then
8              return "allow";
9  return "deny";
```

privileges associated with a principal do not contribute to the satisfaction of the guard in question, it is ignored, and its relationship predicate is not even evaluated. Otherwise, the principal is "relevant", and its relationship predicate is checked to see if the principal is enabled. Whenever a relevant principal is found to be enabled, the authorization engine checks to see if the required privileges are already present. If so, the search for enabled principals will be terminated. In summary, this "lazy" evaluation strategy opportunistically eschews unnecessary computation. The pseudocode listings for liberal-grant and strict-grant authorization using the lazy-match strategy are shown in Algorithms 1 and 2 respectively.

The two strategies produce the same authorization decision for any given access request.

We implemented a web interface for administrators to select between liberal- or strict-grant semantics, and between eager- or lazy-match strategy (i.e., four combinations).

9. ADMINISTRATIVE ACTIONS

Access control relationships in the authorization graph belong solely to the protection state. They are not application data. Their existence serve only the purpose of protection. One way of managing such relationships will be to place the burden entirely on the system administrators. (In our implementation, we have administrative web pages for administrators to manually add or delete edges of the authorization graph.) This, however, is not scaleable. Imagine the task of adding an edge in the authorization graph to indicate that the family doctor of a patient is referring the patient to a cardiologist (and thus the said cardiologist enjoys certain access rights that other cardiologists do not have over the patient's records). Such an action is common in the daily operation of a health service. It is completely impractical to go through the bottleneck of the system administrators every time such a referral is made. One way of making this scaleable is to delegate this operation to qualified users (e.g., the family doctor in the example), so that the latter may add this edge into the authorization graph. Yet, manual addition and deletion of edges can be error prone. First, business logic may dictate that multiple updates to the authorization graph must occur together (e.g., a person may have only one supervisor, and thus the addition of a new supervisor edge must be accompanied by the deletion of an out-of-date supervisor edge). If the user performs one update but forgets another, then the integrity of the authorization graph cannot be maintained. Second, business logic may dictate that an update can only occur if the user performing the update is qualified to do so (e.g., referral can only be made by a family doctor). Undisciplined updates of the authorization graph overlooks such security requirements.

The primary design objective of administrative actions is to provide a structured means for adding and removing access control relationships, so that such tasks can be performed safely by users other than system administrators. In our design, the declaration of an administrative action consists of the following components:

- **Action identifier**: A unique name is used for identifying the administrative action. For example, the referral action is identified by the identifier "Referral".
- **Enabling precondition**: Every administrative action is presumed to be performed by a user against a patient (e.g., a family doctor performing a referral for a patient). So every administrative action has two ***primary participants***, namely, the user who performs that action and the patient to which the action is targeted. The identifiers user and patient are used in the declaration for referring to the primary participants. Whether the action is ***enabled*** (see below) depends on whether the user and the patient satisfy a certain relationship predicate. Such a relationship predicate, called the enabling precondition, is specified as a hybrid logic formula with free variables user and patient. For example, the following hybrid logic formula can be used for requiring that referral can only be conducted by the family doctor of a patient.[10]

$$@_{\mathsf{user}} \langle \mathsf{family\text{-}doctor} \rangle \mathsf{patient}$$

- **Participants**: Other than user and patient, there may be other participants involved in the action. They are called ***auxiliary participants***. The participant list enumerates the identifiers to be used for referring to auxiliary participants in the rest of the declaration. In the example of referral, there is only one auxiliary participant, "specialist", who is the specialist to which the referral is directed.
- **Applicability precondition**: Whether the administrative action is considered ***applicable*** (see below) depends on whether a certain condition holds among all the participants (both primary and auxiliary). Such

---

[10]This is only an illustration. We are fully aware that in real life it is not just the family doctor who can perform referral.

a condition is specified as a hybrid logic formula containing free variables that are user, patient, as well as the identifiers listed in the participant list above. The hybrid logic formula specifies a graph predicate of arity $\ell + 2$, where ℓ is the number of auxiliary participants. In the running example, we require that (a) the specialist is approved by the insurance company of the user, and (b) the user and the specialist must belong to the same health region. The above conditions are captured by the following hybrid logic formula.

$$\left(@_{\text{patient}}\langle \text{insurance} \rangle \langle \text{approves} \rangle \text{specialist}\right) \wedge$$
$$\left(@_{\text{user}}\langle \text{region} \rangle \langle -\text{region} \rangle \text{specialist}\right)$$

- **Effects**: The effects of an administrative action is a list of *updates*. Each update is of the form "**add** $i(x, y)$" or "**del** $i(x, y)$". Here, i is a relation identifier (e.g., supervisor-of), and x and y are identifiers of participants (either primary or auxiliary). The keywords **add** and **del** indicates whether the update is an edge addition or deletion.

For example, the referral action has one update:

add referred-clinician(patient, specialist)

The enabling and applicability preconditions together specify the security constraints that must be met in order for the user to be allowed to perform the administrative action against the patient. The effects may involve updating multiple edges in the authorization graph. Grouping them together in one administrative action ensures that the updates are either performed together, or not at all. This in turn ensures the integrity of the authorization graph, and prevents errors on the part of the user who performs the updates.

At run time, the following sequence of events occur, which gives semantics to administrative actions.

1. When a user retrieves the record of a patient, the two primary participants are tested against the enabling precondition of every declared administrative action. An action for which the enabling precondition is satisfied is said to be *enabled*. The set of enabled actions is computed.

2. When the patient record is displayed, a tab showing the list of all enabled actions is made available to the user. The user may choose to perform any of the enabled actions.

3. When the user signals to perform an enabled action, the list of auxiliary participants (if any) will be displayed to the user. The user must now instantiate each of the participants by selecting a person. This is facilitated by intelligent search features offered by OpenMRS.

4. Once the participants are selected, both the enabling and applicability preconditions are checked. The action is deemed *applicable* if the check succeeds. (We will explain below why the enabling precondition is checked again.)

5. If the action is applicable, then the effects of the action will be executed. Note that deleting a non-existent edge is an error. Similarly, adding an edge that already exists is also considered an error. Either all the updates are executed, or execution fails without any change to the authorization graph.

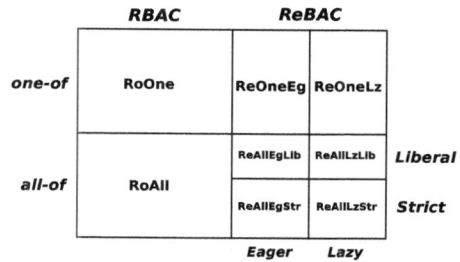

Figure 1: The 8 experimental configurations.

Note that the execution of effects is an atomic operation: either all updates are successfully executed, or else no update is performed. This is achieved by the transaction manager. Actually, the transaction begins at step 4 above. Including the check of both enabling and application preconditions into the transaction prevents time-of-check-to-time-of-use (TOCTTOU) race conditions [7, §6.2.1]. In addition, to prevent unintended roll-back, the preconditions should be crafted in such a way that the presence of an edge is verified in the preconditions if it is deleted in the effects, and the absence of an edge is confirmed in the preconditions if it is added in the effects.

To support policy engineering, we also developed administrative web pages for users to build a library of reusable hybrid logic formulas. Such formulas can be referenced in the declarations of administrative actions.

10. PERFORMANCE EVALUATION

An empirical study has been conducted to evaluate the performance of the various authorization schemes proposed in this paper. As our ReBAC-equipped version of OpenMRS is not yet deployed in any clinical setting, no production data set is available, and thus performance evaluation was conducted with synthetic data. Rather than performing "disembodied" simulation of the various authorization schemes, we measured the performance of those schemes within the infrastructure of OpenMRS, thereby capturing the overhead in a realistic implementation.

We compared the performance of the OpenMRS authorization mechanism in eight different configurations (Fig. 1). The two RBAC configurations (Ro*) correspond to OpenMRS with only the legacy RBAC authorization mechanism (i.e., ReBAC is turned off). These two configurations differ in whether requests are directed against one-of guards (RoOne) or all-of guards (RoAll). ReBAC authorization is turned on (and RBAC is turned off) for the remaining six configurations (Re*). Two of the ReBAC configurations correspond to one-of requests (ReOne*). They differ in whether eager- or lazy-match strategy is implemented. The last four ReBAC configurations correspond to all-of requests (ReAll*). In the case of all-of guards, there are two possible semantics (liberal- or strict-grant), as well as two possible matching strategies (eager or lazy), resulting in four configurations: ReAllEgLib, ReAllEgStr, ReAllLzLib, and ReAllLzStr.

RBAC Protection State. We randomly synthesized an RBAC protection state for the two RBAC configurations (Ro*). OpenMRS pre-compiles the role hierarchy into a flat space of roles. The RBAC protection state therefore con-

Users:	10,000	Privileges:	200	Roles:	67
Privilege-role assignment pairs:					469
User-role assignment pairs:					50,000

Figure 2: RBAC Parameters

tains a user-role assignment and a privilege-role assignment, but not a role hierarchy. Fig. 2 enumerates the parameters used for synthesizing the RBAC protection state. Justifications for the choice of these parameters are given in Appendix A.

ReBAC Protection State. For the six ReBAC configurations (Re*), we constructed an authorization graph out of a social network dataset, soc-Pokec, obtained from the Stanford Large Network Dataset Collection [5]. The graph has 1.6 million nodes and 30 million directed edges. This dataset is thus even bigger than what the OpenMRS community calls a high-density deployment.[11]

To construct the authorization graph, we identified 10,000 nodes with the highest in-degrees, and labelled them as users (i.e., clinicians).[12] The remaining nodes are patients. Consequently, a directed edge in the social graph can be one of four types: user-user, user-patient, patient-user, or patient-patient. According to the type of each directed edge, we then randomly labelled the directed edges using the relation identifiers of the Electronic Health Records System case study in [19, §5]. A detailed list of relation identifiers and the distribution of the edge labels can be found in Appendix B.

ReBAC Policies. The six ReBAC configurations (Re*) presumes the existence of ReBAC policies (authorization principals). We generated an authorization principal for each of the 67 roles. Authorization rules were formulated in such a way that each principal grants the same privileges as its corresponding role. Principal matching rules were in place so that every authorization principal is associated with a randomly generated hybrid logic formula. Specifically, from the two example formulas in the Electronic Health Records System case study in [19, §5], we extracted ten hybrid logic formulas for our experiment. For each principal, a formula was randomly selected from those ten formulas (with equal probability). See Appendix C for details.

Methods, Guards, and Requests. As the existing service-layer methods of OpenMRS will not work with the authorization graph synthesized above, we randomly synthesized service-layer methods for the purpose of this experiment. Each synthesized service-layer method takes a patient as an argument, and is invoked by a user (i.e., clinician). A guard is randomly generated for each method; one-of guards for the *One* configurations, and all-of guards for the *All* configurations. Each method has an empty body as we are only concerned about authorization overhead. For each of the eight configurations, we generated 200 method calls, with randomly selected clinicians and patients. The authorization times of the 200 method calls are then averaged and reported. Details can be found in Appendix D.

Results and Discussions. We conducted the experiment on a desktop machine with AMD FX-8350 8-core Pro-

---

[11]According to a thread in the OpenMRS developer forum [1], the number of patient records in various reported OpenMRS deployments ranges from 8,982 to 741,606.

[12]Our intuition is that clinicians are more connected than patients. Specifically, they have more incoming edges, for example, to indicate who is the attending clinician of whom.

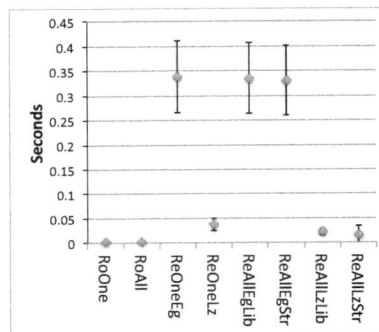

Figure 3: Average time for an authorization check (with 95% confidence interval).

cessor (16 MB cache), 16 GB RAM (1866 MHz, DDR3), and an 840 EVO Solid State Drive running Windows 8 OS. The results are shown in Fig. 3.

The baseline RBAC configurations (Ro*) incur negligible running time. The three eager-match configurations (*Eg*) have authorization time averaging around 0.33 seconds, suggesting that the eager-match strategy is not practical. In contrast, all the lazy-match configurations (*Lz*) have competitive authorization times averaging around 0.016–0.037 seconds. In summary, matching strategy, and not authorization semantics, is the key determinant of performance.

In our experience, the main performance overhead comes not from backtracking within the hybrid logic model checker, but from database accesses. Due to the sheer size of the authorization graph (1.6 million nodes, 30 million edges), simply retrieving the neighbours of a given node takes 0.002 second in our preliminary experiments, resulting in unacceptable authorization times. Noticing this, we stored the access control relationships in a graph database (Neo4j [3]) instead of the original relational database (MySQL [2]), resulting in a 20-fold speed-up in neighbour retrieval time (0.0001 sec) and thus the fast authorization times reported above (Fig. 3).

LESSON 6. *A graph database offers more competitive ReBAC authorization performance than a relational database.*

Further details on the preparation of Neo4j for our experiments are discussed in Appendix E.

11. CONCLUSIONS AND FUTURE WORK

This ReBAC adaptation of OpenMRS is the first implementation of ReBAC in a production-scale electronic medical records system. We reported reusable engineering lessons for ReBAC deployment, presented extensions of advanced ReBAC features recently proposed by Crampton and Sellwood [16], designed and implemented the first administrative model for ReBAC, and evaluated the performance of authorization checks.

Our implementation can serve as a testbed for future extensions of ReBAC. A number of research opportunities are motivated by this implementation exercise. First, the way ReBAC interacts with the legacy RBAC mechanism is by way of conjunction: access is granted if both access control subsystem grant access. What are other ways in which RBAC and ReBAC can interact with one another to deliver advanced access control features? Second, authorization in

OpenMRS is performed through the satisfaction of privilege requirements known as guards. These privilege requirements interact with the design of other access control features (e.g., authorization principals, authorization algorithms, positive and negative permissions, conflict resolution) in an intimate manner. We have opted for simplicity in most of our design choices. Further studies on how advanced access control features can be implemented in the presence of OpenMRS-style privilege requirements is a research challenge. Third, while we have fashioned the first administrative model for ReBAC, the theory of ReBAC administrative models is an unexplored area. How does one perform, say, safety analysis in this administrative model [24]? Fourth, in the original proposal of ReBAC [19] relationships are contextual. For example, a referral relationship is effective only in the context of a certain medical case. Context creation and removal provide a clean mechanism for expiration of tentative relationships. How does one implement contexts in OpenMRS, especially with usability in mind?

Acknowledgments

This work is supported in part by an NSERC Discovery Grant (RGPIN-2014-06611) and a Canada Research Chair (950-229712).

12. REFERENCES

[1] Max number of records in an OpenMRS implementation. http://listarchives.openmrs.org/Max-number-of-records-in-an-OpenMRS-implementation-td4662224.html.

[2] MySQL. http://www.mysql.com/.

[3] Neo4J. http://neo4j.com/.

[4] OpenMRS. http://openmrs.org/.

[5] Stanford Large Network Dataset Collection. http://snap.stanford.edu/data.

[6] AKTOUDIANAKIS, E., CRAMPTON, J., SCHNEIDER, S., TREHARNE, H., AND WALLER, A. Policy templates for relationship-based access control. In *Proceedings of the 11th Annual International Conference on Privacy, Security and Trust (PST'13)* (Tarragona, Catalonia, Spain, July 2013), IEEE, pp. 221–228.

[7] ANDERSON, R. *Security Engineering*, 2nd ed. Wiley, 2008.

[8] ANONYMIZED. ReBAC Java Library.

[9] BEZNOSOV, K. Requirements for access control: US healthcare domain. In *Proceedings of the Fourth ACM Workshop on Role-Based Access Control (RBAC'1998)* (Fairfax, VA, Oct. 1998), p. 43.

[10] BRUNS, G., FONG, P. W. L., SIAHAAN, I., AND HUTH, M. Relationship-based access control: Its expression and enforcement through hybrid logic. In *Proceedings of the 2nd ACM Conference on Data and Application Security (CODASPY'12)* (San Antonio, TX, USA, Feb. 2012).

[11] CARMINATI, B., AND FERRARI, E. Enforcing relationships privacy through collaborative access control in web-based social networks. In *Proceedings of the 5th International Conference on Collaborative Computing: Networking, Applications and Worksharing (CollaborateCom'09)* (Washington DC, USA, Nov. 2009).

[12] CARMINATI, B., FERRARI, E., AND PEREGO, A. Enforcing access control in web-based social networks. *ACM Transactions on Information and System Security 13*, 1 (Oct. 2009).

[13] CHENG, Y., PARK, J., AND SANDHU, R. Relationship-based access control for online social networks: Beyond user-to-user relationships. In *Proceedings of the 4th IEEE International Conference on Information Privacy, Security, Risk and Trust (PASSAT'12)* (Amsterdam, Netherlands, Sept. 2012).

[14] CHENG, Y., PARK, J., AND SANDHU, R. A user-to-user relationship-based access control model for online social networks. In *Proceedings of the 26th Annual IFIP WG 11.3 Working Conference on Data and Applications Security and Privacy (DBSec'12)* (Paris, France, July 2012), vol. 7371 of *LNCS*.

[15] CRAMPTON, J. Why we should take a second look at access control in Unix. In *Proceedings of the 13th Nordic Workshop on Secure IT Systems (NordSec'08)* (Copenhagen, Denmark, Oct. 2008).

[16] CRAMPTON, J., AND SELLWOOD, J. Path conditions and principal matching: A new approach to access control. In *Proceedings of the 19th ACM Symposium on Access Control Models and Technologies (SACMAT'14)* (London, Ontario, Canada, June 2014).

[17] ENE, A., HORNE, W. G., MILOSAVLJEVIC, N., RAO, P., SCHREIBER, R., AND TARJAN, R. E. Fast exact and heuristic methods for role minimization problems. In *Proceedings of the 13th ACM Symposium on Access Control Models and Technologies (SACMAT'08)* (Estes Park, CO, June 2008), pp. 1–10.

[18] FISCHER, J., MARINO, D., MAJUMDAR, R., AND MILLSTEIN, T. D. Fine-grained access control with object-sensitive roles. In *Proceedings of the 23rd European Conference on Object-Oriented Programming (ECOOP'09)* (Genoa, Italy, July 2009), vol. 5653 of *LNCS*, pp. 173–194.

[19] FONG, P. W. L. Relationship-based access control: Protection model and policy language. In *Proceedings of the First ACM Conference on Data and Application Security and Privacy (CODASPY'11)* (San Antonio, Texas, USA, Feb. 2011), pp. 191–202.

[20] FONG, P. W. L., MEHREGAN, P., AND KRISHNAN, R. Relational abstraction in community-based secure collaboration. In *Proceedings of the 20th ACM Conference on Computer and Communications Security (CCS'13)* (Berlin, Germany, Nov. 2013), pp. 585–598.

[21] FONG, P. W. L., AND SIAHAAN, I. Relationship-based access control policies and their policy languages. In *Proceedings of the 16th ACM Symposium on Access Control Models and Technologies (SACMAT'11)* (Innsbruck, Austria, June 2011), pp. 51–60.

[22] GATES, C. E. Access control requirements for Web 2.0 security and privacy. In *IEEE Web 2.0 privacy and security workshop (W2SP'07)* (Oakland, California, USA, May 2007).

[23] GOSLING, J., JOY, B., STEELE, G., BRACHA, G., AND BUCKLEY, A. *The Java Language Specification*, Java SE 8 ed. Oracle America, Inc, Mar. 2014.

[24] HARRISON, M. A., RUZZO, W. L., AND ULLMAN, J. D. Protection in operating systems.

Communications of the ACM 19, 8 (Aug. 1976), 461–471.

[25] Hibernate. http://hibernate.org/.

[26] KICZALES, G., LAMPING, J., MENDHEKAR, A., MAEDA, C., LOPES, C., LOINGTIER, J.-M., AND IRWIN, J. Aspect-oriented programming. In *Proceedings of the European Conference on Object-Oriented Programming (ECOOP'97)* (Jyväskylä, Finland, June 1997), M. Aksit and S. Matsuoka, Eds., vol. 1241 of *LNCS*, Springer, pp. 220–242.

[27] LI, N., BYUN, J.-W., AND BERTINO, E. A critique of the ANSI standard on role-based access control. *IEEE Security and Privacy 5*, 6 (Nov. 2007), 41–49.

[28] MAMLIN, B. Re: Policy based access control for OpenMRS. http://listarchives.openmrs.org/Policy-based-Access-Control-for-OpenMRS-td7220685.html, Jan. 2012.

[29] RØSTAD, L., AND EDSBERG, O. A study of access control requirements for healthcare systems based on audit trails from access logs. In *Proceedings of the 22nd Annual Computer Security Applications Conference (ACSAC'2006)* (Miami Beach, Florida, USA, Dec. 2006), pp. 175–186.

[30] SANDHU, R., BHAMIDIPATI, V., AND MUNAWER, Q. The ARBAC97 model for role-based administration of roles. *ACM Transactions on Information and System Security 2*, 1 (1999), 105–135.

[31] SANDHU, R. S., COYNE, E. J., FEINSTEIN, H. L., AND YOUMAN, C. E. Role-based access control models. *IEEE Computer 19*, 2 (Feb. 1996), 38–47.

[32] Spring framework. http://projects.spring.io/spring-framework/.

[33] TARAMESHLOO, E., AND FONG, P. W. L. Access control models for geo-social computing systems. In *Proceedings of the 19th ACM Symposium on Access Control Models and Technologies (SACMAT'14)* (London, Ontario, Canada, June 2014).

APPENDIX

A. RBAC PROTECTION STATE

We create 10,000 users for our experiments. Since OpenMRS has 184 distinct built-in privileges, we round up and thus create 200 privileges. We deduce several ratios from the "healthcare" database of [17]: (a) role-to-privilege ratio is 1:3; (b) average number of roles per user is 5; (c) average number of privilege per role is 7. From these ratios, we create 67 roles ($\approx 200/3$), 469 privilege-role assignment pairs ($\approx 67 \times 7$), and 50,000 user-role assignment pairs ($\approx 10000 \times 5$).

B. ReBAC PROTECTION STATE

From [19, §5], we extract the following relation identifiers. We indicate below the type of each identifier: e.g., an identifier of the patient-user type is identified by "p-u".

Rel. Id.	Type	Rel. Id.	Type
gp	p-u	register-ward	p-u
referrer	u-u	ward-nurse	u-u
appoint-team	u-u	agent	p-p
team	u-u		

Every directed edge in the social graph belongs to one of the four types: user-user, user-patient, patient-user, patient-patient. Based on the type of a given directed edge, a relation identifier of that type is random selected (with uniform distribution). Note that there is no relation identifier that has the type user-patient. For those edges, a dummy relation identifier is assigned.

C. ReBAC POLICIES

The Electronic Health Records System case study of [19, §5] has two formulas that we can use in our experiments. The first formula, specifying the patient-clinician relation, is constructed incrementally in four stages in [19, §5.1]. We take the subformulas constructed in the various stages as candidate formulas for our experiment.

$$\phi_1 = \langle gp \rangle requestor$$
$$\phi_2 = \langle gp \rangle \langle -referrer \rangle requestor$$
$$\phi_3 = \phi_1 \vee \phi_2$$
$$\phi_4 = \langle gp \rangle \langle -referrer \rangle \langle appoint\text{-}team \rangle requestor$$
$$\phi_5 = \langle gp \rangle \langle -referrer \rangle \langle appoint\text{-}team \rangle (requestor \vee \langle member \rangle requestor)$$
$$\phi_6 = \phi_3 \vee \phi_5$$
$$\phi_7 = \langle register\text{-}ward \rangle requestor$$
$$\phi_8 = \langle register\text{-}ward \rangle (requestor \vee \langle ward\text{-}nurse \rangle requestor)$$
$$\phi_9 = \phi_6 \vee \phi_8$$

The last candidate formula is basically a minor adaptation of the formula expressing the agency relation in [19, §5.2].

$$\phi_{10} = \langle gp \rangle requestor \vee \langle -agent \rangle \langle gp \rangle requestor$$

D. AUTHORIZATION REQUESTS

We generated 400 methods with `all-of` guards, and another 400 with `one-of` guards. The set P of privileges for each guard contains a minimum of one and a maximum of three privileges randomly selected from the 200 available privileges (Fig. 2).[13] In addition to the privileges we randomly generated a list of 400 clinician, and a list of 400 participants, to serve as participants in the authorization requests.

The methods were invoked in order (from 1 to 400) along with the corresponding clinician, patient pair. This process was uniformly conducted for all configurations, with the *One* configurations invoking the methods with the `one-of` guards, and the *All* configurations invoking the methods with the `all-of` guards. The first 200 method invocations were discarded as they were used for warming up the Java Virtual Machine. The performance of the remaining 200 method invocations were recorded.

E. Neo4j WARMUP

Retrieving the neighbourhood of a node in Neo4J normally start out slow then speeds up, and stabilize at an average of 0.0001 seconds after approximately 250 queries. Therefore, we randomly generated 250 distinct neighbourhood retrieval queries that were ran before the method invocations for each test configuration.

---

[13]The service-layer methods of OpenMRS never have a privilege set of size larger three.

Federated Access Management for Collaborative Network Environments: Framework and Case Study

Carlos E. Rubio-Medrano, Ziming Zhao, Adam Doupé and Gail-Joon Ahn
The Laboratory of Secure Engineering for Future Computing (SEFCOM)
Arizona State University
Tempe, AZ, USA
{crubiome, zmzhao, doupe, gahn}@asu.edu

ABSTRACT

With the advent of various collaborative sharing mechanisms such as Grids, P2P and Clouds, organizations including private and public sectors have recognized the benefits of being involved in inter-organizational, multi-disciplinary, and collaborative projects that may require diverse resources to be shared among participants. In particular, an environment that often makes use of a group of high-performance network facilities would involve large-scale collaborative projects and tremendously seek a robust and flexible access control for allowing collaborators to leverage and consume resources, e.g., computing power and bandwidth. In this paper, we propose a federated access management scheme that leverages the notion of *attributes*. Our approach allows resource-sharing organizations to provide distributed *provisioning* (publication, location, communication, and evaluation) of both attributes and policies for federated access management purposes. Also, we provide a proof-of-concept implementation that leverages *distributed hash tables* (DHT) to traverse chains of attributes and effectively handle the federated access management requirements devised for inter-organizational resource sharing and collaborations.

1. INTRODUCTION

Traditionally, collaborative information sharing heavily relies on client-server or email-based systems. By recognizing the inherent deficiencies such as a central point of failure and scalability issues, several alternatives have been proposed to support collaborative sharing of resources, including Grid computing, Peer-to-Peer (P2P) networking [11] and Cloud computing [27]. Given all the diverse contexts of collaboration, achieving effective access control is a critical requirement. The sharing of sensitive information and resources is necessarily to be highly controlled by defining what is shared, who and under which conditions is allowed to share. In particular, users without pre-existing relationships may try to collaborate and request the information. It is required for a resource provider to be able to cope with a large

number of collaborators and guarantee the information and resources be released only to trusted collaborators within the community. In addition, resources are constructed with various types and domain policies, and each collaborating party may enforce security policies in their systems with different degrees of assurance. Therefore, building systematic mechanisms for sharing resources across collaborative network environments is indeed an important challenge.

Furthermore, organizations including private and public sectors have recognized the benefits of being involved with inter-organizational, multi-disciplinary collaborative projects that may require diverse resources shared among participants, e.g., data, computation time, storage, etc. In particular, an environment that often makes use of a group of high-performance network facilities would involve large-scale collaborative projects and tremendously seek a robust and flexible access control for allowing collaborators to leverage and consume resources. For example, under the US Department of Energy (DoE), numerous research laboratories and scientists have collaborated and performed their experiments demanding specific network bandwidth and designated computing resources from each other. They even exchanged data and resources with other foreign researchers, which lead them to utilize high-performance network environments such as ESnet [29], GÉANT [7], and NORDUnet [21]. Despite the necessary administrative tasks such as resource scheduling and provisioning, there is a need to properly mediate the way such resources are to be safely shared in the context of collaborations. Because most of these providers depict their own in-house *authentication* and *authorization* services, a well-defined, inter-organizational and implementation-independent approach is needed. With this in mind, this paper presents our approach to address the aforementioned challenges by leveraging the concept of *attributes*: observable properties that are exhibited by access control entities, e.g., users and protected resources, that become relevant under a given security context [19], focused on DoE networks and their collaborators' networks. Using attributes as an underlying framework, we propose an approach based on the concept of a *federation* between participant organizations, allowing them to *provision*: specify, publish, locate, and communicate attributes for federated access management purposes in a distributed way, thus allowing for the specification and automated evaluation of both local (intra-domain) and federated (inter-domain) policies. With this in mind, this paper makes the following contributions:

- We formulate the main components involved in federated access management. We show how attributes in the *lo-*

cal context can be leveraged in a *federated* context such that access permissions for inter-organizational resource sharing can be properly granted.

- We also provide a well-defined description of attributes, which includes the use of data types, standardized names, and run-time values, so that participants can unambiguously use those to define inter-organizational attributes and policies for federated access management purposes.

- We propose an attribute generation approach by means of a set of so-called *attribute derivation rules* (AD-Rules). Moreover, we also introduce *attribute derivation graphs* (AD-Graphs) that allow to compose AD-rules.

- We provide an initial step toward automated attribute discovery based on *distributed hash tables* (DHT) [28], which allows for efficient discovery and retrieval of attributes within a federated and distributed context. In addition, we provide a *proof-of-concept* implementation of our attribute provisioning scheme, including an evaluation approach that shows the feasibility of our approach for real-life implementations.

This paper is organized as follows: we start by articulating problem statements and technical challenges with respect to federated access management in Section 2. Then, we describe our approach in Section 3 followed by the *proof-of-concept* implementation and evaluation results in Section 4, which shows the practicability of our approach for supporting real-world collaborations among the DoE-affiliated high-performance network facilities. We overview the related work in Section 5 and discuss some relevant topics related to our approach as well as matters for future work in Section 6. Finally, Section 7 provides concluding remarks.

2. BACKGROUND

As previously mentioned, DoE-affiliated high-performance network facilities have identified the need to provide automated means for resource sharing between different administrative (and security) domains. As an example, the Open Grid Forum [9] introduced a multi-organizational effort called the *network services interface* (NSI) [23] that is composed of a set of well-defined protocols that allow participants to collaborate on research endeavors by implementing inter-organizational *services* in an automated way. The protocol devised for a given NSI service is implemented by so-called *network service agents* (NSA) which are expected to support all service-related tasks within the context of a given administrative domain. Fig. 1 shows an example depicting a data transfer between two hosts that are located within the administrative boundaries of two different organizations and whose networking path involves the participation of a third network serving as a bridge. In this example, each participating network implements the protocol devised for the NSI *connection* service by means of a dedicated NSA. Following such a protocol, a connection request R is first serviced by the *local* NSA where R originates (NSA$_1$ in Fig. 1). On each network, the local NSA is in charge of reserving local ports and bandwidth to create a connection within its network boundaries. NSA$_1$ is also in charge of contacting the other NSAs involved in serving R (NSA$_2$ and NSA$_3$) so that they can make reservations within their inner networks. In addition, all involved NSAs must handle network connections

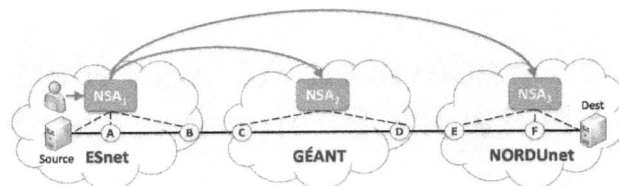

Figure 1: An NSI inter-domain data transfer: An end-user presents credentials to the software agent labeled as NSA$_1$, requesting for data stored in a host under the ESnet domain to be transferred to a host located under the NORDUnet domain, which is in turn managed by the agent known as NSA$_3$. The GÉANT domain (managed by NSA$_2$) serves as a bridge for the connection purpose.

between independent networks by physically interconnecting any relevant *service termination points* (STPs), which are abstract (high-level) representations of actual network ports and are labeled from A to F in Fig. 1. Once the connection path between the source and destination hosts is completed, the requested data transfer takes place.

In this collaborative setting within DoE-affiliated high-performance network facilities, we articulate the following the federated access management requirements that need to be accommodated:

1. Participating organizations should be allowed to define its own set of federated access management policies governing the way a given service, e.g., the aforementioned connection service, is provided in response to both local and external requests. As an example, ESnet may want to give priority over local resources to requests originated within its local domain.

2. Participating organizations may also agree on a set of inter-domain federated access management policies governing a subset of service interactions between them. As an example, ESnet and GÉANT may agree on a policy allowing for a collaborative project between both organizations to be guaranteed with high quality of service by reserving sufficient bandwidth for data transfers.

3. Participating organizations may implement their own in-house federated access management systems, which may in turn handle their own set of local credentials and possibly their own set of locally-relevant attributes. This may potentially result in problems such as attribute incompatibility, or different attributes being assigned to the same access control entity by different domains, e.g., users getting credentials issued by each service in response to their access request, possibly result in a large set of credentials to be handled. However, organizations may not favor a complete replacement of their current authentication and access control modules, as such an effort may involve considerable financial and organizational effort. As an example, ESnet may find it difficult to replace the current set of locally-issued credentials for the more than 40 research institutions currently being served by the network [29].

4. Every access control entity, e.g., end-users and protected resources, involved in serving a given access request is expected to provide a set of security-relevant properties, e.g., user credentials or resource descriptors, which may

have in turn been assigned either by its local security domain or by an external one, in such a way that proper policy evaluation based on such properties can take place. If a given entity fails to show those properties, even when they may have been legitimately assigned beforehand, the evaluation of a relevant access control policy may fail thus causing legitimate access to be denied as a result. In practice, such properties are commonly assumed to exist at policy evaluation time, either locally or remotely, e.g., stored in a dedicated centralized database. In addition, security-relevant properties may be in turn *derived* by processing other related properties. As an example, user credentials may be used to obtain the set of collaborative projects the user is involved in, without requiring the user to explicitly enumerate them, granting access only to the resources those projects are entitled to. However, existing infrastructures are not capable of seamlessly locating and transforming security properties in a distributed setting such as the one depicted in Fig. 1, which is composed of several independently-managed security domains.

5. Finally, existing federated approaches for security, e.g., OpenID [26] or Shibboleth [18], are focused on authentication: support for authorization is limited and is mostly left for third parties to implement from scratch, e.g., attribute and policy definition, discovery, and evaluation.

Consider the example of the three participant organizations on the data transfer requests depicted in Fig. 1. Each organization agrees on an inter-organizational policy P_1 that allows for data transfers between participants, e.g., from STPs A to F, if all of the following conditions are met: first, the requester is a member of a collaborative group labeled as G. Second, the size of the data to be transferred is less than or equal to 10 Tb. Third, the available bandwidth on each network is higher than or equal to 1 Gbit/s.

3. APPROACH

A well-defined approach for the specification and provisioning of both policies and security-relevant properties (attributes) is critical to enable inter-organizational resource collaboration—specifically an approach that goes beyond credential-sharing by including *heterogeneous* attributes obtained from different federated access management entities, which may have been assigned by different security domains. As depicted in a recent report by the *National Institute for Standards and Technology* (NIST) [19], proper provisioning mechanisms may become a crucial component for the successful development of new technologies and new infrastructures based on attributes. Inspired by recent successful approaches for federated authentication, we propose a federated and distributed solution for the specification, location, generation, and communication of both attributes and policies for federated access management purposes that is intended to support automated resource sharing and the establishment of collaborative projects among independent organizations, each possibly implementing their own security domain as well as their own dedicated federated access management infrastructure. A graphical depiction of our approach is shown in Fig. 2: a locally-defined attribute a_1 belonging to a given user is transformed into a series of federation-recognized attributes (a_2, a_3, a_4) that are in turn provided by other organizations engaged in a federation and may be used for access control decisions.

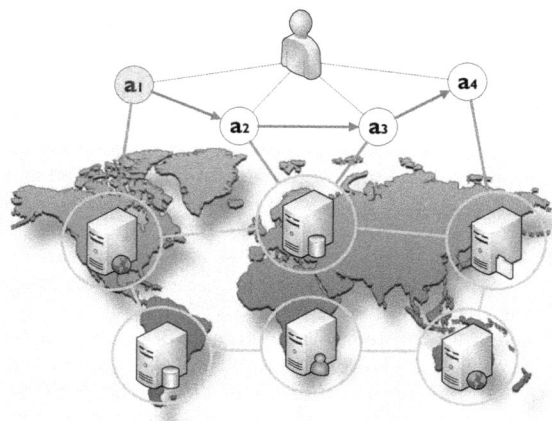

Figure 2: A federated access management framework: the local attribute a_1 is transformed into the federated attributes labeled as a_2, a_3 and a_4 by leveraging *attribute derivation rules* (AD-Rules) implemented by remote peers.

In order to participate in our proposed federation, participating organizations under DoE-affiliated high-performance network facilities must fulfill the following:

1. *Attribute identification*: Participating organizations are to identify security-relevant properties within their local domains that may serve as *local* attributes for federated access management purposes. As an example, in Fig. 1, ESnet should identify any relevant metadata belonging to the data to be transferred that can be used to obtain the properties that are relevant under policy P_1, e.g., its size in bytes.

2. *Attribute mapping*: Participants must *map* local attributes onto a set of publicly-known *federated* attributes to be used in the context of an inter-domain collaboration. Following our running example, a standard definition of an attribute depicting the size of a given chunk of data, e.g. a convention name, size unit, etc., would allow the specification and enforcement of policies across organizational domains. Because participant organizations may in turn have their own in-house definitions for local attributes, e.g., names, data ranges, etc., a consensual inter-organizational definition of federated attributes is needed. With this in mind, existing approaches based on ontological representations such as the one proposed by Paci, et al. [24], may be utilized to mitigate the existence of different attribute definition schemes, also known as *attribute heterogeneity*. Due to the nature of DoE-affiliated network facilities, we assume such a common knowledge base on attributes has been established beforehand.

3. *Attribute discovery*: Participants should allow organizational peers to leverage the federated attributes they provide by means of a discovery service. Following our running example, ESnet and GÉANT should be able to locate each other's attributes when constructing an inter-domain policy for shared connections.

4. *Federated access management administration*: Organizations should implement a proper administrative model for creating, updating, and removing both local as well as federated attributes and federated access management

policies that restrict access to protected resources within collaborative projects.

5. *Policy conflict resolution*: Finally, participants should be able to detect and resolve conflicts when constructing federated access management policies, e.g., contradictory or redundant rules, etc. As an example, let's assume the ESnet domain also provides a local policy P_2 that allows for intra-domain transfers to take place, e.g., from STPs A to B in Fig. 1, if the requesting end-user is a member of a certain local group and the data to be transferred has not been obtained from a particular server storing sensitive data located within the network scope. In such a setting, the inter-organizational policy P_1 depicted in Section 2 may be in conflict with P_2 if the data to be transferred comes from such a data-sensitive server, as P_1 may authorize the transfer but P_2 may deny it.

With respect to the evaluation of federated access management policies, participants are responsible for the following:

1. *Policy retrieval*: Upon receiving a given federated access management request R, participants should retrieve the set L containing local policies relevant to R. Following our running example, ESnet should retrieve the P_2 policy regarding data transfers originating in its local domain.

2. *Attribute provision*: Participants should provision any local and federated attributes as specified in the policies contained in L. To enable this provisioning, participants are to make their federated attributes available for other peers to provision upon request. In addition, participants should make (allowable) attribute transformations available to their peers. Following our running example, GÉANT transforms the credentials presented by an end-user in the ESnet domain into an attribute depicting membership to the federated collaborative project G that is required in the inter-organizational policy P_1.

3. *Policy dispatch*: Participants should dispatch policy evaluation requests for relevant federated policies I that are relevant to R. Conversely, participants should evaluate and provide results for any policy evaluation requests they receive as part of a request evaluation process initiated by a federated peer. Back to our running example, participant networks should retrieve all attributes relative to a connection request that happen to be under the scope of their local security domain and should dispatch both attribute and policy evaluation requests, e.g., P_1, to the other networks involved in the construction of the network path.

4. *Results aggregation*: Finally, the policy decisions for both sets L and I should be derived and combined to produce a final decision for the request R, which is to be communicated to the requesting entity, e.g., the end-user under the ESnet domain in Fig. 1.

3.1 Model Description

We start the discussion of our model for federated access management by defining the following components:

- *actors* are end-users (i.e. human agents) or subjects (i.e. computer processes) acting on behalf of users;
- *targets* are the protected resources within a security domain;

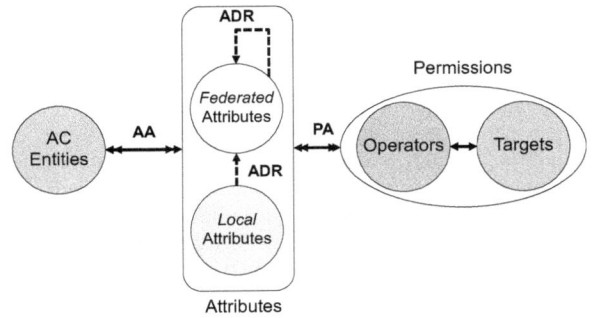

Figure 3: A model for federated access management: attributes are related to entities, e.g., end-users and protected resources, by means of the *attribute assignment* (AA) relation. Attributes (both *local* and *federated*) may be transformed into *federated* attributes by means of AD-Rules (ADR). Permissions are related to attributes by means of the *permission assignment* (PA) relation.

- *context* is the running (executing) environment, e.g. operating system, supporting platform, etc., where a given request is issued and/or served.

Fig. 3 shows a visual representation of our model: attributes are related to access control entities by means of the *attribute assignment* (AA) relation, allowing each entity to exhibit many different attributes and a single attribute to be potentially exhibited by more than one entity. *Federated* attributes are publicly-known attributes that may be relevant in the context of a given collaboration project. *Local* attributes are related to federated attributes through *attribute derivation rules* (AD-Rules), which are shown as directed arrows in a dotted line in Fig. 3. The precise definition of such AD-Rules, e.g., how local attributes are ultimately related to federated ones, is defined by peers within the context of a given collaboration. As we will discuss in Section 3.4, AD-Rules can be organized into a graph-like structure known as an *attribute derivation graph* (AD-Graph), which provides a representation of how attributes are related to permissions, which are in turn related to federated attributes by means of the *permission assignment* (PA) relation. Permissions are depicted as a combination of a protected source (target) and an operation that can be performed on it. A given attribute may be related to one or more permissions, and a given permission may be related to one or more attributes.

A description of our proposed approach is shown in Fig. 4. The basic components are actors (ACT), targets (TAR), and context (CON), which together construct the set E of access control entities. Moreover, we also consider the sets operations (OPER) and permissions (P). We define the sets names (N) and values (V), which are used for defining the sets of attributes (A) and federated attributes (F). The relationships between the elements of our model are described by defining the *attribute assignment* (AA) and *permission assignment* (PA) relations, as well as our proposed AD-Rules.

The definition of AD-Graphs is based on the concepts of graph theory and the definition of AD-Rules. The access control decision process is modeled by functions *provisionedAttributes*, *expectedAttributes*, *relatedPermissions*, and *checkAccess*. Function *provisionedAttributes* calculates the set of attributes that can be provisioned from a given AD-Graph based on the local and federated attributes initially exhibited by a set of access control entities. Function *expectedAttributes* returns the set of attributes that are related to a given permission, by inspecting the PA relation. The mirror function *relatedPermissions* returns the set of all permissions that are associated in the PA relation with a given attribute. Finally, function *checkAccess* implements the authorization checking functionality by first calculating the set of attributes provisioned by the entities in a given access control request and comparing it with the set of attributes that are related to the requested permission, which is only granted if the set of provisioned attributes (obtained from the *provisionedAttributes* function) is a subset of the set of attributes related to such permission, which is obtained from the *expectedAttributes* function.

3.2 Attributes

We define attributes as an abstraction of *security-relevant* properties that are exhibited by access control entities, namely, actors, targets, policies, and any applicable context. Their physical nature, e.g., if the attribute represents a file's metadata or an end-user credential, and the way those attributes are collected from the access control entities remain dependent on each organizational domain.

As shown in Fig. 4, we define attributes to have the following three components: (1) a data *type*, which restricts the nature and the possible range of values defined for the attribute, (2) a *name*, which is later used for defining AD-Rules on them and is defined in the context of a given inter-organizational setting, and (3) a *value*, which is used when evaluating such AD-Rules. Examples of attributes include: <Double, *data.size*, 100.0>, <String, *data.source*, "*server.esnet*">, and <Date, *system.date*, "*10-10-2015*">.

3.3 Federated Attributes

Federated attributes are obtained by processing local attributes from access control entities under a given organizational domain. Such processing is to be modeled through the AD-Rules, thus allowing federated attributes to be related to access rights (permissions).

As an example, AD-Rules may provide functionality intended to validate a given local attribute by inspecting its value component and producing a proper federated attribute as a result. Thus, a validated federated attribute ensures that a given collaboration state remains secure.

As described in Section 3.1, permissions can be assigned to federated attributes, which then serve as a layer of association between local attributes and permissions defined in another organizational domain for collaborative purposes. Such a layer helps identify the local attributes that may be involved in granting a given inter-domain permission, as well as the set of constraints represented by AD-Rules that may be involved in such a process. Moreover, our approach allows for AD-Rules to take federated attributes as an input or may also take both local as well as federated ones as an input to produce federated attributes as a result, as depicted in Fig. 3, thus allowing for expressing richer inter-domain policies based on processing already existing federated attributes.

3.4 Attribute Derivation Rules and Graphs

As introduced in Section 3.1, *attribute derivation rules* (AD-Rules) are expected to provide a mapping between local

- ACT, the set of actors.
- TAR, the set of targets.
- CON, the set of context instances.
- OPER, the set of operations.
- P ⊆ TAR × OPER, the set of permissions.
- E = ACT ∪ TAR ∪ CON, the set of access control entities.
- N, the set of names.
- V, the set of values.
- T, the set of data types.
- A = { a | a = <*type*, *name*, *value*>where *type* ∈ T, *name* ∈ N, *value* ∈ V, the set of attributes.
- F ⊆ A, the set of federated attributes.
- AA ⊆ A × E, the *attribute assignment* relation mapping attributes with a given access control entity.
- PA ⊆ P × A, the *permission assignment* relation mapping permissions and attributes.
- ADR = { r | r: $2^A \to 2^F$ }, the set of attribute derivation rules mapping sets of attributes to sets of federated attributes.
- ADG, the set of directed, weakly connected, and possibly cyclic attribute derivation graphs. A graph g = <NODES, ARCS>∈ ADG if NODES ⊆ 2^A and ARCS ⊆ ADR. We say $(n_1, arc, n_2) \in g$ if n_1, $n_2 \in$ NODES and $arc \in$ ARCS and $n_1 \subseteq domain(arc)$ and $n_2 \subseteq codomain(arc)$.
- *provisionedAttributes*: $2^E \times$ ADG $\to 2^A$, a function mapping a set of entities $E' \subseteq$ E with the set of attributes that the entities in E'can provision from a given ADG g. An attribute f is said to be provisioned by an entity $e \in E'$if there exists a set of attributes A'= { a | a ∈ A, e ∈ E', (a, e) ∈ AA } ⊆ A and a set of paths P = {p | p = x_0, x_1, ...x_n, n ≥ 0} in g such that $\forall$ p ∈ P, $x_0 \in$ A'and $x_n = f$, and $\forall x_i$, x_j in p, $1 \le i < n$, $j = i + 1$, $\exists$ r ∈ ADR such that $r(x_i) = x_j$.
- *expectedAttributes*: P $\to 2^A$, a function returning the set of attributes that are related to a given permission p. Formally, returns all $a \in$ A such that $(p, a) \in$ PA.
- REQ = {req = <*act*, p = <*tar*, *oper*>, *ctx* >| *act* ∈ ACT, $p \in$ P, *ctx* ∈ CON}, the set of access control requests, allowing an actor *act* to request for a permission p to be granted.
- *checkAccess*: REQ × ADG $\to$ {*true*, *false*}, a boolean function that checks if a given request *req* = (*act*, p = (*tar*, *oper*), *ctx*) ∈ REQ should be granted or denied based on a given attribute derivation graph *adg*. Formally, the function returns *true* if *provisionedAttributes*({*act*, *tar*, *ctx*}, *adg*) ⊆ *expectedAttributes*(p), and returns *false* otherwise.

Figure 4: A model description of our approach.

attributes and federated attributes. For this purpose, AD-Rules are said to be *non-injective**, as two or more elements from an input set of attributes (domain) may be mapped to the same element in the output set (co-domain).

In addition, AD-Rules can be *chained* together to produce a graph-like structure showing how attributes can be provisioned. Such *attribute derivation graphs* (AD-Graphs) are *directed*, because AD-Rules represent unidirectional edges (due to their nature as functions). Moreover, AD-Graphs are also *weakly* connected, as there is no requirement for all nodes (attributes) to be connected to each other. Finally, AD-Graphs are also possibly *cyclic*, as a customized

---

*A function f: A $\to$ B is said to be *injective* or *one-to-one*, $\forall$ a, a'∈ A, a ≠ a'⇒ $f(a) \neq f(a')$.

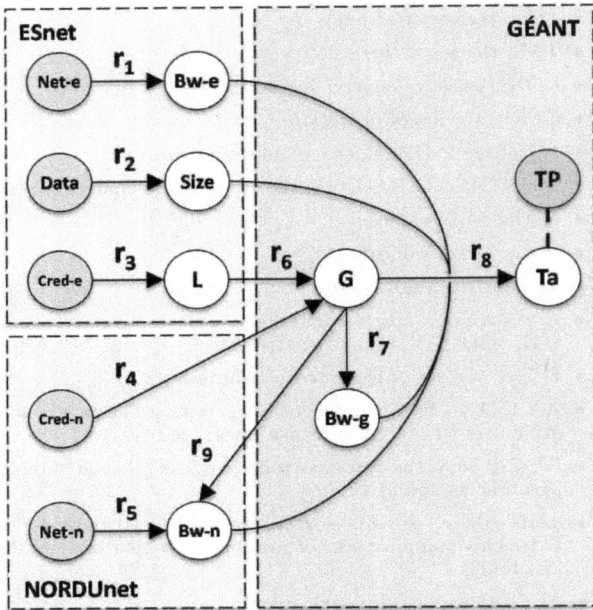

Figure 5: A distributed AD-Graph depicting policy P_1: local attributes (shown in grey) are transformed into federated ones (shown in white). As an example, the AD-Rule labeled as r_8 transforms attributes G (group membership), *Size* (data size) and *Bw-e*, *Bw-g*, *Bw-n* (bandwidth) into the federated attribute *Ta* that is related to the *TP* (data transfer) permission.

chaining of AD-Rules may end up introducing a cycle in the produced AD-Graph.

AD-Graphs may also support collaborative processing by allowing a division into proper subgraphs, each subgraph implemented in a different security domain: as mentioned in Section 2, each participating domain is in charge of defining its own permissions, local and federated attributes, as well as the AD-Rules and AD-Graphs to generate those. AD-Graphs can be modeled as a distributed graph: a given AD-Graph G defined for a federation F may be divided into a set of subgraphs G'_1, G'_2, ... G'_n, such that each G'_i is to be processed by a different domain in F.

As an example, the AD-Graph in Fig. 5 implements the inter-organizational policy P_1 described in Section 2 as follows: the ESnet local attribute *Cred-e*, which depicts a locally-issued credential, is transformed by the AD-Rule labeled as r_3 into the federated attribute L that features membership to a local group within ESnet. L is subsequently processed by the AD-Rule r_6 in the GÉANT domain, producing the federated attribute G, which in turn depicts membership to an inter-organizational collaborative group. Later, G, along with attributes *Size*, *Bw-e*, *Bw-g*, and *Bw-n* are taken as input for the AD-Rule labeled as r_8, producing the *Ta* attribute as a result. This attribute features an access token related to the *TP* permission authorizing the data transferring process shown in Fig. 1. Such a permission is included in Fig. 5 for the illustrative purposes.

Leveraging the previous definitions, the problem of resolving an access request to a shared resource within a federation can be first modeled as a path traversal problem within a distributed graph: determining if there exists a path between a set of starting nodes (local attributes) and a given ending node (federated attribute). Then, determining if such a federated attribute grants the requested permission over the desired resource. A general procedure for resolving an access request, derived from the model shown in Fig. 3: given a federation F, a permission P, and a set of input attributes I the procedure starts by obtaining the set of *expected* federated attributes granting P, e.g., by parsing local and federated access management policies. If the *required* set is found to be a subset of I—that is, I contains the attributes required for P, access is granted. Otherwise, the procedure extracts a set of paths from an AD-Graph in F, each of these paths starting with an attribute in the set I and ending with an attribute in the *required* set. Then, each path is traversed by executing each of the included AD-Rules. If new federated attributes are generated, and such attributes happen to include the attributes in *required*, access is granted and the procedure terminates. Otherwise, access is denied.

3.5 Attribute Provisioning

In our approach, attribute provisioning is crucial to handle federated access management requests in the context of inter-organizational resource sharing. Such a process includes allowing for participating organizations to know about the AD-Rules that are implemented by other organizations and are involved in a given AD-Graph G. Concretely, participants need up-to-date information about G so that they can extract correct paths within G that can produce the desired federated attributes. With this in mind, attribute provisioning can therefore be divided into two process: path discovery and path traversal.

The *path discovery* process allows for each organization to distribute information about its locally-implemented AD-Rules to the federated access management federation, so that they can potentially maintain a representation of G for path calculation. However, there are several practical challenges: first, each organization needs to be notified when changes to G occur, e.g. adding or removing a given AD-Rule, which may create a large set of communication messages between participants. Second, there is an added maintenance cost, e.g. processing time, that participating organizations must incur for handling and maintaining an up-to-date G. Finally, storage efficiency may become an issue when a large G must be locally maintained. An alternative approach would be creating a central database storing G, along with a set of replicas for enhanced availability. However, such a scheme may suffer from service bottlenecks and consistency issues when communicating updates to the replicas. In addition, a centralized server may become the subject of a *denial of service* (DoS) attack, which could certainly limit the availability of the overall attribute provisioning scheme, thus potentially preventing participating organizations from serving federated access management requests. With this in mind, there is a need for a distributed approach that allows for participating organizations to release information about the AD-Rules they implement in such a way that the administration burden, e.g., number of communication messages, is significantly reduced. In addition, such an approach should also prevent organizations from having to store a complete AD-Graph locally for path discovery purposes and should provide support against attacks targeting a single point of failure. We present an implementation tailored for meeting such goals in Section 4.

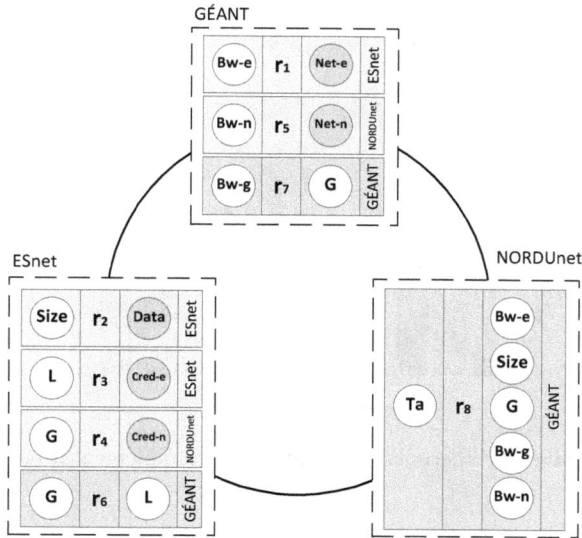

Figure 6: An illustrative DHT *ring* depicting the AD-Graph of Fig. 5: federated peers store *entries* containing information about the AD-Rules implemented by other peers in the context of federated access management.

Following the model described in Fig. 3, the path traversal process allows participating organizations to invoke the AD-Rules included in a given path p in G that may ultimately produce a given federated attribute. Invocation of such AD-Rules should be done by following a sequence starting from the first AD-Rule in p up to the last one. Each time an AD-Rule is executed, the produced set of attributes is added to a set of input attributes for the next AD-Rule in the sequence. In addition, the invocation of an AD-Rule r enables to locate the federated domain implementing r, the set of input attributes, as well as the set of produced attributes. A request for the invocation of r should include the set of attributes that serve as its input. Finally, the attributes produced by r, if any, should be then communicated back to the requesting organization.

4. IMPLEMENTATION AND EVALUATION

In this section, we describe our proof-of-concept implementation and evaluation results. We elaborate how we accommodate the concerns described in Section 3.5. Also, we discuss how the path discovery process was implemented with the concept of *distributed hash tables* (DHT) [28]. In addition, we discuss our implementation on the path traversal process which is based on a client-server architecture for the remote invocation of our proposed AD-Rules.

4.1 Path Discovery

Fig. 6 illustrates the path discovery process based on our running example. We allow for participants in a federation F to join a DHT *ring* to publish and retrieve information about the AD-Rules that may produce federated attributes. This process may be in turn decomposed into two inner components, namely, AD-Rule publishing and AD-Rule retrieval.

The procedure for publishing an AD-Rule is conducted as follows: each domain is in charge of inserting an *entry* into the DHT for each AD-Rule they implement for a given AD-Graph under the context of F. Such an entry should include information about the input attributes (either local

or federated ones), the name of the AD-Rule, and the set of federated attributes to be produced as a result. Moreover, some information on how to *execute* such AD-Rule should be also provided, e.g., a universal resource locator (URL). As an example, the ESnet domain will publish an entry into the DHT containing information about the AD-Rule r_1, including the local input parameter *Net*, which conceptually depicts information about the current state of the local network, and the federated attribute *Bw*, which provides a standard representation of the current bandwidth capacity. In addition, such an entry should contain a valid URL for other federated peers invoking the AD-Rule r_1 remotely. Following the insertion procedure for DHTs [28], such an entry may end up being stored for future location at a different federated peer, following a hashing scheme based on the standardized naming convention for federated attributes introduced in Section 3.2. In Fig. 6, the entry for the AD-Rule labeled as r_1 (published by ESnet) ends up being stored by the DHT node under the scope of the GÉANT domain. Conversely, AD-Rules may be retired from a given AD-Graph by removing their corresponding entries from a given DHT ring. Recall such procedure may not necessarily remove the production of federated attributes in the context of an AD-Graph, as such attributes may be produced by another AD-Rule in the DHT ring, e.g., removing the entry for the AD-Rule r_6 does not prevent an attribute G from being produced by the AD-Rule labeled as r_4.

The retrieval procedure for entries containing information about AD-Rules is to be conducted as follows: a participating domain D interested in producing a given attribute A may retrieve the set S of entries corresponding to A in the DHT ring, e.g., by hashing the A's identifier. Then, by inspecting the information about AD-Rules contained in S, D must determine if there exists a local or federated attribute under its local domain that can be used as an input parameter to an AD-Rule to produce A. If so, information from the corresponding entry in the set S is retrieved and the AD-Rule is invoked. However, if no suitable entry is found, e.g. all input attributes to the entries in S are out of scope or cannot be locally produced, D may attempt to explore the DHT ring once again for entries producing the attributes taken as an input to the entries in S, thus potentially producing a set P of graph paths in an AD-Graph stored in the DHT. Such a process may be repeated up to the point when no more entries can be obtained from the DHT or a cycle in the AD-Graph stored in the DHT is detected, e.g., when an iteration retrieves entries that were previously retrieved in the past, or a path can be traversed. A path in P is traversed, e.g., by calling the sequence of AD-Rules contained in it, only if it starts with an attribute under the scope of D and ends with the desired attribute A. Considering our running example, an entity under the ESnet domain may provision an attribute Ta depicted in Fig. 5 as follows: the DHT featured in Fig. 6 retrieves the entry for the AD-Rule labeled as r_8 from the ring node implemented by NORDUnet. As the input parameters of r_8 are all federated attributes, ESnet inspects the DHT ring once again for determining proper AD-Rules provisioning those attributes. Then, entries generating Bw-e (r_1), Bw-g (r_7), Bw-n (r_5 and r_9), $Size$ (r_2) and G (r_4, r_6), are returned. For the federated attribute Bw-e, ESnet can provide the local attribute Net-e required for r_1, thus creating a *traversable* path within the distributed AD-Graph. In addition, for the federated attribute $Size$,

Table 1: Performance (ms) for policy P_1.

Processing Time	ALT	ATT	OPT
10	411	352	83
50	484	921	1,405
100	531	1,613	2,144
100	492	14,214	14,706
2,500	470	35,201	35,671
5,000	498	85,254	85,652

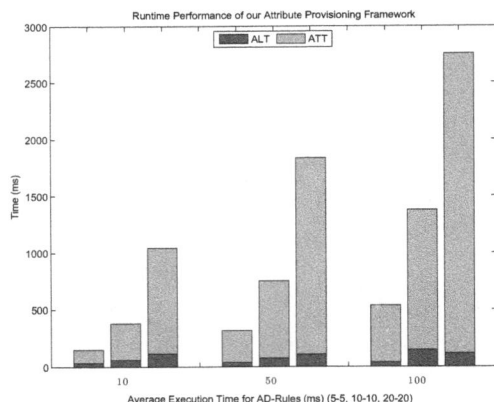

Figure 7: Experimental results for our implementation.

ESnet can also provide the required local attribute *Data* required for r_2, thus creating a path as well. In the case of G, the entry belonging to r_4 may be discarded as its input attribute (*Cred-n*) is local only to NORDUnet. However, in the case of the entry for r_6, ESnet may inspect the DHT ring once again for an entry producing the input attribute L. Next, the entry for r_3 is returned taking *Cred-e* as an input. Since *Cred-e* is local to ESnet, another traversable path is constructed. With respect to an attribute *Bw-n*, the AD-Rules labeled as r_5 can be also discarded as its input attribute (*Net-n*) is local to NORDUnet. However, r_9 can be used as it takes the federated attribute G as an input, and a path producing G has been already obtained. Similarly, an attribute *Bw-g* can be obtained from r_7 as such an AD-Rule takes G as an input. The setting depicted in Fig. 5 and Fig. 6 allows for the AD-Rules labeled as r_7 and r_9 to disclose network-related information, e.g., bandwidth, only when membership to an inter-organizational project (as depicted by the G attribute) can be shown.

4.2 Path Traversal

Our implementation supports the process of path traversal by allowing for each participant domain D to implement a software agent that is capable of handling requests for the invocation of the AD-Rules that are under the scope of D. Information on locating such agent and invoking the implemented AD-Rules should be consistent with the entries published in the DHT ring described in Section 4.1, e.g., ESnet may provide a TCP/IP agent that implements the AD-Rule labeled as r_1 in Fig. 5 and Fig. 6. For a given path P composed of n entries obtained from a DHT ring, the traversal procedure would include requesting for the execution of each entry starting from the entry at the first position and collecting the attributes produced by the AD-Rule being invoked (if any). The process continues as soon as new attributes are produced on every AD-Rule invocation and finishes either when a given AD-Rule depicted by an entry in the path is not able to produce any attributes or the final entry (at position n - 1) has been executed and the final attributes have been produced as a result.

4.3 Experimental Results

We have implemented the DHT functionality discussed before by leveraging the Open Chord 1.0 API [15]: an open source implementation of the Chord DHT [28] that allows for remote peers to implement a DHT ring by communicating with each other over TCP/IP sockets. In addition, our proposed AD-Rules, as discussed in Section 3.4, were implemented by leveraging a client-server architecture over TCP/IP sockets with the standard `java.net` package.

In the first experiment, we examined the inter-organizational policy P_1 shown in Fig. 5 and Fig. 6. Such an AD-Graph is stored in a DHT ring composed of three nodes and each of them simulates three participating organizations in

our running example. In addition, each of these nodes has been augmented with a server module implementing each of the AD-Rules included in the aforementioned AD-Graph. As an example, the ESnet domain was simulated by DHT node as well as a server module implementing the r_1, r_2 and r_3 AD-Rules. In addition, the *processing* time of each AD-Rule included was simulated by introducing a code to halt the execution for a certain period of time. In our experiments, we measured the *average location time* (ALT) for constructing a given path P within the AD-Graph implementing P_1 policy. Also, we measured the *average traversing time* (ATT) for P to return a federated attribute as a result. Finally, we calculated the *overall provisioning time* (OPT) by consolidating both ALT and ATT. Table 1 shows our experimental results when attempting to provision the federated attribute Ta simulating an entity in the ESnet domain holding the local attributes *Cred-e*, *Net-e* and *Data* as shown in our example. Since the *length* (number of DHT entries) of the paths under the experiments remains the same, e.g. the same number of involved attributes and AD-Rules, variation in the OPT for each experiment is mostly due to the preconfigured execution time of the AD-Rules included in such paths, whereas the ALT involved in constructing those paths remains manageable.

In the second experiment, we measured the response time in provisioning attributes over various AD-Graphs. On each experiment, we produced an AD-Graph depicting a varying number of paths (*branches*) and each of them includes the different number of composing nodes (*links*). In addition, we simulated the execution time of each AD-Rule involved in the produced AD-Graph by using a configurable parameter. We maintained the DHT and server configuration as described earlier. On each experiment instance, we attempted to provision the attribute produced by the DHT entry located at the last node of each path in the simulated AD-Graph. As an example, for a path composed of l nodes, we issue a request for the attribute produced by the DHT entry located at position l-1, assuming that we can include the attribute in the request as the input for the entry depicted in position 0 of the path. Fig. 7 shows our results when constructing AD-Graphs of size (b-l) where b stands for the number of branches and l stands for the number of links on each AD-Graph, e.g., the first three-column set shows the evaluation results when setting up an execution time of 10 ms for AD-Rules and constructing AD-Graphs of size (5-5), (10-10) and (20-20) respectively.

As described before, we obtained both the ALT and the ATT on each experiment, which are used to calculate the OPT. In the first experiment, most of the overall provisioning time is spent on the path traversal, which is mostly influenced by both the execution time of each AD-Rule in a given AD-Graph, as well as the length of the path. Similarly the ALT observed in the second experiment, while it was also affected by the length of the path, remains just as a small fraction of the OPT, mostly due to the nature of distributed network settings based on DHTs.

5. RELATED WORK

The problem of providing security guarantees in inter-organizational settings has been largely addressed in literature. In particular, several *federated identity* [4] approaches have been introduced to allow partnering organizations to reuse locally-issued credentials when accessing resources located under the scope of an external security domain. As an example, OpenID [26] and Shibboleth [18] have recently gained acceptance in both industry and academia respectively for user-credential sharing. Our approach builds on this idea by allowing participants to exchange federated *attributes*, thus potentially allowing for such attributes to serve as *tokens* granting access to shared resources, in an approach also inspired by Kerberos [20], OAuth [14] and more recently, Facebook Login [8], which strives to allow third-party applications to leverage the user credentials defined for the popular social network to access application-dependent resources.

Moreover, our AD-Rules are inspired by the idea depicted in the credential-discovery protocol proposed by the RT Framework [17], which allows for credentials issued by independent domains to be located and leveraged for federated access management purposes. Similar to the RAMARS Framework [12], our AD-Rules are depicted in a graph-like structure that allows for user-defined attributes to be transformed into a set of widely-recognized credentials. However, the RAMARS framework assumes each security domain implementing the transformation functions may be *partially* trusted by modeling trust in the range [0,1]. In our approach, we assume all federated peers *fully* trust each other for the implementation of the federation goals as discussed in Section 3 and the model presented in Fig. 4, due to the nature of DoE-affiliated high-performance network facilities.

In addition, recent approaches leveraging federated identity for sharing resources include the work of Broeder et al. [2] and Ananthakrishnan et al. [1]. Moreover, Klingenstein [16] and Chadwick and Inman [5] incorporate the concept of end-user attributes with the federated identity. Our approach includes attributes originated from different access control entities rather than considering attributes and credentials from end-users.

In the context of attribute-based models, Zhang et al. [30] introduced their *attribute-based access control matrix*, which extends classical theory in the field of access control to accommodate attributes as well as the notion of *security state*. Moreover, Priebe et al. [25] presented an approach leveraging the concepts of *ontologies* and the *semantic web* in order to formalize the notion of attributes. An approach close to ours was introduced by Covington and Sastry [6], who presented a *contextual attribute access control* (CABAC) model which was realized in mobile applications. However, our approach goes a step further by describing the way such attributes are mapped to access rights (permissions) by means of AD-Rules and AD-Graphs. Recently, a notable approach was proposed by Jin et al. [13], whose approach formalizes a series of attribute-based model families. However, our approach introduces a notion of security token and AD-Rules to capture the mapping between attributes and corresponding access rights.

6. DISCUSSION AND FUTURE WORK

Attribute Provisioning. As shown in Section 4, efficient provisioning of federated attributes is crucial for processing federated access management policies in order to resolve policies in a timely manner. The attribute provisioning scheme presented in Section 3.5 supports this goal by reducing the number of communication messages between participating domains to determine if a given AD-Graph depicts a path between a pair of attributes. Each participant organization should decide the number of times it will attempt to retrieve new entries from a DHT ring when constructing a given path. As an example, an organization may set a limit of three explorations of the DHT ring while trying to find a set of input attributes for AD-Rules that fall under the scope of its local domain. Setting a low limit of explorations might prevent participants from discovering a potential path in the AD-Graph, however a large limit may increase attribute provisioning time, thus possibly affecting the overall processing time of a given federated access management policy. In addition, due to the fact DHTs require participants to locally store only a subset of all the entries included in a given ring, our scheme allows participants to store only a subset of AD-Rules entries, thus potentially relieving them from storing information related to the complete AD-Graph. In this way, the process of adding and removing AD-Rules is significantly simplified, thus providing a means for modifying a given AD-Graph to better meet the specific goals devised for collaborations, e.g., adding new AD-Rules to handle user credentials from a new participating domain.

Trust Model. Our current approach assumes all participants in our federation *fully* trust each other for the implementation of both the AD-Rules as well as the model defined in Fig. 4. This strong assumption requires that participants faithfully produce federated attributes by providing verified and accurate AD-Rules and communicating those in a timely manner. However, such an assumption may not always hold in practice. As an example, the incorrect implementation of a given AD-Rule may potentially compromise the overall security of a federated environment. Future work may focus on incorporating a trust model among participants and a risk analysis framework such that incidents can be detected and proper countermeasures can be deployed as a result.

Privacy. Following the *fully-trusted* assumption just described, a basic privacy model may be implemented on top of our approach by allowing for sensitive information contained in locally-defined attributes not to be revealed to other organizational peers when producing federated attributes. For instance, in Fig. 5, sensitive information in attribute *Cred*, e.g., a user's full name, may be replaced by a *pseudonym* in the L attribute produced by the AD-Rule labeled as r_3. An alternative approach may allow for end-users to hide sensitive attributes at request time by incorporating techniques such as the *privacy-preserving attribute-based credentials* (PABC) proposed by Camenisch et al. [3].

Policy Language and Conflict Resolution. Efficient discovery and retrieval of policies (as shown in Section 3) may benefit from the use of a standard policy language, in a similar technique to the one used by the XACML *role-based access control* (RBAC) Profile [22]. Moreover, a comprehensive policy specification framework is critical to detect and resolve conflicts that may arise between federated and local policies, or the intersection of the two, e.g., contradictory rules, following an approach similar to the one proposed by Hu et al. [10].

Integration with NSI. Finally, we plan to work on integrating our approach with the NSI effort presented in Section 2, in such a way that the collaborative efforts devised by participant organizations can be better met by securely leveraging DoE-affiliated high-performance facilities.

7. CONCLUDING REMARKS

In this paper, we have explored the problem of implementing well-defined, consistent, and inter-organizational access management for collaborative resource sharing. In our proposed approach and experiments, we also showed that participants could engage in a federation under a well-defined set of responsibilities, including the use of standardized attribute definitions, attribute provisioning, and distributed policy evaluation. We believe our approach may also be applicable to any other collaborative settings beyond high-performance network environments, e.g. collaborative projects in the health-care domain would certainly benefit for automated approaches that allow for information to be safely shared between independently-run organizations, possibly improving the patient experience and encouraging the development of groundbreaking advancements.

8. ACKNOWLEDGEMENTS

We would like to thank the anonymous reviewers for their valuable comments that helped improve the presentation of this paper. This work was partially supported by the grant from the United States Department of Energy (DE-SC0004308). Any opinions, findings, and conclusions or recommendations expressed in this material are those of the authors and do not necessarily reflect the views of the funding agency.

9. REFERENCES

[1] R. Ananthakrishnan, J. Bryan, K. Chard, I. Foster, T. Howe, M. Lidman, and S. Tuecke. Globus nexus: An identity, profile, and group management platform for science gateways. In *Proceedings of 2013 IEEE International Conference on Cluster Computing (CLUSTER)*, pages 1–3, Sept 2013.

[2] D. Broeder, R. Wartel, B. Jones, P. Kershaw, D. Kelsey, S. Lüders, A. Lyall, T. Nyrönen, and H. J. Weyer. Federated identity management for research collaborations. Technical report, CERN, 2012.

[3] J. Camenisch, A. Lehmann, G. Neven, and A. Rial. Privacy-preserving auditing for attribute-based credentials. In *Proceedings of European Symposium on Research in Computer Security (ESORICS)*, pages 109–127, 2014.

[4] D. W. Chadwick. Federated identity management. In *Foundations of Security Analysis and Design V*, pages 96–120. Springer, 2009.

[5] David W Chadwick and George Inman. Attribute aggregation in federated identity management. *IEEE Computer*, 42(5):33–40, 2009.

[6] M. J. Covington and M. R. Sastry. A contextual attribute-based access control model. In *Proceedings of the 2006 International Conference on the Move to Meaningful Internet Systems (OTM)*, pages 1996–2006. Springer, 2006.

[7] Europe's National Research and Education Networks (NRENs). Geánt Project Home, 2015. http://www.geant.net/.

[8] Facebook Inc. Facebook Login, 2015. https://www.facebook.com/about/login/.

[9] Open Grid Forum. An Open Global Forum for Advanced Distributed Computing, 2015. https://www.ogf.org/.

[10] H. Hu, Gail-J. Ahn, and K. Kulkarni. Detecting and resolving firewall policy anomalies. *IEEE Transactions on Dependable and Secure Computing*, 9(3):318–331, 2012.

[11] Jing J. and Gail-J. Ahn. Role-based access management for ad-hoc collaborative sharing. In *Proceedings of 11th Symposium on Access Control Models and Technologies (SACMAT)*, pages 200–209. ACM, 2006.

[12] Jing Jin and Gail-Joon Ahn. Authorization framework for resource sharing in grid environments. *Grid and Distributed Computing*, 63:148–155, 2009.

[13] X. Jin, R. Krishnan, and R. Sandhu. A unified attribute-based access control model covering dac, mac and rbac. In *Proceedings of the 26th Annual IFIP WG 11.3 conference on Data and Applications Security and Privacy (DBSec)*, pages 41–55. Springer, 2012.

[14] M. Jones and D. Hardt. The oauth 2.0 authorization framework: Bearer token usage. Technical report, RFC 6750, October, 2012.

[15] Kaffille, Sven and Loesing, Karsten. Open Chord, 2015. http://sourceforge.net/projects/open-chord/.

[16] N. Klingenstein. Attribute aggregation and federated identity. In *Proceedings of the 2007 International Symposium on Applications and the Internet Workshops (SAINT)*, pages 26–26, Jan 2007.

[17] Ninghui Li, J.C. Mitchell, and W.H. Winsborough. Design of a role-based trust-management framework. In *Proceedings of the 2002 IEEE Symposium on Security and Privacy*, pages 114–130, 2002.

[18] R. L. Morgan, S. Cantor, S. Carmody, W. Hoehn, and K. Klingenstein. Federated Security: The Shibboleth Approach. *EDUCAUSE Quarterly*, 27(4):12–17, 2004.

[19] National Institute of Standards and Technology. Guide to Attribute Based access Control (ABAC) Definition and Considerations, 2013. NIST Special Publication 800-162 Draft.

[20] B.C. Neuman and T. Ts'o. Kerberos: an authentication service for computer networks. *Communications Magazine, IEEE*, 32(9):33–38, Sept 1994.

[21] Nordic Council of Ministers. Nordic Infrastructure for Research & Education (NORDUnet), 2015. https://www.nordu.net/.

[22] OASIS. XACML v3.0 Core and Hierarchical Role Based Access Control (RBAC) Profile Version 1.0, 2014. http://docs.oasis-open.org/xacml/3.0/xacml-3.0-rbac-v1-spec-cd-03-en.html.

[23] Open Grid Forum. Network Services Interface (NSI), 2015. https://redmine.ogf.org/projects/nsi-wg.

[24] F. Paci, R. Ferrini, A. Musci, K. Steuer, and E. Bertino. An interoperable approach to multifactor identity verification. *IEEE Computer*, 42(5):50–57, May 2009.

[25] T. Priebe, W. Dobmeier, and N. Kamprath. Supporting attribute-based access control with ontologies. In *Proceedings of the First International Conference on Availability, Reliability and Security (ARES)*, pages 465–472, Washington, DC, USA, 2006. IEEE.

[26] D. Recordon and D. Reed. Openid 2.0: A platform for user-centric identity management. In *Proceedings of the Second ACM Workshop on Digital Identity Management*, DIM '06, pages 11–16, New York, NY, USA, 2006. ACM.

[27] M. S. Singhalm, S. Chandrasekhar, Ge Tingjian, R. Sandhu, R. Krishnan, Gail-J. Ahn, and E. Bertino. Collaboration in multi-cloud applications: Framework and security issues. *IEEE Computer*, 2013.

[28] I. Stoica, R. Morris, D. Karger, M. F. Kaashoek, and H. Balakrishnan. Chord: A scalable peer-to-peer lookup service for internet applications. In *Proceedings of the 2001 Conference on Applications, Technologies, Architectures, and Protocols for Computer Communications*, pages 149–160, New York, NY, USA, 2001. ACM.

[29] US Department of Energy. Energy Sciences Network (ESnet), 2015. http://www.es.net/.

[30] X. Zhang, Y. Li, and D. Nalla. An attribute-based access matrix model. In *Proceedings of the 2005 ACM symposium on applied computing (SAC)*, pages 359–363, New York, NY, USA, 2005. ACM.

Fine-Grained Business Data Confidentiality Control in Cross-Organizational Tracking

Weili Han, Yin Zhang, Zeqing Guo
Software School, Fudan University
Shanghai Key Laboratory of Data Science
Shanghai, China, 201203
wlhan@fudan.edu.cn

Elisa Bertino
Department of Computer Science
Purdue University
West Lafayette, IN 47907
bertino@cs.purdue.edu

ABSTRACT

With the support of the Internet of Things (IoT for short) technologies, tracking systems are being widely deployed in many companies and organizations in order to provide more efficient and trustworthy delivery services. Such systems usually support easy-to-use interfaces, by which users can visualize the shipping status and progress of merchandise, according to business data which are collected directly from the merchandise through sensing technologies. However, these business data may include sensitive business information, which should be strongly protected in cross-organizational scenarios. Thus, it is critical for suppliers that the disclosure of such data to unauthorized users is prevented in the context of the open environment of these tracking systems. As business data from different suppliers and organizations are usually associated together with merchandise being shipped, it is also important to support fine-grained confidentiality control. In this paper, we articulate the problem of fine-grained business data confidentiality control in IoT-enabled cross-organizational tracking systems. We then propose a fine-grained confidentiality control mechanism, referred to as xCP-ABE, to address the problem in the context of open environment. The xCP-ABE mechanism is a novel framework which makes suppliers in tracking systems able to selectively authorize specific sets of users to access their sensitive business data and satisfies the confidentiality of transmission path of goods. We develop a prototype of the xCP-ABE mechanism, and then evaluate its performance. We also carry out a brief security analysis of our proposed mechanism. Our evaluation and analysis show that our framework is an effective and efficient solution to ensure the confidentiality of business data in cross-organizational tracking systems.

Categories and Subject Descriptors

D.4.6 [**Software**]: Security and Protection—*Access controls*; E.3 [**Data**]: Data Encryption—*Public key cryptosystems*

General Terms

Security

Keywords

Fine-Grained, Access Control, Internet of Things (IoT), Cross-Organizational, Ciphertext-Policy Attribute-Based Encryption (CP-ABE), Tracking System, Electronic Pedigree

1. INTRODUCTION

Recent advances in the Internet of Things (IoT for short) have enhanced the efficiency of current tracking systems [6][13]. Thus, these systems are now being widely deployed. Sensed data in tracking systems are typically sent to end-servers from sensors in the form of events. An information flow of sensed data and transaction data is built following the packages' transfers across the multiple organizations involved in the shipping. By using these data, users including end customers, suppliers and supervisors which are usually governmental agencies can conveniently observe the movements of the merchandise in the tracking systems.

However, a major problem in such tracking systems is represented by security, and especially the security of data in the information flow. To date, only very few papers [25][26][27] have addressed these issues. EPCglobal [15] leverages the digital signature technology to ensure the trustworthiness of the sensed data in the tracking systems, especially for drug supply systems [4]. Furthermore, some extensions have been developed to ensure the trustworthiness of data used for the protection of foods [17] and wine safety [30], and for protecting high-value merchandise from counterfeiting.

Other relevant approaches [8][10][14] have focused on the path authentication of RFID-enabled (Radio-Frequency IDentification) supply chains. Such approaches can support authentication and privacy protection, but as they only have available limited memory, *e.g.,* 120 bits [14] to store the data, they are unable to scale to real business data.

None of the existing approaches has addressed the problem of the confidentiality of sensed data and transaction data, when these data are managed by a supporting information system, such as EPCIS [15]. Two major challenges in such context are represented by the open environment typical of cross-organizational tracking systems and the need for fine-grained control. That is, when users query the electronic pedigrees, which contain business data with trustworthiness assurance, of some merchandise, all the business data of the merchandise in the pedigrees would be available to users in current IoT-enabled tracking systems. Besides, because IoT-enabled tracking systems usually depend on cooperation among multiple organizations, it is difficult to protect the confidentiality of sensed data at a fine-grained level.

Kerschbaum [21] has proposed an access control model for mobile physical objects. Such a model supports two high level policies covering the up-stream and down-stream visibility. However, the Kerschbaum's model supports data access control only in a coarse granularity. Even when Kerschbaum's model is integrated with an attribute-based access control model, the access control granularity remains at the object level. That is, an end-customer can read either all the tracking information associated with merchandise or none.

Our proposed model and methods address three key issues: the open environment, fine-grained control in current cross-organizational tracking systems, and the confidentiality of transmission path of goods. The main contributions of this paper are as follows:

- We articulate the problem of fine-grained business data confidentiality control in IoT-enabled cross-organizational tracking systems, and propose a fine-grained access control model which controls business data in the level of data segment.

- We design a mechanism, called xCP-ABE, for enforcing fine-grained access control policies that are suitable for the context of open environment of cross-organizational tracking. In xCP-ABE, we classify data segment types and user types in IoT-enabled cross-organizational tracking systems. The performance evaluation shows that our framework is promising and efficient.

- Our framework satisfies the confidentiality of transmission path of goods in cross-organizational tracking systems. The security analysis proves the point.

The rest of this paper is organized as follows: Section 2 introduces relevant background. Section 3 formalizes the problem addressed in the paper and introduces our model definitions. Section 4 describes our implementation for the fine-grained control model in IoT-enabled cross-organizational tracking systems. Section 5 describes the experimental evaluation, analyzes the evaluation results, and analyzes the security of our mechanism. Section 6 discusses some issues concerning our proposed framework and prototype. Section 7 investigates related work. Finally, Section 8 summarizes the paper and outlines our future work.

2. BACKGROUND

2.1 Ciphertext-Policy Attribute-Based Encryption (CP-ABE)

CP-ABE [7] is a type of attribute-based encryption scheme, which can enforce fine-grained access control policies [16][24]. In CP-ABE, there is an authority which monitors attributes and distributes keys. Each data owner can encrypt a message with an access control policy (A_c), and specify which data receivers can decrypt the ciphertext. Each data receiver has its own attributes and secret key (sk) which is derived

Table 1: Frequently mentioned notions

Items	Description
pk, mk	The public key and master key
sk	A user's secret key
k_{pr}	An entity's private key in electronic pedigree systems
k_{pu}	An entity's public key in electronic pedigree systems
k_{aes}	The key of AES
u	A user in tracking systems
m	Business data including sensing data and transaction data
A_u	A set of attributes of a user
A_c	An access control policy that data owners define
c_{xcpabe}	The ciphertext of business data after encryption of xCP-ABE
c_{unlink}	The ciphertext of business data with satisfaction of unlinkability
c_k	The ciphertext of k_{aes}

from the attributes of the data receiver at a trusted third party (an authority). Only if a data receiver's attributes satisfy the access control policy attached to the ciphertext, the data receiver is able to decrypt the ciphertext and obtain the corresponding plaintext. The main notation used in this paper is summarized in Table 1.

In CP-ABE, the public key pk and the master key mk are created once at the initialization process of the authority. The secret key sk, which is different for each receiver, is generated once for each data receiver. pk is common to all the users, whereas a data receiver's sk should be kept private.

2.2 Electronic Pedigree in IoT-Enabled Cross-Organizational Tracking Systems

The notion of electronic pedigree has been introduced by EPCglobal [15] into IoT-enabled cross-organizational tracking systems as a trustworthy format of business data. The electronic pedigree can keep track of the manufacturing and shipping processes of merchandise by recording and transmitting all the relevant data in the cyber space. In IoT-enabled cross-organizational tracking systems where suppliers, end customers, supervisors are the main roles, suppliers have rights to manage electronic pedigrees, i.e., they can initialize an electronic pedigree, append data to the pedigree, and sign it. End customers, on the other hand, can check the information of the merchandise by querying electronic pedigrees. Supervisors usually have more powerful privileges to view all sensed information and make statistical analysis to monitor the supplies.

The management of electronic pedigrees is often supported by pedigree servers which store the massive generated electronic pedigrees [32], and provide web interfaces for users to query electronic pedigrees. Users in systems can access electronic pedigrees, and after parsing electronic pedigrees, business data included in pedigrees are available to users.

In order to guarantee the authenticity and integrity of electronic pedigrees, signature chains are used as credentials. Each electronic pedigree is usually digitally signed by the supplier with its private key (k_{pr}). By making use of

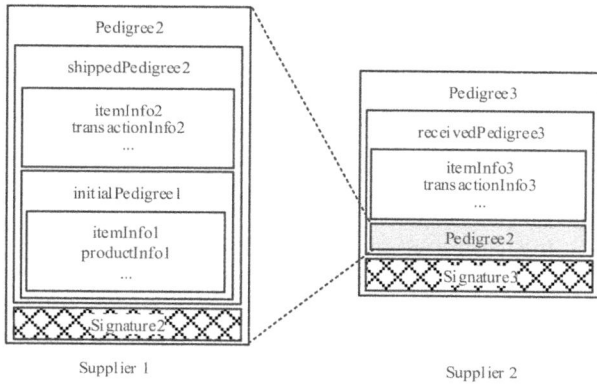

Figure 1: Internal structure of electronic pedigrees as the format of business data in IoT-enabled cross-organizational tracking systems.

the signature and the relevant public key (k_{pu}), the electronic pedigree's receiver can validate the authenticity and integrity of the pedigree.

As is shown in Fig. 1, an electronic pedigree has a nested structure, which means that an electronic pedigree usually contains another one. Every merchandise has a chain of electronic pedigrees, each of which records the situation of the merchandise in a certain component of the whole supply chain. Besides, an electronic pedigree (usually structured according to XML) usually includes multiple data segments, such as product information, item information, transaction information.

IT vendors, including SAP [2] and IBM [3], have developed tracking systems which conform to the EPCGlobal standard [15]. California Board of Pharmacy mandated the E-Pedigree Law Act "E-Pedigree Requirements" which requires that manufacturers, wholesalers and repackagers leverage RFID and electronic pedigrees to help people track each prescription drug [1][23]. In this paper, we thus use electronic pedigrees expressed according to such standard as our concrete format for business data.

3. PROBLEM DESCRIPTION

3.1 Definitions for Cross-Organizational Tracking Systems

A cross-organizational tracking system usually involves several parties (including commercial and shipping organizations, end customers, supervisors), multiple objects (including merchandise) and data segments.

In a cross-organizational tracking system, we model the set of parties related to the object o_j:

$$\mathbb{P}(o_j) := \mathbb{S}(o_j) \cup \mathbb{C}(o_j) \cup \mathbb{V}(o_j)$$

where the parties in $\mathbb{S}(o_j)$ represent the suppliers, including manufacturers, wholesalers and repackagers, who handle the object o_j, and the parties in $\mathbb{C}(o_j)$ represent the end customers who buy the object o_j. The parties in $\mathbb{V}(o_j)$ represent the supervisors who supervise the compliance of the supplies. The parties in $\mathbb{V}(o_j)$ usually have powerful privi-

leges to investigate all business data to validate whether the supplies are compliant with existing laws.

In our model each party is represented by a tuple:

$$p_i := \langle id_i \in \mathbb{ID}, A_i \subset \mathbb{A} \rangle$$

The entities in the set $\mathbb{ID}$ represent all possible identifiers; the entities in the set A_i represent the attributes which are associated with the party p_i; the entities in the set $\mathbb{A}$ represent all the optional attributes in a tracking system. For example, Wal-Mart Shanghai can be expressed as `WalMartSH =`

$$\langle \text{75477469-4}, \{(\text{role},\text{retailer}),(\text{city},\text{SH})\} \rangle$$

Here, the party is `WalMartSH`, its organization's identification in China is `75477469-4`, and it plays a role as a retailer in Shanghai.

We model the object:

$$o_j \in \mathbb{O} := \langle id_j \in \mathbb{ID}, SEG(o_j) \rangle$$

The entities in the set $SEG(o_j)$ represent the data segments of which the object o_j is made up of. For example, if there are data segment seg_p and data segment seg_q in the information flow of an object o_j, $SEG(o_j) = \{seg_p, seg_q\}$.

And we model the data segment

$$seg(o_j) \in \mathbb{SEG} := \langle type_{seg}, s(o_j), content, time \rangle$$

as a data segment related to an object o_j. The $type_{seg}$ represents the type of the data segment $seg(o_j)$, and the party $s(o_j)$ represents the party who creates the data segment $seg(o_j)$. The $content$ represents the content recorded in the data segment $seg(o_j)$. The $time$ represents when the creation/modification of the data segment $seg(o_j)$ happens. For example, a piece of pork can be expressed as:
```
pork_abcd =
⟨ C23E12F43PK,
{⟨ transactionInfo.shipping,
Shandong Luneng Farm, selected pork,
16:00 2015/1/7⟩,
⟨ transactionInfo.receiving,
Huadong WalMart, selected pork,
19:00 2015/1/8⟩}⟩
```
Here, the object is `pork_abcd`, its identification is `C23E12-F43PK`, and there are two data segments whose types are `transactionInfo.shipping` and `transactionInfo.receiving` respectively.

A party can launch a query as:

$$\mathbf{Q1} : (p_i \in \mathbb{P}(o_j), o_j \in \mathbb{O}) \to SEG(o_j)$$

where each party p_i can query all data segments according to an object's identifier.

3.2 An Example Scenario

There is a high risk that the gained information of an object o_j is likely to be abused and business secrets of $\mathbb{S}(o_j)$ may be leaked where a business system provides a service of **Q1**.

In the rest of the paper we will use simple examples based on the following attack scenario:

A retailer R *is selling a high-profit merchandise and offers a tracking service to end customers. A commercial competitor* T *wants to get information about the suppliers of* R *so that it can contact them to establish its own business.*

To achieve the purpose, T can ask some individuals (possibly from its own organization) to act as end customers and buy the merchandise for a period of time. As end customers, these individuals will be able to gain access to the suppliers' information and supply chain information, which for R is sensitive information.

Although the access control model designed by Kerschbaum includes down-stream visibility and up-stream visibility policies [21], this access control model cannot protect against the above threat, because the end customers by T may be granted by the up-stream visibility policy to access all data segments. Otherwise, if end customers are not granted by the up-stream visibility policy, end customers cannot see any tracking data of the object, which could not be an appropriate situation for a tracking system.

3.3 A Fine-Grained Access Control Model

In cross-organizational tracking scenarios, the fine-grained access control system usually considers the attributes of parties and different data segments of the objects. Based on the definitions introduced in Section 3.1, we can define that the fine-grained access control model consists of the following components:

- $\mathbb{P}$, $\mathbb{O}$, $\mathbb{SEG}$ are respectively the party, object, and data segment sets defined in Section 3.1.

- Permission of each object o_j: $PERM(o_j) := o_j.SEG(o_j) \times accesses$. Here, $o_j \in \mathbb{O}$; $SEG(o_j) \subset \mathbb{SEG}$; *accesses* represent the possible actions on the data segments. Usually, *accesses* only include *read* or *view*.

This model enhances the flexibility on the basic of the access control model with attributes. The fine-grained access control model allows policy designers to decide the visibility of each data segment rather than of object level.

Based on the definition of the above model, the fine-grained access control query **Q2** can be described as

$$\textbf{Q2} : (p_i \in \mathbb{P}(o_j), o_j \in \mathbb{O}) \xrightarrow{\Sigma_{seg(o_j) \in SEG(o_j)} f_{seg(o_j)}(ATTR(p_i))}$$
$$\Sigma_{f_{seg(o_j)}(ATTR(p_i))=true} seg(o_j)$$

Here, a function that determines whether a party p_i can access a data segment $seg(o_j)$ is a Boolean function as follows:

$$f_{seg(o_j)}(ATTR(p_i)) : (seg(o_j), ATTR(p_i)) \longrightarrow \{true, false\}$$

When a party $p_i \in \mathbb{P}(o_j)$ asks for the data segments of an object o_j, given the attributes of p_i and all the access control policies of $seg(o_j) \in SEG(o_j)$, then p_i is allowed to access $seg(o_j)$ indicated by the function $f_{seg(o_j)}$ returning *true*.

After a party launches the query **Q2**, all data segments $seg(o_j)$, which are in $SEG(o_j)$ and make $f_{seg(o_j)}(ATTR(p_i))$ = *true* hold, will be returned.

The defined access control model with **Q2** may be configured to avoid the attack risk in Section 3.2, because the visibility of data segments depends on the attributes of parties.

When the retailer R sells a high-profit merchandise, which has multiple suppliers, the fine-grained access control mode can be applied to the supply chain of the merchandise to encrypt the

suppliers' information. The access control policies enforced in the encryption may allow the supervisors to decrypt the sensitive data segments, but the end customers have no right to access them.

As a result, although the commercial competitor T can assign some individuals or its employees to act as end customers and get part of the tracking information of the merchandise, the commercial competitor T cannot find out the commercial secrets of the retailer R because of the fine-grained access control mechanism.

Note that end customers, including the individuals directed by the commercial competitor T, can only know those data segments which do not contain sensitive business data. In contrast, the supervisors have their rights to view all data segments of the merchandise in this case.

4. XML-ORIENTED CP-ABE

4.1 Challenges in Implementing Q2 in Cross-Organizational Tracking Systems

A suitable approach for protecting the confidentiality of business data is to use encryption. However in cross-organizational tracking systems, it is difficult to leverage traditional public key encryption-based schemes, such as RSA, which would require managing and distributing massive amounts of keys because of the large number of data segments, each of which may have associated different fine-grained access control policies.

A more viable solution is represented by the CP-ABE encryption scheme (see Section 2.1) which leverages the attributes associated with the parties and objects. The CP-ABE scheme is suitable for scenarios where the data owners need to define access control policies of ciphertext without being able to determine the complete list of data receivers in advance, and the number of data receivers is very large. In comparison with the traditional public key encryption-based scheme, the main advantage of CP-ABE is less overhead for the key management infrastructure [5].

The application of the CP-ABE scheme to IoT-enabled cross-organizational tracking systems requires addressing some implementation challenges. These challenges arise from the nested architecture of data in electronic pedigrees to the need to store multiple XML policies in one file. In particular, because a pedigree has a nested structure, data in a pedigree may contain parent-child relationships. The implementation of a CP-ABE encryption scheme in IoT-enabled tracking systems should be able to handle the nested encryption and decryption operations.

Besides, the implementation of the property **unlinkability** in cross-organizational tracking systems also needs to be considered for the transmission path confidentiality of goods. The property **unlinkability** means the transmission path of goods is kept secret by default in a tracking system. And only the authorized users can get the information about the transmission path. However, in the current cross-organizational tracking environment, because all the business data generated in a supply chain can be obtained

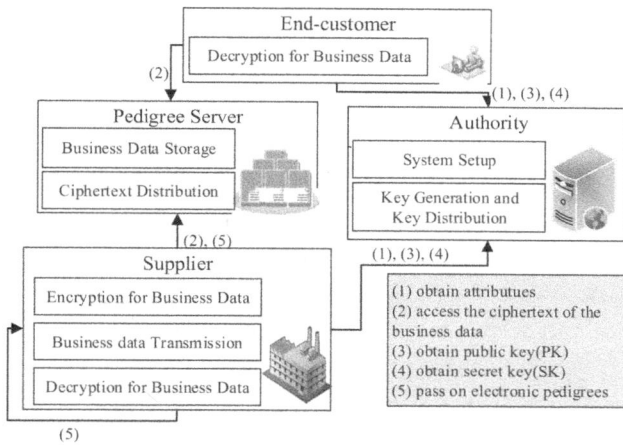

Figure 2: Framework of our proposed xCP-ABE in IoT-enabled cross-organizational tracking systems

by u, the information, which about the transmission path of goods is contained in the business data, will be disclosured.

We thus develop an XML-oriented CP-ABE framework (referred to as xCP-ABE) to implement the fine-grained access control model **Q2** in cross-organizational tracking systems that satisfies the property **unlinkability**. In xCP-ABE, attributes and users' secret keys are delivered in advance by an authority. When suppliers take part in supply chains and insert business data into electronic pedigrees as data owners, they encrypt the business data segments and bind the access control policies to the business data segments. xCP-ABE leverages attributes to specify and manage sets of suppliers and end customers, and leverages attribute-based access control policies to enable suppliers to assign access privileges to business data. According to our analysis of information recorded in the electronic pedigree [15], we divide all the data receivers into several sets which are described by different attributes. We summarize business data segments which need to be encrypted respectively by suppliers on the basis of the EPCglobal standard which introduces different kinds of electronic pedigrees [15]. For implementing the property **unlinkability**, we make use of xCP-ABE to control the users' access to the information about the transmission path of goods, and traditional encryption mechanism is leveraged so that attackers are isolated from getting the transmission path through comparing ciphertext method. We will prove the **unlinkability** of our framework in Section 5.3.

4.2 Enforcement Framework

As is shown in Fig. 2, the proposed xCP-ABE framework consists of the following steps:

System Setup. The authority first initializes pk and mk. It then delivers each user u in the cross-organizational tracking system pk and its own attributes (step (1),(3) in Fig. 2).

Key Generation and Key Distribution. When u needs to receive its secret key, the authority takes pk, mk, u's A_u as inputs and generates sk which is bound to u's attributes. Then sk is returned to u (steps (4) in Fig. 2).

Business Data Encryption. For business data, a supplier can specify a certain access control policy A_c. The xCP-ABE encryption algorithm takes pk, m, and A_c from the supplier as inputs and returns the ciphertext c_{xcpabe}. AES algorithm is used to encrypt c_{xcpabe} and outputs the ciphertext c_{unlink}. Then, the key k_{aes} of the AES algorithm is also encrypted by the xCP-ABE and returns the ciphertext c_k. The access policy of c_k is specified by the supplier, too. Note that, when the supplier is the last component of the supply chain, he will not generate c_{unlink} and c_k.

Here, the xCP-ABE encryption algorithm provides the fine-grained confidentiality control. And the AES algorithm ensures the property unlinkability of the system. The security analysis has been provided in Section 5.3.

Business Data Transmission. After the encryption, the supplier passes the encrypted pedigree c_{unlink} and the encrypted key c_k to the Pedigree Server and suppliers in the next component of the supply chain (step (5) in Fig. 2).

Business Data Decryption. When the supplier pass the encrypted content to the supplier in the next component of the supply chain, the receiver supplier decrypts c_k to get k_{aes} and uses k_{aes} to decrypt c_{unlink} in order to get c_{xcpabe} (step (2) in Fig. 2).

When a user u accesses the encrypted pedigrees through the web interface provided by the pedigree server, the user u will decrypt c_{unlink} as same as the receiver supplier.

Note that we consider the pedigree server to be public. The server can store and retrieve massive electronic pedigrees. But the server cannot protect business data from malicious attacks, *i.e.*, stealing electronic pedigrees stored in the server by adversaries. The transmission between suppliers and the pedigree server is assumed to be secure under existing security protocols such as SSL. The transmission of various keys assumes to be secure under the authority.

4.3 Encryption Scheme for Business Data

In cross-organizational tracking systems, the operation of encrypting business data occurs when suppliers create an electronic pedigree. In the process of encryption, every supplier has the right to authorize users to obtain the business data generated by the supplier according to setting up its own access control policies. These policies determine whether users can decrypt the ciphertext or not. Besides, the encryption scheme also provides the property **unlinkability** for our proposed framework. Any users cannot make use of different ciphertexts to track the transmission path of business data. The process of encrypting the business data in our proposed xCP-ABE is illustrated in Fig. 3.

Step 1: Encryption with CP-ABE. When a supplier generates several data segments, each of which records one piece of business data, the supplier makes use of the encryption scheme of CP-ABE to encrypt the data segments into the encrypted data segments (shown as the grey blocks in Fig. 3).

Step 2: Concatenation into the ciphertext c_{xcpabe}. After generating the encrypted data segments, the supplier concatenates them into one ciphertext c_{xcpabe}.

Step 3 (optional): Concatenation into a complete electronic pedigree. After generating the ciphertext c_{xcpabe}, the supplier concatenates c_{xcpabe} created by himself and the previous electronic pedigree created by previous suppliers together. The step is optional because the step is skipped when there is no previous electronic pedigree.

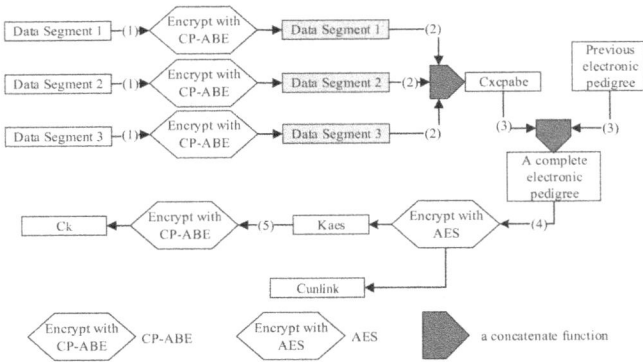

Figure 3: Encryption scheme for business data in our proposed xCP-ABE mechanism

Step 4: Encryption with AES. When generating a complete electronic pedigree, the supplier makes use of the encryption scheme of AES to encrypt the electronic pedigree. The encryption scheme will output the key k_{aes}, and the ciphertext c_{unlink}.

Step 5: Encryption with CP-ABE. When generating the key k_{aes}, the supplier makes use of the encryption scheme of CP-ABE to encrypt the key k_{aes}, and obtains the ciphertext c_k.

The encryption of xCP-ABE outputs the ciphertext c_k of the key k_{aes}, and the ciphertext c_{unlink} of the complete electronic pedigree. Then, the supplier sends these two ciphertext c_k and c_{unlink} to the Pedigree Server (shown in Fig. 2) and the next supplier.

4.4 Decryption Scheme for Business Data

In cross-organizational tracking systems, the operation of decrypting business data occurs when a user, including a supplier or an end-customer, wants to access business data. Before beginning to decrypt the ciphertext of business data, the user needs to get the ciphertext first. An end-customer usually obtains the ciphertext from the Pedigree Server (shown in Fig. 2), while a supplier usually obtains the ciphertext from the previous supplier of the same supply chain.

The ciphertext a user gets contains two parts: c_k, the ciphertext of the key k_{aes}, and c_{unlink}, the ciphertext of the

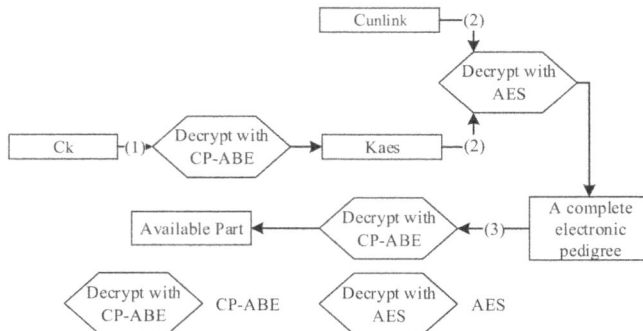

Figure 4: Decryption scheme for business data in our proposed xCP-ABE mechanism

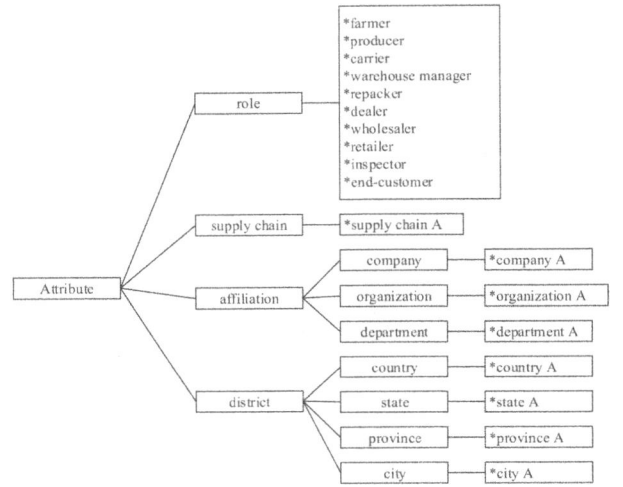

Figure 5: Relationship of attributes defined in cross-organizational tracking systems. A starred string means a possible value in the category

complete electronic pedigree. Then, the process of decrypting the business data in our proposed xCP-ABE is illustrated in Fig. 4.

Step 1: Decryption with CP-ABE. The user makes use of his own secret key sk and the public key pk to decrypt the ciphertext c_k. If the attributes of the user are satisfied with the access policies created by the supplier, the user can obtain the key k_{aes}. Otherwise, the user is not authorized and cannot continue the decryption scheme.

Step 2: Decryption with AES. After the user gets the key k_{aes}, the user inputs the key k_{aes} and the ciphertext c_{unlink} into the decryption scheme of AES so that the user can get the complete electronic pedigree. Here, the complete electronic pedigree is the set of the ciphertext of electronic pedigrees generated by several suppliers.

Step 3: Decryption with CP-ABE. After the user gets the complete electronic pedigree, the user makes use of his own secret key sk and the public key pk again to decrypt the complete electronic pedigree. The attributes of the user determine that how many parts in the complete electronic pedigree can be decrypted and shown as available for the user.

At last, the user, who wants to access business data, can only get the business data which the user is authorized to see.

4.5 Analysis on User Attributes, Access Control Policies and Data Segment Types

We now propose a classification of user attributes in cross-organizational tracking systems based on an analysis of the standard for electronic pedigree [15] and supply chain management. The description of user attributes is shown in Fig. 5. We divide the user attributes into four different categories: roles, supply chains, affiliations, and districts. The attribute *role* represents the data receiver's position in a supply chain. The attribute *supply chain* represents in which supply chain the supplier participates. The attribute *affiliation* represents the commercial entity that the data receiver belongs to, and this attribute contains the attribute *com-*

140

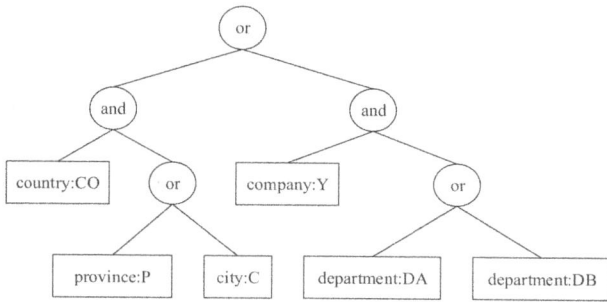

Figure 6: A sample of a common access control policy in cross-organizational tracking systems

pany, the attribute *organization* and the attribute *department*. Last, the attribute *district* represents a data receiver's geographical position or administrative region. There are four attributes including *country*, *state*, *province*, and *city*, under the attribute *district*.

Here, we demonstrate how our framework defines attributes using some concrete examples. Suppose that Bob is a farmer who joins the supply chain for producing pork in Company P, and he is located in Province Y, Country Z. After he asks the authority for his attributes, Bob will receive his attributes *role: pork-farmer, supply chain: pork, company: P, province: Y, country: Z*.

The access control mechanism enables suppliers to show business data to a selected set of data receivers by encrypting the data segments. An access control policy can be represented by an access tree structure in which each interior node is a boolean gate and the leaves are associated with attributes. An example is illustrated in Fig. 6. The access tree structure in Fig. 6 is recorded in electronic pedigrees as follows:

```
country:CO province:P city:C 1of2 2of2 com-
pany:Y department:DA department:DB 1of2 2of2
1of2
```

Because the access tree belongs to the type of binary tree, "AND" and "OR" gates in the access tree structure are represented with "2of2" and "1of2" in the access control policy string respectively.

Data segments in electronic pedigrees have been defined in Section 3.1. As business data may be from different components of a supply chain, different kinds of data segments can be defined. The main data segment types are described in Table 2.

5. EVALUATION

5.1 Experimental Environment

For implementing a prototype of xCP-ABE in an IoT-enabled cross-organizational tracking system, we set up an experimental environment. From the perspective of software environment, we employ Java Version 1.6.0 and Eclipse Version 3.6 as our prototype's developing environments. We also leverage the open-source project *cpabe* in GitHub [29] to implement Ciphertext-Policy Attribute-Based Encryption in our prototype. From the perspective of hardware environment, we employ the same utility for the Pedigree Server,

Table 2: List of main data segment types in IoT-enabled cross-organizational tracking systems

Data Segments	Description
documentInfo	Information about the identifier for the pedigree and the version number of the pedigree scheme.
itemInfo	Information about the physical item which the electronic pedigree represents, such as date of production, quantity of units.
senderInfo	Information about the supplier who is sending the shipment.
recipientInfo	Information about the supplier who is receiving the shipment.
receivingInfo	Information about the receipt of the merchandise which the the electronic pedigree represents.
productInfo	Information about the merchandise which the electronic pedigree represents, such as object name, usage mode.
transactionInfo	Information about the transaction in which the ownership of the merchandise passes from a supplier to another supplier, such as the information of the sender and the receiver.
signatureInfo	Information about the signer and the context of the signature applied to the pedigree.

the Authority, and the Supplier Server. The utility is of HP p7-1035n with 4 Intel Core i5-2500S CPU @2.70GHz, 4 GB memory and 1 TB disk. The operation system is Windows 7 Enterprise.

5.2 Prototype and Simulation Experiments

We implemented a prototype of xCP-ABE in an IoT-enabled cross-organizational tracking system [17] based on the above experimental environment. We simulated a supply chain to generate pedigrees to assess time consumption of the encryption processes and the decryption processes. To better evaluate the influence on business models, we set up two implementations for our fine-grained access control model: the implementation with unlinkability and the one with linkability.

In Section 4.3 and Section 4.4, we introduce our proposed encryption scheme and decryption scheme. Based on these two mechanism, we implement a prototype which is satisfied with unlinkability. Besides, we implement a prototype which is not satisfied with unlinkability. The prototype is linkable so that users can track the transmission path of electronic pedigrees with the help of comparing ciphertext method. Compared with the prototype with unlinkability, the prototype with linkability removes Step 4 and Step 5 mentioned in Section 4.3, and Step 1 and Step 2 mentioned in Section 4.4.

Note that, the experiment of the implementation with linkability aims to show the different performance between two types of implements, because the implementation with linkability can avoid duplicate encryptions which are usually computationally expensive.

The details of our simulated supply chain extended with our encryption protocol are as follows.

Assume a party *p1* that produces an object *o1*. *o1* is first processed at the **Birth Step**, and *p1* creates a *birthpedigree* for *o1*. *p1* then stores a *signatureInfo* into the *birthpedigree* without encryption. *o1* continues the execution of the **Initial Step**, and *p1* needs to create an *initialpedigree* for *o1*. *p1* stores a *productInfo* and an *itemInfo* into the *initialpedigree*. As *p1* considers the *productInfo* of *o1* highly sensitive, *p1* decides to encrypt the *productInfo*.

Then *p1* decides to ship *o1* to another party *p3* with the help of the transport network of *p2*. *o1* is processed at the **Ship Step**, and *p1* creates a *shippedpedigree* for *o1*. *p1* stores a *documentInfo*, an *itemInfo*, a *transactionInfo*, and a *signatureInfo* into the *shippedpedigree*, and defines different access control policies for encrypting these four data segments. When *p2* transports *o1*, *o1* is processed at the **Trans Step**, and *p2* creates a *transpedigree* for *o1*. *p2* stores a *signatureInfo* into the *transpedigree* without encryption.

After *p3* receives *o1* from *p2*, *o1* is processed at the **Received Step**, and *p3* creates a *receivedpedigree* for *o1*. *p3* stores a *documentInfo*, a *receivedInfo*, and a *signatureInfo* into the *receivedpedigree*, and encrypts the *documentInfo*, and the *receivedInfo* respectively. An inspector, who assesses whether a merchanise, *e.g.*, food, is safe, requires to assess *o1*, and *o1* is processed at the **Ciq Step**. The inspector creates a *ciqpedigree* for *o1*. Then *p3* repackages *o1*, and *o1* is processed at the **Repack Step**. *p3* creates a *repackagepedigree* including an encrypted *productInfo* for *o1*.

In order to evaluate the time consumption, we measured the time required for encrypting a pedigree based on some access control policies and the time required by a user for decrypting the pedigree based on its attributes. The results are shown in Fig. 7 and Fig. 8.

Fig. 7 shows the results of the implementation with unlinkability. In the experiments for testing the implementation with unlinkability, the time consumption of encryption ranges from 250ms to 450ms, and the time consumption of decryption ranges from 50ms to 250ms.

Fig. 8 shows the experimental results of the implementation with linkability. In the experiments for testing the implementation with linkability, the time consumption of encryption ranges from 100ms to 300ms, and the time consumption of decryption ranges from 0 to 200ms.

According to Fig. 7 and Fig. 8, we can point out that the time consumption of encryption in each step depends on the amount of business data generated by the supplier. But, the time consumption of encryption in the later step does not depend on the one in the previous step. For example, in the last step RGP, because *repackagepedigree* contains much more business data than other pedigrees in the previous steps, the time consumption of the step RGP is much higher than others.

And the time consumption of decryption is growing with the steps of supply chain, because the process of decryption contains the business data generated by the supplier of current step and all the previous business data. Meanwhile, the time consumption of encryption is independent on the time consumption of decryption.

Besides, not only the implementation with unlinkability but also the implementation with linkability have good performance on time consumption of encryption and decryp-

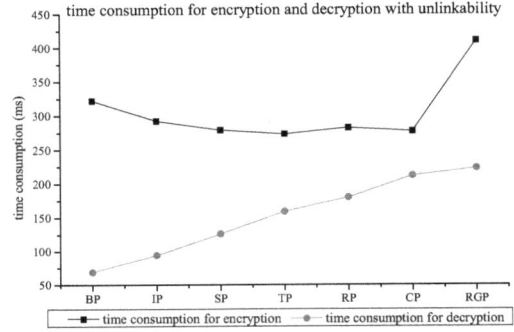

Figure 7: Time consumption of encryption and decryption in each step of the experimental supply chain with the prototype of unlinkability. (Here, BP means *birthpedigree*; IP means *initialpedigree*; SP means *shippedpedigree*; TP means *transpedigree*; RP means *receivedpedigree*; CP means *ciqpedigree*; RGP means *repackagepedigree*.)

tion, and they make little influence on the business model. Between these two implementations, the implementation with linkability is better at the time consumption of encryption and decryption than the one with unlinkability, because the implementation with linkability contains less steps than the one with unlinkability.

5.3 Security Analysis

In this section, we briefly analyze the security properties of our proposed framework from three aspects: fine-grained data confidentiality control, unlinkability, and collusion resistance.

Fine-Grained Data Confidentiality Control. To implement the fine-grained business data control model defined in Section 3.3, our proposed xCP-ABE mechanism is based on CP-ABE [7], and inherits its security strengths which include fine-grained control of the accessed data in the context of open environment of a cross-organizational tracking system. Hence, in our proposed framework, only the supplier is able to obtain a complete control over which party has access to the data that the supplier encrypts according to the access control policy by the supplier. Moreover, because the pedigree server keeps the business data encrypted at all time, even if the pedigree server suffers from malicious attacks, the data is not compromised. Furthermore, because the xCP-ABE sets every XML element as one data element to encrypt, our proposed framework supports fine-grained access control data control at the level of data segment, which provides finer granularity than the object-level access control.

Unlinkability. In order to implement the property **unlinkability**, we make use of xCP-ABE to control the users' access to the information about the transmission path of goods, and traditional encryption mechanism is leveraged so that attackers are isolated from getting the transmission path through comparing ciphertext method.

We denote a segment *info* that is encrypted using CP-ABE with access policy A_c by $[info; A_c]$, and an electronic pedigree p_1 that is encrypted using AES with key k_{aes} by $\{p_1; k_{aes}\}$. And when the key k_{aes} of $\{p_1; k_{aes}\}$ is encrypted

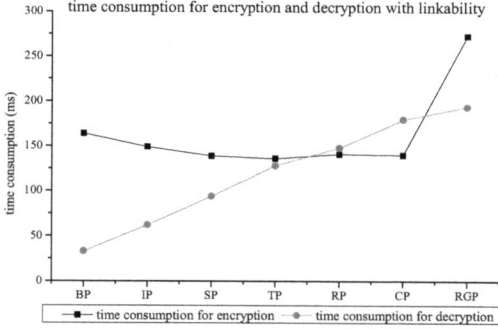

Figure 8: Time consumption of encryption and decryption in each step of the experimental supply chain with the prototype of linkability. (Here, BP means *birthpedigree*; IP means *initialpedigree*; SP means *shippedpedigree*; TP means *transpedigree*; RP means *receivedpedigree*; CP means *ciqpedigree*; RGP means *repackagepedigree*.)

using CP-ABE with access policy A_c, we denote the pedigree p_1 by $\{p_1; [k_{aes}; A_c]\}$.

Assume a pedigree p_0, which stores a segment $info_0$. It can be described as

$$p_0.([info_0; A_{c_{info_0}}])$$

And a nested electronic pedigree p_1, which contains the ciphertext of p_0 and has segments $info_1$, $info_2$. It can be described as

$$p_1.(\{p_0; [k_{aes_0}; A_{c_{k_{aes_0}}}]\}, [info_1; A_{c_{info_1}}], [info_2; A_{c_{info_2}}])$$

We prove that xCP-ABE mechanism supports unlinkability:

1. Attackers cannot get the information about the transmission path stored in the data segments without authorization.

2. Attackers cannot get the transmission path through comparing ciphertext method.

Proof. In the first condition, it is easy to see that if attackers want to get the information about the transmission path stored in the data segments, they must decrypt $\{p_0; [k_{aes_0}; A_{c_{k_{aes_0}}}]\}$ and $\{p_1; [k_{aes_1}; A_{c_{k_{aes_1}}}]\}$. However, because attackers are not authorized and their sk does not satisfy the access policy $A_{c_{k_{aes_0}}}$ and $A_{c_{k_{aes_1}}}$, attackers cannot get knowledge of p_0 and p_1. Hence, attackers cannot get the information about the transmission path stored in the data segments without authorization.

In the second condition, when attackers try to get the transmission path through comparing ciphertext method, they have to look for the same parts between two encrypted electronic pedigrees which are generated by two continuous suppliers:

$$\{p_0.([info_0; A_{c_{info_0}}]); [k_{aes_0}; A_{c_{k_{aes_0}}}]\}$$

$$\{p_1.(\{p_0; [k_{aes_0}; A_{c_{k_{aes_0}}}]\}, ...); [k_{aes_1}; A_{c_{k_{aes_1}}}]\}$$

But in our proposed encryption mechanism, because the pedigree $p_0.([info_0; A_{c_{info_0}}])$ is encrypted with different AES keys (k_{aes_0} and k_{aes_1}) and two different ciphertexts of the

pedigree $p_0.([info_0; A_{c_{info_0}}])$ are generated, there are not two same parts between encrypted electronic pedigrees p_0 and p_1 and merely two ciphertexts of pedigrees are useless for attackers to get the transmission path. Hence, attackers cannot get the transmission path through comparing ciphertext method.

In a word, xCP-ABE mechanism supports unlinkability.

Collusion Resistance. In our prototype, we make use of groups with efficiently computable bilinear maps to establish our private key randomization, which is the same as the technology proposed in the literatures [9][28]. Because this part is the same as the one in CP-ABE and the security analysis of the technology has been provided [7], we do not discuss it here in detail.

6. DISCUSSION

6.1 Policy Conflict in the Duplicated Encryption of xCP-ABE

Policy conflict means two contradictory policies happen at the same time. In our proposed encryption and decryption mechanism, policy conflict occurs. The access policy of c_k generated by the successive supplier may be contradictory to the access policy defined by the previous supplier. Once u cannot satisfy the access policy of c_k, u can read nothing recorded in the electronic pedigrees about the merchandise, even including previous electronic pedigrees. If u has got the authorization from the previous supplier to view the previous electronic pedigree, the policy conflict happens.

In general, there are two conditions of policy conflict as follows:

1. The previous supplier authorizes the party to view data segment *seg*, while the successive supplier bids the party to view the data segment *seg*.

2. The previous supplier bids the party to view data segment *seg*, while the successive supplier authorizes the party to view the data segment *seg*.

The different order in the two conditions for policy conflict can result to different performance. In the first condition, the policy conflict makes the party miss the right to view the data segment *seg*. And, in the second condition, the policy conflict makes no influence on the performance of authorization.

In our proposed mechanism, we allow the policy conflict to exist. There are two reasons for supporting the action:

1. For the first condition of policy conflict, the user can get the available data segments through asking for the previous electronic pedigree from the pedigree server and decrypting it.

2. For the second condition of policy conflict, because the user has been bidden by the previous supplier from viewing data segment, there is no impact for whether the successive supplier authorizes the user to view or not.

6.2 RFID Tags in Cross-Organizational Tracking

Tracking is a *killer-app* of the RFID technology. RFID can usually store a limited data in a tag which is usually enforced by some authentication and pin-based control mechanisms to protect the data. Kerschbaum [21] even used the memory (up to 64k) of tags to store the signatures during the movement of an object.

However, it is difficult to store business data in a tag due to the technical limitations and cost issue. When a reading process between a tag and a reader must be finished in critical time (e.g., 0.5 second), the memory size cannot be enlarged without limitations, but the business data of a mobile object is usually unlimited. Especially, the tags must be attached with all merchandise, the cost of each tag is critical for a tracking system. Thus, it is strongly motivated for a holder of a tracking system to reduce the technical features except for the identification of RFID tags.

As a result, the proposed model and mechanisms in this paper do not depend on other technical features of RFID except for the identification feature. All other information processes happen in servers.

6.3 Extended Framework to Multi-Authority ABE

In this paper, the component of xCP-ABE employs an authority to deliver users their attributes and their own secret keys. Actually, our proposed framework can be easily extended to support MA-ABE (short for Multi-Authority ABE) [11], which allows any polynomial number of independent authorities to monitor attributes and distribute private keys. In cross-organizational tracking systems, suppliers can be divided into several fields naturally according to their roles or affiliations. For every field, one supplier authority is established for managing attributes and secret keys of suppliers in the field. All the end customers are arranged to get services from the customer authority which independently manages attributes and secret keys of end customers. The pedigree server is a central component for suppliers and end customers to ask for querying business data.

The framework extended to MA-ABE is practical in the scenario where suppliers in the supply chain belong to several big organizations or companies. For confidential control, each organization or company requires to manage the attributes and the secret keys of its own suppliers. In this case, suppliers can be divided into several *organization fields*; and the framework leverages an authority in each *organization field*. For example, Wal-Mart itself contains *producers, carriers, warehouse managers,* and *wholesalers* in a supply chain. Thus, the proposed framework extended to MA-ABE can be used. The system admits Wal-Mart to establish an authority so that Wal-Mart can manage the attributes and the secret keys of its own employees, including *producers, carriers, warehouse managers,* and *wholesalers.*

7. RELATED WORK

Security for the IoT has been investigated by several researchers [6][13]. RFID technology [22][31] is used in supply chain management [22] in order to be able to achieve item-level tracking and accountability in the sensing layer of the IoT [26]. IBM has proposed the *smart food program* as a food traceability framework to standardize the supply chain and to improve the accountability in the application layer of the IoT [20]. In addition, in order to ensure the normalization of product data in the drug industry, EPCglobal [15] has defined a standard for electronic pedigrees. Digital signa-

ture technology is leveraged to support the trustworthiness of product data during transmission. Then, on the basis of the EPCglobal's work, Han *et al.* [17][18] made further research and implemented an electronic pedigree system for food safety, which provides a more trustworthy tracking service in the application layer of the IoT. Moreover, the group signature technology [12] is employed in smart grid systems to ensure the privacy protection of users' identifications [19]. Shi *et al.* [27] have proposed SecTTS which uses a policy-based method to allow each supply chain partner to define different relay policies, which are used to determine whether the query is relayed to an EPCIS or not, for information with different sensitivity.

Our framework has major differences with respect to the SecTTS mechanism. The goal of our framework is to support fine-grained access control to business data, while the SecTTS mechanism focuses on the security of the communications among the various supply chain parties.

The research work most closely related to ours is by Kerschbaum [21]. Kerschbaum introduced two high level policies, namely up-stream and down-stream visibility policies for mobile physical objects, and proposed mechanisms for their enforcement. In up-stream visibility policy, a company is allowed (or denied) to access data associated with objects the company has received from its supply chain partners. And in down-stream visibility policy, a company is allowed (or denied) to access data associated with objects shipped to its supply chain partners.

However, Kerschbaum's model only provides object-level protection whereas our approach supports more fine-grained access control. Besides, Kerschbaum's model designs the protocol with standard passive RFID tags whereas our approach is built in the application layer rather than the sensing layer. Compared to Kerschbaum's model, our proposed model leverages CP-ABE as a mechanism to enforce access control and thus meets the requirement of the open environment of cross-organizational tracking systems.

8. CONCLUSION AND FUTURE WORK

Data security is a key issue in cross-organizational tracking systems. To the best of our knowledge, this paper is the first one to address the problem of fine-grained access control for business data in IoT-enabled cross-organizational tracking systems. Leveraging the proposed xCP-ABE scheme, our framework enables suppliers in IoT-enabled tracking systems to selectively authorize users to access fine-grained business data.

As our future work, we will extend xCP-ABE with authorization revocation features in order to deal with useless attributes and illegal users. Besides, we will investigate a richer access control policy model for CP-ABE and design some methods to detect and resolve policy conflicts. Last but not least, we will investigate how to optimize the performance of our implemented prototype.

Acknowledgement

This paper is supported by Twelve.Five National Development Foundation for Cryptography (MMJJ201301008), National Key Science and Technology Program (P01-029-2014 (10)-2.4-02-T-C), Natural Science Foundation of Shanghai (12ZR1402600) and Shanghai Science and Technology Development Funds (13dz2260200, 13511504300). We thank anonymous reviewers for their comments.

9. REFERENCES

[1] California board of pharmacy. california e-pedigree law. http://www.pharmacy.ca.gov/about/e_pedigree_laws.shtml, accessed in 2015.

[2] The center for healthcare supply chain research. sap support of the healthcare supply chain's ongoing effort to ensure patient safety and drive business value. http://www.hcsupplychainresearch.org/WP/SAP_whitepaper.pdf, accessed in 2015.

[3] Frequentz.com. ibm's infosphere traceability server. http://frequentz.com/traceability-server/, accessed in 2015.

[4] Tracelink inc. track and trace products with epcis event exchange and epedigree. http://tracelink.com/product- tracking-for-product-security-patient-safety, accessed in 2015.

[5] S. Alshehri, S. Radziszowski, and R. K. Raj. Designing a secure cloud-based ehr system using ciphertext-policy attribute-based encryption. In *Proceedings of the Data Management in the Cloud Workshop*, Washington, DC, USA, 2012.

[6] L. Atzoria, A. Ierab, and G. Morabitoc. The internet of things: A survey. *Computer Networks*, pages 2787–2805, 2010.

[7] J. Bethencourt, A. Sahai, and B. Waters. Ciphertext-policy attribute-based encryption. In *Proceedings of the IEEE Symposium on Security and Privacy*, pages 321–334, Washington, DC, USA, 2007.

[8] E.-O. Blass, K. Elkhiyaoui, and R. Molva. Tracker: Security and privacy for rfid-based supply chains. In *Proceedings of Network and Distributed System Security Symposium*, 2011.

[9] D. Boneh, X. Boyen, and E.-J. Goh. Hierarchical identity based encryption with constant size ciphertext. In *Proceedings of Advances in Cryptology-EUROCRYPT*, pages 440–456, 2005.

[10] S. Cai, Y. Li, and Y. Zhao. Distributed path authentication for dynamic rfid-enabled supply chains. In *Proceedings of Information Security and Privacy Research*, pages 501–512, 2012.

[11] M. Chase. Multi-authority attribute based encryption. *Journal of Theory of Cryptography*, pages 515–534, 2007.

[12] D. Chaum and E. V. Heyst. Group signatures. In *Proceedings of Advances in Cryptology-EUROCRYPT*, pages 257–265, 1991.

[13] M. Domingo. An overview of the internet of things for people with disabilities. *Journal of Network and Computer Applications*, pages 584–596, 2012.

[14] K. Elkhiyaoui, E.-O. Blass, and R. Molva. Checker: on-site checking in rfid-based supply chains. In *Proceedings of the fifth ACM conference on Security and Privacy in Wireless and Mobile Networks*, pages 173–184, 2012.

[15] EPCglobal. Pedigree ratified standard. http://www.gs1.org/gsmp/kc/epcglobal/pedigree/pedigree_1_0-standard-20070105.pdf, 2007.

[16] V. Goyal, O. Pandey, A. Sahai, and B. Waters. Attribute-based encryption for fine-grained access control of encrypted data. In *Proceedings of the 13th ACM conference on Computer and communications security*, pages 89–98, 2006.

[17] W. Han, Y. Gu, W. Wang, Y. Zhang, Y. Yin, J. Wang, and L. Zheng. The design of an electronic pedigree system for food safety. *Information Systems Frontiers*, 17 (2):275–287, 2015.

[18] W. Han, Y. Gu, Y. Zhang, and L. Zheng. Data driven quantitative trust model for the internet of agricultural things. In *Proceedings of the 4th International Conference on the Internet of Things*, Cambridge, MA, 2014. IEEE.

[19] D. He, C. Chen, J. Bu, S. Chan, Y. Zhang, and M. Guizani. Secure service provision in smart grid communications. *IEEE Communications Magazine*, pages 53–61, 2012.

[20] IBM. Smarter food technology. http://www.ibm.com/smarterplanet/us/en/foodtechnology/ideas/index.html, Accessed in 2015.

[21] F. Kerschbaum. An access control model for mobile physical objects. In *Proceedings of the 15th ACM symposium on Access control models and technologies*, pages 193–202, 2010.

[22] D. M. Lambert and M. C. Cooper. Issues in supply chain management. *Journal of Industrial Marketing Management*, pages 65–83, 2000.

[23] E. Law and S. L. Youmans. Combating counterfeit medications: The california pharmacist perspective. *Journal of Pharmacy Practice*, 24(1):114–121, 2011.

[24] M. Li, S. Yu, Y. Zheng, K. Ren, and W. Lou. Scalable and secure sharing of personal health records in cloud computing using attribute-based encryption. *IEEE Transactions on Parallel and Distributed Systems*, 24:131–143, 2013.

[25] L. Liu, W. Han, T. Zhou, and X. Zhang. Scout: Prying into supply chains via a public query interface. *IEEE Systems Journal*, 2014. doi: 10.1109/JSYST.2014.2337519.

[26] K. Michael and L. McCathie. The pros and cons of rfid in supply chain management. In *Proceedings of International Conference on Mobile Business*, pages 623–629, 2005.

[27] J. Shi, Y. Li, W. He, and D. Sim. Sectts: A secure track & trace system for rfid-enabled supply chains. *Journal of Computers in Industry*, pages 574–585, 2012.

[28] V. Shoup. Lower bounds for discrete logarithms and related problems. In *Proceedings of Advances in Cryptology-EUROCRYPT*, pages 256–266, 1997.

[29] J. Wang. cpabe. https://github.com/wakemecn/cpabe, 2012.

[30] L. Wang, S. K. Kwok, and W. H. Ip. A radio frequency identification-based quality evaluation system design for the wine industry. *International Journal of Computer Integrated Manufacturing*, 25(1):11–19, 2012.

[31] R. Want. An introduction to rfid technology. *Journal of Pervasive Computing*, pages 25–33, 2006.

[32] Y. Zhang, W. Han, W. Wang, and C. Lei. Optimizing the storage of massive electronic pedigrees in hdfs. In *Proceedings of Internet of Things*, pages 68–75, 2012.

A Prototype to Reduce the Amount of Accessible Information

Rainer Fischer
Carl-Zeiss-Promenade 10
07745 Jena, Germany
rainer.fischer@hp.com

ABSTRACT

Authorized insiders downloading mass data via their user interface are still a problem. In this paper a prototype to prevent mass data extractions is proposed. Access control models efficiently protect security objects but fail to define subsets of data which are narrow enough to be harmless if downloaded. Instead of controlling access to security objects the prototype limits the amount of accessible information. A heuristic approach to measures the amount of information is used. The paper describes the implementation of the prototype which is an extension of an SAP system as an example for a large enterprise information system.

Categories and Subject Descriptors

K.6.5 [**Management of Computing and information systems**]: Security and Protection – *unauthorized access*

General Terms

Security

Keywords

Access Control; Data Leakage Protection; SAP security; Security Policy

1. INTRODUCTION

The danger of data being publicized or forwarded to competitors grows with the amount and importance of the data held within an organization. Another factor which increases the risk is the number of authorized users. Addressing the problem of data leakage, this paper presents a prototype concept to lower risks by limiting an authorized user's ability to extract data.

IT applications with a sophisticated access control set boundaries to the user's competencies within an information system. While the user's tasks may require random access to a great variety of authorized data, it is impossible that one can read through more data than the limited human mind can handle. Using this fact, this paper introduces a technology which limits access based on the amount of information rather than its content. The approach is meant as a contribution with a rather simple implementation to the problem of insiders leaking great amounts of data.

The paper is devided into 4 parts. Following this introduction the second section describes the environment of the prototype and its integration into an existing system. The second part of that section describes the architecture of the prototype. Part three describes the implemented rules which are used to control data transfers to users. Section Three then then uses different scenarios to describe the influence of the prototype on the system behavior and furthermore its impact on user behavior. The last section gives a conclusion and an outlook on future work.

2. PROTOTYPE IMPLEMENTATION

2.1 Environment and Integration

The implementation of the prototype is embedded into a SAP ERP system (ECC 6.0) as an example for large information systems. Within this application there is a basic technology called ALV-Grid. It consists of a number of function modules to visualize data in a table providing standard functionality such as sorting, filtering or export to files. While being a widely used technology, ALV-Grid is not the only one. Furthermore, only function module REUSE_ALV_GRID_DISPLAY was manipulated. For a productive use there are several other spots within a SAP system that needed extension if the goal was a system which controls the complete information flow to the SAP GUI. With the data browser (transaction code SE16), one common point of information extraction is covered by the prototype, though.

The implementation within the SAP system is an implementation on application level. This leads to the following advantages and disadvantages. The data sent to the user is known to the application so the potentially visible data can be reduced. The actual visibility, that means which data is on the screen, cannot be determined because there is no information about filtering or scrolling on GUI level. On the other hand data already sent to the user interface can already be considered as unsafe as a SAP GUI cannot count as a safe application.

The SAP system with its underlying framework Netweaver provides several ways to extend the original code provided by SAP. The chosen method is the modification of the original code of the mentioned function module using an object key and adding a function module call. This function module is able to change the content of variable T_OUTTAB which holds the extracted data of a single user request.

2.2 Implementation

The implementation of the prototype in ABAP consists of four function modules with the first one being called by the modification itself to manipulate the selection result. The other function modules calculate the size of a request, log the request and check the rules.

The main function module starts with the loading of the rules from a customizing table. Rules are of three different types. The first type limits the number of symbols for a single data request. The second type limits the number of symbols that a user may extract within a certain timeframe. The third type of rules limits the number of data requests a user is allowed to start within a certain timeframe.

Rules of the third type are checked at the beginning and if the limit of one of these rules is already reached with this new request, the whole data extraction is forbidden so the result is reduced to zero. If this is not the case, the size of each single field of the result table of the data request is calculated and counted. After a line of the table data is counted the rules of type one and two are checked and if a limit is reached, the result is reduced by the current and all following lines of data. At the end, the new result is logged with user name, time and size. If the result was reduced, only the size of the reduced result is logged.

The function modules for checking the rules selects all logged data from a log table. It then compares the logged number (rule type 3) or amount of information (rule type 2) plus the current extraction to the limit given by the rule. If the limit is reached, the return code is set appropriately. For rule type one the current given size is compared to the given limit.

The logging of the data extraction is done by a function module writing the user name, date, time and size of the data extraction into a log table. The data of the log table is used for future checks of rules of the second and third type.

The function module calculating the size is analyzing the type of a given field and determines the size depending on this type. For text and text-like data each symbol is counted. One symbol may be one or two bytes long, depending on the encoding. The length of the text is not counted by the data field definition but by the actual content, which means that space values at the end of a field of characters are not counted. Fields of type date or time are counted as 8 or 6 symbols. For integer and fixed point (packed) values, all digits based on the decimal system are counted as one symbol. Again, only actual content is counted, not the defined maximum length. A problem are floating point values. With the limited accuracy it is not possible to determine the number of decimal digits. One example is value 0.15 which should be two or three symbols, but the saved data in a floating point value in SAP equals 0.149999999 so the number of digits grows. The solution in the prototype uses a constant of 15 for the size of a float value because 15 is the documented accuracy. Floating point values do not play a major role in business data in SAP tables so the compromise has a limited influence.

To take into account that a typical table with business data often contains empty fields, initial values are not counted at all.

2.3 Customized Rules

The customized rules try to represent the limit of the user's ability to read through data on one side and security threatening data extractions on the other side. The used limits can be found in the following table with the limit being the number of symbols for rule types one and two and the number of extractions for rule type three.

While only one rule of the first type makes sense, there are short term and long term limits for rule types two and three. Of course, the short term limits allow far greater numbers per time unit compared to the long term limits, representing short term and long term working abilities of humans.

Rule with ID 1 sets a limit of 40,000 symbols for a single query. That means, no data extraction exceeding this limit is allowed at any time. That also means that no more than 40,000 symbols can be added to the historic data after one data request.

Table 1. Implemented rules

Rule ID	Rule type	Limit	Timeframe DD:HH:MM:SS
1	1	40,000	
2A	2	200,000	00:01:00:00
2B	2	1,000,000	01:00:00:00
2C	2	10,000,000	30:00:00:00
3A	3	5	00:00:00:30
3B	3	50	00:01:00:00
3C	3	200	01:00:00:00
3D	3	3,000	30:00:00:00

The rules of type two set three different limits over timeframes reaching from one hour to thirty days. Rules of type number three limit the number of data requests starting with a timeframe of thirty seconds up to thirty days.

3. Influence on System and User Behavior

For the evaluation of the prototype different examples of data extractions are described. These cases represent typical data extractions mainly used by IT workers since the extractions are aiming for data tables and not end user transactions. IT workers with their typically broad authorizations and access to potentially dangerous transactions represent a high risk group among the users. It is assumed that regular access control allows these actions, which means in particular that access to the mentioned tables is granted. That also means full access to tables on one and the limitation from the prototype on the other side are compared. The influence on the system and the necessary change in user's behavior is described. The used transaction for all cases is the data browser (SE16). The data browser allows a user to show the content of a single table. For each column of the table, selection parameters in the form of single values, intervals and wildcards with the operations equal, greater/lower than or unequal can be used to include or exclude lines of data. For the result columns can be either selected or unselected for visualization.

1. Extract all materials (general view)

Table MARA contains most of the data for the general view of the material master with a structure consisting of more than one hundred columns. Without the prototype the authorization for the table allows a user to extract all data at once. Especially rules of the first type prevent this extraction as only a portion of the selected materials is shown. Extracting all this data is surly a threat to security. On the other hand a typical material master is far greater that what a user is able to handle manually. So if the selection is not meant for further processing in another application the selection of all this data is not necessary. If the user only selected all data to afterwards browse through the result to find one specific line, he will need to change his behavior to a more detailed selection. If the selection criteria were accidentally forgotten, a second, more detailed selection is still possible, because the limit within a timeframe (second rule type) is not yet reached.

2. Get the number of materials.

Getting the number of existing materials is no threat to security. It should add just very little to the counted amount of information. In fact, the prototype does not add anything at all because ALV-Grid is not used to present the number of lines.

3. Extract all materials of a certain type.

Without any limit the selection of all materials of a certain type with all columns is an easy task. If the number of existing materials of a type is small, a user might be able to extract all columns for the materials despite the limits. But he will quickly reach the limit if the number of materials of the selected type is too high. The selection of certain columns, e.g. only the material number, greatly reduces the transferred information compared to all columns. In the test system material numbers have a varying length from 8 to 15 symbols. That means somewhere between two to five thousand material numbers can be selected at once. Since only the material numbers are shown, the threat to security is far smaller compared to an all column selection.

If not all materials were shown due to the limit of rule number one, a later selection for the missing results is possible. In order to not select the same materials again, the first result must be saved to exclude it from the next selection. This leads to a compromised convenience compared to unlimited access.

4. Find the last one hundred materials that were created.

If there is no limit all materials can be selected and sorted afterwards by creation date and time. The then first (or last) one hundred lines are the correct ones. This method is no longer possible if limits forbid to select all materials. Additionally, the data browser does not provide a method for selecting the last one hundred materials by select options. Since it is no longer possible to select all materials it is now necessary for the user to use *greater than* and a specific date for the selection. In various steps a date resulting in slightly more than on hundred lines can be found. The preview of the number of results is very useful finding that certain date before actually starting the request.

5. Find all materials of a certain type that are valid in a certain plant.

The validity of a material in a plant is not found in table MARA (general view) but in table MARC while the material type can only be found in MARA. If the number of materials is small enough to be selected (material number should be sufficient), it is no problem to use this result for a further selection in table MARC. If the number of materials is already too high to select the key values, the data browser cannot accomplish this selection. So in this case the implementation of the limits brings a loss of functionality with it and more sophisticated technologies need to be used such as Quickviewer (SQVI) or Infoset-Queries (SQ02). They provide more detailed select options and the combination of several tables.

The simulation of all five scenarios shows utility in the dimension of security. While security threatening data extractions are effectively hindered, less threatening actions are not influenced. From a user perspective the limits negatively influence the performance on certain tasks. This influence is mainly due to the fact that more information is extracted than what is really necessary. This negative influence can be reduced by the change of user behavior together with methods that allow a fine-grained data selection.

4. CONCLUSION AND FUTURE WORK

In this paper an implantation of the idea to control access by the amount of information rather than the content is described. The implantation uses three classes of rules to prevent the extraction of mass data.

The idea of limiting access by the amount of information has potential for different information systems. A first prototype was implemented into an SAP system. Future research may identify other fields for applying this idea.

Since the prototype hardly fits into existing models of access control an extension of existing models and formal ways to describe rules may be developed in the future.

Furthermore, the ability to process information relies greatly on the type of the requested information, the way of presentation and the task a user is performing. Thus finding values for the limits and timeframes to instantiate the rules is a field for future progress.

The presented rules themselves are quite simple to understand but may lack of functionality within large enterprise applications. Future extension may roughly differentiate by the data objects that lead to result by weighing there influence for the calculation of size. The rules also lack of possibilities to differentiate between users or user groups. Future development could define an integration into existing authorization concepts.

A SMT-based Tool for the Analysis and Enforcement of NATO Content-based Protection and Release Policies

Alessandro Armando
DIBRIS, U. of Genova, Italy
Security and Trust Unit,
FBK-Irst, Trento, Italy
armando@fbk.eu

Silvio Ranise and
Riccardo Traverso
Security and Trust Unit,
FBK-Irst, Trento, Italy
{ranise,rtraverso}@fbk.eu

Konrad Wrona
NATO Communications and
Information Agency
The Hague, Netherlands
konrad.wrona@ncia.nato.int

ABSTRACT

NATO is developing a new IT infrastructure for automated information sharing between different information security domains and supporting dynamic and flexible enforcement of the need-to-know principle. In this context, the *Content-based Protection and Release* (*CPR*) model has been introduced to support specification and enforcement of NATO access control policies. While the ability to define fine-grained security policies for a large variety of users, resources, and devices is desirable, their definition, maintenance, and enforcement can be difficult, time-consuming, and error prone. In this paper, we give an overview of a tool capable of assisting NATO security personnel in these tasks by automatically solving several policy analysis problems of practical interest. The tool leverages state-of-the-art SMT solvers.

Categories and Subject Descriptors

D.4.6 [**Security and Protection**]: Access controls

Keywords

NATO information sharing infrastructure; Attribute-based Access Control; XACML

1. INTRODUCTION

The successful operation of NATO missions requires the effective and secure sharing of information not only among partners of the coalition, but also with external organizations (e.g., the Red Cross). While making as much information as possible available to the various participants involved in a mission, it is crucial to avoid the disclosure of sensitive details to users with insufficient authorization. The tension between confidentiality and availability complicates the task of information sharing: permitting access to partners of the coalition is necessary to ensure their effective involvement, but disclosure to unintended recipients must be avoided.

To meet these challenges, NATO is developing a new IT infrastructure that will enable automated information shar-

ing between different information security domains while providing a strong separation between different communities of interest while supporting dynamic and flexible enforcement of need-to-know principles [8]. In this context, the *Content-based Protection and Release* (*CPR*) model has been introduced in [2] to support the specification and enforcement of access control policies used in NATO and, more generally, in complex organizations. The design goals of the CPR model include supporting *(i)* the specification of fine-grained security policies related to a large variety of users, resources and devices, possibly encompassing multiple security domains and *(ii)* the seamless compositions of policies possibly addressing different concerns. To meet the first goal, CPR builds upon the Attribute Based Access Control (ABAC) model [10] thereby overcoming the limitations of traditional access control models (e.g., RBAC [7]). The second goal is achieved by supporting the composition of *release policies* (defining relationships between subjects and resources) and *protection policies* (describing the technical constraints, e.g. communication channels and terminals under which the information stored in resources can be accessed). This not only simplifies policy specification and management but it also enables a more efficient implementation of the policies and procedures mandated by directives within NATO and other international/governmental organizations. Yet, the task of defining, maintaining, and enforcing fine grained policies of complex organizations is still daunting. This calls for automated support of a number of key activities occurring in the definition and management of CPR policies such as

- *Policy Debugging.* In order to evaluate if a newly created policy matches the intentions of the designers, it is advantageous to construct scenarios in which certain users can or cannot get access to resources according to some expectations.

- *Policy Analysis.* Before deploying a newly developed policy it is important to be assured that it has some fundamental (e.g., safety) properties. For instance, a group of users with the given clearance level will never get access to resources with a given level of sensitivity.

- *Policy Enforcement.* In order to re-use available enforcement mechanisms, CPR policies should be expressed in common policy languages, such as XACML[1].

CPR policies can be specified by means of a high-level policy language (*CPRL*) [2], which is currently being validated

---

[1]http://docs.oasis-open.org/xacml/3.0

within NATO in several use case scenarios (a simplified version of one of these is described below). CPRL is rooted in first-order logic and is therefore endowed with a simple, yet formal semantics—akin to many other logic-based access control languages [3]. CPRL policies are therefore amenable to formal analysis by using automated reasoning techniques and tools. Moreover, many problems of practical interest (such as answering authorization queries and checking for subsumption between policies) can be reduced to *decidable* theorem-proving problems [2], called Satisfiability Modulo Theories (SMT) problems, which extend the Boolean satisfiability (SAT) problem by allowing for a much richer vocabulary when creating formulae. In this paper, we give an overview of the *CPRL Tool* that provides automated support to the aforementioned activities by leveraging state-of-the-art SMT technology. The tool takes a set of CPR policies together with a question and automatically computes an answer together with supporting evidence. For instance, if the question is "Does the CPRL policy satisfy the property that a group G of users can never get access to a set R of resources?" and the answer is "No," then the evidence is a scenario in which a user in the group G is permitted to access a resource in R.

2. THE CPR ACCESS CONTROL MODEL

Modern joint military missions rely on network-centric operations. The future of the NATO information sharing infrastructure [9] is built around an access control component that operates in an open and distributed environment. It has been observed that traditional access control models—such as discretionary (DAC), Mandatory (MAC), and role-based (RBAC) models—are not always adequate in this environment [4]. The Attribute-Based Access Control (ABAC) model (see e.g. [6]) offers a powerful and unifying extension to these well-known models.

In ABAC, requesters are permitted or denied access to a resource based on the properties, called attributes, that may be associated to users, resources, and the context. Examples of attributes are: identity, role, and military rank of users; identifier, and sensitivity of resources; and, for context, time of day and threat level. In ABAC, suitably defined attributes can represent security labels, clearances and classifications (for encoding MAC), identities and access control lists (for DAC), and roles (for RBAC). In this sense, ABAC supplements traditional access control models rather than supplanting them [6]. Policies in ABAC can be seen as conditions on the attribute values of the entities involved in an access decision or, in other words, they are Boolean functions that map the attribute values of the user u, the resource r, and the context c to true ("permit") when u is entitled to get access to r in the context c, and false ("deny") otherwise.

The model underlying CPR policies refines ABAC mainly in two respects. First, in addition to the attributes of users, resources, and the context, those of terminals are considered, i.e. the capabilities of the device through which a user is trying to access a resource. Examples of terminal attributes are the hardware model, the type of encryption used to locally store data and the type of connection to the terminal (e.g., SSL). Second, the CPR (access control) policies are structured in two distinct sub-policies: a *release policy*, taking into account user, resource, and contextual attributes and a *protection policy*, taking into account resource, terminal, and contextual attributes. This enables separation of pol-

icy management roles and reflects the current procedures used within international and governmental organizations, e.g. NATO. For example, consider the situation in which a user wants to access NATO classified information. This requires, on the one hand, connecting to a network infrastructure used for processing NATO classified information. To do this, a terminal must satisfy a number of technical requirements related to hardware and software configuration that are precisely defined in NATO technical directives and guidance documents. On the other hand, the security policy governing user access to the documents stored in the network is defined in a separate set of directives and guidance documents. To summarize, a user u can access a resource r with a terminal t by checking if (i) the attributes of u and r satisfy the release policy and (ii) those of r and t satisfy the protection policy. If checks (i) and (ii) are both positive, "permit" is returned, otherwise the result is "deny."

2.1 CPRL

For lack of space, we describe here the syntax of the CPRL language by using logical expressions; its concrete syntax is illustrated in Section 4 by means of an example. The semantics of CPRL is given in terms of a class of models of First-Order Logic (FOL) [5].

We regard subjects, terminals, resources, actions, and environments (called *entities*) as records whose fields are the attributes of the entities. An entity is uniquely identified by the values associated to its attributes. A *domain* is the set of values that an attribute can take. The semantics of a *CPR policy* α—regardless of the language in which it is written—is given by a collection of structures, each one composed by a universe—a non-empty set of values for the attributes—and a Boolean function (predicate) over the values of the attributes expressing a relation among a user u, a terminal t, a resource r, an action a, and an environment e. We say that user u can execute action a on resource r by using terminal t in environment e according to the CPR policy α iff the Boolean function α returns true when applied to the values associated to the attributes of u, t, r, a, and e.

We say that a structure in the semantics of a CPR policy *satisfies* the policy. We observe that structures in the semantic of a CPR policy correspond to standard interpretations in FOL. This allows us to use the language of FOL for writing CPR policies and standard logical techniques to compositionally express CPR policies by means of simpler logical expressions encoding release and protection policies. Formally, we will use the notion of logical theory $T = (\Sigma, \mathcal{M})$ that fixes the collection $\mathcal{M}$ of the possible interpretations of the symbols in a given set Σ. The idea is that, in certain situations, one is not interested in showing that a formula $x < y \wedge x \not< y + y$ is unsatisfiable for all possible interpretations of the symbols $<$ and $+$, but only for those interpretations in which $<$ is the usual ordering over the integers and $+$ is the addition function. For CPRL policies, let $T_D = (\Sigma_D, \mathcal{M}_D)$ be a theory of the attributes domains characterizing their relevant algebraic properties.

We consider the attributes (fields) $a_1, ..., a_n$ of an entity (record) x as unary functions mapping x to the values of $a_1, ..., a_n$, respectively. So, the operation of dereferencing the attribute a_i of the entity x is simply modelled as function application $a_i(x)$ also written as $x.a_i$.

From now on, we assume $T_D = (\Sigma_D, \mathcal{M}_D)$ given and all the formulae to be built from symbols in $\Sigma_D \cup Att$, i.e. containing both the attributes Att associated to the entities and the algebraic operators Σ_D for the domains on which the attributes take values. The interpretation of the functions in Att is not constrained so that any possible value (in the appropriate domain) can be associated to each attribute of an entity whereas the interpretation of the symbols in Σ_D is constrained by the models in $\mathcal{M}_D$. We define a *release policy expression* as a FOL formula $\rho(\mathsf{u},\mathsf{a},\mathsf{r},\mathsf{e})$—intuitively saying that u can perform action a on resource r in environment e—in which it is possible to dereference at most the attributes of u, a, r or e (while it is prohibited to dereference the attributes of t). We define a *protection policy expression* as a FOL formula $\pi(\mathsf{t},\mathsf{a},\mathsf{r},\mathsf{e})$—intuitively saying that the action a can be performed on resource r by using terminal t in environment e—in which it is possible to dereference at most the attributes of t, a, r or e (while it is prohibited to dereference the attributes of u). A *CPR policy* $\alpha(\mathsf{u},\mathsf{t},\mathsf{a},\mathsf{r},\mathsf{e})$ is the conjunction of a release policy $\rho(\mathsf{u},\mathsf{a},\mathsf{r},\mathsf{e})$ and a protection policy $\pi(\mathsf{t},\mathsf{a},\mathsf{r},\mathsf{e})$; in symbols,

$$\alpha(\mathsf{u},\mathsf{t},\mathsf{a},\mathsf{r},\mathsf{e}) \quad := \quad \rho(\mathsf{u},\mathsf{a},\mathsf{r},\mathsf{e}) \wedge \pi(\mathsf{t},\mathsf{a},\mathsf{r},\mathsf{e}). \quad (1)$$

Before defining queries, we introduce the notion of *abstraction of an entity* x as a formula $Abs(x)$ in which it is possible to dereference only the attributes of x. If entity x^* is such that $Abs(x^*)$, we say that x^* *belongs to* (or, *is in*) Abs. If x^* is the only entity such that $Abs(x^*)$ evaluates to true, we say that Abs is an *attribute assignment of* x^*. Typically, an attribute assignment has the following form

$$x.a_1 = v_1 \wedge \cdots \wedge x.a_n = v_n \quad (2)$$

where $a_1, ..., a_n$ are *all* the attributes of the entity x and $v_1, ..., v_n$ are values in the attribute domains. An *abstract query* $Q(\mathsf{u},\mathsf{t},\mathsf{r},\mathsf{a},\mathsf{e}) := U(\mathsf{u}) \wedge T(\mathsf{t}) \wedge R(\mathsf{r}) \wedge A(\mathsf{a}) \wedge E(\mathsf{e})$ is a conjunction of an abstraction U of users, an abstraction T of terminals, an abstraction R of resources, an abstraction A of actions, and an abstraction E of environments. When all the abstractions in a query Q are attribute assignments, we say that Q is a *standard query*. Below, we use *query* to mean both an abstract and a standard query.

Let $\alpha(\mathsf{u},\mathsf{t},\mathsf{r},\mathsf{a},\mathsf{e})$ be a CPR policy and $Q(\mathsf{u},\mathsf{t},\mathsf{r},\mathsf{a},\mathsf{e})$ a query, a user u in U may execute an action a in A on a resource r in R by using a terminal t in T in an environment e belonging to E iff

$$Q(\mathsf{u},\mathsf{t},\mathsf{r},\mathsf{a},\mathsf{e}) \wedge \alpha(\mathsf{u},\mathsf{t},\mathsf{r},\mathsf{a},\mathsf{e}) \quad (3)$$

is satisfiable modulo the theory $T_D = (\Sigma_D, \mathcal{M}_D)$ of domains, i.e. it evaluates to true in some of the interpretations fixing the meaning of the symbols in Σ_D according to the interpretations in $\mathcal{M}_D$. The satisfiability of (3) is equivalent to that of the following two formulae:

$$Q(\mathsf{u},\mathsf{t},\mathsf{r},\mathsf{a},\mathsf{e}) \wedge \rho(\mathsf{u},\mathsf{r},\mathsf{a},\mathsf{e}) \quad (4)$$

$$Q(\mathsf{u},\mathsf{t},\mathsf{r},\mathsf{a},\mathsf{e}) \wedge \pi(\mathsf{t},\mathsf{r},\mathsf{a},\mathsf{e}) \quad (5)$$

for $\alpha(\mathsf{u},\mathsf{t},\mathsf{r},\mathsf{a},\mathsf{e}) := \rho(\mathsf{u},\mathsf{r},\mathsf{a},\mathsf{e}) \wedge \pi(\mathsf{t},\mathsf{r},\mathsf{a},\mathsf{e})$. It is possible to show [2] that the above satisfiability checks are decidable when queries, release and protection policies are quantifier-free formulae, i.e. formulae obtained by combining atoms with the standard Boolean connectives.

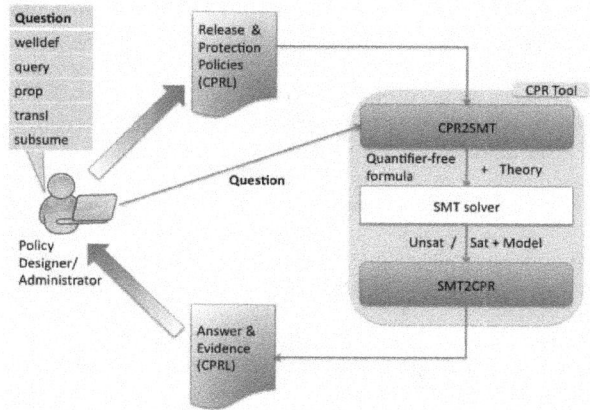

Figure 1: Enforcement and Analysis of CPR Policies

3. ANALYSIS OF CPR POLICIES

Our approach to help policy designers and administrators in the definition, analysis and enforcement of CPR policies is depicted in Figure 1. By using *CPRL*, the designer declares the attributes of the entities, their domains, and the release and protection policies. Additionally, the designer selects a "Question" from those in the table in the top left corner of Figure 1 in order to form one of the following *CPRL (analysis) problems*.

- Single group (R, P) of release and protection policies: "*welldef*(R, P)" checks if there exists (at least) a query that is permitted and (at least) another one that is denied by R and P; "*query*(R, P, Q)" checks if the query Q is permitted or denied by R and P; "*prop*(R, P, O)" asks if property O is verified by R and P; and "*transl*(R, P)" asks to translate R and P to a XACML policy set.

- Two groups (R, P) and (R', P') of release and protection policies: "*query*(R, P, R', P', Q)" checks if query Q is answered in the same way by group (R, P) and group (R', P'); "*prop*(R, P, R', P', O)" checks if property O is verified by group (R, P) and group (R', P'); and "*subsume*(R, P, R', P')" aims to check if group (R, P) subsumes group (R', P'), i.e. if using (R, P) automatically also fulfills (R', P').

These problems are solved by the CPR tool (right of Figure 1) which is composed of a pipeline of three modules: CPR2SMT, SMT Solver, and SMT2CPR. The first module takes as an input the CPRL analysis problem and returns a quantifier-free FOL formula φ together with a theory T_D of the domains of the attributes such that the (un-)satisfiability of φ modulo T_D is equivalent to a positive (negative, resp.) answer to the given problem. The second module, SMT solver, takes as input a quantifier-free FOL formula φ with a theory T_D and returns as a result either unsat(isfiable), or sat(isfiable) respectively, together with an model making φ true. The third and last module, SMT2CPR, takes as an input the output of the SMT solver and returns an answer to the original question. For instance, assume the CPRL analysis problem is "*query*(R, P, Q)" and "unsat" is returned by the SMT solver, then the answer computed by SMT2CPR is "Denied" meaning that the query Q is denied by R and P.

4. APPLICATION TO THE PMD SCENARIO

The goal of the NATO Passive Missile Defence (PMD) system is to minimize the adverse effects of defence against missile attacks; to this end, simulations are run in specific geographic areas, taking into account several parameters (e.g., the type of missile and weather conditions). The result of a simulation is a map of the predicted enemy missile trajectory and debris impact area, annotated with the consequences of the impact at several locations, hazard areas with risk analysis, the trajectories of intercepting missiles, sub-munition locations and descriptions, etc. Maps generated by the PMD system can be used in NATO missions for crisis-response planning, disaster preparation and rescue, and medical operations, including those that require the coordination of NATO coalition partners with civilian organizations such as the Red Cross. Indeed, the various parts of a computed map are subject to different release conditions. For example, a NATO user may see both missile trajectories and public information about the zones of operation, while a Red Cross member must not see the former (because he may be able to infer the location from which the intercepting missile was fired) yet should be allowed to access the public information. In addition, protection requirements should be enforced to guarantee that accessed information can be handled with an adequate level of technical and operational support; e.g., data should be downloaded using an TLS protocol and stored in encrypted form on the laptop of the user. For the sake of brevity, we omit environments.

Figure 2 shows release conditions and protection requirements expressed in CPRL. The first block of declarations (lines 1-11) specifies the attributes of users, resources, and terminals. In particular, the user attributes are **organization** and **clearance** (line 8): the former contains the name of the organization to which the user belongs, for simplicity, only two values are considered (line 7); the latter is the user clearance level (line 1). The terminal attributes are **confidentiality** and **mgauthority** (lines 10-11): the former gives the level of strength of the protection mechanisms to store the data offered by the terminal (line 2) while the latter specifies the name of the organization managing the terminal (line 7). The resource attributes are **category** and **topic** (line 9): the value of the former is the content category associated to the graphical objects in the map— namely **ScenarioDescription**, **COIMetrics** (metrics related to the consequences of the impact between the threatening and intercepting missiles), or **PublicInformation** (line 3); the value of the latter is the content topic, i.e. **HighValue-AssetsOrLists**, **ThreatOperatingAreas**, **ThreatAndInterceptorTrajectoryDetails**, **GeneralHazardAreaLocation**), or **SubmunitionAreaLocation** (lines 4–6).

The second block of declarations (lines 13–28) lists release policies and the third block (lines 30–49) the protection policies. To illustrate the meaning of the specification in Figure 2, let us consider some of the policy declarations. The release policy expression **rP1** (line 13) says that any user can view objects containing public information: that fact that the keyword **user** is not even mentioned in the expression implies that no constraint is imposed on the values of user attributes. Similarly, the protection policy expression **pP1** (line 30) says that objects containing public information can be accessed via any terminal. The more complex release policy expression **rP2** (lines 14–19) can be interpreted as follows: a user belonging to NATO with clearance level **Secret**

can access an object (**resource**) with category **ScenarioDescription** and whose topic can be either **HighValueAssetsOrLists**, **ThreatOperatingAreas**, or **ThreatAndInterceptorTrajectoryDetails**.

The CPRL Tool can be used to analyze the policy specification in Figure 2 as follows. As a preliminary check, it is possible to ask if the policy is well-defined. The answer of the CPR Tool is "Yes" together with the following permitted query (below, **clr**, **cat**, **top**, **con**, and **mga** abbreviate **clearance**, **category**, **topic**, **confidentiality**, and **mgauthority**, respectively):

> **user**.clr=Restricted & **user**.org=NATO_Org & **resource**.cat=COIMetrics & **resource**.topic=SubmunitionAreaLocation & **terminal**.con=High & **terminal**.mga=NATO_Org

meaning that a NATO user with clearance **Restricted** can access a resource with category **COIMetric** and topic **SubmunitionAreaLocation** by using a **High** confidentiality terminal managed by NATO, and the following denied query:

> **user**.clr=Unclassified & **user**.org=NATO_Org & **resource**.cat=ScenarioDescriptions & **resource**.top=GeneralHazardAreaLocation & **terminal**.con=High & **terminal**.mga=NATO_Org

meaning that a NATO user with clearance **Unclassifed** cannot access a resource with category **ScenarioDescriptions** and topic **GeneralHazardAreaLocation** by using a terminal managed by NATO with **High** confidentiality. Then, the CPR Tool can be asked to answer the following authorization query

> **query** q1 = **user**.organization = NATO_Org & **terminal**.mgauthority = NATO_Org & **resource**.topic = GeneralHazardAreaLocation ;

encoding the intuition that a resource whose topic is **GeneralHazardAreaLocation** can be released to NATO users when these use NATO terminals. The output of the tool confirms that query q1 is permitted by the policy in Figure 2 and adds that it is so by either using release policy expression **rP1** with the protection policy **pP1** or release policy expression **rP3** with the protection policy **pP3** (reporting that no other combination of release and protection policy expressions permit the query). Additionally, the CPR Tool "completes" the assignment of values to attributes for users, terminals, and resources that are not mentioned by **q1**. So, e.g., together with the fact that **rP1** with **pP1** permits the query, the following attribute assignments are returned:

> **user**.clr=Unclassified & **user**.org=NATO_Org & **resource**.cat=PublicInformation & **resource**.top=GeneralHazardAreaLocation & **terminal**.con=NoInfo & **terminal**.mga=NATO_Org

A closer look at these assignments gives us a hint about a possible under-specification of the policy since a resource whose topic is **GeneralHazardAreaLocation** cannot have category **PublicInfo**. This suggests to add the constraint

> ! (**resource**.topic = GeneralHazardAreaLocation)

to both **rP1** and **pP1**. If after this change to the policy, we ask again the CPR Tool to answer query **q1** above, we discover that only **rP3** with **pP3** permits it.

This is only a partial account of the use of the CPR Tool in the PMD scenario. For example, it can be used to translate the policy specification in Figure 2 to XACML so that

```
1   type Clearances = { None, Unclassified, Restricted, Confidential, Secret };
2   type Confidentialities = { NoInfo, Basic, Standard, Enhanced, High };
3   type Categories = { PublicInformation, ScenarioDescriptions, COIMetrics };
4   type Topics = { HighValuesAssetsOrLists, ThreatOperatingAreas,
5                   ThreatAndInterceptorTrajectoryDetails,
6                   GeneralHazardAreaLocation, SubmunitionAreaLocation };
7   type Organizations = { NATO_Org, Red_Cross };
8   entity User = [ clearance : Clearances, organization : Organizations ] ;
9   entity Resource = [ category : Categories, topic : Topics ] ;
10  entity Terminal = [ confidentiality : Confidentialities, mgauthority : Organizations ] ;
11  release rP1 = (resource.category = PublicInformation);
12  release rP2 = (user.clearance = Secret) & (user.organization = NATO_Org) &
13      (resource.category = ScenarioDescriptions) &
14      ((resource.topic = HighValuesAssetsOrLists) |
15          (resource.topic = ThreatOperatingAreas) |
16          (resource.topic = ThreatAndInterceptorTrajectoryDetails)) ;
17  release rP3 = (user.organization = NATO_Org) &
18      (resource.category = COIMetrics) &
19      (resource.topic = GeneralHazardAreaLocation) ;
20  release rP4 = (user.organization = NATO_Org) &
21      (resource.category = COIMetrics) &
22      (resource.topic = SubmunitionAreaLocation) &
23      ((user.clearance = Secret)             |
24      (user.clearance = Confidential) |
25      (user.clearance = Restricted)    ) ;
26  protection pP1 = (resource.category = PublicInformation);
27  protection pP2 = (resource.category = ScenarioDescriptions) &
28      (terminal.mgauthority = NATO_Org) &
29      ((resource.topic = HighValuesAssetsOrLists) |
30          (resource.topic = ThreatOperatingAreas) |
31          (resource.topic = ThreatAndInterceptorTrajectoryDetails)) &
32      ((terminal.confidentiality = High) |
33          (terminal.confidentiality = Enhanced)) ;
34  protection pP3 = (resource.category = COIMetrics) &
35      (resource.topic = GeneralHazardAreaLocation) &
36      ((terminal.confidentiality = High)          |
37          (terminal.confidentiality = Enhanced) |
38          (terminal.confidentiality = Standard) |
39          (terminal.confidentiality = Basic)      |
40          (terminal.confidentiality = NoInfo)) &
41      (terminal.mgauthority = NATO_Org) ;
42  protection pP4 = (resource.category = COIMetrics) &
43      (resource.topic = SubmunitionAreaLocation) &
44      !(terminal.confidentiality = NoInfo) &
45      (terminal.mgauthority = NATO_Org) ;
```

Figure 2: PMD scenario: release and protection policy expressions

available policy enforcement mechanisms can be used. This has been exploited to map the full PMD policy specification to XACML for use in the CPR access control system described in [1].

5. REFERENCES

[1] A. Armando, M. Grasso, S. Oudkerk, S. Ranise, and K. Wrona. Content-based Information Protection and Release in NATO Operations. In *SACMAT*, 2013.

[2] A. Armando, S. Oudkerk, S. Ranise, and K. Wrona. Formal Modelling of Content-Based Protection and Release for Access Control in NATO Operations. In *FPS 2013*, volume 8352 of *LNCS*, pages 227–244, 2014.

[3] S. De Capitani di Vimercati, S. Foresti, S. Jajodia, and P. Samarati. Access control policies and languages. *JCSE*, 3(2):94–102, 2007.

[4] S. De Capitani di Vimercati, S. Foresti, S. Jajodia, and P. Samarati. Access control policies and languages in open environments. In *Secure Data Management in Decentralized Systems*. Springer, 2007.

[5] H. B. Enderton. *A Mathematical Introduction to Logic*. Academic Press, Inc., 1972.

[6] X. Jin, R. Krishnan, and R. Sandhu. A Unified Attribute-Based Access Control Model Covering DAC, MAC and RBAC. In *DBSec*, number 7371 in LNCS, pages 41–55, 2012.

[7] R. Sandhu, E. Coyne, H. Feinstein, and C. Youmann. Role-Based Access Control Models. *IEEE Computer*, 2(29):38–47, 1996.

[8] K. Wrona and G. Hallingstad. Controlled information sharing in NATO operations. In *IEEE Military Communications Conference (MILCOM)*, 2011.

[9] K. Wrona and G. Hallingstad. Development of High Assurance Guards for NATO. In *MCC*, 2012.

[10] E. Yuan and T. Jin. Attribute-Based Access Control (ABAC) for Web Services. In *IEEE Int, Conf. on Web Services*, pages 561–569, 2005.

Towards an Automatic Top-down Role Engineering Approach Using Natural Language Processing Techniques

Masoud Narouei
Department of Computer Science and Engineering
University of North Texas
Denton, TX, USA
masoudnarouei@my.unt.edu

Hassan Takabi
Department of Computer Science and Engineering
University of North Texas
Denton, TX, USA
takabi@unt.edu

ABSTRACT

Role Based Access Control (RBAC) is the most widely used model for access control due to the ease of administration as well as economic benefits it provides. In order to deploy an RBAC system, one requires to first identify a complete set of roles. This process, known as role engineering, has been identified as one of the costliest tasks in migrating to RBAC. In this paper, we propose a top-down role engineering approach and take the first steps towards using natural language processing techniques to extract policies from unrestricted natural language documents. Most organizations have high-level requirement specifications that include a set of access control policies which describes allowable operations for the system. However, it is very time consuming, labor-intensive, and error-prone to manually sift through these natural language documents to identify and extract access control policies. Our goal is to automate this process to reduce manual efforts and human errors. We apply natural language processing techniques, more specifically semantic role labeling to automatically extract access control policies from unrestricted natural language documents, define roles, and build an RBAC model. Our preliminary results are promising and by applying semantic role labeling to automatically identify predicate-argument structure, and a set of predefined rules on the extracted arguments, we were able correctly identify access control policies with a precision of 75%, recall of 88%, and F1 score of 80%.

Categories and Subject Descriptors

D.6.5 [**Management of Computing and Information Systems**]: Security and Protection – Access controls

General Terms

Security, access control, classification, natural language processing, algorithms, design, experimentation

Keywords

Role Based Access Control; Role Engineering; Natural Language Processing; Semantic Role Labeling; Privacy Policy

1. INTRODUCTION

In computer security, Access Control Policies (ACPs) are critical to the security of organizations. However, defining proper ACPs is very challenging, especially in large organizations. Higher-level policy frameworks, such as Role Based Access Control (RBAC) promise long-term cost savings through reduced management effort, but manual development of initial policies can be difficult, expensive, and error prone. In RBAC, roles represent functions within a given organization and access permissions are associated with roles instead of users. Users can activate a subset of the roles which they are members of and easily acquire all the required permissions. In order to deploy RBAC, an organization must first identify a set of roles that is complete, correct and efficient, and then assign users and permissions to these roles [6].

There are two general approaches to accomplish the task of role engineering: the top-down approach and the bottom up approach [4]. The top-down approach uses a detailed analysis of business processes: organizational business processes are analyzed, particular job functions are defined and decomposed into smaller units. Once the permissions required to perform specific tasks are identified, they can be grouped into appropriate functional roles. The process is repeated until all the job functions are covered. Because there are large numbers of business processes, users and permissions in an organization, and also as such a process is human-intensive, it is a rather difficult task and hence believed to be slow, expensive, and not scalable.

Most organizations have high-level requirement specifications that determine how information access is managed and who, under what circumstances, may access what information. These documents define security policies and include a set of access control policies which describes allowable operations for the system. All US federal agencies are required to provide information security by the "Federal Information Security Act of 2002" [2], and policy documentation is part of that requirement [4]. Although private industry is not required to provide such documentation, the significant cost associated with cyber-attacks has led many companies to document their security policies as well. Besides, having security policies documented makes it much easier for organizations to transition from access control lists (ACLs) into a more robust RBAC infrastructure. We refer to these documents as Natural Language Access Control Policies (NLACPs) which are defined as "*statements governing management and access of enterprise objects. NLACPs are human expressions that can be translated to machine-enforceable access control policies*". However, NLACPs are normally expressed in human understandable terms and are not directly implementable in an access control mechanism. These documents are unstructured and may be ambiguous and thus hard to convert to formally actionable elements, so the enterprise policy may be difficult to encode in a machine-enforceable form. It is very time consuming, labor-intensive, and error-prone to manually sift through these existing natural language artifacts to identify and extract the buried ACPs. In order to properly enforce the security policies, these ACPs should be translated to machine-readable policies which is done manually and is a very labor intensive and error prone process. Our goal is to automate this process to reduce manual efforts and human errors.

In this paper, we take the first steps towards using natural language processing techniques to extract policies from these natural language requirements documents. We propose techniques and tools that will support effective development of trustworthy access control policies through automatically extracting access control policies from unrestricted natural language documents and transforming them to enforceable policies. Our goal is to allow organizations to use existing, unconstrained natural language texts such as requirements documents for inferring ACPs. Our approach consists of four main steps: (1) applying linguistic analysis to parse natural language documents and annotate words and phrases in sentence, (2) inferring the semantic roles in each sentence using annotated words and phrases, (3) transforming these semantic roles into ACPs, and (4) aggregating the extracted ACPs into roles.

In this paper, we limit our discussions to the linguistic analysis of natural language documents and extracting semantic roles from each sentence. We also present initial results of applying the technique to a sample of our policy dataset. To the best of our knowledge, there is not much work in the literature that addresses this issue and this is the first report on effectiveness of applying semantic role labeling to large and diverse set of ACPs.

The rest of this paper is organized as follows: We start with an overview of previous literature in section 2. In section 3, we present our proposed approach and its components. The experiments and results are presented in section 4, and finally, conclusion and future works wraps up the paper.

2. RELATED WORK

Xiao et al. proposed Text2Policy for automated extraction of ACPs [9]. It first uses shallow parsing techniques with finite state transducers to match a sentence into one of four possible access control patterns. If such a match can be made, Text2Policy uses the annotated portions of the sentences to extract the subject, action, and object from the sentence. *Slankas et al.* proposed Access Control Rule Extraction (ACRE) [7] which applies inductive reasoning to find and extract ACRs while Text2Policy applies deductive reasoning based upon existing rules to find and extract ACRs. While this work these two early works are promising, they suffer from several weaknesses. ACRE uses a supervised learning approach to identify sentences containing ACRs which requires a labeled dataset similar in structure and content to the document being analyzed. This data is hard to come by. Text2Policy does not require a labeled data set but it misses ACRs that do not follow one of its four patterns. It is reported that only 34.4% of the identified ACR sentences followed one of Text2Policy's patterns [6]. Additionally, Text2Policy's NL parser requires splitting longer sentences as the parser cannot handle complicated sentence structures. Neither one of these approaches take into account the presence of contextual

information or environment conditions which is a very challenging task.

3. THE PROPOSED METHODOLOGY

An overall view of the proposed system is shown in Figure 1. In the following sections, we describe each of these steps in details.

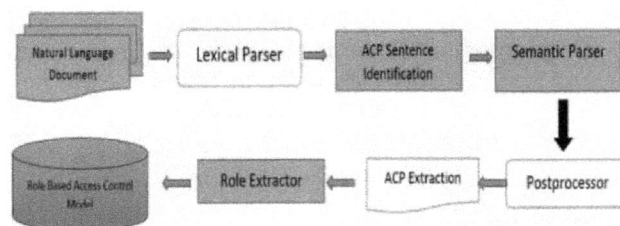

Figure 1. Overview of the proposed system

3.1 Lexical Parser

We first read the entire document and apply a state-of-the-art sentence segmentation and tokenization. Sentence segmentation identifies the boundaries of sentences. Tokenization detects individual words, punctuation, and other items from the text.

3.2 ACP Sentence Identification

Identifying whether a sentence contains access control content or not is an important step in correctly extracting access control policies. Often time ACPs are just a part of requirement documents and the documents have contents that describe functional requirements that are not necessarily related to ACPs. Attempting to extract ACPs from the whole document is an error prone and tedious process. So, we need to determine what sentences have potentially ACP content and then perform further analysis only on those sentences to extract ACP elements. Previous work has used k-Nearest Neighbors (k-NN) classifier to identify sentences containing ACPs [7]. k-NN is an instance based classifier that attempts to locate the k nearest neighbors of an instance in an instance space and labeling that instance with the same class as that of most neighbors. In this paper, our focus is mainly on correctly identifying ACP elements and using those ACPs to create a RBAC system. For this purpose, we adopt the same approach used in [7].

3.3 Semantic Parser

We propose to use semantic role labeling (SRL) to automatically identify predicate-argument structure in ACP sentences. SRL is a task in natural language processing consisting of the detection of the semantic arguments associated with the verb (or more technically, a predicate) of a sentence and their classification into their specific roles. It identifies who did what to whom by assigning roles to constituents of the sentence representing entities related to a specific verb. The following sentence, exemplifies the annotation of semantic roles:

[$_{Arg0}$ John] [$_{ArgM-MOD}$ can] [$_V$ **assign**] [$_{Arg1}$ clerk] [$_{Arg2}$ to users from department A]

Here, the roles for the predicate **assign** (assign.01, that is, the *roleset* of the predicate) are defined in the PropBank Frames scheme as:
V: verb
ArgM-MOD: modal
Arg0: (assigner)
Arg1: (thing assigned)
Arg2: (assigned to)
SRL is very important in making sense of the meaning of a sentence. Such semantic representation is at a higher-level of abstraction than a syntax tree. In general, given any sentence,

the task of SRL consists of analyzing the propositions expressed by all target verbs in a sentence and for each target verb, all the constituents in that sentence which fill a semantic role of the verb, will be extracted. Here, we use the following notation to describe ACPs:

$$\{A; B; C\}$$

Where *A* stands for *Argument0*, *B* stands for *predicate* and *C* stands for *argument1*. *Argument0* usually denotes agent or experiencer for that predicate and *Argument1* denotes theme (where predicate affects).

In this paper, we use Senna semantic role labeler [1], which performs sentence-level analysis. Senna is a multilayer neural network architecture that relies on large unlabeled datasets and allows the training algorithm to discover internal representations that prove useful for the requested task. Senna is fast because it uses a simple architecture, it is self-contained because it does not rely on the output of another system, and it is accurate because it offers state-of-the-art or near state-of-the-art performance.

3.4 Postprocessor

After generating verb-arguments, we need to do additional processing on the output. The requirement documents are typically stated by managers using their own language because they do not have the technical knowledge of the system and this makes ACP extraction from their stated sentences even more complicated. We apply named entity recognition and then argument expansion as described below.

3.4.1 Named Entity Recognition

Named entity recognition (NER) is the task of identifying named entities and sequences of words in a text belonging to predefined categories such as the names of persons, locations, organizations, expressions of times, quantities, monetary values, percentages, etc. The task here is to take an unannotated text and produce an annotated text that highlights the names of entities:

[ORGANIZATION Customer Service Reps], [PERSON Pharmacists], and [ORGANIZATION Billing Reps] can collect and use customer name and [TIME date of birth] to help confirm identity.

In this example, *Customer Service Reps* is an organization consisting of three tokens, *Pharmacists*, is a person consisting of one token, *Billing Reps* is an organization consisting of two three tokens, and finally *date of birth* is a time consisting of three tokens.

3.4.2 Argument Expansion

Another complication is that sometimes more than one ACP is stated in a given sentence. Consider the following sentence for example:

Customer Service Reps and Billing Reps can collect customer name to help confirm identity.

There are 4 different ACPs associated with this sentence:

- {customer service rep; collect; customer name}
- {billing rep; collect; customer name}
- {customer service rep; confirm; identity}
- {billing rep; confirm; identity}

Now consider the following list of the extracted semantic roles for each predicate collect:

[Arg0 Customer Service Reps and Billing Reps] [ArgM-MOD can] [v **collect**] [Arg1 customer name] [ArgM-PNC to help confirm identity].

SRL's output can be interpreted as an abstract form for ACPs, so we have to expand this abstract form to generate all of the related ACPs. This expansion could be in the form of extracting all named entities or other standalone nouns in Arg0 as the possible agents and also extracting independent entities from Arg1 as themes. After extracting all of these entities, we list all of the combinations of these entities based on each predicate. For example, the listing for the first predicate can be expanded as the following rules:

- {customer service rep; collect; customer name}
- {billing rep; collect; customer name}

3.5 Role Extractor

Once the ACP elements are extracted using SRL and postprocessing is done, role extractor uses this information to define roles from the extracted ACPs. The extracted ACPs are in the form of {subject, object, operation} and many of the extracted subjects are associated with job functions within organization (e.g. doctor, pharmacist, nurse, etc.) which could represent roles. A naïve approach would be to just look at the ACPs and find the ones with the same subject and group them together in one role and use all the ACPs with that subject to build the role permission assignment relationships. The object and operation elements of the ACPs are used to define permissions in RBAC and then assign those permissions to roles based on that specific subject using ACP associations. Another approach is to use classifier such as *k*-Nearest Neighbors (*k*-NN) classifier or Naive Bayes classifier to extract roles from the ACPs. However, we leave the implementation of role extractor to future work as it is not focus of this paper.

4. EXPERIMENTAL RESULTS

We conduct experiments to answer research question of how effectively the subject, object, and operation elements of ACPs are extracted. As ACPs exist in numerous domains, we use multiple domains for the evaluation. We use documents from the electronic healthcare, educational, and conference management domains. For the electronic health care domain, we use iTrust [3], an open source healthcare application that includes various features such as maintaining medical history of patients, identifying primary caregivers, storing communications with doctors, and sharing satisfaction results. For the educational domain, we employ use cases from the IBM Course Registration System [5] and for the conference management system, we use documents from CyberChair [8]. For our evaluation we use the iTrust data set that was used by *Xiao et al.* [9], which has 418 sentences identified as containing ACP content. The second dataset, IBM Course Registration System consists of eight use cases and there are 169 ACP sentences and the CyberChair data set consists of 139 ACP sentences.

Evaluation Criteria: To evaluate results, we use several measures such as *recall*, *precision*, and the *F1* score.

To compute these values, we categorize the extractions into four categories: false positives (FP) are cases where we mistakenly identify a word as an ACP element when it is not, false negatives (FN) occur when we fail to correctly extract an actual ACP element, true positives (TP) are correct extractions, and true negatives (TN) are cases where we correctly identified that a word in the sentence was not an ACP element. From these values, we define precision as the proportion of correctly extracted ACP elements against all extractions against the test data. We also define recall as the proportion of ACP elements found for the current data under test. The F_1 score is the

Table 1. Comparison of ACP extraction between ACRE and the proposed system

Dataset	ACRE			SRL		
	Precision	Recall	F_1	Precision	Recall	F_1
iTrust	80%	75%	77%	75%	88%	80%
IBM Course Management	81%	62%	70%	54%	87%	58%
CyberChair	75%	30%	43%	46%	84%	59%

harmonic mean—a weighted average of precision and recall—giving an equal weight to both recall and precision.

In order to evaluate the effectiveness of our proposed approach, we use the data sets that were manually labeled by *Slankas et al.* [7] for this purpose. The evaluation results as well as comparison with the most recent system (ACRE) are presented in Table 1.

As the results show, our approach based on semantic role labeling performs very well and outperforms the ACRE approach in most cases. In terms of recall, our approach significantly outperforms the ACRE across all the data sets. The algorithm used in ACRE requires repetition in sentence structure as well as subjects and resources throughout the document to perform well. This algorithm performed best on iTrust because it contained repetitions throughout the document but performed poor on the CyberChair. That's because there are not enough repetition in that document for finding initial set of known subjects and resources and expanding the patterns. However, semantic role labeling does not require repetition as every sentence will be considered separately, independent of the other sentences. As long as there are role sets defined for that predicate, semantic role labeling can find most of the arguments. This is why the results for semantic role labeling are stable throughout all documents and it provides good results regardless of the structure of the document. In terms of precision, however, our approach does not perform very well. One issue with using semantic role labeling is that it extracts all arguments for all of the verbs in a sentence. Sometimes only a portion of these verbs such as (set, add, etc) describe access control policies. Consider the following example:

*Only the manager [$_v$ **is**] [$_v$ **allowed**] to [$_v$ **add**] a new resident to the system and to [$_v$ **start**] or [$_v$ **update**] the care plan of a resident.*

Here, there are five verbs but ACPs are only associated with three of them, namely *add*, *start* and *update*. Often times there are other verbs that do not express ACPs such as *click, include, etc,* and they generate too many false positives, impacting the performance of the systems. To solve this issue, we plan to create a dictionary of the verbs that are usually associated with access control policies and only consider those verbs which improve the results significantly.

Although our approach does not perform well in terms of precision, if we look at F1 scores, which considers both recall and precision, we can see that our approach outperforms the ACRE. For the IBM Course Management data set, our approach is outperformed by ACRE and it is because precision is very low which leads to lower F1 score. In addition to offering better recall and F1 score, another advantage of our approach over the ACRE is that it does not require any labeled data set whereas ACRE uses a supervised learning approach and requires a labeled dataset similar in structure and content to the document being analyzed to setup the classifiers.

5. CONCLUSION AND FUTURE WORK

We proposed a top-down role engineering approach using semantic role labeling technique to extract policies from natural language requirements documents. The semantic role labeling allowed us to identify predicate-argument structure and applying a set of predefined rules on the extracted arguments allowed us to correctly identify ACPs with a recall of 88%, precision of 75%, and F1 score of 80%. In the future, we plan to create a dictionary of the verbs that are usually associated with access control policies and only consider those verbs to improve the results. We are also working on implementing the complete system including implementing ACP sentence identification step and role extractor components to improve role engineering results.

6. REFERENCES

[1] Collobert, R., Weston. J., Bottou, L., Karlen, M., Kavukcuoglu. K., and Kuksa P. 2011. Natural Language Processing (Almost) from Scratch, *Journal of Machine Learning Research (JMLR)*, 2011.

[2] Federal information security management act of 2002, 2002. Title III of the E-Government Act of 2002.

[3] Meneely, A., Smith, B., Williams, L., 2011. iTrust Electronic Health Care System: A Case Study. *Software System Traceability.*

[4] Takabi, H. and Joshi, J., StateMiner: an efficient similarity-based approach for optimal mining of role hierarchy. In *Proceedings of the 15th ACM symposium on Access control models and technologies* (SACMAT '10). ACM, New York, NY, USA, 55-64.

[5] *Multilingual Information Extraction and Summarization.* T. Poibeau, eds. Springer Berlin Heidelberg. 23–50.

[6] Sinha, A., SuttonJr, S. M., and Paradkar, A. 2010. Text2test: Automated inspection of natural language use cases. In *Proc. ICST*, pages 155–164, 2010.

[7] Slankas, j., Xiao, X., Williams, L., and Xie, T. 2014. Relation Extraction for Inferring Access Control Rules from Natural Language Artifacts. In *Proceedings of the of 2014 Annual Computer Security Applications Conference* (ACSAC 2014), New Orleans, LA.

[8] Socher, R., Bauer, J., Manning, C. D., Y. Ng. A, 2013. Parsing with Compositional Vector Grammars. *In Proc. ACL.* (2013).

[9] Xiao, X., Paradkar, A., Thummalapenta, S., and Xie. T. 2012 Automated extraction of security policies from natural-language software documents. In *Proc. 20th FSE*, November 2012.

Hard Instances for Verification Problems in Access Control

Nima Mousavi[*]
Google, Inc.
Waterloo, Canada
nima.mousavi@gmail.com

Mahesh Tripunitara
ECE, University of Waterloo
Waterloo, Canada
tripunit@uwaterloo.ca

ABSTRACT

We address the generation and analysis of hard instances for verification problems in access control that are **NP**-hard. Given the customary assumption that $\mathbf{P} \neq \mathbf{NP}$, we know that such classes exist. We focus on a particular problem, the user-authorization query problem (UAQ) in Role-Based Access Control (RBAC). We show how to systematically generate hard instances for it. We then analyze what we call the structure of those hard instances. Our work brings the important aspect of systematic investigation of hard input classes to access control research.

Categories and Subject Descriptors

D.4.6 [**Operating Systems**]: Security and Protection—*Access controls*; D.2.4 [**Software Engineering**]: Software/Program Verification

General Terms

Theory, Verification

Keywords

Intractability; Hard instances; User Authorization Query; Role-Based Access Control

1. INTRODUCTION

Access control is a fundamental area of research in security. In many contexts that principles from access control are applied, optimization and verification problems arise — see, for example, [4, 5, 6, 9, 11, 12, 17, 18, 19, 22]. In many cases, software tools are proposed for addressing instances of the problem that may arise in practice.

Part of the reason such empirical work is interesting is that such tools appear to perform well notwithstanding the underlying intractability of the problem. A reason such

[*]Nima Mousavi's contributions to this work were made when he was a Ph.D. student at the University of Waterloo.

tools perform well is that **NP**-hardness is a characterization of worst-case only. Therefore, one expects that there exist classes of inputs that are easy. However, such easy instances are not the only ones that may arise in practice. Under the customary assumption that $\mathbf{P} \neq \mathbf{NP}$, if a problem is **NP**-hard, we know that given any tool for it, instances exist that are hard for it. An important nuance is that a given class of instances is not necessarily hard for all tools.

Suppose a problem is **NP**-hard. What does a hard instance for it look like? As we mention above, there is no universal answer to this question. It depends on (a) the problem, and, (b) the tool under consideration. An FAQ for MiniSat [1], a constraint-solver for CNF-SAT instances, is instructive in this regard. It observes that MiniSat performs poorly for, "... a problem whose unknown variables are almost all true..." (A reasoning is provided there, which we do not reproduce here.) Notwithstanding this subjectivity, there is research on some canonical problems in identifying hard instances. Our intent is to bring such a mindset and such research to access control.

We adopt a concrete problem that has been considered in recent research in access control: the User-Authorization Query problem (UAQ) [2, 3, 4, 14, 19, 22]. Tools have been proposed for it. In a piece of work that proposes a tool, most classes of instances that are considered are shown to be easy for the tool. Also, there has been no systematic approach to identifying what classes of UAQ instances are hard for a particular tool.

Contributions   We provide a systematic approach to generating hard instances for UAQ. We then study what we call the structural properties of such instances. While we focus on UAQ, our work is more broadly applicable, and provides a blueprint for other problems and tools for them.

2. UAQ

UAQ is an optimization problem which, like many other such optimization problems, has natural decision versions. When we use the acronym "UAQ," we typically refer to the decision version we discuss below. This is the same version that has been addressed in prior work. When we wish to refer to the optimization version, we say so.

The decision version of UAQ takes the following inputs. (1) An authorization policy, which is Role-Based Access Control (RBAC) [16]. In RBAC, a user acquires permissions via membership in roles. In the context of UAQ, the policy is a pair, $\langle RH, PA \rangle$, where RH is a role-hierarchy, that organizes the roles into a reflexive partial order, and PA is the role-permission assignment relation. The mindset is that

n	CPU Time (sec)	$|R|$	$|P_{lb}|$
25	34	125	963
30	43	150	1167
35	110	210	2139
40	259	240	2371
45	472	315	3811
50	1135	350	45075

Table 1: Instances of UAQ generated from the model RD for CSP that we discuss in Section 3. Complete data is provided by Mousavi [13]. The CPU times are significantly more than the running times for the inputs in the work that proposes the tool [14] (see Table 2.)

this policy pertains to a user, who may activate a subset of the roles to which he is authorized in a session, subject to the constraints that are the other inputs.

(2) A set of Separation of Duty (SoD) constraints, D, each of the form $\langle R, t \rangle$ where R is a set of roles each of which appears in RH above and $t \in [2, |R|]$ is an integer. Its semantics is that the user is not allowed to activate t or more roles from R in any session. (3) Two sets of permissions, P_{lb} and P_{ub}, where $P_{lb} \subseteq P_{ub}$. The "lb" is for "lower bound," and the "ub" is for "upper bound." Each of the two sets is a subset of the permissions that appear in PA above. Their semantics is that the user requires that the set of roles he activates in the session authorized him to all the permissions in P_{lb}. The set of roles should not authorize him to any permission outside P_{ub}. He may be authorized to permissions from $P_{ub} \setminus P_{lb}$ subject to the constraint k_p below.

(4) Two integers, k_r, k_p. The UAQ instance is true if and only if there exists a set of roles of size at most k_r that satisfies all of the SoD constraints in D, and all the permissions in P_{lb}, but only at most k_p permissions from $P_{ub} \setminus P_{lb}$.

A software tool UAQ is known to be **NP**-complete [3, 19, 22]. There is an open-source software tool for it [14]. As we mention in Section 1, when we refer to a class of hard instances, we really need to put it in the context of a problem (UAQ, in our case), and a tool. This tool is our choice. The tool is based on reduction to CNF-SAT, and the use of an off-the-shelf SAT solver such as MiniSat [1]. This makes our work particularly interesting because MiniSat represents several years of research progress on SAT solvers.

3. HARD INSTANCES OF UAQ

We now consider the question: is it possible to devise a systematic approach to generating hard instances for UAQ? In this section, we provide the answer, 'yes.' Our proof is by construction — we provide an approach. Our approach is based on the Constrained Satisfaction Problem (CSP), which we introduce next.

CSP A CSP (i.e., an instance of CSP) comprises a set of variables $x_1, x_2, \cdots, x_n$, where the variable x_i takes a value from a nonempty domain d_i, and a set of constraints $C_1, C_2, \cdots, C_m$. Each constraint C_i is an associative relation specifying the allowable values for the variables involved in C_i. A solution to a CSP is an assignment of values to all variables such that it satisfies all the constraints. A CSP is satisfiable if and only if there is a solution to it.

As an example, the graph coloring problem can be posed as a CSP. A decision-version of the graph coloring problem is: given as input an undirected graph G and an integer k, color the vertices of G such that no two adjacent vertices receive the same color, and at most k colors are used in total. As a CSP, we would adopt the vertices as the variables. Each of the domains would be the set of k colors that are allowed. The constraints would then express the edges, i.e., if $\langle v_i, v_j \rangle$ is an edge, then the corresponding variables x_i, x_j should not receive the same color. One way to do this is for each pair $\langle x_i, x_j \rangle$, we specify the pairs of colors that are allowed.

A model for generating hard instances of CSP, called RD, has been proposed by Xu et al. [20, 21]. Our method for generating hard UAQ instances is based on their model, which we now discuss.

DEFINITION 1. *[20, 21] A class of random CSP instances of model RD is denoted by $RD(k, n, \alpha, r, p)$ where:*

- $k \geq 2$ *denotes the arity of each constraint,*

- n *denotes the number of variables,*

- $\alpha > 0$ *determines the size of the domain of each variable. We set it to n^α,*

- $r > 0$ *determines the number of constraints that is $rn \log n$,*

- $1 > p > 0$ *is a probability that is called the tightness of each constraint.*

An instance of $RD(k, n, \alpha, r, p)$ is constructed as follows. Given n variables, we first construct $rn \ln n$ constraints. Each constraint is formed by selecting k variables at random. For each constraint, each tuple of possible values is selected to be incompatible with probability p.

Xu et al. [20, 21] have shown that for $p = 1 - e^{-\alpha/r}$, instances generated by model RD, $RD(k, n, \alpha, r, p)$, are hard if $\alpha > 1/k$ and $p \leq \frac{k-1}{k}$.

CSP to UAQ To create an instance of UAQ based on model RD that we discuss above, we first construct an RBAC policy ρ as follows.

- Generate n sets of roles $R_1, R_2, \cdots, R_n$, where each set comprises n^α distinct roles.

- Set $RH = \{\langle r, r \rangle : r \in R\}$ where $R = \bigcup_i R_i$.

- For every pair of roles in the same set, $r_k^i, r_l^i \in R_i$, define a permission to which only r_k^i and r_l^i are authorized.

- Randomly select two sets of roles R_i and R_j, and for each pair of roles $r_k^i \in R_i$ and $r_l^j \in R_j$, define a permission to which only r_k^i and r_l^j are authorized. Perform this step $rn \ln n$ times.

We create an instance of UAQ in which we set $P_{lb} = P_{ub} = P$ (where P is the set of all permissions defined above). The input k_p is then inconsequential. We set the of SoD constraints, $D = \emptyset$. We show how an instance of UAQ with $k_r = n^{\alpha+1} - n$ generated as above is an instance of $RD(k, n', \alpha, r, p)$ when $k = 2$ and $n' = n$. We observe that

162

		Prior work [14]		Increased $|P_{lb}|$	
$|R|$	$|P|$	$|P_{lb}|$	Time (sec)	$|P_{lb}|$	Time (sec)
200	500	7	0.097	500	16.121
200	500	5	0.105	500	0.126
100	500	7	0.283	500	0.287
300	1000	7	0.803	1000	5.326
100	500	6	0.174	500	> 1000
100	500	11	0.060	500	0.136

Table 2: CPU times for six inputs from each class from prior work [14], and those six inputs with the P_{lb} set to P, i.e., its size increased to be all of P.

		Tree width	
n	Time (sec)	lower-bound	upper-bound
32	260	24	63
39	291	25	71
43	588	30	98
47	825	33	117
50	1135	32	117

Table 3: A portion of our data for the lower-bound and upper-bound tree-widths of the CSPs for some our hard UAQ instances. The complete data is provided by Mousavi [13].

if there exists a set of $n^{\alpha+1} - n$ roles that activates all the permissions, then the remaining n roles, denoted by R', are such that no two roles are authorized to the same permission. Since every pair of roles in the same role-set R_i shares a permission, R' must have exactly one role from each set. That is, $|R' \cap R_i| = 1$ for all i.

An instance of UAQ that we generate can be seen as an instance of model RD, i.e., $RD(2, n, \alpha, r, p)$, by defining a variable x_i for each set of roles R_i. The domain of each variable x_i consists of n^α values $v_1, v_2, \cdots, v_{n^\alpha}$. For each permission p to which $r_k^i \in R_i$ and $r_l^j \in R_j$ are authorized, there is a constraint that disallows values v_k and v_l for x_i and x_j respectively. There is a satisfying assignment for $x_1, x_2, \cdots, x_n$ if and only if there exist a set of $n^{1+\alpha} - n$ roles that activates all the permissions in P_{lb}.

We generated hard UAQ instances with $\alpha = 0.5, p = 0.5, r = 0.72$, and $n \in \{25, 26, \cdots, 50\}$, and used the open-source tool on which we focus [14] to address them. Table 1 shows the CPU time for some of the instances as well as the size of each instance. The CPU times for this experiment, and all the others we discuss in this paper, were measured on a standard desktop PC with an Intel Dual Core E8400 CPU, each of which clocks at 3 GHz and has a 6 MB cache. The machine runs 64-bit Ubuntu 14.04 LTS operating system and has 8 GB RAM.

The CPU times in Table 1 are significantly larger than the CPU time that our prior work that proposes the tool reports [14]. We report the CPU time and the sizes for six of those instances in Table 2.

Preliminary observations It is clear that the instances in Table 1 take significantly more CPU time than those from prior work that we report in Table 2. When one looks at the corresponding sizes, an immediate observation regards the size of P_{lb}. The P_{lb} sizes in Table 1 are much higher than those in Table 2. We may conclude that the size of P_{lb} is the source of hardness in UAQ.

We repeated our measurements for the six instances from prior work by increasing $|P_{lb}|$ to the maximum, i.e., we set $P_{lb} = P$. The results are shown in Table 2. The data shows that for half of the cases, the CPU time did indeed increase by at least two orders of magnitude. However, in the other half, it had negligible impact. This suggests that P_{lb} size alone cannot explain the hardness of UAQ.

4. STRUCTURE OF HARD INSTANCES

In this section, we study what we call the structural property of hard UAQ instances. In this work, we discuss our approach that first reduces UAQ to CSP, and then studies the resultant CSP instances. Two other approaches, (a) two graphs associated with hard UAQ instances, and, (b) via reduction to CNF-SAT, are discussed by Mousavi [13].

Given a UAQ instance, we construct a CSP instance as follows. We define a variable for each role and each permission. Each variable is either zero or one, denoting whether the corresponding role or permission is active. Let v_r and v_p denote the variables corresponding to $r \in R$ and $p \in P$. We define the following constraints.

- for each permission $p \in P$, we define a constraint involving v_p and all v_r's corresponding to the roles authorized to p. The constraint allows only assignments in which v_p is one if and only if at least one of the v_r's is one.

- for each SoD constraint $\langle R_i, t_i \rangle \in D$, we define a constraint involving variables v_r's for all $r \in R_i$ that allows at most $t_i - 1$ of the variables to be one.

- for each $\langle r_i, r_j \rangle \in RH$, we define a constraint where the allowable combination values for (r_i, r_j) are $\{(one, one), (zero, one), (zero, zero)\}$.

- for each $p \in P_{lb}$, the only allowed value for v_p is one.

- for each $p \in P - P_{ub}$, the only allowed value for v_p is zero.

- a constraint involving variables v_p for $p \in P_{ub} - P_{lb}$ that allows at most k_p of the variables to be one.

- a constraint involving variables in $\{v_r : r \in R\}$ that allows at most k_r of the variables to be one.

A CSP instance can be further represented by a constraint graph where there is a vertex for each variable and each constraint. There is an edge between a variable-vertex and a constraint-vertex if and only if the corresponding variable occurs in the corresponding constraint.

We assert that each CSP is solvable in $O(nd^{w+1})$-time where n is the number of variables, d is the maximum domain size of each variable, and w is the tree width of the corresponding constraint graph [15]. (The tree width of a graph is defined for the tree decomposition of the graph. The tree decomposition of a graph is a tree whose nodes are clusters of nodes from the original graph. Two nodes in the tree, n_1 and n_2 have an edge only if the intersection of the node-clusters that n_1 and n_2 are of nodes from the original graph, is non-empty. The tree width is then one less than the minimum sized node-cluster across all tree decompositions of the graph. We refer the reader to Halin [8] for a deeper discussion.)

Therefore, the tree width is a structural property of the CSP problem that is closely related to its hardness. In fact, the tree width provides an upper bound for the difficulty of a CSP problem. For each instance of hard UAQ's, we first reduce it to a CSP instance as explained above, and then compute the upper bound and lower bound of the tree width of the associated constraint graph. We do this because, in general, computing the tree width for a CSP instance is itself **NP**-hard. Mousavi [13] shows lower- and upper-bounds for the tree width of the constraint graph that corresponds to the hard UAQ instances from Section 3. We use the Minor-Min-Width algorithm [7] for computing the lower-bounds and the Greedy-Fill-In algorithm [10] for the upper-bounds.

5. CONCLUSIONS

We have provided an approach to generating, and analyzing the structure of, hard instances for a verification problem in access control, UAQ. For this, we have leveraged existing work on hard instances of CSP. Our intent is to demonstrate that there exists a systematic approach to both, and to bring such work to access control research. More details and discussions are provided by Mousavi [13].

6. REFERENCES

[1] MiniSat. `http://minisat.se/`, Feb 2015.

[2] A. Armando, S. Ranise, F. Turkmen, and B. Crispo. Efficient Run-time Solving of RBAC User Authorization Queries: Pushing the Envelope. In *Proceedings of the ACM Conference on Data and Applications Security and Privacy (CODASPY'12)*. ACM, Feb. 2012.

[3] L. Chen and J. Crampton. Set covering problems in role-based access control. In *Proceedings of the 14th European conference on Research in computer security*, ESORICS'09, pages 689–704. Springer-Verlag, 2009.

[4] S. Du and J. B. D. Joshi. Supporting authorization query and inter-domain role mapping in presence of hybrid role hierarchy. In *Proceedings of the eleventh ACM symposium on Access control models and technologies*, SACMAT '06, pages 228–236. ACM, 2006.

[5] A. Ene, W. Horne, N. Milosavljevic, P. Rao, R. Schreiber, and R. E. Tarjan. Fast Exact and Heuristic Methods for Role Minimization Problems. In *Proceedings of the 13th ACM Symposium on Access Control Models and Technologies*, SACMAT '08, pages 1–10. ACM, 2008.

[6] M. Gofman, R. Luo, A. Solomon, Y. Zhang, P. Yang, and S. Stoller. RBAC-PAT: A Policy Analysis Tool for Role Based Access Control. In S. Kowalewski and A. Philippou, editors, *Tools and Algorithms for the Construction and Analysis of Systems*, volume 5505 of *Lecture Notes in Computer Science*, pages 46–49. Springer Berlin Heidelberg, 2009.

[7] V. Gogate and R. Dechter. A Complete Anytime Algorithm for Treewidth. In *Proceedings of the 20th Conference on Uncertainty in Artificial Intelligence*, UAI '04, pages 201–208. AUAI Press, 2004.

[8] R. Halin. S-functions for graphs. *Journal of Geometry*, 8(1-2):171–186, 1976.

[9] K. Jayaraman, M. Tripunitara, V. Ganesh, M. Rinard, and S. Chapin. Mohawk: Abstraction-Refinement and Bound-Estimation for Verifying Access Control Policies. *ACM Trans. Inf. Syst. Secur.*, 15(4):18:1–18:28, Apr. 2013.

[10] A. Koster, H. Bodlaender, and S. Van Hoesel. Treewidth: Computational experiments. Technical report, Universiteit Utrecht, 2001.

[11] N. Li and M. V. Tripunitara. Security Analysis in Role-based Access Control. *ACM Trans. Inf. Syst. Secur.*, 9(4):391–420, Nov. 2006.

[12] N. Li, M. V. Tripunitara, and Q. Wang. Resiliency Policies in Access Control. In *Proceedings of the 13th ACM Conference on Computer and Communications Security*, CCS '06, pages 113–123. ACM, 2006.

[13] N. Mousavi. Algorithmic Problems in Access Control. Ph.D. thesis, University of Waterloo, 2014. Available from `https://uwspace.uwaterloo.ca/`.

[14] N. Mousavi and M. V. Tripunitara. Mitigating the Intractability of the User Authorization Query Problem in Role-Based Access Control (RBAC). In L. Xu, E. Bertino, and Y. Mu, editors, *Proceedings of the 6th International Conference on Network and System Security (NSS)*, volume 7645 of *Lecture Notes in Computer Science*, pages 516–529. Springer, 2012.

[15] S. J. Russell and P. Norvig. *Artificial Intelligence - A Modern Approach (3rd ed.)*. Pearson Education, 2010.

[16] R. S. Sandhu, E. J. Coyne, H. L. Feinstein, and C. E. Youman. Role-Based Access Control Models. *IEEE Computer*, 29(2):38–47, February 1996.

[17] J. Vaidya, V. Atluri, and Q. Guo. The Role Mining Problem: Finding a Minimal Descriptive Set of Roles. In *Proceedings of the 12th ACM Symposium on Access Control Models and Technologies*, SACMAT '07, pages 175–184. ACM, 2007.

[18] Q. Wang and N. Li. Satisfiability and Resiliency in Workflow Authorization Systems. *ACM Trans. Inf. Syst. Secur.*, 13(4):40:1–40:35, Dec. 2010.

[19] G. T. Wickramaarachchi, W. H. Qardaji, and N. Li. An efficient framework for user authorization queries in RBAC systems. In *Proceedings of the 14th ACM symposium on Access control models and technologies*, SACMAT '09, pages 23–32. ACM, 2009.

[20] K. Xu, F. Boussemart, F. Hemery, and C. Lecoutre. A simple model to generate hard satisfiable instances. In *Proceedings of the 19th international joint conference on Artificial intelligence (IJCAI'05)*, pages 337–342. Morgan Kaufmann Publishers Inc., 2005.

[21] K. Xu and W. Li. Many Hard Examples in Exact Phase Transitions. *Theor. Comput. Sci.*, 355(3):291–302, Apr. 2006.

[22] Y. Zhang and J. B. D. Joshi. UAQ: a framework for user authorization query processing in RBAC extended with hybrid hierarchy and constraints. In *Proceedings of the 13th ACM symposium on Access control models and technologies*, SACMAT '08, pages 83–92. ACM, 2008.

Initial Encryption of Large Searchable Data Sets using Hadoop

Feng Wang
SAP SE
Karlsruhe, Germany
feng.wang02@sap.com

Mathias Kohler
SAP SE
Karlsruhe, Germany
mathias.kohler@sap.com

Andreas Schaad
SAP SE
Karlsruhe, Germany
andreas.schaad@sap.com

ABSTRACT

With the introduction and the widely use of external hosted infrastructures, secure storage of sensitive data becomes more and more important. There are systems available to store and query encrypted data in a database, but not all applications may start with empty tables rather than having sets of legacy data. Hence, there is a need to transform existing plaintext databases to encrypted form. Usually existing enterprise databases may contain terabytes of data. A single machine would require many months for the initial encryption of a large data set. We propose encrypting data in parallel using a Hadoop cluster which is a simple five step process including the Hadoop set up, target preparation, source data import, encrypting the data, and finally exporting it to the target. We evaluated our solution on real world data and report on performance and data consumption. The results show that encrypting data in parallel can be done in a very scalable manner. Using a parallelized encryption cluster compared to a single server machine reduces the encryption time from months down to days or even hours.

Categories and Subject Descriptors

H.2.0 [**Database Management**]: General – *security;* H.3.4 [**Information Storage and Retrieval**]: Systems and Software – *Distributed systems, Performance evaluation.*

General Terms

Performance, Security

Keywords

Database; Searchable Encryption; Hadoop; Performance

1. INTRODUCTION

Storing data externally with a hosted provider becomes more and more attractive to companies which want to save costs on their own physical infrastructure. Since the cloud service providers have access to all data, clearly, storing sensitive data externally asks for solutions providing respective privacy precautions such that only the data owner is able to access the data.

Inspired by CryptDB [1], we developed a system to encrypt and store data on a database, all happening transparently to the

application. Hence, it can be used in the same way traditional databases are accessed to execute a large set of queries over the encrypted data. Introducing such an encrypted database solution to an existing application landscape requires an initialization phase where all unencrypted data is transferred and encrypted into the new database.

Since most of the encryption operations are slow, encrypting a plaintext table is very time-consuming, especially when the table is large. Using tables enabled for adjustable encryption [13] having multiple encryption layers for one database entry adds significantly to the computation time for the initial encryption. We show how to make the initial table encryption an automated process and much more efficient using a Hadoop cluster for parallelized data processing.

The rest of the report is structured as follows. Section 2 describes the technical details. In Section 3, we discuss the performance test and its result, and conclude with Section 4.

2. IMPLEMENTATION

In this section, we will discuss the technical details of how to encrypt the database in parallel.

2.1 Search over Encrypted Data

Inspired by CryptDB [1], we implemented a JDBC driver for connecting to database containing encrypted data. The goal of the driver is to realize accessing encrypted data transparently to the client application, which means a large set of regular SQL queries can be used to search over encrypted data.

SQL operations (equality search, range search, aggregations, etc.) require that data is stored with different encryption schemes. When encrypting a database, each plaintext data item is encrypted using multiple schemes, depending on the SQL operations to be executed on the data. In total there are five types of encryption schemes we use:

- Random (RND): RND has the highest security level. Two same plaintexts result in different ciphertexts. This scheme is used for secure data storage and retrieval only, no other SQL operation is supported on these ciphertexts. We use AES in CBC mode (with Padding).

- Deterministic (DET): For DET holds $DET(x) = DET(y)$, if $x = y$. Hence, equality operations on the ciphertext is supported. AES in ECB mode (with padding) is used.

- Order-preserving encryption (OPE): For OPE, if $x < y$, then $OPE(x) < OPE(y)$ holds. It supports SQL range queries on the ciphertext. We use the algorithm introduced by Boldyreva et al. [2].

- Additive homomorphic encryption (HOM): We use the Paillier algorithm [3] for aggregating encrypted values as it holds: $HOM(x) \cdot HOM(y) = HOM(x + y)$.

- Re-encryption (JOIN): For maximum security, all columns are encrypted with different keys. Joining two columns, however, requires them to be deterministically encrypted with the same key. With the encryption scheme introduced by Pohlig and Hellman [4] we support on demand re-encryption of a column to be on the same key as another column for join operations (see [13] for more details).

For the support of an initial maximum security and storage optimization, we use adjustable encryption [13]. This means a plaintext item x is encrypted in a layered approach with multiple encryption schemes such that, for instance, *RND(DET(OPE(x)))* holds. If during an SQL execution an in-between-layer is required, top layers are removed on demand to reveal the respective layer.

Obviously, even if stacked, we want the encryption schemes to keep their characteristics we listed above. Hence, schemes on a lower layer must have the same characteristics required for the layer stacked on top of it (e.g., OPE must be deterministic, if DET is stacked on top). We use four stack structures to support multiple SQL operations in one query (e.g., aggregation and a range condition). Moreover, we provide two stack structures for integers and one stack structure for strings. Table 1 gives an overview.

In Table 1, the row "Types" stands for the type of plaintext data the characteristics of the encryption schemes are actually applicable. For example, for integer or decimal values, the additive homomorphic encryption scheme is required, to actually enable aggregations; it is, however, not required for strings. For sorting items (with OPE) different paddings are used for integer and string values; moreover, in our use cases joins are only done with integer values such that we omit this layer for strings. Stack structure 1 is used for data retrieval to the client and group by selections only. Having AES-based encryption schemes in this stack is a very fast solution for decrypting result sets on the client.

Table 1 Encryption Structure

	Stack 1	Stack 2	Stack 3	Stack 4
Layer 1	DET	OPE	OPE	HOM
Layer 2	RND	RND	JOIN	
Layer 3			RND	
Types	Integer, String, Date, Decimal	String	Integer, Date, Decimal	Integer, Decimal
Usage	Retrieval, Group By	Range queries with strings	Joins, Equality, Range queries w/ numbers	Aggregation

2.2 Encryption

We use the implemented JDBC driver and a Hadoop cluster to encrypt the plaintext table. There are five steps in total for the complete process. The basic workflow is shown in Figure 2.

2.2.1 Set up

Firstly the cluster to encrypt the data needs to be set up. We use Apache Hadoop [5], Apache Sqoop [6], and Apache Oozie [7]. These tools are installed in the cluster.

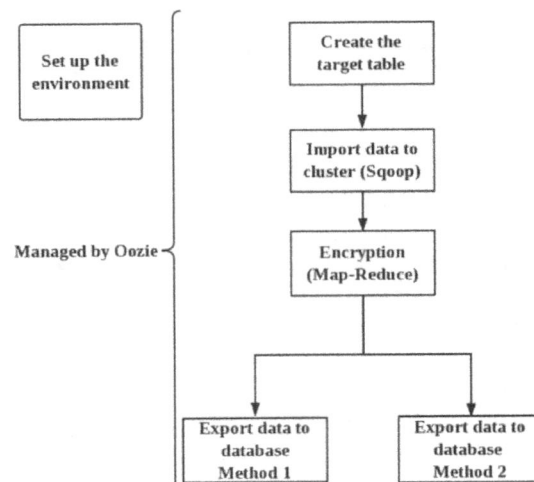

Figure 2. Workflow

Table 2 Plaintext Tables

Table Name	Number of Columns	Number of Entries	Size on Disk (KB)
BKPF	111	9,737,795	1,059,148
ORDERS	10	1,280,000	98,308
KNA1	175	14,554	3,076
KNB1	77	10,269	620
T001	79	269	448
T003	38	132	212
T005T	8	2,531	132
T016T	4	40	56
TBSLT	5	1,049	72

Table 3 Experiment Result

Table Name	Import data to cluster	Encryption	Export data to database	
			Method 1	Method 2
BKPF	1h42m	27h41m	About 24h	About 5d4h
ORDERS	1m40s	2h1m	23m	1h40m
KNA1	40s	19m	2m	10m
KNB1	1m	4m	50s	3m
T001	30s	2m	30s	40s
T003	30s	2m	30s	30s
T005T	30s	4m	30s	2m
T016T	30s	1m	30s	1m
TBSLT	30s	1m	30s	1m

Table 4 Encrypted Tables

Table Name	Number of Columns	Number of Entries	Size on Disk (KB)	Size vs. Plain-text
ENC_BKPF	227	9,737,795	~153,135k	144x
ENC_ORDERS	26	1,280,000	3,011,868	30x
ENC_KNA1	353	14,554	289,992	94x
ENC_KNB1	160	10,269	116,944	188x
ENC_T001	159	269	1,800	4x
ENC_T003	77	132	444	2x
ENC_T005T	17	2,531	4,324	33x
ENC_T016T	9	40	268	5x
ENC_TBSLT	11	1,049	516	7x

2.2.2 Create target table

We use the above mentioned stack structures to prepare and create the target table. Given the source table, for each of its plaintext columns, one or more encrypted columns will exist in in the encrypted table; each of these columns corresponds to exactly one stack. There will always be an encrypted column corresponding to Stack 1 for retrieving data. Which other stacks are created in addition is either selected automatically according to the source column's data type or is manually selected by the user. For instance, a plaintext integer column would have three encrypted columns in the target table, storing the encrypted data according to stack 1, 3, and 4. If it is an identifier column, the user might manually omit the column with HOM encryption (stack 4) as identifiers are usually not aggregated.

2.2.3 Import data to cluster

The third step is to import the plaintext data from the database to the cluster's file system called HDFS. To achieve this goal, we use Apache Sqoop. Sqoop is a tool for transferring data between Apache Hadoop and the relational database. The relational database can be from any database vendor. In our case, SAP HANA [9] is used. The imported data is stored in a CSV file type-like structure, which means each line in the file represents an entry of the table.

The performance of this step mainly depends on the database itself and the network between database and cluster. The data imported to the HDFS will be the input for next step.

2.2.4 Encryption

The forth step is to do the encryption on the cluster. It is a map-reduce process. As we have mentioned above, the imported data is in CSV file type, which means each line in the file represents an entry of the plaintext table. So in the map stage, the imported file is read line by line, and each line is encrypted using the encryption algorithms mentioned above. This step does not need the reduce stage. The output of this step is also CSV file(s) which is according to the encrypted table structure previously created.

The performance of this step mainly depends on the performance of the cluster.

2.2.5 Export data to database

The last step is to export the data from the cluster to the database. We implemented this step by two different methods.

The first method is to use Sqoop which is similar to Section 2.2.2. Sqoop export uses the INSERT SQL statement, which means it will use a statement like *INSERT INTO <TABLE> VALUES (<ROW>)* to export data from the Hadoop cluster to the target table. Since this method needs to iterate through all data line by line, it is quite slow. For some relational databases a batch mode is supported. Each time multiple lines can be inserted by using *INSERT INTO <TABLE> VALUES (<ROW1>), (<ROW2>), etc.*, and obviously this will make the exporting faster. As a result, the performance of the first method highly depends on if the database supports the batch mode INSERT. Moreover, it also depends on the condition of the network. And for some large tables, this exporting process requires the cluster connecting to the database for a long time, which may result in the connection being closed during the process.

The second method we implemented deals with exporting the data in a naïve way. This method requires the cluster having the Hadoop NameNode Web Interface installed. After the previous step (map-reduce encryption) is finished, the database server can directly download the output file(s) from the NameNode Web Interface. Then it obviously depends on the database which commands to be used to import the data into the database. In our case, using SAP HANA, the IMPORT FROM FILE [10] command is used.

The performance of the second method depends on the network and the database IMPORT performance.

2.2.6 Workflow management

The previous steps (Section 2.2.2 to Section 2.2.5) are all scheduled and managed by Apache Oozie. Oozie is a workflow scheduler tool to manage the Hadoop jobs. The reason to use Oozie is that it can make the implementation "cleaner", easier to modify, and more reliable.

3. EVALUATION

In this section, we will discuss our experiments with the above described setup and its performance.

3.1 Environment setup

SAP HANA is used as database. Typically for this database, all data is stored in memory in tables using column-based storage.

The Hadoop cluster resides on an internal virtual hosting environment. There is one master, twelve slaves, and one Ambari server [8]. The master machine has 8 CPUs, and 31.6 GB memory. The slave machines have each 8 CPUs, and 16 GB memory. All have between 100 and 300 GB available space.

3.2 Plaintext Tables

We have chosen 9 plaintext tables in total to test the performance. All the tables are standard SAP ERP tables and mainly come from the application of sFIN [11]. The details are shown in Table 3.

3.3 Time

The tables listed in Table 3 are encrypted one by one. There is only one job running in parallel, and before a new job is started, the cluster is cleaned. For all columns we create encrypted columns (stacks) according to the type of the plaintext column given with Table 1. We report on both methods to export the data to database (see Section 2.2.4). The results are showed in Table 4.

From Table 4, it is clear that the direct export using INSERT statements is much faster if it comes to large tables rather than using method 2 with CSV files. Method 2 takes about 5 times as much for processing then method 1. A reason we see is that in method 2 all encrypted data has to be extracted and copied from Hadoop's file system to the database server where it then has to be processed a second time for importing it with the IMPORT command.

3.4 Encrypted Tables

After the encryption, there are 9 encrypted tables corresponding to the plaintext tables. Their information is shown in Table 5.

3.5 Scalability test

We test the scalability of our solution with a midsized table ORDERS. We report on the scalability of the encryption with respect to the size of the table as well as with the size of the Hadoop cluster, i.e., number of working nodes.

3.5.1 Different table size

Firstly we use a fixed number of nodes (1 master server, 12 slave nodes) in cluster and change the table's size by randomly selecting a predefined number of entries from table ORDERS. And for exporting, we use method 1. The results are shown in Table 5.

Table 5 Scalability test for different table size

Number of entries	Time (m)			
	Import	Encryption	Export	Total
1,280,000	1.6	121	23	145.6
1,120,000	1.3	98.3	32	131.6
960,000	1.5	87.3	22	110.8
800,000	2.1	73.25	10.6	85.95
640,000	1.5	59.3	10.5	71.3
480,000	1	43	7	51
320,000	0.8	33	4.5	38.3
160,000	0.5	16	2.5	19
10,000	0.5	5.3	0.6	6.4

A more intuitive result is showed in Figure 3. From it, it is clear that with the linear increasing table size, the computation time also increases linearly.

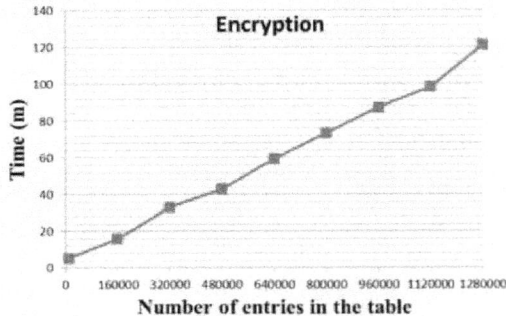

Figure 3: Computation time for different table sizes

3.5.2 Different number of nodes in cluster

We also test the influence of the number of nodes in cluster on the computation time. Because in the cluster only slave nodes store the data and do the computation, we increased the number of slave nodes from one node to 12 nodes in total. The complete table ORDERS is used for each encryption, remaining stable in its size. For exporting, again method 1 is used. The results are shown in Table 6.

Table 6 Scalability test for different number of nodes

Number of slave nodes	Time (m)			
	Import	Encryption	Export	Total
12	1.6	121	23	145.6
9	4	150	34	188
6	1.6	213.9	33	248.5
3	1.5	432.25	21.3	455.05
1	1.5	1498.5	25	1525

A more intuitive result is showed in Figure 4. From it, we can see the number of slave nodes affects the computation time and correlates directly with the number of nodes used. The time roughly drops to a third by using 3 nodes instead of only one. And it drops roughly to 1/12 when using 12 nodes.

4. CONCLUSION

In this report, we mainly talk about how to encrypt tables in parallel. After the environment setup, the idea is to divide the

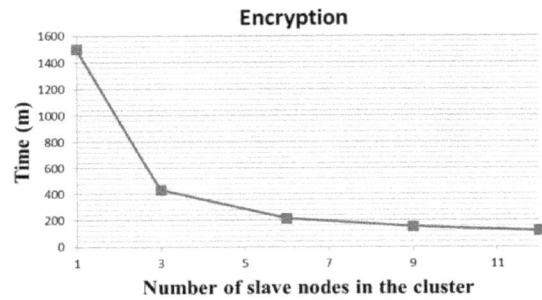

Figure 4: Computation time for different node numbers

process in three main steps: import data to cluster, encryption, and export data to database. For step "import data to cluster", Apache Sqoop is used. For step "encryption", Map-Reduce is used. In step "export data to database", there are two potential methods. The first one uses Sqoop too, and the second one is a naïve method where the data is copied to the database with a database-specific import command.

We have run tests using real world tables. The results show that an automated encryption solution is feasible and using a Hadoop cluster reduces encryption time drastically in a very scalable manner.

5. REFERENCES

[1] Popa, R. A., Redfield, C., Zeldovich, N., & Balakrishnan, H. 2011. Cryptdb: protecting confidentiality with encrypted query processing. In *Proceedings of the Twenty-Third ACM Symposium on Operating Systems Principles*.

[2] Boldyreva, A., Chenette, N., Lee, Y., & O'neill, A. 2009. Order-preserving symmetric encryption. In *Advances in Cryptology – EUROCRYPT*.

[3] Paillier, P. 1999. Public-key cryptosystems based on composite degree residuosity classes. In *Advances in cryptology – EUROCRYPT*.

[4] Pohlig, S. C., Hellman, M. E. 1978. An improved algorithm for computing logarithms over and its cryptographic significance (corresp.). In *Transactions on Information Theory*.

[5] *Apache Hadoop*. http://hadoop.apache.org/.

[6] *Apache Sqoop*. http://sqoop.apache.org/.

[7] *Apache Oozie*. http://oozie.apache.org/.

[8] *Apache Ambari*. http://ambari.apache.org/.

[9] *SAP HANA*. http://hana.sap.com/abouthana.html.

[10] *SAP HANA 'IMPORT FROM'*. http://help.sap.com/saphelp_hanaplatform/helpdata/en/20/f71 2e175191014907393741fadcb97/content.htm.

[11] *SAP Simple Finance aka sFIN*. http://scn.sap.com/docs/DOC-59882.

[12] Kerschbaum et al. 2013. Optimal Re-Emcryption Strategy for Joins in Encrypted Databases. In *Working Conference on Data and Applications Security and Privacy (DBSec)*.

[13] Florian Kerschbaum et al. 2013. Adjustably encrypted in-memory column-store. In *ACM Conference on Computer and Communications Security*.

Generating Secure Images for CAPTCHAs through Noise Addition

David Lorenzi[§], Pratik Chattopadhyay[†], Emre Uzun[§],
Jaideep Vaidya[§], Shamik Sural[†], Vijayalakshmi Atluri[§]
[§]Rutgers University, 1 Washington Park, Newark, NJ 07102, USA
{dlorenzi, emreu, jsvaidya, atluri}@rutgers.edu
[†]School of Information Technology, Indian Institute of Technology, Kharagpur, India
{pratikc, shamik}@sit.iitkgp.ernet.in

ABSTRACT

As online automation, image processing and computer vision become increasingly powerful and sophisticated, methods to secure online assets from automated attacks (bots) are required. As traditional text based CAPTCHAs become more vulnerable to attacks, new methods for ensuring a user is human must be devised. To provide a solution to this problem, we aim to reduce some of the security shortcomings in an alternative style of CAPTCHA - more specifically, the image CAPTCHA. Introducing noise helps image CAPTCHAs thwart attacks from Reverse Image Search (RIS) engines and Computer Vision (CV) attacks while still retaining enough usability to allow humans to pass challenges. We present a secure image generation method based on noise addition that can be used for image CAPTCHAs, along with 4 different styles of image CAPTCHAs to demonstrate a fully functional image CAPTCHA challenge system.

Categories and Subject Descriptors

K.4.4 [**Computers and Society**]: Electronic Commerce—*Security*; H.6.5 [**Management of Computing and Information Systems**]: Security and Protection—*Authentication*

1. INTRODUCTION

CAPTCHAs play an important role in guarding online assets from automated attacks and bots. They have been around in some form since the late 90's, and were popularized with the rise in public "free" online services such as hotmail or yahoo mail. The most common type of CAPTCHA in use is the text based CAPTCHA. This is due in part to its ease of implementation (generate random strings of alphanumeric characters) and scalability/robustness (large sample space of possible character combinations). However, many successful attacks that leverage various image processing techniques and computer vision techniques have been tar-

geted against this form of access control. Recently [3], convolutional neural networks (CNN), a deep-learning method, have been able to break the standard (at that time) reCAPTCHA challenges with 99% accuracy. As a result, the difficulty of the challenges served has increased, to the point that users have to frequently solve a few challenges due to the challenges being too distorted to decipher correctly, thus making them user unfriendly.

Image CAPTCHAs offer potential solutions to many of the shortcomings currently faced by text based CAPTCHAs [7, 11]. Their challenges lend themselves well to mobile and touch based devices, as well as traditional forms of human-computer interaction. However, image based CAPTCHAs are not without their own set of problems [10, 9], with scalability being a primary problem. The idea of a "secure" image CAPTCHA is not new, however in most cases the style of challenge question is different [12] such that the image is no longer the focus of security, as it normally is with image labeling or object recognition based image CAPTCHAs. Image based CAPTCHAs have also been used to crowdsource image labels while providing security [1]. It is difficult to find large archives of unique images that are tagged correctly. Image processing and computer vision tools can and have been used to perform attacks against image CAPTCHAs with results strong enough to keep image CAPTCHAs from being a premier method of access control [2, 4].

In [8], we presented a generalized methodology to transform existing images by applying various noise generation algorithms into variants that are resilient to image recognition attacks. As such, the "secure" image we generate utilizing noise algorithms are designed to thwart Reverse Image Search (RIS) engines [5] from finding exact matches of an image that can potentially lead to associated metadata compromising the integrity of the CAPTCHA challenge. The noise addition procedure also alters the image to the point where various computer vision (CV) algorithms have trouble performing their operations on the image. While it is true that the image becomes more distorted, it is still comprehensible to a human eye and can be used as a challenge question in an image CAPTCHA. The following section demonstrates how the images are generated and then used in the creation of an image CAPTCHA.

2. PROPOSED SYSTEM

It is worth noting that as a result of adding noise, the images produced are very "grainy" or "pixelated" in appearance – very similar to a snowy TV picture. Since the noise

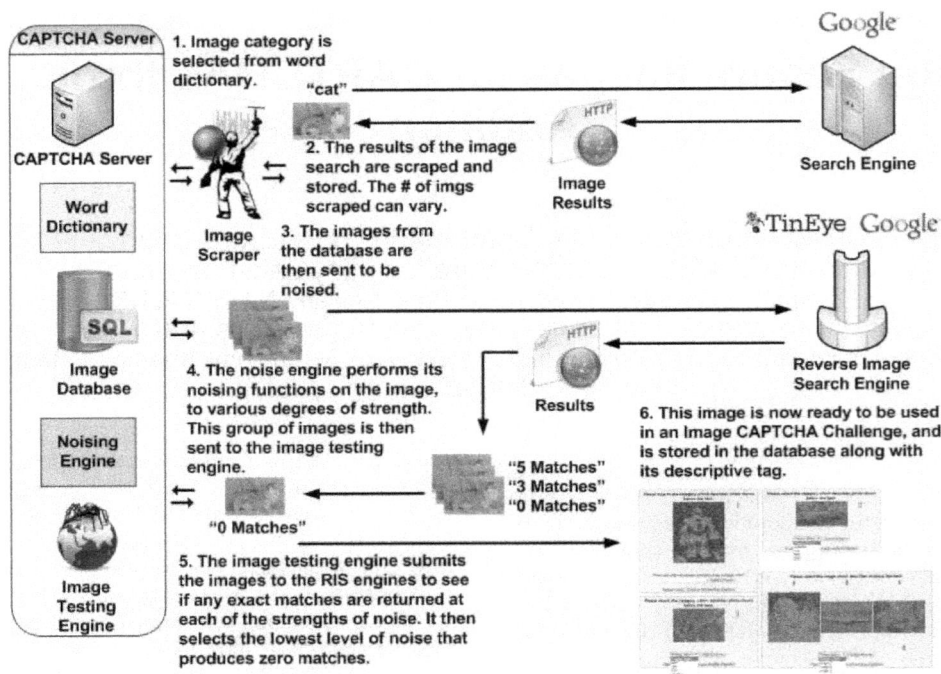

Figure 2: Image generation for CAPTCHA challenge

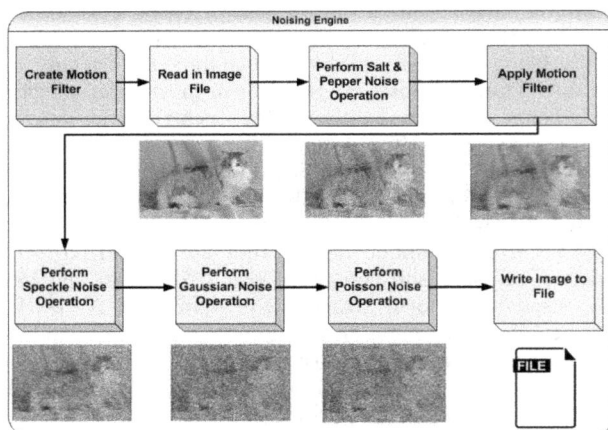

Figure 1: Procedure for producing a noisy image

introduced is primarily additive and multiplicative in nature, color values in various pixels get shifted around. When viewed as a number matrix, the original image and the produced image are widely different, and from the perspective of an automated attacker the pixel intensities of the noised image differ significantly from that of a structured image. However, when viewed by a human eye (along with a human mind behind it), the colors blend into an image that is coherent and cognizable (the "Pointillism effect"). Interestingly, this side effect of enhancing security actually does not impact usability negatively (to a point). In general, this effect is easier to achieve the further away your eye is from the image, or if the image is small in dimensions (scaled down). In honor of one of the co-creators of the Pointillism technique,

19th century French neo-impressionist painter Paul Signac, we name the procedure, SIGNAC (Secure Image Generation Noise Algorithms for CAPTCHAs).

SIGNAC is implemented using the MATLAB Image Processing Toolbox [6]. The basic idea is to use the function imnoise to add noise to the input image. The noise functions utilized in the method are the four generalized noise functions available in the MATLAB IPT (Gaussian, Speckle, Salt & Pepper, Poisson). While noising alone is sufficient to meet the criteria of security, frequently it requires an amount of noise that is near or exceeds the limits for a human to be able to comprehend what is depicted in the image. To improve usability, image filters can be applied to provide additional alterations, lowering the amount of noise required to meet the security criteria. Figure 1 demonstrates the noising process, while the script below gives an idea of the method in action. X is the image at the initial starting point when it is read into the IPT. $c1$ through $c5$ represent the image at various stages of its alteration. Note that this example is a multimethod output, as different noise and filter functions are being used to generate an image at each step. It is important to note that ordinality plays a large factor in the outcome of the image's success or failure in defeating an RIS engine. This script is designed to create the image filter, read in the image file, apply noise, filter the image, then apply noise 3 more times before writing the image out.

```
f=fspecial('motion',11,3)
x=imread('1.jpg')
c1=imnoise(x,'salt & pepper',0.35)
c2=imfilter(c1,f)
c3=imnoise(c2,'speckle',0.35)
c4=imnoise(c3,'gaussian',0,0.35)
c5=imnoise(c4,'poisson')
imwrite(c5,'1', 'jpg');
```

One of the more challenging aspects to generating secure images is that the level of noise required to prevent the RIS engine from returning a match varies with each individual image. As such, we have devised a system to handle the testing of images created with the noising process to ensure that any image used in a challenge will return zero RIS matches. The image testing engine provides feedback to the noising engine when generating the challenge images by submitting the noised image to an RIS engine and seeing if any matches are returned. The noising engine generates images in a stepwise manner (starting from 0.10 mean noise), incrementing the mean noise in the image by 0.05 each time until zero matches are achieved or a value of 0.45 mean noise is reached (the image is discarded if it goes higher, as humans will be unable to understand it). If desired, the image testing engine can have the noising engine stepwise decrements the mean noise by 0.01 until a match is returned again and then increase that value by 0.01 - providing the finest granularity for the minimum amount of noise required to defeat the RIS engine for that image. This gives the human user the best chance at comprehending the image while still meeting the security requirements. Figure 2 demonstrates the overall process flow.

3. DEMONSTRATION SCENARIO

For our live demonstration scenario, we provide an example security and usability analysis of an image found online using an image search engine with our image challenge testing script (this script is analogous to the image testing engine described in the system architecture section). We use MATLAB as a tool in conjunction with Tineye to test prospective images to be used as challenges in one of the four CAPTCHA schemes. The script is designed to provide a quick visual overview of the incrementalism required for testing various images against the "zero matches" security requirement to stop reverse image search attacks and hinder computer vision attacks. Figure 3 shows the results of the testing script for one image. One benefit of having such a script is that it allows image CAPTCHA researchers to test and look for features, styles, and composition in various images that lend themselves better for security use. This method of presentation also makes it easier to have a mechanical turk or other human method of verification provide answers to the "usability" of a particular noised image.

3.1 CAPTCHA Challenge Styles

We have created four different styles of CAPTCHA to test various levels of information revealed by what each challenge presents to the user. Thus, some challenges can be considered more difficult to answer because they provide fewer contextual clues for the test subject to determine what exactly it is that is being depicted in the image. In figures 4 - 7 the different styles are each demonstrated. Style 1 asks the user to enter a string of text that best describes the image. This occurs as a freeform response with no textual clues and is the most difficult of the challenges to answer correctly. Style 2 provides a dropdown box with 4 options for a user to choose. Style 3 provides a dropdown box with 5 options, one always being a "Not Here" (correct answer not listed) response. Style 4 presents a user with three images, and asks for them to select the image that is best described by the word given to them.

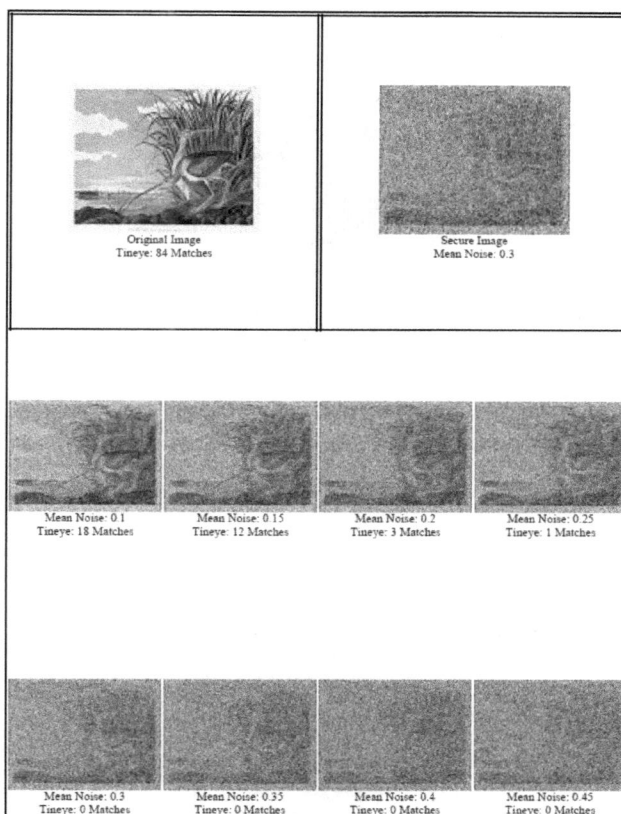

Figure 3: Image Analysis for CAPTCHA challenge

3.2 Future Work

Since RIS engines and CV tools can be accessed via online services, a clever CAPTCHA designer could write scripts that test images on various online tools to see if they meet the designer's security criteria - if they fail, the image can be discarded or reused later on at a higher level of noise. One can create a set of "blended" noised images where each image has just enough noise, for that particular image, to make it return zero matches. In order to achieve this, the noising algorithm can be stepped up or down depending on how the RIS engine responds. The script starts this testing process at 0.10 mean noise and increments by 0.10 depending on the number of returned matches. After no matches are returned, the noise can be stepped down by 0.05 until a match is returned again. The goal is reached when a granularity of +/- 0.01 is achieved with zero matches. For example, one image requires a mean of 0.12, another 0.17 and another 0.24 etc. This would then provide the optimum usability possible from this method. A similar method for noise can be used along with the CV algorithms as well. However, we feel this method would be required if these CAPTCHAs were to be deployed at a public usage scale.

4. REFERENCES

[1] P. Faymonville, K. Wang, J. Miller, and S. Belongie. Captcha-based image labeling on the soylent grid. In *Proceedings of the ACM SIGKDD Workshop on Human Computation*, HCOMP '09, pages 46–49, New York, NY, USA, 2009. ACM.

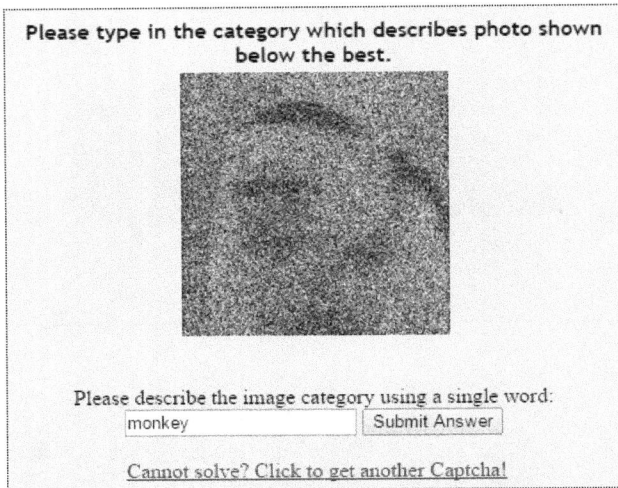

Figure 4: Image CAPTCHA Style 1

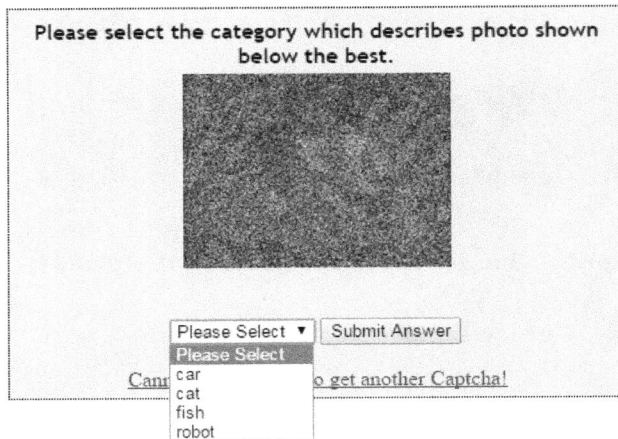

Figure 6: Image CAPTCHA Style 3

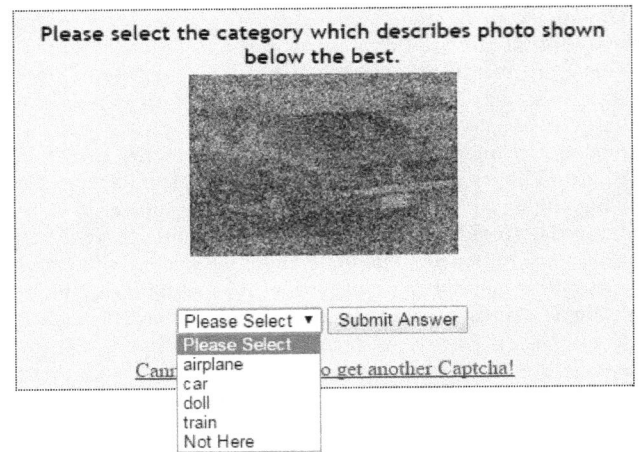

Figure 5: Image CAPTCHA Style 2

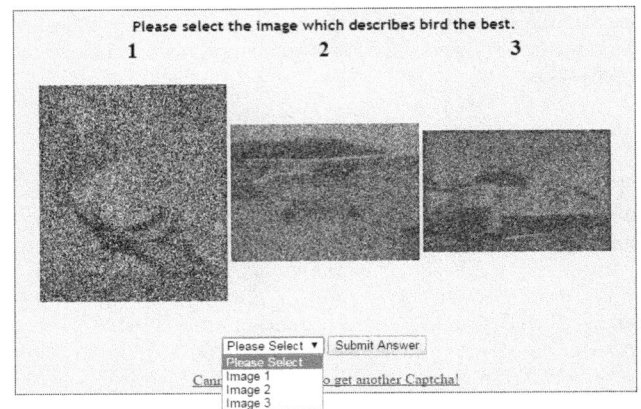

Figure 7: Image CAPTCHA Style 4

[2] C. Fritsch, M. Netter, A. Reisser, and G. Pernul. Attacking image recognition captchas. In S. Katsikas, J. Lopez, and M. Soriano, editors, *Trust, Privacy and Security in Digital Business*, volume 6264 of *Lecture Notes in Computer Science*, pages 13–25. Springer Berlin Heidelberg, 2010.

[3] I. J. Goodfellow, Y. Bulatov, J. Ibarz, S. Arnoud, and V. Shet. Multi-digit number recognition from street view imagery using deep convolutional neural networks. *CoRR*, abs/1312.6082, 2013.

[4] C. J. Hernandez-Castro, A. Ribagorda, and Y. Saez. Side-channel attack on the humanauth captcha. In *Security and Cryptography (SECRYPT), Proceedings of the 2010 International Conference on*, pages 1–7, July 2010.

[5] I. Inc. Tineye reverse image search. https://www.tineye.com/, Sept 2014.

[6] M. Inc. Documentation center - imnoise. http://www.mathworks.com/help/images/ref/imnoise.html, Sept 2014.

[7] S. R. Lang and N. Williams. Impeding captcha breakers with visual decryption. In *AISC '10*, pages 39–46, 2010.

[8] D. Lorenzi, E. Uzun, J. Vaidya, S. Sural, and V. Atluri. Enhancing the security of image captchas through noise addition. In *Proceedings of the 30th IFIP International Conference on Information Security and Privacy*, 2015.

[9] D. Lorenzi, J. Vaidya, S. Sural, and V. Atluri. Web services based attacks against image captchas. In *Information Systems Security*, volume 8303 of *Lecture Notes in Computer Science*, pages 214–229, 2013.

[10] D. Lorenzi, J. Vaidya, E. Uzun, S. Sural, and V. Atluri. Attacking image based captchas using image recognition techniques. In *Information Systems Security*, volume 7671 of *Lecture Notes in Computer Science*, pages 327–342, 2012.

[11] P. Matthews, A. Mantel, and C. C. Zou. Scene tagging: Image-based captcha using image composition and object relationships. In *ASIACCS '10*, pages 345–350, 2010.

[12] R. Ur-Rahman, D. Tomar, and S. Das. Dynamic image based captcha. In *CSNT 2012*, pages 90–94, May 2012.

A Logic of Trust for Reasoning about Delegation and Revocation

Marcos Cramer
University of Luxembourg

Diego Agustín Ambrossio
University of Luxembourg

Pieter Van Hertum
KU Leuven

ABSTRACT

In ownership-based access control frameworks with the possibility of delegating permissions and administrative rights, chains of delegated accesses will form. There are different ways to treat these delegation chains when revoking rights, which give rise to different revocation schemes. Hagström et al. [8] proposed a framework for classifying revocation schemes, in which the different revocation schemes are defined graph-theoretically; they motivate the revocation schemes in this framework by presenting various scenarios in which the agents have different reasons for revocating. This paper is based on the observation that there are some problems with Hagström et al.'s definitions of the revocation schemes, which have led us to propose a refined framework with new graph-theoretic definitions of the revocation schemes. In order to formally study the merits and demerits of various definitions of revocation schemes, we propose to apply the axiomatic method originating in social choice theory to revocation schemes. For formulating an axiom, i.e. a desirable property of revocation frameworks, we propose a logic, *Trust Delegation Logic (TDL)*, with which one can formalize the different reasons an agent may have for performing a revocation. We show that our refined graph-theoretic definitions of the revocation schemes, unlike Hagström et al.'s original definitions, satisfy the desirable property that can be formulated using TDL.

Categories and Subject Descriptors

K.6.5 [**Management of Computing and Information Systems**]: Security and Protection

Keywords

delegation, revocation, trust, logic, access control

1. INTRODUCTION

In ownership-based frameworks for access control, it is common to allow principals (users or processes) to grant both permissions and administrative rights to other principals in the system. Often it is desirable to grant a principal the right to further grant permissions and administrative rights to other principals. This may lead

to delegation chains starting at a *source of authority* (the owner of a resource) and passing on certain permissions to other principals in the chain.

Furthermore, such frameworks commonly allow a principal to revoke a permission that she granted to another principal. Depending on the reasons for the revocation, different ways to treat the chain of principals whose permissions depended on the second principal's delegation rights can be desirable. For example, if one is revoking a permission given to an employee because he is moving to another position in the company, it makes sense to keep in place the permissions of principals who received their permissions from this employee; but if one is revoking a permission from a user who has abused his rights and is hence distrusted by the user who granted the permission, it makes sense to delete the permissions of principals who received their permission from this user. Any algorithm that determines which permissions to keep intact and which permissions to delete when revoking a permission is called a *revocation scheme*. Revocation schemes are usually defined in a graph-theoretical way on the graph that represents which authorizations between the principals are intact.

Hagström et al. [8] have presented a framework for classifying possible revocation schemes along three different dimensions: the extent of the revocation to other grantees (propagation), the effect on other grants to the same grantee (dominance), and the permanence of the negation of rights (resilience). Since there are two options along each dimension, there are in total eight different revocation schemes in Hagström et al.'s framework. This classification was based on revocation schemes that had been implemented in database management systems [7, 6, 2, 3]. The framework's design decisions are carried over from these database management systems and are often not fully motivated. Furthermore, the behaviour of the revocation schemes is dependent on the conflict resolution policy of the system, which is not integrated into the framework.

We identify a number of problems with Hagström et al.'s framework and the definitions of the revocation schemes included in the framework. This motivates our refined framework, in which the conflict resolution policy is integrated into the framework, and in which the graph-theoretic definitions of the revocation schemes have been modified.

In order to avoid that our refined framework turns out to have undesirable properties like those we identified in Hagström et al.'s framework, we propose to formally study the merits and demerits of various definitions of revocation schemes using the axiomatic method originating in social choice theory. Which behaviour is desirable for a revocation scheme depends on the reasons for performing the revocation. So in order to formulate an axiom, i.e. a desirable property of revocation schemes, we propose a logic, *Trust Delegation Logic (TDL)*, with which one can formalize the different reasons an agent may have for performing a revocation. We show that our modified graph-theoretic definitions of the revocation schemes, unlike Hagström et al.'s original definitions, satisfy the desirable property that can be formulated using TDL.

The rest of the paper is structured as follows. In Section 2, we discuss related work, giving an overview of Hagström et al.'s framework as well as of the conflict resolution policies proposed in the literature. In Section 3 we motivate and define a refinement to Hagström et al.'s framework. In Section 4, we consider the diverse reasons for revocating on some example scenarios, and sketch how these reasons can be used to formulate the desirable behaviour of the revocation schemes. In Section 5, we motivate and define Trust Delegation Logic (TDL). In Section 6 we illustrate how the scenarios discussed in Section 4 can be formalized in TDL. In Section 7 we use TDL to formally formulate a desirable property for revocation frameworks, which our revocation framework satisfies. After discussing possible further work on the topic of this paper in Section 8, we conclude the paper in Section 9.

2. RELATED WORK

Hagström et al. [8] have introduced three dimensions according to which revocation schemes can be classified. These are called *propagation*, *dominance* and *resilience*:

Propagation. The decision of a principal i to revoke an authorization previously granted to a principal j may either be intended to affect only the direct recipient j or to propagate and affect all the other users in turn authorized by j. In the first case, we say that the revocation is *local*, in the second case that it is *global*.

Dominance. This dimension deals with the case when a principal losing a permission in a revocation still has permissions from other grantors. If these other grantors' revocation rights are dependent on the revoker, the revoker can dominate over these grantors and revoke the permissions from them. This is called a *strong* revocation. The revoker can also choose to make a *weak* revocation, where permissions from other grantors to a principal losing a permission are kept.

Resilience. This dimension distinguishes revocation by removal (deletion) of positive authorizations from revocation by issuing a negative authorization which just inactivates positive authorizations. In the first case another principal may grant a similar authorization to the one that had been revoked, so the effect of the revocation does not persist in time. In the second case a negative authorization will overrule any (new) positive permission given to the same principal, so its effect will remain until the negative permission is revoked. We call a revocation of the first kind a *delete* or *non-resilient* revocation, and a revocation of the second kind a *negative* or *resilient* revocation.

Since there are two possible choices along each dimension, Hagström et al.'s framework allows for eight different revocation schemes.

Delegation frameworks that allow issuing negative authorization can bring about a state in which a conflict may arise. If a principal is granted both a positive and a negative authorization for the same object, then we say that these two authorizations *conflict* each other. A system's *conflict resolution policy* determines how to resolve such a conflict. Here is a list of possible conflict resolution policies as described by Ruan and Varadharajan [11]:

Negative-takes-precedence: If there is a conflict occurring on the authorization for some object, the negative authorizations will take precedence over the positive one.

Positive-takes-precedence: Positive authorizations from i to j take precedence over negative authorizations from k to j for all $k \neq i$. This means that a negative authorization from i to j directly

inactivates only positive authorizations from i to j, and leaves other permission to j active.

Strong-and-Weak: Authorizations are categorized in two types, strong and weak. The strong authorizations always take precedence over the weak ones. Conflicts among strong authorizations are not allowed. In conflicts between weak authorizations negative ones take precedence. Note that the intended meaning of *strong* and *weak* in this policy differs from their meaning in Hagström et al.'s dominance dimension.

Time-takes-precedence: New authorizations take precedence over previously existing ones. Note that this policy will make negative authorizations non-resilient.

Predecessor-takes-precedence: If the principal i delegates (possibly transitively) some right to principal j, then authorizations issued by i to some other principal k concerning that right will take precedence over authorizations issued by j to k. In other words, the priority of subjects decreases as the privilege is delegated forward.

Hagström et al. assume the system to have either a negative-takes-precedence or a positive-takes-precedence conflict resolution policy. Note that under a negative-takes-precedence policy, a negative revocations on principal k dominates all positive authorizations to k, so that the difference between weak and stron negative revocations disappears.

3. REFINING THE REVOCATION FRAMEWORK

In this section we first analyze some problems with the revocation framework by Hagström et al. [8]. While analyzing the problems, we already informally sketch how we propose to solve them. Next we define a refined revocation framework in which all of these problems have been solved.

3.1 Problems with Hagström et al.'s framework

(1) In Hagström et al.'s framework, strong global revocations will propagate forward dominating over all the existing delegation chains, making them even stronger than desired. We illustrated this by an example:

EXAMPLE 1. *User A issues an authorization to users B and C. B also grants this authorization to C. If a strong global delete revocation (in Hagström et al.'s sense) is performed over the authorization from A to B, then the authorization A granted to C is also deleted. But since A granted this authorization to C independently from B, it seems unjustified to delete it (Hagström et al. give no motivation for this behaviour).*

(2) In Hagström et al.'s framework, the choice of a conflict resolution policy is not incorporated into the revocation framwork, even though it affects the behaviour of the dominance dimension. We extend the dominance dimension to incorporate the choice of how to resolve conflicts between positive and negative authorizations in the revocation framework. In our refined framework, there are three choices along the dominance dimension:

- **weak:** The principal performing the revocation only dominates over direct authorizations granted by herself, authorizations from other grantors are kept intact.
- **predecessor-takes-precedence (p-t-p):** The principal performing the revocation dominates over other grantors' authorizations that are dependent on her.
- **strong:** The principal performing the revocation dominates over all other grantors' authorizations.

Note that we now use the terminology from conflict-resolution policies as presented in [11] and in Section 2 for the choices on the dominance dimension. Hence "strong" now has a different meaning than in Hagström et al.'s framework: As long as Hagström et al.'s framework is combined with a positive-takes-precedence policy, the strong revocations in their framework have the same force as our p-t-p revocations. The strength of our strong revocations can only be achieved in Hagström et al.'s framework by combining it with a negative-takes-precedence policy.

It is not desirable to allow all users who have a delegation right to perform strong revocations. Hence we include in our framework the possibility for a principal to grant to another principal a special right to perform strong revocations to other users.

(3) In Hagström et al.'s framework, delete revocations are supposed be non-resilient, which according to Hagström et al. means that "another user may issue the same permission that was just revoked, and the effect of the revocation disappears". This property fails to be satisfied in global deletion revocations, as illustrated by this example:

EXAMPLE 2. *User A issues an authorization to user B, and B further grant this authorization to C. If A deletes the authorization given to B, then the authorization from B to C is also deleted. Reissuing the authorization from A to B will not re-instate the authorization from B to C as before the revocation.*

To avoid this problem in our framework, when a delete is performed, we do not delete the forward chain, but just inactivate it.

(4) Hagström et al. motivate the distinction between delete and negative revocations mainly through the notion of resilience as defined in Section 2. However, in weak revocations there can be no difference between a resilient and a non-resilient revocation, since a weak revocation does not affect authorizations issued by others than the revoker. They motivate the usage of weak negatives by pointing out that they are useful for temporary revocations. But since in our framework the forward chain does not get deleted in a delete revocation (see point (3)), a delete can also be easily undone, so that a delete revocation is a sensible choice even when the revocation is likely to be only temporary. Hence we do not need weak negative revocations.

Furthermore, p-t-p and strong deletes would have undesirable effects, as illustrated by the following example:

EXAMPLE 3. *User A issues an authorization to user B, and gives user C the right to perform strong revocations. User C performs a strong delete on B, removing without traces the authorization provided to B by A. Later A realizes that C cannot be trusted to perform strong revocations, and takes away B's right to do so. Even though C can no longer perform strong revocations, the effect of his strong delete persist: B does not have the right originally issued to him by A until someone issues a new authorization to him.*

Hence we do not have a p-t-p or strong delete revocation in our framework, but instead have the distinction between a resilient and a non-resilient negative for p-t-p and strong revocations.

To conclude, if the dominance of a revocation is p-t-p or strong, there are two options along the resilience dimension, non-resilient and resilient. But if the dominance is weak, there is no choice along the resilience dimension, and the revocation is characterized as a "weak delete". So there are five possible choices to be made along the dominance and resilience dimensions: weak delete, p-t-p non-resilient, p-t-p resilient, strong non-resilient, and strong resilient.

(5) Hagström et al. do not allow negative authorizations to be inactivated. The reason they give is that they "do not want a revocation to result in a subject having more permissions than before the revocation". However, the deletion of negative authorizations is allowed, even though it may have the same effect. We do allow

negative authorizations to be inactivated, but the only kind of revocation that can result in a subject having more permissions than before is a revocation of someone's right to perform strong revocations, and in this case this is a desirable property.

3.2 The refined framework

Let **S** be the set of principals (subjects) in the system, let **O** be the set of objects in the system and let **A** be the set of access types. For every object $o \in \mathbf{O}$, there is a *source of authority* (SOA), i.e. the manager of object o.

For any $\alpha \in \mathbf{A}$ and $o \in \mathbf{O}$, the SOA of o can grant the right to access α on object o to other principals in the system. Secondly, the SOA can delegate this granting right further. Thirdly, the SOA can grant the right to perform strong revocations and to delegate this right further. Accordingly we have three *permissions*: *access right* (A), *delegation right* (D) and *strong revocation right* (S). We assume that delegation right implies access right. The set $\{A, D, S\}$ of permissions is denoted by **P**.

Additionally to positive authorizations ($+$), our framework admits four different types of negative authorizations, *p-t-p resilient negative* ($-_{\mathrm{PR}}$), *p-t-p non-resilient negative* ($-_{\mathrm{PN}}$), *strong resilient negative* ($-_{\mathrm{SR}}$) and *strong non-resilient negative* ($-_{\mathrm{SN}}$). The set $\{+, -_{\mathrm{PR}}, -_{\mathrm{PN}}, -_{\mathrm{SR}}, -_{\mathrm{SN}}\}$ of authorization types is denoted by **T**.

DEFINITION 1. *An authorization is a tuple* $(i, j, \alpha, o, \tau, \pi, t)$, *where* $i, j \in S$, $\alpha \in A$, $o \in O$, $\tau \in T$, $\pi \in P$, $t \in \mathbb{Z}$.

The meaning of an authorization $(i, j, \alpha, o, \tau, \pi, t)$ is that at time point t principal i has granted to principal j an authorization of type τ for permission π concerning access type α on object o. We assume that all authorizations in the system are stored in an *authorization specification*. There is no interaction between the rights of principals concerning different access-object pairs (α, o). For this reason, we can consider α and o to be fixed for the rest of the paper, and can simplify $(i, j, \alpha, o, \tau, \pi, t)$ to (i, j, τ, π, t).

Since delegation right implies access right, an authorization $(i, j, +, D, t)$ can only be issued if an authorization $(i, j, +, A, t)$ is also issued. By taking the contrapositive, the connection is reversed for negative authorizations: For $\tau \neq +$, an authorization (i, j, τ, A, t) can only be issued if an authorization (i, j, τ, D, t) is issued.

We visualize an authorization specification by a labelled directed graph, as in Example 4, in which A is the SOA. For every authorization (i, j, τ, π, t) in the authorization specification, this graph contains an edge from i to j labelled τ, π, t. We refrain from showing the authorizations that can be implied to exist by the rules specified in the previous paragraph.

EXAMPLE 4. *An authorization specification*

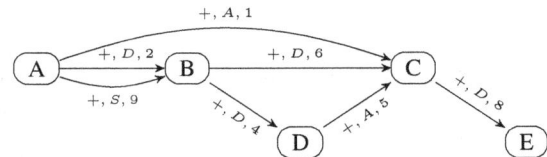

A negative authorization can inactivate other authorizations in the authorization specification. Which authorizations get inactivated by a negative authorization depends on which type of negative authorization it is. There are three basic ideas governing the inactivation of authorizations: Firstly, non-resilient authorizations can only inactivate previously issued authorizations, whereas resilient authorizations can also inactivate authorization issued after the negative authorization. Secondly, a strong negative authorization from i to j inactivates every positive authorization from some principal k to j, whereas a p-t-p authorization from i to j only inactivates an authorizations from k to j if k is dependent on i. Thirdly, any authorization that is no longer connected back to the SOA through active authorizations is inactivated.

In order to formally specify which authorizations get inactivated when issuing a negative authorization, we simultaneously define the notions of an authorization being *active* and an authorization being *directly inactivated* in Definitions 2 and 3.[1] The auxiliary notion of a directly inactivated authorization captures the idea of an authorization from k to j being inactivated by a strong negative authorization from i to j.

DEFINITION 2. *An authorization* (i, j, τ, π, t) *is* active *if it is* not *directly inactivated and there are principals* $p_1, \ldots, p_n, p_{n+1}$ *and integers* $t_1, \ldots, t_n$ *satisfying the following properties:*
(i) $p_1 = SOA$, $p_n = i$, $p_{n+1} = j$ and $t_n = t$;
(ii) *for* $1 \leq l < n$ *there is an authorization* $(p_l, p_{l+1}, +, \pi', t_l)$ *that is* not *directly inactivated, where* $\pi' = S$ *if either* $\tau \in \{-SR, -SN\}$ *or* $\pi = S$, *and* $\pi' = D$ *otherwise;*
(iii) *there do not exist* l, m *with* $1 \leq l \leq m \leq n$ *and an authorization* $(p_l, p_{m+1}, \tau', \pi'', t')$ *such that* $\pi'' = \pi$ *and* $\tau = +$ *if* $m = n$, *and* $\pi'' = \pi'$ *otherwise, and such that either* $\tau' = -PN$ *and* $t' > t_m$ *or* $\tau' = -PR$.

DEFINITION 3. *An authorization* $(i, j, +, \pi, t)$ *is* directly inactivated *if there is an* active *authorization* $(k_1, j, -SR, \pi, t_1)$ *or there is an* active *authorization* $(k_2, j, -SN, \pi, t_2)$ *with* $t_2 > t$.

A principal j has the right to access of type α on object o iff j is the SOA or there is an active authorization of the form $(i, j, \alpha, o, +, A, t)$ or $(i, j, \alpha, o, +, D, t)$. j has the right to perform strong revocations concerning action α on object o iff j is the SOA or there is an active authorization of the form $(i, j, \alpha, o, +, S, t)$. Strong negative authorizations towards the SOA are disallowed.

In Definition 4, we define the ten revocation schemes of our refined framework. We use W, P, S, L, G, N, R and D as abbreviations for *weak, p-t-p (predecessor-takes-precedence), strong, local, global, non-resilient, resilient* and *delete* respectively. Note that when defining the revocation schemes, we do not need to specify which of the authorizations get inactivated, because Definition 2 already tells us what to inactivate. Hence we just specify which authorizations get added and/or deleted.

DEFINITION 4. *Let* i, j *be principals, and* $\pi \in \{A, D, S\}$.
- *A WGD revocation for permission* π *from* i *to* j *at time* t *consists of deleting any authorization of the form* $(i, j, +, \pi, t')$.
- *For* $\delta \in \{P,S\}$ *and* $\rho \in \{N,R\}$, *a* $\delta G\rho$ *revocation for permission* π *from* i *to* j *at time* t *consists of issuing the negative authorization* $(i, j, -\delta\rho, \pi, t)$.
- *For* $(\delta, \rho) \in \{(W,D), (P,N), (P,R), (S,N), (S,R)\}$, *a* $\delta L\rho$ *revocation for permission* π *from* i *to* j *at time* t *consists of deleting and adding the same revocations as in a* $\delta G\rho$ *revocation from* i *to* j, *and* – *if* π *is* D *or* S – *additionally adding an authorization* (i, l, τ, π', t') *for every authorization* (j, l, τ, π', t') *such that* $\pi' = S$ *if* $\pi = S$, *and* π' *is either* D *or* A *if* $\pi = D$.

Since delegation right implies access right, a revocation for permission A can only be performed if the corresponding revocation for permission D is performed at the same time.

---

[1]These definitions inductively depend on each other. They should be read as an inductive definition with the well-founded semantics [5]. In Appendix A we discuss some of the issues resulting from the inductive interdependence of these definitions.

3.3 Examples of revocations

Here are three examples for different revocations from B to C on the authorization specification from Example 4. Examples for the other seven revocation schemes of our framework can be found in Appendix B. In all examples, we show the effect of simultaneous revocations for permissions A and D. In order to illustrate better the difference between resilient and non-resilient revocations, we show the state of the authorization specification after C reissues the previously issued authorization to D after the revocation.

EXAMPLE 5. *Weak Local Delete revocation from* B *to* C

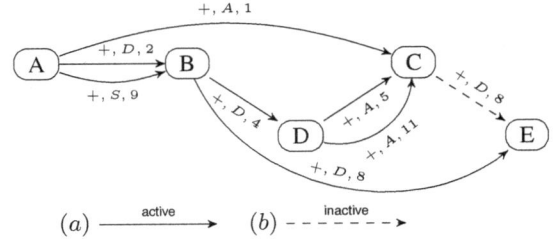

EXAMPLE 6. *P-t-p Global Non-resilient revocation from* B *to* C

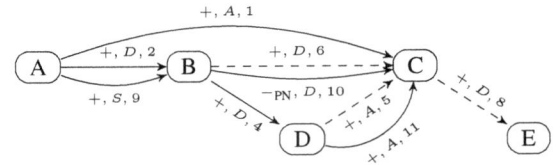

EXAMPLE 7. *Strong Global Resilient revocation from* B *to* C

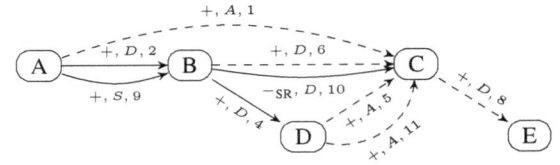

4. REASONS FOR REVOCATING

Hagström et al. have motivated the variety of revocation schemes by sketching various scenarios in which the principals performing the revocation have different reasons for revocating, so that different behaviour of the revocation is desirable. In order to study the desirable behaviour of the various revocation schemes, in this section we first present some scenarios, which we use to illustrate the different reasons the revocator has to perform the revocation, based on her level of trust or distrust towards the revokee. Having presented the scenarios, we informally sketch how we want to define the desirable behaviour of the various revocation schemes. These ideas will be formalized in subsequent sections.

4.1 Four scenarios

SCENARIO 1. *User A caught user C leaking information to a third-party. A revokes C's rights, ensuring that C cannot be given access by other users in the system.*

In this scenario user A had trusted user C in the past, thus issuing him an authorization, but now A distrusts principal C due the fact that he has leaked information to a third-party. So A will perform a *P-t-p Global Resilient* revocation, and – if she has strong revocation

176

right – additionally a *Strong Global Resilient* revocation, both in order to remove the authorization she had granted and to forbid as many other principals as possible to grant new authorizations to C.

SCENARIO 2. *User C is leaving to join the rival company. When user A notices the situation, she preemptively blocks C's capabilities (but keeping the authorizations previously issued by C).*

In this scenario user A had trusted user C in the past, thus issuing him an authorization. Since C is leaving to the rival company, A now distrusts C to access files or to newly delegate access right to others, but since A never misused any rights, A still has trust in the delegation authorization previously issued by C. So A will perform a *P-t-p Local Resilient* revocation and – if possible – a *Strong Local Resilient* revocation, in order to remove the authorizations that had been granted to C and to forbid as many other principals as possible to grant new authorizations to C, at the same time preserving the effect of authorizations that C had previously delegated.

SCENARIO 3. *User A hears the rumour that user B has received a bribe, but A does not know whether the rumour is true. Upon informing other users, A revokes B's rights, allowing other users to re-issue them.*

In this scenario, A no longer trusts B since she has heard the rumour about B, so she will revoke B's rights. But since A does not know whether the rumour is true, A allows other users to give the rights back to B (A will tell others about the rumour and trusts them to only give the rights back to B if they know the rumour to be false). So A will perform a *P-t-p Global Non-resilient* revocation and – if possible – a *Strong Global Non-resilient* revocation, in order to inactivate the previously issued authorizations granted to B, at the same time allowing other users to newly grant authorizations to B.

SCENARIO 4. *User A is revising the authorizations she had granted in the past. During the process A finds an authorization to user C, whom A does not remember.*

In this scenario user A had trusted user C in the past, thus issuing him an authorization, but now A neither trusts nor distrusts C, as she has no recollection of who C is or why the authorization had been granted. So A will perform a *Weak Global Delete* in order to remove the authorization she had granted to C without affecting authorizations granted to C by other users.

4.2 Desirable behaviour of revocation schemes

When explaining the above scenarios, we referred to the level and manner of trust or distrust between the revoker and the revokee in order to motivate the choice of different revocation schemes in different scenarios. The main novel idea of this paper is to formalize this reasoning about trust, delegation and revocation in such a way that we can formulate desirable properties that graph-theoretic definitions of revocation schemes should satisfy. Before we present this formalization, we will – for the rest of this section – first sketch the ideas behind this formalization and these desirable properties.

In Section 5, we will define *Trust Delegation Logic* (TDL), a logic that allows us to reason about the different levels and manners of trust or distrust that we find in the above four scenarios. One central idea in this logic is that A grants B the right to further delegate some right only if A trusts B to make correct judgments about who should be given that right. By expressing her trust in B to make correct judgments about something, A commits herselves to the truth of judgments that she has not made herself, namely the judgments that B has committed himself to. When A makes a judgment herself, we say that A has *explicit belief* in the judgment,

whereas a judgment that A is committed to in the light of a principal trusted by A believing the statement is an *implicit belief* of A. Trust of principal A in principal B is modelled as A's belief in B's trustworthy. Depending on whether A's belief is explicit or implicit, we can also call this trust explicit or implicit. For example, if A expresses trust in B concerning the action of expressing trust in other principals, and B expresses trust in C, then A explicitly trusts B and implicitly trusts C.

A further central idea is that a principal A should have access right of access type α iff the SOA of that object trusts A, either explicitly or implicitly, concerning access α. Delegation chains correspond to chains of principals along whom an implicit trust in some principal can project upwards towards the SOA. A revocation takes place when at some point along such a chain of principals, a principal stops trusting in the next principal on the chain, thus disabling this upward projection of implicit trust.

TDL allows us to model different ways in which a principal can stop trusting or start distrusting another principal. Some of these ways have been illustrated in the above four scenarios. The various revocation schemes correspond to these various ways of stopping to trust.

Given these explanations, we can now sketch how TDL allows us to formulate a desirable property for graph-theoretic definitions of revocation schemes: The graph-theoretic definitions of the revocation schemes should be such that for any given delegation and revocation interaction between the principals, an active authorization to a principal A should exist in a graph if and only if – translating the delegation and revocation behaviour to TDL – the SOA believes A to be trustworthy for the access in question.

5. A LOGIC FOR REASONING ABOUT DELEGATION AND REVOCATION

In this section we present a logic for formalizing the reasons for revoking delegations. This logic, which we call *Trust Delegation Logic* (TDL), is a first-order multi-modal logic with both classical negation and negation-as-failure. TDL formalizes both the relation of trust between principals and the action of announcing one's trust in another principal by delegating some right to him/her/it. In developing TDL, we have taken over some ideas from [4] and [1].

We first define the syntax of TDL. Next we motivate its constructs and some of its axioms by sketching how we apply TDL for modelling delegation and revocation. After that we formally define the proof theory of TDL, briefly motivating the remaining axioms. TDL is only defined proof-theoretically, i.e. it does not have a formal semantics, since this is not needed for the application that we have in mind.

5.1 TDL syntax

There are five types of objects, *principal, access, time point, set of principal-time-pairs* and *announcement modality*. SOA is a constant symbol of type *principal*, $\emptyset$ is a constant symbol of type *set of principal-time-pairs*, B, $\mathcal{B}$, K and $\mathcal{K}$ are constants of type *announcement modality*, and ∞ and all integers are constants of type *time point*. *scons* is a ternary function symbol taking a term of type *principal*, a term of type *time* and a term of type *set of principal-time-pairs*, and returning a term of type *set of principal-time-pairs*. We use t, t', t_2, t_3 as *time point* variables, i, j, k as *principal* variables, $\Sigma, \Sigma', \Sigma_2$ as variables of type *set of principal-time-pairs*, α as an *action* variable, m as an *announcement modality* variable, and x as a variable of arbitrary type. Formulae of TDL are defined by the following EBNF rule:

$$\varphi ::= \neg\varphi \mid \sim\varphi \mid (\varphi \wedge \varphi) \mid \forall x\, \varphi \mid T_i\alpha \mid T_i^t\varphi \mid T_i\mathbb{D}\alpha \mid T_i\mathbb{S}\alpha \mid$$
$$B_{i,\Sigma}^t\varphi \mid K_{i,\Sigma}^t\varphi \mid I_i^t m\varphi \mid R_{i,\Sigma}^t m\varphi \mid r_i^t a \mid t > t' \mid (i,t) \in \Sigma$$

We write $\varphi \rightarrow \psi$ for $\neg(\varphi \wedge \neg\psi)$, $\varphi \leftrightarrow \psi$ for $(\varphi \rightarrow \psi) \wedge (\psi \rightarrow \varphi)$, $\exists t > t'\, \varphi$ for $\exists t\, (t > t' \wedge \varphi)$, and $\exists x\, \varphi$ for $\neg\forall x\, \neg\varphi$. We drop brackets according to usual conventions. If φ is of the form $\neg\psi$, $\bar\varphi$ denotes ψ. Else $\bar\varphi$ denotes $\neg\varphi$.

While $\neg\varphi$ is the classical negation of φ, $\sim\varphi$ is negation as failure, i.e. $\sim\varphi$ is provable when φ is not provable.

$\emptyset$ refers to the empty set, and given a set Σ of principal-time-pairs, $scons(i,t,\Sigma)$ refers to the set $\Sigma \cup \{(i,t)\}$ ($scons$ stands for *set constructor* [9]). The following two axioms model this behaviour of $\emptyset$ and $scons$:

$$(\emptyset)\; \forall i\, \forall t\, \neg(i,t) \in \emptyset$$
$$(scons)\; \forall i,j,t,t',\Sigma\, ((i,t) \in scons(j,t',\Sigma) \leftrightarrow$$
$$(i = j \wedge t = t') \vee (i,t) \in \Sigma)$$

For the sake of readability, we abuse notation by using common set-theoretic notation in TDL formulas, writing for example $\Sigma \cup \{(i,t)\}$ instead of $scons(i,t,\Sigma)$, and $\{(i,t),(j,t')\}$ instead of $scons(j,t',scons(i,t,\emptyset))$.

5.2 Motivating TDL

The formula $r_i^t\alpha$ intuitively means that at time t, i has access right of access type α (the object o which may be accessed with access type α is not made explicit in TDL).

As [4], we make a distinction between *belief* and *strong belief*: A principal who *believes* φ at time t (denoted $B_{i,\Sigma}^t\varphi$) has some justification for φ but believes that the justification might be wrong. A principal i who *strongly believes* φ at time t (denoted $K_{i,\Sigma}^t\varphi$) on the other hand believes that his/her/its justification for φ is correct. The Σ in the subscript of the belief operators indicates whether the belief is explicit or implicit (see Section 4.2 for this distinction): If Σ is $\emptyset$, it is explicit belief. If Σ is a non-empty set, the belief is implicit, and Σ indicates the principals who mediate this implicit belief together with the time points of their beliefs that mediate this belief. For example, if i trusts j at time t, j trusts k at time t', and k believes φ at time t_2, then i implicitly believes φ at time t, and this implicit belief is mediated by j and k through their beliefs at time t' and t_2 respectively: $B_{i,\{(j,t'),(k,t_2)\}}^t\varphi$.

Similarly as in [1], the fact that a principal i trusts a principal j on access α is formalized in TDL by a formula of the form $K_{i,\Sigma}^t T_j\alpha$. Here $T_j\alpha$ can be read intuitively as "j is trustworthy on access α". This way of formalizing the trust relation between two agents has the advantage of formally clarifying the difference between not trusting someone and actively distrusting someone, the first being formalized by $\neg K_{i,\Sigma}^t T_j\alpha$ (i.e. i lacks a strong belief about the trustworthiness of j), and the second by $K_{i,\Sigma}^t \neg T_j\alpha$ (i.e. i believes that j not trustworthy). Furthermore, weak distrust ($B_{i,\Sigma}^t \neg T_j\alpha$) is a useful formalization for the reserved kind of distrust that we have in Scenario 3.

TDL allows us to model five different levels of trust between a principal i and a principal j: *Strong trust*, where i strongly believes that j is trustworthy ($K_{i,\Sigma}^t T_j\alpha$), *weak trust* ($B_{i,\Sigma}^t T_j\alpha \wedge \neg K_{i,\Sigma}^t T_j\alpha$), *lack of trust* ($\neg B_{i,\Sigma}^t T_j\alpha \wedge \neg B_{i,\Sigma}^t \neg T_j\alpha$), *weak distrust* ($B_{i,\Sigma}^t \neg T_j\alpha \wedge \neg K_{i,\Sigma}^t \neg T_j\alpha$), and *strong distrust* ($K_{i,\Sigma}^t a \neg T_j\alpha$). The distinction between weak trust and lack of trust will not be relevant for modelling the reasoning about delegation and revocation, but the distinction between the remaining four levels of trust will be relevant.

Additionally to trust in someone on an action, the logic can also express epistemic trust: $K_{i,\Sigma}^t T_j^{t'}\varphi$ intuitively means that i trusts j not to make mistakes in judgements about the truth value of φ, if the judgement is made before time point t'. The time point at which the judgement was made needs to be considered in order to correctly model local revocations, in which an agent still trusts the authorizations previously produced by the revokee, but does not trust new authorizations issued by the revokee (see Scenario 2).

The action of granting to j the right to perform action α is modelled in TDL by the action of publicly announcing one's trust in j on action α. Whenever one makes a public announcement, the announcement gets marked as an announcement of belief (B), strong belief (K), lack of belief ($\mathcal{B}$) or lack of strong belief ($\mathcal{K}$). [4] uses the letter I for the action of informing someone, which is similar to the action of public announcement; so we have decided to use the letter I to denote public announcements: For example, $I_i^t K\varphi$ intuitively means that i publicly announces its strong belief in φ at time t. $I_i^t K T_j\alpha$ means that i announces its strong trust in j on action α, and corresponds to i issuing a positive authorization for j with permission α at time t. Performing a Weak Global Delete revocation for permission α is achieved by the public announcement $I_i^t \mathcal{B} T_j\alpha$, with which i retracts its trust in j by announcing that it no longer believes j to be trustworthy.

If i wanted to give j the right to give any principal k the right to perform access α, i could achieve this by publicly announcing its strong trust in j concerning judgements about the trustworthiness of other principals: $I_i^t K\; \forall k\; T_j^\infty T_k\alpha$. If i was trusted by the SOA to make such an announcement, then j would now be trusted by the SOA to announce its trust in any principal k on access α, i.e. to grant the right to perform access α to any principal. However, j would not yet be permitted to delegate to someone else the right to grant this right. To give j this right, the i's announcement would have to be $I_i^t K\; \forall k_1 {}^\infty\; \forall k_2\; T_{k_1}^\infty T_{k_2}\alpha$. After this announcement, j can make an announcement of the form $I_j^{t'} K\; \forall k_2\; T_{k_1}^\infty T_{k_2}\alpha$, i.e. j can grant to some principal k_1 the right to grant to some further principal k_2 the right to perform access α.

This method can be used to model delegation with an arbitrary bound on the length for the delegation chain. But both Hagström et al.'s framework and our refinement of it do not put any bound on the length of delegation chains. In order to use this method for modelling delegation with no bound on the length of the delegation chain, we would have to allow principals to make infinitely many public announcements at once. In order to avoid this complication, we have introduced a third kind of trust, denoted $T_i\mathbb{D}\alpha$. Its intuitive meaning is that i is trusted to delegate the right to perform access α. Formally, its intended semantics is that $T_j\mathbb{D}\alpha$ should imply every formula in the infinite set $\{T_j\alpha,\; \forall k\; T_j^\infty T_k\alpha,\; \forall k_1 T_j^\infty\; \forall k_2\; T_{k_1}^\infty T_{k_2}\alpha,\; \dots\}$. This is achieved by the following axiom governing the behaviour of $T_i\mathbb{D}\alpha$:

$$(T\mathbb{D})\; T_i\mathbb{D}\alpha \rightarrow T_i\alpha \wedge T_i^\infty T_j\mathbb{D}\alpha$$

Using this new kind of trust, we can use the public announcement $I_i K T_j\mathbb{D}\alpha$ to model i's issuing a positive authorization for j with permission D at time t. $I_i^t \mathcal{B} T_j\mathbb{D}\alpha$ models i's performing a Weak Global Delete revocation on j for permission $\mathbb{D}$.

Performing a P-t-p Global Resilient revocation can be modelled by announcing strong distrust in another principal: $I_i^t K \neg T_j\alpha$ or $I_i^t K \neg T_j\mathbb{D}\alpha$. If i explicitly announces its distrust j in this way, i thereby prevents an implicit belief in the trustworthiness of j to be passed through i to the SOA. Hence j will need to be connected to the SOA via some trust chain that is independent of i in order to get access or delegation right.

If i's strong distrust in j corresponds to a p-t-p revocation, what will correspond to a strong revocation? The answer is that for a strong revocation i needs to make an announcement that will ensure that the SOA does not trust j. For if the SOA is ensured not to trust j, then j's rights are blocked, just as after a strong revocation. Of course, in blocking j's rights in this way, i will have to make use of the fact that the SOA has – either directly or indirectly – granted i the right to perform a strong revocation. As a first attempt at modelling strong revocation and the right to perform strong revocations in TDL, it therefore makes sense to consider the following approach (for simplicity, we restrict ourselves to strong revocations for permission α):

APPROACH 1. $I_i^t K \neg T_j \alpha$ models not only p-t-p revocation, but also strong revocation. The stronger effect of strong revocation is achieved by having the SOA believe in i's judgements of other principals non-trustworthiness when i has the strong revocation right. So i's issuing a positive authorization to j for permission S should be modelled by i announcing j to be trusted on distrusting other principals: $I_i^t K \forall k \; T_j^\infty \neg T_k \alpha$.

The problem with this approach is that it would lead to blocked access in some situations where access should be granted. Suppose for example that the SOA grants A strong revocation right, A grants this right further to B, and B uses this right to issue a strong negative authorization to C. Furthermore, the SOA grants simple access right to A, who grants this further directly to C. So far, C does not have access, since its access is blocked by the strong negative authorization issued by B. But suppose next that the SOA globally revokes A's strong revocation right. Then B also loses its strong revocation right, so that the negative authorization issued by B becomes inactive. Hence C should now have access. But with the above approach, the fact that A granted B the strong revocation right means that A trusts B on distrusting other principals. Since B still distrusts C, this would mean that A implicitly distrusts C, so that C cannot have access based on a trust chain going through A.

To solve this problem, we model i's performing a Strong Global Resilient revocation on j for permission α by i announcing that the SOA should strongly distrust j: $I_i^t K \forall t \; K_{SOA,\emptyset}^t \neg T_j \alpha$. Note that nested belief modalities are interpreted in a deontic way: $K_{i,\emptyset}^t K_{j,\emptyset}^t \varphi$ means that i strongly believes that j *should* strongly believe that φ. Granting i strong delegation right should make i being trusted on judgements about the SOA's strong distrust in other principals. In order to also be able to model performing a Strong Global Resilient revocation for permission S, we need to introduce a fourth kind of trust denoted $T_i \mathbb{S} \alpha$, for reason similar as the reasons for introducing $T_i \mathbb{D} \alpha$. The intuitive meaning of $T_i \mathbb{S} \alpha$ is that i is trusted in judgements about the SOA's strong distrust in other principals; here we need to allow for public announcements of distrust of various kinds: $\neg T_j \alpha$, $\neg T_j \mathbb{D} \alpha$ and $\neg T_j \mathbb{S} \alpha$. Furthermore, $T_i \mathbb{S} \alpha$ should imply that i is trusted to delegate the right to perform strong revocations, i.e. to consider another principal k trustworthy for performing strong revocations. The following axiom captures all this:

$$(T\mathbb{S}) \; T_i \mathbb{S} \alpha \rightarrow T_i^\infty T_j \mathbb{S} \alpha \wedge T_i^\infty \forall t \; K_{SOA,\emptyset}^t \neg T_j \alpha \; \wedge$$

$$T_i^\infty \forall t \; K_{SOA,\emptyset}^t \forall k \; \forall t_2 \; \neg T_j^{t_2} T_k \mathbb{D} \alpha \wedge T_i^\infty \forall t \; K_{SOA,\emptyset}^t \neg T_j \mathbb{S} \alpha$$

A principal i may epistemically trust both a principal who believes φ and a principal who believes $\neg \varphi$. In such a situation we do not want i to implicitly hold the inconsistent beliefs that φ and that $\neg \varphi$, because we want implicit belief to stay consistent. Instead, we want i to implicitly believe neither φ nor $\neg \varphi$. So the principle that i's epistemic trust in j concerning φ and j's belief in φ together imply i's implicit belief in φ cannot hold without exception. Instead,

we say that if i epistemically trusts j concerning φ and j believes φ, then i has a *reason* to believe φ. To deduce that i believes φ from the fact that i has a reason to believe φ we additionally require there to be no reason for i to believe $\neg\varphi$. In TDL, $R_{i,\Sigma}^t B\varphi$ (respectively $R_{i,\Sigma}^t K\varphi$) denotes the fact that at time t, i has a reason to believe (respectively to strongly believe) φ implicitly, mediated by Σ. In order for the absence of a reason for i to believe $\neg\varphi$ to be provable, it needs to be formulated using negation-as-failure rather than classical negation: $\sim \exists \Sigma \; R_{i,\Sigma}^t B \neg \varphi$.

5.3 TDL proof theory

In order to correctly capture the intended functioning of negation-as-failure in TDL's proof theory, we need TDL's deducibility relation $\Gamma \vdash \varphi$ to be defined in such a way that $\Gamma \nvdash \varphi$ in general implies $\Gamma \vdash \sim \varphi$. This can be achieved by defining this deducibility relation inductively[2] as follows:

DEFINITION 5. *We define $\Gamma \vdash \varphi$ to be the case if one of the following conditions holds:*

- $\varphi \in \Gamma$
- φ *is an axiom of TDL*
- *For some formula ψ, $\Gamma \vdash \psi$ and $\Gamma \vdash \psi \rightarrow \varphi$ (modus ponens)*
- φ *is of the form $K_{i,\Sigma}^t \psi$ and $\vdash \psi$ (necessitation for strong belief)*
- φ *is of the form $R_{i,\Sigma}^t K \psi$ and $\vdash \psi$ (necessitation for reasons for strong belief)*
- φ *is of the form $\sim \psi$, where ψ is not of the form $\sim \chi$, and $\Gamma \nvdash \psi$ (negation-as-failure)*

The axioms of TDL include the axioms of the standard Hilbert system for first-order logic (as described for example in subchapter 3.6 of [10]) as well as all axioms mentioned in section 5.2 and in the rest of this section.

The axioms governing the behaviour of the two belief modalities and their interaction are taken over from Demelombe [4]. Both belief modalities obey the system (KD):

$$(K_B) \; B_{i,\Sigma}^t \varphi \wedge B_{i,\Sigma}^t (\varphi \rightarrow \psi) \rightarrow B_{i,\Sigma}^t \psi$$

$$(D_B) \; \neg(B_{i,\Sigma}^t \varphi \wedge B_{i,\Sigma}^t \neg \varphi)$$

$$(K_K) \; K_{i,\Sigma}^t \varphi \wedge K_{i,\Sigma}^t (\varphi \rightarrow \psi) \rightarrow K_{i,\Sigma}^t \psi$$

$$(D_K) \; \neg(K_{i,\Sigma}^t \varphi \wedge K_{i,\Sigma}^t \neg \varphi)$$

Furthermore, strong belief satisfies the axiom schema (KT), which intuitively says that a principal strongly believes that what it strongly believes is true:

$$(KT) \; K_{i,\Sigma}^t (K_{i,\emptyset}^t \varphi \rightarrow \varphi)$$

Strong belief implies weak belief:

$$(KB) \; K_{i,\Sigma}^t \varphi \rightarrow B_{i,\Sigma}^t \varphi$$

We need axioms similar to these axioms about the two belief modalities for the reason-for-belief modality:

$$(K_{RB}) \; R_{i,\Sigma}^t B\varphi \wedge R_{i,\Sigma}^t B(\varphi \rightarrow \psi) \rightarrow R_{i,\Sigma}^t B\psi$$

$$(K_{RK}) \; R_{i,\Sigma}^t K\varphi \wedge R_{i,\Sigma}^t K(\varphi \rightarrow \psi) \rightarrow R_{i,\Sigma}^t K\psi$$

$$(KT_R) \; R_{i,\Sigma}^t K K_{i,\emptyset}^t K\varphi \rightarrow R_{i,\Sigma}^t K\varphi$$

$$(RKRB) \; R_{i,\Sigma}^t K\varphi \rightarrow R_{i,\Sigma}^t B\varphi$$

---

[2]Since Definition 5 is an inductive definition, it can – similarly to Definitions 2 and 3 discussed in Appendix A – in some contexts lead to the relation $\vdash$ being undefined. However, as follows from the proof of Theorem 1 sketched in Appendix C, $\Gamma \vdash \varphi$ is defined whenever Γ is a set of announcement formulas corresponding to a authorization specification free of strong S-revocation loops.

Recall that $B_{i,\Sigma}^t B_{j,\Sigma'}^{t'} \varphi$ is interpreted to mean that i believes that j *should* believe that φ. It is reasonable to assume that i believes that someone else should believe φ iff i herself believes φ. This is captured by the following four axiom schemas:

$$(BB_1)\ B_{i,\Sigma}^t \varphi \rightarrow B_{i,\Sigma}^t \forall t' B_{j,\emptyset}^{t'} \varphi$$

$$(BB_2)\ B_{i,\Sigma}^t B_{j,\emptyset}^{t'} \varphi \rightarrow B_{i,\Sigma}^t \varphi$$

$$(KK_1)\ K_{i,\Sigma}^t \varphi \rightarrow K_{i,\Sigma}^t \forall t' K_{j,\emptyset}^{t'} \varphi$$

$$(KK_2)\ K_{i,\Sigma}^t K_{j,\emptyset}^{t'} \varphi \rightarrow K_{i,\Sigma}^t \varphi$$

The action of asserting a strong belief is always also considered an action of asserting the corresponding weak belief, and the action of denying a weak belief is always also considered an action of denying the corresponding strong belief:

$$(IKB)\ I_i^t K\varphi \rightarrow I_i^t B\varphi$$

$$(IBK)\ I_i^t \not{B}\varphi \rightarrow I_i^t \not{K}\varphi$$

Since the SOA has the ultimate authority over the object in question, every principal has the right to perform an action iff it is trusted by the SOA on that action:

$$(SOA)\ r_i^t a \leftrightarrow \exists \Sigma\ K_{SOA,\Sigma}^t T_i \alpha$$

If at time t, i has epistemic trust in j concerning the judgements about φ made before time point t', this means that if j believes φ at time $min(t, t')$, i generally has a reason to believe φ. However, this reason to believe φ cannot be inferred if j believes φ only implicitly, mediated by the belief of some principal k at time t, and i has a reason to distrust k concerning judgements about φ held at time t. This is formalized in the *axiom schemas of epistemic trust*:

$$(ET_B)\ B_{i,\emptyset}^t T_j^{t'} \varphi \wedge ((t' > t \wedge t_2 = t) \vee (\neg t' > t \wedge t_2 = t')) \wedge$$
$$B_{j,\Sigma}^{t_2} \varphi \wedge \sim \exists k, t_3, \Sigma'\ (k \in \Sigma \wedge R_{i,\Sigma'}^t B \neg T_k^{t_3} \varphi)$$
$$\rightarrow R_{i,\Sigma \cup \{(j,t_2)\}}^t B\varphi$$

$$(ET_K)\ K_{i,\emptyset}^t T_j^{t'} \varphi \wedge ((t' > t \wedge t_2 = t) \vee (\neg t' > t \wedge t_2 = t')) \wedge$$
$$K_{j,\Sigma}^{t_2} \varphi \wedge \sim \exists k, t_3 \Sigma'\ (k \in \Sigma \wedge R_{i,\Sigma'}^t B \neg T_k^{t_3} \varphi)$$
$$\rightarrow R_{i,\Sigma \cup \{(j,t_2)\}}^t K\varphi$$

The following axioms govern the relationship between belief and reason to belief that we already explained at the end of Section 5.2:

$$(RB)\ R_{i,\Sigma}^t B\varphi \wedge \sim \exists \Sigma'\ R_{i,\Sigma'}^t B \neg \varphi \rightarrow B_{i,\Sigma}^t \varphi$$

$$(RK)\ R_{i,\Sigma}^t K\varphi \wedge \sim \exists \Sigma'\ R_{i,\Sigma'}^t B \neg \varphi \rightarrow K_{i,\Sigma}^t \varphi$$

$$(BR)\ B_{i,\Sigma}^t \varphi \rightarrow R_{i,\Sigma}^t B\varphi$$

$$(BR)\ K_{i,\Sigma}^t \varphi \rightarrow R_{i,\Sigma}^t K\varphi$$

We assume that principals are sincere, in the sense that in general a principal believes what he/she/it has previously announced. However, this principle needs some restrictions: Firstly, a principal can distance itself from a previous annoncement by making an announcement with the same content as before but with opposite announcement modality (e.g., to distance itself from its previous announcement of belief in φ, a principal can announce its non-belief in φ). Secondly, an announcement of weak belief in φ can be made obsolete by an announcement of strong belief in $\bar{\varphi}$ by a trustworthy principal. Thirdly, an announcement of strong belief only implies that the principal has reasons for strong belief; strong belief can be implied using axiom (RK) in the absence of reasons

for the negation. This is formalized in the *sincerity axiom schemas*:

$$(Sin_B)\ I_i^{t'} B\varphi \wedge t > t' \wedge \sim \exists t_2 > t'\ (t > t_2 \wedge I_i^{t_2} \not{B}\varphi) \wedge$$
$$\sim \exists j, \Sigma\ \exists t_3 > t\ (t > t_3 \wedge B_{i,\Sigma}^{t_3} T_j^t \bar{\varphi} \wedge I_j^{t_3} K\bar{\varphi}) \rightarrow B_{i,\emptyset}^t \varphi$$

$$(Sin_K)\ I_i^{t'} K\varphi \wedge t > t' \wedge \sim \exists t_2 > t'\ (t > t_2 \wedge I_i^{t_2} \not{K}\varphi) \rightarrow R_{i,\emptyset}^t K\varphi$$

$$(Sin_{\not{B}})\ I_i^{t'} \not{B}\varphi \wedge t > t' \wedge \sim \exists t_2 > t'\ (t > t_2 \wedge I_i^{t_2} B\varphi) \rightarrow \neg B_{i,\emptyset}^t \varphi$$

$$(Sin_{\not{K}})\ I_i^{t'} \not{K}\varphi \wedge t > t' \wedge \sim \exists t_2 > t'\ (t > t_2 \wedge I_i^{t_2} K\varphi) \rightarrow \neg K_{i,\emptyset}^t \varphi$$

We assume that all principals trust themselves, as stated by the *axiom of self-trust*:

$$(ST)\ K_{i,\emptyset}^t T_i \alpha$$

Since $T_k^t \varphi$ means that k's judgements made before time point t about φ are trusted, $T_k^t \varphi$ should clearly imply $T_k^{t'} \varphi$ if t' is an earlier time point than t:

$$(T^t)\ T_k^t \varphi \wedge t > t' \rightarrow T_k^{t'} \varphi$$

In order for the binary relation $>$ to function properly in the logic, we need the following axiom scheme. For any two time point constants $c_1, c_2 \in \mathbb{Z} \cup \{\infty\}$, if $c_1 < c_2$ in the natural ordering of $\mathbb{Z} \cup \{\infty\}$ (in which ∞ is larger than any integer), the following formula is a TDL axiom:

$$(>)\ c_1 < c_2 \wedge \neg c_2 < c_1 \wedge \neg c_1 < c_1$$

6. SCENARIOS IN TDL

In this section we show how TDL can be used to model the reasoning about trust and distrust involved in justifying the choices of revocation schemes in the scenarios from section 4.1.

In order to formalize scenario 3, we need to add some details to the description of the scenario: Suppose that A is the SOA and that at time point 1, A grants C delegation right concerning the access α, i.e. $I_A^1 KT_C \mathbb{D}\alpha$. At time 2, C grants B this delegation right: $I_C^2 KT_B \mathbb{D}\alpha$. Later, let's say at time point 9, A finds out that C is leaving to join the rival company, and hence now distrusts C concerning access α or to grant delegation right concerning access a to anyone else: $I_A^9 K \neg T_C \alpha$ and $I_A^9 K \neg T_C \mathbb{D}\alpha$. A also explicitly denies her previous trust statement to make clear it is no longer in place: $I_A^9 \not{K} T_C \mathbb{D}\alpha$. But since C never misused any rights, A still trusts the delegation authorizations issued by C before time point 9: $I_A^9 K\ \forall k\ T_C^9 T_k \mathbb{D}\alpha$. We expect that C loses his access and delegation rights at time point 9, but that B retains these rights.

We now explain how this expected result is actually attained in TDL: By axiom (Sin_K), $I_A^1 KT_C \mathbb{D}\alpha$ and the fact that A does not deny this announcement before time point 9 imply that for $1 \leq t \leq 8$, $K_{A,\emptyset}^t T_C \mathbb{D}\alpha$, which by $(T\mathbb{D})$ and (K_K) further implies $K_{A,\emptyset}^t T_C a$. Since $A = SOA$, axiom (SOA) implies $r_C^t a$ and $r_C^t \mathbb{D}\alpha$, i.e. C has access and delegation rights from time point 2 until time point 8. But since $I_A^9 \not{K} T_C \mathbb{D}\alpha$, we cannot deduce $r_C^9 a$ and $r_C^9 \mathbb{D}\alpha$ in this way: At time point 9, C no longer has access and delegation right, as expected. However, for $2 \leq t \leq 9$, we can deduce $r_B^t a$ and $r_B^t \mathbb{D}\alpha$, i.e. that B has access and delegation rights: First, note that for $1 \leq t \leq 9$ we have $K_{A,\emptyset}^t\ \forall k\ T_C^9 T_k \mathbb{D}\alpha$ (which by (K_K) implies $K_{A,\emptyset}^t T_C^9 T_B \mathbb{D}\alpha$). In case $1 \leq t \leq 8$, this follows from $K_{A,\emptyset}^t T_C \mathbb{D}\alpha$, $(T\mathbb{D})$ and (K_K); in case $t = 9$, it follows from $I_A^9 K\ \forall k\ T_C^9 T_k \mathbb{D}\alpha$ and (Sin_K). $I_C^2 KT_B \mathbb{D}\alpha$ and (Sin_K) imply that for $2 \leq t \leq 9$, $K_{C,\emptyset}^t T_B \mathbb{D}\alpha$, so using (ET_K), we can derive $K_{A,\emptyset}^t T_B \mathbb{D}\alpha$, which similarly as in the above proofs of $r_C^t a$ and $r_C^t \mathbb{D}\alpha$ implies $r_B^t a$ and $r_B^t \mathbb{D}\alpha$.

Here is how the other scenarios discussed in Section 4 can be formalized in TDL (we assume that the revocation always takes place at time point 9):

Scenario 1. User A distrusts user C concerning access and delegation: $I_A^9 K \neg T_C \mathbb{D}\alpha$. This implies not only $K_{A,\emptyset}^9 \neg T_C \mathbb{D}\alpha$, but by axiom (KK_1) also $K_{A,\emptyset}^9 \forall t\ K_{SOA,\emptyset}^t \neg T_C \mathbb{D}\alpha$. According to the explanations about strong revocations in section 5.2, if the SOA trusts A on strong revocations ($\exists \Sigma\ K_{SOA,\Sigma}^9 T_A \mathbb{S}\alpha$), the latter formula has the same effect as a Strong Global Resilient revocation.

Scenario 3. The reserved kind of distrust resulting from hearing a rumour for which one does not know whether it is true is modelled in TDL as weak distrust, i.e. weak belief in the non-trustworthiness of the principal in question: $I_A^9 B \neg T_B \mathbb{D}\alpha$. Since axiom (Sin_B) blocks the inference of $B_{i,\emptyset}^t B \neg T_B \mathbb{D}\alpha$ from $I_A^9 B \neg T_B \mathbb{D}\alpha$ if some trusted principal announces trust in j (i.e. delegates to j), $I_A^9 B \neg T_B \mathbb{D}\alpha$ loses its effect as soon as such an anouncement takes place. Hence we have the effect of a non-resilient revocation, as desired.

Scenario 4. User A neither trusts nor distrusts user C: $I_A^9 \not{B} T_C \mathbb{D}\alpha$ and $I_A \not{B}^9 \neg T_C \mathbb{D}\alpha$. These announcements remove the effect of any previous announcement made by A about the trustworthiness of C, i.e. the situation is now practically the same as if A had never trusted C. This corresponds to a Weak Global Delete, in which a positive authorization is removed, leaving no trace of it ever having been there.

7. DESIRABLE BEHAVIOUR OF REVOCATION SCHEMES

In this section we show how TDL can be used to formally formulate a desirable property for a graph-theoretically defined revocation framework. This allows us to study revocation frameworks using the axiomatic method originating in social choice theory.

There are different revocation schemes because there are different reasons for revocating. We start this section by exhibiting a correspondence between revocation schemes and reasons for revocating formalizable in TDL. The main idea behind the desirable property of revocation frameworks that we define is that if performing revocation schemes and granting rights was replaced by publicly announcing one's formal reasons for revocating or granting, then these public announcements should logically imply (in TDL) a principal's access right iff that principal is actually granted access based on the delegation graph.

7.1 Matching reasons for revocating to revocation schemes

As explained in Section 5, there are five levels of trust that an agent can have in another agent, of which four need to be distinguished in modelling delegation and revocation. But even when i explicitly strongly distrusts j concerning delegation right ($K_{i,\emptyset}^t \neg T_j \mathbb{D}\alpha$), i may still trust j's previous judgements concerning $T_k \mathbb{D}\alpha$ for other principals k ($K_{i,\emptyset}^t \forall k T_j^t T_k \mathbb{D}\alpha$). So the level of trust in another agent concerning delegation right can be different from the level of trust concerning previously granted authorizations. However, these two levels of trust are not completely independent of each other: For example, $K_{i,\emptyset}^t T_j \mathbb{D}\alpha$ implies $K_{i,\emptyset}^t \forall k T_j^t T_k \mathbb{D}\alpha$. More generally, the second level of trust must be at least as high as the first level of trust. This means that only 10 of the 16 ensuing combinations of trust levels are actually possible.

Table 1 shows which granting-revocation behaviour corresponds to each of these ten possible combinations of trust levels. Some cells contain multiple revocation schemes. This means that the granting-revocation behaviour corresponding to the combination of trust levels represented by that cell consists of performing multiple revocation schemes at the same time. For an agent without strong revocation rights, the granting-revocation behaviour corresponding to some combination of trust levels is determined by dropping the strong revocations from the revocations in the cell that represent that combination of trust levels.

The formulas in the table have $\bar{\pi}$ in place of α, $\mathbb{D}\alpha$ or $\mathbb{S}\alpha$. $\bar{\pi}$ is defined as follows:

DEFINITION 6. *For $\pi \in \{A, D, S\}$, we define $\bar{\pi}$ by setting $\bar{\pi} := \alpha$ if $\pi = A$, $\bar{\pi} := \mathbb{D}\alpha$ if $\pi = D$, and $\bar{\pi} := \mathbb{S}\alpha$ if $\pi = S$.*

The revocation schemes in the table should always be for the same π that is used in the $\bar{\pi}$ in the formulas.

We consider the pair of levels of trust that i has in j to be the reason i has for granting a right to j or revoking a right from j. Hence the graph-theoretic definitions of the revocation schemes should be such that access is granted whenever this is justifiable on the basis of these trust-based reasons for granting and revocating. We use deducibility in TDL as our formal criterion for justifiablity.

These explanations already determine the desirable property for a set of graph-theoretic definitions of revocation schemes. We now proceed to formalizing this desirable property.

7.2 Formal desirable property

We first define a set **C** corresponding to the ten meaningful cells of Table 1:

DEFINITION 7. $\mathbf{C} := \{(m,n) \in \{1,2,3,4\}^2 \mid m \geq n\}$.

Next we define a *granting-revocation action* corresponding to a cell in the table:

DEFINITION 8. *For $i, j \in \mathbf{S}$, $(m,n) \in \mathbf{C}$ and $\pi \in \mathbf{P}$, define $\mathbf{GR}(i, j, (m,n), \pi)$ to be the granting-revocation behavior in the cell in row m and column n of Table 1 performed by i onto j for permission π.*

For example, $\mathbf{GR}(A, B, (2,2), D)$ is a Weak Global Delete revocation from A to B for permission D.

Next we define a *public announcement* corresponding to a cell in the table:

DEFINITION 9. *For $i, j \in \mathbf{S}$, $(m,n) \in \mathbf{C}$ and $\pi \in \mathbf{P}$, define $\mathbf{I}(i, j, (m,n), \pi)$ to be the set of public announcements by i in trust in j for permission π according to the level of trust of row m and column n of Table 1.*

For example, $\mathbf{I}(A, B, (4,1), \alpha)$ is $\{I_A^t K \forall k T_B^t T_k \bar{\pi}, I_A^t K \neg T_B \bar{\pi}\}$.

We now need to define the notion of an authorization specification resulting from a sequence of granting-revocation-actions.

DEFINITION 10. *Given a sequence σ of elements of $\mathbf{S} \times \mathbf{S} \times \mathbf{C} \times \mathbf{P}$, we define the authorization specification $\mathbf{A}(\sigma)$ inductively as follows:*

- $\mathbf{A}(\langle\rangle) = \emptyset$
- $\mathbf{A}(\langle(i_1,j_1,a_1,r_1),\ldots,(i_n,j_n,a_n,r_n)\rangle)$ *is the authorization specification resulting from performing $\mathbf{GR}(i_n,j_n,a_n,r_n)$ on $\mathbf{A}(\langle(i_1,j_1,a_1,r_1),\ldots,(i_{n-1},j_{n-1},a_{n-1},r_{n-1})\rangle)$.*

Now we need to define which sequences of granting-revocation-actions are actually valid in our system:

DEFINITION 11. *A sequence $\langle(i_1,j_1,a_1,r_1),\ldots,(i_n,j_n,a_n,r_n)\rangle$ of elements of $\mathbf{S} \times \mathbf{S} \times \mathbf{C} \times \mathbf{P}$ is called a valid granting-revocation pattern iff for every $k < n$, the authorization specification $\mathbf{A}(\langle(i_1,j_1,a_1,r_1),\ldots,(i_k,j_k,a_k,r_k)\rangle)$ is free of strong S-revocation loops and authorizes i to perform $\mathbf{GR}(i_k,j_k,a_k,r_k)$.*

	$K_{i,\emptyset}^t \forall k T_j^t T_k \bar{\pi}$	$\neg B_{i,\emptyset}^t \forall k T_j^t T_k \bar{\pi} \wedge$ $\neg B_{i,\emptyset}^t \forall t' \forall k \neg T_j^{t'} T_k \bar{\pi}$	$B_{i,\emptyset}^t \forall t' \forall k \neg T_j^{t'} T_k \bar{\pi} \wedge$ $\neg K_{i,\emptyset}^t \forall t' \forall k \neg T_j^{t'} T_k \bar{\pi}$	$K_{i,\emptyset}^t \forall t' \forall k \neg T_j^{t'} T_k \bar{\pi}$
$K_{i,\emptyset}^t T_j \bar{\pi}$	grant permission π	X	X	X
$\neg B_{i,\emptyset}^t T_j \bar{\pi} \wedge \neg B_{i,\emptyset}^t \neg T_j \bar{\pi}$	WLD	WGD	X	X
$B_{i,\emptyset}^t \neg T_j \bar{\pi} \wedge \neg K_{i,\emptyset}^t \neg T_j \bar{\pi}$	PLN ∘ SLN	WGD ∘ PLN ∘ SLN	PGN ∘ SGN	X
$K_{i,\emptyset}^t \neg T_j \bar{\pi}$	PLR ∘ SLR	WGD ∘ PLR ∘ SLR	PGN ∘ PLR ∘ SGN ∘ SLR	PGR ∘ SGR

Table 1: The correspondence between the revocation framework and reasons for revocating formalized in TDL

The notion of being free of strong S-revocation loops is explained and formally defined in Appendix A.

The following theorem, whose proof is sketched in Appendix C, now formally expresses that our refined revocation framework has the desirable property that we have previously already explained and motivated:

THEOREM 1. *Let $n \in \mathbb{N}$, and let σ be a valid granting-revocation pattern of length n. Then for all $i \in \mathbf{S}$, $\mathbf{I}(\sigma) \models r_i^n \alpha$ iff i is the SOA or there is an active authorization of the form $(p, i, +, \alpha, t)$ in $\mathbf{A}(\sigma)$.*

Note that if we had refrained from implementing in our revised framework one of the five changes to Hagström et al.'s framework discussed in section 3.1, the resulting framework would not satisfy this desirably property.

8. FUTURE WORK

In this paper we studied revocation for a version of delegation that does not have any bound on the length of delegation chains. However, TDL lends itself very well also to delegation with such a bound. Indeed, for this purpose a somewhat reduced version of TDL, which lacks the $T_i \mathbb{D}$ and $T_i \mathbb{S}$ trust operators, would be sufficient. It would be interesting to study the possibility to define a systematic revocation framework for such bounded delegation that satisfies a desirable property analogous to the one that our framework for revoking unbounded delegation has been shown to satisfy.

Some reasons for revoking rights cannot be captured in TDL: User A may revoke B's rights just because she does not consider it to be useful for B to have the right in question, even though she strongly trusts B. And A may choose a certain kind of revocation scheme based on considerations of responsibility, not just considerations of trust. Our preliminary investigations into this topic suggest that our refined framework also corresponds well to these not trust-based reasons for revoking, but further investigations are due in order to develop an extension of TDL that can formalize such reasons and proof our system to satisfy a desirable property based on this extended logic.

In order to develop an axiomatic theory of revocation schemes similar to the application of the axiomatic method in social choice theory, other desirable properties of revocation schems or revocation frameworks need to be identified an compared to the desirable property that we proposed.

9. CONCLUSION

After identifying some problems with Hagström et al.'s [8] revocation framework, we presented a refined framework that avoids these problems. In order to ensure that our refined framework does not itself suffer from similar problems, we systematically studied the relation between the reasons for revoking and the graph-theoretic definitions of revocation schemes. In order to formalize reasons for revoking based on trust and distrust, we developed Trust Delegation Logic (TDL). TDL allowed us to formulate a desirable property that a graph-theoretically defined revocation framework should satisfy. This desirable property is based on a correspondence between revocation schemes and reasons for revocating, and requires the revocation schemes to be defined in such a way that access is granted whenever this is justifiable on the basis of the reasons for granting and revoking. The main theorem of the paper asserts that our refined framework does satisfy this desirable property.

10. ACKNOWLEDGEMENTS

This work was supported by the FNR-FWO project *Specification logics and Inference tools for verification and Enforcement of Policies*.

11. REFERENCES

[1] G. Aucher, S. Barker, G. Boella, V. Genovese, and L. van der Torre. Dynamics in Delegation and Revocation Schemes: A Logical Approach. In Y. Li, editor, *Data and Applications Security and Privacy XXV*, volume 6818 of *Lecture Notes in Computer Science*, pages 90–105. Springer Berlin, 2011.

[2] E. Bertino, S. Jajodia, and P. Samarati. A Non-timestamped Authorization Model for Data Management Systems. In *Proceedings of the 3rd ACM Conference on Computer and Communications Security*, CCS '96, pages 169–178, New York, NY, USA, 1996. ACM.

[3] E. Bertino, P. Samarati, and S. Jajodia. An extended authorization model for relational databases. *Knowledge and Data Engineering, IEEE Transactions on*, 9(1):85–101, Jan 1997.

[4] R. Demolombe. Reasonig about trust: A formal logical framework. In C. Jensen, S. Poslad, and T. Dimitrakos, editors, *Trust Management*, volume 2995 of *Lecture Notes in Computer Science*, pages 291–303. 2004.

[5] M. Denecker. The Well-Founded Semantics Is the Principle of Inductive Definition. In J. Dix, L. del Cerro, and U. Furbach, editors, *Logics in Artificial Intelligence*, volume 1489 of *Lecture Notes in Computer Science*, pages 1–16. Springer Berlin Heidelberg, 1998.

[6] R. Fagin. On an Authorization Mechanism. *ACM Trans. Database Syst.*, 3(3):310–319, Sept. 1978.

[7] P. P. Griffiths and B. W. Wade. An Authorization Mechanism for a Relational Database System. *ACM Trans. Database Syst.*, 1(3):242–255, Sept. 1976.

[8] Å. Hagström, S. Jajodia, F. Parisi-Presicce, and D. Wijesekera. Revocations-A Classification. In *Proceedings of the 14th IEEE Workshop on Computer Security Foundations*, CSFW '01, pages 44–, Washington, DC, USA, 2001. IEEE Computer Society.

[9] B. Jayaraman and D. Jana. Set constructors, finite sets, and logical semantics. *The Journal of Logic Programming*, pages 55–77, 1999.

[10] W. Rautenberg. *A Concise Introduction to Mathematical Logic*. Springer, 2006.

[11] C. Ruan and V. Varadharajan. Resolving Conflicts in Authorization Delegations. In L. M. Batten and J. Seberry, editors, *ACISP*, volume 2384 of *Lecture Notes in Computer Science*, pages 271–285. Springer, 2002.

APPENDIX

A. INDUCTIVE INTERDEPENDENCE OF DEFINITIONS 2 AND 3

Definitions 2 and 3, in which we define the notions of an authorization being *active* and being *directly inactivated*, depend one on another. This interdependence looks similar to a problematic circular definition, but can actually be understood as an inductive definition, which can be formally interpreted using the well-founded semantics [5]. In this appendix we briefly sketch the theory of inductive definitions under the well-founded semantics, and comment about what practical consequences follow from using an inductive definition for defining wthe notion of an *active* authorization.

An *inductive definition* of predicates $P_1, \ldots, P_n$ consists of rules of the form $\forall \bar{x} \ P(\bar{x}) \leftarrow \psi$, where $P \in \{P^1, \ldots, P^n\}$ and ψ may itself refer to predicates in $\{P^1, \ldots, P^n\}$. In such a rule, $P(\bar{x})$ is called the *head* of the rule, and ψ the *body* of the rule.

An inductive definition may have a form, which makes it impossible to interpret the defined predicates in a way that is consistent with the rules. For example, the inductive definition $\{P \leftarrow \neg P\}$, which defined P to be the case if $\neg P$ is the case is problematic: If we assume P is false, then $\neg P$ is true, so by the single rule of this definition, P should be true. So P cannot be false. However, since P is defined through this inductive definition, it can only be true if some rule in the inductive definition is true. But the only rule in this definition cannot make P true.

One approach to avoid such problems is to define some syntactic restrictions on the set of rules that ensure that such problems cannot arise. However, such syntactic restrictions are usually to restrictive, barring some inductive definitions that we can intuitively and formally make sense of.

Another approach to avoid such problems is that of using the *well-founded semantics* for inductive definitions, which is a partial semantics, i.e. for problematic definitions like the above, it does not define a truth function for the predicates that were purported to be defined by the inductive definition. But whenever an inductively defined predicate has an intuitively meaningful interpretation, the well-founded semantics formally assigns this interpretation to the predicate [5].

The well-founded semantics is defined through an inductive process which involves adding new information about the defined predicates at each step of the induction based on the rules in the inductive definition: This information consists of an assignment of truth values to *domain atoms*; a *domain atom* is a pair $(P, \bar{a})$ – usually written as $P(\bar{a})$ – where P is an n-ary predicate symbol defined in the inductive definition, and $\bar{a} \in D^n$, where D is the domain of the structure. At the first step of the induction, no truth values are assigned to domain conditions. At every subsequent step, the truth value $\mathbf{t}$ may be assigned to a domain atom $P(\bar{a})$ if applying the rules for P to the *previous* assignment of truth values to domain atoms establishes that $P(\bar{a})$ is true; the truth value $\mathbf{f}$ may be assigned to domain atoms $P_1(\bar{a_1}), \ldots, P_k(\bar{a_k})$ if applying the rules for $P_1, \ldots, P_k$ to the *resulting* assignment of truth values to domain atoms establishes that $P_1(\bar{a_1}), \ldots, P_k(\bar{a_k})$ are false. This different treatment of the two truth values reflects the inductive nature of the definition, according to which a domain atom can only

be true if some rule makes it true, whereas a domain atom should be considered false in the absense of a rule making it true. The *well-founded model* of an inducive definition is defined to be the limit assignment of truth values to domain atoms in such an induction [5]. If the well-founded model does not assign either $\mathbf{t}$ or $\mathbf{f}$ to every domain atom of the defined predicates, it is a partial model.

The inductive definition of authorizations being *active* and *directly inactivated* can in some contexts lead to a partial well-founded model, i.e. to the notions of *active* and *directly inactivated* not having a coherently determinable meaning. Consider for example the following authorization specification:

EXAMPLE 8.

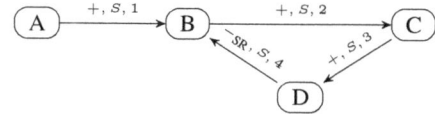

If we assume that the negative authorization from D to B is active, it directly inactivates the authorization from A to B. But then there is no active chain of authorizations that supports the authorization from D to B, so it would have to be inactive. If on the other hand we assume that the authorization from D to B is inactive, then the authorization from A to B is not directly inactivated, an the chain of authorization from A via B and C to D is active, thus ensuring that the authorization from D to to B is active. So either way we run into a contradiction. This means that the interpretation of "active" under the well-founded semantics is partial in the context of this authorization specification.

In this example, the problem was caused by principal D using its power to perform strong revocations in order to remove the rights from B, even though D's right to perform strong revocations depended on a delegation chain including B. The problem can be avoided by adding a constraint to the system that disallows principals from using their strong revocation right to remove the strong revocation right from a principal on whom they depend for their strong revocation right.

This constraint needs to be formulated in both a more formal and a more general way. For this we first need the notion of a $+-S$-chain, which formalizes the notion of a potentially active chain of positive S-authorizations followed by a strong negative S-authorization, which can only be inactivated if attacked by another $+-S$-chain. The time stamp of a $+-S$-chain indicates the least time stamp that a positive authorization must have in order not to be affected by the $+-S$-chain.

DEFINITION 12. *A $+-S$-chain with time stamp t is a chain of authorizations* $(p_0, p_1, +, S, t_1)$, $(p_1, p_2, +, S, t_2)$, $\ldots$, $(p_{n-1}, p_n, +, S, t_n)$, $(p_n, p_{n+1}, \tau, S, t_{n+1})$ *satisfying the following properties:*

- $p_0 = SOA$
- *Either $\tau = -_{SR}$ and $t = \infty$, or $\tau = -_{SN}$ and $t = t_{n+2}$.*
- *There are no i, j with $0 \le i < j \le n$ such that there is an authorization $(p_i, p_j, -_{PR}, S, t')$.*
- *There are no i, j with $0 \le i < j \le n$ such that there is an authorization $(p_i, p_j, -_{PN}, S, t')$ with $t' < t_j$.*

We say that a $+-S$-chain C_1 with time stamp t *attacks* a $+-S$-chain C_2 iff C_1 ends in a principal that has issued one of the authorizations in C_2 at some time $t' > t$.

Now the formalized and generalized constraint can be formulated as follows: We require that the $+-S$-chain in the authorization specification can be partially ordered in such a way that a $+-S$-chain C_1 attacks a $+-S$-chain C_2 only if $C_1 < C_2$ in the partial ordering. Informally, this means that there should be no loops of $+-S$-chains under the attack relation. An authorization specification satisfying this constraint is called *free of strong S-revocation loops*.

B. FURTHER REVOCATION EXAMPLES

EXAMPLE 9. *Weak Global Delete revocation from* B *to* C

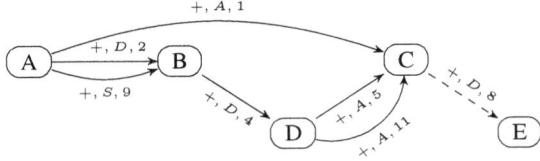

EXAMPLE 10. *P-t-p Global Resilient revocation from* B *to* C

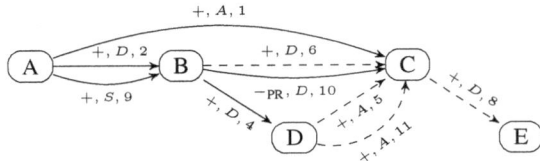

EXAMPLE 11. *P-t-p Local Resilient revocation from* B *to* C

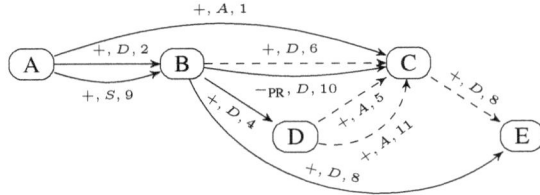

EXAMPLE 12. *P-t-p Local Non-resilient revocation from* B *to* C

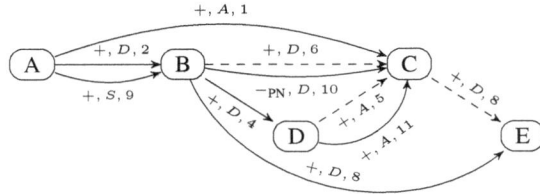

EXAMPLE 13. *Strong Global Non-resilient revocation from* B *to* C

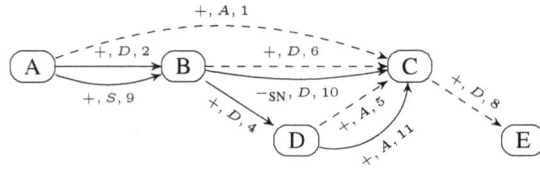

EXAMPLE 14. *Strong Local Resilient revocation from* B *to* C

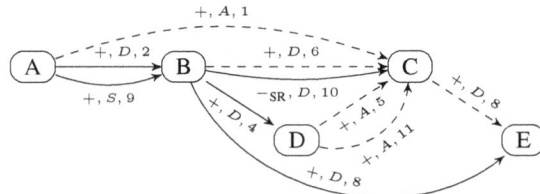

EXAMPLE 15. *Strong Local Non-resilient revocation from* B *to* C

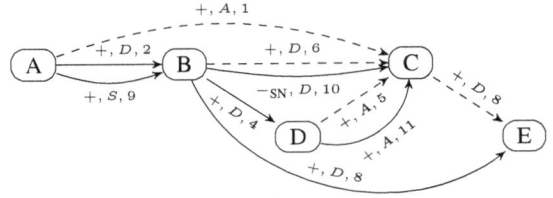

C. SKETCH OF PROOF OF THEOREM 1

We prove Theorem 1 by first exhibiting a procedure for determining which authorizations in $\mathbf{A}(\sigma)$ are active, and then exhibiting a correspondence between statements about the activeness of authorization in $\mathbf{A}(\sigma)$ and statements about the deducibility of certain TDL formulas from $\mathbf{I}(\sigma)$.

First we need to define the notion of a π-chain for $\pi \in \mathbf{P}$:

DEFINITION 13. *A π-chain is a chain of authorizations* $(p_0, p_1, +, \pi', t_1)$, $(p_1, p_2, +, \pi', t_2)$, ..., $(p_{n-1}, p_n, +, \pi', t_n)$, $(p_n, p_{n+1}, +, \pi, t_{n+1})$ *satisfying the following properties:*
- *$p_0 = SOA$*
- *$\pi' = D$ if $\pi = A$, and $\pi' = \pi$ otherwise.*
- *There are no i, j with $0 \leq i < j \leq n+1$ such that there is an authorization $(p_i, p_j, -_{PR}, \pi'', t')$, where $\pi'' = \pi$ if $j = n+1$, and $\pi'' = \pi'$ otherwise.*
- *There are no i, j with $0 \leq i < j \leq n+1$ such that there is an authorization $(p_i, p_j, -_{PN}, \pi'', t')$ with $t' < t_j$, where $\pi'' = \pi$ if $j = n+1$, and $\pi'' = \pi'$ otherwise.*

Note that a $+-S$-chain is an S-chain followed by negative S-authorization.

σ is a valid granting-revocation pattern, so $\mathbf{A}(\sigma)$ is free of strong S-revocation loops, i.e. there is a partial ordering $<$ on the set of $+-S$-chains over $\mathbf{A}(\sigma)$. Since the set of $+-S$-chains over $\mathbf{A}(\sigma)$ is finite, $<$ is a well-ordering, and we can perform induction along $<$. This allows us to determine which $+-S$-chains are active: A $+-S$-chain C_1 is active iff it is not attacked by an active $+-S$-chain $C_2 < C_1$.

Next we can establish which positive S-authorizations are active: A positive S-authorization is directly inactivated iff its end node is attacked by an active $+-S$-chain. A positive S-authorization is active iff it is an element of an S-chain whose authorizations are not directly inactivated.

Next we can establish that a strong negative authorizations is active iff it starts at some principal at which some active S-chain ends. This allows us to establish which other authorizations are directly inactivated: $(i, j, +, \pi, t)$ is directly inactivated iff there is an active authorization (k, j, τ, π, t') such that either $\tau = -_{SR}$ or $\tau = -_{SN}$ and $t < t'$. Finally, we can establish that a positive π-authorization is active iff it is an element of a π-chain whose authorizations are not directly inactivated.

In a similar way as one can show in a step-by-step way the correctness of this procedure for determining the activeness of authorizations in $\mathbf{A}(\sigma)$, one can prove the following three equivalences:
1. For $\tau = -_{SR}$ or $\tau = -_{SN}$, (i, j, τ, π, t) is active at time t' iff $\mathbf{I}(\sigma) \vdash \exists \Sigma \, K_{SOA,\Sigma}^{t'} T_i \mathbb{S} \alpha$.
2. $(i, j, +, \pi, t)$ is directly inactivated at time t' iff $\mathbf{I}(\sigma) \vdash \exists \Sigma \, R_{SOA,\Sigma}^{t'} B \neg T_j \bar{\pi}$.
3. $(i, j, +, \pi, t)$ is active at time t' iff $\mathbf{I}(\sigma) \vdash \exists \Sigma \, K_{SOA,\Sigma}^{t'} T_i \bar{\pi}$ and $\mathbf{I}(\sigma) \not\vdash \exists \Sigma \, R_{SOA,\Sigma}^{t'} B \neg T_j \bar{\pi}$.

The theorem now follows from equivalence 3 together with TDL axioms (SOA), (RK) and (ST).

Towards Attribute-Based Authorisation for Bidirectional Programming

Lionel Montrieux
lionel@nii.ac.jp

Zhenjiang Hu
hu@nii.ac.jp

National Institute of Informatics
Tokyo, Japan

ABSTRACT

Bidirectional programming allows developers to write programs that will produce transformations that extract data from a source document into a view. The same transformations can then be used to update the source in order to propagate the changes made to the view, provided that the transformations satisfy two essential properties.

Bidirectional transformations can provide a form of authorisation mechanism. From a source containing sensitive data, a view can be extracted that only contains the information to be shared with a subject. The subject can modify the view, and the source can be updated accordingly, without risk of release of the sensitive information to the subject. However, the authorisation model afforded by bidirectional transformations is limited. Implementing an attribute-based access control (ABAC) mechanism directly in bidirectional transformations would violate the essential properties of well-behaved transformations; it would contradict the principle of separation of concerns; and it would require users to write and maintain a different transformation for every subject they would like to share a view with.

In this paper, we explore a solution to enforce ABAC on bidirectional transformations, using a policy language from which filters are generated to enforce the policy rules.

Categories and Subject Descriptors

D.4.6 [**Security and Protection**]: Access Controls; H.2.7 [**Database Administration**]: Security, integrity, and protection

General Terms

Security

Keywords

authorization, access control, bidirectional transformation

SACMAT'15, June 1–3, 2015, Vienna, Austria.
Copyright is held by the owner/author(s). Publication rights licensed to ACM.
ACM 978-1-4503-3556-0/15/06 ...$15.00.
http://dx.doi.org/10.1145/2752952.2752963.

1. INTRODUCTION

A bidirectional transformation is a pair of functions, *get* and *put* that maintain consistency between a source and a view [10]. The source and view are typically graphs, or structured documents such as XML documents. The *get* function takes a source document, and produces a view document. On the contrary, the *put* (or *putback*) function takes both the source and an updated view, and produces an updated source, where the changes made to the view have been propagated. The transformation from source to view is called a *forward* transformation, while the transformation from view to source is called a *backward* transformation.

Bidirectional transformations have recently received a lot of attention, both from the programming languages community [2, 4, 11, 17, 20, 36, 27] and from the software engineering community, where they have been used in contexts as varied as model-driven engineering [19, 35], consistent website updating [25], parallel programming [24], and many others [6]. Since 2012, a workshop dedicated to bidirectional transformations is organised every year [16].

A particularly interesting class of bidirectional transformations is the class of *well-behaved* transformations, which must obey two laws: the *GetPut* law, and the *PutGet* law. Intuitively, a well-behaved transformation will return identical views before and after a backward transformation using an unmodified view (*GetPut* law), and will return the same view after a backward transformation using a modified view (*PutGet* law). A lot of the work in bidirectional transformations focuses on well-behaved transformations.

Bidirectional transformations, and especially well-behaved ones, are notoriously difficult to write and maintain. Bidirectional *programming* attempts to solve that issue by providing programming languages that allow developers to define transformations in a way that is easier to write and maintain, often at the cost of a loss of expressive power [20].

Security views have been used to restrict access to data [29, 9]. Subjects may access views that will extract the data they are allowed to read from a source that also contains data that they should not have access to. These views are often not editable (except for Foster et al.'s updatable security views [11]), but they highlight the fact that views can be used as an authorisation mechanism.

We show in this paper that bidirectional programs can also be used as a form of authorisation mechanism. We show that implementing Attribute-Based Access Control (ABAC) directly using a put-based bidirectional programming language causes three types of problems:

- The laws of well-behaved transformations make it difficult to use runtime attribute values to implement ABAC using *only* bidirectional transformations.

- Including access control into a bidirectional program goes against the idea of separation of concerns.

- Including access control into bidirectional programs prevents the reuse of the same program with subjects with different access policies.

We then propose an architecture that combines put-based bidirectional programs with ABAC policies. View-centric authorisation policies are used to generate filters that sanitise views after forward transformations and before backward transformations are applied, therefore enforcing ABAC rules on the views and their corresponding sources. Those policies are written in a policy language that focuses on the specificities of bidirectional transformations over XML documents. We demonstrate our solution using a calendar sharing example.

The rest of this paper is organised as follows: in Section 2, we formally introduce bidirectional transformations, as well as the laws that govern "well-behaved" transformations. We also discuss and compare the different types of bidirectional transformation engines available. In Section 3, we use an example to illustrate the relationship between bidirectional transformations and authorisation, and highlight how put-based bidirectional programs are limited in their ability to express authorisation constraints. Section 4 is an overview of our approach to express and enforce ABAC on bidirectional programs. We present our policy language in Section 5, and authorisation filters in Section 6. In Section 7, we discuss our implementation of the approach, as well as our proof of concept to demonstrate the approach's feasability. Section 8 presents related work. We conclude this paper in Section 9, where we also discuss future work.

2. BACKGROUND

In this section, we formally introduce well-behaved bidirectional transformations, as well as different types of bidirectional programming languages.

2.1 Bidirectional transformations

A bidirectional transformation is a pair of functions that can transform a *source* into a *target*, and update the source to reflect changes made to the target [6], as illustrated on Figure 1. The *get* function produces a target from a source, in what is called a *forward transformation*. The *put* function updates the source according to changes made to the target, in what is called a *backward transformation*. The target is also often called a *view*, especially in transformations concerned with the view-update problem.

Formally [11], a bidirectional transformation is a mapping between a set of sources S and a set of views V, where we can define the *get* function as:

$$get : s \rightarrow v \qquad (1)$$

and the *put* function as:

$$put : s \rightarrow v \rightarrow s \qquad (2)$$

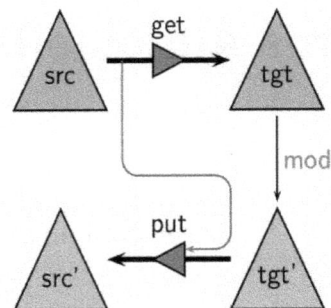

Figure 1: Get and put functions

2.2 Laws of well-formed transformations

A transformation is said to be *well-formed* when it satisfies two important laws, *GetPut* and *PutGet* [11, 20].

The *GetPut* law is the identity law. It mandates that, if a view is left unchanged since its extraction from the source (using *get*), then a backward transformation (*put*) will not alter the source. Formally, we can describe *GetPut* as:

$$put \ s \ (get \ s) = s \qquad (3)$$

The *PutGet* law mandates that all changes made to the view are reflected fully to the source (during *put*), such that a subsequent *get* will preserve all the changes. Formally, we can describe *PutGet* as:

$$get \ (put \ s \ v) = v \qquad (4)$$

2.3 Bidirectional programming languages

Bidirectional programming languages can be classified in two families: get-based languages and put-based languages.

2.3.1 Get-based languages

Several programming languages have been proposed that allow developers to write programs that produce bidirectional transformations. The majority of these languages are *get-based* languages, where the developer writes a *get* function, and the language's tools can derive a *put* function that, when combined with the *get* function, form a well-behaved bidirectional transformation. Examples of such languages include GRoundTram [17], Boomerang [4], and others.

However, for a given *get* function, there may be many *put* functions that would form a well-behaved bidirectional transformation. Get-based programming tools that automatically generate a *put* function given a *get* function will therefore not necessarily generate a *put* function that suits the developer's needs. A simple example illustrates the issue. We consider a rectangle, represented by its height h and width w, as the source. The *get* function returns the rectangle's height only, which is the view:

$$get(w, h) = h \qquad (5)$$

Many *put* functions exist that would produce a well-behaved transformation. For example, the rectangle's original width could be used:

$$put1 \ (w, h) \ h' = (w, h') \qquad (6)$$

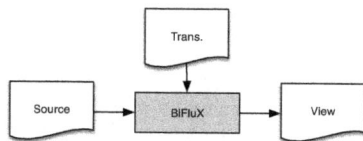

(a) Forward transformation

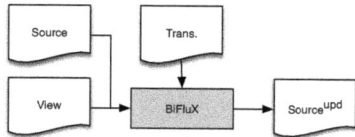

(b) Backward transformation

Figure 2: Bidirectional transformations in BiFluX

But many alternative *put* functions would also be acceptable, e.g.:

$$put2\ (w, h)\ h' = (w * h/h', h') \quad (7)$$

Both these *put* functions, and infinitely more, will produce a well-behaved bidirectional transformation, but not all of them will be acceptable for the developer. This is a limitation of get-based languages.

To mitigate this issue, several extensions of *get* functions have been proposed, such as quotient lenses [12], matching lenses [2], or Edit lenses [18].

2.3.2 Put-based languages

More recently, *put-based* languages (sometimes also called *putback* languages) have been proposed, such as BiFluX [27, 36]. Put-based languages ask the developer to provide a *put* function, and derive the *get* function automatically. Since it can be shown that, for a given *put* function, there is only one *get* function that produces a well-behaved bidirectional transformation [27, 36], developers have better control over the behaviour of their transformations.

BiFluX is a *putback* language for bidirectional transformations over XML files. Figure 2 shows how transformations work with BiFluX, with Figure 2a representing a forward transformation, and Figure 2b representing a backward transformation. Developers can write a program in BiFluX's language, and the compiler, implemented in Haskell [3], produces both a forward and a backward transformation, also in Haskell, that are guaranteed to form a well-behaved bidirectional transformation.

3. BIDIRECTIONAL PROGRAMMING AND ABAC

In this section, we use a calendar example to implement authorisation using bidirectional programming. We highlight and discuss the limitations of well-behaved bidirectional transformations as a way of implementing an ABAC authentication mechanism. Our example is a modified version of Foster's calendar sharing problem [11]. Appendix A shows the example in more detail. This example is a simple projection of the source into a view, chosen for its simplicity. However, bidirectional programming languages such as BiFluX can handle much more than projections, as they are able to change the structure of the data between the source and the view.

Alice maintains an online calendar, in which she records both her personal and work appointments (events). For each event, she records a start and end date and time, a location, a description, and a note. She would like to share her calendar with her colleague Bob. In order to balance her desire for privacy with Bob's need to access her calendar, she elicits the following requirements:

- Bob should be given access to Alice's work events, but not to her private events (*Req. 1*);

- Bob should only be given access to the following fields of Alice's work events: start time, end time, name, and location (*Req. 2*).

```
1   UPDATE $event IN $source/event BY
2     MATCH ->
3       REPLACE $event/starttime WITH
            $starttime;
4       REPLACE  $event/endtime WITH
            $endtime;
5       REPLACE  $event/location WITH
            $location
6   | UNMATCHV -> CREATE VALUE
7       <event>
8         <starttime/>
9         <endtime/>
10        <name/>
11        <note>nothing</note>
12        <location/>
13        <private>False</private>
14      </event>
15  | UNMATCHS -> DELETE .
16  FOR VIEW event[$starttime AS v:
        starttime,
17    $endtime AS v:endtime, $name AS v:
        name,
18    $location AS v:location] IN $view/*
19  MATCHING SOURCE BY $event/name VIEW BY
        $name
20  WHERE private/text() = 'False'
```

Listing 1: BiFluX transformation for the calendar example

Alice's calendar is an XML document. She wants to write a bidirectional program to share her calendar with Bob, and use BiFluX to generate a bidirectional transformation from it. She writes a bidirectional program that satisfies *Reqs. 1* and *2* (Listing 1). The program features well-separated CRUD operations: the *UNMATCHV* definition, on lines 6-14, defines the *Create* permissions; the *view* definition, on lines 16-20, defines the *Read* permissions; the *MATCH* definition, on lines 2-5, defines the *Update* permissions; and finally, the *UNMATCHS* definition, on line 15, defines the *Delete* permissions.

The program satisfies Alice's requirements. Line 20 restricts the view to Alice's work events only, ensuring that Bob cannot read her personal events. Since only work events are available in the view, the *UNMATCHS* directive can only apply to work events, and therefore Bob will not be able to delete any of Alice's private events. Similarly, the *MATCH* directive guarantees that Bob will not be able to update any of Alice's private events. And finally, the *UN-MATCHV* directive prescribes, on line 13, that any event created by Bob will be added to Alice's calendar as a work event. Hence, Bob is not able to create new private events on Alice's calendar. This satisfied *Req. 1*. The view definition, on lines 16-20, stipulates which fields of Alice's events Bob can access, which satisfies *Req. 2*.

```
1  <?xml version="1.0"?>
2  <calendar>
3    <event>
4      <starttime>2014-11-20_14:00</
         starttime>
5      <endtime>2014-11-20_15:00</endtime>
6      <name>Group meeting</name>
7      <note>Prepare some slides</note>
8      <location>Room 1611</location>
9      <private>False</private>
10   </event>
11   <event>
12     <starttime>2014-11-21_20:00</
         starttime>
13     <endtime>2014-11-20_22:00</endtime>
14     <name>Dinner</name>
15     <note>Meet with Mr. Creosote</note>
16     <location>Restaurant</location>
17     <private>True</private>
18   </event>
19 </calendar>
```

Listing 2: Alice's calendar

Listing 2 shows an example of Alice's calendar (the source of the transformation, which conforms to the source DTD in Appendix A.1). There are two events in the calendar, and only one of those is a work event. The forward transformation produces the view on Listing 3, which only contains the work event. The *note* field, which Bob is not authorised to see, does not appear on the view.

```
1  <?xml version="1.0"?>
2  <calview>
3    <event>
4      <starttime>2014-11-20_14:00</
         starttime>
5      <endtime>2014-11-20_15:00</endtime>
6      <name>Group meeting</name>
7      <location>Room 1611</location>
8    </event>
9  </calview>
```

Listing 3: Bob's view of Alice's calendar (XML)

Bob can update or delete events in his view, and he can create new events, as long as his changes produce an updated view that still conforms to the view DTD (see Appendix A.2). Bob's changes can be reflected to Alice's source with a backward transformation. Listings 4 and 5 show an example. Listing 4 contains a new event that Bob added to his view. Listing 5 is the event as it is added to Alice's source as a result of the backward transformation. The fields created by Bob are added to Alice's source, as well as the default value for the *note* field. The *private* field is set to *false*, which indicates a work event. BiFluX has verified that the bidirectional transformation is well-behaved.

```
1  [...]
2  <event>
3    <starttime>now</starttime>
4    <endtime>later</endtime>
5    <name>New Meeting</name>
6    <location>The Office</location>
7  </event>
8  [...]
```

Listing 4: Addition to Bob's view

```
1  [...]
2  <event>
3    <starttime>now</starttime>
4    <endtime>later</endtime>
5    <name>New Meeting</name>
6    <location>The Office</location>
7    <note>Nothing</note>
8    <private>False</private>
9  </event>
10 [...]
```

Listing 5: Propagated event in Alice's source

Alice, however, is not satisfied with her program. She thinks that Bob's access to her calendar is too broad, and that her data may be at risk. To mitigate the risk she decides to incorporate a form of ABAC to her transformation. She elicits the following additional requirements:

- Bob should be able to create new or update existing events, but only during working hours[1] (*Req. 3*);

- Bob should be able to delete existing events from Alice's calendar, but only if he is at work, as determined by his IP address (*Req. 4*).

Alice wants to update her program to satisfy these requirements. In ABAC terminology, the time of the day is an environment attribute, and Bob's location is a subject attribute. For simplicity, Alice wants the value of these attributes to be evaluated when transformations are performed, as opposed to when Bob is actually making the changes. In BiFluX, Alice could simply pass the values of these two attributes to the main procedure, and use conditional statements to implement authorisation. Listing 6 shows an excerpt of the calendar program, where *Req. 3* is implemented. Alice has added, on line 2, an **if** statement, that will create a new event in the source only if the variable $workingHours evaluates to *true* when the transformation is run. *Req. 4* can be implemented in a similar way.

---

[1]We assume working hours to be Mon-Fri, 09:00am - 07:00pm

```
1   [...]
2   | UNMATCHV -> IF ($workingHours == true
      ) THEN {
3     CREATE VALUE
4       <event>
5         <starttime/>
6         <endtime/>
7         <name/>
8         <note>nothing</note>
9         <location/>
10        <private>False</private>
11      </event>
12  } ELSE {}
13  [...]
```

Listing 6: Updated transformation (portion)

Unfortunately, the transformation produced from Alice's modified program does not satisfy *PutGet* for some combination of the attributes' values. For example, if Bob creates a new event (Listing 4) during his working hours, the source will be updated just like in Alice's initial program (Listing 5). Any new forward transformation will produce a source with the added event, which will be identical to Bob's updated view. This is *PutGet*. However, if the backward transformation happens *outside* of Bob's working hours, then the new event will *not* be added to Alice's source, and any subsequent forward transformation will not include the event, and will therefore be different from Bob's view, which violates *PutGet*. *GetPut*, however, is still satisfied since it involves no changes in the view, but the introduction of rules based on the values of attributes to govern what Bob can read will cause the same issue.

The issue is more easily highlighted by considering a very simple bidirectional transformation in Haskell, that could have been produced by a simple BiFluX program. The following *get* function takes a list as its source, and returns the first element of the list as the view. The *put* function replaces the first element of the source with its single element:

```
1   get :: Source -> View
2   get (x:xs) = x
3
4   put :: Source -> View -> Source
5   put y (x:xs) = y:xs
```

It is obvious that both *GetPut* and *PutGet* hold. We then refine the two functions, so that the *get* function will only return the first element of the source list if an attribute a evaluates to true, and an empty list otherwise. Similarly, the *put* function will only update the source with its view element if a evaluates to true, and leave the source otherwise unchanged:

```
1   get :: Bool -> Source -> View
2   get a (x:xs) = if a then x
3                      else []
4
5   put :: Bool -> Source -> View -> Source
6   put a y (x:xs) = if a then y:xs
7                        else x:xs
```

In this case, *GetPut* and *PutGet* only hold if the value of a does not change between operations. This is a significant issue for our example, as it would force Bob to get a new view right before updating Alice's calendar every time he wants to update it. Another issue arises if we modify the

functions a bit more. Now, *get* is unchanged, but *put* takes b instead of a as an argument. The functions become:

```
1   get :: Bool -> Source -> View
2   get a (x:xs) = if a then x
3                      else []
4
5   put :: Bool -> Source -> View -> Source
6   put b y (x:xs) = if b then y:xs
7                        else x:xs
```

If the values of a and b are independent, then it is not possible to guarantee that *GetPut* and *PutGet* hold anymore, even if their respective values are fixed. *GetPut* is then expressed as:

$$put \ b \ s \ (get \ a \ s) = s$$

PutGet is then expressed as:

$$get \ a \ (put \ b \ s \ v) = v$$

Let us consider a to be true and b false. Given the list [1,2] as a source, and considering that we update the view, when appropriate, with the value 4, Table 1 shows whether *GetPut* and *PutGet* hold for each value of a and b.

The second line, where a is true and b is false, can be detailed as follows. For *GetPut*, we first run `get true [1,2]`, which returns 1. We then run `put false [1,2] 1`, which returns [1,2]. *GetPut* holds. For *PutGet*, we first run `put false [1,2] 4`, which returns [1,2]. We then run `get true [1,2]`, which returns 1. *PutGet* does not hold. The other combinations of values of a and b can be developed in the same way.

This example highlights the limitation to the expressivity of authorisation rules implemented as part of a bidirectional transformation. If a transformation uses attributes whose value may vary, then the transformation will not be well-behaved for some combinations of the attributes' values.

Another issue with this solution is that the authorisation code (*what* can be done, under which conditions) is mixed with the implementation (*how* it can be done), which violates the principle of separation of concerns [7].

Finally, a third issue has to do with reuse and maintainability. It is possible that Alice may want to share the same data with more people than just Bob, but with slightly different requirements. For example, she may want to give read-only access to her work-related events to some of her subordinates, or give write access to somebody else, but only for events related to a particular project. If Alice integrates the authorisation constraints directly into the program, she will have to write a program for each of those people that she wants to share a view with. If the structure of Alice's calendar, or of the views, must change, then she will have to edit many transformations.

In the next section, we propose an approach that solves these three issues. A separation of the authorisation rules from the program achieves separation of concerns, and also allows one to define well-behaved transformations that BiFluX can run.

4. OVERVIEW OF THE APPROACH

To address the issues discussed above, we propose an approach that separates the expression and enforcement of the

Table 1: Status of *GetPut* and *PutGet* for values of a and b

a	b	GetPut	Holds?	PutGet	Holds?
T	T	put true [1,2] (get true [1,2]) = [1,2]	Y	get true (put true [1,2] 4) = 4	Y
T	F	put false [1,2] (get true [1,2]) = [1,2]	Y	get true (put false [1,2] 4) = 1	N
F	T	put true [1,2] (get false [1,2]) = [[],2]	N	get false (put true [1,2] 4) = []	N
F	F	put false [1,2] (get false [1,2]) = [1,2]	Y	get false (put false [1,2] 4) = []	N

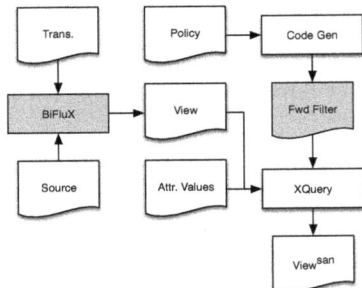

Figure 3: Forward transformation, with authorisation filter

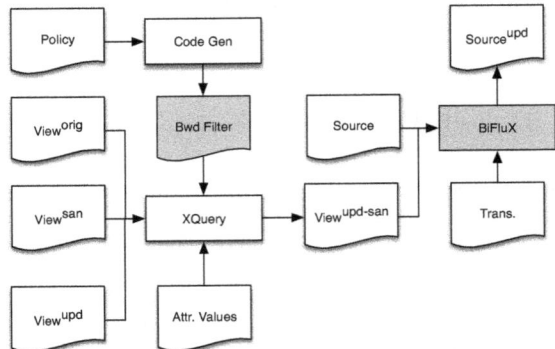

Figure 4: Backward transformation, with authorisation filter

authorisation policy from the program. In our approach, the program is written without consideration for authorisation attributes: all changes to the view (creation, update and deletion of elements) are authorised, and the view contains all the information that could ever be read. The part of the program that defines the view acts as a "best scenario" *read* policy, while the *MATCH*, *UNMATCHS* and *UNMATCHV* parts of the program define *how* the update, delete and create operations are carried on, respectively, if they were to be authorised. The program must produce a well-behaved bidirectional transformation. An authorisation policy is written separately, to specify the conditions under which create, read, update and delete operations can be reflected to the source. The policy is then used to produce two filters, one for forward transformations, and one for backward transformations. Figures 3 and 4 show how the filters are used in conjunction with BiFluX for the generation of the view (forward transformation), and the propagation to the source (backward transformation), respectively.

The policy (*Policy*) is first compiled into a forward filter (*Fwd Filter* in Figure 3) and a backward filter (*Bwd Filter* in Figure 4).

To get the view from the source (Figure 3), the forward transformation is run first. It uses the source (*Source*) and produces a view (*View*). Then, the view is passed through the forward filter (*Fwd Filter*) using the current values of the attributes involved (*Attr. Values*), which produces a sanitised view ($View^{san}$), which can be shared with the recipient (e.g., Bob).

To reflect the changes made to the view back into the source (Figure 4), the view originally produced ($View^{orig}$), the view shared with the recipient after the forward filter ($View^{san}$) and the view as updated by the recipient ($View^{upd}$) are passed through the backward filter (*Bwd Filter*), together with the current values of the attributes involved (*Attr. Values*). Any change that is not allowed at that moment will be reverted by the backward filter. Alternatively, one could reject the update entirely if some unauthorised changes are detected. The resulting view

($View^{upd-san}$) is then passed, together with the original source (*Source*), to BiFluX to run the backward transformation. The result is an updated source ($Source^{upd}$), that has only been updated with the authorised changes.

This approach separates the authorisation rules from the program. It allows for a clearer expression of the authorisation policy, as well as a clearer expression of the program. The separation also allows one to define complex, attribute-based authorisation policies that would otherwise result in transformations that are not well-behaved.

Because the policy is defined over a *view*, the same program can be reused to share views with multiple subjects, by defining a different policy for each of them, or each group of them that can be governed by the same policy.

Our approach applies to simple projections of a source onto a view (Alice's calendar sharing requirements define an example of a simple projection), where bidirectional transformations are a way of addressing the view-update problem. But it also applies to more complex transformations where the structures of the source and view are different. For example, a source for an online store may contain a set of products, each of then containing stock information and the details of all orders of the product; while the view would be a set of orders from customers, each order containing details about the products ordered. In both cases, the authorisation policy will determine which parts of the view can be created, read, updated or deleted.

5. A POLICY LANGUAGE FOR BIDIRECTIONAL TRANSFORMATIONS

BXauthZ is a simple policy language to express attribute-based rules on XML views. BXauthZ allows one to define rules for CRUD operations. The resources on which rules apply are defined as XPath expressions [34]. The language

⟨Policy⟩	::=	'policy' ⟨id⟩ '{' ⟨subject⟩ ⟨transformation⟩ ⟨rule⟩ '}'
⟨Subject⟩	::=	'subject' ⟨id⟩
⟨Transformation⟩	::=	'transformation' ⟨id⟩
⟨Rules⟩	::=	⟨Rule⟩ ⟨Rules⟩
	|	⟨Rule⟩
⟨Rule⟩	::=	'rule' ⟨id⟩ '{' ⟨Actions⟩ ⟨Resources⟩ ⟨Conditions⟩ '}'
	|	'rule' ⟨id⟩ '{' ⟨Actions⟩ ⟨Resources⟩ '}'
⟨Actions⟩	::=	⟨Action⟩ ⟨Actions⟩
	|	⟨Action⟩
⟨Resources⟩	::=	⟨Resource⟩ ⟨Resources⟩
	|	⟨Resource⟩
⟨Conditions⟩	::=	⟨Condition⟩ ⟨Conditions⟩
	|	⟨Condition⟩
⟨Action⟩	::=	'action' 'create'
	|	'action' 'read'
	|	'action' 'update'
	|	'action' 'delete'
⟨Resource⟩	::=	'resource' ⟨XPathExpression⟩
	|	'resource' ⟨XPathExpression⟩ 'matching-by' ⟨Name⟩
⟨Condition⟩	::=	'condition' ⟨BooleanExpression⟩

Figure 5: Grammar of BXauthZ (abbreviated)

is loosely based on Axiomatics' ALFA syntax[2], which is a concise DSL to write policies that can be compiled into eXtensible Access Control Markup Language (XACML) [26] (note that BXauthZ does not compile to XACML).

5.1 Grammar

Figure 5 shows an abbreviated version of BXauthZ's grammar. A policy in BXauthZ describes authorisation permissions for one or several subjects to perform CRUD operations over XML data in a view. A policy has a unique name, and includes the subjects and the transformation that produces the view on which the policy applies (both mandatory), as well as a set of rules (optional, though an empty set of rules would not produce a very useful policy). Any action on any resource is forbidden, unless explicitly permitted by a rule.

Each rule has a unique name, and is made of three parts: a set of actions (mandatory), a set of resources (mandatory), and a set of conditions (optional). Each rule's effect is *Permit*, as long as *all* the conditions are satisfied. The actions can be *create*, *read*, *update* or *delete*. The resources are expressed as XPath expressions [34]. If the resource is an XML node, then the permission applies to the node as

[2] http://www.axiomatics.com/alfa-plugin-for-eclipse.html, accessed January 2015

well as all its contents, including descendant nodes. Conditions are boolean expression. Resources for *create*, *update*, and *delete* actions also have a `matching-by` statement which denotes the child element or attribute that is used to match elements, in order to tell the difference between an update and a creation or deletion of an element.

There is no rule combination algorithm in BXauthZ, unlike policy languages such as XACML. Since all the rules define *Permit* effects, and since anything that is not explicitly permitted is denied, there can not be any conflicting answers, and therefore the order in which the rules are evaluated does not matter. If several rules use the same XPath expression, then the satisfaction of any of the rules will allow for the action defined by that rule.

5.2 Example

Listing 7 shows a sample policy written by Alice, to regulate Bob's access to the view generated by the program Alice created on Listing 1. The policy conforms to the 4 requirements elicited by Alice in Section 3.

```
1  policy BobCalendar {
2        subjects {Bob}
3        transformation calendar
4        rule CalRead {
5              action read
6              resource /calview/*
7        }
8        rule CalCreate {
9              action create
10             action update
11             resource /calview/*
                     matching-by name/
                     text()
12             condition $workingHours
13       }
14       rule CalUpdateDelete {
15             action delete
16             resource /calview/*
                     matching-by name/
                     text()
17             condition $atOffice
18       }
19 }
```

Listing 7: Policy for Bob's access to Alice's calendar

The policy's only subject is Bob (line 2), and the policy applies to views produced by the program on Listing 1 (line 3). There are four rules in the policy. The first one (lines 4-7) defines the read actions (line 5). Bob is allowed to read everything, at all times (line 6). Therefore, the forward filter generated by this policy will leave the generated view intact. Because the view definition in the program already excludes private events from the view, and because it already restricts the elements of each events that can be accessed, *Reqs. 1* and *2* are satisfied.

The second rule (lines 8-13) has two actions, create (line 9) and update (line 10). The resources are all the events in the view (line 11). This rule has a condition (line 12), which states that the rule only applies if `$workingHours` evaluates to *true*, which will only be the case during working hours, as defined by Alice. This rule satisfies *Req. 3*.

The third rule (lines 14-18) has only one action, delete (line 15). The resources are all the events in the view (line 16), like the other two rules. The rule has one condition (line

17), which states that the rule only applies if `$atOffice` evaluates to *true*, which will only be the case if Bob's IP address shows that he is located on the company premises. The rule satisfies *Req. 4*.

5.3 Remark

Nodes that are not covered by any rule, and who do not have at least one ancestor covered by a rule, will not always be removed from the view. If such a node has at least one descendant covered by a rule, then the node will be conserved in the filtered view, but without its content, except for the descendants that must be conserved as well. Let us consider this simple view as an example:

```
1  <a>
2     <b/>
3     <c>
4        <d/>
5     </c>
6  </a>
```

There could be a policy that applies to that view, and defines only one rule, with /a/c/d as a resource. While the a and c elements are not covered by the rule, they are ancestors of d, which is captured by the rule. b, however, is not an ancestor of d. Therefore, the sanitised view that would result from the application of the policy would be:

```
1  <a>
2     <c>
3        <d/>
4     </c>
5  </a>
```

6. AUTHORISATION FILTERS

The BXauthZ compiler produces, for each policy, a pair of XQuery filters. The forward filter, which is run after the forward transformation, sanitises the view according to the *read* actions in the policy, so it can be shared with its recipient. The backward filter, which is run before the backward transformation, sanitises the view according to the *create*, *update* and *delete* actions in the policy, to guarantee that no unauthorised changes are propagated to the source. Both filters will use the values of the attributes defined in the rules' conditions. Those values should be obtained securely, for example through a Policy Information Point (PIP). Determining which values can be collected from the client (e.g. Bob) without verification is out of the scope of this paper.

6.1 The forward filter

The forward filter takes two inputs: the view generated by the forward transformation, and the values of the attributes involved in the filter. The filter outputs a sanitised view. We call the view generated by the forward transformation, $view^{orig}$, and the sanitised view produced by the forward filter, $view^{sanV}$. Using the XPath expressions defined in the policy, the filter removes from the view the elements to which access is not granted at the time the filter is run.

6.2 The backward filter

The backward filter takes three inputs. The first one is the view updated by the user, which we call $view^{upd}$. The second one is the original view, $view^{orig}$. The third one is the view produced by the forward filter, $view^{sanV}$. The filter outputs a sanitised view that we call $view^{sanS}$. The filter also takes as an input the values of all the attributes involved in *create*, *update*, and *delete* decisions.

This backward filter is more complex than the forward filter. Indeed, it needs to merge the changes made by the user, as well as the elements that have been hidden from the user by the forward filter. First, the filter uses $view^{sanV}$, $view^{sanS}$, and the attributes' values to revert the changes made to the view that are not permitted by the policy. Then, the filter uses this product together with $view^{orig}$ to add the elements that had been remove by the forward filter. The resulting view can them be used by the backward transformation to reflect the user's changes back to the source.

7. IMPLEMENTATION AND PROOF OF CONCEPT

Our implementation of the approach described in this paper, as well as the calendar example, are available online.

7.1 Policy language and filter generation

BXauthZ[3] has been implemented as a Domain-Specific Language (DSL) using Xtext[4], an Eclipse-based framework for developing DSLs and programming languages. BXauthZ offers a complete IDE based on eclipse, as well as code generation capabilities that generate both the forward and the backward filters for any policy.

7.2 Filter evaluation

The filters are generated by BXauthZ in XQuery 3.0 [33]. Any product that complies with the XQuery 3.0 recommendation should be able to execute the filters. To conduct our tests, we used Zorba 3.0[5], an open source, multi-platform XQuery and JSON query processor.

7.3 Proof of concept

To evaluate our approach, we have developed a proof of concept based around the calendar example used throughout this paper. Bob's policy, as well as a few alternatives, were created using BXauthZ, and the corresponding filters were generated using BXauthZ's code generator[6].

8. RELATED WORK

Secure XML views [29] have been studied in detail as a means to provide access to confidential information. Fan et al. have proposed an approach to support XPath queries over security views [9]. Kuper et al. generalised the notion of security views where authorisation policies are specified over DTDs [23]. Rota et al. integrate XACML with OWL [31] ontologies to provide semantic authorisation for XML documents [28].

As far as we are aware, the only work that addresses the view-update problem in security views is Foster's updatable security views [11, 10], for which there is no implementation. Foster introduces secure lenses as an extension of his previous work on lenses [13], with a type system to ensure integrity and confidentiality of the data in the source [11]. While the calendar example in this paper is inspired by Foster's, secure lenses are very different from the solution we

---

[3] https://github.com/lmontrieux/bxauthz
[4] http://www.xtext.org
[5] http://www.zorba.io
[6] https://github.com/lmontrieux/biflux-filters-poc

propose, in the sense that he uses annotations on the source to enforce the confidentiality and integrity of some of the source data, while we devise policies on the view to ensure confidentiality and integrity, and implement them around a bidirectional transformation engine, rather than extending its semantics to support it, which Foster does (although with Boomerang [4] instead of BiFluX).

Access control for XML documents is also a field that has been widely researched. For example, Kudo and Hada proposed XML Access Control Language (XACL), a language that provides authorisation for XML documents, based on a provisional authorisation model, and using XPath expressions [21, 22]. Gabillon and Bruno transform authorisation policies into XSLT sheets [32], that are used to extract a secure view from XML documents [14]. Auntariya et al. propose a rule-based access control model that provides declarative policy rules on XML documents, as well as conflict resolution and default authorisation [1]. Gowadia and Farkas use RDF statements with authorisation properties to represent XML access control rules [15]. Zhang et al. use XML Schemas to represent Role-Based Access Control (RBAC) models for XML data [37]. Byun and Park introduce a two phase filtering approach to modify queries on XML databases in order to ensure that the results will not violate access control policies [5]. Duong and Zhang describe an access control model for XML that supports both read and write authorisation, allowing authorised users to change the structure of the XML documents [8]. Finally, Thimma et al. introduce Hybrid XML Access Control (HyXAC), a hybrid access control approach that provides secure queries on XML documents while improving its performance over other solutions [30].

9. CONCLUSION

In this paper, we highlighted the strong connection between authorisation and bidirectional transformations, as transformations themselves can provide a simple form of access control. We provided a solution that allows for the enforcement of attribute-based authorisation on bidirectional programs, without compromising on the laws of well-behaved bidirectional transformations. Our approach uses a custom policy language that is used to generate filters that sanitise views after a forward transformation and before a backward transformation. The former guarantees that no unauthorised data is leaked to the recipient of the view, while the latter guarantees the integrity of the source. Our approach enforces a clear separation of concerns between the programs and the authorisation policies, therefore allowing one to reuse the same transformation to share information with several subjects, simply by creating a different policy for each subject or group of subjects.

A first direction for future work would be to derive the entire program from the policy alone, which would allow users such as Alice to share data in what we hope would be a much easier way, while still conserving the advantages of bidirectional transformations. Our experience shows that writing non-trivial, well-behaved programs can be very challenging. However, such a solution would reduce the user's ability to control the update, and in particular may restrict the view to a projection of the source.

Another direction for future work is the exploration of other bidirectional transformation engines, in particular get-based solutions. Because get-based solutions do not require

the user to explicitly define a put strategy, it is the engine itself that selects a strategy that, given a forward transformation, will satisfy both the *PutGet* and *GetPut* laws. If authorisation is considered in the approach, the choice of a *put* function should satisfy the authorisation policy.

Yet another direction is the implementation of ABAC constructs directly into bidirectional transformation languages, with the goal of making the transformations more efficient. This may require us to relax the laws of well-behaved transformations in order to allow for attribute-based authorisation, while still offering strong guarantees that transformations behave as expected.

Finally, issues of conflicts and performance should be studied. Sharing data using multiple views, that are shared to different subjects, will lead to conflicts that will need to be resolved. For example, if a view deletes a node whilst another one modifies it, a conflict resolution strategy will be necessary. Performance should also be considered. Efficient bidirectional transformation engines will allow for practical use over large documents.

10. ACKNOWLEDGEMENTS

This work is supported financially by the Nation Basic Research Program (973 Program) of China (grant No. 2015CB352201) and by JSPS Grant-in-Aid for Scientific Research (A) No. 25240009 in Japan.

11. REFERENCES

[1] C. Anutariya, S. Chatvichienchai, M. Iwiahara, V. Wuwongse, and Y. Kambayashi. A rule-based XML access control model. In M. Schröder and G. Wagner, editors, *Rules and Rule Markup Languages for the Semantic Web*, number 2876 in Lecture Notes in Computer Science, pages 35–48. Springer, 2003.

[2] D. M. Barbosa, J. Cretin, N. Foster, M. Greenberg, and B. C. Pierce. Matching lenses: Alignment and view update. In *Proceedings of the 15th ACM SIGPLAN International Conference on Functional Programming*, ICFP '10, pages 193–204, New York, NY, USA, 2010. ACM.

[3] R. Bird. *Introduction to Functional Programming using Haskell*. Prentice Hall, London; New York, 2nd edition, May 1998.

[4] A. Bohannon, J. N. Foster, B. C. Pierce, A. Pilkiewicz, and A. Schmitt. Boomerang: Resourceful lenses for string data. In *Proceedings of the 35th Annual ACM SIGPLAN-SIGACT Symposium on Principles of Programming Languages*, POPL '08, pages 407–419, New York, NY, USA, 2008. ACM.

[5] C. Byun and S. Park. Two phase filtering for XML access control. In W. Jonker and M. Petković, editors, *Secure Data Management*, number 4165 in Lecture Notes in Computer Science, pages 115–130. Springer, Jan. 2006.

[6] K. Czarnecki, J. N. Foster, Z. Hu, R. Lämmel, A. Schürr, and J. F. Terwilliger. Bidirectional transformations: A cross-discipline perspective. In R. F. Paige, editor, *Theory and Practice of Model Transformations*, number 5563 in Lecture Notes in Computer Science, pages 260–283. Springer, Jan. 2009.

[7] P. D. E. W. Dijkstra. On the role of scientific thought. In *Selected Writings on Computing: A personal Perspective*, Texts and Monographs in Computer Science, pages 60–66. Springer, 1982.

[8] M. Duong and Y. Zhang. An integrated access control for securely querying and updating XML data. In A. Fekete and X. Lin, editors, *Nineteenth Australasian*

Database Conference (ADC 2008), volume 75 of *CRPIT*, pages 75–83, Wollongong, NSW, Australia, 2008. ACS.

[9] W. Fan, C.-Y. Chan, and M. Garofalakis. Secure XML querying with security views. In *Proceedings of the 2004 ACM SIGMOD International Conference on Management of Data*, SIGMOD '04, pages 587–598, New York, NY, USA, 2004. ACM.

[10] J. Foster, B. Pierce, and S. Zdancewic. Updatable security views. In *22nd IEEE Computer Security Foundations Symposium, 2009. CSF '09*, pages 60–74, July 2009.

[11] J. N. Foster. *Bidirectional Programming Languages*. PhD thesis, University of Pensylvania, Dec. 2009.

[12] J. N. Foster, T. J. Green, and V. Tannen. Annotated XML: Queries and provenance. In *Proceedings of the Twenty-seventh ACM SIGMOD-SIGACT-SIGART Symposium on Principles of Database Systems*, PODS '08, pages 271–280, New York, NY, USA, 2008. ACM.

[13] J. N. Foster, M. B. Greenwald, J. T. Moore, B. C. Pierce, and A. Schmitt. Combinators for bi-directional tree transformations: A linguistic approach to the view update problem. In *Proceedings of the 32Nd ACM SIGPLAN-SIGACT Symposium on Principles of Programming Languages*, POPL '05, pages 233–246, New York, NY, USA, 2005. ACM.

[14] A. Gabillon and E. Bruno. Regulating access to XML documents. In M. S. Olivier and D. L. Spooner, editors, *Database and Application Security XV*, number 87 in IFIP — The International Federation for Information Processing, pages 299–314. Springer, Jan. 2002.

[15] V. Gowadia and C. Farkas. RDF metadata for XML access control. In *Proceedings of the 2003 ACM Workshop on XML Security*, XMLSEC '03, pages 39–48, New York, NY, USA, 2003. ACM.

[16] F. Hermann and J. Voigtländer. First international workshop on bidirectional transformations (BX 2012): Preface. *Electronic Communications of the EASST*, 49(0), July 2012.

[17] S. Hidaka, Z. Hu, K. Inaba, H. Kato, K. Matsuda, and K. Nakano. Bidirectionalizing graph transformations. In *Proceedings of the 15th ACM SIGPLAN International Conference on Functional Programming*, ICFP '10, pages 205–216, New York, NY, USA, 2010. ACM.

[18] M. Hofmann, B. Pierce, and D. Wagner. Edit lenses. In *Proceedings of the 39th Annual ACM SIGPLAN-SIGACT Symposium on Principles of Programming Languages*, POPL '12, pages 495–508, New York, NY, USA, 2012. ACM.

[19] B. Hoisl, Z. Hu, and S. Hidaka. Towards co-evolution in model-driven development via bidirectional higher-order transformation. pages 466–471, Jan. 2014.

[20] Z. Hu, H. Pacheco, and S. Fischer. Validity checking of putback transformations in bidirectional programming. In C. Jones, P. Pihlajasaari, and J. Sun, editors, *FM 2014: Formal Methods*, number 8442 in Lecture Notes in Computer Science, pages 1–15. Springer, Jan. 2014.

[21] M. Kudo and S. Hada. XML document security based on provisional authorization. In *Proceedings of the 7th ACM Conference on Computer and Communications Security*, CCS '00, pages 87–96, New York, NY, USA, 2000. ACM.

[22] M. Kudo and N. Qi. Access control policy models for XML. In T. Yu and S. Jajodia, editors, *Secure Data Management in Decentralized Systems*, number 33 in Advances in Information Security, pages 97–126. Springer, Jan. 2007.

[23] G. Kuper, F. Massacci, and N. Rassadko. Generalized XML security views. In *Proceedings of the Tenth ACM Symposium on Access Control Models and Technologies*, SACMAT '05, pages 77–84, New York, NY, USA, 2005. ACM.

[24] K. Morita, A. Morihata, K. Matsuzaki, Z. Hu, and M. Takeichi. Automatic inversion generates divide-and-conquer parallel programs. In *Proceedings of the 2007 ACM SIGPLAN Conference on Programming Language Design and Implementation*, PLDI '07, pages 146–155, New York, NY, USA, 2007. ACM.

[25] K. Nakano, Z. Hu, and M. Takeichi. Consistent web site updating based on bidirectional transformation. *International Journal on Software Tools for Technology Transfer*, 11(6):453–468, Dec. 2009.

[26] OASIS. eXtensible access control markup language (XACML) version 3.0, Jan. 2013.

[27] H. Pacheco, T. Zan, and Z. Hu. BiFluX: A bidirectional functional update language for XML. In *6th International Symposium on Principles and Practice of Declarative Programming (PPDP 2014)*, 2014.

[28] A. Rota, S. Short, and M. A. Rahaman. XML secure views using semantic access control. In *Proceedings of the 2010 EDBT/ICDT Workshops*, EDBT '10, pages 5:1–5:10, New York, NY, USA, 2010. ACM.

[29] A. Stoica and C. Farkas. Secure XML views. In E. Gudes and S. Shenoi, editors, *Research Directions in Data and Applications Security*, number 128 in IFIP — The International Federation for Information Processing, pages 133–146. Springer, 2003.

[30] M. Thimma, T. K. Tsui, and B. Luo. HyXAC: A hybrid approach for XML access control. In *Proceedings of the 18th ACM Symposium on Access Control Models and Technologies*, SACMAT '13, pages 113–124, New York, NY, USA, 2013. ACM.

[31] W3C. OWL web ontology language reference, Feb. 2004.

[32] W3C. XSL transformations (XSLT) version 2.0, Jan. 2007.

[33] W3C. XML XPath language (XPath) 3.0, Apr. 2014.

[34] W3C. XQuery 3.0: An XML query language, Apr. 2014.

[35] Y. Yu, Y. Lin, Z. Hu, S. Hidaka, H. Kato, and L. Montrieux. Maintaining invariant traceability through bidirectional transformations. In *2012 34th International Conference on Software Engineering (ICSE)*, pages 540–550, June 2012.

[36] T. Zan, H. Pacheco, and Z. Hu. Writing bidirectional model transformations as intentional updates. In *Companion Proceedings of the 36th International Conference on Software Engineering*, ICSE Companion 2014, pages 488–491, New York, NY, USA, 2014. ACM.

[37] X. Zhang, J. Park, and R. Sandhu. Schema based XML security: RBAC approach. In S. D. C. d. Vimercati, I. Ray, and I. Ray, editors, *Data and Applications Security XVII*, number 142 in IFIP International Federation for Information Processing, pages 330–343. Springer, 2004.

APPENDIX

A. CALENDAR SHARING EXAMPLE

Due to space constraints, the calendar sharing example in this paper had to be kept short. We present an expanded version in this section.

A.1 Source DTD

This is the DTD to which the source file, i.e. Alice's entire calendar, has to conform.

```
1  <!DOCTYPE calendar [
2  <!ELEMENT calendar (event*)>
3  <!ELEMENT event(starttime, endtime,
     name, note,
4  location, private)>
5  <!ELEMENT starttime (#PCDATA)>
6  <!ELEMENT endtime (#PCDATA)>
7  <!ELEMENT name (#PCDATA)>
8  <!ELEMENT note (#PCDATA)>
9  <!ELEMENT location (#PCDATA)>
10 <!ELEMENT private (#PCDATA)>
11 ]>
```

A.2 View DTD

This is the DTD to which the view file, i.e. Bob's view of Alice's calendar, has to conform.

```
1  <!DOCTYPE calview [
2  <!ELEMENT calview (event*)>
3  <!ELEMENT event (starttime, endtime,
     name,
4  location)>
5  <!ELEMENT starttime (#PCDATA)>
6  <!ELEMENT endtime (#PCDATA)>
7  <!ELEMENT name (#PCDATA)>
8  <!ELEMENT location (#PCDATA)>
9  ]>
```

A.3 Transformation without Access Control

This is the transformation written by Alice to share a view of her calendar with Bob. The transformation mandates how changes to Bob's view must be reflected to Alice's source. It also shows that only private events will appear in Bob's view, and that the note field will be hidden.

```
1  UPDATE $event IN $source/event BY
2  MATCH  ->
3    REPLACE $event/starttime WITH
       $starttime;
4    REPLACE  $event/endtime WITH
       $endtime;
5    REPLACE  $event/location WITH
       $location
6  | UNMATCHV -> CREATE VALUE
7    <event>
8      <starttime/>
9      <endtime/>
10     <name/>
11     <note>nothing</note>
12     <location/>
13     <private>False</private>
14   </event>
15 | UNMATCHS -> DELETE .
16 FOR VIEW event[$starttime AS v:
     starttime,
17   $endtime AS v:endtime, $name AS v:
       name,
18   $location AS v:location] IN $view/*
```

```
19  MATCHING SOURCE BY $event/name VIEW BY
      $name
20  WHERE private/text() = 'False'
```

A.4 Policy

This is the policy written by Alice to further restrict what Bob is allowed to do with his view of her calendar.

```
1  policy BobCalendar {
2         subjects {Bob}
3         transformation calendar
4         rule CalRead {
5             action read
6             resource /calview/*
7         }
8         rule CalCreate {
9             action create
10            action update
11            resource /calview/*
                matching-by name/
                text()
12            condition $workingHours
13        }
14        rule CalUpdateDelete {
15            action delete
16            resource /calview/*
                matching-by name/
                text()
17            condition $atOffice
18        }
19 }
```

A.5 Source XML

This is Alice's calendar at the beginning of our example. This XML file conforms to the DTD in Section A.1.

```
1  <?xml version="1.0"?>
2  <calendar>
3    <event>
4      <starttime>2014-11-20_14:00</
         starttime>
5      <endtime>2014-11-20_15:00</endtime>
6      <name>Group meeting</name>
7      <note>Prepare some slides</note>
8      <location>Room 1611</location>
9      <private>False</private>
10   </event>
11   <event>
12     <starttime>2014-11-21_20:00</
         starttime>
13     <endtime>2014-11-20_22:00</endtime>
14     <name>Dinner</name>
15     <note>Meet with Mr. Creosote</note>
16     <location>Restaurant</location>
17     <private>True</private>
18   </event>
19 </calendar>
```

A.6 View XML

This is Bob's view of Alice's calendar after a forward transformation, using the transformation in Section A.3. Since the access control policy in Section A.4 allows for Bob to read the entire view under any circumstances, this view is also the view obtained after the forward filter.

```
1  <?xml version="1.0"?>
2  <calview>
3    <event>
```

```
4      <starttime>2014-11-20_14:00</
          starttime>
5      <endtime>2014-11-20_15:00</endtime>
6      <name>Group meeting</name>
7      <location>Room 1611</location>
8    </event>
9  </calview>
```

A.7 Updated view

This is Bob's view after he has modified it. Bob has added a new event, and deleted the existing one. The new event can only be reflected in Alice's source during working hours, while the deleted event can only be removed from Alice's source when Bob is at the office.

```
1  <?xml version="1.0"?>
2  <calview>
3    <event>
4      <starttime>2015-02-11_16:00</
          starttime>
5      <endtime>2015-02-11_18:00</endtime>
6      <name>Performance review</name>
7      <location>Room 2005</location>
8    </event>
9  </calview>
```

A.8 Updated views, after backward transformation

The view in the previous section is then passed to the backward filter. Depending on the time of the day and Bob's location, the resulting, sanitised view could take one of four forms. The first possible sanitised view results from running the backward transformation during working hours, and while Bob is at the office. In this case, the sanitised view is identical to the view in Section A.7.

Another possibility, if the backward filter is run during working hours but while Bob is not at the office, is that the newly created event is still present, but the deleted event has been reinstated in the view:

```
1  <?xml version="1.0"?>
2  <calview>
3    <event>
4      <starttime>2014-11-20_14:00</
          starttime>
5      <endtime>2014-11-20_15:00</endtime>
6      <name>Group meeting</name>
7      <location>Room 1611</location>
8    </event>
9    <event>
10     <starttime>2015-02-11_16:00</
          starttime>
11     <endtime>2015-02-11_18:00</endtime>
12     <name>Performance review</name>
13     <location>Room 2005</location>
14   </event>
15 </calview>
```

The other two possible views are omitted due to space constraints.

A.9 Updated sources

Once the backward filter has been run, BiFluX can then safely reflect the changes to the view back to the source. The previous section showed to possible sanitised views. The first one, where both changes made by Bob were accepted, will produce the following updated source:

```
1  <?xml version="1.0"?>
2  <calendar>
3    <event>
4      <starttime>2015-02-11_16:00</
          starttime>
5      <endtime>2015-02-11_18:00</endtime>
6      <name>Performance review</name>
7      <note>Nothing</note>
8      <location>Room 2005</location>
9      <private>False</private>
10   </event>
11   <event>
12     <starttime>2014-11-21_20:00</
          starttime>
13     <endtime>2014-11-20_22:00</endtime>
14     <name>Dinner</name>
15     <note>Meet with Mr. Creosote</note>
16     <location>Restaurant</location>
17     <private>True</private>
18   </event>
19 </calendar>
```

The second one, where only the newly created event was accepted, will produce the following updated source:

```
1  <?xml version="1.0"?>
2  <calendar>
3    <event>
4      <starttime>2014-11-20_14:00</
          starttime>
5      <endtime>2014-11-20_15:00</endtime>
6      <name>Group meeting</name>
7      <note>Prepare some slides</note>
8      <location>Room 1611</location>
9      <private>False</private>
10   </event>
11   <event>
12     <starttime>2014-11-21_20:00</
          starttime>
13     <endtime>2014-11-20_22:00</endtime>
14     <name>Dinner</name>
15     <note>Meet with Mr. Creosote</note>
16     <location>Restaurant</location>
17     <private>True</private>
18   </event>
19   <event>
20       <starttime>2015-02-11_16:00</
          starttime>
21     <endtime>2015-02-11_18:00</endtime>
22     <name>Performance review</name>
23       <note>Nothing</note>
24     <location>Room 2005</location>
25       <private>False</private>
26   </event>
27 </calendar>
```

Privacy and Access Control: How are These Two Concepts Related?

Anna Squicciarini
College of Information Sciences and
Technology
Pennsylvania State University
asquicciarini@ist.psu.edu

Ting Yu
Qatar Computing Research Institute
Doha, Qatar
tyu@qf.org.qa

Categories and Subject Descriptors

C.2 [**COMPUTER-COMMUNICATION NETWORKS**
]: Security and protection (e.g., firewalls)

Keywords

Security, Privacy, Access Control

1. PANEL DESCRIPTION

Privacy issues are increasingly becoming important for many domains and applications. Many of such issues arise from the constant streaming of personal and sensitive data made available from lay users online, and also from the emerging widespread of highly ubiquitous and content-rich, personalized applications. Further, strong regulatory frameworks are now in place to ensure that users' data is properly managed and protected. For instance, the responsible management of sensitive data is explicitly being mandated through laws such as the Sarbanes-Oaxley Act and the Health Insurance Portability and Accountability Act (HIPAA). Accordingly, data and user privacy have received substantial research attention over the past years. Several technical challenges have been tackled, including how to balance utility with the need to preserve privacy of individual data, and how to protect data from unwanted and unauthorized parties [5, 1, 6, 2]. In parallel, in response to several privacy outcries, many companies and organizations involved with users' data collection and management (particularly online) have also made an effort toward introducing stronger privacy and access control solutions. Yet these efforts have been shown to be inadequate or insufficient [7].

Among the various methods and mechanisms to ensure users' privacy, access control techniques are a well-established building block to protect users' data. Historically, the mechanism for access control was considered only a support provided by database systems for sensitive structured data. Such a model of authorization is intuitive to application developers and users of the database system, but it only

addresses a small portion of the complex issues underlying users' and data privacy. It is now clear that emerging applications require access control to be applied and managed in a more flexible and yet rigorous way [4, 3].

Further, access control represents only a small piece in the complex puzzle of users' privacy. Even when access control systems are successful in blocking out unwanted viewers, they are ineffective as privacy protection for a large, decentralized system like the World Wide Web, where it is easy to copy or aggregate information.

This panel will examine the challenges we face in adapting access control models, techniques, and tools produced thus far to address today's and tomorrow's privacy issues. We will discuss whether these issues may require our approach to access control to change in light of important changes in the way users adopt computing and data sharing. In many common new applications, users' data is no longer structured, nor well organized, nor centralized; a vast population of users operating mobile and other new devices has very little education in their use; and users' information is ubiquitous to the point where users themselves are often unaware of the amount of information they make available. These changes make achieving privacy much more challenging.

The panel will also examine the role of access control in the broader context of a variety of privacy protection methods. Whereas access control models rely on security properties and technical guarantees, privacy has a strong subjective component that is hard to quantify and properly measured. The extent to which the subjective privacy needs of a user can be met by an access control system is still unclear. Further, what techniques and approaches can we develop to help users, both experts and non-experts, protect the massive amount of data available about them and at everybody's reach? The panel will identify and rank specific challenges within these areas. It will discuss the important aspects that research should address, but maybe does not today.

2. REFERENCES

[1] A. Blum, K. Ligett, and A. Roth. A learning theory approach to noninteractive database privacy. *Journal of the ACM (JACM)*, 60(2):12, 2013.

[2] J.-W. Byun, E. Bertino, and N. Li. Purpose based access control of complex data for privacy protection. In *Proceedings of the tenth ACM symposium on Access control models and technologies*, pages 102–110. ACM, 2005.

SACMAT'15, June 1–3, 2015, Vienna, Austria.
ACM 978-1-4503-3556-0/15/06.
http://dx.doi.org/10.1145/2752952.2752980.

[3] J. Camenisch, S. Mödersheim, G. Neven, F.-S. Preiss, and D. Sommer. A language enabling privacy-preserving access control. SACMAT, 2010.

[4] D. W. Chadwick and K. Fatema. A privacy preserving authorisation system for the cloud. *Journal of Computer and System Sciences*, 78(5):1359–1373, 2012.

[5] C. Dwork. Differential privacy: A survey of results. In *Theory and Applications of Models of Computation*, pages 1–19. Springer, 2008.

[6] M. J. May, C. A. Gunter, and I. Lee. Privacy apis: Access control techniques to analyze and verify legal privacy policies. In *Computer Security Foundations Workshop, 2006. 19th IEEE*, pages 13–pp. IEEE, 2006.

[7] H. J. Smith, T. Dinev, and H. Xu. Information privacy research: an interdisciplinary review. *MIS quarterly*, 35(4):989–1016, 2011.

Mitigating Access Control Vulnerabilities through Interactive Static Analysis

Jun Zhu, Bill Chu, Heather Lipford, Tyler Thomas
University of North Carolina at Charlotte
Charlotte, NC 28223, USA
{jzhu16, billchu, Heather.Lipford, tthoma81}@uncc.edu

ABSTRACT

Access control vulnerabilities due to programming errors have consistently ranked amongst top software vulnerabilities. Previous research efforts have concentrated on using automatic program analysis techniques to detect access control vulnerabilities in applications. We report a comparative study of six open source PHP applications, and find that implicit assumptions of previous research techniques can significantly limit their effectiveness. We propose a more effective hybrid approach to mitigate access control vulnerabilities. Developers are reminded in-situ of potential access control vulnerabilities, where self-review of code can help them discover mistakes. Additionally, developers are prompted for application-specific access control knowledge, providing samples of code that could be thought of as static analysis by example. These examples are turned into code patterns that can be used in performing static analysis to detect additional access control vulnerabilities and alert the developer to take corrective actions. Our evaluation of six open source applications detected 20 zero-day access control vulnerabilities in addition to finding all access control vulnerabilities detected in previous works.

Categories and Subject Descriptors

D.4.6 [**Security and Protection**]

General Terms

Security, Human Factors

Keywords

Access Control Vulnerability; Secure Programming; Static Analysis

1. INTRODUCTION

Many computer security problems are caused by software vulnerabilities in applications that can be exploited by attackers. A common cause for such vulnerabilities is flaws introduced by developers during program construction. Secure programming practices to prevent such flaws have been well documented [1-5], yet developers continue to make the same mistakes. For example,

SACMAT'15, June 1–3, 2015, Vienna, Austria
Copyright © 2015 ACM 978-1-4503-3556-0/15/06...$15.00
http://dx.doi.org/10.1145/2752952.2752976

in 2013 WhiteHat Security analyzed over 600 corporate web sites and found that 86% of them contain serious security vulnerabilities, and it took on average 193 days to resolve vulnerability from the time it was discovered [6]. Access control vulnerabilities due to developer mistakes have been consistently ranked amongst top software vulnerabilities [7].

Static source code analysis is the leading method, in both academic research as well as commercial tools, to detect security vulnerabilities in program code [8-11]. Yet research suggests that software developers do not use commercial static analysis tools regularly [12]. One explanation for this usage gap is that using static analysis tools requires special training, so they are instead utilized by members of an organization's Software Security Group (SSG) [13]. Performing static analysis effectively to detect access control vulnerabilities often requires application-specific knowledge. Customized rules must be written in order for static analyzers to detect missing access control checks. As a result, using static analysis to detect access control vulnerabilities can be expensive in practice because it requires close collaboration between software developers and software security specialists trained to use static analysis tools.

Previous research efforts have primarily concentrated on using automatic program analysis techniques to detect access control vulnerabilities [14-19]. While these works have led to discovery of access control vulnerabilities in open source projects, there has not been any study evaluating their limits. We conducted a comparative study using six open source PHP applications, many of them used by related works as part of their evaluations. We found that the implicit assumptions made by these previous research techniques have significant limitations. Detecting access control vulnerabilities automatically is hard because it is difficult to infer intention of the developer based on source code alone.

We propose a hybrid approach based on **interactive static analysis** [20], which helps to mitigate vulnerabilities in two ways. First, developers are reminded in-situ of potential vulnerabilities, where self-review of code can help developers discover their own mistakes. Additionally, developers are prompted for application-specific access control knowledge, providing samples of code that could be thought of as static analysis by example. These examples are turned into code patterns that can be used in performing static analysis to detect additional vulnerabilities and alert the developer to take corrective action.

We implemented a prototype and evaluated its effectiveness in detecting access control vulnerabilities in six open source projects including a large-scale web application, Moodle [30]. Our results indicate that interactive static analysis outperforms automatic analysis techniques and that this can be used without imposing excessive interruption to developer workflow.

2. OUTCOME COMPARISON

To detect access control vulnerabilities, one must first have a correct access control model. Since usage of formal access control model specification languages are not widespread, such a model could be constructed either manually or inferred using data mining techniques. Previous researchers have attempted to automatically learn a correct access control model from source code and use it to detect likely vulnerabilities [14-19]. We collectively refer to these approaches *auto detection*.

Tan et al. [15] detects access control vulnerabilities through mining the program for program-wide patterns and considers deviations or anomalies as bugs. Dalton et al [16] detects authentication and access control vulnerabilities by performing dynamic information flow tracking on user credentials. It ensures that only properly authenticated user could access privileged resources, and prevents authentication bypass and access control attacks based on untrusted user credentials.

Son et al. [17] attempted to detect access control vulnerabilities automatically by exploiting several heuristics about the way programs are structured. First, code that implements distinct user role functionality and its access control checks reside in distinct methods and files. They compute commonality values between different files and partition the files into roles using a commonality threshold. Second, they compute branch asymmetry values, the ratio of statements in the successful branch vs. failed branch. The heuristic is that a security check is likely to have a large asymmetry number. So an asymmetry threshold value might suggest candidate access control checks. Based on the above two heuristics, they then infer correct access control checks as repetition of access control checks above a certain threshold in the same role.

Gauthier et al. [18] proposed to detect security weaknesses and vulnerabilities based on the heuristic that syntactically similar security-sensitive code fragments should be protected by similar checks. They first detect security-sensitive code clones based on a query-radius threshold value, and then based on the heuristic that access control checks are usually correctly enforced in majority cases within these code clones while wrongly enforced in minority cases, they identify the minority cases as security weaknesses or vulnerabilities.

Monshizadeh et al. [19] defines a four-tuple authorization context representing the access control rules, including developer identification of (global) access control variables. It detects privilege escalation vulnerabilities based on the consistency analysis on authorization contexts. Inconsistencies in authorization context are regarded as vulnerabilities.

2.1 Vulnerability Taxonomy

To better characterize the approaches for vulnerability detection, we now describe a taxonomy of access control software flaws. We use the term Security Sensitive Operation (SSO) to refer to an operation that requires access control checks (e.g. updating a database table). The types of access control vulnerabilities targeted by previous research can be described by the following taxonomy. (1) *Missing*: If there is no access control checks on an execution path leading to an SSO. (2) *Inconsistent*: There exist duplicate instances of the same SSO in the code but the control checks for them are not implemented consistently while their intended control policy should be equivalent. (3) *Untrusted data*: access control check is based on untrusted variables, including uninitialized variables and variables coming from untrusted data

sources that can be manipulated by an attacker. (4) *Logic errors*: Other logic errors in an access control check.

Table 1 summarizes types of errors addressed by previous research. The ASIDE column represents our work, which will be discussed in detail later in the paper.

Table 1. Types of access control vulnerabilities that each technique could solve.

	ASIDE	[16]	[17]	[18]	[19]
Missing	□				
Inconsistent	□		□	□	□
Untrusted data	□	□			□
Logic errors					

Most auto detection approaches learn correct access control model based on observed access control patterns. Throughout this paper, we use the term *access control check* to refer to a fragment of code that implements an access control policy. An *access control pattern* is a tuple of *(access control check, SSO)* representing a code instance where the access control check is performed for the SSO. Inferring the correct access control model for a given SSO requires multiple access control patterns. Once the access control model for an SSO is learned, one can easily identify vulnerability as code instances where the correct access control check does not appear. Therefore in [17-19] detecting missing access control is a special case of inconsistent access control checks. A natural question then arises: do applications have sufficiently large number of access control patterns to support learning of an accurate access control model? We conducted a study of six open source projects to find out.

2.2 Empirical Data on Duplicates

We selected six open source PHP-based projects for this evaluation. They are summarized in Table 2. References next to each project indicate the papers in which a given project has been used as part of their evaluation.

Table 2. Projects used in evaluation

Project	LOC	Description
Mybloggie 2.1.3 [19]	8,874	Blogging system
SCARF 1.0 [19]	1,318	Conference discussion forum
Wheatblog 1.1 [17]	4,032	Blogging system
Bilboblog 0.2.1 [16]	2,000	Blogging system
PhpStat 1.5 [16]	12,700	Application presenting IM statistics
Moodle [18]	625,000	Course management

We focused our evaluations on SSOs that are database operations. The techniques discussed here can be easily extended to other type of SSOs such as file operations. Besides Moodle, all other projects have easy to understand functions and a small number of database tables so it is fairly straightforward to identify security sensitive database operations through code reviews. We manually examined each SSO instance and identified access control checks in the source code. Table 3 summarizes our findings for projects MyBloggie, SCARF, Biboblog, Wheatbog, and PhpStat. Numbers in the table are access control patterns found. Columns headed with insert, update, delete, and select represent types of SSOs involved in these access control patterns. For example, for project SCARF, there are five access control patterns involving database delete operations. One pattern is repeated twice while the rest are not repeated. It is clear that in majority cases, an SSO either appears only once in an access control pattern or the number of patterns it appears in is very small.

Table 3. Distribution of access control patterns

Project	Insert	Update	Delete	Select
Mybloggie 2.1.3	2,2,2,1,1	2,2,1,1,1	2,2,1,1	
SCARF 1.0	1,1,1,1,1,1,1	4,3,2,2,1,1,1	2,1,1,1,1	
Bilboblog 0.2.1	1	1	1	
Wheatblog 1.1	1,1,1,1,1,1	2,1,1,1,1,1,1	1,1,1,1,1	2,2,1
PhpStat 1.5	2,1,1,1,1,1	6,6,3,2,1,1	2,1,1	

Because of the large number of tables in Moodle (over 250) as well as Moodle's large code base, we identified SSOs as database operations involved in known access control vulnerabilities (details described in Section 4.1). We believe this gives us an accurate estimated list of SSOs because Moodle is professionally maintained and has very good documentation of security fixes. We identified 31 SSOs in Moodle following this method and two of the authors manually annotated access control logic associated with each of them. Figure 1 shows our results on the distribution of access control patterns involving these 31 SSOs. Each bar represents the number of repeated access control patterns. The median number of repetitions for an access control pattern is one.

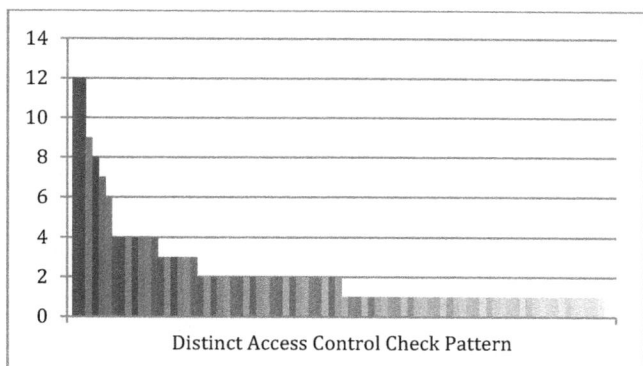

Figure 1. Distribution of access control patterns in Moodle.

Low repetitions of access control patterns limit the performance of auto detection approaches. At one extreme, consider the case that an access control pattern only appears once in the code. The auto detection approach will not be able to construct a correct access control model for such a case. More generally, the confidence of the constructed access control model depends on the size of repeated access control patterns as well as "noise" in code instances. Here "noise" refers to branching logic that may look like access control but is in fact not related to access control (e.g. business logic to select what table to update depending on application context). If code instances contain much non-security related branching logic in addition to access control checks, a larger number of code pattern repetitions are needed to "learn" how to separate the two kinds of branching logic. Threshold values were used by auto detection approaches to make these decisions. However, it is not clear how the combination of size of access control pattern repetition and branching complexity affect the accuracy of access control model extraction. It is not clear either how thresholds tuned for one project can be applied to another project.

Furthermore, auto detection techniques typically assume that there is only one unique access control check for a given SSO. This is however not always the case. We will provide concrete examples where an application may have multiple access control checks for the same SSO in Section 4.3.

At the observed level of repetition of access control patterns, auto detection approaches will have large false negatives (details in Section 4.2). We are thus motivated to take a hybrid approach in which we seek developer input to identify access control models for SSOs. We argue that such an approach will be more effective provided that it does not cause too much distraction to the developers.

3. INTERACTIVE STATIC ANALYSIS

Interactive tool support for secure programming in IDE [21-23] has been proposed to remind developers to write secure code as they construct the application, similar to how a grammar checker helps someone writing in a word processor. Initial user studies showed the promise of this approach for validating untrusted input to prevent injection attacks [23]. Zhu et al. generalized this approach to interactive static analysis [20] by refining the concept of interactive annotation [22] and hypothesized that it could be applicable for detecting access control vulnerabilities. Our work significantly improves upon the notion of interactive static analysis in the following areas: (a) providing a proof of concept implementation for access control vulnerability detection (b) evaluation of interactive static analysis's impact on developer workflow, and (c) evaluating its effectiveness with six open source projects and comparing our results with related works.

3.1 Interactive Static Analysis Example

We refer to our prototype implementation as ASIDE for PHP (Application Security plug-in for the Integrated Development Environment for PHP), or ASIDE in short. In this section we use an example from the open source project Moodle to illustrate key concepts of interactive static analysis and how it might work in practice. A Moodle chat room is created by a teacher for a specific course. Only logged-in users with required chat capability should send messages to the chat room. Listing 1 shows two code snippets from two different Moodle files that we use for this example. Listing 1.b has an access control vulnerability, which we will explain below.

```
require_login($course->id, false, $cm);
require_capability('mod/chat:chat', $context);
$DB->insert_record('chat_messages', $newmessage);
$DB->insert_record('chat_messages_current',
$newmessage);
```

a. Code snippet from /mod/chat/gui_basic/index.php of Moodle

```
require_login($course, false, $cm);
if(isguestuser()){print_error('noguests','chat');}
//chat_login_user() calls database insertion //to
tables chat_messages, chat_messages_current
if (!$chat_sid = chat_login_user($chat->id,
'sockets', $groupid, $course)) {
    print_error('cantlogin');}
```

b. Code snippet from /mod/chat/gui_sockets/index.php of Moodle

Listing 1. Example code snippets from Moodle. Code in 1.b is vulnerable. Access control checks are shown in *italics*.

Identifying SSOs is an important step in a secure software development lifecycle (SSDLC) [24] because knowing which data elements have security implications is critical for threat modeling [25]. A Software Security Group (SSG) within organizations often coordinates the SSDLC activities with development teams. In such an environment, security sensitive operations (e.g. operations SELECT, INSERT, UPDATE, DELETE on specific database tables) will be identified. This is the primary information required as input to interactive static analysis. Our example involves two Moodle database SSOs: INSERT to *chat_messages* and *chat_message_current*.

ASIDE continuously analyzes the source code in the background as the developers write code in Eclipse. When an SSO is detected, a yellow notification is placed alongside line 50 in Figure 2. The developer can hover over or click on the notification to interact with ASIDE. In this example, ASIDE is asking for the developer to highlight access control logic for inserting data into tables *chat_messages* and *chat_messages_current*. The function called on line 50 in Figures 2 and 3 invokes those database insertion operations.

The developer performs the annotation by highlighting the code containing the intended access control logic as shown in Figure 3 (lines 27 and 29 in green). This process is referred to as *interactive annotation* because no additional language syntax is required and it is integrated into the IDE. By providing the annotation, the developer is reminded to write code for access control checks, and will have an opportunity to reflect on the checks as they are being annotated. This reflection provides an additional opportunity for developers to self-review their code and notice mistakes they or others may have made. One nice effect of interaction annotation is that it can quickly identify cases where the developer has inadvertently left out the access control logic for a SSO entirely (the *missing* error type discussed in Section 2.1).

ASIDE uses static analysis techniques to detect vulnerabilities. In this example, ASIDE noticed that both code snippets from Listing 1 perform the same SSOs: inserting records to tables *chat messages* and *chat_messages_current*, but the two access control checks are different. This is an example of using duplication of access control checks to find inconsistent access control checks for the same SSO. ASIDE alerts the developer that there is a likely vulnerability, as shown by the red mark besides line 50 in Figure 3. This example is indeed a known Moodle vulnerability, CVE-2013-2242, where an unauthorized user can insert messages to a chat room. The vulnerable code in Listing 1.b only checks to make sure a user is not a guest user but did not ensure the user has the authorization for a particular chat room.

This example demonstrates key components of the interactive static analysis approach. First, vulnerability detection and mitigation is aimed at the developer, with the goal of providing assistance to help developers with this task. The notifications also provide developers in-situ reminders of the security implications of their code. Static analysis utilizes application specific access control knowledge requested from the developer, to aid in the detection of vulnerabilities. Together, this approach could potentially reduce the cost of vulnerability detection through earlier detection and reduced demand on software security experts.

3.2 ASIDE Overview

Figure 4 provides an overview of major components of ASIDE, which takes as input: (a) Abstract Syntax Trees (ASTs) of the application generated by Eclipse PDT [26], and (b) a set of security sensitive operations (SSOs) specified by the Software Security Group (SSG). ASIDE then uses these to generate annotation requests to the developer. With the annotations

provided by the developer, static analysis is used to detect vulnerabilities.

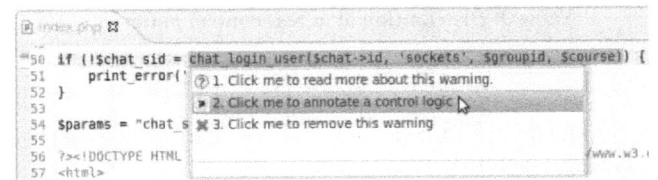

Figure 2. Explanation for interactive annotation

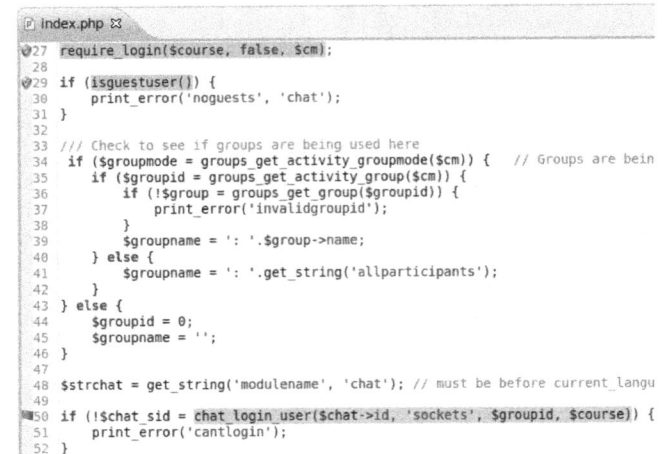

Figure 3. Access control checks (above green highlight), and a vulnerability warning (lower red highlight).

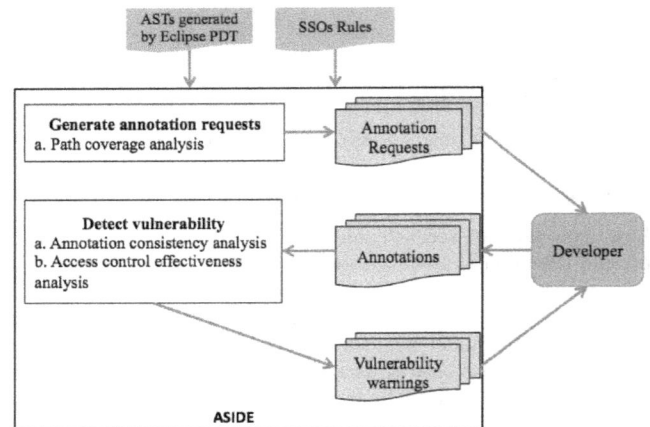

Figure 4. ASIDE architecture

Related auto detection approaches have avoided studying access control related to SELECT operations for database tables [17, 19], because they may lead to overwhelming false positives. Applications often read sensitive information from tables without the need of performing access control checks. For example, password may be read from a database table as part of the login process without access control checks. We overcome this limitation by considering sensitive SELECT operations only when sensitive data retrieved from the SELECT operation flows to a page-displaying API, for example echo() or print() in PHP. Frequently used page-displaying APIs for major web application development platforms are well known. They are often

202

represented as default sinks by commercial static analysis tools to detect cross-site scripting vulnerabilities. If, instead of being displayed, a sensitive information read impacts other SSOs, access control checks would be performed for these SSOs.

ASIDE then performs *path coverage analysis* [20] to generate annotation requests, which are displayed to a developer as shown in Figure 2, details are described in section 3.3. The developer could interact with these requests and make annotations through ASIDE. Based on new annotations, ASIDE performs static analysis to detect vulnerabilities and display warnings to developers. Static analysis can be performed in a background thread, and should not block the developer's interaction with the IDE. While the current implementation is not yet optimized for efficiency, we believe these techniques can be efficiently implemented because they fit nicely with multi-core computer architecture.

3.3 Interactive Annotation

Web applications differ from other applications in that they do not have a unique program entry point, or "main program". One can identify program entry points for web applications. For example, we distinguish two types of files with .PHP extensions. First, a file may contain only class and/or function definitions. Second, a file may contain executable code outside of function and class definitions. The second type of file is referred to as a program entry as a URL can invoke it.

ASIDE requests interactive annotation at the program entry level because it most likely corresponds to an application use case. Access control policies are often defined for use cases. Placement of an annotation request at this level makes it easier for a developer to identify intended access control code. ASIDE expects annotations for access control logic to consist of statements that could divert the execution path away from performing the SSO. For example, in Listing 1.a, method invocation *require_capability('capability_name')* throws an exception if the capability indicated by *capability_name* is not satisfied. More specifically, annotated code should satisfy several requirements: (1) it must be on the execution path from the program entry point to the SSO; (2) it must consist of either (2.a) a set of Boolean expressions[1] in a branch/conditional statement that lead to altering the execution path leading to the SSO involved, or (2.b) method invocations that could either throw exceptions or terminate the execution.

ASIDE enumerates all the execution paths from every program entry point to every SSO by computing program call graphs. This process is referred to as *path coverage analysis* [20] because it ensures that for every execution path thus identified, there must be at least one annotation for an access control check "covering" this path. ASIDE generates an annotation request for the developer for each path without an annotation. For example, in Figure 2, there exists an execution path from the program entry point *index.php* to the SSO INSERT to *chat_messages*, via function call *chat_login_user($chat->id, 'sockets', $groupid, $course)* on line 50. ASIDE thus generates an annotation request for line 50, shown as a yellow notification beside the code line.

3.4 Vulnerability Detection

Vulnerability detection in ASIDE is based on three mechanisms. First, the interactive annotation process encourages developers to

---

[1] PHP does not have static typing. We determine Booleans based on statement context.

self-review the access control logic and detect errors. This is particularly effective to help discover cases of missing access control checks. The second mechanism is based on the observation that the same SSOs normally require the same access control checks. The third mechanism is based on the observation that the annotated control checks should be (access) *control effective,* meaning they rely on trusted data for control decisions, rather than untrusted data or uninitialized variables.

3.4.1 Annotation consistency analysis

Differences in access control checks for the same SSOs often indicate a mistake. We adapted a method proposed by Son et al. [27] to determine whether two annotations match. We briefly summarize the steps of this process below and explain it through an example.

1. Obtain the calling context of an annotated check, using program slicing [28, 29], containing all statements to which the annotated check has data dependency. Listing 2 shows slices of code with annotations for control checks represented in *italics*.
2. Given the annotated check and its calling context, extract the access control template (ACT) of the annotated check, an abstract representation of the access control check along with its data dependencies for determining matches.
3. Given two ACTs, ACT_a and ACT_b, for each statement in ACT_a, check if there exists only one statement in ACT_b that matches it, and vice versa. The order of statements does not matter, because we consider their data dependency as part of the matching. Two statements match iff (a) their AST structures and operators are isomorphic, and (b) their data dependencies also match.

Consider the examples in Listing 2. The code in Listing 2.a matches code in Listing 2.c because the annotated access control checks refer to the same function call *has_capability()*. The first parameters in both instances match as both refer to the same constant. The second parameters are variables but both can be traced to the same constant "admincontext." On the other hand, Listing 2.b and 2.c do not match because the second parameters are traced to different values.

```
$context = "admincontext";
if(has_capability('moodle/blog:create',
$context)){ //annotated check
$DB->insert_record('blog'); //SSO
}
```

a. This access control check matches c but not b.

```
$context = "studentcontext";
if(has_capability('moodle/blog:create',
$context)){
$DB->insert_record('blog'); //SSO
}
```

b. This check does not match with either a or c.

```
$newcontext = "admincontext";
if(has_capability('moodle/blog:create',
$newcontext)){
$DB->insert_record('blog'); //SSO
}
```

c. This access control check matches a but not b.

Listing 2. Matching of annotated access control checks

3.4.2 Access control effectiveness analysis

Access control decisions must be made based on trusted data such as constant or data validated by the application (e.g. values in a web session). We use an example from SCARF to motivate our discussions. In Listing 3, the developer may annotate the Boolean expression *WHERE session_id='$id'* as a check for the SSO DELETE FROM sessions. ASIDE analyzes the annotated expression *session_id='$id'*, and identifies it is constraining the *session_id* field with a variable *$id*. ASIDE performs data flow analysis for *$id* and finds it is from a common untrusted data source *$_GET*, and therefore ASIDE regards the annotated access control check to have no access control effectiveness, and reports it as an access control vulnerability.

```
$id=(int)$_GET['session_id']; //untrusted data
query("DELETE FROM sessions WHERE
session_id='$id'"); //SSO
```

Listing 3. editsession.php in SCARF

Given an annotated access control check, ASIDE performs taint propagation data flow analysis. We use default taint sources in commercial static analysis tools (e.g. $_GET). ASIDE generates a vulnerability warning if any variable used in an annotated access control check can be traced to a taint source.

4.   EVALUATION

We evaluate ASIDE's effectiveness using six open source PHP applications. Five of the six applications, Mybloggie, SCARF, Bilboblog, Wheatblog, and PhpStat, were used by auto detection research discussed in Section 2. We thus use them to compare ASIDE's performance. In addition we chose Moodle to find out how ASIDE performs in a large-scale complex application. Moodle is an open source e-learning platform with thirteen stable releases and over 73 million users across 273 countries [30]. Moodle has over 625,000 LOC and 2,000 PHP files.

We evaluated ASIDE against these projects with the following research questions: (a) How would ASIDE impact the developer's work flow? (b) How effective is ASIDE at mitigating known vulnerabilities? (c) What is the number of false positives? (d) How does ASIDE's ability to detect vulnerabilities compare with related work? (e) What are the limitations of ASIDE in detecting access control vulnerabilities?

3.5 Setup

We described our evaluation set up briefly in Section 2. Projects Mybloggie, SCARF, Bilboblog, Wheatblog, and PhpStat have relatively simple functions so we performed manual code review to identify security sensitive operations. We could not perform a thorough code review of Moodle because of its size. Moodle has 199 documented vulnerabilities for all versions. We selected Moodle version 2.1.0 released in 2011 because it contains the largest number (19) of known access control vulnerabilities in any stable release. Based on bug fix logs, we determined that 13 of them were connected with access control vulnerabilities for database tables: CVE-2013-2242, 2012-4408, 2012-3392, 2012-0797, 2012-2356, 2012-2367, 2012-3397, 2012-2354, 2012-2355, 2012-2358, 2012-3391, 2012-2359, and 2012-5473. Three vulnerabilities, CVE-2011-4293, 2012-4407 and 2012-3390, were access control vulnerabilities related to file access. We were not able to determine the source of failed access control in the remaining three cases: CVE-2012-0798, 2011-4309, and 2011-4303. Since our prototype implementation is targeting sensitive operations on database tables, we focused our efforts on examining the 13 CVEs connected with database tables. Our approach can be extended to cover many file accesses as well. Read and write operations on sensitive files could be considered as SSOs. It is straightforward to specify file paths of the sensitive files and the file read and write APIs. For example, *"$sensitiveFile = fopen("customers", "w"); fwrite($sensitiveFile,*

$txt);"* writes *$txt into the file specified by the *sensitiveFilePath*, so we can specify an SSO: *fwrite* into file *customers*. This approach will work as long as file name can be determined via data flow analysis

Thirty-one database table operations are connected with the 13 selected CVEs, as shown in Table 4. Because these 13 CVEs are classified as access control vulnerabilities, we assume that the 31 database table operations are SSOs. We ran ASIDE against the Moodle 2.1.0 code base with the 31 identified SSOs. Two of the authors simulated developers by making interactive annotations of access control checks responding to ASIDE requests. This effort spanned 70 files with an average of 223 lines of code per file. We used the following types of clues in identifying access control checks: (a) Developer comments, (b) Function and variable names, (c) Reported security fixes to access control vulnerabilities, and (d) Context and flow of the program.

Table 4. Known access control vulnerabilities in Moodle 2.1.0 and associated security sensitive operations

Brief Description	SSOs
Unauthorized chat room access (CVE-2013-2242)	Insert: chat_messages, chat_messages_current, chat_users
Unauthorized reset (CVE-2012-4408)	Delete: event, role_capabilities, role_assignments, groupings, comments, grade_outcomes, grade_settings, assignment, course_completion_crit_compl, groups_members, groupings_groups Update: event
Unauthorized forum deletion (CVE-2012-3392)	Delete: forum_subscriptions
Deleted user can maintain access (CVE-2012-0797)	Insert: external_tokens
Unauthorized access to question-bank (CVE-2012-2356)	Insert: question Update: question
Unauthorized addition of calendar event (CVE-2012-2367)	Insert: event Update: event
Unauthorized access to group information (CVE-2012-3397)	Select: groups
Unauthorized reading of messages (CVE-2012-2354)	Select: message, message_read
Unauthorized addition of quiz questions (CVE-2012-2355)	Insert: quiz_question_instances
Unauthorized database modifications (CVE-2012-2358)	Insert: data_records, data_content Update: data_records
Unauthorized read of forums (CVE-2012-3391)	Select: forum
Privilege escalation (CVE-2012-2359)	Insert: role_capabilities Update: role_capabilities
Unauthorized information access (CVE-2012-5473)	Select: user

3.6 Vulnerability Detection

Table 5 summarizes vulnerabilities discovered by ASIDE across all six projects. The column "known vulnerability" includes reports from other approaches discussed in Section 2 and the 13 known access control vulnerabilities from Moodle. In the table, [M] represents missing checks, [I] represents 'inconsistent', [UT] represents 'untrusted data', and [L] stands for 'other logic error'.

Table 5. Vulnerability detection results

Project	Known Vul.	Known Vul. by ASIDE	0-day Vul. by ASIDE
Moodle 2.1.0	6[I], 7[L]	6[I]	1[I]
Mybloggie 2.1.3	3[M], 3[UT]	3[M], 3[UT]	14[M], 1[I]
SCARF 1.0	1[M], 10[UT]	1[M], 10[UT]	
Bilboblog 0.2.1	1[UT]	1[UT]	
Wheatblog 1.1	1[M]	1[M]	
PhpStat 1.5	1[M]	1[M]	4[M]

Except for 7 logic errors in Moodle, ASIDE was able to discover all 26 known vulnerabilities. We will discuss these 7 logic errors in a later section. ASIDE discovered 20 zero-day access control vulnerabilities. Listing 4 shows a zero-day example where a developer created a comment "Added security", from which we can infer that the developer intended to add a control check for the SSO, but wrote it incorrectly. With ASIDE, this issue will be detected right at the point of annotation. Once the developer annotates the expression *!isset($_SESSION['username']) && !isset($_SESSION['passwd']* as access control. ASIDE will identify that this is an invalid check because function *echo()* does not generate an exception. This check will not alter the execution path leading to the SSO. ASIDE will notify the developer to write a valid check so that this vulnerability could be mitigated.

```php
<?php
// Added security
if (!isset($_SESSION['username'])&&
!isset($_SESSION['passwd'])) {
     echo"<metahttp-equiv=\"Refresh\"
content=\"2;url=".self_url()."/login.php\" />";}
sql_query("DELETE FROM ".POST_TBL." WHERE
post_id='$post_id'"); //SSO
?>
```

Listing 4. Vulnerable code in del.php in Mybloggie 2.13

Listing 5 illustrates another zero-day finding confirmed and patched by the Moodle development team (CVE-2014-0122). The SSOs involved are insertions into database tables *chat_messages*, and *chat_messages_current*, the same operations as involved in the example in Listing 1. The vulnerable code is in file "chat_ajax.php". It was discovered by comparing this code instance with the code instance shown in Listing 1.a.

```php
if (!$chatuser = $DB->get_record('chat_users',
array('sid'=>$chat_sid))) { throw new
moodle_exception('notlogged', 'chat');}
if (!isloggedin()) {
   throw new moodle_exception('notlogged',
'chat'); }
$DB->insert_record('chat_messages', $message);
$DB->insert_record('chat_messages_current',
$message);
```

Listing 5. Vulnerable code in chat_ajax.php in Moodle 2.1.0

Moodle requires that only logged in users with access to a particular chat room can insert chat messages. Moodle maintains a

temporary table of users currently in chat rooms. The vulnerable code checks the temporary table as a proxy for the fact that a given user has the appropriate chat authorization. It did not account for the case where a user's chat privilege may be revoked after he entered the chat room.

In addition, using the same technique, ASIDE found two other zero-day Cross-site Request Forgery vulnerabilities in Moodle 2.1.0 affecting the most recent release of Moodle. They have been confirmed and patched by the Moodle development team (CVE-2014-0010, CVE-2014-0126).

3.7 False Positive for Vulnerability Detection

False positive warnings arise when ASIDE incorrectly alerts the developer of a potential vulnerability. We found false positives resulting from vulnerability detection based on annotation inconsistency. Table 6 summarizes the false positives for warnings generated by annotation inconsistency. For example, in Moodle 2.1.0, 19 warnings were generated because there exist 19 sets of inconsistencies where different access control checks were annotated for the same SSO. Among them, 12 are true positives leading to the discovery of 7 vulnerabilities, including a zero-day. Note that ASIDE may generate multiple warnings per vulnerability. This is because multiple sensitive operations are often grouped together. It is possible to have more than one form of valid access control check for the same SSO and it is impossible to detect semantic equivalency in general. An SSO may appear to have multiple forms of associated access control checks for several reasons. First, SSOs often occur in groups. For example in Moodle, insertions into the following tables often occur together: *chat_messages*, *chat_messages_current*, *chat_users*. Two such groups may require different access control authorities even when they share some common SSOs. Therefore, from the perspective of a given SSO, it has different access control checks when it belongs to different groups.

Table 6. False positives for warnings.

Project	Warnings generated by inconsistency	False positives for warnings	Why false positives?
Moodle 2.1.0	19	7	Group difference, Context difference
Mybloggie 2.1.3	1	0	N/A
SCARF 1.0	0	0	N/A
Bilboblog 0.2.1	0	0	N/A
Wheatblog 1.1	1	1	Context difference
PhpStat 1.5	1	1	Context difference

Second, a given access control policy may have semantically equivalent but syntactically different implementations. The third cause is due to application context difference as illustrated in Listing 6. In this example both function calls *role_change_permission()* in Listing 6.a and *reset_role_capabilities()* in listing 6.b insert information into the security sensitive table *role_capabilities*. Thus, they both have the same SSO. However, changing role permission requires the "review role" whereas resetting role capabilities requires the "manage role" as indicated in the code. We found similar situations in Wheatblog and PhpStat where the same SSO may use a different access control check depending on either an administrator context or a user context.

```
require_login($course, false, $cm);
require_capability('moodle/role:review',
$context);
role_change_permission($roleid, $context,
$capability->name, CAP_PREVENT);
```
a. Code snippet from /moodle210/admin/roles/permissions.php.

```
require_login();
require_capability('moodle/role:manage',
$systemcontext);
reset_role_capabilities($roleid);
```
b. Code snippet from /moodle210/admin/roles/manage.php

Listing 6. Different access control checks for the same SSO

3.8 Impact on Developers

Developer adoption is critical for the success of interactive static analysis. One way to measure developer usability is to look at interactive annotation requests per file because it diverts a developer's attention from writing code. In an IDE environment a file is always the focus of the developer's attention. Table 7 summarizes annotations requests for all six projects.

Results from Moodle only have an estimated range because we estimated the set of SSOs using a process described in Section 4.1. A total of 186 annotation requested were generated based on identified SSOs for Moodle. Average annotation request per file is estimated between 0.093 and 2.67. Many Moodle files will not contain any SSOs at all. The lower number is based on total files in Moodle while the higher number is based on files containing at least one SSO. For the other five projects we were able to get a more precise estimate of the number of annotation requests because we have identified all the SSOs through code review. The data suggest that a developer will receive no more than 2 annotations requests per file.

Table 7. Total number of annotation requests

Project	Total annotation requests	Annotations per file
Moodle 2.1.0	186	(0.093, 2.67)
Mybloggie 2.1.3	21	0.32
SCARF 1.0	27	1.42
Bilboblog 0.2.1	2	0.08
Wheatblog 1.1	24	0.49
PhpStat 1.5	30	2

A false positive in annotation requests (aka. False requests) arises when there is no access control check needed. An example for such a situation is code for system installation, during which security sensitive database tables are initialized. Such a situation is different from online system maintenance functions, which require appropriate authorization checks. System installation often is run in a special setting before the system is brought online. In such a mode explicit access control checks in the source code are not necessary. Such false positives are generated because it is difficult for ASIDE to differentiate online system maintenance functions and offline system initialization functions as both of them are contained in files with .php extensions. Excluding the small group of PHP files performing installation functions from the interactive static analysis process can easily eliminate these false requests. Another example of false request involves user

registration, login and password recovery functions where sensitive tables are accessed but no access control checks are needed. Table 8 summarizes our false positive findings.

Overall, ASIDE generated 290 requests for annotation for all six projects. We identified 29 of these requests as unnecessary requests. 23 out of the 29 false requests belongs to code performing system installation. One can eliminate these requests quite easily by excluding the group of PHP files performing installation from the interactive static analysis process. For example in Moodle, six of the 70 files we studied are dedicated to installation. Five out of the 29 false requests occurs in login, registration and password recovery.

Table 8. False positives for annotation requests

Project	Total annotation requests	False requests	Why false positives for requests?
Moodle 2.1.0	186	20	Install
Mybloggie 2.1.3	21	3	Install
SCARF 1.0	27	3	Install, registration, password recovery
Bilboblog 0.2.1	2	0	N/A
Wheatblog 1.1	24	3	Registration, login
PhpStat 1.5	30	0	N/A

Automatic Annotation could be used to reduce the number of annotation requests at a risk of somewhat reduced capacity on vulnerability detection. This may be a viable choice if minimizing developer interruption is a high priority.

In our evaluation of the six applications, we had two observations. First, given an access control check for an SSO, if the exact same code pattern is found associated with the same SSO in a different file, then there is a very high probability that this code pattern is the access control check in that second file. We thus could with high confidence make an automatic annotation.

Our second observation is that multiple SSOs in one file often share access control checks. For example, in Listing 7, SSO_1 and SSO_2 shares the same check $require\_admin()$. Thus once a developer finishes making an access control check annotation for SSO_1, it is likely to be the access control check for all other $SSOs$ on the execution path (e.g. SSO_2 in Listing 7), and thus ASIDE automatically annotates $require\_admin()$ as the check for SSO_2 in Listing 7 as well.

```
require_admin(); //control check
if (isset($_GET['delete'])) {
query("DELETE FROM comments WHERE
comment_id='$comment_id'");//SSO_1
} else if (isset($_GET['approve'])) {
query("UPDATE comments SET approved='1' WHERE
comment_id='$comment_id'");} //SSO_2
```
Listing 7. Example code of applying auto-annotation

Table 8 shows the results of reductions in annotation requests if automatic annotation heuristics were used. The average number of requests per file can be reduced to well below one. However, with auto annotation, we may not detect one of the known vulnerabilities discussed in Section 4.2, shown in Listing 5. We found that vulnerability by comparing two duplicates of access control checks for the same SSO. One of the duplicates is a proper subset of the other, the correct access control check. If the developer annotated the vulnerable check without noticing his mistake, the duplicated one would be incorrectly annotated automatically, thus missing the opportunity of finding this vulnerability. However, if the correct access control check had been annotated first, we would still be able to find the vulnerability.

3.9 Comparison with Auto Detection

ASIDE is able to detect all 26 vulnerabilities found by related work auto detection approaches. In addition ASIDE found 20 zero-day vulnerabilities that were missed by related work. This supports our claim that auto detection has significant limitations in detecting access control vulnerabilities because there are insufficient access control patterns for them to learn access control models for SSOs. ASIDE performs better because it relies on developer input to identify access control models.

Table 9. Annotations needed with or without auto-annotation

Project	Total annotation requests	Annotation requests per file	Annotation requests with auto annotation	Annotation requests per file with auto annotation
Moodle 2.1.0	186	0.093, 2.67	48	0.024, 0.69
Mybloggie 2.1.3	21	0.32	15	0.23
SCARF 1.0	27	1.42	11	0.58
Bilboblog 0.2.1	2	0.08	2	0.08
Wheatblog 1.1	24	0.49	17	0.37
PhpStat 1.5	30	2	4	0.27

None of the related work provided false negative analysis. Our analysis suggests that they are likely to have high false negatives. For example, in Mybloggie and Wheatblog we found more zero-days than vulnerabilities reported by related work that used the same applications for evaluation. Moodle provides an additional source for false negative analysis as it has well documented vulnerability findings. Seven of the 13 Moodle vulnerabilities could not be discovered by any of the methods discussed in this paper. We examined all 7 cases in detail. Each case can be attributed to subtle logic errors. In each case, there are no other access control patterns one can compare. It is not surprising that logic errors are unavoidable in a large complex application. Thus, there is unlikely to ever be an automated method to identify all access control vulnerabilities. The best industry practice to discover logic errors is still through manual code reviews [31].

ASIDE can offer useful assistance to manual code reviews by saving annotations in IDE. First, through interactive annotation, it encourages developers to self-review the code. They may be able to detect and quickly correct access control vulnerabilities even in cases where the access control code pattern is not repeated. Second, interactive annotation can reduce the cost of manual code review by capturing developer's design rationale and helping a reviewer to highlight access control concerns during code review. It can help reviewer zoom in on critical parts of the code quickly. It can also be incorporated into a team development environment where peer review of critical access control logic can be tracked to reduce human errors.

In addition to new projects, interactive static analysis can be applied effectively to projects with a large legacy code base as well. Developers will be requested to provide interactive annotations either upon addition of new code, or modifications of existing code. Such annotations can be used to trigger automatic annotation and detect vulnerabilities in the legacy code.

Interactive static analysis is not without challenges, including: (a) how to motivate developer adoption, and (b) how to deal with annotation errors, which may be unavoidable. Developer adoption should be addressed first by designing a tool that is easy to use and provides the least possible disruption to developer's normal workflow. For example, in Section 4.4 we illustrated that unnecessary developer interruption could be minimized. There is a strong incentive for organizations to adopt a low cost and effective secure programming tool, and influence their developers to use it.

While developer input is the most reliable source of application knowledge, human errors are unavoidable. Incorrect annotations may lead to false negatives. Our prototype implementation does not contain any mechanism to account for human errors. A number of strategies may be used to detect human errors, including:

Identify omissions. We observed that access control checks for different SSOs often have shared parts. So if a term (e.g. a Boolean expression or function call) which has been part of an annotation for an access control check for one SSO and is not part of an annotation for another SSO even though it is along an execution path from a program entry point, this may be pointed out as a possible annotation omission.

Peer review. An annotation may be reviewed by a second developer working on related pieces of code.

It is important to remember that vulnerabilities found by any tool ultimately are subject to the review of a developer. Final actions depend on the developer, the same people interactive analysis rely on for providing interactive annotations.

3.10 Comparison with Commercial tools

Writing custom rules is the approach adopted by most commercial static analysis tools, such as Fortify SCA [32]. We take the code snippet shown in Listing 8 as an example and write a custom rule, in Fortify SCA, for its access control requirements. The security sensitive operation $DB->insert_record(...)$ requires the access control check require_permission(...) before its execution. To write an access control custom rule for it, one first needs to model this requirement as a finite state machine, as shown in Figure 5. Each box represents a state; each arrow represents a transition between two states triggered by certain code patterns. In this example, the program must be in the checkState state before the security sensitive operation can be carried out securely. BrokenAccess represents the state when a broken access control vulnerability occurs, upon which Fortify SCA will report a warning. With this model in mind, one can write a custom rule as illustrated in Listing 9 where one first defines all the states shown in Figure 5 and then defines the transitions between the states.

```
require_permission(…);
$DB->insert_record(…);
```

Listing 8. Example code snippet with SSO and control check

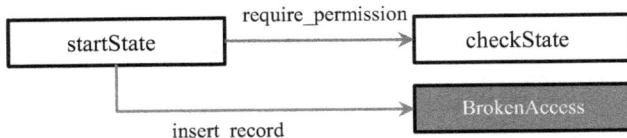

Figure 5. Finite state transition machine for the control flow

This example illustrates the disadvantage of writing custom rules, in that it requires learning of new concepts and specification languages. Such training is unlikely to be widely available for average developers. This type of analysis is typically performed by software security experts collaborating with developers who would provide the required application specific knowledge. Such an arrangement contributes to the high cost of writing custom rules.

```
</ControlflowRule>
<ControlflowRule formatVersion="3.2"
language="PHP">
<VulnCategory>Broken Access Control</VulnCategory>
<!--Definitions for require_permission,
insert_record are omitted -->
<Definition><![CDATA[

state startState(start);
state checkState;
state sensitiveState(error); //BrokenAccess
startState->checkState {$require_permission(…)}
startState->sensitiveState {$insert_record(…) }]]>

</Definition>
</ControlflowRule>
```

Listing 9. A custom control flow rule for Fortify SCA

4. CONCLUSION

There is wide agreement that the IT industry must do more to reduce software vulnerabilities, and that secure programming must be fully integrated into the software development process. Providing interactive support to developers for secure programming is a logical step given the successful history of using interactive tools, most notably Integrated Development Environments such as Eclipse and Visual Studio, to increase programmer productivity by reducing errors. In this paper, we demonstrate the potential of using interactive static analysis as a hybrid approach to mitigate access control vulnerabilities by soliciting input from developers. We demonstrated promising results in vulnerability detection in six open source applications. We found 20 zero-day access control vulnerabilities missed by related approaches. Vulnerability detection can be achieved without adverse impacts on developer workflow.

We believe interactive static analysis is more cost effective compared to existing commercial tools because it does not rely on writing custom rules. It is also more effective at detecting vulnerabilities than auto detection approaches because it relies directly on developer input as opposed to either heuristics or statistical inference. Furthermore, interactive static analysis is designed to fit into the best practices of secure software development lifecycles and encourage developers to fix vulnerabilities during code construction.

No automated tools can detect all access control vulnerabilities. The hybrid approach outlined here can support effective code review and help highlight developer attention to access control issues. Future research is needed in at least the following two areas. First, because developer adoption is a critical success factor for interactive static analysis, one must design an appropriate user interface and interaction for developers. To this end, the design must be intuitive, fit seamlessly into developer workflow, and minimize unnecessary distractions. We are currently exploring and evaluating interface designs to meet this goal [33]. Second, we need to explore more hybrid heuristics, involving developer input as well as program analysis, to discover new types of access control vulnerabilities.

5. ACKNOWLEDGEMENT

This research is support in part by NSF grants: 1129190, 1318854. We acknowledge S. E. Dog for his contributions in reviewing Moodle codes. We acknowledge HP for giving us an education license of Fortify SCA static analyzer.

6. REFERENCES

[1] Howard, M. and Leblanc, D., 2009. Writing secure code. O'Reilly Media, Inc.

[2] Oracle.com, 2012. Secure coding guidelines for the Java programming language, version 4.0, http://www.oracle.com/technetwork/java/seccodeguide-139067.html%3E.

[3] Owasp.org, 2013. OWASP secure coding practices quick reference guide, version 2.0, https://http://www.owasp.org/images/0/08/OWASP_SCP_Quick_Reference_Guide_v2.pdf.

[4] Seacord, R.C., 2008. The CERT C secure coding standard. Pearson Education.

[5] Van Wyk, K.R., 2003. Secure coding: principles and practices. O'Reilly Media, Inc.

[6] WhiteHat Security, 2013. WhiteHat Security website security statistics report, https://http://www.whitehatsec.com/assets/WPstatsReport_052013.pdf.

[7] OWASP.org, 2013. Top Ten Vulnerabilities. https://www.owasp.org/index.php/Top_10_2013-Top_10

[8] Balzarotti, D. Cova, M., Felmetsger, V. Jovanovic, N., Kirda, E., Kruegel, C., and Vigna, G. (2008) Saner: Composing static and dynamic analysis to validate sanitization in web applications. *In Proceedings of the 2008 IEEE Symposium on Security and Privacy*, pages 387-401.

[9] Chaudhuri, A. and Foster, J. S.. Symbolic security analysis of Ruby-on-Rails web applications. (2010) *In Proceedings of the 17th ACM conference on Computer and Communications Security*, pages 585-594.

[10] Chess, B. and McGraw, G. (2014, November) Static analysis for security. *IEEE Security and Privacy*, 2:76-79.

[11] Chess, B. and West, J. (2007) Secure programming with static analysis. Addison-Wesley Professional, first edition.

[12] Johnson, B., Song, Y., Murphy-hill, E., and Bowdidge, R., 2013. Why don't software developers use static analysis tools to find bugs? *In 2013 35th International Conference on Software Engineering (ICSE)*, IEEE, 672-681.

[13] McGraw G., Migues S. and West J., 2013. Building Security in Maturity Model. http://bsimm.com/download/BSIMM-V.pdf.

[14] Son, S. and Shmatikov, V., 2011. SAFERPHP: Finding semantic vulnerabilities in PHP applications. *In Proceedings*

of the ACM SIGPLAN 6th Workshop on Programming Languages and Analysis for Security, ACM.

[15] Tan, L., Zhang, X., Ma, X., Xiong, W., and Zhou, Y., 2008. AutoISES: Automatically Inferring Security Specification and Detecting Violations. *In USENIX Security Symposium,* 379-394.

[16] Dalton, M., Christos K., and Nickolai Z.. "Nemesis: Preventing Authentication & Access Control Vulnerabilities in Web Applications." *USENIX Security Symposium.* 2009.

[17] Son, S., Mckinley, K.S., and Shmatikov, V., 2011. Rolecast: finding missing security checks when you do not know what checks are. *In ACM SIGPLAN Notices,* ACM, 1069-1084.

[18] Gauthier, F., Lavoie, T., and Merlo, E. (2013, December). Uncovering access control weaknesses and flaws with security-discordant software clones. *In Proceedings of the 29th Annual Computer Security Applications Conference* (pp. 209-218).

[19] Monshizadeh, M., Prasad N., and Venkatakrishnan V. N., 2014. "Mace: Detecting privilege escalation vulnerabilities in web applications." *In Proceedings of the 2014 ACM SIGSAC Conference on Computer and Communications Security.* ACM, 2014.

[20] Zhu, J. Xie, J. Lipford, H. and Chu, B. December 2013. Support Secure Programming In Web Applications through Interactive Static Analysis. *Journal of Advanced Research.* Elsevier.

[21] Xie, J., Chu, B., and Lipford, H.R., 2011. Idea: interactive support for secure software development. *In Engineering Secure Software and Systems,* Springer, 248-255.

[22] Xie, J., Chu, B., Lipford, H.R., and Melton, J.T., 2011. ASIDE: IDE support for web application security. *In Proceedings of the 27th Annual Computer Security Applications Conference* ACM, 267-276.

[23] Xie, J. Lipford, H. and Chu,B. 2012. Evaluating Interactive Support for Secure Programming. *ACM Conference on Human Factors in Computing Systems* (CHI).

[24] Howard, M., and Lipner, S. (2006) The Security Development Lifecycle. Microsoft Press.

[25] Shostack, A. Threat Modeling, Design for Security. 2014 John Wiley & Sons Inc.

[26] Eclipse.org, 2012. Eclipse PHP Development Environment, http://projects.eclipse.org/projects/tools.pdt.

[27] Son, S., Mckinley, K.S., and Shmatikov, V., 2013. Fix Me Up: Repairing access-control bugs in web applications. *In Network and Distributed System Security Symposium,* ACM.

[28] Weiser, M. Program slicing (1981, March). *In Proceedings of the 5th International Conference on Software Engineering,* pp 439–449.

[29] Weiser, M. Program slicing (1984, July). *In IEEE Transactions on Software Engineering,* Volume 10, Issue 4, pp 352–357.

[30] Moodle.org, 2014. Moodle Statistics, http://moodle.org/stats/.

[31] Guo, P. "Small-Group Code Reviews for Education" in *Communications of the ACM (CACM),* vol. 57 no. 09, pp. 10-11, September 2014.

[32] HP, 2013. HP Fortify Static Code Analyzer, http://www8.hp.com/us/en/software-solutions/software.html?compURI=1338812 - .UUnHuVthvUY.

[33] Lipford, H., Thomas, T., Chu, B., and Murphy-Hill, E. 2014. Interactive Code Annotation for Security Vulnerability Detection. In *Proceedings of the 2014 ACM Workshop on Security Information Workers* (pp 17-22). ACM

Towards a General Framework for Optimal Role Mining: A Constraint Satisfaction Approach

Jafar Haadi Jafarian
Department of Software and
Information Systems
University of North Carolina at
Charlotte
Charlotte, NC, USA
jjafaria@uncc.edu

Hassan Takabi
Department of Computer
Science and Engineering
University of North Texas
Denton, TX, USA
takabi@unt.edu

Hakim Touati
Department of Software and
Information Systems
University of North Carolina at
Charlotte
Charlotte, NC, USA
htouati@uncc.edu

Ehsan Hesamifard
Department of Computer
Science and Engineering
University of North Texas
Denton, TX, USA
hesamifardehsan@my.unt.edu

Mohamed Shehab
Department of Software and
Information Systems
University of North Carolina at
Charlotte
Charlotte, NC, USA
mshehab@uncc.edu

ABSTRACT

Role Based Access Control (RBAC) is the most widely used advanced access control model deployed in a variety of organizations. To deploy an RBAC system, one needs to first identify a complete set of roles, including permission role assignments and role user assignments. This process, known as role engineering, has been identified as one of the costliest tasks in migrating to RBAC. Since many organizations already have some form of user permission assignments defined, it makes sense to identify roles from this existing information. This process, known as role mining, has gained significant interest in recent years and numerous role mining techniques have been developed that take into account the characteristics of the core RBAC model, as well as its various extended features and each is based on a specific optimization metric. In this paper, we propose a generic approach which transforms the role mining problem into a constraint satisfaction problem. The transformation allows us to discover the optimal RBAC state based on customized optimization metrics. We also extend the RBAC model to include more context-aware and application specific constraints. These extensions broaden the applicability of the model beyond the classic role mining to include features such as permission usage, hierarchical role mining, hybrid role engineering approaches, and temporal RBAC models. We also perform experiments to show applicability and effectiveness of the proposed approach.

SACMAT'15, June 1-3, 2015, Vienna, Austria.
Copyright © 2015 ACM 978-1-4503-3556-0/15/06 ...$15.00.
http://dx.doi.org/10.1145/2752952.2752975.

Categories and Subject Descriptors

K.6.5 [**MANAGEMENT OF COMPUTING AND INFORMATION SYSTEMS**]: Security and Protection; D.4.6 [SECURITY AND PROTECTION]: Access Controls

Keywords

Access Control; RBAC; Role Mining; Constraint Satisfaction Problem; SMT Solver

1. INTRODUCTION

Role-based access control (RBAC) is widely used in enterprise security management and enterprise identity management products as an authorization model in which access decisions are based on the roles that users hold within an organization. Contrary to discretionary access control models, users are associated with roles and each role is associated with specified permissions. In fact, roles represent functions within a given organization and access permissions are associated with roles instead of users. In order to deploy RBAC, an organization must first identify a set of roles that is complete, correct and efficient, and then assign users and permissions to these roles [1]. This process is known as role engineering and is the costliest component of an RBAC implementation [2].

There are two general approaches to construct an RBAC system: the top-down approach and the bottom-up approach. In the top-down approach, a human expert performs a detailed analysis of business processes and derives roles from such analysis. However, this top-down analysis is human-intensive and it is believed to be slow and expensive. To overcome the drawbacks of top-down approaches, researchers have proposed to use bottom-up data mining techniques to discover roles. These bottom-up approaches utilize the existing system configuration data (in particular, the user permission assignments) to define roles. It first considers the existing users' permissions before RBAC is implemented, and aggregates them into roles. Such a bottom-up approach is called role mining.

The role mining problem can be formalized as follows: given an access control configuration shown as $\rho = \langle U, P, UP \rangle$, where U is a set of users, P is a set of permissions, and UP is the user permission assignments relation, we want to generate an RBAC state shown as $\gamma = \langle R, UA, PA, RH \rangle$ where R is a set of roles, $UA \subseteq U \times R$ is the user role assignments relation, $PA \subseteq R \times P$ is the role permission assignments relation, and $RH \subseteq R \times R$ is a partial order over R, called a role hierarchy.

Role mining has raised significant interest in the research community and there have been several attempts to propose bottom-up approaches to mining roles [3, 4, 5, 6, 7, 8, 9, 10]. Since for a specific user permission assignments set, several consistent RBAC states can be generated, the main concern in role mining pertains to the goodness of the generated role set. However, there is no formal notion of goodness of a generated role set. *Vaidya et al.* have formally defined the role mining problem using the notion of minimality [10], and *Molloy et al.* [6] define a full-fledged metric for the goodness of an RBAC state. However, none of the proposed methods in the literature allows the administrator to generate a customized RBAC state based on a customized metric. Each approach assumes a specific goodness measure and strives to provide a heuristic/greedy approach to generate a locally optimal role set based on the measure.

In this paper, we propose the concept of converting the role mining problem into a constraint satisfaction problem such that the goodness measure can be defined by the administrator, and various context-aware or environmental requirements can also be considered in the generation of the RBAC model. To do this, we formally define the original role mining problem, and define our goodness measure as a variation of the weighted structural complexity [6]. Conversion of role mining problem to a constraint satisfaction problem has several advantages. **Firstly**, it allows one to discover the optimal RBAC state based on the defined goodness measure. For instance, for the optimization metric defined based on the number of roles, as in Section 4 a solution to the role mining constraint satisfaction problem is proven to be the most optimal solution. **Secondly**, it allows one to define customized constraints either to generate better roles based on some metrics (such as permission usage), or to restrict the generated RBAC state based on application specific constraints. **Thirdly**, the use of constraint satisfaction enables definition of customized goodness measures. In other words, any goodness measure can be written as a constraint and added to the model.

For formal description of the problem, we use propositional logic and take advantage of satisfiability modulo theories (SMT) solvers to discover the desired RBAC states. Although the Boolean satisfiability (SAT) problem is NP-complete, efficient and scalable algorithms for SAT that were developed over the last decade have contributed to dramatic advances in our ability to automatically solve problem instances involving tens of thousands of variables and millions of constraints.

The rest of the paper is organized as follows. In Section 2 we review the preliminary concepts of SAT and SMT solvers. Section 3 provides a summary description of related works in this area and an overview of the goodness measures that are suggested in the literature. In Section 4, we provide a basic formalization for the role mining problem and describe the basis of our approach. We then describe some of the important extensions to the original role mining problem that can be expressed and solved using our proposed approach. Section 5 evaluates our approach and Section 6 concludes the paper.

2. BACKGROUND

In complexity theory, the satisfiability problem (SAT) is a decision problem, whose instance is a Boolean expression written using only AND, OR, NOT, variables, and parentheses. A formula of propositional logic is said to be satisfiable if logical values can be assigned to its variables in a way that makes the formula true. The Boolean satisfiability problem, also known as propositional satisfiability problem, is NP-complete and there is no known algorithm that can solve SAT efficiently, correctly, and for all possible input instances. However, many instances of SAT are of central importance in various areas of computer science and can be solved rather efficiently using heuristical SAT-solvers.

A literal is either a variable or the negation of a variable (the negation of an expression can be reduced to negated variables by De Morgan's laws). For example, x_1 is a positive literal and $\neg x_2$ is a negative literal. A clause is a disjunction of literals. For example, $x_1 \wedge \neg(x_2)$ is a clause.

There are several special cases of the Boolean satisfiability problem in which the formula are required to be conjunctions of clauses (*i.e.*, formulae in conjunctive normal form). Determining the satisfiability of a formula in conjunctive normal form where each clause is limited to at most three literals, known as "3SAT", "3CNFSAT", or "3-satisfiability", is NP-complete. Determining the satisfiability of a formula in which each clause is limited to at most two literals, known as "2SAT", is NL-complete. Determining the satisfiability of a formula in which each clause is a Horn clause (i.e. it contains at most one positive literal) is called Horn-satisfiability and is P-complete.

The Cook-Levin theorem states that the Boolean satisfiability problem is NP-complete. However, beyond this theoretical significance, efficient and scalable algorithms for SAT that were developed over the last decade have contributed to dramatic advances in our ability to automatically solve problem instances involving tens of thousands of variables and millions of constraints. SAT solvers provide heuristic approaches to find a solution, or prove that none exists, relatively quickly, even though the instance has thousands of variables and tens of thousands of constraints.

An extension that has gained significant popularity is satisfiability modulo theories (SMT) that can enrich CNF formulas with linear constraints, arrays, all-different constraints, uninterpreted functions, etc. Such extensions typically remain NP-complete, but very efficient solvers are now available that can handle many such kinds of constraints.

3. RELATED WORK

The first major work in role mining is *ORCA* [11]. This algorithm performs hierarchical clustering on permissions. Initially, each permission forms a cluster by itself. That is, it starts with the set of clusters $S = \{\{p_1\}, \{p_2\}, ..., \{p_m\}\}$ where $p_1, p_2, ..., p_m$ are permissions. Iteratively, it finds a pair $s_i, s_j \in S$ such that the number of users having s_i and s_j is the largest among all such pairs, and updates S by adding $s_i \cup s_j$ and removing s_i and s_j. The process continues until $|S| = 1$ or until no user has the permissions in any two clusters in S. The paper also presents a tool that visualizes the cluster hierarchy on a coordinated system based on the cluster membership size. The tool also presents a visual method for marking organizational unit quotas and marking membership differences. This method can aid the expert user in finding the correlations between cluster hierarchies and small deviations in the membership of neighboring clusters. However, each permission is only part of one role which is very unrealistic.

CompleteMiner was proposed by *Vaidya et al.* [9]. It starts by creating an initial set of roles $R_{initial}$ from the distinct user permission sets. It then computes all possible intersection sets of the initial roles. The time complexity of CompleteMiner is exponential to the size of $R_{initial}$. CompleteMiner practically generates all possible roles and prioritizes them based on the number of users associated with them. To reduce the computational complexity of the algorithm, [9] presented *FastMiner* which is similar to CompleteMiner except that it computes only intersection sets between pairs of initial roles. This heuristic approach may result in omission of some significant roles. However, it reduces the computational complexity of the algorithm to $O(n^2m)$. The authors also propose a role prioritization method of a candidate role r as $|e(r)| * \alpha + |n(r)|$, where $e(r)$ denotes the set of users that have exactly the permissions in r, $n(r)$ is the number of users whose permissions are a superset of r, and α is a tunable parameter to favor initial roles. *Molloy et al.* presented a novel prioritization approach for the algorithm, named *DynamicMiner* [6] which considers the inter-relation of generated roles in creation of new ones.

The *Graph Optimization* algorithm was proposed by *Zhang et al.* [7]. It considers role mining as a graph optimization problem. The optimization objective is to minimize the number of roles and edges. Contrary to ORCA, initially the permission set for each user forms a role. Then, the algorithm iteratively finds two roles such that the restructuring results in an improvement in terms of optimization objective. The restructuring is done using the split and merge operations according to the set relationship between permission set of the roles. It is unclear how many iterations the algorithm would need before stopping; but one can set a limit on the number of iterations to limit the running time. However, this limit may easily disrupt results of the algorithm, since it may impede the generation of some good candidate roles.

In [3], the authors proposed a sophisticated role mining algorithm based on minimizing the number of roles. For simplicity, a user u's permission set is denoted as $P(u)$. All users that have all of u's permissions form the set $U(u)$. Similarly for each permission p, the set of users that have p is denoted as $U(p)$ and the set of permissions that are assigned to all users in $U(p)$ is denoted as $P(p)$. In each step, the algorithm selects a user u and finds a pair $\langle U(u); P(u) \rangle$ which forms a role. All user-permission assignments between $U(u)$ and $P(u)$ are then removed and the remaining user-permission assignments will be considered in subsequent iterations. The selected user is the one with the fewest (but non-zero) uncovered permissions (or users). The computational complexity of the algorithm is $O(mn)$. The paper also proposes another algorithm, called edge concentration, with the optimization objective of minimizing the number of edges. The algorithm

starts by using the previous role minimizing algorithm to find a set of roles. It then greedily improves the objective function using several transformations until no further improvement is possible. The restructuring process is similar to the algorithm in [7] and the time complexity depends on the number of iterations it takes the algorithm to terminate.

Vaidya et al. have formally defined the role mining problem as a matrix decomposition problem, which they refer to as the RMP (Role Mining problem) problem [10]. They show that the RMP problem is NP-complete and there is a close relationship between RMP and several existing data mining problems such as the minimal tiling problem and the discrete basis problem. Furthermore, they have proposed several variants of the basic-RMP. The N-approximate RMP allows a limited amount of inexactness, which may result in less number of roles. The min-noise RMP allows administrators to specify the number of roles yet mine the best possible set of roles. All these techniques are limited to mining RBAC systems that do not have a role hierarchy. Lu *et al.* use binary integer programming to model the basic RMP and its variants [8].

Molloy et al. in [5] proposed a hierarchical role mining algorithm based on the ontology of formal concept analysis. A concept is a pair $\langle P, U \rangle$ such that U contains all the users that have all permissions in P, and P contains all the permissions that are shared by all users in U, and both U and P are maximal. The family of these concepts obeys the mathematical axioms defining a lattice, and is called a concept lattice. The *reduced concept lattice* (obtained by removing redundancies caused by inheritance in the concept lattice) can be viewed as an RBAC state. The sub-concept relation corresponds to the role inheritance relation. The algorithm uses the reduced concept lattice as the initial role hierarchy, and heuristically prunes it. The algorithm is similar in spirit to *Graph Optimization* of [7] in that both algorithms start from some RBAC state and then performs local optimizations. The former starts from the permission sets of users, while the latter starts from the reduced concept lattice.

Takabi et al. in [12] propose a hierarchical role mining algorithm, called state miner, which generates an RBAC state based on an existing RBAC state. The objective of the paper is to generate a good RBAC state with minimal perturbation from the existing state. The paper formally defines a criteria for evaluating the perturbation between two RBAC states, and provides a heuristic approach for generating a good RBAC state based on the weighted structural complexity (WSC) [6] and with minimal perturbation.

With regard to goodness measure, several metrics have been defined in the literature to measure goodness of identified roles. *Vaidya et al.* [9] suggest to minimize the number of roles. *Zhang et al.* [7], *Ene et al.* [3], and *Lu et al.* [8] aim to minimize the number of user-role assignment and permission-role assignment relations. In [13] *Colantino et al.* describe a measure that minimize the administration cost of the resulting RBAC model. In [6] *Molloy et al.* propose the notion of weighted structural complexity (WSC) that sums up the number of relationships in an RBAC state, with adjustable weights for different kinds of relationships. In [4] *Guo et al.* suggest to minimize the number of roles and edges in role hierarchy graph. They argue that including UA and PA in weighted structural complexity is redundant, because the role hierarchy incorporates the information represented by them. We believe that this argument does not hold as role hierarchy represents only relations between roles, while UA and PA are part of administration cost as well.

Considering all aforementioned metrics, the weighted structural complexity is the most general and most flexible measure that covers other measures as well. The weighted structural complexity (WSC) is formally defined as follows:

Given $W = \langle w_r, w_u, w_p, w_h \rangle$, where $w_r, w_u, w_p, w_h \in Q^+ \cup \infty$, the weighted structural complexity of an RBAC state, which is denoted as $wsc(\gamma, W)$ is computed as follows:

$$wsc(\gamma, W) = w_r * |R| + w_u * |UR| + w_p * |RP| + w_h * |t\_r(RH)| \quad (1)$$

where Q^+ is the set of all non-negative rational numbers, $|.|$ indicates the size of the set or relation, and $t\_r(RH)$ indicates the transitive reduction of role-hierarchy. Note that unlike the approach by *Molloy et al.* in [6], we do not allow direct user permission assignments because it is not clear when we should use roles and when we should use direct assignment of permissions to users; moreover, it defeats the purpose of RBAC.

It is possible to adjust the weights of wsc to limit RBAC states to meet different objectives. For example, by setting w_h to ∞, we can force a flat RBAC state since each role inheritance relation costs ∞ or by setting $w_r = 1$, $w_u = wp = 0$, and $w_h = \infty$, we can minimize the number of roles.

4. FORMALIZING ROLE MINING PROBLEM AS SATISFIABILITY PROBLEM

Role mining is the problem of identifying a set of roles from an initial access control configuration to build an RBAC state. We transform the role engineering problem from a role mining problem to a constraint satisfaction problem. We aim to build the most optimal RBAC state satisfying all the RBAC principles and goals. We first define a goodness measure for an RBAC state, and then we model them as constraints and use a constraint satisfiability solver such as SMT to come up with the best possible RBAC state. Our original optimization metric and goodness measure for validity and optimality of an RBAC state is defined as follows:

- The RBAC state must maintain the initial user to permission assignment.

- The RBAC state should have the minimum possible number of roles.

- The roles should have the maximum possible number of permissions.

- The users should have the minimum possible number of roles.

[leftmargin=*]

An initial access control configuration with **n** users and **m** permissions is represented by a user permission assignment in the form of $n \times m$ Boolean matrix UP. Each $up_{i,j}$ in the matrix $UP \in \{0,1\}^{n \times m}$ represents user i access decision for permission j.

$$UP_{n \times m} = \begin{pmatrix} up_{1,1} & up_{1,2} & \ldots & up_{1,m} \\ \ldots & \ldots & \ldots & \ldots \\ up_{n,1} & up_{n,2} & \ldots & up_{n,m} \end{pmatrix} \quad (2)$$

where $up_{i,j}$ is 1 if the user i has permission j and 0 otherwise.

Given a set of user permissions assignments, we strive to build the most optimal RBAC state based on the defined goodness measure. The RBAC state is in the form of two Boolean matrices, a user role $n \times k$ Boolean variable matrix $UA \in \{0,1\}^{n \times k}$ where each variable $ua_{i,j}$ represents assignment of the role j to the user i, and a role permission $k \times m$ Boolean variable matrix $PA \in \{0,1\}^{k \times m}$ where each variable $pa_{i,j}$ represents assignment of the permission j to the role i. The two matrices are represented as follows:

$$UA_{n \times k} = \begin{pmatrix} ua_{1,1} & ua_{1,2} & \ldots & ua_{1,k} \\ \ldots & \ldots & \ldots & \ldots \\ ua_{n,1} & ua_{n,2} & \ldots & ua_{n,k} \end{pmatrix} \quad (3)$$

where $ua_{i,j}$ is 1 if the user i is assigned the role j and 0 otherwise.

$$PA_{k \times m} = \begin{pmatrix} pa_{1,1} & pa_{1,2} & \ldots & pa_{1,m} \\ \ldots & \ldots & \ldots & \ldots \\ pa_{k,1} & pa_{k,2} & \ldots & pa_{k,m} \end{pmatrix} \quad (4)$$

where $pa_{i,j}$ is 1 if the role i has the permission j and 0 otherwise.

We model the RBAC state as a constraint satisfiability problem. In this paper, we define a set of constraints that the RBAC state must satisfy based on the principles previously described. However, more constraints can be added and some examples are described in the Section 4.2.

Role engineering aims to build an RBAC state maintaining the user to permission assignment. In other words, if a user u_i has the permission p_j ($up_{i,j} = 1$) assigned to him, he should have at least one role r_k ($ua_{i,k} = 1$) such that r_k is assigned the permission p_j ($pa_{k,j} = 1$). Similarly, if a user u_i does not have the permission p_j ($up_{i,j} = 0$) assigned to him, he should not have any role r_k containing the permission p_j. This is the most basic constraint an RBAC state should maintain. We call this constraint the **stability Constraint**.

Definition 1. *(Boolean Matrix Multiplication). Given three matrices UP, UA, and PA, the Boolean matrix multiplication is described by $UA \times PA = UP$, where UP is represented in the space $\{0,1\}^{n \times m}$.*

Definition 2. *(Boolean Matrix Decomposition): Given a matrix $UP \in \{0,1\}^{n \times m}$, the Boolean matrix decomposition is derived by solving the Boolean system of equation $UP = UA \times PA$ for each user i permission j.*

The stability constraint is represented in the logical model by the Boolean disjunctions using propositional logic, representing the Boolean matrix decomposition of the user to permission Boolean matrix and is described by:

$$up_{i,j} = \left(\bigvee_{l=1,k} (ua_{i,l} \wedge pa_{l,j}) \right) \quad (5)$$

A Boolean matrix might have several decompositions that hold the stability constraint. From the second principle of goodness measure, we define a new constraint on minimizing the number of roles in the RBAC state. This constraint aims to find the minimal user-role and role-permission decomposition and is called **minimal decomposition constraint**.

Definition 3. *(Minimal Matrix Decomposition): Given a matrix $UP \in \{0,1\}^{n \times m}$, the minimum matrix decomposition derives two matrices $UA \in \{0,1\}^{n \times k}$ and $PA \in \{0,1\}^{k \times m}$ such that* k *is minimal.*

Another possible constraint aims to maximize the number of permissions assigned to a role. This constraint is more an optimization factor than a necessary constraint to an optimal RBAC state. It is modeled using the average number of permissions assigned to a role in the generated RBAC state. Using the SMT solver, one can iteratively specify a range for the average number of permissions assigned to a role variable. This constraint introduces an overhead in terms of processing time since we introduce integer programming. This constraint is called the **permission maximization constraint**.

Similarly, a constraint on minimizing the number of roles assigned to a user can be modeled to optimize the search space. This constraint is evaluated and modeled in the same way as the permission maximization constraint. This constraint is called the **role minimization constraint**.

The constraint satisfiability model allows users to define more constraints to the system to minimize the search space of the SAT solver. For example, a constraint evaluation and prioritization can be defined based on the weighted structural complexity [6] described in Section 3 to cover all components of an RBAC system.

Our constraint satisfiability approach models snapshots of the system. However, an iterative approach is needed to check against iterative constraints such as the minimal decomposition constraint. An example of such iterative approach is explained below.

4.1 An Iterative Approach for Constraint Satisfiability

Since the Minimal Decomposition Constraint is modeled as an iterative constraint, we first start modeling the system with an initial fixed number of roles and then iteratively decrease the number of roles and remodel the system until we reach an unsatisfiable state. The last state before the unsatisfiable state is the most optimal state for the current constraints. The initial number of roles cannot be higher than the number of permissions since the worst case is that each role is assigned exactly one permission. We describe a more sophisticated approach to selecting the initial number of roles using matrix decomposition properties. To solve a system of equations, the number of unknown variables must be at least the same as the number of equations (constraints). This is a necessary condition that we can apply in some cases.

In addition, using binary search we can decrease the number of iterations until we reach an unsatisfiable state. We can then backtrack to the last satisfiable state and use the number of roles as starting point and use the sequential verification.

Using the stability constraint and the minimal decomposition constraint with an initial fixed number of roles, we generate an initial RBAC state. This initial RBAC state represents any possible user role assignment and role permission assignment and is generated using the **SMT** solver under the two constraints. The remaining constraints can be modeled in our system in a similar way. The following algorithm describes how the stability constraint is asserted and

how the minimal decomposition constraint is enforced in the iterative selection of role numbers, as shown in algorithm 1.

Algorithm 1 Iterative Algorithm for Constraint Satisfiability

---

$U \leftarrow numberofusers$;
$P \leftarrow$ number of permissions;
$R \leftarrow$ P;
$prev \leftarrow$ P;
$UP \leftarrow$ initialize with user to permission;
$stop \leftarrow sat$;
while $stop \neq sat$ **do**
  $UAR \leftarrow$ initialize with $U \times R$ variable names;
  $PA \leftarrow$ initialize with $R \times P$ variable names;
  Assert($UP = UA \times PA$);
  $stop \leftarrow Evaluate(UP = UA \times PA)$;
  if $stop ==$ sat **then**
    $prev \leftarrow R$
    $R \leftarrow R/2$
  end if
end while
while $stop \neq sa'$ **do**
  $UAR \leftarrow$ initialize with $U \times R$ variable names;
  $PA \leftarrow$ initialize with $R \times P$ variable names;
  Assert($UP = UA \times PA$);
  $stop \leftarrow Evaluate(UP = UA \times PA)$;
  if $stop ==$ sat **then**
    $prev \leftarrow R$
    $R \leftarrow R - 1$
  end if
end while

As we mentioned, the proposed constraint satisfiability model allows users to define more constraints. In the next section, we describe some extensions of the original role mining problem and how then can be modeled as constraint satisfiability problems.

4.2 Role Mining Problem Extensions

In this section, we describe several extended formalizations to highlight the effectiveness, flexibility and expressiveness of our approach in providing additional properties for the original role mining problem.

4.2.1 Permission Usage as Optimization Metric

In Section 4 we described how the role mining problem can be transformed into a satisfiability problem and solved using SMT. However, the number of roles may not be the only optimization metric in generation of an RBAC state. One very important optimization metric is the usage pattern of permissions by users. If a user has two permissions p_1 and p_2 among other permissions, and uses p_1 far more often than p_2, one optimization metric is to place p_1 and p_2 in different roles. In other words, the optimization metric would be to generate roles that include permissions with similar usage patterns. Our approach to role mining is an iterative optimization approach that uses the active learning paradigm. We use the usage pattern as an optimization factor, and we proceed iteratively to select the most suitable role set. By iteratively detecting the least suitable roles and adding role constraints, we reduce the possible role space and greedily converge to the most suitable RBAC state.

Given a user permission usage matrix $UUP_{u \times p}$, we build an initial RBAC state. The permission usage matrix includes non-negative integers where 0 values in $UUP_{i,j}$ represent that the permission p_j does not belong to user u_i and non-zero values denotes that the user has the permission.

The RBAC state is in the form of two matrices, a user role $u \times r$ Boolean matrix assignment $UA_{u \times r}$ and a role usage $r \times p$ matrix $UPA_{r \times p}$. The initial RBAC state is generated using the following formula:

$$UUP_{u \times p} = UA_{u \times r}.UPA_{r \times p} \qquad (6)$$

To generate such matrices, we need to choose the number of roles r. Since minimization of the number of roles is not an optimization factor here (although it can be), we choose a good-enough lower bound for the number of roles equal to half of the number of permissions: $r = p/2$.

The UUP matrix includes pre-assigned variables while the UA and UPA matrices consist of unassigned variables that must be satisfied by the SMT. The UA matrix includes integer variables constrained to the range $[0, 1]$, and the UPA matrix is comprised of variables that must be non-negative. The equation 6 can be rewritten in terms of integer linear constraints as:

$$
\begin{aligned}
& r = p/2 \\
& \forall i,j \left(UUP_{i,j} = \sum_{k=1}^{r} UA_{i,k} * UPA_{k,j} \right) \\
& 1 \le i \le u; 1 \le j \le p \\
& \forall i,k (0 \le ua_{i,k} \le 1); 1 \le k \le r \\
& \forall k,j (upa_{k,j} \ge 0); 1 \le k \le r
\end{aligned} \qquad (7)
$$

where $ua_{i,k}$ denotes the variables in UA matrix, and $upa_{k,j}$ denotes the variables in UPA.

By solving the above integer constraints with SMT, Boolean and integer values will be assigned to variables in matrices UA and UPA respectively. The UA matrix denotes the roles assigned to each user, while the UPA matrix includes non-negative integers. If the SMT does not find a satisfiable solution for the equation 7, we increase r and re-execute the SMT.

The generated RBAC state does not necessarily reflect the best possible assignment based on usage. The SMT might generate some roles that cannot be considered as good roles in terms of permission usage. We refer to such roles as *taboo roles* and generate constraints that exclude such roles and try to find a new satisfaction based on the initial constraints and newly added constraints of taboo roles.

Since our approach is an iterative approach that strives to minimize the distance between the permission usage for users and the permission usage for their roles, we compute the usage distance between roles and their users. This distance can be computed using different algorithms such as RBF kernel, and nearest neighbor. Suppose $UUP[i]$ represents the ith row of matrix UUP. Generally speaking, for all users u_i that have the role r_j, we calculate the distance between $UUP[i]$ and $UPA[j]$ and determine if the role R_j is a suitable role for the system. We use active learning to select the least suitable role assignment, that is we select the role with the highest distance to its users. Assuming the distance of a role r_k is represented by $dist_k$, and the distance of a permission p_j in r_j is represented by $dist_{k,j}$, the

distance of a role r_k can be calculated based on algorithm 8.

Algorithm 2 Calculating Distance for Taboo Role based on Usage

---
for $k = 1 \to r$ **do**
    for $i = 1 \to u$ **do**
        if $ur_{i,k}$ **then**
            for $j = 1 \to p$ **do**
                $dist_{k,j} = dist_{k,j} + (|uup_{i,j} - urp_{k,j}|)$
            end for
        end if
    end for
    $dist_k = 0$
    for $j = 1 \to p$ **do**
        $dist_k = dist_k + dist_{k,j}$
    end for
    $dist_k = dist_k/p$
end for
if there exists any role k with $dist_k > \Gamma$ **then**
    return r_k with maximum $dist_k$
end if

Γ defines the acceptable distance threshold. This role's permissions are then added to the set of constraints initially specified to the SMT solver as conflicting permissions that cannot be grouped together in a role. For example, assume role has non-zero assignments for m variables; i.e. $r_j = (rp_{j,1}, \ldots, rp_{j,m})$ and it is chosen as a taboo role. The following constraint is added to the constraint of equation 8.

$$
\begin{aligned}
& \forall j \left(\neg ((UPA_{j,1} > 0) \wedge \ldots \wedge (UPA_{j,p} > 0)) \right) \\
& 1 \le j \le r
\end{aligned} \qquad (8)
$$

This new constraint will reduce the possible role combinations. We then run the SMT against this new set of constraints, and iterate this process until we reach the optimal RBAC state where each role distance is below the pre-defined threshold Γ.

4.2.2 Hierarchical RBAC

The hierarchical RBAC defines a relation $RH \subseteq Roles \times Roles$ such that $(r_i, r_j) \in RH$ means r_i dominates r_j: $r_i \ge r_j$. The partial ordering *dominate* relation denotes that r_i practically contains all permissions of r_j. Specifically, if $P(r_i)$ denotes the permission set of r_i, then $P(r_j) \subseteq P(r_i)$. Assume RP_i denotes the vector of permissions assigned to role r_i. Role r_i dominates (i.e. includes) role r_j if:

$$\forall k (UA_{j,k} \le UA_{i,k}); 1 \le k \le p \qquad (9)$$

In a hierarchical RBAC state, each role is either dominated by another role, and/or dominates another role.

$$
\begin{aligned}
\bigwedge_{i=1}^{r} (\bigvee_{j=i+1}^{r} ((\bigwedge_{k=1}^{p} (UA_{j,k} \le UA_{i,k})) \\
\vee (\bigwedge_{k=1}^{p} (UA_{j,k} \ge UA_{i,k}))))
\end{aligned} \qquad (10)
$$

The equation 10 denotes the constraint that each role should either dominate or be dominated by another role.

As mentioned in Section 3, based on the weighted structural complexity (WSC) presented [6], the number of relations in role hierarchy after transitive reduction, denoted by $t_r(RH)$ is an important measure for goodness of an RBAC state. A transitive reduction is the minimal set of relationships that describes the same hierarchy. For example, $t\_r(\{(r_1, r_2), (r_2, r_3), (r_1, r_3)\} = \{(r_1, r_2), (r_2, r_3)\}$ as $(r1, r3)$ can be inferred.

Minimization of transitively reduced role hierarchy can be formalized as minimization of the following equation:

$$\sum_{\forall j} \sum_{\forall i((r_i \geq r_j) \wedge (\neg \exists k(r_k \geq r_j \wedge r_i \geq r_k)))} 1 \qquad (11)$$

The minimization can be solved by upper-bounding equation 11 and tightening the bound until the model becomes unsatisfiable.

4.2.3 Reconfiguration of RBAC State

Takabi et al. [12] provide an approach that aims to reconfigure the existing hierarchical RBAC state with minimal perturbation and present a heuristic algorithm to discover an RBAC state as similar as possible to the existing state and the optimal state.

To define minimal perturbation, the paper defines a flexible and general measure for similarity between roles and role sets that takes into account users and permissions associated with roles as well as relations in role hierarchy with adjustable weights. For similarity between two roles, the authors first define similarity based on permissions, users and relations in the role hierarchy individually, and then combine them to get a composite similarity measure as defined below.

Permission centric similarity between roles r_1 and r_2 is defined based on authorized permissions for roles as: $PermSim(r_1, r_2) = \frac{|rp_1 \cap rp_2|}{|rp_1 \cup rp_2|}$ where rp_1 is the set of all permissions authorized for role r_1 ($authorized\_permissions(r_1)$) and rp_2 is the set of all permissions authorized for role r_2 ($authorized\_permissions(r_2)$).

User centric similarity between roles r_1 and r_2 is defined based on authorized users for roles as: $UserSim(r_1, r_2) = |\frac{ru_1 \cap ru_2}{ru_1 \cup ru_2}|$ where ru_1 is the set of all users authorized for role r_1 ($authorized\_users(r_1)$) and ru_2 is the set of all users authorized for role r_2 ($authorized\_users(r_2)$).

Hierarchy relation centric similarity between roles r_1 and r_2 is defined based on hierarchy relations for roles as:

$$RelSim(r_1, r_2) = \frac{min(|Sen(r1)|, |Sen(r_2)|)}{max(|Sen(r_1)|, |Sen(r_2)|)} * \frac{1}{2}$$
$$+ \frac{min(|Jun(r1)|, |Jun(r_2)|)}{max(|Jun(r_1)|, |Jun(r_2)|)} * \frac{1}{2} \qquad (12)$$

where $Sen(r)$ and $Jun(r)$ are the sets of immediate seniors and immediate juniors of role r respectively.

The paper combines these measure to define similarity between two roles as a value between 0 and 1 as follows:

Role-role similarity. For any two roles r_1 and r_2, the paper defines similarity measure between them as: $sim(r_1, r_2) = PermSim(r_1, r_2)*w_{sp} + UserSim(r_1, r_2)*w_{su} + RelSim(r_1, r_2)*w_{sh}$ where $w_{sp} + w_{su} + w_{sh} = 1$.

Furthermore, the paper defines an algorithm for computing similarity between two role sets, denoted by $sim(rs_1, rs_2)$. Dissimilarity of two role sets is defined as $dissim(rs_1, rs_2) = 1 - sim(rs_1, rs_2)$. It also defines a global optimization function of WSC of the generated RBAC state, defined in equation 1, and dissimilarity of currently deployed role set and generated role set:

$$GOF(wsc, dissim) = (1-wf)*wsc + wf*wsc*dissim \qquad (13)$$

where $wf \in [0, 1]$ is a weighting factor for the similarity and shows the significance of WSC in optimization of the RBAC state.

The paper then provides a heuristic approach for the problem. We can define a heuristic approach based on our formal model to provide a greedy solution for the problem. Initially, we generate an optimal RBAC state based on the WSC formula using the presented methods in Sections 4, and 4.2.2. We call the role set of currently deployed RBAC state as R_{dpl} and the role set of generated RBAC state as R_{new}. We define a taboo role as a role in R_{new} which has the least similarity with all the roles in R_{dpl}. Algorithm 3 can be used to detect the taboo role. For each role r_i in R_{new}, the algo-

---

Algorithm 3 Determining a Taboo Role based on Role Similarity

---
for $i = 1 \rightarrow |R_{new}|$ **do**
  $maxSim(R_i) = 0$
  for $j = 1 \rightarrow |R_{dpl}|$ **do**
    if $sim(r_i, r_j) < maxSim(r_i)$ **then**
      $maxSim(r_i) = sim(r_i, r_j)$
    end if
  end for
end for
if there exists any role k with $maxSim(r_i) < \Gamma$ **then**
  return r_k with minimum $maxSim(r_k)$
end if

---

rithm finds a distinct role r_j in R_{dpl} which is most similar to r_i and stores the minimum similarity in $maxSim(r_i)$. Then it finds a role in R_{new} which has a similarity less than an acceptable threshold and chooses the role r_k with minimum similarity. Based on the definition, this role is the taboo role. In each iteration, we remove one taboo role using constraint of equation 8 and use SMT to generate a new RBAC state by considering the new constraints. If the newly generated RBAC state increases the GOF, we repeat the process; otherwise, we stop. This greedy approach allows us to generate an RBAC state with optimized GOF.

4.2.4 Hybrid Role Engineering Approach

The top-down role engineering approach begins with defining a particular job function and then creating a role for this job function by associating required permissions. With tens of business processes, tens of thousands of users and millions of authorizations, this is seemingly a difficult task. Therefore, relying on a top-down approach in most cases is not viable. In contrast, the bottom-up approach starts from the existing permissions before RBAC is implemented and aggregates them into roles. While the top-down model is likely to ignore the existing permissions, a bottom-up model may not consider business functions of an organization. The hybrid role engineering approaches have been proposed to combine both top-down and bottom-up approaches [9, 14, 15, 16]. The necessity for proposing such approach can be justified by noting that in each organization there are always some very well-defined straightforward roles that can easily be recognized. Therefore, the bottom-up role engineering can be initiated from a partial RBAC state and discovers the complete RBAC state based on user permission assignments.

Our approach can be effectively used to model hybrid approaches. Assume from the top-down role engineering we know that there are m roles $r_1, \ldots, r_m$ in the system, and we also know which users have any of these roles. For each known role r_k we choose a role in the RBAC state and do the assignments to variable $(pa_{k,1}, \ldots, pa_{k,p})$ where each $pa_{k,j}$ is a Boolean value. Furthermore, the user role assignment extracted from the top-down approach are reflected in the UP matrix. The initial number of roles, r, is defined as $r = u - m$, and we proceed the bottom-up approach as explained in Section 4.

4.2.5 Temporal RBAC (TRBAC)

The temporal roles based access control (TRBAC) model is as an extension of RBAC model that addresses the temporal aspects of roles and trigger-based role enabling [17]. In this model, the role enabling base (REB) defines temporal intervals during which a specific role is active (or inactive). To generate a TRBAC state from a DAC state, we require an extended user to permission assignment which determines the intervals during which each assignment is active. Such schema includes tuples of the form $(u_i, \{p_1, \ldots, p_m\}, [l, u])$. $[l, u]$ determines the temporal interval during which user u_i is allowed to use permissions $\{p_1, \ldots, p_m\}$. To generate a TRBAC state, we initially define a set of temporal intervals in the following manner: for each two intervals $[l_1, u_1]$ and $[l_2, u_2]$, if $l_2 < u_1$ we generate three intervals: $[l_1, l_2]$, $[l_2, u_1]$, and $[u_1, u_2]$.

Next, we sort the intervals based on the number of user permission assignments in them. Then SMT is used to generate an RBAC state for the interval with the highest number of permissions (denoted by $[l'_1, u'_1]$). For the second highest interval, initially we use the generated roles in the first step and remove user permission assignments that are already covered in the first RBAC state. Then, we again use the SMT to generate an RBAC state for the second interval. The initial RBAC state is extended with the second interval. We continue this process until all user permission assignments are taken into account and scheduling for all intervals is accomplished. The REB is generated based on the distinct intervals during which roles are active. For example if role r_i is active only during interval $[l'_i, u'_i]$ we generate two periodic events:

- A periodic event $([l'_i, u'_i], i, enable\ r_i)$ where i is the name of the period and $enable\ r_i$ is an event expression.

- A periodic event $([u'_i, l'_i], i, disable\ r_i)$

5. EVALUATION AND EXPERIMENTAL RESULTS

In this section, we evaluate the proposed approach by performing several experiments to show its effectiveness. We use both real world datasets that have been used in previous role mining papers as well as newly generated synthetic data. We will start by describing the real world datasets and the top down approach used to generate the synthetic data. Then we describe our experimental settings, and the parameters used. We will also analyze our experimental results.

Algorithm 4 Synthetic Data Generation Algorithm

$R \leftarrow$ number of roles;
$U \leftarrow$ number of users;
$P \leftarrow$ number of permissions;
$UA \leftarrow$ initialize at zero;
$PA \leftarrow$ initialize at zero;
for $k = 1 \rightarrow R$ **do**
  $numberUsers \leftarrow Rand(U)$;
  for $i = 1 \rightarrow numberUsers$ **do**
    $user \leftarrow Rand(U)$;
    $UA_{user,k} \leftarrow 1$;
  end for
  $numberPerms \leftarrow Rand(P)$;
  for $j = 1 \rightarrow numberPerms$ **do**
    $perm \leftarrow Rand(P)$;
    $PA_{perm,k} \leftarrow 1$;
  end for
end for

5.1 Synthetic Data Generation

We use a top down approach to generate our synthetic data set for evaluation. Given a predefined number of roles, along with number of users and number of permissions present in the organization, we generate a random RBAC state. We use a top down approach where we assume the following scenario: a company with n users and m permissions identified k roles for its access control configuration. We follow the rational process a company uses to assign users to roles and permissions to roles, and we randomize all the assignments. Each role r_i has a randomly generated number of users n_i that are in turn randomly picked out of the total number of users n. Similarly, each role r_i has a randomly generated number of permissions m_i, that are randomly picked out of the total number of permissions m. Algorithm 4 was used to generate the data set.

5.2 Experimental Settings

We developed our prototype using Microsoft Z3-Library with Microsoft Visual Studio .NET. For the synthetic data set, we performed the experiments on a Core-i5 with 6 gigabyte of memory. We explored multiple scenarios including varying number of users, permissions, overall variables, and initial roles. We evaluated the number of iterations and the average execution time needed for each scenario.

5.3 Experimental Results Analysis

Figure 1 represents the number of original roles used for generating the data set against the number of generated roles. As shown, the number of generated roles is always smaller than the number of roles used for original data set generation. This shows that our approach is very close to the optimal solution with regards to the constraints modeled. In this experiment, we changed the number of users and permissions, and initial roles used in data set generation.

Figure 2 shows the time complexity required to solve the model against the number of variables. As expected, the execution time is exponential in terms of the number of variables. However, recent advances in SMT solvers allow a large number of variables. We noticed that the execution time for each satisfiable assignment is very low. However, unsatisfiable states consume a large amount of time, because

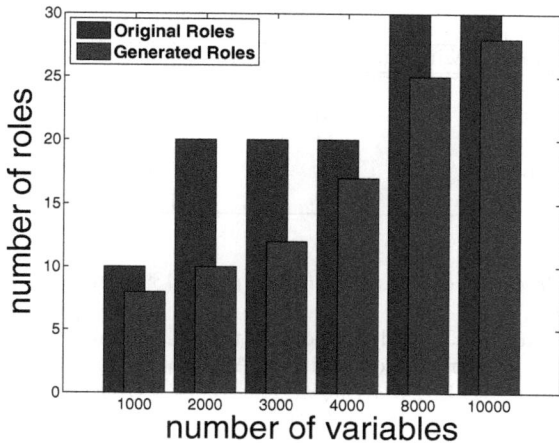

Figure 1: Initial vs. Generated Roles Comparison

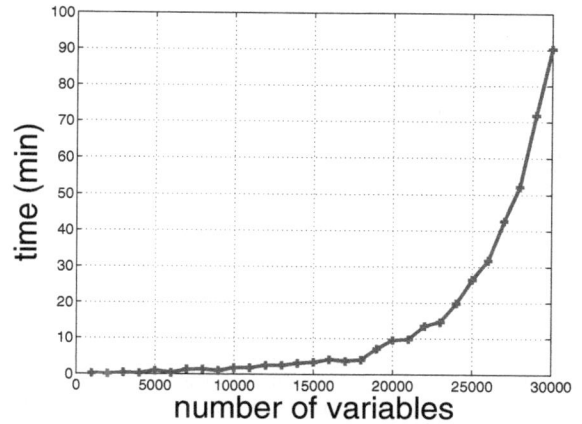

Figure 2: Time vs. Variables Number Comparison

the SMT solver has to go through all the possible assignments. Usually, in SMT solvers a *timeout* can be defined for the SMT such that the solver stops searching after the timeout predefined threshold. In future work, we will take advantage of previous execution times to adjust the timeout dynamically and improve the overall time complexity.

In Section 4, we introduced a method for determining the initial number of roles and the number of iterations. However, we believe that this can be further improved using more context-aware information such as user inputs. Another possible improvement is to model all the iterations as a single asserted constraint such that solution to this model provides the optimal RBAC state without any need for iteration. This model can be developed using the notion of constraint ordering.

5.4 Real World Datasets

The datasets that have been used in the literature were obtained from researchers at HP Labs and used for evaluation in [3]. The healthcare data was from the US Veteran's administration; the domino data was from a Lotus Domino server; EMEA data was from Cisco firewalls used to provide external users access to HP resources. We also use their firewall 1 and firewall 2 policies. More detailed information about these datasets (*e.g.*, number of users, permissions, user permission assignments) can be found in Table 1.

For these experiments, we use rank of the UP matrix as starting point instead of the iterative approach in the Algorithm 1. The maximum number of linearly independent rows in a matrix is called the row rank of the matrix, and the maximum number of linearly independent columns in a matrix is called the column rank of that matrix. For every matrix, the column rank is equal to the row rank.

Suppose $UP_{n \times m} = UA_{n \times r} \times PA_{r \times m}$ where r is the number of roles. First, we calculate rank of matrices. It can be shown that [18]

$$
\begin{aligned}
rank(UP) =& rank(UA \times PA) \\
&\leq min\{rank(UA), rank(PA)\} \\
&\leq rank(UA) \leq min\{r, m\} \leq r \quad (14)
\end{aligned}
$$

So, we have $rank(UP) \leq r$. The number of roles cannot be less than $rank(UP)$. On the other hand, we also have $r \leq n$, where n is the number of users. We conclude that $Rank(UP) \leq r \leq n$.

The UP matrix typically has some rows and columns with exact same values. We remove these rows and columns from matrix in order to lower its size. These columns and rows increase the number of variables and equations without providing any other benefit. Note that since these rows and columns are repetitive, their removal from the matrix does not affect the final result. We use SAGE v. 6.4.1, a free open-source mathematics software system, to calculate rank of the matrix UP. It is clear that the rank of matrix does not change after removing repeated rows and columns.

As we mentioned before, the minimum number of roles cannot be less than the rank of matrix UP. Therefore, we set number of roles, r, to be equal to $rank(UP)$. Based on equation $UP = UA \times PA$, we generate our equations set with variables set that includes all elements of two matrices: $UA_{n \times r}$ and $PA_{r \times m}$. We use SMT-Lib form for our equations set because most SMT solvers support this format. The number of variables in the generated equation set is $n * r + r * m$, and we have $n * m$ equations. Then we use SMT solvers Z3 (v. 4.3.2) to solve the generated equations set.

All the experiments were performed on a Ubuntu (v. 14.04) virtual machine (Intel Corei5, with 3Gb RAM). The results are shown in Table 1. The results show that we were able to find a solution with the minimum number of roles and also report the time it takes to solve the equation set.

6. CONCLUSION AND FUTURE WORK

In this paper, we transformed the role mining problem into a constraint satisfaction problem. To this aim, we provided a formal definition of the role mining problem based on propositional logic. We provided an optimal approach for solving the described model using the SMT. We also extended the original problem to include several other constraints. One extension was based on the permission usage where we defined how the permission usage can be used as an optimization metric to extract an RBAC state which

Table 1: The real world datasets

Dataset	$|U|$	$|P|$	$|UP|$	Density	Reduced Size ($|U|*|P|$)	Rank	Minimum number of roles	Time
Healthcare	46	46	1486	0.702	18*19	14	14	0.232 s
Domino	79	231	730	0.040	23*38	20	20	1.299 s
EMEA	35	3046	7220	0.068	34*263	34	34	5 min 43.353 s
Firewall 1	365	709	31951	0.123	90*86	68	68	3 min 17.149 s
Firewall 2	325	590	6428	0.190	11*11	10	10	0.092 s

preserves the way permissions are used by users. We also extended our model such that it generates an optimal hierarchical RBAC state. We also described how our approach allows to combine top-down and bottom-up approaches in an effective manner. Another contribution of our work was to describe how the problem of reconfiguring the RBAC state can be formally described and solved using our approach. Also, we included an extension for role mining based on TRBAC model.

For future works, we intend to further study different aspects and properties of our model. Firstly, we want to analyze the effectiveness of our model in generating an optimal model including all metrics of WSC. Also, we want to present a usage-based model based on the constraint satisfaction which includes adaptive learning and role recommendation. Another extension to the model is to consider incremental states where a user, or permission is added to RBAC state. Furthermore, we will attempt to improve the performance of our model using more innovative approaches in description of constraints and by reducing the number of required variables.

7. REFERENCES

[1] Edward J. Coyne. Role engineering. In *Proceedings of the first ACM Workshop on Role-based access control*, RBAC '95, New York, NY, USA, 1996. ACM.

[2] Michael P. Gallaher, Alan C. Oconnor, and Brian Kropp. The Economic Impact of Role-Based Access Control, March 2002.

[3] Alina Ene, William Horne, Nikola Milosavljevic, Prasad Rao, Robert Schreiber, and Robert E. Tarjan. Fast exact and heuristic methods for role minimization problems. *Proceedings of the 13th ACM symposium on Access control models and technologies - SACMAT '08*, (June):1, 2008.

[4] Qi Guo, J. Vaidya, and V. Atluri. The role hierarchy mining problem: Discovery of optimal role hierarchies. In *Computer Security Applications Conference, 2008. ACSAC 2008. Annual*, pages 237 –246, dec. 2008.

[5] Ian Molloy, Hong Chen, Tiancheng Li, Qihua Wang, Ninghui Li, Elisa Bertino, Seraphin Calo, and Jorge Lobo. Mining roles with semantic meanings. *Proceedings of the 13th ACM symposium on Access control models and technologies - SACMAT '08*, page 21, 2008.

[6] Ian Molloy, Ninghui Li, Tiancheng Li, Ziqing Mao, Qihua Wang, and Jorge Lobo. Evaluating role mining algorithms. *Proceedings of the 14th ACM symposium on Access control models and technologies - SACMAT '09*, page 95, 2009.

[7] Dana Zhang, K. Ramamohanarao, and Tim Ebringer. Role engineering using graph optimisation. In *Proceedings of the 12th ACM symposium on Access control models and technologies*, pages 139–144. ACM, 2007.

[8] Haibing Lu, J. Vaidya, and V. Atluri. Optimal boolean matrix decomposition: Application to role engineering. In *Data Engineering, 2008. ICDE 2008. IEEE 24th International Conference on*, pages 297 –306, april 2008.

[9] Jaideep Vaidya, V. Atluri, and J. Warner. RoleMiner: mining roles using subset enumeration. In *Proceedings of the 13th ACM conference on Computer and communications security*, pages 144–153. ACM, 2006.

[10] Jaideep Vaidya, Vijayalakshmi Atluri, and Qi Guo. The role mining problem: Finding a minimal descriptive set of roles. In *In Symposium on Access Control Models and Technologies (SACMAT)*, pages 175–184, 2007.

[11] J. Schlegelmilch and Ulrike Steffens. Role mining with ORCA. In *Proceedings of the tenth ACM symposium on Access control models and technologies*, pages 168–176. ACM, 2005.

[12] Hassan Takabi and James Joshi. Stateminer: An efficient similarity-based approach for optimal mining of role hierarchy. In *In Symposium on Access Control Models and Technologies (SACMAT)*, pages 55–64, 2010.

[13] Alessandro Colantonio, Roberto Di Pietro, and Alberto Ocello. A cost-driven approach to role engineering. In *Proceedings of the 2008 ACM symposium on Applied computing*, SAC '08, pages 2129–2136, New York, NY, USA, 2008. ACM.

[14] Ludwig Fuchs and Günther Pernul. Hydro — hybrid development of roles. In *Proceedings of the 4th International Conference on Information Systems Security*, ICISS '08, pages 287–302, Berlin, Heidelberg, 2008. Springer-Verlag.

[15] Mario Frank, Andreas P. Streich, David Basin, and Joachim M. Buhmann. A probabilistic approach to hybrid role mining. In *Proceedings of the 16th ACM Conference on Computer and Communications Security*, CCS '09, pages 101–111, New York, NY, USA, 2009. ACM.

[16] S. Mandala, M. Vukovic, J. Laredo, Yaoping Ruan, and M. Hernandez. Hybrid role mining for security service solution. In *Services Computing (SCC), 2012 IEEE Ninth International Conference on*, pages 210–217, June 2012.

[17] James B. D. Joshi, Elisa Bertino, Usman Latif, and Arif Ghafoor. Trbac: A temporal role -based access control model. *ACM Transactions on Information and System Security (TISSEC*, 2001.

[18] L. Hogben. *Handbook of linear algebra*. Chapman & Hall/CRC, 2007.

SPA: Inviting Your Friends to Help Set Android Apps

Zeqing Guo[1], Weili Han[1,3], Liangxing Liu[1], Wenyuan Xu[2], Ruiqi Bu[1], Minyue Ni[1]

1. Software School, Fudan University, Shanghai, China
2. Department of Electronic Engineering, Zhejiang University, Hangzhou, China
3. Shanghai Key Laboratory of Data Science, Fudan University, Shanghai, China
{wlhan@fudan.edu.cn, xuwenyuan@zju.edu.cn}

ABSTRACT

More and more powerful personal smart devices take users, especially the elder, into a disaster of policy administration where users are forced to set personal management policies in these devices. Considering a real case of this issue in the Android security, it is hard for users, even some programmers, to generally identify malicious permission requests when they install a third-party application. Motivated by the popularity of mutual assistance among friends (including family members) in the real world, we propose a novel framework for policy administration, referring to Socialized Policy Administration (SPA for short), to help users manage the policies in widely deployed personal devices. SPA leverages a basic idea that a user may invite his or her friends to help set the applications. Especially, when the size of invited friends increases, the setting result can be more resilient to a few malicious or unprofessional friends. We define the security properties of SPA, and propose an enforcement framework where users' friends can help users set applications without the leakage of friends' preferences with the supports of a privacy preserving mechanism. In our prototype, we only leverage partially homomorphic encryption cryptosystems to implement our framework, because the fully homomorphic encryption is not acceptable to be deployed in a practical service at the moment. Based on our prototype and performance evaluation, SPA is promising to support major types of policies in current popular applications with acceptable performance.

Categories and Subject Descriptors

D.4.6 [**Software**]: Security and Protection—*Access controls*

General Terms

Security

Keywords

Policy based Management, Policy Administration, Socialized Policy Administration, Android, Social Computing

1. INTRODUCTION

Recently, users are faced with smarter and smarter personal devices, *e.g.*, smartphones, which contain large amounts of information and powerful sensors. According to the report of Techinasia [26], 1.3 billion smartphones, containing over 0.7 million third-party applications, have been shipped to customers since 2014. That is, over one out of six persons in the world got a new smart phone in the past year. Unfortunately, these users, even applications' developers, are usually unprofessional to manage these applications in devices [6][2][8][17][7].

Friends (including family members) are indeed supports for security in both the real world and the cyberspace. In real life, people who are not good at security management may invite their friends (including family members) who are professional to help set their devices and applications. For example, a woman could invite her husband to set electronic devices; an elder could ask grandson to provide a configured smart phone. The invitation would be possible among friends if they agree to share their privacy. This is very common in current social network services. In this paper, we extend this idea into the cyberspace, which means, a user may ask for help from his or her friends to set their devices via Social Network Services (SNSs for short) on the Internet. Although this extension looks very intuitional, some technical challenges, such as privacy preservation, should be resolved. When a user asks his or her friends some sensitive settings and the friends cannot control the responses, or the framework cannot protect the responses from personal information leakage, the framework can be maliciously used to gather privacy from the friends.

Existing methods of collaborative policy authoring [30] or administration [12] are far from the protection of friends' privacy. The work of [30] aims to protect the privacy with the supports of nominated friends (co-owners of content) when a user shares his or her personal content on a SNS, such as Facebook. It requires friends' interactions, and does not consider friends' privacy. In addition, CPA (Collaborative Policy Administration) proposed in the work of [12] leverages other similar settings of applications to set users' application. CPA is not required to consider the privacy protection issue of the applications, because the settings of these applications are in public. However, in our extension, the privacy of these involved friends can be very critical, because the responses would implicitly include some sensitive information. Once the information is automatically gathered, more sensitive personal profiles would be exposed to the public.

This paper, therefore, articulates the problem of socialized policy administration and proposes an enforcement framework. The main contributions are as follows:

- We articulate the methodology of socialized policy administration where a user can request his or her friends to help automatically set sensitive policies. We design a model family, including *Basic SPA* which includes essential elements of SPA, *m-SPA* which supports multiple friends groups of a user, *w-SPA* which supports the user labels weights for friends, and *Composite SPA* which merges the features of *m-SPA* and *w-SPA*. We also design a framework for a mobile scenario where the privacy of friends is preserved. To the best of our knowledge, this is the first paper to enable unprofessional users with the help of their friends to set sensitive policies with privacy preservation.

- We find out that partially homomorphic encryption algorithms which we leverage in SPA can support major policy types in popular mobile applications. In SPA, homomorphic encryption will run in a semi-trusted service, where the SPA responses from friends will be merged together. A thin client, such as a smart phone, can decrypt the merged result, then set the policy in the client. Due to the performance of current fully homomorphic encryption, although the under-developed fully homomorphic encryption may support more types of policies, several practical algorithms which support one or several types of homomorphic encryption are leveraged in our implementation. We analyze the possible supported types of policies in SPA by these homomorphic encryption algorithms based on our downloaded popular third-party applications.

Note that, although the policies of devices can be automatically set by SPA, users can modify the policies in their devices by themselves. As a result, professional users may also obtain useful references from their friends.

The rest of this paper is organized as follows: Section 2 introduces the background knowledge and our target problem. Section 3 describes the security assumptions and defines SPA models. Section 4 describes the design and implementation of SPA. We then present our experimental process and evaluation results in Section 5. Next, we have a discussion about vulnerabilities of SPA and security of homomorphic encryption in Section 6. Section 7 introduces related work. Finally, Section 8 summarizes this paper and outlines our future work.

2. BACKGROUND AND MOTIVATION

2.1 Homomorphic Encryption

Homomorphic encryption is a form of encryption which allows specific types of computations to be carried out on ciphertext and generate an encrypted result which, when decrypted, matches the result of operations performed on the plaintext [28]. That is, A may encrypt his message m and send the ciphertext $\mathbb{E}(m)$ to B. B may then take the ciphertext $\mathbb{E}(m)$ and evaluate a function $\mathbb{F}$ on the underlying m obtaining the encrypted result $\mathbb{E}(\mathbb{F}(m))$. B may decrypt this result, and achieve the wanted functionality on data m, but B learns nothing about the data that it has operated on.

Although the fully homomorphic encryption (FHE) which supports an arbitrary function $\mathbb{F}$ on ciphertexts was proposed several years ago [3][25][27], its performance is hard to meet the requirements for a practical business service. Gentry showed the first fully homomorphic encryption scheme using lattice-based cryptography in 2009 [10][11]. Such a scheme allows one to compute arbitrary functions over encrypted data without the decryption key, *i.e.*, given encryptions $\mathbb{E}(m_1)$, ..., $\mathbb{E}(m_t)$, one can efficiently compute a composite ciphertext that encrypts $\mathbb{F}(m_1, ..., m_t)$ for any efficiently computable function $\mathbb{F}$.

As a result, partially homomorphic cryptosystems are the good choices in practical. Some partially homomorphic cryptosystems are as follows.

- **Paillier (Additive):** The Paillier cryptosystem, invented by Pascal Paillier in 1999, is a probabilistic asymmetric algorithm for public key cryptography [18]. The cryptographic algorithm generates a key pair, consisting of a public key and a private key. The public key is used to encrypt plaintext; whereas the private key is used to decrypt ciphertext.

  The scheme is an additive homomorphic cryptosystem [4]. The additive homomorphic properties can be represented as follows:

  $$\mathbb{F}(\mathbb{E}(m_1), \mathbb{E}(m_2)) = \mathbb{E}(m_1 + m_2)$$

  Here, $\mathbb{E}$ refers to encryption function, and $\mathbb{F}$ is a function defined by the partially homomorphic cryptosystem whose value is the encryption of the sum of m_1 and m_2. And m_1, m_2 are two plaintexts.

- **RSA (Multiplicative):** RSA is one of the first practicable public-key cryptosystems and is widely used for secure data transmission. RSA stands for Ron Rivest, Adi Shamir and Leonard Adleman, who first publicly described the algorithm in 1977 [19]. In such a cryptosystem, the encryption key is public and differs from the decryption key which is kept secret.

  The scheme is a multiplicative homomorphic cryptosystem [9]. The multiplicative homomorphic properties can be represented as follows:

  $$\mathbb{F}(\mathbb{E}(m_1), \mathbb{E}(m_2)) = \mathbb{E}(m_1 \cdot m_2)$$

  Here, the definitions of $\mathbb{E}$, $\mathbb{F}$, m_1, m_2 are the same as those in **Paillier**.

- **ElGamal (Multiplicative):** The ElGamal encryption system is an asymmetric key encryption algorithm for public-key cryptography. It was described by El-gamal in 1985 [5]. The scheme is also a multiplicative homomorphic cryptosystem, and its multiplication homomorphic properties is the same with **RSA's**.

2.2 Motivated Scenario in Mobile Application Setting

A user, *e.g.*, Alice, may set her applications with little professional knowledge, assisted by her friends whose settings can be kept secret without privacy leakage:

Alice, Bob, Cindy, Dale, Eric are in a Facebook *group named "Classmates". Alice downloads* Instagram, *which is recommended by her classmates.*

However, after she finishes the initially installing process, she is confused about how to configure these settings, because she never used Instagram. At the moment, Alice has no choice but to finish these settings independently, which is obviously very hard and time-consuming to understand all guides to set Instagram's policies.

What Alice expects is the following scene. She sends a request to her classmates in the Facebook group respectively. Her classmates receive the request, and tell her their configurations CONFIDENTIALLY. Then Alice can set her Instagram according to her classmates' configurations. E.g., if the majority of her classmates set "Like Notification" as "off", then she sets it "off". In addition, if Alice applies a high-level policy, e.g., follow major settings in "Classmates", the settings in Instagram can be automatically finished without click by click.

Alice can modify the setting by herself if she has her different preferences after the automatically setting by SPA. But she can immediately set Instagram without the deep professional knowledge of application settings.

We define this process as "socialized policy administration" where the social relations are leveraged to help users set sensitive policies. This requirement would become more and more important when the mobile technologies, especially when smartphones and wearable smart devices are widely equipped by those who lack security awarenesses and experiences of policy administration.

3. SPA MODELS

3.1 Security Assumptions

In the above scenario, SPA is designed to protect Alice from malicious or harmful policies in her devices. That is, her unprofessional settings in security management seriously affect on the system security. we can conclude the following security assumptions:

- The major friends (Bob, Cindy, Dale, Eric) set correct security and management policies of applications. And their settings should be protected during SPA processes. That is, the user and the cloud service should know the least information of the user's friends' settings.

- The cloud service which helps SPA to merge the responses from friends (Bob, Cindy, Dale, Eric) is semi-trust. That is, details of the friends' responses cannot be viewed through the cloud service. But when the cloud service colludes with the user, they can get privacy data of friends. The assumption is reasonable in the major secure cloud-based applications[13].

The privacy concern in SPA will lead that if Alice has only one friend, SPA will be ceased.

3.2 SPA Models

As is shown in Figure 1, we define a family of SPA models where (1) *Basic SPA* includes the essential elements of

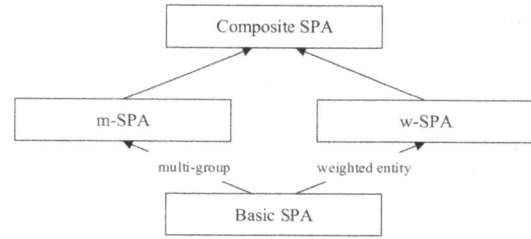

Figure 1: SPA Models

SPA; (2) *m-SPA* supports multiple friend groups when a user launches SPA requests; (3) *w-SPA* allows the user to set the weight according to each friend's ability of managing policy; (4) *Composite SPA* supports multiple features of *m-SPA* and *w-SPA*. The above four models are proposed to meet different requirements of application scenarios.

3.2.1 Basic SPA Model

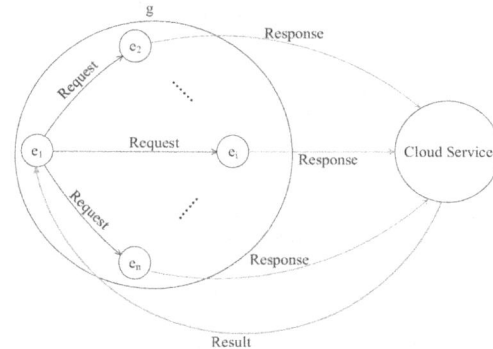

Figure 2: Basic SPA Model

As is shown in Figure 2, the formal definition of Basic SPA is as follows.

Definition 1. Basic SPA Model:

$$Basic\ SPA := (E, g, R, P, SPAPolicy)$$

Here, E, g, R, P, $SPAPolicy$ refer to a set of entities, a group, a set of roles, a set of processes, a high level policy respectively:

- **Entity (E)** refers to the user who has their customized setting for applications (such as Android apps). Let $e := (id, policies)$ denote an entity, where id is the unique identification of e, $policies$ consist of every application's setting policy, each of which includes attributes as well as values. E.g., $e_{Alice} = (id_{Alice}, policies)$ represents that e_{Alice} is an entity assigned to Alice with identification id_{Alice}, and her setting policies are represented by $policies$. In the motivated scenario, there are five entities: Alice, Bob, Cindy, Dale, Eric. We hide the applications' policies of these entities here.

- **Group (g)** is created by a user (e.g., Alice in the motivated scenario) to implement the Socialized Policy Administration. Let $g = \{e_1, e_2, \ldots, e_n\}$ denote a group, where each element e_i is an entity. In *Basic SPA* model, a user, *e.g.*, Alice, can send requests to a sole selected $g_i \subseteq \{g | e_{Alice} \in g\}$. In the motivated scenario, $g = \{$Alice, Bob, Cindy, Dale, Eric$\}$. Note that, $|g| \geq 3$.

- **Role (R)** refers to the entity's role in *Basic SPA* Model. There are two types of roles: *requester*, and *respondent*. The *requester* refers to the one who sends SPA request and asks his or her friends for help about policy setting, and the *respondent* refers to the one who receives SPA request. *E.g.*, if Alice asks her friends for help, Alice is a *requester* and her friends are *respondents*.

- **Process (P)** denotes either an SPA request or an SPA response in *Basic SPA* model. There are two types of processes: *request* and *response*. Both *request* and *response* can be described as a tuple $(e, r, policy)$, where e refers to an entity, r refers to a role, and *policy*, which is the setting policy that the user asks for, is a part of *e.policies*. *E.g.*, in the motivated scenario, Alice is confused about how to configure settings on *Instagram*. Thus, she sends *request* to entities in her classmate group, including Bob, Cindy, Dale, Eric, for help. This *request* can be represented by (Alice, *requester*, *Instagram*). And these *responses* responded by her friends in the group can be represented by (Bob, *respondent*, *Instagram₁*), (Cindy, *respondent*, *Instagram₂*), etc.

- **SPAPolicy** refers to the high level policy supported by *Basic SPA* model. For instance, *Basic SPA* supports **Average value** policy where the *requester* can obtain the average number based on all *respondents'* settings. For a sound volume setting, each *respondent* can report their value to a *requester* with *confidentiality*, then the *requester* can leverage **Average value** to set his or her sound volume.

There exists a relation between the entity and the role. Let $roles(e_i) = \{r | (e_i, r, policy) \in P\}$ denote a function mapping each entity to a role. For example, Alice is an entity and in a process. We can use the function $roles(e_{Alice})$ to find the role of e_{Alice}.

In order to ensure the *confidentiality* of *respondents*, more than one *response* is required before the result is sent back to the *requester* to prevent him or her from identifying the settings of *respondent*. In addition, *requester* knows only "a little", "some", "most" of the *respondents* instead of the exact number of *respondents* who response his *request*, which can avoids the *requester* knowing the choices of all *respondents* when all *respondents* happen to make the same *responses* to a *request*.

3.2.2 *Multi-group – m-SPA Model*

As is shown in Figure 3, *m-SPA* is extended from *Basic SPA*. It allows *requesters* to send *requests* to multiple groups. The formal definition of *m-SPA* is as follows.

Definition 2. m-SPA Model:

$$m\text{-}SPA := (E, MG, R, P, SPAPolicy)$$

Here, E, MG, R, P, $SPAPolicy$ refers to a set of entities, a multi-group, a set of roles, a set of processes, a high level policy respectively.

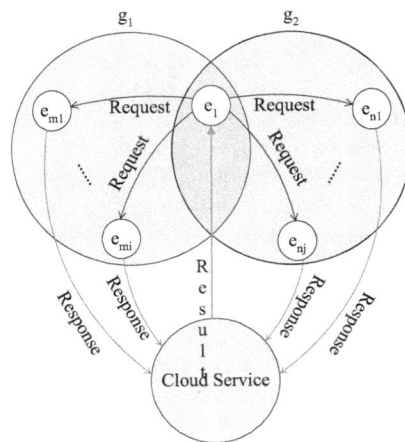

Figure 3: m-SPA Model

- **Multi-group (MG)** is a set of several groups of friends. Let $MG = \{g_1, \ldots, g_n\}$, where $n \geq 1$, denote a multi-group. If and only if an entity $e \in g_1 \cup \ldots \cup g_n$, where $g_1, \ldots, g_n \in MG$, $roles(e)$ can be a *respondent* of MG. If and only if an entity $e \in g_1 \cap \ldots \cap g_n$, where $g_1, \ldots, g_n \in MG$, $roles(e)$ can be a *requester* of MG. *E.g.*, Alice owns two groups that are named *highschool* and *university* in *m-SPA* Model. The set $\{g_{highschool}, g_{university}\}$ is a multi-group. She is allowed to be a *requester* in this multi-group and other entities in this multi-group are *respondents*.

Comparing with *Basic SPA*, the definitions of entity, role, process, and SPAPolicy do not change in *m-SPA*, whereas multi-group is a set of several groups selected by the *requester*.

3.2.3 *Weighted entity – w-SPA Model*

The structure of *w-SPA* is extended from *Basic SPA* shown in Figure 2, while the structure of entity is different. Considering the facts that *respondents'* knowledge about managing privacy determines the reliability of the result and a *requester* is familiar with *respondents*, the result is more reliable if the *requester* gives each *respondent* a weight corresponding to each friend's ability of managing policy. The following definition reflects this idea.

Definition 3. w-SPA Model:

$$w\text{-}SPA := (E_w, g, R, P, SPAPolicy)$$

w-SPA Model is unchanged from *Basic SPA* model expect the structure of entity E_w.

- **Weighted Entity (E_w)** defines an entity, which includes an additional attribute *weight* (the value of weight is 100 by default), and a *requester* can change it before sending *requests*. Let $e_w := (id, policies, weight)$ denote an entity in *w-SPA*, where *id* and *policies* are the same as those in *Basic SPA*, and *weight* is a number determined by a *requester*.

3.2.4 Composite SPA

Composite SPA contains all features of both multi-group and weighted entity, as it combines *m-SPA* and *w-SPA*. *Composite SPA* remains unchanged from *m-SPA* except the structure of entity E, which is the same as the entity in *w-SPA*.

3.3 Correctness and Robustness of SPA Models

We begin with *Composite SPA*, which is the most general case of these four SPA models, and formalize the correctness and robustness of *Composite SPA* model. Here, we only analyze the high level policy of **Average value**. Some hypotheses during the analysis are as follows:

- A user is a *requester* in $g_1, \cdots, g_m$, and $|g_1 \cup \cdots \cup g_m - e_{requester}| = n$. That is, there are n different friends in the *requester's* groups. These friends of the *requester* may be professional users, unprofessional users, or malicious users. And let $n_{pro}, n_{unpro}, n_{mal}$ denote the number of professional, unprofessional, and malicious users respectively, so $n_{pro} + n_{unpro} + n_{mal} = n$.

- The *requester* is confused about a setting policy, which is a continuous type in the range $[0, 100]$, for a certain application. *SPAPolicy* for the continuous type is **Average value** in *Composite SPA*. Suppose that there exist four non-negative integers e_1, e_2, e_3, e_4, where e_1, $e_2, e_3, e_4 \in [0, 100]$ and $e_1 < e_2 < e_3 < e_4$, and the setting values in $[e_1, e_2]$ may be harmful for the *requester*, while $[e_3, e_4]$ is the appropriate choice interval for him or her.

- Each friend may respond to the *request* with a setting value, and can be attached with a weight value. To simplify the proof, we assume that each friend will respond with a setting value, and setting values of professional, unprofessional, malicious users are in $[e_3, e_4]$, (e_2, e_3), $[e_1, e_2]$ repectively. The setting value function and weight function can be defined as follows:

$$setting(e) = \begin{cases} x, & \text{if } e \text{ is professional} \\ y, & \text{if } e \text{ is unprofessional} \\ z, & \text{if } e \text{ is malicious} \end{cases} \quad (1)$$

Here, $x \in [e_3, e_4]$, $y \in (e_2, e_3)$, $z \in [e_1, e_2]$ refer to expectations of setting values of professional users, unprofessional users, malicious users repectively.

$$weight(e) = \begin{cases} w_{pro}, & \text{if } e \text{ is professional} \\ w_{unpro}, & \text{if } e \text{ is unprofessional} \\ w_{mal}, & \text{if } e \text{ is malicious} \end{cases} \quad (2)$$

Here, $w_{pro}, w_{unpro}, w_{mal}$ are three positive integers, where $w_{pro} \geq w_{unpro}$, $w_{mal} \geq w_{unpro}$. This assumption is reasonable as malicious users should masquerade as professional users. Therefore, the user ranks them with a higher value than the ones of unprofessional users.

Based on **Average value** policy, the correctness of *Composite SPA* can be described by the proximity of the expectation of setting values to x:

$$correctness(n_{pro}, n_{unpro}, n_{mal}) = \frac{\sum_{e \in g_1 \cup \cdots \cup g_n} weight(e) \cdot setting(e)}{\sum_{e \in g_1 \cup \cdots \cup g_n} weight(e) \cdot x} \quad (3)$$

Replacing each $setting(e)$, $weight(e)$ with equation (1) and (2), we get

$$correctness(n_{pro}, n_{unpro}, n_{mal}) = 1 - \frac{(x - y) \cdot w_{unpro} \cdot n_{unpro} + (x - z) \cdot w_{mal} \cdot n_{mal}}{x \cdot (w_{pro} \cdot n_{pro} + w_{unpro} \cdot n_{unpro} + w_{mal} \cdot n_{mal})} \quad (4)$$

Then, we calculate the partial differential of *correctness* function:

$$\frac{\partial correctness}{\partial n_{pro}}(n_{pro}, n_{unpro}, n_{mal}) = \frac{(x - y) \cdot w_{unpro} \cdot n_{unpro} + (x - z) \cdot w_{mal} \cdot n_{mal}}{x(w_{pro} \cdot n_{pro} + w_{unpro} \cdot n_{unpro} + w_{mal} \cdot n_{mal})^2} \quad (5)$$

Considering $x > y$ and $x > z$, the inequality $\frac{\partial correctness}{\partial n_{pro}} > 0$ holds, which means when the proportion of the number of professional users increase, the correctness of *Composite SPA* will increase.

The robustness of *Composite SPA* can be described by $\frac{\partial Expectation}{\partial n_{mal}}$. We focus on the influence of changing n_{mal} on the expectation of setting value. The relation of n_{unpro} and the expectation of setting value can be expressed similarly by the following equation.

$$robustness(n_{pro}, n_{unpro}, n_{mal}) = \frac{((z - x)w_{pro} \cdot n_{pro} + (y - z)w_{unpro} \cdot n_{unpro}) \cdot w_{mal}}{(w_{pro} \cdot n_{pro} + w_{unpro} \cdot n_{unpro} + w_{mal} \cdot n_{mal})^2} \quad (6)$$

Let a, b, c denote the percentage of professional, unprofessional, malicious users, where a, b, c are non-negative constants and $a + b + c = 1$. Then we have $a \cdot n = n_{pro}$, $b \cdot n = n_{unpro}$, $c \cdot n = n_{mal}$. The *robustness* can be converted to a function with independent variable n:

$$robustness(n) = -\frac{((x - z) \cdot w_{pro} \cdot a + (y - z) \cdot w_{unpro} \cdot b) \cdot w_{mal}}{(w_{pro} \cdot a + w_{unpro} \cdot b + w_{mal} \cdot c)^2 \cdot n} \quad (7)$$

It is easy to see that $\frac{\partial robustness}{\partial n} > 0$ and $robustness < 0$ for any positive integers n. Therefore, when the n increases, the robustness increases. That is, when the n increases, the decreasing trend of expectation of setting value will decrease.

Composite SPA is the most general SPA model among these four SPA models defined in section 3.2, and *m-SPA*, *w-SPA*, *Basic SPA* are the special cases of *Composite SPA*. When the m of $g_1, \cdots, g_m$ equals to 1 in *Composite SPA*, *Composite SPA* and *w-SPA* will be equivalent. In the case where $w_{pro} = w_{unpro} = w_{mal}$ in Composite SPA, *Composite SPA* are equivalent to *m-SPA*. When $m = 1$ and $w_{pro} = w_{unpro} = w_{mal}$ in *Composite SPA*, *Composite SPA* and *Basic SPA* are equivalent. So the correctness and robustness of these three SPA models can also be represented by above equations.

Table 1: Mappings from Policies and Merging Policies to Homomorphic Properties

Privacy Policies	Merging Policies	Homomorphic Properties	Example
Switch	Majority/Minority preferred	Additive	Paillier
Single Select	Majority/Minority preferred	Additive	Paillier
		Multiplicative	RSA
Multiple Select	Majority/Minority preferred	Additive	Paillier
		Multiplicative	RSA
Continuous	Average value	Additive	Paillier
	Maximum/Minimum value	Fully Homomorphic	Not pratical

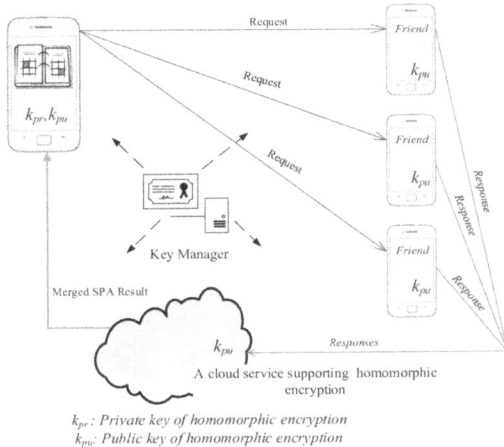

k_{pe}: Private key of homomorphic encryption
k_{pu}: Public key of homomorphic encryption

Figure 4: SPA Framework

4. DESIGN OF BASIC SPA FRAMEWORK

4.1 Basic SPA Framework

The key flow of the proposed framework is illustrated in Figure 4. Before the *processes*, a key management server will disseminate the public and private keys of homomorphic encryption algorithms, such as **Paillier** to the entities in the group. To simplify the implementation, we only propose the framework to support *Basic SPA*. The framework is easily to be extend to other models proposed in Section 3. The security concerns of these models are different from *Basic SPA* and we analyze their security in Section 6.1.

A socialized policy administration process includes the following steps:

1. A *requester* sends a *request* to all friends in the friend group.

2. A *respondent* receives the *request*, and sends a *response* encrypted with the public key of homomorphic encryption to a semi-trusted *cloud* service.

3. The *cloud* merges corresponding *responses*. Then the *cloud* sends an encrypted result to the *requester*. If the number of corresponding *responses* is one, the *cloud* will return an error to the *requester*.

4. The *requester* receives data that *cloud* sends and decrypts it with the private key of homomorphic encryption to get the final result.

In our SPA framework, we define four types of policies as follows.

- **Switch**. The status of a setting consists of "on" and "off", *e.g.*, "find me through email address".

- **Single Select**. There is more than one choice for a setting, but only one choice can be selected. *E.g.*, there are 3 choices ("Off", "From People I Follow", "From Everyone") for the setting "Comment Notifications" on Instagram.

- **Multiple Select**. There is more than one choice for a setting, and more than one choice can be selected at the same time.

- **Continuous**. The numeric value of a setting is continuous.

We also define three types of high-level policies to merge *responses* as follows.

- **Majority/Minority preferred**. This type of merging policies applies to **Switch**, **Single Select** and **Multiple Select** types of policies. When a **Majority preferred** merging policy is set, the final merging result is the majority of choices made by friends.

- **Average value**. This type applies to the **Continuous** type of policies. The final merging result is the average value of choices made by friends.

- **Maximum/Minimum value**. This type also applies to the **Continuous** type of policies. When a **Maximum value** merging policy is set, the final merging result is the maximum value of choices made by friends.

Table 1 shows the mappings from a combination of policies and merging policies to required homomorphic properties and example algorithms.

4.2 Data Structures in SPA

4.2.1 Request

The structure of a *request* is shown in Table 2. The *id* field works as an identifier of a *request*, and the *requester* field describes the entity who starts the *request*. The *SPA-Policy* field describes a high-level policy to merge *responses* corresponding to a *request*. The *policy* field describes the targeted application name and the related setting which includes information about a specific personal setting. *Name*, *type*, *content*, and *value* denote the name of the setting, the type of the setting, the content of an option, and the selected status of an option, respectively. For **Single Select** and **Multiple Select** types of policies, there may be multiple parallel *setting* elements in a *request*.

Table 2: Structure of a _Request_

Field	Description
id	the unique identifier of a _request_
requester	the entity that starts the _request_
SPAPolicy	the policy to merge _response_
policy	app's policy that _requester_ confuses with

4.2.2 _Response_

The structure of a _response_ is shown in Table 3. The _id_ field works as an identifier of a _response_. The _respondent_ field describes the entity which makes the _response_, and the _request_ field is used so that _cloud_ knows which _responses_ are supposed to be merged together to get a final result.

Table 3: Structure of a _Response_

Field	Description
id	the unique identifier of a _response_
respondent	the entity that responds the _request_
request	the corresponding _request_
policy	app's policy that the _requester_ confuses with

4.2.3 _Result_

The structure of an SPA result is shown in Table 4. An SPA result is the result of merging _responses_. The _cloud_ sends an SPA _result_ to the corresponding SPA _requester_. The _policy_ field includes the name of application that need to be set as well as the setting that describes how to set the application concretely.

Table 4: Structure of an SPA Result

Field	Description
id	unique identifier of a result
requester	the entity that starts the _request_
policy	app's policy that the _requester_ confuse with

4.3 Key Algorithms

In this section, we introduce two key algorithms in SPA: a _response_ encryption algorithm and a _response_ merging algorithm.

4.3.1 _Response Encryption Algorithm_

The pseudocode of _response_ encryption algorithm is shown in Algorithm 1.

The method _getSettingSize()_ returns the number of _setting_ elements in a _response_. The method _homomorphicEncrypt()_ operates a homomorphic encryption on the _value_ of a setting. The _value_ of a setting is decided in the following scheme:

- For **Switch** type of a setting, _value_ is 1 for "on", and 0 for "off".

- For **Single Select** and **Multiple Select** types of a setting, _value_ is 1 when the option is selected, otherwise _value_ is 0.

- For **Continuous** type of a setting, _value_ is the corresponding integer value of the setting bar.

Algorithm 1 _Response_ Encryption Algorithm.

Input: r: a _response_
Output: $r_{encrypted}$: an encrypted _response_
1: $m = getSettingSize(r)$
2: **for** $i=1$ to m **do**
3:      $r_{encrypted}.policy.setting_i.value$
4:      $\leftarrow$ **homomorphicEncrypt**($r.policy.setting_i.value$)
5: **end for**
6: **return** $r_{encrypted}$

4.3.2 _Response Merging Algorithm_

The pseudocode of _response_ merging algorithm is shown in Algorithm 2.

Algorithm 2 _Response_ Merging Algorithm.

Input: r_1: a encrypted _response_; r_2: another _encrypted response_
Output: _result_: a merging result
1: **if** $r_1.request.id = r_2.request.id$ **then**
2:      $result.requester \leftarrow r_1.requester$
3:      **Create** a new _policy_ element p
4:      $p.application \leftarrow r_1.policy.application$
5:      $m = getSettingSize(r_1)$
6:      **for** $i=1$ to m **do**
7:          **Create** a new _setting_ element s
8:          $s.name \leftarrow r_1.policy.setting_i.name$
9:          $s.type \leftarrow r_1.policy.setting_i.type$
10:         $s.content \leftarrow r_1.policy.setting_i.content$
11:         $s.value \leftarrow$ **homomorphic**
12:         ($r_1.setting_i.value, r_2.setting_i.value$)
13:         **Apend** s to p
14:      **end for**
15:      **Apend** p to _result_
16: **end if**
17: **return** _result_

When a _response_ comes, the _cloud_ deals with the _response_ as follows:

- When the _cloud_ receives a _response_ corresponding to a new _request_, _cloud_ generates a new record in the database, storing the response related to the specific _request_.

- When the _cloud_ receives a _response_ corresponding to an existing _request_. The _cloud_ starts a merging process, which merges the newcome response with an existing _response_, and updates the record in the database.

Algorithm 2 shows how to merge two _responses_. If the number of _responses_ from friends over two, algorithm 2 can process them iteratively. The method _getSettingSize()_ returns the number of _setting_ elements in a _response_. The method _homomorphic()_ operates a homomorphic addition/multiplicative on two encrypted values. The time complexity of Algorithm 2 is $\mathcal{O}(m)$, where m is the number of _setting_ elements in a _response_.

5. EVALUATION

5.1 Prototype Implementation

In our work, we implemented the SPA framework which builds on a partially homomorphic encryption algorithm,

Paillier. The SPA framework consists of the client and server application.

- The server application forwards requests and responses between entities. It also functions as a semi-trusted *cloud* service to merge responses corresponding to a *request*.

- The client application is released as an *.apk* file. After installing the application on a smartphone, a user can log on to it using a registered account, and perform the SPA functionality when he or she wants to set privacy-aware policies.

5.2 Completeness of Supporting Policy Types

When the implementation of SPA leverages a partial homomorphic encryption algorithm due to performance concerns, we concern how many types of policies in mobile applications can be supported. In this section, we try to find out the completeness of supporting policy types of the implemented SPA.

We conduct experiments to evaluate the completeness of the implemented SPA by measuring the fraction of policies it can handle over the total number of policies. Firstly, we download the top 50 applications of each category on the ranking list of Google Play Store. These 22 categories include social network services, sports, finance and so on. Then we install these 1,100 applications on Android smartphones. For each application, we click to find out the settings related to privacy or security and calculate the number of policies in each type manually.

We conduct the first experiment to learn the percentage of policies that the implemented SPA can support in these 1,100 applications. We do the statistics work in the following two ways. One is to count the total number of applications that contain policies of each type (denoted as m), and we calculate the percentage as m over M, where M is the number of usable applications for statistical analysis among 1,100 applications. The other is to count the total number of policies in each type (denoted as n), and we calculate the percentage as n over N, where N is the total number of policies appearing in the 1,100 applications.

Not all the 1,100 applications contain privacy or security settings. For example, applications related to books and references rarely contain settings. There are also some applications we cannot even open due to the issue of Internet. There are 479 applications of these two kinds in total, and the rest 721 applications are usable for statistical analysis.

Table 5 shows the number and percentage of applications that contain policies of each type. About half of the usable applications contain policies of **Switch** type. Since the implemented SPA can support the defined four types of settings, the percentage of applications that SPA cannot completely support is 27.18%.

Table 6 shows the number and percentage of policies of each type. Nearly half of the total policies are of **Switch** type. As the implemented SPA supports the defined four types of settings, the percentage of policies that the implemented SPA cannot support accounts for 16.48%.

In the second experiment, we select a specific SNSs application as the test case, to learn the percentage of policies that the implemented SPA supports. We conduct the experiment on *WeChat*, a mobile text and voice messaging communication service developed by Tencent in China [29].

Table 5: Number of Applications Containing Policies of Each Type among Usable Applications

Type	Number	Percentage
Switch	339	47.01%
Single Select	124	17.19%
Multiple Select	41	5.68%
Continuous	23	3.19%
Others	196	27.18%

Table 6: Number of Policies of Each Type among Usable Applications

Type	Number	Percentage
Switch	1130	63.77%
Single Select	213	12.02%
Multiple Select	95	5.36%
Continuous	42	2.37%
Others	292	16.48%

It is a very popular instant messaging service in Chinese community. The version we employ here is *WeChat* 5.3 for Android. The policies appear in *WeChat* are shown in Table 7. We simulate these settings in the implemented SPA.

In our experiment, the SPA works well except when the type of policies is **List**. There are two types of policies in *WeChat*: **Switch** and **List**. We have not defined the **List** type, so the implemented SPA cannot deal with this kind of policies. However, we think this kind of policies is not appropriate for policy recommendation. The reason is that users can take advantage of blocked list or hidden friends to know who are less popular in the friend group, which leads to privacy problems.

5.3 Performance Evaluation

In order to provide an acceptable security strength of the SPA framework, there is much computational work on both the client and server application. For the client application, it needs to encrypt a *response* before sending it to the server; For the server application, it takes time and space to do a homomorphic merging operation.

We conduct the first experiment to evaluate the performance of the server application. The server application runs on a PC running Windows 7 professional with 4.00 GB memory and Intel(R) Core i5-2400 CPU @ 3.10GHz processor. We vary the number of *responses* that the server application receives at the same time, and record the time that the server application needs to process these *responses*. The experimental result is shown in Figure 5.

In Figure 5, the horizontal axis represents the number of *responses* that the server receives at the same time, and the vertical axis represents the time that the server needs to deal with these *responses*. The main time costs lie on merging *responses*.

We conduct the second experiment to evaluate the performance of the client application. The two metrics of performance are: time to process *requests* and CPU occupancy rate on Android smartphones. We conduct the experiment on different kinds of smartphones running Android 4.2. These smart phones include a *Nexus 4* with a 8.00G memory, a *Galaxy S4* with a 16.00G memory, and an HTC Desire 816w

Table 7: Policies in WeChat

Setting	Meaning	Type
Friend Confirmation	Confirmation before becoming friends	Switch
Find *QQ* Contacts	Recommend friends on *QQ* to me	Switch
Find Me by *QQ* ID	Find me by searching my *QQ* ID	Switch
Find Me by Phone Number	Find me by searching my phone number	Switch
Find Mobile Contacts	Recommend friends in mobile contacts to me	Switch
Find Me by *WeChat* ID	Find me by searching my *WeChat* ID	Switch
Blocked List	List of friends who cannot send messages to me	Others (List)
Do Not Share My Moments	List of friends who cannot see my *WeChat* status	Others (List)
Hidden Friends	List of friends whose *WeChat* status I do not want to see	Others (List)
Public Moments	Whether strangers can visit my *Wechat* status	Switch

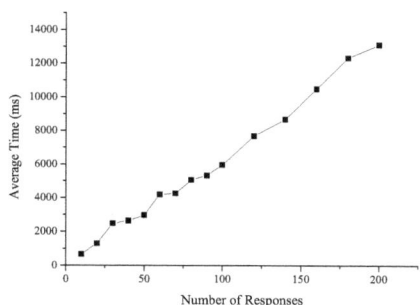

Figure 5: Server Performance

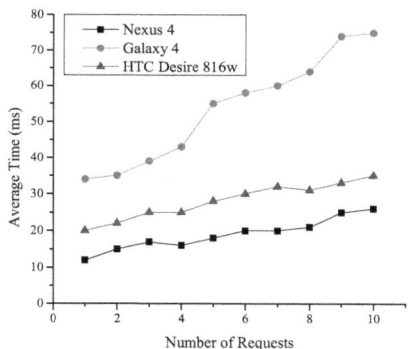

Figure 6: Client Performance

with a 8.00G memory. The experimental result is shown in Figure 6.

In Figure 6, the horizontal axis represents the number of requests that a client application receives at the same time, and the vertical axis represents the time that the client application needs to deal with the requests. The main time costs lie on encrypting a *response* before sending it out.

We further measure the performance of the client by connecting the smartphone device to a computer, and executing "adb shell top" command to view ongoing tasks running on the device. We monitor the status on a Google Nexus 4 running Android 4.2 several times. We can see that the peak value of CPU usage of the client application does not exceed 7%, including encrypting a *response* before sending it out.

Based on the above experiments, we can see that the implemented SPA supports major types of policies of the current popular applications with acceptable performance.

6. DISCUSSION

6.1 Vulnerabilities in SPA

One vulnerability exists when the *requester* acts as an attacker. The *requester* sends a *request* to only one friend and other accounts which are also managed by the *requester* himself. When the only friend makes a *response*, it is possible for the *requester* to reason the settings of the friend based on the final merging result and his own settings. The vulnerability also exists when a *requester* colludes with other friends to crack into the settings of a targeted friend.

There exist several vulnerabilities in *w-SPA*. According to the SPA framework in subsection 4.1, a *requester* sends *requests* to *respondents* directly. Thus, weights, which are the privacy of the *requester*, is sent to *respondents*. If *respondents* exploit this, they could get *requester's* personal judgments of them. It is also possible for a *requester* to get all settings from *respondents* who send *responses* respectively. The *requester* can use carefully designed weights to store all responded *respondents'* setting values in different digits of weighted sum. *E.g.*, Alice wants to get each friend's setting value, which ranges 0 to 100, from **Bob**, **Cindy**, **Dale**, who are her friends. She can set **Bob's** weight to 1, **Cindy's** weight to 1000, and **Dale's** weight to 1000000, and send *requests* to them. These three weight values ensure Alice's friends' setting values store in weighted sum respectively. (If there are some friends who do not respond Alice's *request*, the value will be 0, and it will not affect others setting values) The cloud server will send the encrypted average value of weighted sum to Alice. Then Alice can get setting values from *respondents* who responded her *request*. As a result, the mechanism to support *w-SPA* requires more concerns to protect friends' privacy.

6.2 Using Fully Homomorphic Encryption to Support More Types of Policies

Although there is still no effective and efficient solution, we believe the SPA framework can support more types of policies using fully homomorphic encryption. Our work has implemented SPA framework using a partially homomorphic encryption algorithm, **Paillier**. Experimental results show that the implemented SPA supports the majority of policies in current popular Android applications. However, the limitation of **Paillier** is that it only supports additive operation on data. Fully homomorphic encryption is an efficient way to address this limitation. For example, if a fully homomorphic encryption supports value comparison on ciphertexts, it is possible to get the maximum or minimum value among choices made by friends.

6.3 Security of Homomorphic Encryption

The security of homomorphic encryption affects the security strength of the SPA framework. Shannon formalized the security of encryption schemes for the first time in the literature [21]. Shannon introduced the notion of *perfect secrecy/unconditional security*, which characterized encryption schemes in which the knowledge of a ciphertext does not give any information about either the corresponding plaintext or the key [9]. The highest security level a homomorphic encryption can reach is IND-CPA [9]. IND stands for indistinguishability whereas CPA are acronyms for chosen plaintext attack. A chosen plaintext attack (CPA) is an attack model for cryptanalysis which presumes that the attacker has the capability to choose arbitrary plaintexts to be encrypted and obtain the corresponding ciphertexts [1].

RSA cannot achieve a security level of IND-CPA, but **Paillier** and **ElGamal** achieve the highest security level for homomorphic encryption schemes. However, RSA is still considered strong enough.

7. RELATED WORK

This paper proposes a novel policy administration framework, socialized policy administration (SPA) to manage personal policies, where users can invite their friends to help set sensitive policies.

Policy administration is an effective approach to protect and operate information systems [23][15]. The literature [16] specifies four core components in a traditional framework of policy-based management: Policy Decision Point (PDP), Policy Enforcement Point (PEP), Policy Administration Point (PAP), and Policy Repository (PR). In the traditional administration model, a professional expert or group will take charge of the policy administration, whose functions include policy design, policy verification, and policy deployment [12]. Many researchers proposed their policy administration methods [20][14]. However, smarter phones and mobile applications challenge the existing trust model in the policy administration, where common users do not possess professional knowledge of policy-based management.

Therefore, much work has been done to meet new requirements in policy administration. In the literature [24], Squicciarini *et al.* pointed out, in spite of the fact that content sharing represents one of the prominent features of existing Social Network sites, Social Networks yet do not support any mechanism for collaborative management of settings for shared content. Squicciarini *et al.* modeled the problem of collaborative enforcement of privacy policies on shared data by using game theory. In particular, they proposed a solution that offers automated ways to share images based on an extended notion of content ownership. The approach makes use of the concept of shared ownership of data. This is achieved by having the originator of the data, that is the user responsible for uploading the data, specify other potential owners of that data. The system then holds an auction on the possible privacy policy to apply to the data in which all the owners submit a vote for their desired policy. The

literature claims to be the first research to discuss a novel model for privacy management across social networks, where data may belong to many users.

In the literature [30], Wishart *et al.* pointed out content sharing on social network services may lead to privacy problems. The literature proposes a privacy-aware social networking service and then introduced a collaborative approach to authoring privacy policies for the service. The approach permits the originators of content on the social network to specify policies for the content they upload. The conditions under which the policy applies can then be edited by nominated users of the social networking service.

The literature [22] proposes policy recommendation. Mohamed Shehab and Said Marouf proposed a multicriteria recommendation model that utilizes application-based, user-based, and category-based collaborative filtering mechanisms. Collaborative filtering mechanisms are based on previous user decisions, and application permission requests to enhance the privacy of the overall site's user population.

In the literature [12], Han *et al.* proposed a policy administration mechanism, referred to as collaborative policy administration (CPA for short), to simplify the policy administration. In CPA, a policy administrator can refer to other similar policies to set up their own policies to protect privacy and other sensitive information. To obtain similar policies more effectively, a text mining-based similarity measure method is presented.

Existing approaches of collaborative policy authoring or administration involve cooperators or friends. However, these methods rarely focus on protection of privacy of who participate in the collaborative policy administration process. Instead, this paper pays attention to the privacy of friends who help set our applications. We implemented an enforcement SPA framework by using homomorphic encryption, and experimental results show that the proposed mechanism can supports major types of policies with acceptable performance.

8. CONCLUSION AND FUTURE WORK

To the best of our knowledge, this paper is the first research to study privacy-preserving solutions to enable unprofessional users to set sensitive policies with the help of their friends on social network services. We firstly articulate the problem of socialized policy administration (SPA for short), where a user can request his or her friends to help set sensitive policies. We then propose an SPA framework for a mobile scenario, and implement the SPA framework using a partially homomorphic encryption, Paillier. We conduct experiments to evaluate the completeness and performance of the proposed SPA framework. The results show that the framework supports the majority of policies in current popular Android applications, and the performance is promising to support these policies.

In our future work, we will leverage some formal methods to analyze the security of the SPA framework. In addition, we will design a new schema to support *w-SPA* with privacy preserving. We will focus on the implementation of a practical SPA component for users to integrate into their applications. Last but not least, we will investigate a method for a user to find other users who may have similar usage scenario with him or her to make the result more suitable for the *requester*'s usage scenario.

Acknowledgement

This paper is supported by National Key Science and Technology Program (P01-029-2014(10)-2.4-02-T-C), Natural Science Foundation of Shanghai (12ZR1402600), Twelve.Five National Development Foundation for Cryptography (MMJJ 201301008), and Shanghai Science and Technology Development Funds (13dz2260200, 13511504300). We thank anonymous reviewers for their comments.

9. REFERENCES

[1] R. Anderson. Security engineering: A guide to building dependable distributed systems. 2001.

[2] D. Barrera, H. G. Kayacik, P. C. van Oorschot, and A. Somayaji. A methodology for empirical analysis of permission-based security models and its application to Android. In *Proceedings of the 17th ACM conference on Computer and communications security*, pages 73–84. ACM, 2010.

[3] Z. Brakerski and V. Vaikuntanathan. Efficient fully homomorphic encryption from (standard) LWE. In *Proceedings of 2011 IEEE 52nd Annual Symposium on Foundations of Computer Science (FOCS)*, pages 97–106. IEEE, 2011.

[4] I. Damgård and M. Jurik. A generalisation, a simpli. cation and some applications of Paillier's probabilistic public-key system. In *Public Key Cryptography*, pages 119–136. Springer, 2001.

[5] T. ElGamal. A public key cryptosystem and a signature scheme based on discrete logarithms. In *Advances in Cryptology*, pages 10–18. Springer, 1985.

[6] W. Enck, M. Ongtang, P. D. McDaniel, et al. Understanding Android security. *IEEE Security & Privacy*, 7(1):50–57, 2009.

[7] Z. Fang, W. Han, and Y. Li. Permission based android security: Issues and countermeasures. *Computers & Security (COSE)*, 43:205–218, 2014.

[8] A. P. Felt, E. Chin, S. Hanna, D. Song, and D. Wagner. Android permissions demystified. In *Proceedings of the 18th ACM conference on Computer and communications security*, pages 627–638. ACM, 2011.

[9] C. Fontaine and F. Galand. A survey of homomorphic encryption for nonspecialists. *EURASIP Journal on Information Security*, 2007, 2007.

[10] C. Gentry. *A fully homomorphic encryption scheme*. PhD thesis, Stanford University, 2009.

[11] C. Gentry. Fully homomorphic encryption using ideal lattices. In *Proceedings of the Forty-first Annual ACM Symposium on Theory of Computing*, STOC '09, pages 169–178, New York, NY, USA, 2009. ACM.

[12] W. Han, Z. Fang, L. T. Yang, G. Pan, and Z. Wu. Collaborative policy administration. *IEEE Transactions on Parallel and Distributed Systems (TPDS)*, 25(2):498–507, 2014.

[13] M. Li, S. Yu, K. Ren, and W. Lou. Securing personal health records in cloud computing: Patient-centric and fine-grained data access control in multi-owner settings. In *Proceedings of SecureComm 2010*, pages 89–106. Springer, 2010.

[14] N. Li and Z. Mao. Administration in role-based access control. In *Proceedings of the 2nd ACM symposium on Information, computer and communications security*, pages 127–138. ACM, 2007.

[15] L. Lymberopoulos, E. C. Lupu, and M. S. Sloman. An adaptive policy-based framework for network services management. *Journal of Network and Systems Management*, 11(3):277–303, September 2003.

[16] B. Moore, E. Ellesson, J. Strassner, and A. Westerinen. Policy core information model–version 1 specification. Technical report, RFC 3060, February, 2001.

[17] M. Nauman, S. Khan, and X. Zhang. Apex: extending Android permission model and enforcement with user-defined runtime constraints. In *Proceedings of the 5th ACM Symposium on Information, Computer and Communications Security*, pages 328–332. ACM, 2010.

[18] P. Paillier. Public-key cryptosystems based on composite degree residuosity classes. In *Advances in cryptology—EUROCRYPT' 99*, pages 223–238. Springer, 1999.

[19] R. L. Rivest, A. Shamir, and L. Adleman. A method for obtaining digital signatures and public-key cryptosystems. *Communications of the ACM*, 21(2):120–126, 1978.

[20] R. Sandhu and Q. Munawer. The arbac99 model for administration of roles. In *Proceedings of the 15th Annual Computer Security Applications Conference (ACSAC'99)*, pages 229–238. IEEE, 1999.

[21] C. E. Shannon. Communication theory of secrecy systems. *Bell system technical journal*, 28(4):656–715, 1949.

[22] M. Shehab and S. Marouf. Recommendation models for open authorization. *IEEE Transactions on Dependable and Secure Computing*, 9(4):583–596, 2012.

[23] M. S. Sloman. Policy driven management for distributed systems. *Journal of Network and Systems Management*, 2(4):333–360, December 1994.

[24] A. C. Squicciarini, M. Shehab, and F. Paci. Collective privacy management in social networks. In *Proceedings of the 18th international conference on World wide web*, pages 521–530. ACM, 2009.

[25] D. Stehlé and R. Steinfeld. Faster fully homomorphic encryption. In *Advances in Cryptology-ASIACRYPT 2010*, pages 377–394. Springer, 2010.

[26] Techinasia. 1.3 billion smartphones shipped in 2014; xiaomi ends year ranked 5th globally. https://www.techinasia.com/idc-smartphones-shipped-2014-apple-samsung-xiaomi/, Jan 2015.

[27] M. Van Dijk, C. Gentry, S. Halevi, and V. Vaikuntanathan. Fully homomorphic encryption over the integers. In *Advances in Cryptology-EUROCRYPT 2010*, pages 24–43. Springer, 2010.

[28] Wikipedia. Homomorphic encryption, 2014. [Online; accessed 7-June-2014].

[29] Wikipedia. Wechat, 2014. [Online; accessed 18-June-2014].

[30] R. Wishart, D. Corapi, S. Marinovic, and M. Sloman. Collaborative privacy policy authoring in a social networking context. In *POLICY*, pages 1–8, 2010.

Author Index